Mexico's Beach Resorts
FOR
DUMMIES®
1ST EDITION

by Lynn Bairstow

Wiley Publishing, Inc.

Mexico's Beach Resorts For Dummies™

Published by
Wiley Publishing, Inc.
909 Third Avenue
New York, NY 10022
www.wiley.com

Copyright © 2002 by Wiley Publishing, Inc., Indianapolis, Indiana

Published simultaneously in Canada

For general information on our other products and services or to obtain technical support, please contact our Customer Care Department within the U.S. at 800-762-2974, outside the U.S. at 317-572-3993, or fax 317-572-4002.

Wiley also publishes its books in a variety of electronic formats. Some content that appears in print may not be available in electronic books.

Library of Congress Cataloging-in-Publication Data:

Library of Congress Control Number: 2002108115

ISBN: 0-7645-6262-2

ISSN: 1537-8144

Manufactured in the United States of America

10 9 8 7 6 5 4 3 2 1

About the Author

For **Lynne Bairstow,** Mexico has become more home to her than her native United States. After living in Puerto Vallarta for most of the past eleven years and exploring Mexico, she's developed not only an appreciation but also a true love for this country and its complex, colorful culture. Her travel articles on Mexico have been published in the *New York Times, San Francisco Chronicle, Los Angeles Times, Frommer's Budget Travel* magazine, and *Alaska Airlines Magazine.* In 2000, the Mexican government awarded Lynne the Pluma de Plata, a top honor granted to foreign writers, for her work in the Frommer's guidebooks to Mexico.

Dedication

This book is dedicated to my many friends in Mexico who, through sharing their insights, anecdotes, knowledge, and explorations of Mexico, have shared their love of this country. In particular, Carlos, Silver, Claudia, and Ricardo have shared with me and have shown me what a magical place Mexico is and how much more I have to discover and enjoy.

Author's Acknowledgments

Many thanks to all of the many people who helped me gather the information, tips, and treasures that have made their way into this book. I am especially grateful for the assistance of Claudia Velo and Tori Weathers and their tireless work in ensuring that the information in this book is correct and for their valuable ideas and contributions.

Publisher's Acknowledgments

We're proud of this book; please send us your comments through our Dummies online registration form located at www.dummies.com/register/.

Some of the people who helped bring this book to market include the following:

Editorial

Editors: Linda Brandon, Project Editor; Amy Lyons, Development Editor

Copy Editor: Mike Baker

Cartographer: John Decamillis

Editorial Manager: Jennifer Ehrlich

Editorial Assistant: Carol Strickland

Senior Photo Editor: Richard Fox

Assistant Photo Editor: Michael Ross

Cover Photos: Front: Glenn McLaughlin/Corbis-Stock Market; Back: Mark Lewis/Getty Images

Production

Project Coordinator: Ryan Steffen

Layout and Graphics: Sean Decker, Carrie Foster, Kristin McMullan, Laurie Petrone, Julie Trippetti

Proofreaders: Laura Albert, David Faust, Andy Hollandbeck, Susan Moritz, Carl Pierce, Dwight Ramsey, TECHBOOKS Production Services

Indexer: TECHBOOKS Production Services

Special Help

Michelle Hacker

Publishing and Editorial for Consumer Dummies

    Diane Graves Steele, Vice President and Publisher, Consumer Dummies

    Joyce Pepple, Acquisitions Director, Consumer Dummies

    Kristin A. Cocks, Product Development Director, Consumer Dummies

    Michael Spring, Vice President and Publisher, Travel

    Brice Gosnell, Publishing Director, Travel

    Suzanne Jannetta, Editorial Director, Travel

Publishing for Technology Dummies

    Andy Cummings, Acquisitions Director

Composition Services

    Gerry Fahey, Executive Director of Production Services

    Debbie Stailey, Director of Composition Services

Contents at a Glance

Cartoons at a Glance

By Rich Tennant

page 9

page 255

page 49

page 343

page 85

page 295

page 433

page 145

page 379

page 189

Cartoon Information:
Fax: 978-546-7747
E-Mail: richtennant@the5thwave.com
World Wide Web: www.the5thwave.com

Maps at a Glance

Table of Contents

Introduction

Mexico not only offers travelers some of the best beaches in the world, but it also presents a rich, thousand-year-old culture and amazing natural wonders to explore. Whether it's the desert caves of Los Cabos or the Caribbean reefs off Cancún and Cozumel, Mexico's largely untouched coastline is a virtual playground for travelers. In addition to the many natural attractions, Mexican beach resorts have added golf, tennis, diving, and abundant watersports to their lures. But can the rest of your knowledge about this vast country fit inside a mango seed? For many people, Mexico is both familiar and a mystery, and some opinions of this land are influenced by inaccurate or out-dated stereotypes. If you're a traveler who is more attuned to the culture, you may have visited one or two Mexican beach resorts, but you're probably curious about some of the others.

How do you sift through the destination choices — and then all of the hotel options — without throwing in the beach towel in a daze of confusion? How do you plan a vacation that's perfect for you — not one that simply follows the recommendations of a friend or travel agent? You've come to the right place. This guide rescues you from both information overload and detail deficit — those annoying syndromes that afflict far too many would-be travelers. I give you enough specifics to help you figure out and plan the type of trip you want and steer clear of the type of trip you don't want.

Sure, plenty of other guidebooks are available that cover Mexico and its beach destinations, but many of them may as well be encyclopedias: They include practically everything you can possibly see and do. When the time comes to decide upon accommodations, attractions, activities, and meals, you have a tough time finding the best options because they're buried in with the rest of the mediocre to not-so-hot suggestions.

Mexico Beach Resorts For Dummies is a whole new enchilada. In the following pages, I streamline the options, focusing on the high points (and warning you about the low points) of each vacation spot. I leave out the less-visited, harder-to-reach beach resorts so that I can concentrate on the most popular (and most exciting) destinations. With the straight-forward tips that I offer — how to get there, what to expect when you arrive, where to stay, where to eat, and where to have big fun — arranging your dream vacation can't be easier.

About This Book

You can use this book in three ways:

- ✔ **As a trip planner:** Whether you think you know where you want to go in Mexico, or you don't have a clue, this book helps you zero in on the ideal beach resort for you. It guides you through all the necessary steps of making your travel arrangements, from finding the cheapest airfare and considering travel insurance to figuring out a budget and packing like a pro. Chapters are self-contained, so you don't have to read them in order. Just flip to the chapters as you need them.

- ✔ **As a beach-resort guide:** Pack this book along with your sunscreen — it will come in just as handy while you're away. Turn to the appropriate destination chapters whenever you need to find the best beaches, a good place to eat, a worthwhile boat cruise, a challenging golf course, the lowdown on a hot nightspot, or tips on any other diversions.

- ✔ **For an enjoyable overview:** If you want a feel for Mexico's most popular beach resorts, read this book from start to finish to get a taste of all the highlights.

Travel information is subject to change at any time — call ahead for confirmation when making your travel plans. Your safety is important to me (and to the publisher), so I encourage you to stay alert and be aware of your surroundings. Keep a close eye on cameras, purses, and wallets — all favorite targets of thieves and pickpockets.

Conventions Used in This Book

In this book I, include reviews of my favorite hotels and restaurants, as well as information about the best attractions at each of Mexico's top beach resorts. As I describe each, I use abbreviations for commonly accepted credit cards. Here's what those abbreviations stand for:

AE (American Express)

DC (Diners Club)

MC (MasterCard)

V (Visa)

I also include some general pricing information to help you as you decide where to unpack your bags or where to dine on the local cuisine. I use a system of dollar signs (U.S. dollars) to show a range of costs so that you can make quick comparisons.

Unless I say otherwise, the lodging rates that I give are for two people spending one night in a standard double room. Prices are provided for both high season — the most popular travel time that runs roughly from Christmas to Easter — and the generally lower-priced summer season (or low season). I use the dollar sign pricing system to indicate the high season rates. Some hotel rates are much higher than others no matter what time of year it is. Don't be too quick to skip an accommodation that seems out of your price range, though. Some rates include breakfast, both breakfast and dinner, or even three meals per day. Other resorts are *all-inclusive*. This means that after you pay for your room, you never have to dip into your pocket again for meals, beverages, tips, taxes, most activities, or transportation to and from the airport. So, although a price tag may seem sky-high at first, you may actually find it affordable upon second glance. The dining rates are for main courses only.

Check out the following table to decipher the dollar signs:

Cost	Hotel	Restaurant
$	Less than $75	Less than $15
$$	$75–$125	$15–$30
$$$	$125–$175	$30–$50
$$$$	$175–$250	$50 and up
$$$$$	More than $250 per night	

Foolish Assumptions

As I wrote this book, I made some assumptions about you and what your needs may be as a traveler. Here's what I assumed about you:

- ✔ You may be an inexperienced traveler looking for guidance when determining whether to take a trip to a Mexican beach resort and how to plan for it.

- ✔ You may be an experienced traveler who hasn't had much time to explore Mexico or its beaches and wants expert advice when you finally do get a chance to enjoy some time in the sun.

- ✔ You're not looking for a book that provides all the information available about Mexico or that lists every hotel, restaurant, or attraction available to you. Instead, you're looking for a book that focuses on the places that offer the best or most unique experiences in these beach resorts.

How This Book Is Organized

I divide this book into ten parts. The chapters within each part cover specific subjects in detail. Skip around as much as you like. You don't have to read this book in any particular order. In fact, think of these pages as a buffet. You can consume whatever you want — and no one cares if you eat the flan for dessert before you have the enchiladas.

For each beach resort, I include a section called "Fast Facts." You can find these sections at the end of "Settling into" chapters. These sections give you handy information that you may need when traveling in Mexico, including phone numbers and addresses to use in an emergency, area hospitals and pharmacies, names of local newspapers and magazines, locations for maps, and more.

Part 1: Getting Started

In this part, I compare and contrast Mexico's most popular beach resorts so that you can decide which place best suits your tastes and needs. Sure, they all have gorgeous beaches, but that's where the similarities end. To help you plan a vacation that's tailored to your preferences, this part guides you through the process of figuring out which resort or resorts are best for you.

I also give you a brief overview of local customs, cuisines, and fiestas and celebrations. I take you through the best — and worst — times of year to travel, and I explain the differences between high season and low season. I also tell you about special holidays that may help you decide when to visit Mexico. I offer up some budget-planning tips, and finally, I offer special trip-planning advice for families, singles, gay and lesbian travelers, seniors, and travelers who are physically challenged.

Part 11: Ironing Out the Details

This section is where I lay out everything you need to know about making all the arrangements for your trip. I help you decide whether to use a travel agent, a packager, or the Internet. I offer advice on finding the best airfare — and airline — for your destination. Likewise, I explain how to estimate the total cost of your vacation and how to stay within your budget. Finally, I take you through all the ins and outs of other vacation essentials, from getting a passport and considering travel insurance to staying safe and packing like a pro.

Part 111: Cancún

Welcome to Mexico's most popular beach resort. This area is a great destination for first-time travelers to Mexico. Why? Because it has all the comforts of home — familiar restaurant and hotel chains along with great shopping — plus easy access to diverse cultural and geographical activities — excursions to the ancient ruins of Tulum, world-class scuba diving, and plenty of Mexican fiestas. I provide all the details for getting to, eating at, staying in, and playing at all of Cancún's hot spots.

Part IV: Cozumel and the Riviera Maya

Staying on a tropical island is a dream for many, and Cozumel offers a distinctive island destination for a laid-back vacation with a myriad of water activities, many centered around the famous reef that outlines the southwest coast. Back on the mainland, the Riviera Maya provides a stunning stretch of pristine beaches, unique towns, and mega-resorts from Cancún to Tulum. Check out the up-and-coming town of Playa del Carmen or visit one of the eco-parks. There's plenty here for everyone. In this part, I cover all the information you need to travel to and around these two beach resorts.

Part V: Puerto Vallarta and the Central Pacific Coast

Turn to this part for the inside scoop (I'm a long-time resident!) on visiting the beautiful city of Puerto Vallarta. From viewing historic landmarks to dining in world-class restaurants to finding the perfect beach along the 50 miles of coastline surrounding Banderas Bay, a trip to this part of Mexico is sure to please even the most discriminating vacationer.

Part VI: Ixtapa and Zihuatanejo

Who says you can't get it all in one destination? Traveling to the towns of Ixtapa and Zihuatanejo provide the best of two worlds: Ixtapa gives you high-class hotels along a beautiful strip of sand and nearby Zihuatanejo wraps you in the warmth of its small-town charms. This part offers advice on staying and dining in both of these great vacations spots.

Part VII: Acapulco

The grande dame of Mexico's west coast, Acapulco draws many visitors to its glittering bay and glamorous nightlife. Enjoy the excitement of a bustling city combined with the amenities of a beachfront resort. This part gives you the lowdown on vacationing in Mexico's first beach resort.

Part VIII: Huatulco and the Southern Pacific Coast

For details on a vacation that centers on the natural beauty of the land and the sea, turn to Part VIII. This part offers a close-up look at two towns along the Southern Pacific Coast: Huatulco and Puerto Escondido.

Part IX: Los Cabos and Southern Baja

Want to take time out for a great golf vacation? Ready to reel in a big one? Or, just need to let your hair down and enjoy some super-charged nightlife? Then turn to Part IX for all the details on vacationing in Los Cabos and on the Baja Peninsula.

Part X: The Part of Tens

Every *For Dummies* book has a Part of Tens. In this section, I take a look at the ten most common myths about Mexico, and I share with you my ten favorite Mexico experiences. I also have some timely advice for those of you planning a honeymoon.

In the back of the book, I also include appendixes, one of which is a Quick Concierge. It contains lots of handy information you may need when traveling in Mexico, like phone numbers and addresses of emergency personnel or area hospitals and pharmacies, contact information for babysitters, lists of local newspapers and magazines, protocol for sending mail or finding taxis, and more. Check out this appendix when searching for answers to lots of little questions that may come up as you travel.

Also included is an appendix with useful toll-free numbers and Web sites, another that directs you to other sources of information, and finally, a helpful glossary of Spanish words and phrases.

Worksheets to help make your travel planning easier are located at the very back of the book. You can find them easily because they're printed on yellow paper.

Icons Used in This Book

Throughout this book, helpful icons highlight particularly useful information. Here's a look at what each symbol means:

Keep an eye out for the Bargain Alert icon as you look for money-saving tips and great deals.

Watch for the Heads Up icon to identify annoying or potentially danger-ous situations such as tourist traps, unsafe neighborhoods, budgetary rip-offs, and other things to avoid.

Look to the Kid Friendly icon for attractions, hotels, restaurants, and activities that are particularly hospitable to children or people travel-ing with kids.

The Romance icon signals the most romantic restaurants, hotels, and attractions that Mexico's beach resorts have to offer.

The Tip icon alerts you to practical advice and hints to make your trip run more smoothly.

Note the ¡Viva Mexico! icon for food, places, or experiences that offer a true taste of the spirit of Mexico.

Where to Go from Here

There's nothing like a beach vacation — whether you spend it lazing in the sun or pursuing active, water-bound activities — and it's even better when planned with the right advice and insider tips. Whether you're a veteran traveler or new to the game, *Mexico's Beach Resorts For Dummies* helps you put together just the kind of trip you have in mind. So, start turning these pages, and before you know it, you'll feel those balmy beach breezes on your face!

Part I
Getting Started

The 5th Wave   By Rich Tennant

"Do you mind __NOT__ practicing your 'Olé's!' while I'm vacuuming?"

In this part . . .

*P*lanning a trip can be daunting — so I'm here to help give you a sense of the place you're considering visiting. Mexico is a vast and varied country with a bevy of unique beach resorts. I introduce you to the highlights of the most popular ones, so you can pick the destination that best matches your idea of the perfect seaside getaway.

In Part I, I cover the basics: Each of Mexico's beach resorts has a charm all its own, so deciding which one best suits your preferences is the first step in planning your ideal vacation. Next come the details — like when to go and which type of hotel is best for you. I also give tips and tricks for accurately planning your vacation budget. Nothing will take away the pleasure of lazy days faster than worries about spending too much money, so spend some time here to ward away those stressful thoughts and stay in the green. Finally, I offer some tips for travelers with special needs — whether you're a solo traveler or a family — in order to help ensure that you pick exactly the right place that fulfills both your personal requirements and your expectations.

Chapter 1

Discovering Mexico's Beach Resorts and Deciding Where to Go

● ●

In This Chapter

▶ Introducing Mexico's beach resorts

▶ Deciding which area you'd like to visit

▶ Examining the pros and cons of each destination

● ●

My first visit to Mexico was a weekend getaway in Puerto Vallarta, and as I was flying above the country, I started to wonder how I'd ever communicate with anyone when I didn't know a word of Spanish. Lucky for me, English is commonly spoken, and it didn't take me long to fall into the town's tropical rhythms and friendly ways. My second visit to this country was to Mexico City. I brought a suitcase full of sundresses only to find myself in a sophisticated urban environment, with temperatures rivaling New York in November. With a country as large and diverse as Mexico, it helps to know a bit about where you're headed so that you can make the most of your time in this colorful, multi-faceted country.

Mexico has a lot going for it in terms of attracting travelers — warm weather, miles and miles of coastline, and a location so close to the United States that sometimes it almost seems like a part of it. Although the official language is Spanish, the use of English is almost as common as Spanish in resort areas. A visit to Mexico can offer the experience of visiting a foreign country accompanied by many of the familiarities of home.

Generally speaking, the beaches of Mexico are spectacular. But they're also as varied as the country itself. Deciding which one is right for you depends a lot on what you're looking for in a vacation. As you read this chapter, think about what you really want in a destination. Romantic? Family fun? Lively singles scene? And consider how you want to travel.

Budget? Luxury? Somewhere in between? These considerations will help narrow down your planning. One thing's for certain — no matter what you're seeking, there's at least one Mexican beach resort that fits the bill . . . perfectly.

Because of Mexico's sheer size, it's not practical to cover more than one of its beach resorts in a single trip, with the exception of the Riviera Maya, found south of Cancún. In this chapter, I help you decide which resort best matches your wish list. Although there are many more beaches to explore in Mexico, in this book, I only include those with the easiest air access and the best services and facilities for tourism.

If you don't know where to begin in choosing between Acapulco and Cancún, or Los Cabos and Puerto Vallarta, don't worry. In this book, I tell you everything you need to know about each of the destinations that I cover in order to help decide which one is right for you. In this chapter, I give you a rundown of the highlights and drawbacks of each of Mexico's most popular beach resorts. Because the type of accommodations you want may determine where you go — or don't go — I also explain the different types of lodging available at each destination.

Understanding the Lay of the Land

Mexico is a country known for both its geographical and cultural diversity. And, as a country with over 130,000 miles of shoreline, you can choose between a quiet stretch of sand, a pounding surf break, or a dynamic beach resort with nonstop nightlife.

Mexico's beach resorts are located in one of three main regions of the country: the Caribbean coast, along the eastern seaboard; the Pacific coastline; or on Mexico's Baja peninsula, an extension of California which is almost completely separated from mainland Mexico.

The eastern destinations are known for their crystalline waters, which border the coral reefs of the Caribbean, and flat, scrubby landscapes. This area was the land of the ancient Maya, and their impressive remains are close enough to the popular beach destinations to explore. The Pacific beach resorts tend to have mountainous backdrops and dramatic tropical jungles bordering cobalt blue waters. Baja's beach resorts combine a stunning desert landscape with oceans teeming with sea life.

Picking the Right Beach Resort

While Acapulco was Mexico's first beach to attract international travelers, the white-sand beaches and nearby ruins of Cancún make it the most popular choice today. Puerto Vallarta and Huatulco offer a strong dose of natural charm and eco-tourism, and Los Cabos has become Mexico's mecca for golfers and fishermen. Zihuatanejo and Cozumel both offer a laid-back retreat beneath palm fronds and sunny skies. In a nutshell, each resort has its own look, character, and special something. The following sections are snapshots to help you focus on the resort that's right for you.

Also see "Mexico's Beach Resorts: The Score Card" at the end of this chapter for a concise rating of each aspect of the resort areas that I cover in this book.

Choosing Cancún

Cancún is Mexico's most popular beach resort — and the reason most people travel to Mexico. Simply stated, it perfectly showcases both the country's breathtaking natural beauty and the depth of its thousand-year-old history. Cancún is also especially comforting for first-time visitors to Mexico, as it offers a taste of life back home that makes foreigners feel instantly at ease in this beach resort.

Cancún offers an unrivaled combination of high-quality accommodations, dreamy beaches, and diverse, nearby shopping, dining, and nightlife. The added lure of ancient culture is also evident in all directions. And the best part? Cancún is also a modern mega-resort. Even if you're a bit apprehensive about visiting foreign soil, you'll feel completely at home and at ease in Cancún. English is spoken, dollars are accepted, roads are well paved, and lawns are manicured. Malls are the place for shopping and dining, and you'll quickly spot recognizable names for dining, shopping, nightclubbing, and sleeping.

Two principal parts comprise Cancún: **Isla Cancún** (Cancún Island), with a 14-mile-long strip of beachfront hotels reminiscent of Miami Beach, and **Ciudad Cancún** (Cancún City), on the mainland, with hotels as well as the functional elements of any community.

Cancún, located on the Yucatan Peninsula, is also the departure point for wonderful day-trips to the nearby islands of Cozumel and Isla Mujeres (meaning Island of Women), where you can enjoy first-class diving, as well as the inland remains of ancient cultures.

If you're looking for an incredible introduction to Mexico's beaches and wish to experience a Mexican-lite vacation while enjoying world-class shopping in a pampered environment, Cancún is your beach. (Check out the chapters in Part III for more detailed information on this resort.)

Mexico

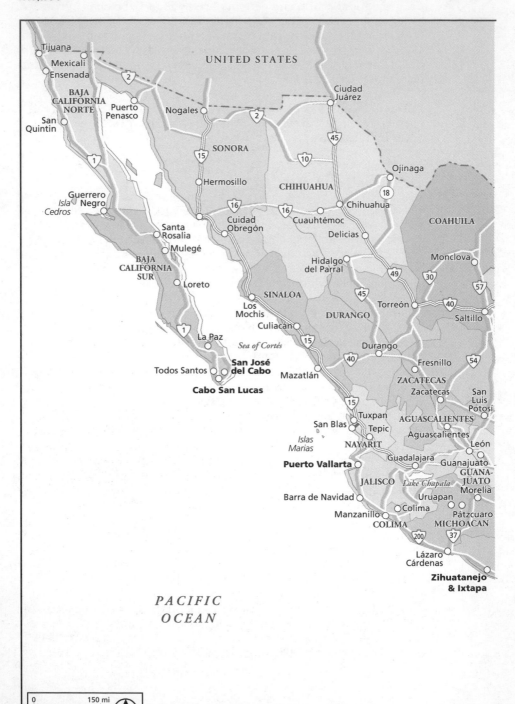

UNITED STATES

Tijuana
Mexicali
Ensenada
BAJA CALIFORNIA NORTE
Puerto Penasco
San Quintin
Nogales
Ciudad Juárez
SONORA
Hermosillo
CHIHUAHUA
Ojinaga
Chihuahua
Cuauhtémoc
Guerrero Negro
Isla Cedros
Santa Rosalia
Mulegé
Cuidad Obregón
Delicias
COAHUILA
BAJA CALIFORNIA SUR
Loreto
Hidalgo del Parral
Monclova
SINALOA
Los Mochis
Culiacán
DURANGO
Torreón
Saltillo
La Paz
Sea of Cortés
Durango
San José del Cabo
Todos Santos
Mazatlán
Fresnillo
Cabo San Lucas
ZACATECAS
Zacatecas
San Luis Potosí
Tuxpan
AGUASCALIENTES
San Blas
Tepic
Aguascalientes
León
Islas Marias
NAYARIT
Puerto Vallarta
Guadalajara
Guanajuato
GUANA-JUATO
JALISCO
Lake Chapala
Morelia
Barra de Navidad
Uruapan
Manzanillo
Colima
Pátzcuaro
MICHOACAN
COLIMA
Lázaro Cárdenas
Zihuatanejo & Ixtapa

PACIFIC OCEAN

0   150 mi
0   150 km
N

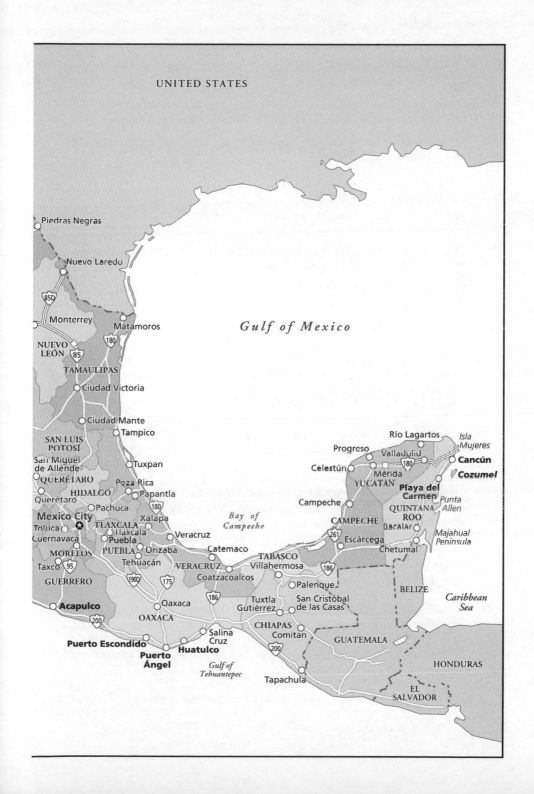

UNITED STATES

Piedras Negras

Nuevo Laredo

Gulf of Mexico

85D

Monterrey   Matamoros

NUEVO
LEÓN   180

85

TAMAULIPAS

Ciudad Victoria

Ciudad Mante

Tampico

Río Lagartos   *Isla
Mujeres*

SAN LUIS
POTOSÍ   Progreso   Valladolid

Cancún

San Miguel
de Allende   Tuxpan   Celestún   180   Mérida   **Cozumel**

QUERÉTARO   YUCATÁN

Poza Rica   **Playa del
Carmen**   *Punta
Allen*

Querétaro   HIDALGO   Papantla   180   Campeche   QUINTANA
ROO

Pachuca   Bacalar

Mexico City   Xalapa   *Bay of
Campeche*   CAMPECHE   *Majahual
Peninsula*

Toluca   TLAXCALA

Tlaxcala   261   Escárcega   Chetumal

Cuernavaca   Puebla   Veracruz

MORELOS   PUEBLA   Orizaba   Catemaco   TABASCO

Taxco   95   Tehuacán   VERACRUZ   Villahermosa   186

GUERRERO   190D   175   Coatzacoalcos   Palenque   BELIZE   *Caribbean
Sea*

Acapulco   Oaxaca   186

Tuxtla   San Cristóbal   GUATEMALA

200   OAXACA   Gutiérrez   de las Casas

Salina   CHIAPAS
Cruz   Comitan

Puerto Escondido   **Huatulco**

**Puerto
Ángel**   *Gulf of
Tehuantepec*   200   HONDURAS

Tapachula   EL
SALVADOR

Top aspects of a vacation in Cancún include:

- Great beaches of powdery, white sand and turquoise-blue water
- First-class facilities, modern accommodations, and tons of shopping and dining options
- Numerous outdoor activities including jungle tours, visits to Mayan ruins, and eco-oriented theme parks
- No need to worry about communication — an English language-friendly destination

But also consider the following:

- It's so easy to forget that you're in Mexico that you may miss the Mexican experience altogether.
- Built for tourism, the prices in Cancún are higher than in most other Mexican beach resorts.
- Its popularity means you'll have lots of company here!

Diving into Cozumel

If underwater beauty is your most important criteria for choosing a beach, then Cozumel will dazzle you. Considered by many to be one of the top-ten diving spots in the world, few places can top the aquatic splendor of the waters surrounding this island.

And when you come up for air, or if you're a non-diver, Cozumel has several inland attractions, a variety of watersports, a brand new golf course, and ample choices for dining and libations. As Mexico's most important port of call for cruise ships, Cozumel also has the best duty-free shopping and one of the largest selections of fine-jewelry shops in the country. The island's one town, San Miguel, has a charming old-Mexico feel to it.

Cozumel has more budget-friendly accommodations and places to dine than newer, nearby Cancún. However, while the island is really active during the day, it's generally a very quiet place at night.

Just a 45-minute ferry ride away from mainland Mexico, Cozumel makes for a great jumping-off point for explorations along the Yucatan's coastline. Just across the channel from Cozumel is captivating Playa del Carmen, quickly growing in popularity due to its central location and funky-sophisticated charms.

In addition to being a diver's dream destination, staying in Cozumel can be like enjoying multiple beach resorts in one vacation! (Take a look at Chapter 12 for more on Cozumel.)

Top aspects of a vacation in Cozumel include:

- ✔ World-class diving
- ✔ Secluded beaches to get away from it all
- ✔ Relaxed island atmosphere
- ✔ A short ferry trip away from the mainland's cultural and historical attractions

But also consider the following:

- ✔ The nightlife is almost non-existent.
- ✔ Cozumel is super-casual; there's not a dress-up place on the island.
- ✔ Stores tend to be more expensive than elsewhere because they cater to cruise-ship visitors.
- ✔ When the cruise ships arrive, the towns are very crowded.

Exploring the Riviera Maya

Cancún's popularity has given rise to a growing curiosity and desire to explore other parts of the pristine coastline to the south. New venues started popping up along the shoreline heading south to Tulum. Now officially dubbed the Riviera Maya, this stretch of peaceful places to stay is ideal for either more adventurous travelers or those who simply want to stay put in an all-inclusive enclave.

The hottest spot along the Riviera Maya is Playa del Carmen, which lies just over 40 miles south of Cancún. Playa — as locals refer to it — is a small town that's both funky and sophisticated. In the early '80s, Playa del Carmen was nothing more than the ferry landing for Cozumel, but it has since developed into an engaging resort town of its own merit, with powdery-sand beaches and an eclectic collection of lodging, dining, and shopping.

Playa seems to attract younger visitors who are looking for a combination of simplicity and variety. Recently, though, Playa has also attracted developers. As they rapidly change the beachscape to the north and south with the addition of mega-resorts, they're also changing Playa's previously playful vibe. But Playa still has enough of its original flavor to make it different from any other resort in the area.

South of Playa del Carmen lie a succession of commercial nature parks, planned resort communities, and a few rustic beach hideaways including Xcaret, Puerto Aventuras, Xpu-Ha, Akumal, Xel-Ha, and Tulum. This stretch of coast is also sprinkled with newly developed, all-inclusive resorts.

If you love getting away from it all, the Riviera Maya is a natural choice for exploration and relaxation. (See Chapter 13 for more details.)

Top aspects of a vacation in the Riviera Maya include:

- Beautiful beaches and an array of eco-parks ideal for nature lovers
- Favored by more adventurous travelers, some of whom have settled here to offer eclectic accommodations, shopping, and dining options
- Smaller crowds and lower prices
- All-inclusive heaven with great savings if traveling with children

But also consider the following:

- Limited shopping and dining exist outside of Playa del Carmen.
- Nightlife? What nightlife? Unless you consider stargazing an aspect of nightlife.
- Without a rental car, you'll be stuck where you stay.

Playing in Puerto Vallarta

Puerto Vallarta is the place to go for those looking to experience a beach resort with authentic Mexican flavor. Unlike other resorts, such as Cancún, Ixtapa, and Huatulco, Puerto Vallarta grew up around an original beach community. To this day, it has a seductively simple pace of life that's reflected in the warmth of its people and the spirit of the place itself.

Puerto Vallarta, with its traditional Mexican architecture and gold-sand beaches bordered by jungle-covered mountains, is currently the second most visited resort in Mexico (trailing only Cancún). Vallarta, as locals prefer to call it, maintains a small-town charm despite being home to sophisticated hotels, great restaurants, a thriving arts community, an active nightlife, and a growing variety of eco-tourism attractions that range from mountain biking the Sierra foothills to whale watching.

Natural beauty and modern infrastructure aside, Puerto Vallarta is remarkable for the number of options it offers for different types of tourists. Whether you're a couple looking for a romantic getaway, a family trying to find a great value, or senior travelers in search of new shores to explore, Vallarta has something to fit everyone. This resort is also known for being very gay-friendly, and it has a selection of hotels, excursions, and nightlife options that caters specifically to same-sex couples.

If you're an avid golfer with family members that don't share your passion for the links, Vallarta is also a great option. You can take advantage of the six championship-quality courses that are now available for play, making Vallarta an up-and-coming golf resort, while the resort provides ample activities for the non-golfers in your group.

With an ideal mix of modern services and traditional charms, Puerto Vallarta is both a great first-time introduction to Mexico and a wonderful place for those looking to explore more of this country's natural and cultural riches. (Look at the chapters in Part V for more on this area.)

Top aspects of a vacation in Puerto Vallarta include:

- Considered Mexico's friendliest beach resort
- An authentic sense of community
- Ideal combination of natural beauty and modern infrastructure
- An epicurean's delight with more than 250 restaurants, as well as a varied nightlife and great shopping
- Wide variety of lodging options to fit all tastes and pocketbooks
- Countless activities, including mountain biking, hiking, birdwatching, jungle trekking in ATVs, diving, snorkeling, ocean kayaking, and surfing
- Excellent — and uncrowded — golf courses

But also consider the following:

- The beaches, at least those in central Puerto Vallarta, are not the best in Mexico. They feature a golden sand that's darker than most. However, the northern and southern shores offer exquisite options, and they're only a short distance away.
- The presence of numerous beach vendors and timeshare salespeople means that you'll have plenty of practice saying, "No, gracias!"
- The town is jam-packed during the major Mexican holidays — Easter, September 16, November 20, and Christmas — which means higher prices, fewer lodging opportunities, and tangled traffic.

Introducing Ixtapa/Zihuatanejo

If you can't decide between a modern beach resort and a typical Mexican seaside village, then you should consider Ixtapa/Zihuatanejo, located north of Acapulco on Mexico's Pacific Coast. These side-by-side destinations offer the best of both worlds less than five miles from one another. Although they share common geography, they couldn't be more different in character. Ixtapa is a model of modern infrastructure, services, and luxury hotels, while Zihuatanejo — or Zihua, to the locals — is the quintessential Mexican beach village.

If you favor luxury over charm, you should opt for Ixtapa and take advantage of the well-appointed rooms in this pristine setting of great natural beauty. You can easily and quickly make the four-mile trip into Zihuatanejo for a sampling of the simple life in this *pueblo* (small town) by the sea. However, if you prefer a more rustic retreat with real personality, you should settle in Zihuatanejo.

Though this dual destination is a good choice for the traveler looking for a little of everything, from resort-style indulgence to unpretentious simplicity, you should keep in mind that these two resorts are more welcoming to couples and adults than families with small children. A number of places are off-limits to children under the age of 16 — something of a rarity in Mexico.

Ixtapa and Zihuatanejo offer active days and relaxed evenings. During the day, you can choose between scuba diving, deep-sea fishing, bay cruises to remote beaches, and golf. The nightlife in both towns borders on the subdued, but Ixtapa is the livelier of the two. The favored evening activity here tends to be a late dinner on the beach.

Enjoy a sense of two-for-one in this dual destination that's truly an optimal combo of the best of Mexico beach resorts. (See the chapters in Part VI for more on these two destinations.)

Top aspects of a vacation in Zihuatanejo include:

- ✔ Beautiful beaches within a bay that ensures calm waters with ample stretches of sand for sun worshipers

- ✔ Traditional Mexican beach-town atmosphere

- ✔ Smaller, more unique accommodations in a variety of price ranges

- ✔ A casual, relaxed atmosphere

- ✔ One of the best-priced destinations in Mexico

But also consider the following:

- ✔ The nightlife is very quiet.

- ✔ Beach-going sums up the daytime activity; however, you can take short trips to find horseback riding, bird-watching, and other, more active endeavors.

- ✔ It's among the least kid-friendly destinations in Mexico.

- ✔ The summers are extremely hot, and air conditioning is not prevalent.

Top aspects of a vacation in Ixtapa include:

- ✔ Modern infrastructure and expansive beaches
- ✔ Larger chain hotels and nicely-appointed accommodations
- ✔ Two good golf courses with some of the lowest greens fees in Mexico
- ✔ Enough variety in the nightlife — especially fun for the twenty- and thirty-year-old crowd

But also consider the following:

- ✔ It lacks the true "feeling" of being in Mexico.
- ✔ Mexican tourists can make the Easter and Christmas holidays crowded.
- ✔ Summers are very hot.

Getting acquainted with Acapulco

Acapulco is known for its sultry beaches for tanning during the day and its glitzy discos for partying at night. To this day, Acapulco has a nonstop, 24-hours-a-day energy, which clearly demonstrates why it was the largest and most renowned Mexican resort from the 1940s to the 1970s, when movie stars made it their playground. Although golf and tennis are played here with intensity, the real participant sport is the nightlife, which has made this city famous for decades.

Despite the seemingly decadent, nocturnal attractions, Acapulco is also a charmingly ideal place for a fun-filled family vacation. Many activities and destinations cater to children, including water parks, zoos, and exciting tours down a nearby river. Accommodations fit every budget, and children are welcome almost everywhere in town — in the true spirit of Mexican family hospitality.

In addition to the broadest range of late-night entertainment in Mexico, this beach resort also has excellent airline connections, outstanding dining, and a wide array of daytime activities. You can stay at luxurious hillside villas, resort hotels, or modest inns on the beach and in the old center of Acapulco. It's got something for everyone.

Although the view of the bay is stunning, the bay's cleanliness is still somewhat in question, despite valiant efforts by the city officials. This is an important consideration if your ideal beach getaway includes lots of time in the ocean. If you plan on spending your afternoons in the sea, you may want to choose a different resort or, at least, a place located south of town in one of the areas fronting the Pacific Ocean rather than Acapulco Bay.

Acapulco is for you if you want to dine at midnight, dance until dawn, and sleep all day on a sun-soaked beach. (For more information, check out the chapters in Part VII.)

Top aspects of a vacation in Acapulco include:

- Nightlife so hot it rivals the sunshine
- Unforgettable views of the breathtakingly beautiful bay
- An average of 360 days of sunshine per year
- Wide variety of lodging options
- Excellent air-travel connections

But also consider the following:

- The cleanliness of the bay remains questionable.
- The most popular resort with residents of Mexico City, it tends to fill up with city dwellers on weekends and major holidays.
- Acapulco has a somewhat outdated feel to it, and as a big city, it can seem less clean than other Mexican beach resorts.

Hanging out in Huatulco

The resort found furthest south along Mexico's Pacific Coastline, Huatulco is the perfect place for those travelers who want to enjoy pristine beaches and jungle landscapes but would rather view them from a luxury-hotel balcony. If you want to enjoy the beauty of nature during the day and then retreat to well-appointed comfort by night, Huatulco is for you.

The area offers undeveloped stretches of pure, white sands. Isolated coves lie in wait for the promised growth of Huatulco, which luckily, isn't occurring as rapidly as Cancún's expansion. Huatulco is a FONATUR development project that aims to cover 52,000 acres of land. Of that area, over 40,000 acres are to remain as ecological preserves. (FONATUR is a government agency that develops strategic plans and assists in arranging financing for tourism development projects. It is the agency responsible for the site selection and planning of Cancún and both Ixtapa and Los Cabos are other FONATUR destinations.)

Huatulco has developed a name because of its eco-tourism attractions — river rafting, rappelling, and jungle hiking, to name a few. However, the shopping, the nightlife, and even the dining options outside the hotels are scarce, and what is available is high priced for the quality.

If you're especially drawn to snorkeling, diving, boat cruises to virgin bays, and simple relaxation, Huatulco fits the bill. (See Chapter 26 for more information.)

Top aspects of a vacation in Huatulco include:

- ✔ Magnificent, unspoiled beaches where you can get away from it all
- ✔ Beautifully appointed accommodations
- ✔ Slow-paced, small-town atmosphere with modern infrastructure
- ✔ Plenty of eco-oriented activities like river rafting, rappelling, and jungle hiking
- ✔ Water-lovers paradise with lots of snorkeling, diving, and boating
- ✔ Superb service and friendliness from the locals

But also consider the following:

- ✔ The nightlife is almost nonexistent.
- ✔ The dining and shopping options are limited.
- ✔ It's harder to reach than many resorts, and a limited number of direct flights service the area.
- ✔ It's slightly more expensive than other beach resorts in Mexico.

Partying in Puerto Escondido

Puerto Escondido — usually referred to as Puerto — is known for its great surf, breathtaking beaches, friendly locals, and inexpensive prices. Located just north along the Pacific Mexico coastline from Huatulco, Puerto Escondido is another "real" place — not a planned development — which gives it a unique and authentic character. And it almost seems as though the locals would rather keep the place small.

In addition to its legendary surf break, Puerto is increasingly gaining a reputation with travelers seeking both spiritual and physical renewal. Abundant massage and bodywork services, yoga classes, and exceptional and varied vegetarian dining options — not to mention seaside tranquility — are hallmarks of this resort. I consider it the single best beach value in all of Mexico.

European travelers make up a significant number of the visitors, and it's common to hear a variety of languages on the beach and in the bars. Puerto is also a place that younger travelers favor — and one of the few resorts that offers welcoming options for the backpack- and hammock-type of traveler.

Puerto is definitely the place for surf lovers, but it's also great for those who are looking for a funky, relaxed beach attitude infused with a cosmopolitan appreciation for espresso drinks and world music. (See Chapter 27 for details on Puerto Escondido.)

Top aspects of a vacation in Puerto Escondido include:

- ✔ The best surfing beaches in Mexico
- ✔ The best overall value
- ✔ Vibrant nightlife with lots of live music
- ✔ Simple atmosphere with no pretensions of being a grand place
- ✔ Plenty of healthful and healing-oriented services

But also consider the following:

- ✔ Accommodations are generally in independent inns that feature fewer services.
- ✔ Puerto Escondido is not a resort that caters to children. That aspect, combined with a concern about the powerful ocean surf, makes this destination not recommendable for family travelers.
- ✔ Challenging air access is the rule. It usually involves complicated connections through Mexico City and/or Oaxaca, which makes travel time lengthy.

Lazing in Los Cabos

What was once considered an offbeat outpost for only the most rugged of sportsmen and vagrants has somehow evolved into Mexico's most posh beach resort. Los Cabos, located on the Baja Peninsula just south of California, actually refers to three areas: the quaint town of **San Jose del Cabo,** the high-energy tourist enclave of **Cabo San Lucas,** and the 18-mile-long stretch of highway connecting the two, known as **the Corridor,** which is lined with luxury resorts.

Each town has its own distinct personality: San Jose is a gentrified version of a small Mexican town, and Cabo San Lucas is a party place that attracts the most visitors. Alternately known as "the end of the line" and "the last resort," Cabo San Lucas boasts a let-loose nightlife that frequently goes until breakfast the next morning. Cabo San Lucas, in particular, is so American-friendly that you may find you rarely get the chance to practice your Spanish, and dollars are accepted as readily as pesos. In fact, many visitors find that it feels more like an extension of Southern California than Mexico.

Although sport fishing originally took credit for putting Los Cabos on the map, golf is now the stronger attraction. The Corridor that connects the two "Cabos" has an impressive collection of championship golf courses interspersed at respectable distances among the gorgeous resorts dotting the coastline. Accommodations in the two bookend towns range from smaller inns to larger chain hotels.

The beaches are breathtaking — cobalt-blue ocean meeting terra-cotta desertscapes speckled with cacti. Surfing is challenging here, and the numerous inlets seem custom-made for sea kayaking. Favored land-bound activities beyond golf include ATV tours and horseback riding.

In terms of everything from taxis to dining out, Los Cabos is much more expensive than other Mexican beach resorts. One contributing factor is its remote location — other than the abundant seafood caught offshore, almost everything else needs to be trucked down the long peninsula to make it here. (The chapters in Part IX go into detail about Los Cabos.)

Top aspects of a vacation in Los Cabos include:

- The sheer beauty of the combination desert and seascapes
- Outstanding sporting opportunities, from the legendary sport fishing to premier golf, plus exceptional spas to take out the kinks
- No need to worry about speaking Spanish — an English language and U.S. currency-friendly destination

But also consider the following:

- It's indisputably Mexico's most expensive beach resort.
- If you plan on doing any exploring, you may need to consider renting a car because the distance from one "Cabo" to another is significant.
- You may feel more like you're in Southern California than Mexico; Los Cabos has become very Americanized.
- Despite the level of sophistication of the hotels (especially along the Corridor), the region's dining and nightlife options are lacking, and they're likely to appeal to a college-age crowd at best.

Mexico's Beach Resorts: The Score Card (3 points indicate the highest rating)

Points for:	Cancún	Cozumel	Riviera Maya	Puerto Vallarta	Ixtapa	Zihuatanejo	Acapulco	Huatulco	Puerto Escondido	Los Cabos
Luxury	3	1	1	2	3	2	2	2	1	3
Nightlife	3	1		3	1	1	3	1	2	3
Great Food	2	1	1	3	2	1	3	1	2	2
Beaches	3	3	3	1	1	2	2	3	1	2
Bargain Rates	1	2	2	3	1	3	2	1	3	1
Local Color	1	2	1	3	1	3	3	1	3	1
Mexican Culture	2	1	2	3	1	2	3	1	1	
Golf	1	1	1	3	1	1	1	1		3
Senior Appeal	2	1	1	3	1	1	1	1		3
Hiking	1	1	1	3	1	1	2	3	3	3
Natural Beauty	2	3	3	3	1	2	1	3	3	3
Sightseeing	3	1	3	2	1	1	3	3	2	3
Diving/Snorkeling	3	3	3	1	1	1	1	3	1	3
Watersports	3	2	2	3	3	3	2	3	3	3
Peace and Quiet	1	2	3	1	2	3	1	3	3	2
Family Friendly	3	1	3	3	3	2	3	2	2	3
Easy Access	3	1	1	3	2	2	2	1	1	3

Chapter 2

Deciding When to Go

exico's beach resorts enjoy sun-drenched and moderate winters, and they logically attract the most visitors when the weather at home is cold and dreary. However, almost any time of the year has its pros and cons for travel. In this chapter, I review what you can expect from the weather during different months of the year. I also highlight some of Mexico's most festive celebrations that you may want to plan your trip around.

Forecasting the Weather

Mexico has two main climatic seasons: a **rainy season** (May to mid-October) and a **dry season** (mid-October through April). The rainy season can be of little consequence in the dry, northern region of the country, but the southern regions typically receive tropical showers, which begin around 4 or 5 p.m. and last a few hours. Though these rains can come on suddenly and be quite strong, they usually end just as quickly as they began, and they cool the air for the evening. I personally favor the rainy season because that's when the landscape is at its most lush and tropical flowers are everywhere. The lightning flashes offshore also make for a spectacular show.

Hurricane season — June through October — particularly affects the Yucatán Peninsula and the southern Pacific coast.

June, July, and August are very hot and humid on the Yucatán Peninsula, with temperatures rising into the mid-80s (30° C) and 90s (33° C). Most of coastal Mexico experiences temperatures in the 80s in the hottest months. Very high summer temperatures are reserved for Mexico's northern states that border the United States. During winter months, temperatures average 70–75 (22°–25° C) during the days, and about 55–65 (12°–18° C) in the evenings, in most of the resorts covered. Los Cabos is often cooler (50° F/10° C) during winter months.

Looking at Travel Seasons

Mexico has two principal travel seasons: high and low. The **high season** begins around December 20 and continues to Easter, although in some places the high season can begin as early as mid-November. The **low season** begins the day after Easter and continues to mid-December; during the low season, prices may drop between 20% and 50%. At beach destinations popular with Mexican travelers, such as Acapulco, the prices revert back to high-season levels during July and August, the traditional, national summer vacation period. Prices in inland cities seldom fluctuate from high to low season, but they may rise dramatically during the weeks of **Easter** and **Christmas.** In Isla Mujeres and Playa del Carmen, both on the Yucatán Coast, the high season starts in mid-November as well, but also has a "second" high season, in August, when many European visitors arrive. All of these exceptions and others are mentioned in the relevant chapters that follow.

I find **November** to be the best month to travel to Mexico: The scenery is still green from the recently-ended rainy season, and temperatures are just beginning to turn a bit cooler, which can produce crystal-clear skies. Crowds are also at a minimum, and you're likely to find some good deals.

One time you may want to avoid is **spring break.** The highest concentration of high-octane party crowds is found in Cancun and Mazatlan, but Puerto Vallarta also gets its fair share of craziness. Frankly, why travel to see American youth behaving badly? Other times you may want to avoid are the weeks of Christmas and Easter. During these traditional Mexican holiday periods, both crowds and prices are at their highest, but the crowds consist more of families and couples than young and rowdy revelers.

Mexico's Calendar of Events

Mexicans are known for throwing a great party — *fiesta!* — and their love of fireworks is legendary. You may choose to plan your visit around a colorful national or religious celebration. Watersports enthusiasts may consider visiting during one of the numerous regattas and sport-fishing festivals held at many of the resorts. Remember that, during national holidays, Mexican banks and government offices — including immigration — are closed.

Christmas and Easter are celebrated similarly to the way they're celebrated in the United States, but Christmas is much more religiously oriented, and less emphasis is placed on Santa and the exchange of gifts.

January/February/March

Día de Reyes (Three Kings Day) commemorates the three kings bringing gifts to the Christ child. On this day, children receive gifts, much like
the traditional exchange of gifts that accompanies Christmas in the
United States. Friends and families gather to share the *Rosca de Reyes,* a
special cake. A small doll representing the Christ child is placed within
the cake; whoever receives the doll in his or her piece must host a
tamales-and-*atole* (meat or sweet filling wrapped in a corn husk and a
hot drink) party the next month. January 6.

Music, dances, processions, food, and other festivities are features of
Día de la Candelaria (Candlemass) and lead up to a blessing of seed
and candles in a celebration that mixes pre-Hispanic and European traditions marking the end of winter. All those who attended the three
kings celebration reunite to share *atole* and *tamales* at a party hosted
by the recipient of the doll found in the *rosca.* February 2.

Día de la Constitución (Constitution Day) is a celebration in honor of
the current Mexican constitution that was signed in 1917 as a result of
the Mexican Revolution of 1910. If you're in Mexico on this day, you'll
see a parade wherever you are. February 5.

Carnaval (Carnival) is the last celebration before Lent, and it's celebrated with special gusto in Cozumel and in Mazatlan, north of Puerto
Vallarta. Here, the celebration resembles New Orleans's Mardi Gras
with a festive atmosphere and parades. Transportation and hotels are
packed, so it's best to make reservations six months in advance and
arrive a couple of days before the beginning of celebrations. Three
days preceding Ash Wednesday and the beginning of Lent.

Benito Juárez was a reformist leader and president of Mexico who
became a national hero. The national holiday honoring **Benito Juárez's
Birthday** is the same date of the **spring equinox,** an important celebration of the ancient Mexicans. In Chichén-Itzá (chee-*chin* eat-*zah*), the
ancient Mayan city located 112 miles/179km from Cancun, the celebration of the first day of spring is particularly impressive. The Temple of
Kukulcan — Chichén-Itzá's main pyramid — aligns with the sun, and
the shadow of the body of it's plumed serpent moves slowly from the
top of the building downward. When the shadow reaches the bottom,
the body joins the carved-stone snake's head at the base of the pyramid. According to ancient legend, at the moment that the serpent is

whole, the earth is fertilized to assure a bountiful growing season. Visitors come from around the world to marvel at this sight, so advance arrangements are advisable. Elsewhere, festivals and celebrations to welcome spring mark the equinox. In the custom of the ancient Mexicans, dances are performed and prayers to the elements and the four cardinal points (north, south, east, west) are said in order to renew their energy for the upcoming year. It's customary to wear white with a red ribbon. March 21. (The serpent's shadow at Chichén-Itzá can be seen from March 19 to 23.)

April/May/June

Semana Santa (Holy Week) celebrates the last week in the life of Christ from Palm Sunday through Easter Sunday with somber religious processions, spoofs of Judas, and reenactments of specific biblical events, plus food and craft fairs. Businesses close during this traditional week of Mexican national vacations. If you plan on traveling to or around Mexico during Holy Week, make your reservations early. Airline seats on flights into and out of the country are reserved months in advance. Buses to almost anywhere in Mexico are always full, so try arriving on the Wednesday or Thursday prior to the start of Holy Week. Easter Sunday is quiet. The week following is a traditional vacation period. Week before Easter.

Labor Day is a national holiday celebrating workers. It features countrywide parades and fiestas. May 1.

Cinco de Mayo is a national holiday that celebrates the defeat of the French at the Battle of Puebla in 1862. May 5.

July/August/September

Mexico begins **Día de Independencia (Independence Day)** — the holiday that marks Mexico's independence from Spain — at 11 p.m. on September 15, with the president of Mexico's famous independence *grito* (shout) from the National Palace in Mexico City. The rest of the country watches the event on TV or participates in local celebrations, which mirror the festivities at the national level. September 16 is actually Independence Day and is celebrated with parades, picnics, and family reunions throughout the country. September 15 to 16.

During the **fall equinox,** Chichén-Itzá once again takes center stage as the same shadow play that occurs during the spring equinox repeats itself for the fall equinox. September 21 and 22.

October/November/December

What's commonly called the **Día de los Muertos** (Day of the Dead) is actually two days: All Saints Day, honoring saints and deceased children, and All Souls Day, honoring deceased adults. Relatives gather at cemeteries countrywide, carrying candles and food and often spend the night beside the graves of loved ones. Weeks before, bakers begin producing bread formed in the shape of mummies and round loaves decorated with bread "bones." Decorated sugar skulls emblazoned with glittery names are sold everywhere. Many days ahead, homes and churches erect special altars laden with bread, fruit, flowers, candles, photographs of saints and of the deceased, and favorite foods and photographs of the deceased. On these two nights, children walk through the streets dressed in costumes and masks, often carrying mock coffins and pumpkin lanterns, into which they expect money to be dropped. November 1 and 2.

Puerto Vallarta goes all out during **Fiestas del Mar** (SeaFest), a month-long calendar of activities that includes art festivals, sports competitions, the Governor's Cup golf tournament, and an outstanding gourmet-dining festival, which features guest chefs from around the world working with local chefs in select restaurants. Among the sporting events are sailing regattas, windsurfing exhibitions, and beach volleyball competitions. November 10 to 30.

Día de Revolución (Revolution Day) is a national holiday commemorating the start of the Mexican Revolution in 1910 with parades, speeches, rodeos, and patriotic events. November 20.

During the **Día de Nuestra Señora de Guadalupe (Feast of the Virgin of Guadalupe),** the patroness of Mexico is honored throughout the country with religious processions, street fairs, dancing, fireworks, and masses. It's one of Mexico's most moving and beautiful displays of traditional culture. In December 1531, the Virgin of Guadalupe appeared to a young man, Juan Diego, on a hill near Mexico City. He convinced the bishop that he had seen the apparition by revealing his cloak, upon which the Virgin was emblazoned. In Puerto Vallarta, the celebration begins on December 1 and extends through December 12, with traditional processions to the church for a brief mass and blessing. In the final days, the processions and festivities take place around the clock. There's a major fireworks exhibition on December 12 at 11 p.m. December 12.

Christmas Posadas celebrates the Holy Family's trek to Bethlehem. On each of the nine nights before Christmas, it's customary to reenact the Holy Family's search for an inn with door-to-door candlelit processions in cities and villages nationwide. December 15 to 24.

Chapter 3

Planning Your Budget

• •

In This Chapter

▶ Checking out hotel, transportation, and dining costs

▶ Finding out when and what to tip

▶ Considering taxes

▶ Figuring out those extra expenses: activities, attractions, and shopping

▶ Discovering budget-saving tips

• •

*T*he brochures are in front of you, and visions of lazy, sunny days fill your thoughts — so who wants to think about money? Trust me — take a few minutes to figure out your expected expenses now, so you can enjoy a worry-free vacation later.

Your budget is greatly affected by your choice of beach resort. A room in Los Cabos is considerably more expensive than one in Puerto Vallarta, and ditto for all the other expenses down the line. After you have your hotel and airfare down, it's a good idea to calculate the other estimated costs associated with your trip to plan a proper budget.

Using the worksheets at the back of this book to jot down anticipated costs can help you see whether you need to trim any of your expenses. Or even better, you may discover that you can afford to slip into that oceanfront room or plan that sunset sail you've been dreaming of.

To make certain that you don't forget any expenses, try taking a mental stroll through your entire trip. Start with the costs of transportation from your home to the airport, your airline tickets, and transfers to your hotel. Add your daily hotel rate (don't forget taxes!) meals, activities, entertainment, taxis, tips, your return to the airport, and finally, your return trip home from the airport and any parking fees you may have incurred. Just to be safe, add an extra 15% to 20% for extra, unexpected costs that may pop up.

Calculating Your Hotel Cost

The biggest part of your vacation budget will go towards your hotel and airfare, so I suggest getting those expenses down as low as possible. In the various destination chapters, I use dollar signs ($–$$$$$) to indicate the price category of each hotel. (Check out the Introduction for a rundown on the price categories and their corresponding dollar signs.) You can get a room for $30 a night, or you can get a room for $700 a night! Keep in mind that some room rates include breakfast — or all meals, beverages, and entertainment — so be sure to compare mangos with mangos. Also, when finalizing your reservations, be sure to check if the total cost includes taxes and tips. Even within a resort, the price of rooms can vary widely. Room location — oceanfront versus a view of a dumpster — is one differential. Ask yourself how much your room location matters. Do you view your room as simply a place to sleep, shower, and dress? Or will you not feel officially "on vacation" unless you can fall asleep to the sound of the surf? If so, a pricier room may well be worth it. However, remember that many "garden view" rooms in my recommendations are only steps away from the beach and possibly even more tranquil than their oceanfront counterparts.

When it comes to rates, the most common term is **rack rate.** The rack rate is the maximum rate that a resort or hotel charges for a room. It's the rate you get if you walk in off the street and ask for a room on a night that the place is close to being full.

The rack rate is the first rate a hotel offers, but you usually don't have to pay it. Always ask if a lower rate or special package is available — it can't hurt, and you may at least end up with a free breakfast or spa service.

In this book, I use rack rates as a guidepost, not expecting that you'll have to pay them. Minimum night stays, special promotions, and seasonal discounts can all go a long way in bringing the rack rate down. Also, be sure to mention your frequent-flier or corporate-rewards programs if you book with one of the larger hotel chains. Please note that rates change very often, so the prices quoted in this book may be different from the prices you're quoted when you make your reservation.

Room rates also rise and fall with occupancy rates. If your choice of hotels is close to empty, it pays to negotiate. Resorts tend to be much more crowded during weekends.

Feeling romantic? Special packages for **honeymooners** are really popular in Mexican beach resorts. Even if you've been hitched for a while, it could be a second honeymoon, right? If you ask, you may end up with a complimentary bottle of champagne and flower petals on your bed.

Mexico couldn't be more accommodating to travelers with children. Many of the larger chains don't charge extra for children staying in the same room as their parents, and some offer special meal programs and other amenities for younger travelers. While rollaway beds are common, you may have a challenge finding a crib. Ask about this contingency when making your reservation.

Totaling Transportation Costs

After taking care of your airfare (for tips on lowering airfares see Chapter 5), your transportation costs vary depending upon your choice of Mexican beach resorts. While some resort areas — like Cancún — offer economical shuttles and great public transportation options, others — like Los Cabos — have such expensive local transportation that getting around may cost even more than getting there.

One advantage of a **package** tour (when you make one payment that covers airfare, hotel, round-trip transportation to and from your accommodations, and occasionally meals or tours) is that the round-trip ground transportation between the airport and your hotel is usually included. If you're not certain if your package covers ground transportation, ask. Note that the taxi union inside Mexico is strong, so you're unlikely to find any shuttle transportation provided by your hotel.

 Generally, it doesn't make sense to rent a car, with the noted exceptions being in Los Cabos and possibly Cozumel, if you're looking to explore the far side of the island there. Renting a small car runs about $70 a day on average, including insurance, so you may want to squeeze your car-dependent explorations into a day or two at the most. It's also wise to plan your rental-car excursions to coincide with your arrival or departure so you can use your wheels for either leg of your airport-hotel transportation needs.

As a rule, taxis tend to be the most economical and efficient transportation for getting around the other beach destinations, such as Puerto Vallarta, Cancún, Acapulco, and Huatulco. In each of the chapters detailing these resorts, I provide taxi rates for getting around town.

Estimating Dining Dollars

In each resort's dining section, Parts III through IX, I describe my favorite restaurants, all of which include dollar signs ($–$$$$$) to give you an idea of the prices you can expect to pay. Refer to the Introduction of this book for a detailed explanation of these price categories.

The prices quoted refer to main courses at dinner, unless otherwise specified. I eliminated the most expensive shrimp and lobster dishes from my estimates to avoid pre-trip sticker shock. In most cases, you can find additional entrees above and below my quoted price range. To estimate your total dining expenses, add in estimated costs for beverages, appetizers, desserts, and tips as well.

Hotels increasingly are offering dining plans. To help you wade through the terminology, here's a review of the basics:

- **Continental plan (CP):** Includes a light breakfast — usually juices, fruits, pastries or breads, and coffee.

- **Breakfast plan (BP):** Includes a full, traditional American-style breakfast of eggs, bacon, French toast, hash browns, and so forth.

- **Modified American plan (MAP):** Includes breakfast (usually a full one) and dinner.

- **Full American plan (FAP):** Includes three meals a day.

- **All-inclusive:** Includes three all-you-can-eat meals a day, plus snacks, soft drinks, and alcoholic beverages. Sometimes, additional charges apply for premium liquors or wines.

- **European Plan (EP):** No meals are included.

Mexican beach-resort hotels are known for their expansive breakfast buffets. But the buffets can also be expensive, averaging about $20, even for small children. If breakfast is your main meal or only meal of the day, these all-you-can-eat extravaganzas may be worthwhile; otherwise, you're probably better off sleeping in or finding breakfast elsewhere.

Note that the highest dining-out prices are found in Los Cabos. Because almost all ingredients need to be transported from the mainland, the costs are much higher.

Be sure to explore restaurants away from your hotel. You're likely to get a much better dining value, and you can truly savor the diverse flavors of Mexico. For eateries that best represent the flavorful (and I don't mean spicy) cuisine of Mexico, look for the Viva Mexico icon that accompanies some of the restaurant reviews throughout this book.

While you're in Mexico, be sure to try the local beers. Corona is the best-known brew, but other excellent choices are Bohemia, Modelo Especial, Pacifico, Indio, and Dos Equis Negro. Beer in Mexico is often cheaper than soft drinks! Your vacation is looking better and better, isn't it?

Tipping Tips

Many travelers skimp on tips in Mexico, but please don't. Most of the employees in this country's hospitality industry receive the majority of their income from tips. For bellmen or porters, the equivalent of $1 per bag is appropriate. For hotel housekeeping, tip between $1 and $2 per night, depending upon the type of hotel you're staying in. For restaurant service, 15% is standard, but consider 20% if the service is particularly noteworthy. Oddly enough, the one area you don't need to consider is tips for taxis — it's not customary to tip taxi drivers here unless they help with baggage or you've hired them on an hourly basis and they double as a tour guide.

You'll no doubt run into all sorts of enterprising young boys looking for a tip to point you in the direction of your restaurant, help you into a parking spot, or do some other sort of unnecessary favor. In cases like these, tip as you see fit, or as the spirit moves you.

Spending Wisely on Activities, Attractions, and Shopping

You're going to a beach resort, so regardless of your budget, you always have the option of simply soaking up the tropical sun during the day and then taking in the moonlit nights. It's the most economical plan and a relaxing and enjoyable option for many. Still, with so much to do and see, you're likely to want to spend some time and money getting out and enjoying the many treasures of Mexico.

Pricing for **sightseeing tours** varies by the destination, the length of time of the excursion, whether or not a meal and beverages are included, and other extras. However, there are some pretty typical ranges you can use as a guideline. A city tour generally runs from $12 to $20; half-day boat cruises that include lunch can cost between $40 and $60; and full-day excursions to neighboring areas run between $60 and $150.

If you plan to take part in any **sports-related activities** like golf, diving, or sport fishing, you may find the prices to be higher than back home, but you're also apt to find a bargain relative to the other beach-resort venues. For example, greens fees at the Acapulco Princess Golf Club are $63, but the fees at Cabo del Sol in Los Cabos are over $200 for 18 holes. Dives range from around $50 to $70 for a two-tank dive, but here, you tend to really get what you pay for in terms of quality of equipment and dive guides, so it's best to pay up. Cozumel has the greatest selection of expert dive shops, and the competition makes Cozumel's prices the most reasonable for the quality of experience. Going fishing? There are variables beyond your point of departure, including size of boat, charter options, and type of gear and refreshments, but count on between $50 and $75 per person for a half-day charter.

As for **nightlife,** the cost depends more on your personal tastes. The "hot" nightlife areas, such as Acapulco and Cancún, are pricier than others, and $20 cover charges are common during busier times. Puerto

Vallarta and Los Cabos have more casual and less expensive, but just as lively, nightlife options. You're not bound to spend too much cash in Ixtapa, Cozumel, or Huatulco, either, simply because there's not much to do after dark in these locations. When you're out on the town, beer is the best bargain and costs about $1 to $3 per beer. National-branded drinks can run you around $3 to $5 each. Ladies can easily find bargains like "two-for-one" or "all-you-can-drink" specials.

Shopping is your call — you can plan to spend or save here. Besides silver jewelry and other souvenirs, the best excuse for shopping in Mexico are the great prices on duty-free perfumes, watches, and other goods in Cancún and along the Riviera Maya. Other destinations have less to offer in the duty-free area, but each resort's shopping specialties are discussed in greater detail within their respective chapters, in Parts III through IX.

Taxing Issues

There's a 15% **value-added tax (IVA)** on goods and services in most of Mexico, and it's supposed to be included in the posted price. This tax is 10% in Cancún, Cozumel, and Los Cabos. Unlike other countries (Canada and Spain, for example) Mexico does not refund this tax when visitors leave the country, so you don't need to hang on to those receipts for tax purposes.

All published prices you encounter in your travels around Mexico's beaches are likely to include all applicable taxes, except for hotel rates, which are usually published without the 15% IVA and the 2% lodging tax.

An **exit tax** of approximately $18 is imposed on every foreigner leaving Mexico. This tax is usually — but not always — included in the price of airline tickets. Be sure to reserve at least this amount in cash for your departure day if you're not certain that it's included in your ticket price.

Cutting Costs

While planning your trip, there are certain things to keep in mind that may help you save some money. Before you leave for vacation, don't forget to consider the incidentals that can really add up — hotel taxes, tips, and telephone surcharges.

Here are a few other suggestions to help keep a lid on expenses so they don't run amuck and blow your vacation budget:

- ✔ **Travel in the off-season.** If you can travel at non-peak times (September through November, for example) you can usually find better hotel bargains.

✔ **Travel on off days of the week.** If you can travel on a Tuesday, Wednesday, or Thursday, you may find cheaper flights to your destination. When you inquire about airfares, ask if it's cheaper to fly on a different day.

✔ **Try a package tour.** With one call to a travel agent or packager you can book airfare, hotel, ground transportation, and even some sightseeing for many of these destinations for a lot less than if you tried to put the trip together yourself. (See Chapter 5 for specific suggestions of package tour companies to contact.)

✔ **Always ask for discount rates.** Membership in AAA, frequent-flyer plans, AARP, or other groups may qualify you for a discount on plane tickets and hotel rooms if you book them in the United States. In Mexico, you can generally get a discount based on how full the hotel is at the time you show up; however, you're also taking a chance on a vacancy not being available.

✔ **Get a room off the beach.** Accommodations within walking distance of the shore can be much cheaper than those right on the beach. Beaches in Mexico are public, so you don't need to stay in a hotel that's on the sand to spend most of your vacation at the beach.

✔ **Share your room with your kids.** In Mexico, this setup is usually the norm rather than the exception, so book a room with two double beds. Most hotels won't charge extra for up to two children staying in their parent's room.

✔ **Use public transportation whenever practical.** Not only will you save taxi fare, but simply getting to where you're going can be like a mini-excursion as you enjoy the local scene! In Cancún, you're apt to run into mostly tourists on the clean, public buses of the hotel zone. In Puerto Vallarta, you may be serenaded along the bus route — it's part of the charm!

✔ **Cut down on the souvenirs.** It's too much to expect you to return home without any local treasures, but think hard about whether that oversized sombrero will be as charming back home. Your photographs and memories are likely to be your best momentos.

✔ **Use public phones and pre-paid phone cards to call home.** Avoid using the phone in your hotel room to call outside the hotel. Charges can be astronomical, even for local calls. Rather than placing the call yourself, it's better to ask the concierge to make a reservation for you — they do it as a service. You'll even be charged a surcharge for using your own calling card and its 800 number. Remember: Most 800 numbers are not toll-free when dialed from Mexico. Also avoid using the public phones that urge you, in English, to call home using their 800 number. This is the absolute most expensive way to call home, and the sevice charges the call to your home phone. The best option? Buy a Ladatel (brand name for Mexico's public phones) phone card, available at most pharmacies, and dial direct using the instructions in Appendix A of this book.

✔ **Steer clear of the minibar and room service.** Those little bottles can really add up! Consider buying your own supplies and bringing them to your room, and you'll save a bundle. Likewise, room service is the most expensive way to dine — a service charge and tip are added on top of generally inflated prices. Also, some hotels provide complimentary bottled water, but others can charge as much as $5 per bottle, so be sure you know what you're drinking.

✔ **Drink local.** Imported labels can be twice the price as the locally popular brands, which often are also imported but just different brands than the ones you may be accustomed to seeing. At least ask what's being served as the house brand — you may be pleasantly surprised.

✔ **Follow Mexican custom and have lunch as your main meal.** If the restaurant of your dreams is open only for dinner, save that one for your one "splurge" evening and try out the others for your midday meal. Lunch tabs are usually a fraction of their dinner counterparts, and they frequently feature many of the same specialties.

✔ **Skimp on shrimp and lobster.** Sure, I know — you're sitting seaside and dreaming of that tasty lobster. Just understand that they're the priciest items on the menu and the less expensive, local, fresh fish is often just as good or better.

✔ **Buy Mexican bottled water.** Forget the water labels that you know — Mexico's bottled waters are just as good as the imports and about half the price.

Chapter 4

Tips for Travelers with Special Interests

In This Chapter

▶ Bringing the kids along

▶ Traveling tips for folks with special needs

▶ Getting hitched in Mexico

*W*e all consider ourselves unique and as having special needs, but some types of travelers really do warrant a little extra advice. In this chapter, I cover information that's helpful to know if you're traveling with children. If you're a senior traveler or you're traveling solo, there are plenty of tips for you too. Individuals with disabilities can also mine this chapter for useful info. Gay and lesbian travelers can find a section devoted to them as well. And for those of you planning a wedding, I include a section on tying the knot in Mexico. Throughout the chapter, I clue you in on what to expect, offer some useful tips, and whenever possible, steer you to experts concerning your particular circumstances.

Vacationing with Children

Children are considered the national treasure of Mexico, and Mexicans warmly welcome and cater to your children. Although many parents were reluctant to bring young children to Mexico in the past, primarily due to health concerns, I can't think of a better place to introduce children to the exciting adventure of exploring a different culture. Some of the best destinations for children include Puerto Vallarta, Cancún, and Acapulco. Hotels can often arrange for a babysitter. Some hotels in the moderate-to-luxury range have small playgrounds and pools for children and hire caretakers who offer special-activity programs during the day, but few budget hotels offer these amenities. All-inclusive resorts make great options for family travel because, as a rule, they offer exhaustive activities programs. They also make mealtime easy by offering buffet-style meal services almost around the clock.

Before leaving for your trip, check with your pediatrician or family doctor to get advice on medications to take along. Disposable diapers cost about the same in Mexico as they do in the United States, but the quality is poorer. You can get brand-name diapers identical to the ones sold in the United States, but you'll pay a higher price. Familiar, brand-name baby foods are sold in many stores. Dry cereals, powdered formulas, baby bottles, and purified water are all easily available in midsize and large cities or resorts.

Cribs, however, may present a problem; only the largest and most luxurious hotels provide them. However, rollaway beds to accommodate children staying in a room with their parents are often available. Child seats or high chairs at restaurants are common, and most restaurants go out of their way to accommodate the comfort of your children. You may want to consider bringing your own car seat along because they're not readily available to rent in Mexico.

I recommend you take coloring books, puzzles, and small games with you to keep your children entertained during the flight or whenever you're traveling from one destination to the next. Another good idea is to take a blank notebook, in which your children can paste little souvenirs from the trip like the label from the beer Daddy drank on the beach or small shells and flowers that they collect. And don't forget to carry small scissors and a glue stick with you, or the blank notebook may remain blank.

The following is a list of Web sites where you can find helpful advice on traveling with children:

- **Family Travel Network** (www.familytravelnetwork.com) offers travel tips and reviews of family-friendly destinations, vacation deals, and thoughtful features such as "What to Do When Your Kids Are Afraid to Travel" and "Kid-Style Camping."

- **Travel with Your Kids** (www.travelwithyourkids.com) is a comprehensive site offering sound advice for traveling with children.

- **The Busy Person's Guide to Traveling with Children** (http://wz.com/travel/TravelingWithChildren.html) offers a "45-second newsletter" where experts weigh in on the best Web sites and resources for tips on traveling with children.

Seeking Specials for Seniors

People over the age of 60 are traveling more than ever before. And why not? Being a senior citizen entitles you to some terrific travel bargains. If you're not a member of **AARP** (601 E St. NW, Washington, DC 20049; ☎ **800-424-3410** or 202-434-AARP; Internet: www.aarp.org), formerly the American Association of Retired Persons, do yourself a favor and join. AARP offers members a wide range of benefits, including *Modern Maturity* magazine and a monthly newsletter. Anyone over 50 can join.

Mature Outlook (P.O. Box 9390, Des Moines, IA 50322; ☎ **800-336-6330**) is a similar organization, offering discounts on car rentals and hotel stays. The $19.95 annual membership fee also gets you $200 in Sears coupons and a bi-monthly magazine. Membership is open to all Sears customers 18 and over, but the organization's primary focus is on the 50-and-over market.

In addition, most of the major domestic airlines, including American Airlines, United, Continental Airlines, US Airways, and TWA all offer discount programs for senior travelers — be sure to ask whenever you book a flight. *The Mature Traveler,* a monthly newsletter on senior citizen travel, is a valuable resource. It's available by subscription ($30 a year). For a free sample, send a postcard with your name and address to GEM Publishing Group, P.O. Box 50400, Reno, NV 89513, or you can e-mail the folks at *The Mature Traveler* at maturetrav@aol.com. Another helpful publication is *101 Tips for the Mature Traveler,* available from **Grand Circle Travel** (347 Congress St., Suite 3A, Boston, MA 02210; ☎ **800-221-2610;** Internet; www.gct.com)

Grand Circle Travel is also one of the hundreds of travel agencies that specialize in vacations for seniors. But beware: Many agencies are of the tour-bus variety, with free trips thrown in for those who organize groups of 20 or more. Seniors seeking more independent travel should probably consult a regular travel agent. **SAGA International Holidays** (222 Berkeley St., Boston, MA 02116; ☎ **800-343-0273**) offers inclusive tours and cruises for those 50 and older.

Mexico is a popular country for retirees and for senior travelers. For decades, North Americans have been living indefinitely in Mexico by returning to the border and re-crossing with a new tourist permit every 6 months. Mexican immigration officials have caught on, and they now limit the maximum time you can spend in the country to six months in any given year. This measure is meant to encourage even partial residents to comply with the proper documentation procedures.

AIM (Apdo. Postal 31–70, 45050 Guadalajara, Jalisco, Mexico) is a well-written, candid, and very informative newsletter for prospective retirees. Recent issues evaluated retirement in Puerto Vallarta, Puerto Ángel, Puerto Escondido, and Huatulco. Subscriptions are $18 to the United States and $21 to Canada. Back issues are three for $5.

Sanborn Tours (2015 South 10th St., Post Office Drawer 519, McAllen, TX 78505-0519; ☎ **800-395-8482**) offers a "Retire in Mexico" orientation tour.

Puerto Vallarta resident and author Polly Vicars's *Tales of Retirement in Paradise* offers an entertaining account of the pleasures of "retired" life in this seaside town — a very popular beach resort with senior travelers. All proceeds from the book go to the America-Mexico Foundation (Internet: www.puerto-vallarta.com/amf), which provides scholarships to needy and deserving Mexican students. You can buy the $20 book online through Amazon.com (www.amazon.com) or purchase it directly from the author via e-mail at phvicars@pvnet.com.mx. The book is also available for sale in Puerto Vallarta at bookstores and various shops.

Ensuring Access for Travelers with Disabilities

A disability needn't stop anybody from traveling. There are more options and resources out there than ever before. *A World of Options,* a 658-page book of resources for travelers with disabilities, covers everything from biking trips to scuba outfitters. It costs $35 and is available from **Mobility International USA** (P.O. Box 10767, Eugene, OR 97440; ☎ 541-343-1284 voice and TTY; Internet: www.miusa.org). Another source to check out is **Access-Able Travel Source** (Internet: www.access-able.com), a comprehensive database of travel agents who specialize in disabled travel; it's also a clearinghouse for information about accessible destinations around the world.

However, I need to honestly say that Mexico does fall far behind other countries when it comes to accessible travel. In fact, it may seem like one giant obstacle course to travelers in wheelchairs or on crutches. At airports, you may encounter steep stairs before finding a well-hidden elevator or escalator — if one exists. Airlines often arrange wheelchair assistance for passengers to the baggage area. Porters are generally available to help with luggage at airports and large bus stations after you clear baggage claim.

In addition, escalators (and there aren't many in the beach resorts) are often non-operational. Stairs without handrails abound. Few restrooms are equipped for travelers with disabilities, and when one is available, access to it may be via a narrow passage that won't accommodate a wheelchair or a person on crutches. Many deluxe hotels (the most expensive) now have rooms with baths for people with disabilities. Budget travelers may be best off looking for single-story motels, although accessing showers and bathrooms may still pose a problem outside of specially equipped deluxe hotels. Generally speaking, no matter where you are, someone will lend a hand, although you may have to ask for it.

Few airports offer the luxury of boarding an airplane from the waiting room. You either descend stairs to a bus that ferries you to a waiting plane that you board by climbing stairs, or you walk across the airport tarmac to your plane and climb up the stairs. Deplaning presents the same problems in reverse.

In my opinion, the wide, modern streets and sidewalks of Cancún make it the most "accessible" resort. In addition to the superior public facilities, you can find numerous accommodation options for travelers with disabilities.

Travelers with disabilities may also want to consider joining a tour that caters specifically to them. One of the best operators is **Flying Wheels Travel** (P.O. Box 382, Owatonna, MN 55060; ☎ 800-535-6790; Internet: www.flyingwheelstravel.com). They offer various escorted tours and cruises, as well as private tours in minivans with lifts. Another good company is **FEDCAP Rehabilitation Services** (211 W. 14th St., New York, NY 10011). Call ☎ 212-727-4200 or Fax 212-727-4373 for information about membership and summer tours.

Accessible Journeys (☎ 800-TINGLES or 610-521-0339; Internet: www.disabilitytravel.com) caters specifically to slow walkers and wheelchair travelers and their families and friends. **Access Adventures** (☎ 716-889-9096), a Rochester, New York-based agency, offers customized itineraries for a variety of travelers with disabilities. **The Moss Rehab Hospital** (☎ 215-456-9603; Internet: www.mossresourcenet.org) provides friendly, helpful phone assistance through its **Travel Information Service. The Society for Accessible Travel and Hospitality** (☎ 212-447-7284; Fax: 212-725-8253; Internet: www.sath.org) offers a wealth of travel resources for people with all types of disabilities and informed recommendations on destinations, access guides, travel agents, tour operators, vehicle rentals, and companion services. Annual membership costs $45 for adults; $30 for seniors and students.

Vision-impaired travelers should contact the **American Foundation for the Blind** (11 Penn Plaza, Suite 300, New York, NY 10001; ☎ 800-232-5463; Internet: www.afb.org) for information on traveling with seeing-eye dogs.

Gathering Advice for Gays and Lesbians

Mexico is a conservative country with deeply-rooted Catholic religious traditions. Public displays of same-sex affection are rare, and it's still considered shocking for two men to display such behavior, especially outside the major resort areas. Women in Mexico frequently walk hand in hand, but anything more would cross the boundary of acceptability. However, gay and lesbian travelers are generally treated with respect and shouldn't experience any harassment, assuming the appropriate regard is given to local culture and customs. Puerto Vallarta, with its selection of accommodations and entertainment oriented especially toward gay and lesbian travelers, is perhaps the most welcoming and accepting destination in Mexico. **Vicki Skinner's Doin' it Right in Puerto Vallarta** is a special travel service that rents gay-friendly condos and villas for individuals and groups. She also has a newsletter that offers travel specials, tips, and information about special events and activities. To subscribe, write to 1010 University Ave., #C113-741, San Diego, CA 92103 or call ☎ **800-936-3646** or 619-297-3642. You can also subscribe to the newsletter by e-mail at info@doinitright.com.

The International Gay & Lesbian Travel Association (IGLTA) (☎ **800-448-8550** or 954-776-2626; Fax: 954-776-3303; Internet: www.iglta.org) can provide helpful information and additional tips. The **Travel Alternatives Group (TAG)** maintains a database and a gay-friendly accommodations guide. For details, call ☎ **415-437-3800** or e-mail the group at info@mark8ing.com. **Arco Iris** is a gay-owned, full-service travel agency and tour operator specializing in Mexico packages and special group travel. Contact the agency by phone (☎ **800-765-4370** or 619-297-0897; Fax: 619-297-6419) or through their Web site at www.arcoiristours.com. **Now, Voyager** (☎ **800-255-6951**; Internet: www.nowvoyager.com) is a San Francisco-based, gay-owned and operated travel service. **Olivia Cruises & Resorts** (☎ **800-631-6277** or 510-655-0364; Internet: http://oliviatravel.com) charters entire resorts and ships for exclusive lesbian vacations all over the world.

Traveling Solo

Mexico is a great place to travel on your own without really being or feeling alone. Although identical room rates for single and double occupancy are slowly becoming a trend in Mexico, many of the hotels mentioned in this book still offer singles at lower rates.

Mexicans are very friendly, and it's easy to meet other foreigners. But if you don't like the idea of traveling alone, try **Travel Companion Exchange (TCE)** (P.O. Box 833, Amityville, NY 11701; ☎ **800-392-1256** or 631-454-0880; Fax: 631-454-0170; Internet: www.whytravelalone.com), which brings prospective travelers together. Members complete a profile and then place an anonymous listing of their travel interests in the newsletter. Prospective traveling companions then make contact through the exchange. Membership costs $99 for 6 months or $159 for a year. TCE also offers an excellent booklet, for $3.95, on avoiding theft and scams while traveling abroad.

As a female traveling alone, I can tell you firsthand that I generally feel safer traveling in Mexico than in the United States. But I use the same common-sense precautions I use when traveling anywhere else in the world, and I stay alert to what's going on around me.

Mexicans, in general, and men, in particular, are nosy about single travelers, especially women. If taxi drivers or anyone else with whom you don't want to become friendly ask about your marital status, family, and so on, my advice is to make up a set of answers (regardless of the truth): "I'm married, traveling with friends, and I have three children."

Saying you're single and traveling alone may send out the wrong message about availability. Face it — whether you like it or not, Mexico is still a macho country with the double standards that a macho attitude implies. Movies and television shows exported from the United States have created an image of sexually aggressive North American women. If someone bothers you, don't try to be polite — just leave or head into a public place.

You may even consider wearing a ring that resembles a wedding band. Most Mexican men stay away at the sight of a ring, and it also deters many uncomfortable questions.

Planning a Wedding in Mexico

Mexico's beaches may be old favorites for romantic honeymoons, but have you ever considered taking the plunge in Mexico? A destination wedding saves money and can be less hassle compared with marrying back home. Many hotels and attractions offer wedding packages, which can include everything from booking the officiant to hiring the videographer. Pick the plan you want and, presto, your wedding decisions are done! Several properties also provide the services of a wedding coordinator (either for free or at a reasonable cost) who not only scouts out sweetheart pink roses but can also handle marriage licenses and other formalities. A destination wedding can be as informal or as traditional as you like. After returning from their honeymoon, many couples hold a reception for people who couldn't join them. At these parties, couples sometimes continue the theme of their wedding locale (decorate with piñatas or hire a mariachi band, for example) and show a video of their ceremony so that everyone can share in their happiness.

If you invite guests to your destination wedding, find out about group rates for hotels and airfare, which can save 20 percent or more off regular prices. Plan as far ahead as possible so that people can arrange their schedules and join you.

Under a treaty between the United States and Mexico, Mexican civil marriages are automatically valid in the U.S. You need certified copies of birth certificates, driver's licenses, or passports; certified proof of divorce or the death certificate of any former spouses (if applicable); tourist cards (provided when you enter Mexico); and results of blood tests performed in Mexico within 15 days before the ceremony.

Check with a local, on-site wedding planner through your hotel to verify all the necessary requirements and obtain an application well in advance of your desired wedding date. Contact the **Mexican Tourism Board** (☎ **800-446-3942;** Internet: www.visitmexico.com) for information. For some honeymoon advice, turn to Chapter 35.

For more information, see *Honeymoon Vacations For Dummies* (Wiley Publishing, Inc.).

Part II
Ironing Out the Details

In this part . . .

Ready to travel to Mexico? Well then, it's probably time to do a little planning. In the next three chapters, I help you with all the things you need to consider when booking your ideal trip to one of Mexico's beach destinations. I help you decide whether to use a travel agent or take care of the arrangements on your own. I cover the pros and cons of package deals. I point you in the direction of the best places to find the information you need to accurately plan and budget your trip. Finally, I cover all the details — from getting your passport to packing your bags — you need to enjoy a hassle-free vacation.

Chapter 5

Making Your Travel Arrangements

● ●

In This Chapter

▶ Planning your own trip

▶ Knowing what to expect from a travel agent

▶ Understanding package tours

▶ Taking a look at airlines and airfares

▶ Finding the best room for your needs

▶ Booking on a Web site

● ●

Mexico is known for its simplicity of life and easy-going ways, so why should getting there be any more complicated? Whether you're a do-it-yourselfer or a person who prefers to let someone else take care of all the details, reading this chapter can save you time, money, and confusion. I point you in the direction of travel agents — and Internet tools — and explain the benefits and limitations of traveling on a package tour. I offer tips on getting the best airfares and choosing the best airline to whisk you away to your dreamy Mexican beach.

Using a Travel Agent versus Planning on Your Own

Deciding whether to use the services of a travel agent or do your own planning comes down to basically one component: time. If you don't have a lot of time, seeking a travel agent may be the way to go. If you've got some time to spare, you may enjoy planning your own trip. Either way, both options have their benefits.

Going with a travel agent

The best way to find a good travel agent is the same way you find a good plumber, mechanic, or doctor — through word of mouth. The similarities don't end there. Travel agents can be as valuable as these other pros in your life, especially if you're a frequent traveler.

In fact, today, one of the main benefits of using a travel agent is that he or she can save you time. If a travel agent specializes in Mexico, it's even better. They're likely to have personal insights or to be able to tell you things about a destination or hotel that simply can't come through in a brochure.

Any travel agent can help you find a bargain airfare, hotel, or rental car. A good travel agent will stop you from ruining your vacation by trying too hard to save a few dollars at the expense of a good experience. The best travel agents can tell you how much time you should budget for a destination, find a cheap flight that doesn't require you to change planes multiple times, get you a better hotel room for about the same price, arrange for a competitively priced rental car, and even give recommendations on restaurants.

Using a travel agent is the right choice if:

- ✔ You're not too Internet savvy.
- ✔ You prefer discussing things with a live person.
- ✔ You may need to make changes in your itinerary.
- ✔ You're traveling with a group, coming together from several parts of the country.
- ✔ You're departing from one city, but returning to a different city.

Opting to plan on your own

The Internet has given us mere mortals many of the same tools that used to be the exclusive domain of travel agents. Now it's possible to find as good a deal — or perhaps an even better deal — on travel as an agent can usually find. The key to this self-guided, money-saving process? You must be willing to invest the time and patience it takes to uncover the best deals.

Don't underestimate the value of a first-hand recommendation from a friend or coworker. Talk to whoever you know that has been to the place you're thinking of visiting for a fresh assessment and a first-hand opinion. Then, after taking all of your "research" into consideration, make your own decisions and plans based on your own experiences and preferences.

Getting the Most from Your Travel Agent

To get the most out of your travel agent, do a little homework. Read up on your destination (you've already made a sound decision by buying this book) and pick out some accommodations and attractions you think you may like. If necessary, get a more comprehensive — yet compact — travel guide like *Frommer's Portable Cancún; Los Cabos & Baja; Puerto Vallarta, Manzanillo & Guadalajara;* or *Acapulco, Ixtapa & Zihuatanejo* (Hungry Minds, Inc.), after you narrow down the choice of your destination.

If you have access to the Internet, check prices on the Web before meeting with an agent to get a sense of ballpark prices (see the "Finding the Best Airline and Airfare" section later in this chapter). Then take your guidebook and Web information to the travel agent and ask him or her to make the arrangements for you. Because travel agents have access to more resources than even the most complete Web travel site, they may be able to get you a better price than you could get by yourself. And they can issue your tickets and vouchers right there at the office. If they can't get you into the hotel of your choice, they can recommend an alternative, and you can look for an objective review in the guidebook that you conveniently brought with you.

Try to find a travel agent who recently has been to the beach resort in Mexico that interests you. Even if the agent has traveled there, be aware that it's likely he or she stayed at only one or two hotels, probably one of the larger hotels that may have provided the agent with a complimentary room.

Before you call or meet with your travel agent, it's probably best if you have one or two places in mind to compare. *Mexico's Beach Resorts For Dummies* should be a useful tool in narrowing down your choices. I've done the preliminary research to help you choose a place that has the features you're most interested in, and I've weeded out the mediocre hotels and restaurants from my selections to give you a head start. Jot down your preferences and maybe check the Web for some ideas of seasonal promotions and prices so that you have a ballpark idea of what to expect.

Keep in mind, travel agents work on commission. The good news is that *you* don't pay the commission; the airlines, accommodations, and tour companies do. The bad news is that unprincipled travel agents often try to persuade you to book the vacations that provide them with the most money in commissions. Over the past few years, some airlines and resorts have begun to limit or eliminate travel-agent commissions altogether. The immediate result has been that travel agents don't even bother booking certain services unless the customer specifically requests them. And some travel agents have started charging customers for their services. Don't be too put off by this — if you're working with a pro with real, hands-on knowledge of your resort, it could be well worth the extra fee to truly enjoy your vacation.

Deciding If an Escorted Tour or a Package Tour is Right For You

First, bear in mind that there's a big difference between an escorted tour and a package tour. With an escorted tour, the tour company takes care of all the details and tells you what to expect at each attraction. You know your costs up front, and an escorted tour can take you to the maximum number of sights in the minimum amount of time with the least amount of hassle. Package tours generally consist of round-trip airfare, ground transportation to and from your hotel, and your hotel room price, including taxes. Some packages also include all food and beverages and most entertainment and sports, when booked at an all-inclusive resort. You may find that a package tour can save you big bucks and is an ideal vacation option.

Evaluating escorted tours

When choosing an escorted tour, ask a few simple questions before you buy:

- **What is the cancellation policy?** Do you have to put a deposit down? Can they cancel the trip if they don't get enough people? How late can you cancel if you're unable to go? When do you pay? Do you get a refund if you cancel? If *they* cancel?

- **How jam-packed is the schedule?** Do they try to fit 25 hours into a 24-hour day, or will you have ample time to relax by the pool or shop? If getting up at 7 a.m. every day and not returning to your hotel until 6 or 7 p.m. at night sounds like a grind, certain escorted tours may not be for you.

- **How big is the group?** The smaller the group, the less time you spend waiting for people to get on and off the bus. Tour operators may be evasive about this because they may not know the exact size of the group until everybody has made their reservations. But they should be able to give you a rough estimate. Some tours have a minimum group size and may cancel the tour if they don't book enough people.

✔ **What exactly is included?** Don't assume anything. You may have to pay to get yourself to and from the airport. A box lunch may be included in an excursion but drinks might cost extra. Beer might be included but not wine. How much flexibility do you have? Can you opt out of certain activities, or does the bus leave once a day, with no exceptions? Are all your meals planned in advance? Can you choose your entree at dinner, or does everybody get the same chicken cutlet?

Picking a package tour

For popular destinations like Mexico's beaches, package tours are the smart way to go. In many cases, a package that includes airfare, hotel, and transportation to and from the airport costs less than just the hotel alone if you booked it yourself. That's because packages are sold in bulk to tour operators who resell them to the public. It's kind of like buying your vacation at one of those large, members-only discount stores — except the tour operator is the one who buys the 1,000-count box of garbage bags and resells them 10 at a time at a cost that undercuts what you'd pay at your average, neighborhood supermarket.

Package tours can vary as much as those garbage bags, too. Some offer a better class of hotels than others. Some offer the same hotels for lower prices. Some offer flights on scheduled airlines; others book charter planes (which are known for having the absolute minimal amount of conceivable legroom). In some packages, your choice of accommodations and travel days may be limited. Some let you choose between escorted vacations and independent vacations; others allow you to add on just a few excursions or escorted day-trips (also at discounted prices) without booking an entirely escorted tour.

Each destination usually has one or two packagers that are better than the rest because they buy in even bigger bulk. The time you spend shopping around will be well rewarded.

The best place to start looking is the travel section of your local Sunday newspaper. Also check the ads in the back of national travel magazines like *Travel + Leisure, National Geographic Traveler,* and *Condé Nast Traveler.* **Liberty Travel** (☎ 888-271-1584 to find the store nearest you; Internet: www.libertytravel.com) is one of the biggest packagers in the Northeast and usually boasts a full-page ad in Sunday papers. **American Express Vacations** (☎ 800-346-3607; Internet: http://travel.americanexpress.com/travel/) is another option.

When comparing packages, here are a few tips:

- ✔ **Read the fine print.** Make sure you know *exactly* what's included in the price you're being quoted, and what's not.

- ✔ **Don't compare Mayas and Aztecs.** When you look at different packagers, compare the deals that they offer on similar properties. Most packagers can offer bigger savings on some hotels than others.

- ✔ **Know what you're getting yourself into — and if you can get yourself out of it.** Before you commit to a package, make sure you know how much flexibility you have. Often, packagers offer trip-cancellation insurance for around $25–$30, which guarantees return of your payment if you need to change your plans.

- ✔ **Use your best judgment.** Stay away from fly-by-night and shady packagers. Go with a reputable firm with a proven track record. This is where your travel agent can come in handy.

You can even shop for these packages online — try these sites for a start:

- ✔ For one-stop shopping on the Web, go to `www.vacationpackager.com,` an extensive search engine that links you to more than 30 packagers offering Mexican beach vacations and even lets you custom design your own package.

- ✔ Check out `www.2travel.com` and find a page with links to a number of the big-name Mexico packagers, including several of the ones listed in this chapter.

- ✔ For last-minute, air-only packages or package bargains, check out **Vacation Hotline** at `www.vacationhotline.net`. After you find your "deal," you need to call them to make final booking arrangements, but they offer packages from both the popular Apple and Funjet vacation wholesalers.

Another good resource is the airlines themselves, which often package their flights with accommodations. When you pick the airline, you can choose one that has frequent service to your hometown and the one on which you accumulate frequent-flyer miles. Among the airline packages, your options include:

- ✔ **Aeromexico Vacations** (☎ **800-245-8585;** Internet: `www.aeromexico.com`) offers year-round packages to almost every destination they fly to, including Acapulco, Cancún, Cozumel, Ixtapa/Zihuatanejo, Los Cabos, and Puerto Vallarta. Aeromexico has a large selection of over 100 resorts in these destinations and others in a variety of price ranges. The best deals are from Houston, Dallas, San Diego, Los Angeles, Miami, and New York, in that order.

- ✔ **Alaska Airlines Vacations** (☎ **800-468-2248;** Internet: `www.alaskaair.com`) sells packages to Ixtapa/Zihuatanejo, Los Cabos,

Manzanillo/Costa Alegre, Mazatlán, and Puerto Vallarta. Alaska flies direct to Mexico from Los Angeles, San Diego, San Jose, San Francisco, Seattle, Vancouver, Anchorage, and Fairbanks. The Web site offers unpublished discounts that are not available through the phone operators.

✔ **American Airlines Vacations** (☎ 800-321-2121; Internet: www. aavacations.com) has year-round deals to Acapulco, Cancún, Los Cabos, Puerto Vallarta, and the Riviera Maya. You don't have to fly with American if you can get a better deal on another airline; land-only packages include hotel, airport transfers, and hotel room tax. American's hubs to Mexico are Dallas/Fort Worth, Chicago, and Miami, so you're likely to get the best prices — and the most direct flights — if you live near those cities. Their Web site offers unpublished discounts that are not available through the phone operators.

✔ **America West Vacations** (☎ 800-356-6611; Internet: www.america westvacations.com) has deals to Acapulco, Ixtapa, Mazatlán, Manzanillo, Los Cabos, and Puerto Vallarta, mostly from its Phoenix gateway. Many of their packages to Los Cabos also include car rentals. The America West Web site offers featured specials at added discounts that are not available through the phone operators. You can also book hotels without air by calling their toll-free number. Golfers can book golf vacations to Los Cabos through their specialized site at www.awagolf.com or by calling ☎ 888-AWA-GOLF.

✔ **Continental Vacations** (☎ 800-634-5555 and 888-989-9255; Internet: www.continental.com) has year-round packages available to Cancún, Cozumel, Puerto Vallarta, Cabo San Lucas, Acapulco, Ixtapa, and Mazatlán, and the best deals are from Houston; Newark, New Jersey; and Cleveland. You have to fly Continental. The Internet deals offer savings not available elsewhere.

✔ **Delta Vacations** (☎ 800-872-7786; Internet: www.deltavacations. com) has year-round packages to Acapulco, Puerto Vallarta, Los Cabos, Cozumel, and Cancún. Atlanta is the hub, so expect the best prices from there.

✔ **Mexicana Vacations** (☎ 800-531-9321; Internet: www.mexicana. com) offers getaways to all the resorts buttressed by Mexicana's daily direct flights from Los Angeles to Los Cabos, Mazatlán, Cancún, Puerto Vallarta, Manzanillo, and Ixtapa/Zihuatanejo.

✔ **US Airways Vacations** (☎ 800-455-0123; Internet: www.usairways vacations.com) offers packages to Cancún, Cozumel, and the Riviera Maya. Charlotte, N.C. is the hub, and will likely offer the best deals.

Several companies specialize in packages to Mexico's beaches; they usually fly in their own, chartered airplanes, which allows them to offer greatly discounted rates. Here are some of the packagers I prefer:

- **Apple Vacations** (☎ 800-365-2775; Internet: `www.apple vacations.com`) offers inclusive packages to all the beach resorts and has the largest choice of hotels in Acapulco, Cancún, Cozumel, Huatulco, Ixtapa, Los Cabos, Manzanillo, Mazatlán, Puerto Vallarta, and the Riviera Maya. Apple perks include baggage handling and the services of an Apple representative at the major hotels.

- **Funjet Vacations** (bookable through any travel agent, with general information available on their Web site at `www.funjet.com`) is one of the largest vacation packagers in the United States. Funjet has packages to Acapulco, Cancún, Cozumel, the Riviera Maya, Huatulco, Los Cabos, Mazatlán, Ixtapa, and Puerto Vallarta.

- **GOGO Worldwide Vacations** (☎ 888-636-3942; Internet: `www.gogowwv.com`) has trips to all the major beach destinations, including Acapulco, Cancún, Mazatlán, Puerto Vallarta, and Los Cabos, offering several exclusive deals from higher-end hotels. Bookable through any travel agent.

- **Pleasant Mexico Holidays** (☎ 800-448-3333; Internet: `www.pleasantholidays.com`) is another of the largest vacation packagers in the United States with hotels in the Acapulco, Cancún, Cozumel, Ixtapa/Zihuatanejo, Los Cabos, Mazatlán, and Puerto Vallarta.

The biggest hotel chains and resorts also offer packages. If you already know where you want to stay, call the hotel or resort and ask if they offer land/air packages.

Finding the Best Airline and Airfare

The first step for the independent travel planner is finding the airlines that fly to your desired beach resort. Mexico is becoming more easily accessible by plane. Many new regional carriers offer scheduled service to areas previously not served. In addition to regularly scheduled service, direct charter services from U.S. cities to resorts are making it possible to fly direct to most beach resorts from the largest airports in the United States. However, if you find that no direct flights are available, you can always reach your destination through an almost painless connection in Mexico City.

 If you're booked on a flight through Mexico City, always try to check your luggage to your final destination. This is possible if you are flying with affiliated or code-share airlines — separate airlines that work closely together to help travelers reach final destinations via connecting flights. This way, you don't have to lug your bags through the Mexico City airport, and it saves some time during the connecting process.

For information about saving money on airfares using the Internet, see "Researching and Booking Your Trip Online," later in this chapter.

The main airlines operating direct or nonstop flights to points in Mexico include:

✔ **Aeromexico** (☎ 800-237-6639; Internet: www.aeromexico.com). Flights to: Cancún, Puerto Vallarta, Ixtapa/Zihuatanejo, Acapulco, Los Cabos, Huatulco.

✔ **Air Canada** (☎ 888-247-2262; Internet: www.aircanada.ca). Flights to: Puerto Vallarta.

✔ **Alaska Airlines** (☎ 800-426-0333; Internet: www.alaskaair.com). Flights to: Cancún, Puerto Vallarta, Los Cabos.

✔ **American Airlines** (☎ 800-433-7300; Internet: www.im.aa.com). Flights to: Cancún/Cozumel, PuertoVallarta, Acapulco, Los Cabos.

✔ **America West** (☎ 800-235-9292; Internet: www.americawest. com). Flights to: Puerto Vallarta, Acapulco, Los Cabos.

✔ **American Trans Air** (☎ 800-225-2995; Internet: www.ata.com). Flights to: Cancún, Puerto Vallarta.

✔ **British Airways** (☎ 800-247-9297, ☎ 0345-222-111 or 0845-77-333-77 in Britain; Internet: www.british-airways.com). Flights from London to Cancún.

✔ **Continental Airlines** (☎ 800-525-0280; Internet: www. continental.com). Flights to: Cancún/Cozumel, Puerto Vallarta, Acapulco, Los Cabos.

✔ **Delta** (☎ 800-221-1212; Internet: www.delta.com). Flights to: Cancún/Cozumel (serviced through Aeromexico), Puerto Vallarta, Acapulco, Los Cabos, Ixtapa/Zihuatanejo, Huatulco.

✔ **Mexicana** (☎ 800-531-7921; Internet: www.mexicana.com). Flights to: Cancún, Cozumel, Puerto Vallarta, Ixtapa, Zihuatanejo, Acapulco, Huatulco, Los Cabos.

✔ **Northwest Airlines** (☎ 800-225-2525; Internet: www.nwa.com). Seasonal flights to: Cancún/Cozumel, Puerto Vallarta, Acapulco, Los Cabos.

✔ **US Airways** (☎ 800-428-4322; Intnernet: www.usairways.com). Flights to: Cancún/Cozumel.

Competition among the major U.S. airlines is unlike that of any other industry. A coach seat is virtually the same from one carrier to another, yet the difference in price may run as high as $1,000 for a product with the same intrinsic value.

Business travelers, who need flexibility to purchase their tickets at the last minute, change their itinerary at a moment's notice, or who want to get home before the weekend, pay the premium rate, known as the full fare. Passengers who can book their ticket long in advance, who don't mind staying over Saturday night, or who are willing to travel on a Tuesday, Wednesday, or Thursday pay the least — usually a fraction of the full fare. On most flights, even the shortest hops, the full fare is close to $1,000 or more, but a 7- or 14-day advance purchase ticket is closer to $200–$300. Obviously, it pays to plan ahead.

The airlines also periodically hold sales, in which they lower the prices on their most popular routes. These fares have advance purchase requirements and date-of-travel restrictions, but you can't beat the price: usually no more than $400 for a cross-country flight. Keep your eyes open for these sales as you're planning your vacation. The sales tend to take place in seasons of low travel volume. You almost never see a sale around the peak summer vacation months of July and August or around Thanksgiving or Christmas, when people have to fly, regardless of what the fare is.

Consolidators, also known as bucket shops, are a good place to check for the lowest fares. Their prices are much better than the fares you can get yourself and are often even lower than what your travel agent can get you. You can see their ads in the small boxes at the bottom of the page in your newspaper's Sunday travel section. Some of the most reliable consolidators include **Cheap Tickets** (☎ **800-377-1000;** Internet: www.cheaptickets.com), **1-800-FLY-CHEAP** (Internet: www.flycheap.com), and **Travac Tours & Charters** (☎ **877-872-8221;** Internet: www.thetravelsite.com). Another good choice, **Council Travel** (☎ **800-226-8624;** Internet: www.counciltravel.com), especially caters to young travelers, but their bargain-basement prices are available to people of all ages.

Here are some travel tips — tested and true — for getting the lowest possible fare:

- ✔ **Timing is everything:** If you can, avoid peak travel times. In Mexico, the weeks surrounding the Christmas/New Year holidays and Easter are so jam-packed that I find it not very enjoyable to be at a beach resort anyway. Airfares are relatively expensive anytime between January and May, with September through mid-November offering up the best deals. Specials pop up throughout the year, however, based on current demand, and last-minute specials on package tours are an increasingly popular way to travel.

- ✔ **Advantage — advance:** Forgetting what I said in the previous sentence, you can also save big by booking early — with excellent fares available for 30-, 60-, or even 90-day advance bookings. Note that if you need to change your schedule, a penalty charge of $75 to $150 is common.

✔ **Choose an off-peak travel day:** Traveling on a Tuesday, Wednesday, or even Thursday can also save you money. Even if you can't travel both ways on these lower-fare days, you can still save if you fly off-peak at least one way.

✔ **The midnight hour:** In the middle of the week, just after midnight, many airlines download cancelled low-priced airfares into their computers, so this is a great time to buy newly discounted seats. Midnight is the cutoff time for holding reservations. You may benefit by snagging cheap tickets that were just released by those who reserved — but never purchased — their tickets.

Choosing the Room That's Right For You

Whether you've chosen a package deal or you're planning your trip on your own, getting a room is a crucial part of your vacation planning. In this section, I help you decipher the various rates and provide some tips on how to get the best one. I also compare the pros and cons of different types of places to stay.

From small inns to large all-inclusives, most Mexican beach resorts offer every type of vacation accommodation. And the prices can vary even more! Recommendations for specific places to stay are in the chapters devoted to the individual beach towns. I try to provide the widest range of options — both in types of hotels as well as budgets — but I always keep comfort in mind. What you find in this book is what I believe to be the best value for the money. Here are the major types of accommodations:

✔ **Resorts:** These accommodations tend to be the most popular option — especially with package tours — because they offer the most modern amenities, including cable TV, hairdryers, in-room safes, and generally, a selection of places to dine or have a drink. Large by definition, they may also boast various types of sporting facilities, spa services, shopping arcades, and tour-desk services. These places also tend to be the most expensive type of accommodation, but they can be heavily discounted if your timing is right.

✔ **Hotels:** These quarters tend to be smaller than resorts, with fewer facilities. In terms of style, look for anything from hacienda-style villas to all-suite hotels or sleek, modern structures. All hotels at Mexican beach resorts have at least a small swimming pool, and if they're not located directly on a beach, hotels frequently offer shuttle service to a beach club or an affiliate beachfront hotel.

✔ **All-inclusives:** In Mexico, all-inclusives are gaining rapidly in popularity, and they seem to be getting larger and larger in size. As the name implies, all-inclusives tie everything together in one price — your room, meals, libations, entertainment, sports activities, and sometimes, off-site excursions. The advantage that many travelers find with this option is an expected fixed price for their vacation — helpful if you need to stay within a strict budget. Many all-inclusives have their own nightclubs or, at least, offer evening shows and entertainment, such as theme nights, talent contests, or costume parties. As for the food, you may never go hungry, but you're unlikely to go gourmet either. Food quality can be an important variable, about which it helps to have talked to someone who's recently been to the particular all-inclusive.

✔ **Condos, apartments, and villas:** One of these accomodations can be a good option, especially if you're considering a stay longer than a week, and the reach of the Internet has made these lodging options extremely viable. Many condos, apartments, and villas come with housekeepers or even cooks. It's hard to know exactly what you're getting — and often it's futile to complain after you arrive — so again, word of mouth can be helpful here. At the very least, ask for references or search on the Internet to see if anyone can offer up an experience. In addition to the Internet, select options are always advertised in the major metropolitan newspapers, such as the *Los Angeles Times, Chicago Tribune,* and the *New York Times.* My recommendation? Save this option for your second visit when you have a better idea about the various parts of town and the area in general.

Researching and Booking Your Trip Online

More and more savvy travelers turn to the Internet when planning the perfect vacation to find out where the good deals are. Sites such as **Travelocity** (www.travelocity.com), **Microsoft Expedia** (www.expedia.com), and **Orbitz** (www.orbitz.com) allow consumers to comparison shop for airfares, book flights, learn of last-minute bargains, and reserve hotel rooms and rental cars. With most sites requiring you to complete some sort of one-time registration form, Internet research can be a rather time-consuming task, but the benefits of researching your trip online can be well worth the effort:

✔ Airlines offer **last-minute specials,** such as weekend deals or Internet-only fares, to fill empty seats. Most of these E-savers are announced on Tuesday or Wednesday and must be purchased online.

✔ Some sites send you e-mail notification when a cheap fare to your favorite destination becomes available, and some let you know when fares to a particular destination are at their lowest.

✔ All major airlines offer **incentives** — bonus frequent-flier miles, Internet-only discounts, or sometimes, free cellphone rentals — when you purchase online or buy an E-ticket.

✔ Advances in mobile technology provide travelers with **the ability to check flight statuses, change plans, or get specific directions** from handheld computing devices, mobile phones, and pagers. Some sites e-mail or page a passenger if a flight is delayed.

Sign up for weekly e-mail alerts at airline Web sites or check mega-sites that compile comprehensive lists of E-savers, such as Smarter Living (`www.smarterliving.com`) or WebFlyer (`www.webflyer.com`).

The good news is that you don't even have to book your trip online to reap the research benefits of the Web. The Internet can be a valuable tool for comparison shopping, for approaching a travel agent with a base of knowledge, and even for chatting with other travelers to truly rate the quality of the buffets at that all-inclusive you're considering.

Qixo (`www.qixo.com`) allows you to search for flights and hotel rooms on 20 other travel-planning sites (such as Travelocity) at once. Qixo sorts results by price, after which you can book your travel directly through the site.

When it comes to looking for great deals on **hotel rooms,** it's best to use a Web site devoted primarily to lodging because you may find properties that aren't listed on more general online travel sites. Some lodging sites specialize in a particular type of accommodation, such as bed-and-breakfasts, which you won't find on the more mainstream booking services. Others such as TravelWeb offer weekend deals on major chain properties, as discussed later in this section.

✔ Although the name **All Hotels on the Web** (`www.all-hotels.com`) is something of a misnomer, the site *does* have tens of thousands of listings throughout the world. Bear in mind each hotel has paid a small fee ($25 and up) to be listed, so it's less of an objective list and more like a book of online brochures.

✔ **hoteldiscount!com** (`www.180096hotel.com`) lists bargain room rates at hotels in more than 50 U.S. and international cities. The cool thing is that hoteldiscount!com pre-books blocks of rooms in advance, so sometimes it has rooms — at discount rates — at hotels that are "sold out." Select a city and input your dates, and you get a list of the best prices for a selection of hotels. This site is notable for delivering deep discounts in cities where hotel rooms are expensive. The toll-free number is printed all over this site (☎ **800-96-HOTEL**); call it if you want more options than are listed online.

- ✔ **InnSite** (www.innsite.com) has B&B listings in all 50 U.S. states and more than 50 countries around the globe. Find an inn at your destination, see pictures of the rooms, and check prices and availability. This extensive directory of bed-and-breakfasts only includes listings if the proprietor submitted one (it's free to get an inn listed). The descriptions are written by the innkeepers, and many listings link to the inns' own Web sites. Also check out the **Bed and Breakfast Channel** (www.bedandbreakfast.com).

- ✔ **Places to Stay** (www.placestostay.com) lists one-of-a-kind places, with a focus on resort accommodations, in the United States and abroad that you might not find in other directories. Again, listing is selective: This isn't a comprehensive directory, but it can give you a sense of what's available at different destinations.

- ✔ **TravelWeb** (www.travelweb.com) lists more than 26,000 hotels in 170 countries, focusing on chains such as Hyatt and Hilton, and you can book almost 90 percent of these listings online. The site's Click-It Weekends, updated each Monday, offers weekend deals at many leading hotel chains.

- ✔ Specific to Mexico, **Mexico Boutique Hotels** (http://mexico boutiquehotels.com) has listings of small, unique properties that are unlikely to show up on the radar screens of most travel agents or large Web travel sites. In addition to very complete descriptions, the site also offers an online booking service.

- ✔ Another site specializing in Mexico accommodations is www.mexicohotels.com.

- ✔ Check the Web sites of Mexico's top hotel chains for special deals. These include www.caminoreal.com, www.hyatt.com, www.starwood.com, and www.fiestaamericana.com.

Avoid online auctions. Sites that auction airline tickets and frequent-flier miles are the number-one perpetrators of Internet fraud, according to the National Consumers League.

Chapter 6

Money Matters

Most of us save all year to be able to enjoy a wonderful vacation, so in this chapter I share with you the finer points of stretching your dollars into pesos. I tell you about the nuances of changing currency to get more for your money and present the pros and cons of traveler's checks, credit cards, and cash. Finally, I tell you how to regroup after your wallet is lost or stolen.

Making Sense of the Peso

The currency in Mexico is the **Mexican peso,** and in recent years, economists have been talking about its amazing recovery and resiliency against the U.S. dollar. At this book's time of print, each peso is worth close to 11 U.S. cents, which means that an item costing 9 pesos would be equivalent to US$1. Like most things in Mexico, the paper currency is colorful, and it comes in denominations of 20 (blue), 50 (pink), 100 (red), 200 (green), and 500 (burgundy) pesos. Coins come in denominations of 1, 2, 5, 10, and 20 pesos and 50 **centavos** (100 centavos equals 1 peso).

New 50- and 500-peso bills look very similar, but 50-peso bills have a slightly pinkish hue and are smaller in size. However, always double-check how much you're paying and your change to avoid unpleasant surprises. The same applies to 10- and 20-peso coins. Twenty-peso coins are slightly larger than the 10-peso coins, but they look very similar.

Getting change continues to be a problem in Mexico. Small-denomination bills and coins are hard to come by, so start collecting them early in your trip and continue as you travel. Shopkeepers — and especially taxi drivers — always seem to be out of change and small bills; that's doubly true in a market. In other words, don't try to pay with a 500-peso bill when buying a 20-peso trinket.

Before you leave your hotel, it's a good idea to get a hundred pesos — a little over US$11 — in change, that way you're sure to have change for cab and bus fares.

In this book, I use the universal currency sign ($) to indicate both U.S. dollars and pesos in Mexico. When you're in Mexico, you'll notice the common use of the currency symbol ($), generally indicating the price in pesos. It is okay to ask if you're not sure because some higher-end places do tend to price their goods in U.S. dollar. Often, if a price is quoted in U.S. dollars, the letters "USD" follow the price.

The rate of exchange fluctuates a tiny bit daily, so you're probably better off not exchanging too much of your currency at once. Don't forget, however, to have enough pesos to carry you over a weekend or Mexican holiday, when banks are closed. In general, avoid carrying the U.S. $100 bill, the bill most commonly counterfeited in Mexico, and therefore, the most difficult to exchange, especially in smaller towns. Because small bills and coins in pesos are hard to come by in Mexico, the U.S. $1 bill is very useful for tipping. A tip of U.S. coins is of no value to the service provider because they can't be exchanged into Mexican currency.

To make your dollars go further, remember that ATMs offer the best exchange rate; however, you need to consider any service fees. Mexican banks offer the next-best fare, and they don't charge commission, unless you're cashing traveler's checks, in which case they usually charge a small commission. After banks, *casas de cambio* (houses of exchange) are your next-best option, and they usually charge a commission. You can almost always get a lower exchange rate when you exchange your money at a hotel front desk.

Traveler's Checks, Credit Cards, or Cash?

You need to think about *what kind* of money you're going to spend on your vacation before you leave home

Relying on ATMs and cash

These days, all of the Mexico beach resorts detailed in this book have 24-hour ATMs linked to a national network that almost always includes your bank at home. **Cirrus** (☎ 800-424-7787; Internet: www.mastercard.com/cardholderservices/atm/ and **Plus** (☎ 800-843-7587; Internet: www.visa.com/atms) are the two most popular networks; check the back of your ATM card to see which network your bank belongs to. The 800-numbers and Web sites will give you specific locations of ATMs where you can withdraw money while on vacation. Using ATMs permits you to withdraw only as much cash as you need for a few days, which eliminates the insecurity (and the pick-pocketing threat) of carrying around a wad of cash. Note, however, that a daily maximum of about US$1,000 is common.

One important reminder: Many banks now charge a fee ranging from 50 cents to *three dollars* when a non-account-holder uses their ATMs. Your own bank may also assess a fee for using an ATM that's not one of their branch locations. This means, in some cases, you get charged *twice* just for using your bankcard when you're on vacation. Although an ATM card can be an amazing convenience when traveling in another country (put your card in the machine and out comes foreign currency at an extremely advantageous exchange rate), banks are also likely to slap you with a "foreign currency transaction fee" just for making them do the pounds-to-dollars-to-pesos conversion math.

Using a credit card

Credit cards are invaluable when traveling. They're a safe way to carry "money," and they provide a convenient record of all your travel expenses when you arrive home.

Travel with at least two different credit cards if you can. Depending on where you go, you may find MasterCard accepted more frequently than Visa (or visa versa), American Express honored or refused, and so on.

You can get **cash advances** from your credit card at any bank, and you don't even need to go to a teller — you can get a cash advance at the ATM if you know your **PIN number.** If you've forgotten your PIN number or didn't even know you had one, call the phone number on the back of your credit card and ask the bank to send it to you. It usually takes five to seven business days, though some banks will do it over the phone if you tell them your mother's maiden name or some other security clearance.

There's a hidden expense to contend with when borrowing cash from a credit card: Interest rates for cash advances are often significantly higher than rates for credit-card purchases. More importantly, you start paying interest on the advance *the moment you receive the cash.* On an airline-affiliated credit card, a cash advance does not earn frequent-flyer miles.

Traveling with traveler's checks

Traveler's checks are something of an anachronism from the days when people wrote personal checks instead of going to an ATM. Because traveler's checks could be replaced if lost or stolen, they were a sound alternative to filling your wallet with cash at the beginning of a trip.

Still, if you prefer the security of traveler's checks, you can get them at almost any bank. **American Express** offers checks in denominations of $20, $50, $100, $500, and $1,000. You pay a service charge ranging from 1 to 4%, though AAA members can obtain checks without a fee at most AAA offices. You can also get American Express traveler's checks over the phone by calling ☎ **800-221-7282.**

Visa (☎ **800-227-6811**) also offers traveler's checks, available at Citibank locations across the country and at several other banks. The service charge ranges between 1.5 and 2%; checks come in denominations of $50, $100, $500, and $1,000. **MasterCard** also offers traveler's checks; call ☎ **800-223-9920** for a location near you.

Although traveler's checks are very safe, you should consider that:

- ✔ You usually get charged a commission to cash your traveler's checks, and when you add that to the exchange-rate loss, you end up getting fewer pesos for your money.

- ✔ Many smaller shops won't take traveler's checks, so if you plan to shop, it's best to cash the traveler's checks before you embark on your shopping expedition.

Knowing What to Do If Your Wallet Gets Stolen

Odds are that if your wallet is gone you've seen the last of it, and the police aren't likely to recover it for you. However, after you realize it's gone and you cancel your credit cards, call to inform the police. You may need the police-report number for credit card or insurance purposes later. After you've covered all the formalities and before you head to the nearest bar to drown your sorrows, retrace your steps — you may be surprised at how many honest people are in Mexico, and it's likely that you may find someone trying to find you to return your wallet.

Almost every credit-card company has an emergency toll-free number you can call if your wallet or purse is stolen. They may be able to wire you a cash advance off your credit card immediately; in many places, they can get you an emergency credit card within a day or two. The issuing bank's toll-free number is usually on the back of the credit card, but that won't help you much if the card was stolen. Write down the number on the back of your card before you leave, and keep it in a safe place just in case.

If your credit card is stolen, major credit-card companies have emergency 800-numbers. Here's a list of numbers to call in the United States as well as internationally:

- ✔ **American Express** cardholders and traveler's check holders should call ☎ **800-327-2177** (U.S. toll free); ☎ **336-393-1111** (international direct-dial) for gold and green cards.

- ✔ The toll-free, U.S. emergency number for **Visa** is ☎ **800-336-8472**; from other countries, call ☎ **410-902-8012.** Your card issuer can also provide you with the toll-free, lost/stolen-card number for the country or countries you plan to visit.

- ✔ **MasterCard** holders need to dial ☎ **800-826-2181** in the United States or 800-307-7309 from anywhere in the world; or ☎ 314-542-7111. Also check with your card issuer for the toll-free, lost/stolen-card number for the country or countries you want to visit.

To dial a U.S. toll-free number from inside Mexico, you must dial 001-880 and then the last seven digits of the toll-free number.

If you opt to carry **traveler's checks,** be sure to keep a record of their serial numbers so you can handle this type of emergency.

Chapter 7

Tying Up the Loose Ends

● ●

In This Chapter

▶ Getting your entry and departure documents in order

▶ Considering travel and medical insurance

▶ Ensuring a safe vacation

▶ Deciding whether to rent a car or not

▶ Packing wisely

● ●

Are you ready? Really ready? Before you can string that hammock between the palms, you need to take care of a few more details to get to your personal paradise. In this chapter, I cover the essentials and the requirements of getting into Mexico — then back home again. I also review the ins and outs of dealing with travel insurance, ensuring a safe trip, deciding whether you should rent a car, and making sure you pack everything you need for your Mexican beach vacation.

Arriving In and Departing From Mexico

All travelers to Mexico are required to present **proof of citizenship**, such as an original birth certificate with a raised seal, a valid passport, or naturalization papers. Travelers using a birth certificate should also have a current form of photo identification, such as a driver's license or an official ID card. If your last name on the birth certificate is different from your current name (women using a married name, for example), you should also bring a photo identification card *and* legal proof of the name change, like the *original* marriage license or certificate.

When reentering the United States, you must prove both your citizenship *and* your identification, so always carry a picture ID such as a driver's license or valid passport.

Birth certificates will enable you to enter Mexico, but alone, will not enable you to reenter the United States. And although you can enter Mexico using a driver's license as identification, this alone is not acceptable identification for reentering the United States. While in Mexico, you must also obtain a **Mexican tourist permit (FMT),** which is issued free of charge by Mexican border officials after proof of citizenship is accepted. These forms are generally provided by the airline aboard your flight into Mexico.

The tourist permit is more important than a passport in Mexico, so guard it carefully. If you lose it, you may not be permitted to leave the country until you can replace it — a bureaucratic hassle that can take anywhere from a few hours to a week. (If you do lose your tourist permit, get a police report from local authorities indicating that your documents were stolen; having one *might* lessen the hassle of exiting the country without all your identification.) You should also contact the nearest consular office to report the stolen papers so that they can issue a reentry document.

Note that children under the age of 18 traveling without parents or with only one parent must have a notarized letter from the absent parent or parents authorizing the travel. The letter must include the duration of the visit, destination, names of accompanying adults, parents' home addresses, telephone numbers, and so forth. A picture of the child must also be attached to this letter.

Obtaining a Passport

Although you can enter Mexico without a passport, the only legal form of identification recognized around the world is a valid passport, and for that reason alone, it's a good idea to have yours whenever you travel abroad. In the United States, you're used to your driver's license being the all-purpose ID card. Abroad, it only proves that some American state lets you drive. Getting a passport is easy, but it takes some time to complete the process.

The U.S. State Department's Bureau of Consular Affairs maintains an excellent Web site (www.travel.state.gov) that provides everything you need to know about passports (including downloadable applications and locations of passport offices). In addition, the Web site provides extensive information about foreign countries, including travel warnings about health and terrorism. You can also call the National Passport Information Center at ☎ **900-225-5674** (35¢ per minute) or ☎ **888-362-8668** ($4.95 per call).

Applying for a U.S. passport

Apply for a passport at least a month, preferably two, before you leave. Although processing generally takes three weeks, during busy periods it can run longer (especially in spring). For people over the age of 15, a passport is valid for ten years.

If you're a U.S. citizen applying for a first-time passport and you're 13 years of age or older, you need to apply in person at one of the following locations:

✔ **A passport office:** An appointment is required for a visit to one of the following facilities, and your departure date must be within two weeks: Boston, Chicago, Houston, Los Angeles, Miami, New York City, Philadelphia, San Francisco, Seattle, Stamford (Connecticut), and Washington, D.C. No appointments are required at the offices in Honolulu and New Orleans.

✔ **A federal, state, or probate court.**

✔ **A major post office, some libraries, and a number of county and municipal offices:** Not all accept applications; call your local post office or log on to the Web site at www.usps.com for more information.

When you go to apply, bring the following items with you:

✔ **Completed passport application:** To apply for your first passport, fill out form DSP-11 (available online at www.travel.state.gov and www.usps.com). You can complete this form in advance to save time. However, *do not sign* the application until you present it to the person at the passport agency, court, or post office.

✔ **Application fee:** For people age 16 or older, a passport costs $60 ($45 plus a $15 handling fee).

✔ **Proof of U.S. citizenship:** Bring your old passport if you're renewing (see the following section); otherwise, bring a certified copy of your birth certificate with registrar's seal, a report of your birth abroad, or your naturalized citizenship documents.

✔ **Proof of identity:** Among the accepted documents are a valid driver's license, a state or military ID, an old passport, or a naturalization certificate.

✔ **Two identical 2-inch-by-2-inch photographs with a white or off-white background:** You can get these pictures taken in just about any corner photo shop; these places have a special camera to make the photos identical. Expect to pay up to $15 for them. You *cannot* use the strip photos from one of those photo vending machines.

Renewing a U.S. passport by mail

You can renew an existing, non-damaged passport by mail if it was issued within the past 15 years, *and* you were over age 16 when it was issued, *and* you still have the same name as the passport (or you can legally document your name change).

Include your expired passport, renewal form DSP-82, two identical photos (see the preceding section), and a check or money order for $40 (no extra handling fee). Mail everything (certified, return receipt requested, just to be safe) in a padded envelope to National Passport Center, P.O. Box 371971, Pittsburgh, PA 15250-7971.

Allow at least one month to six weeks for your application to be processed and your new passport to be sent.

Getting your passport in a hurry

Although processing usually takes about three weeks, it can actually take far longer, especially during busy times of year, such as the spring. If you're crunched for time, consider paying an extra $35 (plus the express mail service fee) to have your passport sent to you within seven to ten working days. In even more of a hurry? Try **Passport Express** (☎ **800-362-8196** or 401-272-4612; Internet: www.passportexpress.com), a nationwide service that can get you a new or renewed passport within 24 hours. Getting a new passport with this service costs $150 plus the $95 government fees if you need it in one to six days, or $100 plus the $95 government fees if you need it in seven to ten days. If you're renewing your passport, the government fees drop to $75. For a rushed passport, you must have proof of travel (your tickets).

For more details about getting a passport, call the **National Passport Agency** (☎ **202-647-0518**). To locate a passport office in your area, call the **National Passport Information Center** (☎ **900-225-5674,** 35¢ per minute). The Web page of the **U.S. State Department** (www.travel.state.gov) also offers information on passport services, and you can download an application. In addition, many post offices and travel agencies keep passport applications on hand.

Applying for passports from other countries

The following list offers more information for citizens of Canada, the United Kingdom, Ireland, Australia, and New Zealand.

Canadian citizens

Passport information and applications are available from the central **Passport Office** in Ottawa (☎ **800-567-6868;** Internet: www.dfait-maeci.gc.ca/passport/). Regional passport offices and travel agencies also offer applications. Valid for five years, a passport costs $60 Canadian. Applications must include two identical passport-sized photographs and proof of Canadian citizenship. Allow five to ten days for processing if you apply in person or about three weeks if you submit your application by mail.

Residents of the United Kingdom

To pick up an application for a ten-year passport, visit your nearest passport office, major post office, or travel agency. You can also contact the **London Passport Office** at ☎ **0171-271-3000** or search its Web site at www.ukpa.gov.uk/. Passports are £28 for adults.

Residents of Ireland

You can apply for a ten-year passport, costing IR£45, at the **Passport Office** (Setanta Centre, Molesworth St., Dublin 2; ☎ **01-671-1633;** Internet: www.irlgov.ie/iveagh). You can also apply at 1A South Mall, Cork (☎ **021-272-525**) or over the counter at most main post offices. Those under age 18 and over age 65 must apply for a IR£10 three-year passport.

Residents of Australia

Apply at your local post office, search the government Web site at www.passports.gov.au/, or call toll-free ☎ **131-232.** Passports for adults are A$128 and, for those under age 18, A$64.

Residents of New Zealand

You can pick up a passport application at any travel agency or Link Centre. For more info, contact the **Passport Office** (P.O. Box 805, Wellington; ☎ **0800-225-050;** Internet: www.passports.govt.nz). Passports for adults are NZ$80 and, for those under age 16, NZ$40.

Dealing with lost passports

Keep your passport with you at all times, preferably secured in a money belt. The only times to give it up are at the bank or money exchange, for tellers to verify information when you change traveler's checks or foreign currency, or to airline reservations agents and immigration officials when entering or leaving a country.

If you lose your passport in a foreign country, go directly to the nearest U.S. embassy or consulate. Bring all forms of identification you have, and they can start arranging for a new passport. This is a huge hassle that should be avoided at all costs.

Always carry a photocopy of the first page of your passport with you when you travel. Doing so greatly speeds up the paperwork in case your passport goes missing.

Clearing U.S. Customs

You *can* take it with you — up to a point. Technically, no limits exist on how much loot U.S. citizens can bring back into the United States from a trip abroad, but the customs authority *does* put limits on how much

you can bring in for free. (This is mainly for taxation purposes, to separate tourists with souvenirs from importers.)

U.S. citizens may bring home $400 worth of goods duty-free, providing
you've been out of the country at least 48 hours and haven't used the
exemption in the past 30 days. This includes one liter of an alcoholic
beverage (you must, of course, be over 21), 200 cigarettes, and 100
cigars. Anything you mail home from abroad is exempt from the $400
limit. You may mail up to $200 worth of goods to yourself (marked "for
personal use") and up to $100 to others (marked "unsolicited gift")
once each day, so long as the package does not include alcohol or
tobacco products. You'll have to pay an import duty on anything over
these limits.

Note that buying items at a **duty-free shop** before flying home does *not*
exempt them from counting toward U.S. customs limits (monetary or
otherwise). The "duty" that you're avoiding in those shops is the local
tax on the item (like state sales tax in the United States), not any
import duty that may be assessed by the U.S. customs office.

If you have further questions, or for a list of specific items you cannot
bring into the United States, look in your phone book (under U.S.
Government, Department of the Treasury, U.S. Customs Service) to find
the nearest customs office. Or check out Customs Service Web site at
www.customs.ustreas.gov/travel/travel.htm.

Considering Insurance

There are three primary kinds of travel insurance: trip-cancellation
insurance, medical insurance, and lost-luggage insurance.

Trip-cancellation insurance is a good idea if you have paid a large portion of your vacation expenses up front, such as for an air/hotel package
deal, an all-inclusive resort, or a cruise. You should strongly consider
this coverage particularly if you have young children because you never
know when accidents or illnesses will crop up.

But the other two types of insurance — **medical** and **lost luggage** —
don't make sense for most travelers. Your existing health insurance
should cover you if you get sick while on vacation. (Although, if you
belong to an HMO, check to see whether you are fully covered when
away from home.) Homeowner's insurance should cover stolen luggage
if you have off-premises theft. Check your existing policies before you
buy any additional coverage. The airlines are responsible for $2,500 on
domestic flights (and $9.07 per pound, up to $640, on international
flights) if they lose your luggage; if you plan to carry anything more
valuable than that, keep it in your carry-on bag.

Some credit cards (American Express and certain gold and platinum Visa and MasterCards, for example) offer automatic flight insurance against death or dismemberment in case of an airplane crash. If you still feel you need more insurance, try one of the companies listed below. But don't pay for more insurance than you need. For example, if you only need trip-cancellation insurance, don't purchase coverage for lost or stolen property. Trip-cancellation insurance costs approximately 6% to 8% of the total value of your vacation.

Among the reputable issuers of travel insurance are

- **Access America** (6600 W. Broad St., Richmond, VA 23230; ☎ **800-284-8300;** Fax: 800-346-9265; Internet: www.accessamerica.com)

- **Travelex Insurance Services** (11717 Burt St., Ste. 202, Omaha, NE 68154; ☎ **800-228-9792;** Internet: www.travelex-insurance.com)

- **Travel Guard International** (1145 Clark St., Stevens Point, WI 54481; ☎ **800-826-1300;** Internet: www.travel-guard.com)

- **Travel Insured International, Inc.** (P.O. Box 280568, 52-S Oakland Ave., East Hartford, CT 06128-0568; ☎ **800-243-3174;** Internet: www.travelinsured.com)

Getting Sick Away From Home

Apart from how getting sick can ruin your vacation, it also can present the problem of finding a doctor you trust when you're away from home. Bring all your medications with you, as well as a prescription for more — you may run out. Bring an extra pair of contact lenses in case you lose one. And don't forget the Pepto-Bismol for common travelers' ailments like upset stomach or diarrhea.

If you have health insurance, check with your provider to find out the extent of your coverage outside of your home area. Be sure to carry your identification card in your wallet. And if you worry that your existing policy won't be sufficient, purchase medical insurance (see the "Buying Travel and Medical Insurance," section earlier in this chapter) for more comprehensive coverage.

If you suffer from a chronic illness, talk to your doctor before taking the trip. For such conditions as epilepsy, diabetes, or a heart condition, wearing a **Medic Alert identification tag** will immediately alert any doctor to your condition and give him or her access to your medical records through Medic Alert's 24-hour hotline. Membership is $35, with a $15 renewal fee. Contact the Medic Alert Foundation (2323 Colorado Ave., Turlock, CA 95382; ☎ **800-432-5378;** Internet: www.medicalert.org).

Avoiding turista!

It's called "travelers' diarrhea" or *turista,* the Spanish word for "tourist." I'm talking about the persistent diarrhea, often accompanied by fever, nausea, and vomiting, that used to attack many travelers to Mexico. Some folks in the United States call this affliction "Montezuma's revenge," but you won't hear it referred to this way in Mexico. Widespread improvements in infrastructure, sanitation, and education have practically eliminated this ailment, especially in well-developed resort areas. Most travelers make a habit of drinking only bottled water, which also helps to protect against unfamiliar bacteria. In resort areas, and generally throughout Mexico, only purified ice is used. Doctors say this ailment isn't caused by just one "bug," but by a combination of consuming different foods and water, upsetting your schedule, being overtired, and experiencing the stresses of travel. A good high-potency (or "therapeutic") vitamin supplement and extra vitamin C can help. And yogurt is good for healthy digestion. If you do happen to come down with this ailment, nothing beats Pepto-Bismol, readily available in Mexico.

Preventing turista: The U.S. Public Health Service recommends the following measures for preventing travelers' diarrhea:

- Get enough sleep.

- Don't overdo the sun.

- Drink only purified water. This means tea, coffee, and other beverages made with boiled water; canned or bottled carbonated beverages and water; or beer and wine. Most restaurants with a large tourist clientele use only purified water and ice.

- Choose food carefully. In general, avoid salads, uncooked vegetables, and unpasteurized milk or milk products (including cheese). However, salads in a first-class restaurant, or in a restaurant that serves a lot of tourists, are generally safe to eat. Choose food that's freshly cooked and still hot. Peelable fruit is ideal. Don't eat undercooked meat, fish, or shellfish.

- In addition, something as simple as clean hands can go a long way toward preventing *turista.*

Since **dehydration** can quickly become life threatening, be especially careful to replace fluids and electrolytes (potassium, sodium, and the like) during a bout of diarrhea. Do this by drinking Pedialyte, a rehydration solution available at most Mexican pharmacies, sports drinks, or glasses of natural fruit juice (high in potassium) with a pinch of salt added. Or try a glass of boiled, pure water with a quarter teaspoon of sodium bicarbonate (baking soda) and a bit of lime juice added.

If you do get sick, ask the concierge at your hotel to recommend a local doctor — even his or her own doctor if necessary. Another good option is to call the closest consular office and ask them to refer you to a doctor. Most consulates have a listing of reputable English-speaking doctors. Most beach destinations in Mexico have at least one modern facility staffed by doctors used to treating the most common ailments of tourists. In the case of a real emergency, a service from the United States can fly people to American hospitals: **Air-Evac** (☎ **888-554-9729,** or call collect 510-293-5968) is a 24-hour air ambulance. You can also contact the service in Guadalajara (☎ **01-800-305-9400,** 3-616-9616, or 3-615-2471). Several companies offer air-evac service; for a list, refer to the U.S. State Department Web site at http://travel.state.gov/medical.html.

From my ten years' experience of living in and traveling throughout Mexico, I can honestly say that most health problems that foreign tourists to Mexico encounter are self-induced. If you take in too much sun, too many margaritas, and too many street tacos within hours of your arrival, don't blame the water if you get sick. You'd be surprised how many people try to make up for all the fun they've missed out on in the past year on their first day on vacation in Mexico.

Staying Safe and Healthy: Words For the Wise

If you find yourself getting friendly with the locals — and I mean friendly to the point of a fling — don't be embarrassed to carry or insist on stopping for condoms — then use them! Too many vacationing men and women are filled with morning-after regrets because they didn't protect themselves. Don't allow your fear of being judged make you do something that's frankly stupid. Also know that Mexico's teen-to-20-something population has a rapidly escalating **AIDS** rate — especially in resort areas — due to the transient nature of the population and poor overall education about this disease.

And when it comes to **drugs,** many outsiders have the impression that the easy-going nature of these tropical towns means an equally laid-back attitude exists toward drug use. Not so. Marijuana, cocaine, Ecstasy, and other mood-altering drugs are illegal in Mexico. In some resorts, such as Puerto Vallarta, police will randomly search people — including obvious tourists — who are walking the streets at night. However, unless you seek drugs out, whatever behind-the-scenes action there is won't likely affect you.

If you do choose to indulge, don't expect any special treatment if you're caught. In fact, everything bad you've ever heard about a Mexican jail is considered to be close to the truth — if not a rose-colored version of it. Mexico employs the Napoleonic Code of law, meaning that you're guilty until proven innocent. Simply stated, it's not worth the potential high. That's what tequila's for!

If you're traveling with **infants and/or children** in Mexico, be extra careful to avoid anything that's not bottled. Infant formulas, baby foods, canned milk, and other baby supplies can be readily purchased from grocery stores. Your best bet is to carry extra baby eats when you go out. Most Mexican restaurants will cheerfully warm bottles and packaged goods for your child.

Be especially careful of sun exposure because **sunburn** can be extremely dangerous. Protect the little ones with special SPF bathing suits and cover-ups and regularly apply a strong sunscreen.

Dehydration can also make your child seriously ill. Make sure your child drinks plenty of water and juices throughout the day. Especially when they're in the pool or at the beach having fun, they may not remember that they're thirsty, so it's up to you to remind them. Sunburn also contributes to and complicates dehydration.

Renting a Car

The first thing you should know is that car-rental costs are high in Mexico because cars are more expensive here. However, the condition of rental cars has improved greatly over the years, and clean, comfortable, new cars are the norm. At press time, the basic cost for a one-day rental of a Volkswagen (VW) Beetle, with unlimited mileage (but before the 15% tax and $15 to $25 daily for insurance), was $45 in Cancún, $40 in Puerto Vallarta, and $40 in Acapulco. Renting by the week gives you a lower daily rate. Avis was offering a basic seven-day weekly rate for a VW Beetle (before tax or insurance) of $220 in Cancún and Puerto Vallarta and $200 in Acapulco. Prices may be considerably higher if you rent in these same cities around a major holiday.

Car-rental companies usually write up a credit-card charge in U.S. dollars.

Be careful of deductibles, which vary greatly in Mexico. Some deductibles are as high as $2,500, which immediately comes out of your pocket in case of car damage. Hertz has a $1,000 deductible on a VW Beetle; the deductible at Avis is $500 for the same car.

A word to the wise: Always get the insurance. Insurance is offered in two parts. Collision and damage insurance covers your car and others if the accident is your fault, and personal accident insurance covers you and anyone in your car. Read the fine print on the back of your rental agreement and note that insurance may be invalid if you have an accident while driving on an unpaved road.

Personally, I think that Los Cabos is the only destination that is really enjoyed best if you have a car to get around. For all other beach destinations, I prefer to use taxis, which are reasonably priced except in Los Cabos.

Finding the best car-rental deal

Car-rental rates vary even more than airline fares. The price depends on the size of the car, the length of time you keep it, where and when you pick it up and drop it off, where you take it, and a host of other factors.

Asking a few key questions could save you hundreds of dollars. For example, weekend rates may be lower than weekday rates. Ask if the rate is the same for pickup Friday morning as it is for Thursday night. If you're keeping the car five or more days, a weekly rate may be cheaper than the daily rate. Some companies may assess a drop-off charge if you don't return the car to the same renting location; others, notably National, do not. Ask if the rate is cheaper if you pick up the car at the airport or a location in town. Don't forget to mention membership in AAA, AARP, frequent-flyer programs, and trade unions. These memberships usually entitle you to discounts ranging from 5% to 30%. Ask your travel agent to check any and all of these rates. And most car rentals are worth at least 500 miles on your frequent flyer account!

As with other aspects of planning your trip, using the Internet can make comparison shopping for a car rental much easier. All the major booking Web sites — **Travelocity** (www.travelocity.com), **Expedia** (www.expedia.com), **Yahoo Travel** (www.travel.yahoo.com), and **Cheap Tickets** (www.cheaptickets.com), for example — have search engines that can dig up discounted car-rental rates. Just enter the size of the car you want, the pickup and return dates, and the city where you want to rent, and the server returns a price. You can even make the reservation through these sites.

In addition to the standard coverage, car-rental companies also offer additional liability insurance (if you harm others in an accident), personal accident insurance (if you harm yourself or your passengers), and personal effects insurance (if your luggage is stolen from your car). If you have insurance on your car at home, you're probably covered for most of these unlikelihoods. If your own insurance doesn't cover you for rentals, or if you don't have auto insurance, you should consider the additional coverage. But weigh the likelihood of getting into an accident or losing your luggage against the cost of these insurance options (as much as $20 per day combined), which can significantly add to the price of your rental.

Some companies also offer refueling packages, in which you pay for an entire tank of gas up front. The price is usually fairly competitive with local gas prices, but you don't get credit for any gas remaining in the tank. If you reject this option, you pay only for the gas you use, but you have to return the car with a full tank or face charges of $3 to $4 a gallon for any shortfall. If a stop at a gas station on the way to the airport will make you miss your plane, by all means take advantage of the fuel purchase option. Otherwise, skip it.

Remembering safety comes first

If you decide to rent a car and drive in Mexico, there are a few things you need to keep in mind:

✔ Most Mexican roads are not up to U.S. standards of smoothness, hardness, width of curve, grade of hill, or safety markings.

✔ Driving at night is dangerous — the roads aren't good, and they're rarely lit; trucks, carts, pedestrians, and bicycles usually have no lights; and you can hit potholes, animals, rocks, dead ends, or uncrossable bridges without warning.

✔ Never turn left by stopping in the middle of a highway with your left signal on. Instead, pull off the highway onto the right shoulder, wait for traffic to clear, and then proceed across the road.

✔ No credit cards are accepted for gas purchases.

✔ Places called *vulcanizadora* or *llantera* repair flat tires. It's common to find such places open 24 hours a day on the most traveled highways. Even if the place looks empty, chances are you'll find someone who can help you fix a flat.

✔ When possible, many Mexicans drive away from minor accidents, or try to make an immediate settlement, to avoid involving the police.

✔ If the police arrive while the involved persons are still at the scene, everyone may be locked up until responsibility is determined and damages are settled. If you were in a rental car, notify the rental company immediately and ask how to contact the nearest adjuster. (You did buy insurance with the rental, right?)

Packing For Mexico's Beaches

Start packing by taking out everything you think you need and laying it out on the bed. Then get rid of half of it.

It's not that the airlines won't let you take it all — they will, with some limits — but why would you want to get a hernia from lugging half your house around with you? Suitcase straps can be particularly painful with sunburned shoulders.

So what are the bare essentials? Comfortable walking shoes, a camera, a versatile sweater and/or jacket, a belt, a swimsuit, toiletries and medications (pack these in your carry-on bag so you have them if the airline loses your luggage), and something to sleep in. Unless you're attending a board meeting, a funeral, or one of the city's finest restaurants, you probably won't need a suit or a fancy dress. Even the nicest restaurants tend to be casual when it comes to dress, especially for men. Women, on the other hand, tend to enjoy those sexy resort dresses, and they're definitely appropriate in any of the resorts covered in this book. But when it comes to essentials, you get more use out of a pair of jeans or khakis and a comfortable sweater.

Electricity runs on the same current in Mexico as in the United States and Canada, so feel free to bring a hairdryer, personal stereo, or whatever else you'd like to plug in. Don't bother to bring a travel iron — most hotels offer irons and ironing boards, or they offer the service at a very reasonable rate.

When choosing your suitcase, think about the kind of traveling you're doing. If you'll be walking with your luggage on hard floors, a bag with wheels makes sense. If you'll be carrying your luggage over uneven roads or up and down stairs, wheels won't help much. A fold-over garment bag will help keep dressy clothes wrinkle-free, but it can be a nuisance if you'll be packing and unpacking a lot. Hard-sided luggage protects breakable items better, but it weighs more than soft-sided bags.

When packing, start with the biggest, hardest items (usually shoes) and then fit smaller items in and around them. Pack breakable items in between several layers of clothes or keep them in your carry-on bag. Put things that could leak, like shampoos or suntan lotions in resealable plastic bags. Lock your suitcase with a small padlock (available at most luggage stores if your bag doesn't already have one) and put a distinctive identification tag on the outside so your bag will be easy to spot on the carousel.

You're allowed one to two pieces of carry-on luggage, both of which must fit in the overhead compartment or the seat in front of you. These bags should contain a book, any breakable items you don't want to put in your suitcase, a personal headphone stereo, a snack in case you don't like the airline food, a bottle of water, any vital documents you don't want to lose in your luggage (like your return ticket, passport, wallet, and so on), and some empty space for the sweater or jacket that you won't want to be wearing while you're waiting for your luggage in an overheated terminal. You should also carry aboard any prescription medications, your glasses or spare contact lenses, and your camera. I always carry a change of clothes (shorts, T-shirt, and swimsuit) — just in case. If the airline loses your luggage, you're likely to have it within 24 hours, but having these essentials can get you right into vacation fun anyway.

Tips on what to wear to church

Whenever you visit a church in Mexico, no matter how casual the town is, or how close the church is to the ocean, you should never enter wearing just a swimsuit or a pareo. Women should wear something other than short shorts and halter tops. Men should always wear some sort of shirt, even if it's just a tank top.

Because lost-luggage rates have reached an all-time high, consumers are trying to divert disaster by bringing all of their possessions on board. But planes are more crowded than ever, security measures have been increased, and overhead compartment space is at a premium. Most airlines now limit you to a single carry-on for crowded flights and impose size restrictions on the bags you do bring on board. The dimensions vary, but the strictest airlines say carry-ons must measure no more than 22 x 14 x 9 inches, including wheels and handles, and weigh no more than 40 pounds. Many airports are already furnished with x-ray machines that literally block any carry-on bigger than the posted size restrictions. It sounds drastic, but keep in mind that many of these regulations are enforced only at the discretion of the gate attendants. However, if you plan to bring more than one bag aboard a crowded flight, be sure your medications, documents, and valuables are consolidated in one bag in case you're forced to check the second one.

Here's a quick checklist of items you don't want to forget:

- At least two swimsuits
- Sunglasses
- Comfortable walking shoes
- Sandals
- Hat or cap
- Sunscreen
- Driver's license (if you plan to rent a car)
- Scuba certification (if you plan to dive)
- Casual slacks other than jeans (for men, especially if you plan on hitting the trendiest discos, some of which don't allow shorts or jeans)
- A pareo that can double as a long or short skirt, or a wrap (for women)

Part III
Cancún

"Of all the stuff we came back from Mexico with, I think these adobe bathrobes were the least well thought out."

In this part . . .

The most popular of Mexico's beach resorts, Cancún perfectly showcases the country's breathtaking natural beauty and the depth of its thousand-year-old history. Cancún is both the peak of Caribbean splendor and a modern mega-resort. It boasts translucent turquoise waters, powdery white-sand beaches, and a wide array of nearby shopping, dining, and nightlife choices, in addition to a ton of other activities. Most resorts are offered at exceptional value, and Cancún is easily accessible by air.

Many travelers who feel apprehensive about visiting foreign soil feel completely at home and at ease here: English is spoken, dollars are accepted, roads are well paved, and lawns are manicured. A lot of the shopping and dining takes place in malls, and I swear that some hotels seem larger than a small town. Simply stated, Cancún is the reason why most people travel to Mexico. In the following chapters, I introduce you to this Caribbean-coast jewel and offer up lots of tips for making the most of your stay on this nonstop island.

Chapter 8

The Lowdown on Cancún's Hotel Scene

*I*n 1974, a team of Mexican-government computer analysts selected Cancún as an area for tourism development because of its ideal combination of features to attract travelers — and they were right on the money. Cancún is actually an island, a 14-mile-long sliver of land shaped roughly like the number "7." Two bridges, spanning the expansive Nichupté Lagoon, connect Cancún to the mainland. (Cancún means "Golden Snake" in the Mayan language.)

With more than 24,000 hotel rooms in the area to choose from, Cancún has something for every taste and every budget. Here, I review the two main areas — **Cancún Island (Isla Cancún)** and **Cancún City (Ciudad Cancún),** located inland, to the west of the island.

Cancún is definitely the destination to try out an air-hotel package. Although the rack rates at Cancún's hotels are among the highest in Mexico, the package deals are among the best because of the large number of charter companies operating here. I should also point out that if you do arrive without a hotel reservation — not recommended during peak weeks surrounding the Christmas and Easter holidays — you're likely to be able to bargain your way into a great rate.

Choosing a Location

Island hotels are stacked along the beach like dominoes; almost all of them offer clean, modern facilities. Extravagance reigns in the more recently built hotels, many of which are awash in a sea of marble and glass. However, some hotels, although they are exclusive, affect a more relaxed attitude.

Living *la vida* local

For condo, home, and villa rentals as an alternative to hotel stays, check with **Cancún Hideaways,** a company specializing in luxury properties, downtown apartments, and condos — many offered at prices much lower than comparable hotel accommodations. Owner Maggie Rodriguez, a former resident of Cancún, has made this niche market her specialty. You can preview her offerings at www.cancun-hideaways.com.

The water is placid on the upper end of the island facing Bahía de Mujeres, while beaches lining the long side of the island facing the Caribbean are subject to choppier water and crashing waves on windy days. Be aware that the farther south you go on the island, the longer it takes (20 to 30 minutes in traffic) to get back to the "action spots," which are primarily located between the Plaza Flamingo and Punta Cancún on the island — close to the point that connects the two parts of the 7 — and along Avenida Tulum on the mainland.

Almost all major hotel chains are represented along **Isla Cancún,** also known as the **Hotel Zone,** so my selections can be viewed as a representative summary, with a select number of notable places to stay. The reality is that Cancún is so popular as a package destination from the United States that prices and special deals are often the deciding factor for vacationers traveling here.

 Ciudad Cancún is the more authentic Mexican town of the two locations, where the workers in the hotels live and day-to-day business is conducted for those not on vacation. The area offers independently owned, smaller, and much less expensive stays — the difference in prices between these accommodations and their island counterparts is truly remarkable. And many hotels in Ciudad Cancún offer a shuttle service to sister-properties in Isla Cancún, meaning you can still access the beach, and for a fraction of the price in return for a little extra travel time. In my opinion, many of the best restaurants are located here, especially if you're looking for a meal in a type of restaurant other than those you can find back home. It also goes without saying that you get the best value for your meal dollar or peso in Ciudad Cancún.

Cancún's Best Accommodations

Each hotel listing includes specific rack rates for two people spending one night in a standard room, double occupancy during high season (Christmas to Easter), unless otherwise indicated. Rack rates simply mean published rates and tend to be the highest rate paid — you can do better, especially if you're purchasing a package that includes airfare (see Chapter 6 for tips on avoiding paying rack rates). The rack

Accommodations in Ísla Cancún (Hotel Zone)

To Puerto Juárez ↑
and Punta Sam
180

Playa las
Perlas
Playa
Juventud

*Bahía
de Mujeres*

Camino Real Cancún
& Maria Bonita

Cancún
City

Av. López Portillo

Ave. Bonampak

Ferry to Isla Mujeres

Km 3
Playa Linda
Blue Bay Getaway
Cancún

Playa
Lagosta Playa
Tortugas

Fiesta Americana
Grand Coral Beach

Calinda Viva
Cancún

Punta
Cancún

Km 3.5
Km 4
Km 5

La
Fisheria/Savio's

*see Accommodations
in Ciudad Cancún map*

La Boom

Presidente
Inter-Continental

Plaza
Caracol

307
Avenida Tulum

Carlos 'n' Charlies

Paseo Kukulkán

Km 7

Km 7.5

Km 8

Convention
Center

Km 9

Forum by
the Sea/
Coco Bongo

*Canal
Nichupté*

Pok-Ta-Pok
Golf Course

Dady'O/Dady Rock
Bar & Grill

Km 9.5
Playa
Gaviota

Paseo Mujeres

*Laguna
Bojórquez*

Km 10

Miramar Misión
Cancún Park
Plaza

To Tulum
& Chetumal

Lorenzillo's

Plaza Flamingo

Señor
Frog's

Playa Chacmool

Plantation
House

Laguna de Nichupté

Km 11.5

Km12

Flamingo Cancun

Aristos Hotel

*Laguna
del Amor*

La Isla
Shopping Village

Plaza Kukulkán

Ritz Carlton & Club Grill

Km 14

Le Méridien Cancún
Resort & Spa/Côte Sud

Mango Tango

Captain's Cove

Marriott Casa Magna

La Dolce Vita

Paseo Kukulkán

Hilton Cancún Beach & Golf Resort

Ruinas del Rey

Km 16

*Laguna
Inglé*

*Canal
Nizuc*

El Pueblito

Caribbean Sea

Westin
Regina Cancún

Km 20

To Airport

Paseo Kukulkán

Punta
Nizuc

Beach
Golf
Ruins

0   2 mi
0   2 km

N

UNITED STATES

MEXICO
Mexico
City

*Gulf of
Mexico*

Cancún

THE YUCATÁN
PENINSULA

0   500 mi
0   500 km

*PACIFIC
OCEAN*

Aristos Hotel **km 12**	Hilton Cancún Beach & Golf Resort **km 17**
Blue Bay Getaway Cancún **km 3.5**	Le Méridien Cancún Resort & Spa **km 14**
Calinda Viva Cancún **km 8.5**	Marriott Casa Magna **km 14.5**
Camino Real Cancún **km 9.5**	Miramar Misión Cancún Park Plaza **km 9.5**
El Pueblito **km 17.5**	Presidente Inter-Continental Cancún **km 7.5**
Fiesta Americana Grand Coral Beach **km 9.5**	Ritz-Carlton Hotel **km 13.5**
Flamingo Cancún **km 11.5**	Westin Regina Cancún **km 20**

rate prices quoted here include the 12% room tax — note that this is 5% lower than in most other resorts in Mexico, where the standard tax is 17%. Please refer to the Introduction for an explanation of the price categories.

Hotels often double the normal rates during Christmas and Easter weeks, but low-season rates can be anywhere from 20% to 60% below high-season rates. Some rates may seem much higher than others, but many of these higher rates are *all-inclusive* — meaning that your meals and beverages are included in the price of your stay. All tips and taxes and most activities and entertainment are also included in all-inclusive rates.

All hotels listed here have air-conditioning, unless otherwise indicated. Parking is available at all island hotels.

Antillano
$ Ciudad Cancún

A quiet and very clean choice, the Antillano is close to the Ciudad Cancún bus terminal. Rooms overlook either the main downtown street, Avenida Tulum, the side streets, or the interior lawn and pool. The last choice is the most desirable because these rooms are the quietest. Each room has coordinated furnishings, one or two double beds, a sink area separate from the bathroom, and red-tile floors. A bonus: This inexpensive hotel provides guests the use of its beach club on the island. To find Antillano from Avenida Tulum, walk west on Claveles a half block; it's opposite the restaurant Rosa Mexicana. Parking is on the street.

Av. Claveles 1 (corner of Av. Tulum). ☎ *998-884-1532. Fax: 998-884-1878. Internet:* www.hotelantillano.com. *48 units. Street parking. Rack rates: High season $70 double; low season $52 double. AE, MC, V.*

Aristos Hotel
$$ Isla Cancún

Aristos is my pick for an inexpensive hotel on Isla Cancún. One of the island's first hotels, it continues to welcome repeat guests, especially younger (spring breakers), European, and senior travelers. As one of the original hotels, its location is also prime — near to the central shopping, dining, and nightlife centers. Rooms are kept updated and feature wood furnishings. Though the rooms are small, they're very clean and cool, with red-tile floors and small balconies. All rooms face either the Caribbean or the *paseo* (avenue) and lagoon; the best views are the Caribbean side (and no noise from the *paseo*). A central pool overlooks the ocean and a wide stretch of beach one level below the lobby. The hotel has a restaurant and three bars, plus two lighted tennis courts and a small marina with watersports equipment.

Accommodations in Ciudad Cancún (Cancún City)

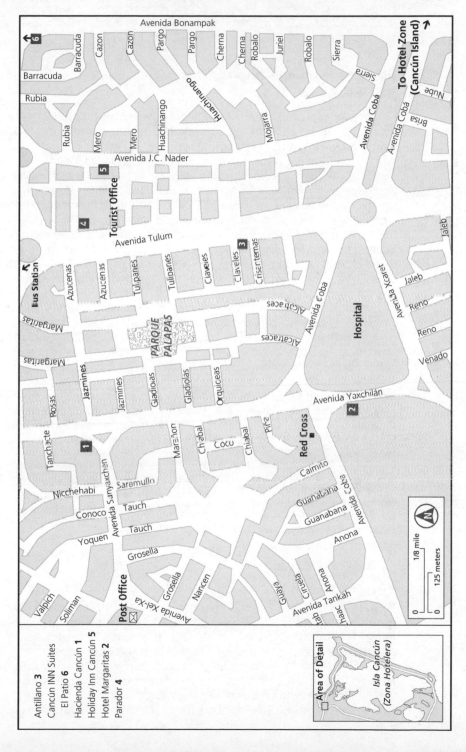

Antillano **3**
Cancún INN Suites
El Patio **6**
Hacienda Cancún **1**
Holiday Inn Cancún **5**
Hotel Margaritas **2**
Parador **4**

Av. Kukulkán, Km 12. ☎ *800-527-4786 in the U.S., or 998-883-0011. Fax: 998-883-0078. E-mail:* aristcun@prodigy.net.mx. *245 units. Free, unguarded parking. Rack rates: High season $120 double; low season $100 double. For all-inclusive option for three meals and drinks, add $36 daily. AE, MC, V.*

Blue Bay Getaway Cancún

$$$ Isla Cancún

Blue Bay is a spirited yet relaxing all-inclusive resort for adults only — no kids under 16 are allowed — that's favored by young adults in particular. One of its best features is its prime location — right at the northern end of the Hotel Zone, close to the major shopping plazas, restaurants, and nightlife, with a terrific beach with calm waters for swimming. Surrounded by acres of tropical gardens, the comfortable, clean, and modern guest rooms are located in two sections: the central building, where rooms are decorated in rustic wood, and the remaining nine buildings, which feature rooms in a colorful Mexican décor. The main lobby, administrative offices, restaurants, and Tequila Sunrise bar are all located in the central building, meaning you're close to all the action — and more noise — if your room is in this section. Included are all of your meals, served at any of the four restaurants, and libations, which you can find in the four bars. During the evenings, guests may enjoy a variety of theme-night dinners, nightly shows, and live entertainment in an outdoor theater with capacity for 150 guests. Activities and facilities include two swimming pools, a tennis court, an exercise room, windsurfing, kayaks, catamarans, boogie boards, complimentary snorkeling and scuba lessons, and a marina. Safes are available for an extra charge, as is dry-cleaning and laundry service. Blue Bay allows guests to use the amenities and facilities at its sister resort, the Blue Bay Club and Marina (a resort for families), located just outside Ciudad Cancún, near the ferry to Isla Mujeres. A free bus and boat shuttle service is provided between both Blue Bay resorts.

Paseo Kukulkán, Km 3.5. ☎ *800-BLUE-BAY in the U.S., or 998-848-7900. Fax: 998-848-7994. Internet:* www.bluebayresorts.com. *216 units. Free parking. Rack rates: High season $280 double; low season $180 double. Rates are all-inclusive (room, food, beverages, and activities). AE, MC, V.*

Calinda Viva Cancún

$$$ Isla Cancún

From the street, the Calinda Viva may not be much to look at, but the location is ideal because it's set on Cancún's best beach for safe swimming. The ocean side has a small but pretty patio garden and pool. Calinda is close to all the shops and restaurants clustered near Punta Cancún and the convention center. You can choose between rooms with either a lagoon or ocean view. The rooms are large and undistinguished in decor, but they're comfortable. They feature marble floors and either two double beds or a king-size bed. Several studios with kitchenettes are also available upon request. In addition to a restaurant and three bars, you also have two lighted tennis courts, watersports equipment rental, and a small marina with its own fishing fleet.

Paseo Kukulkán, Km 8.5, next to the Playa Linda dock. ☎ *800-221-2222 in the U.S., or 998-883-0800. Fax: 998-883-2087. 216 units. Free parking. Rack rates: High season $145–250 double; low season $138–158 double. AE, MC, V.*

Camino Real Cancún
$$$$ Isla Cancún

The Camino Real is among the island's most appealing places to stay, located on 4 acres right at the tip of Punta Cancún. The setting is sophisticated, but the hotel is very welcoming to children. Camino Real is a favored name within Mexico, where vacations are synonymous with family. The architecture of the hotel is trademark Camino Real — contemporary and sleek, with bright colors and strategic angles. Rooms in the newer 18-story Camino Real Club have extra services and amenities, including a complimentary full breakfast each day in the Beach Club lobby. The lower-priced rooms have lagoon views. In addition to the oceanfront pool, the Camino Real has a private saltwater lagoon with sea turtles and tropical fish. Three lighted tennis courts, a fitness center, beach volleyball, a sailing pier, and a watersports center keep things active. The hotel's three restaurants — including the popular María Bonita (see Chapter 10) — and the lively Azucar Cuban dance club are all onsite.

Av. Kukulkán, Punta Cancún. ☎ *800-722-6466 in the U.S., or 998-848-7000. Fax: 998-848-7001. Internet:* www.caminoreal.com/cancun. *389 units. Daily fee for guarded parking adjacent to hotel. Rack rates: High season $275 standard double, $320 Camino Real Club double; low season $195 standard double; $230 Camino Real Club double. AE, DC, MC, V.*

Cancún INN Suites El Patio
$ Ciudad Cancún

A European-style guesthouse, Cancún INN Suites El Patio caters to travelers looking for more of the area's culture. Many of the guests at this small hotel stay for up to a month and enjoy its combination of excellent value and warm hospitality. You won't find any bars, pools, or loud parties in this place; what you do find is excellent service and impeccable accommodations. Rooms face the plant-filled interior courtyard, dotted with groupings of wrought-iron chairs and tables. Each room has a slightly different decor and set of amenities, but all have white-tile floors and rustic wood furnishings in their various configurations. Some rooms have light kitchenette facilities, and there's also a common kitchen area with purified water and a cooler for stocking your own supplies. A small restaurant — actually closer to a dining room — serves breakfast and dinner. While a public phone is located in the entranceway, the staff can also arrange for a cellular phone in your room. The game and TV room has a large-screen cable TV, a library stocked with books on Mexican culture, backgammon, cards, and board games. The hotel offers special packages for lodging and Spanish lessons and discounts for longer stays.

*Av. Bonampak 51 and Cereza, SM2A, Centro. ☎ **998-884-3500**. Fax: 998-884-3540. Internet:* www.cancun-suites.com. *12 units. Rack rates: $50 double. Ask for discounts for longer stays. AE, MC, V.*

El Pueblito
$$$ Isla Cancún

The El Pueblito looks like a traditional Mexican hacienda and has the gracious, hospitable service to match. Several three-story buildings (no elevators) are terraced in a V-shape down a gentle hillside toward the sea, with a meandering swimming pool with waterfalls running between them, to a beachside, thatched-roof restaurant. Consistent renovations and upgrades and a changeover to an all-inclusive concept have made this hotel more appealing than ever and another exceptional all-inclusive value. Rooms are very large and have rattan furnishings, travertine marble floors, large bathrooms, and either a balcony or terrace facing the pool or sea. In addition to a constant flow of buffet-style meals and snacks, there's also the choice of a nightly theme party, complete with entertainment. Miniature golf and a water slide, plus a full program of kid's activities, make this place an ideal choice for families with children. Babysitting services are available for $10 per hour. The hotel is located toward the southern end of the island past the Hilton Resort.

*Paseo Kukulkán, Km 17.5, past the Hilton Resort. ☎ **998-885-0422**, 998-881-8800. Fax: 998-885-2066. Internet:* www.pueblitohotels.com. *349 units. Free parking. Rack rates: High season $300 double, low season $240 double. Rates are all-inclusive. AE, MC, V.*

Fiesta Americana Grand Coral Beach
$$$$$ Isla Cancún

A spectacularly grand hotel, the Fiesta Americana has one of the best locations in Cancún with its 1,000 feet of prime beachfront and proximity to the main shopping and entertainment centers — perfect for the traveler looking to be at the heart of all that Cancún has to offer. The great Punta Cancún location (opposite the convention center) has the advantage of facing the beach to the north, meaning that the surf is calm and perfect for swimming. When it comes to the hotel itself, the operative word here is *big* — everything at the Fiesta Americana seems oversized, from the lobby to the rooms. Service is gracious, if cool, as the hotel aims for a more sophisticated ambience. The finishings of elegant dark-green granite and an abundance of marble extend from the lobby to the large guest rooms, all of which have balconies facing the ocean. Two swimming pools border the beach, including a 660-foot-long free-form swimming pool with swim-up bars and a casual poolside snack bar, plus a full watersports equipment rental service on the beach. Two additional restaurants, plus five bars, are inside the hotel, along with a mini shopping center. If tennis is your game, this hotel has the best facilities in Cancún. Three indoor tennis courts with stadium seating are part of an extensive fitness center and spa.

Paseo Kukulkán, Km 9.5. ☎ ***800-343-7821*** *in the U.S., or 998-881-3200. Fax: 998-881-3263. Internet:* www.fiestaamericana.com.mx. *602 units. Rack rates: High season $328–555 double, $529–650 Club Floors double; low season $222–424 double, $381–504 Club Floors double. AE, MC, V.*

Flamingo Cancún
$$$ Isla Cancún

The Flamingo seems to have been inspired by the dramatic, slope-sided architecture of the Camino Real, but it's considerably smaller and less expensive. I find it a friendly, accommodating choice for families. The clean, comfortable, and modern guest rooms — all with balconies — border a courtyard facing the interior swimming pools and palapa pool bar. A second pool with a sundeck overlooks the ocean. The Flamingo is in the heart of the island hotel district, opposite the Flamingo Shopping Center and close to other hotels, shopping centers, and restaurants.

Blvd. Kukulkán, Km 11.5. ☎ ***998-883-1544***. *Fax: 998-883-1029. Internet:* www.flamingocancun.com. *221 units. Free, unguarded parking across the street in the Plaza Flamingo. Rack rates: High season $170 double; low season $120 double. AE, MC, V.*

Hacienda Cancún
$ Ciudad Cancún

An extremely pleasing little hotel — and a great value — Hacienda Cancún is perfect for travelers on a budget. The facade has been remodeled to look like a hacienda, and rooms continue the theme, with their rustic-style Mexican furnishings. Guest rooms are clean and very comfortable; all have two double beds and windows (but no views). There's a nice, small pool and cafe under a shaded palapa in the back. To find it from Avenida Yaxchilán, turn west on Sunyaxchen; it's on your right next to the Hotel Caribe International, opposite 100% Natural. Parking is on the street.

Sunyaxchen 39–40. ☎ ***998-884-3672***. *Fax: 998-884-1208. E-mail:* hhda@Cancun.com.mx. *35 units. Rack rates: High season $45 double; low season $38 double. MC, V.*

Hilton Cancún Beach & Golf Resort
$$$$ Isla Cancún

The Hilton in Cancún is especially perfect for anyone whose motto is "the bigger the better." Grand, expansive, and fully equipped, this is a true resort in every sense of the word. The Hilton Cancún, formerly the

1994-vintage Caesar Park Resort, is situated on 250 acres of prime Cancún beachfront property with its own 18-hole, par-72 golf course across the street and a location that gives every room a sea view (some have both sea and lagoon views). Like the sprawling resort, rooms are grandly spacious and immaculately decorated in a minimalist style. Marble floors and bathrooms throughout are softened with area rugs and pale furnishings. The more elegant Beach Club rooms are set off from the main hotel in two- and three-story buildings (no elevators) and have their own check-in and concierge service, plus nightly complimentary cocktails. The hotel is especially appealing to golfers because it's one of only two hotels in Cancún with an onsite course. (The other is the Mélia, which has an 18-hole executive course.) The seven interconnected pools with a swim-up bar, two lighted tennis courts, a large, fully equipped gym, and a beachfront watersports center make the Hilton Cancún a good choice for those looking for an action-packed stay. Their Kids Club program is one of the best on the island, making it great for families.

Paseo Kukulkán, Km 17, Retorno Lacandones. ☎ *800-228-3000 in the U.S., or 998-881-8000. Fax: 998-881-8080. Internet:* www.hiltoncancun.com.mx. *426 units. Rack rates: High season $305–380 standard double, $385–585 Beach Club double; low season $220–300 standard double, $300–500 Beach Club double. AE, DC, MC, V.*

Holiday Inn Cancún
$$–$$$ Ciudad Cancún

The nicest hotel in downtown Cancún, the Holiday Inn Cancún is also one of the very best values in the area. It offers all the expected comforts of a chain like Holiday Inn, yet in an atmosphere of Mexican hospitality. Resembling a Mexican hacienda, rooms are set off from a large rotunda-style lobby, lush gardens, and a pleasant pool area, which has a separate wading section for children. All rooms have Talavera tile inlays and brightly colored fabric accents; views of the garden, the pool, or the street; and a small sitting area and balcony. Bathrooms have a combination tub and shower. For the price, I found the extra in-room amenities of a coffeemaker, hairdryer, and iron to be nice pluses. In addition to two restaurants, there's also a generally lively lobby bar, as well as tennis courts and a small gym. Guests of the Holiday Inn may enjoy the facilities of the Melía Cancún Beach Club with complimentary shuttle service. The hotel is located right behind the state government building and within walking distance of downtown Cancún dining and shopping.

Av. Nader 1, SM2, Centro. ☎ *998-887-4455. Fax: 998-884-7954. Internet:* www.holiday-inn.com. *248 units. Rack rates: High season $125 standard, $140 jr. suite; low season $105 standard, $126 jr. suite. AE, MC, V.*

Hotel Margaritas
$–$$ Ciudad Cancún

Located in downtown Cancún, this four-story hotel (with elevator) is comfortable and unpretentious, offering one of the best values in Cancún.

Rooms have white tile floors and a small balcony, and they're exceptionally clean and bright and pleasantly decorated. The attractive pool is surrounded by lounge chairs and has a wading section for children. The hotel offers complimentary safes at the front desk and more services than most budget hotels, including babysitting.

Av. Yaxchilán 41, SM22, Centro. ☎ 998-884-9333. Fax: 998-884-1324. 100 units. Rack rates: High season $80 double; low season $65 double. AE, MC, V.

Le Méridien Cancún Resort & Spa
$$$$$ Isla Cancún

Of all the luxury properties in Cancún, I find Le Méridien the most inviting, with a polished yet welcoming sense of personal service. Although other hotels tend to overdo a sense of formality in striving to justify their prices, Le Méridien has an elegantly casual style that makes you comfortable enough to thoroughly relax. From the intimate lobby and reception area to the most outstanding concierge service in Cancún, guests feel immediately pampered upon arrival. The hotel itself is smaller than others and feels more like an upscale boutique hotel than an immense resort — a welcome relief to those overstressed by activity at home. The decor throughout the rooms and common areas is one of understated good taste — both classy and comforting, not overdone. Rooms are generous in size, and most have small balconies overlooking the pool with a view to the ocean. There's a very large marble bathroom with a separate tub and a glassed-in shower. The hotel attracts many Europeans and younger, sophisticated travelers, and is ideal for a second honeymoon or romantic break. Certainly, a highlight of — or even a reason for — staying here is time spent at the **Spa del Mar,** one of Mexico's finest and most complete European spa facilities, featuring two levels and more than 15,000 square feet of services dedicated to your body and soul. A complete fitness center with extensive cardio and weight machines is found on the upper level. The spa is located below and comprised of a healthy snack bar, a full-service salon, and 14 treatment rooms, as well as separate men's and women's steam rooms, saunas, whirlpools, cold plunge pools, inhalation rooms, tranquility rooms, lockers, and changing areas.

The health club may become a necessity if you fully enjoy the gourmet restaurant, **Côté Sud,** with its specialties based on Mediterranean and Provençal cuisines (check out Chapter 10 for a detailed listing of this restaurant). The menu is simply delicious — not pretentious. Adjoining the spa is a large swimming pool that cascades down three levels. Above the spa is a tennis center with two championship tennis courts with lights. Watersports equipment is available for rent on the beach. There's also a supervised children's program with its own Penguin Clubhouse, play equipment, and a wading pool.

Retorno del Rey, Km 14, Zona Hotelera. ☎ 800-543-4300 in the U.S., or 998-881-2200. Fax: 998-881-2201. Internet: www.meridiencancun.com.mx. *213 units. Free* *parking. Rack rates: High season $290 standard, $450 suite; low season $220 standard, $350 suite. Ask for special spa packages. AE, DC, MC, V. Small pets accepted, with advance reservation.*

Marriott Casa Magna

$$$$ Isla Cancún

This property is quintessential Marriott. Travelers who are familiar with the chain's standards feel at home here and appreciate the hotel's attention to detailed service. In fact, if you're on your first trip to Mexico, and you're looking for a little familiarity of home, this is a great choice because it feels like a slice of the United States transported to a stunning stretch of Caribbean beach. Guest rooms have contemporary furnishings, tiled floors, and ceiling fans; most have balconies. All suites occupy corners and have enormous terraces, ocean views, and TVs in both the living room and the bedroom. The Marriott Casa Magna offers five on-site restaurants to choose from, plus a lobby bar with live music. Alongside the meandering oceanfront pool are two lighted tennis courts. The hotel caters to family travelers with specially priced packages (up to two children can stay free with parents) and the Club Amigos supervised children's program. A more deluxe offering from Marriott, the 450-room luxury **JW Cancún,** recently opened on the beach next to the Casa Magna. Its hallmark is a 20,000-square-foot spa and fitness center.

Paseo Kukulkán, Km 14.5. ☎ 800-228-9290 in the U.S., or 998-881-2000. Fax: 998-881-2071. Internet: www.marriott.com. *452 units. Rack rates: High season $225–254 double, $350 suite; low season $139–160 double, $300 suite. Ask about available packages. AE, MC, V.*

Miramar Misión Cancún Park Plaza

$$$ Isla Cancún

Another good choice for travelers looking for well-priced rooms right on the beach, the ingeniously designed Miramar offers partial views of both the lagoon and ocean from all of its rooms. A notable feature is the large, rectangular swimming pool that extends through the hotel and down to the beach and contains built-in, submerged sun chairs. There's also an oversized whirlpool (the largest in Cancún), a sundeck, and a snack bar on the seventh-floor roof. Rooms are on the small side but are bright and comfortable with a small balcony and bamboo furniture; bathrooms have polished limestone vanities. In addition to three restaurants, there's also the popular nightclub **Batacha,** featuring live music for dancing from 9 p.m. to 4 a.m. Tuesday to Sunday.

Av. Kukulkán, Km 9.5. ☎ 998-883-1755. Fax: 998-883-1136. Internet: www.hoteles mision.com. *266 units. Rack rates: High season $180; low season $140 double. AE, MC, V.*

Parador

$ Ciudad Cancún

The convenient location and rock-bottom prices make this otherwise nondescript hotel among the most popular downtown hotels. Guest rooms, located on one of three floors, are arranged around two long, narrow garden courtyards leading back to a small pool (with an even smaller, separate children's pool) and grassy sunning area. The rooms are contemporary and basic, each with two double beds and a shower. The hotel is next to Pop's restaurant, almost at the corner of Uxmal. Street parking is limited.

Av. Tulum 26. ☎ *998-884-1043, 998-884-1310. Fax: 998-884-9712. 66 units. Rack rates: High season $56 double; low season $38 double. Ask about promotional rates. MC, V.*

Presidente Inter-Continental Cancún

$$$–$$$$ Isla Cancún

On the island's best beach facing the placid Bahía de Mujeres, the Presidente's location is reason enough to stay here, and it's just a two-minute walk to Cancún's public Pok-Ta-Pok Golf Club. Cool and spacious, the Presidente sports a postmodern design with lavish marble and wicker accents and a strong use of color. Guests have a choice of two double beds or one king-size bed. All rooms have tastefully simple unfinished pine furniture. The expansive pool has a pyramid-shaped waterfall and is surrounded by cushioned lounge chairs. In addition to lighted tennis courts and a small fitness center, the marina has watersports equipment rentals. Coming from Cancún City, the Presidente is on the left side of the street before you get to Punta Cancún. For its ambience, I feel that the Presidente is an ideal choice for a romantic getaway or for couples who enjoy indulging in golf, tennis, or even shopping.

Av. Kukulkán, Km 7.5. ☎ *800-327-0200 in the U.S., or 998-848-8700. Fax: 998-883-2602. Internet:* www.interconti.com. *299 units. Rack rates: High season $240–300 double; low season $190–230 double. Ask about special promotional packages. AE, MC, V.*

Ritz-Carlton Hotel

$$$$$ Isla Cancún

The grand-scale Ritz-Carlton is a fountain of formality in this casual beach resort, perfect for someone who wants a Palm Beach-style experience in Mexico. The decor — in both public areas as well as guest rooms — is sumptuous and formal with thick carpets, elaborate chandeliers, and fresh flowers throughout. The hotel fronts a 1,200-foot white-sand beach, and all rooms overlook the ocean, pool (heated during winter months), and tropical gardens. In all rooms, marble bathrooms have telephones, separate tubs and showers, and lighted makeup mirrors. Ritz-Carlton Club floors offer guests five mini-meals a day, private butler service, and Hermés bath products. **The Club Grill,** a fashionable English pub, is one of the best restaurants in the city, and the **Lobby Lounge** is the original home of proper tequila tastings, featuring one of the world's most extensive menus of fine tequilas, as well as Cuban cigars. I love their white-draped cabañas for two on the beach! There's a very good fitness center with spa services, plus three lighted tennis courts. The Ritz Kids program has supervised activities for children, and babysitting services are also available. The hotel has won countless recognitions and accolades for service, although I've been hearing that the hotels' attention to detail has slipped in recent years. Special packages for golfing, spa, and weekend getaways are worth exploring.

Retorno del Rey 36, off Paseo Kukulkán, Km 13.5. ☎ *800-241-3333 in the U.S. and Canada, or 998-885-0808. Fax: 998-881-0815. Internet:* www.ritzcarlton.com. *365 units. Free guarded parking. Rack rates: High season $369–475 double, $389–850 Club floors; low season $189–279 double, Club floors $295–429. AE, MC, V.*

Westin Regina Cancún

$$$$$ **Isla Cancún**

A stunning hotel, the Westin Regina is great for anyone wanting the beauty of Cancún's beaches and a little distance between them and the more boisterous, flashy parts of Cancún's hotel strip. The strikingly austere but grand architecture of the Westin Regina is the stamp of leading Latin-American architect Ricardo Legorreta. A series of five swimming pools front the beach, and the Westin offers two lighted tennis counts and a small fitness center with limited spa services. The hotel is divided into two sections, the main building and the more exclusive six-story, hot-pink, tower section. Standard rooms are unusually large and beautifully furnished with cool, contemporary furniture. The rooms on the sixth floor have balconies, and first-floor rooms have terraces. Rooms in the tower all have ocean or lagoon views and extensive use of marble, furniture with Olinalá lacquer accents, Berber-carpet area rugs, oak tables and chairs, and terraces with lounge chairs. It's important to note that this hotel is a 15- to 20-minute ride from the lively strip that lies between the Plaza Flamingo and Punta Cancún, so it's a better choice for those who want to relish a little more seclusion than Cancún typically offers. However, you can easily join the action when you're so inclined — buses stop in front and taxis are readily available.

Paseo Kukulkán, Km 20. ☎ *800-228-3000 in the U.S., 800-215-7000 in Mexico, or 998-848-7400. Fax: 998-885-0296. Internet:* www.westin.com. *293 units. Rack rates: High season $285–450 double; low season $180–299 double. AE, DC, MC, V.*

Chapter 9

Settling into Cancún

● ●

● ●

Yes, you need a passport or other appropriate credentials (see Chapter 7) to enter Cancún, but after that, you couldn't be in a more American-friendly foreign destination if you tried. If this is your first trip to Mexico — or to a foreign country — you'll probably find that the ensuing culture shock is practically nonexistent. But there are still a few details that you'll be more comfortable knowing before you arrive. In this chapter, I take you from the plane, through the airport, and to your hotel, helping you quickly get your bearings in this easy-to-navigate resort. I continue with tips on everything from taxis to taxes.

Arriving in Cancún

Cancún has one of Mexico's most modern and busiest airports, which seems to be in a constant state of construction to improve and expand its services. Still, it's very easy to navigate — both international and national flights are under the same roof. After checking in with immigration, collecting your bags, and passing through the customs checkpoint, you're ready to enjoy your holiday!

Navigating passport control and customs

Immigration check-in can be a lengthy wait, depending on the number of planes arriving at the same time, but is a generally easy and unremarkable process in which officials ask you to show your passport and complete a tourist card, known as the **FMT** (check out Chapter 7 for more information).

Your FMT is an important document, so take good care of it. You're supposed to keep the FMT with you at all times, as you may be required to show it should you run into any sort of trouble. You also need to turn the FMT back in upon departure, or you may be unable to leave without replacing it.

Next up is the baggage claim area. Here, porters stand by to help with your bags, and they're well worth the price of the tip — about a dollar a bag. After you collect your luggage, you pass through another checkpoint. Something that looks like a traffic light awaits you here. You press a button, and if the light turns green, you're free to go. If it turns red, you need to open each of your bags for a quick search. It's Mexico's random search procedure for customs. If you have an unusually large bag, or an excessive amount of luggage, you may be searched regardless of the traffic-light outcome.

Just past the traffic light, you exit to the street, where you can find transportation to your hotel. Choose between a *colectivo* (shared minivan) and a private taxi. If three or more of you are traveling together, you're probably better off opting for the private cab service. With so many hotels for the collective van to stop at, it can easily take an hour to get to your room, and believe me, the drivers wait until the vans are fully packed before departing! Check out the Cancún orientation map in Chapter 8 to see where your hotel is positioned relative to the airport.

If you do choose the *colectivo* service, which consists of air-conditioned vans, buy your ticket at the booth that's located to the far right as you exit the baggage claim area. Tickets for private cab service can be purchased at a booth inside the airport terminal. Tickets for both the *colectivo* vans and the private taxis are based on a fixed rate depending on the distance to your destination. A taxi ticket is good for up to four passengers.

Getting to your hotel

The airport (CUN) is on the mainland, close to the southern end of the Cancún area. It's about nine miles to downtown **Ciudad Cancún** (Cancún City), which is located on the mainland. The start of the **Zona Hotelera (Hotel Zone),** located on **Isla Cancún** (Cancún Island), is 6½ miles from the airport — about a 20-minute drive east from the airport along wide, well-paved roads.

Hiring a taxi

Rates for a **private taxi** from the airport are around $20 to downtown Cancún or $28 to $40 to the Hotel Zone, depending on your destination. The *colectivos* run from Cancún's international airport into town and the Hotel Zone and cost about $8 per person. There's minibus transportation (for $9.50) from the airport to the Puerto Juárez passenger ferry that takes you to Isla Mujeres. A private taxi can also be hired for this trip for about $40.

No *colectivo* service returns to the airport from Ciudad Cancún or the Hotel Zone, so you must hire a taxi, but the rate should be much less than the trip from the airport. The reason? Only federally chartered taxis may take fares *from* the airport, but any local taxi may bring passengers *to* the airport. Ask for a fare estimate at your hotel, but expect to pay about half what you were charged to get from the airport to your hotel.

Renting a car

Most major car-rental firms have outlets at the airport, so if you're renting a car, consider picking it up and dropping it off at the airport to save on airport-transportation costs. Another way to save money is to arrange for the rental before you leave home. If you wait until you arrive, the daily cost of a rental car may be around $65 to $75 for a Volkswagen Beetle.

Major car rental services include:

- ✔ **Avis** (☎ **800-331-1212** in the U.S., or 998-883-0803; Internet: www.avis.com)

- ✔ **Budget** (☎ **800-527-0700** in the U.S., or 998-884-4812; Fax: 998-884-5011; Internet: https://rent.drivebudget.com/)

- ✔ **Dollar** (☎ **800-800-4000** in the U.S., or 998-886-0775; Internet: www.dollar.com)

- ✔ **Hertz** (☎ **800-654-3131** in the U.S. and Canada, or 998-884-4692; Internet: www.hertz.com)

- ✔ **National** (☎ **800-328-4567** in the U.S., or 998-886-0655; Internet: www.nationalcar.com)

Although you certainly don't have to rent a car here — taxis and buses are plentiful — this is one destination where having a car might make sense for a day or two. First, it can be a convenience, although it's not likely to save you bundles on transportation costs, based on the high relative prices of car rentals in Cancún. The roads in and around Cancún are excellent, and parking is readily available in most of the shopping/entertainment malls. The main reason for renting a car, however, is the flexibility that it provides in exploring the surrounding areas — a day-trip down the coast or to nearby sights is definitely recommended. But if you're not comfortable driving, you can easily cover this ground in one of the many sight-seeing tours available.

If you do rent a car, keep any valuables out of plain sight. Although Cancún's crime rate is very low, the only real problem tends to be rental-car break-ins.

Looking for more information?

Here's a list of the best Web sites for additional information about Cancún:

✔ **All About Cancún** (www.cancunmx.com)

Before taking off on a vacation, every traveler has a few questions. If Cancún is your destination, this site is a good place to start. It contains a database of answers to the most commonly asked questions. Just look for "The Online Experts" section. The site can be slow, but it has input from lots of recent travelers to the region.

✔ **Cancún Convention and Visitors Bureau** (www.gocancun.com)

The official site of the Cancún Convention and Visitor's Bureau provides excellent information on events and area attractions. The site's hotel guide is one of the most complete listings I've seen, and it also offers online booking.

✔ **Cancún Online** (www.cancun.com)

Cancún Online is a comprehensive guide that has lots of information about things to do and see in Cancún. Just remember that advertisers pay to be included and provide most of the details. Highlights include forums, live chats, property-swaps, and bulletin boards, plus information on local Internet access, news, and events. You can even reserve a golf tee time or plan your wedding online.

✔ **Cancún Travel Guide** (www.go2cancun.com)

This group specializing in online information about Mexico has put together an excellent resource for Cancún rentals, hotels, and area attractions. Note that only paying advertisers are listed, but you can find most of the major players here.

✔ **Mexico Web Cancún Chat** (www.mexicoweb.com/travel/chat.html)

This site features one of the more active online chats specifically about Cancún with several different topics to select from. The users share inside information on everything from the cheapest beers to the quality of food at various all-inclusive resorts.

Getting Around Cancún

As I discuss a bit in the "Getting to your hotel" section earlier in this chapter, there are really two Cancúns: **Isla Cancún** (Cancún Island) and **Ciudad Cancún** (Cancún City). The latter, on the mainland, has restaurants, shops, and less-expensive hotels, as well as all the other establishments that make life function — pharmacies, dentists, automotive shops, banks, travel and airline agencies, car-rental firms, and so on — which are all located within an approximately nine-square-block area. The city's main thoroughfare is **Avenida Tulum.** Heading south, Avenida Tulum becomes the highway to the airport, Playa del Carmen, and Tulum. (It actually runs all the way down to Belize.) Heading north, Avenida Tulum intersects the highway to Mérida and the road to Puerto Juárez and the Isla Mujeres ferries.

The famed **Zona Hotelera** (Hotel Zone, also called the **Zona Turística,** or Tourist Zone) stretches out along Isla Cancún, which is a sandy strip of land 14 miles long and shaped like a "7." The Playa Linda Bridge, at the north end of the island, and the Punta Nizuc Bridge, at the southern end, connect Isla Cancún to the mainland. Between these two bridges lies **Laguna Nichupté.** Avenida Cobá from Cancún City becomes Paseo Kukulkán, the island's main traffic artery. Actually, Paseo Kukulkán is the only main road on the island, so getting lost here would really take some effort! To get the hang of pronouncing it quickly enough, say koo-cool-*can,* as in, *can*-cun is sooo cool! Cancún's international airport is located just inland from the south end of the island.

Ciudad Cancún's street-numbering system is a holdover from its early days. Addresses in the city are still expressed by the number of the building lot and the *manzana* (block) or *supermanzana* (group of city blocks). The city is still relatively compact, and the downtown commercial section can be covered easily on foot. Streets here are named after famous Mayan cities, Chichén-Itzá, Tulum, and Uxmal are the names of the boulevards downtown Cancún, as well as nearby archeological sites.

On the island, addresses are given by their kilometer (km) number on Paseo Kukulkán or by reference to some well-known location. The point on the island closest to Ciudad Cancún is km 1; km 20 is found at the very bottom of the "7" at Punta Nizuc, where the Club Med is located.

Taking a taxi

Taxi prices in Cancún are clearly set by zone, although keeping track of what's in which zone can take some work. Taxi rates within the Hotel Zone are a minimum fare of $5 per ride, making it one of the most expensive taxi areas in Mexico.

In addition, taxis operating in the Hotel Zone feel perfectly justified in having a discriminatory pricing structure: Local residents pay about half of what tourists pay, and guests at higher-priced hotels pay about twice the fare that guests in budget hotels are charged. You can thank the taxi union for this bit of fun — they establish the rate schedule.. Rates should be posted outside your hotel; however, if you have a question, all taxi drivers are required to have an official rate card in their taxi, although it's generally in Spanish.

Within the downtown area, the cost is about $1.50 per cab ride (not per person); within any other zone it's $5. Traveling between two zones also costs $5. If you cross two zones the cost is $7.50. Settle on a price in advance, or check at your hotel where destinations and prices are generally posted. Trips to the airport from most zones cost $14. Taxis also have a rate of $18 per hour for travel around the city and Hotel Zone, but you can generally negotiate this rate down to $10 to $12. If you want to hire a taxi to take you to Chichén-Itzá or along the Riviera Maya, expect to pay about $30 per hour — many taxi drivers feel that they're also providing guide services.

Catching a bus

Bus travel within Cancún continues to improve and is increasingly the most popular way of getting around for both residents and tourists. Air-conditioned and rarely crowded, the Hotel Zone buses run 24 hours a day. You can easily spot the bus stops using the signs posted along the road that have a bus on them. Bus stops are in front of most of the main hotels and shopping centers. Most buses cost 50¢. In town, almost everything is within walking distance. Ruta 1 and Ruta 2 (*"Hoteles"*) city buses travel frequently from the mainland to the beaches along Avenida Tulum (the main street) and all the way to Punta Nizuc at the far end of the Hotel Zone on Isla Cancún.

Ruta 8 buses go to Puerto Juárez/Punta Sam, where you can catch ferries to Isla Mujeres. The buses stop on the east side of Avenida Tulum. These buses operate between 6 a.m. and 10 p.m. daily. Beware of private buses along the same route; they charge far more than the public ones. The public buses have the fare amount painted on the front; at the time of publication, the fare was five pesos (50¢).

Zipping around on a moped

Mopeds are a convenient and popular way to cruise around through the very congested traffic, but they can be dangerous. Rentals start at $25 for a day, and the shops require a credit card voucher as security for the moped.

When you rent a moped, you should receive a crash helmet (it's the law) and instructions on how to lock the wheels when you park. Be sure to read the fine print on the back of the rental agreement regarding liability for repairs or replacement in case of accident, theft, or vandalism.

Fast Facts: Cancún

American Express

The local office is located in Ciudad Cancún at Avenida Tulum 208 and Agua (☎ 998-881-4000, 998-881-4040; Internet: www.americanexpress.com/mex/), one block past the Plaza México. The office is open Monday to Friday 9 a.m. to 6 p.m. and Saturday 9 a.m. to 2 p.m.

Area Code

The telephone area code is **988. Note:** The area code changed from 9 in November 2001.

Babysitters

Most of the larger hotels can easily arrange for babysitters, but many sitters speak limited English. Rates range from $3 to $10 per hour.

Banks, ATMs, and Currency Exchange

Most banks are downtown along Avenida Tulum and are usually open Monday to Friday 9:30 a.m. to 5:00 p.m., and many now have automatic teller machines for after-hours cash withdrawals. In the Hotel Zone, banks can be found in the Plaza Kukulkán and next to the convention center. There are also many *casas de cambio* (exchange houses) in the hotel zone, in the plazas, and near the convention center. Avoid changing money at the airport as you arrive, especially at the first exchange booth you see — its rates are less favorable than any in town or others farther inside the airport concourse. In general, the best exchange rates are found at ATMs, casas de cambio, and hotels.

Business Hours

Most downtown offices maintain traditional Mexican hours of operation (9 a.m. to 2 p.m. and 4 p.m. to 8 p.m., daily), but shops remain open throughout the day from 10 a.m. to 9 p.m. Offices tend to close on Saturday and Sunday, but shops are open on Saturday, at least, and increasingly offer limited hours of operation on Sunday. Malls are generally open from 10 a.m. to 10 p.m. or later.

Climate

It's hot but not overwhelmingly humid. The rainy season is May through October. August through October is the hurricane season, which brings erratic weather. November through February is generally sunny but can also be cloudy, windy, somewhat rainy, and even cool, so a sweater and rain protection is handy.

Consular Agents

The **U.S. consular agent** is located in the Playa Caracol 2, 3rd level, rooms 320–323, Boulevard Kukulkán, Km 8.5 (☎ 998-883-0272). The office is open Monday to Friday 9 a.m. to 1 p.m. The **Canadian** consulate is located in the Plaza México 312 (☎ 998-883-3360). The office is open from Monday to Friday 9 a.m. to 5 p.m.

Emergencies/Hospitals

To report an emergency, dial ☎ **060,** which is supposed to be similar to 911 emergency service in the United States. For first aid, the **Cruz Roja** (Red Cross; ☎ 998-884-1616; Fax: 998-884-7466) is open 24 hours a day on Avenida Yaxchilán between avenidas Xcaret and Labná, next to the Telmex building. **Total Assist,** a small, nine-room emergency hospital with English-speaking doctors (Claveles 5, SM 22, at Avenida Tulum; ☎ 998-884-1058, 998-884-1092; E-mail: htotal@prodigy.net.mx), is also open 24 hours. American Express, MasterCard, and Visa are accepted. Desk staff may have limited command of English. An **air ambulance service** is also available by calling ☎ 800-305-9400 (toll-free within Mexico). *Urgencias* means "Emergencies."

Information

The **State Tourism Office** (☎ 998-884-8073) is centrally located downtown on the east side of Avenida Tulum 26, next to Banco Inverlat, immediately left of the Ayuntamiento Benito Juárez building, between avenidas Cobá and Uxmal. The office is open daily 9 a.m. to 9 p.m., and it has maps, brochures, and information on the area's popular sights, including Tulum, Xcaret, Isla Mujeres, and Playa del Carmen. A second tourist information office, the Convention and Visitors Bureau (☎ 998-884-6531, 998-884-3438), is located on Avenida Cobá at Avenida Tulum, next to Pizza Rolandi, and is open Monday to Friday

9 a.m. to 8 p.m. Hotels and their rates are listed at each office, as are ferry schedules. For information prior to your arrival in Cancún, call ☎ 800-CANCUN-8 from the United States or visit the Convention Bureau's Web site at www.gocancun.com.

Pick up copies of the free monthly **Cancún Tips** or the Cancun Tips booklet which is published 4 times a year. Both contain lots of useful information and great maps. The publications are owned by the same people who own the Captain's Cove restaurants, a couple of sightseeing boats, and time-share hotels, so the information, though good, is not completely unbiased.

Internet Access

C@ncunet (☎ 998-885-0055), located in a kiosk on the second floor of Plaza Kukulkán (Paseo Kukulkán Km 13), offers Internet access for $4 per 15 minutes or $16 per hour from 10 a.m. to 10 p.m. In downtown Cancún, **Sybcom** (☎ 998-884-6807) offers Internet access for $3.80 per hour, $2 for 30 minutes, or $1 for 15 minutes. It is located in the Plaza Alconde, Local 2, at Avenida Náder, just in front of Clinica AMAT and is open from 9 a.m. to 11 p.m., Monday to Saturday.

Maps

One of the best around is the free American Express map, usually found at the tourist information offices and the local American Express office. *Cancún Tips* (see "Information") also have excellent maps and are generally available through your hotel concierge.

Newspapers/Magazines

For English-language newspapers and books, go to **Fama** (Avenida Tulum between Tulipanes and Claveles; ☎ 998-884-6586). The shop is open daily from 8 a.m. to 10 p.m. and has a new upstairs coffee shop. American Express, MasterCard, and Visa are accepted. Most hotel gift shops and newsstands also carry English-language magazines and English-language Mexican newspapers.

Pharmacy

Next to the Hotel Caribe Internacional, **Farmacia Canto** (Avenida Yaxchilán 36, at Sunyaxchen; ☎ 998-884-9330) is open 24 hours. American Express, MasterCard, and Visa are accepted. Plenty of drugstores are in the major shopping malls, open until 10 p.m., in the Hotel Zone. You can stock up on Retin-A, Viagra, and many other prescription drugs, without a prescription.

Police

To reach the **police** *(seguridad pública),* dial ☎ 998-884-1913 or 998-884-2342.

Post Office

The **main post office** (☎ 998-884-1418) is downtown at the intersection of avenidas Sunyaxchen and Xel-Ha. It's open Monday to Friday 8 a.m. to 5 p.m. and Saturday 9 a.m. to 12 p.m.

Safety

There is very little crime in Cancún. People are generally safe late at night in tourist areas; just use ordinary, common sense. As at any other beach resort, don't take money or valuables to the beach.

Swimming on the Caribbean side presents a danger from undertow. Pay attention to the posted flag warnings on the beaches.

Car break-ins are about the only crimes here, although they do happen frequently, especially around the shopping centers in the Hotel Zone. VW Beetles and Golfs are frequent targets.

Special Events

The annual **Cancún Jazz Festival,** featuring internationally known musicians, is held each year over the U.S. Memorial Day weekend in late May. The **Cancún Marathon** takes place each December and attracts world-class athletes as well as numerous amateur competitors. Additional information is available through the Convention and Visitors Bureau.

Taxes

There's a 10% value-added tax (IVA) on goods and services, and it's generally included in the posted price. Cancún's IVA is 5% lower than most of Mexico due to a special exemption that dates back to its origins as a duty-free port.

Taxis

Taxi prices in Cancún are set by zone, although keeping track of what's in which zone can take some work. Taxi rates within the Hotel Zone are a minimum fare of $5 per ride, making it one of the most expensive taxi areas in Mexico. Rates within the downtown area are between $1.50 and $2. Taxis can also be hired by the hour or day for longer trips, when you'd prefer to leave the driving to someone else. Rates run between $12 and $18 per hour with discounts available for full-day rates, but an extra charge applies when the driver doubles as a tour guide. Always settle on a price in advance, or check at your hotel, where destinations and prices are generally posted.

Telephone

Avoid the phone booths that have signs in English advising you to call home using a special 800 number — these are absolute rip-offs and can cost as much as $20 per minute. The least expensive way to call is by using a Mexican pre-paid phone card called Telmex (LADATEL), available at most pharmacies and mini-supermarkets, using the official public phones, Telmex (Lada). Remember, in Mexico, you need to dial 001 prior to a number to reach the United States, and you need to preface long-distance calls within Mexico by dialing 01.

Time Zone

Cancún operates on central standard time, but Mexico's observance of daylight savings time varies somewhat from that in the United States.

Chapter 10

Dining in Cancún

· ·

In This Chapter

▶ Discovering Cancún's best restaurants

▶ Finding a restaurant with true Mexican ambiance

· ·

The restaurant scene in Cancún is populated in large part by U.S.-based franchise chains, which really need no introduction. These chains include Hard Rock Cafe, Planet Hollywood, Rainforest Cafe, Tony Roma's, TGI Fridays, Ruth's Chris Steak House, and the gamut of fast-food burger places. Contrary to common travelers' wisdom, many of Cancún's best restaurants are located either in hotels or shopping malls.

The majority of restaurants are located in the Hotel Zone in Isla Cancún, which is logical because that's where most of the tourists who come to dine out are located. However, don't dismiss the charms of dining in Ciudad Cancún. You're likely to find a great meal — at a fraction of the price of an Isla Cancún eatery — accompanied by a dose of local color.

As in may of Mexico's beach resorts, even the finest restaurants in town can be comfortably casual when it comes to dress. Men rarely wear jackets, although ladies are frequently seen in dressy resort wear — basically, everything goes.

For those traveling with kids, Cancún has no shortage of options. From Johnny Rockets to McDonalds, this destination has plenty of kid-friendly — and kid-familiar — places.

Prices in Cancún can cover an extended range, boosted by shrimp and lobster dishes, which can top $20 for an entree. If you're watching your budget, even the higher-priced places generally have less-expensive options — just avoid the premium seafood dishes. Remember that tips generally run about 15%, and most wait-staff really depend on tips for their income, so be generous if the service warrants.

Cancún's Best Restaurants

The restaurants listed here are either locally owned, one-of-a-kind restaurants or exceptional selections at area hotels. Many feature live music as an accompaniment to the dining experience. I arrange the restaurants alphabetically and note their location and general price category. Please refer to the Introduction of *Mexico's Beach Resorts For Dummies* for an explanation of the price categories.

Please see Appendix E for more information on Mexican cuisine.

Captain's Cove

$$ **Isla Cancún** **INTERNATIONAL/SEAFOOD**

Recognized for its consistent value — think heaping servings, friendly service, and great sunset views from the upper deck — Captain's Cove regularly packs customers into its several dining levels. Diners face big, open windows overlooking the lagoon and Royal Yacht Club Marina. For breakfast, there's an extremely popular all-you-can-eat buffet that beats the price and quality of most hotel buffets. Main courses of USDA Angus steak and seafood are the norm at lunch and dinner, and a menu catering especially to children is available. Dessert standouts include flaming coffees, crêpes, and Key lime pie. Captain's Cove sits almost at the end of Paseo Kukulkán, on the lagoon side opposite the Omni Hotel.

Paseo Kukulkán, Km 15. ☎ *998-885-0016. Reservations recommended. Main courses: $16–$20; breakfast buffet $7.95. AE, MC, V. Open: Daily 7 a.m.–11 p.m.*

Club Grill

$$$$ **Isla Cancún** **INTERNATIONAL**

Cancún's most elegant and stylish restaurant, located in the Ritz-Carlton Hotel, is also among its most delicious. The gracious service starts and the old-world charm begins the moment you enter the anteroom with its comfortable couches and chairs and selection of fine tequilas and Cuban cigars. The scene continues into a candlelit dining room with padded side chairs and tables shimmering with silver and crystal. Elegant plates of peppered scallops, truffles, and potatoes in tequila sauce; grilled lamb; or mixed grill arrive at a leisurely pace after the appetizer. The restaurant has both smoking and non-smoking sections. After dinner, take a turn on the dance floor, as a band plays romantic music from 8 p.m. on. Club Grill is the place for that truly special night out. A dress code is enforced: No sandals or tennis shoes, and gentlemen must wear long pants.

Ritz-Carlton Hotel, Blvd. Kukulkán, Km 13.5. ☎ *998-885-0808. Reservations required. Main courses: $11–$40. AE, DC, MC, V. Open: Tues–Sun 7–11 p.m.*

Isla Cancún (Hotel Zone) Dining

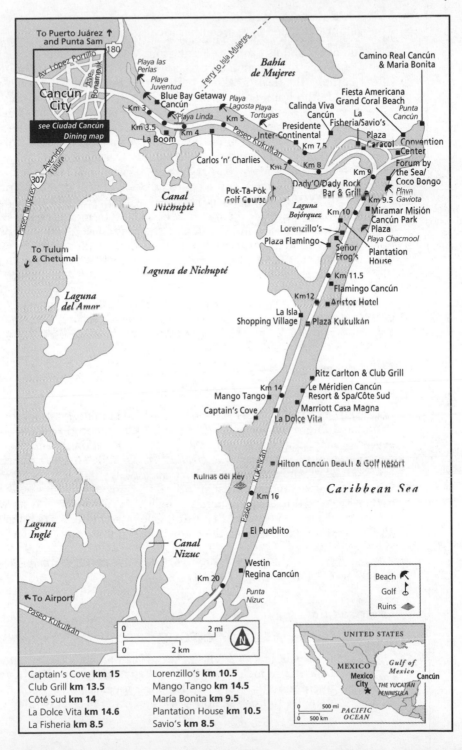

To Puerto Juárez
and Punta Sam

180

Av. López Portillo

Cancún City

Ave. Bonampak

see Ciudad Cancún Dining map

Playa las Perlas

Playa Juventud

Blue Bay Getaway Cancún

Km 3

Playa Linda

Km 3.5

Km 4

La Boom

Carlos 'n' Charlies

Playa Lagosta

Playa Tortugas

Km 5

Paseo Kukulkán

Km 7.5

Km 7

Presidente Inter-Continental

Km 8

307

Av. Tulum

Canal Nichupté

Pok-Ta-Pok Golf Course

Ferry to Isla Mujeres

Bahía de Mujeres

Calinda Viva Cancún

Km 9

Laguna Bojórquez

Laguna de Nichupté

Laguna del Amor

To Tulum & Chetumal

Paseo Nizuc

Paseo Mujeres

Camino Real Cancún & Maria Bonita

Fiesta Americana Grand Coral Beach

Punta Cancún

La Fisheria/Savio's

Plaza Caracol

Convention Center

Forum by the Sea/ Coco Bongo

Playa Gaviota

Dady'O/Dady Rock Bar & Grill

Km 9.5

Km 10

Miramar Misión Cancún Park

Lorenzillo's

Plaza

Plaza Flamingo

Playa Chacmool

Señor Frog's

Plantation House

Km 11.5

Flamingo Cancún

Km 12

Aristos Hotel

La Isla Shopping Village

Plaza Kukulkán

Ritz Carlton & Club Grill

Km 14

Le Méridien Cancún Resort & Spa/Côte Sud

Mango Tango

Marriott Casa Magna

Captain's Cove

La Dolce Vita

Hilton Cancún Beach & Golf Resort

Ruinas del Rey

Caribbean Sea

Km 16

Laguna Inglé

Canal Nizuc

El Pueblito

Westin Regina Cancún

Km 20

Punta Nizuc

To Airport

Paseo Kukulkán

0   2 mi

0   2 km

N

Beach
Golf
Ruins

Captain's Cove **km 15**	Lorenzillo's **km 10.5**
Club Grill **km 13.5**	Mango Tango **km 14.5**
Côté Sud **km 14**	María Bonita **km 9.5**
La Dolce Vita **km 14.6**	Plantation House **km 10.5**
La Fisheria **km 8.5**	Savio's **km 8.5**

UNITED STATES

MEXICO

Gulf of Mexico

Mexico City

THE YUCATÁN PENINSULA

Cancún

PACIFIC OCEAN

0   500 mi

0   500 km

Côté Sud

$$$$ Isla Cancún FRENCH

In Le Méridien Hotel, the Provençal — but definitely not provincial — Côté Sud offers simply exquisite French and Mediterranean gourmet specialties served in a warm and cozy country French setting. Though it offers perhaps the best breakfast buffet in Cancún (for $15), most visitors outside the hotel enjoy it only for dinner, when low lighting and superb service make it a top choice for a romantic dinner. Starters include the traditional pâtés and a delightful escargot served in the shell with a white wine and herb butter sauce. A specialty is duck breast served in a honey and lavender sauce. Equally scrumptious is the rack of lamb, prepared in a Moroccan style and served with couscous. Pan-seared grouper is topped with a paste of black olives, crushed potato, and tomato, and the bouillabaisse is laden with an exceptional array of seafood. Desserts are decadent in true French style, including the signature "Fifth Element," a sinfully delicious temptation rich with chocolate. For the quality and the originality of the cuisine, coupled with the excellence in service, Côté Sud gets my top pick for the best value in fine dining in Cancún.

Le Méridien Hotel, Retorno del Rey, Km 14. ☎ *998-881-2225. Internet:* www. meridencancun.com.mx. *Free parking. Reservations required. Main courses: $14–$30. AE, DC, MC, V. Open: Mon–Sun 6:30 a.m.–11:00 p.m.*

El Pescador

$$ Ciudad Cancún SEAFOOD

Locals all seem to agree: El Pescador is the best spot for fresh seafood in Cancún. A line often forms here for the well-prepared fresh seafood served in a street-side patio and upstairs venue. Feast on shrimp cocktail, conch, octopus, *camarones à la criolla* (Creole-style shrimp), charcoal-broiled lobster, and stone crabs. Can't decide? Try a little of everything in the *Zarzuela* combination seafood plate, cooked in white wine and garlic. El Pescador also features a Mexican specialty menu as well. Another branch, **La Mesa del Pescador,** is located in the Plaza Kukulkán on Cancún Island and is open the same hours, but it's more expensive.

Tulipanes 28, off Av. Tulum. ☎ *998-884-2673. Fax: 998-884-3639. Main courses: $5–$12. AE, MC, V. Open: Daily 11 a.m.–11 p.m.*

La Dolce Vita

$$$ Isla Cancún ITALIAN/SEAFOOD

The casually elegant La Dolce Vita is known as Cancún's favorite Italian restaurant. Appetizers include pâté of quail liver and carpaccio in vinaigrette or mushrooms Provençal. The chef specializes in homemade pastas combined with fresh seafood. You can order green tagliolini with

Ciudad Cancún (Cancún City) Dining

El Pescador **3**
La Habichuela **2**
Los Almendros **7**
Périco's **1**
Rolandi's Pizza **5**
Rosa Mexicana **4**
Stefano's **6**

lobster medallions, linguine with clams or seafood, or rigatoni Mexican-style (with *chorizo*, mushrooms, and chives) as a main course, or as an appetizer for half price. You can dine in air-conditioned comfort or on an open-air terrace with a view of the lagoon. Dinner is accompanied by live jazz from 7:00 to 11:30 p.m., Monday through Saturday.

Av. Kukulkán, Km 14.6, on the lagoon, opposite the Marriott Casamagna. ☎ *998-885-0150, 998-885-0161. Fax: 998-885-0590. Internet:* www.cancun.com/dining/dolce. *Reservations required for dinner. Main courses: $9–$29. AE, MC, V. Open: Daily noon to midnight.*

La Fisheria

$$ Isla Cancún   SEAFOOD

La Fisheria is one of the exceptions to the rule about never finding good food in a shopping mall eatery. The expansive menu at La Fisheria includes shark fingers with a jalapeño dip, grouper fillet stuffed with seafood in a lobster sauce, Acapulco-style ceviche (in a tomato sauce), New England clam chowder, steamed mussels, grilled red snapper with pasta — you get the idea. The menu changes daily, but there's always *tikin xik,* that great Yucatecan grilled fish marinated in *achiote* sauce (made from the paste of the achiote chile). And for those not inclined toward seafood, a wood-burning, oven-made pizza may do, or perhaps one of the grilled chicken or beef dishes. If you're at the mall shopping, La Fisheria is your best bet — and a reason to stop by if you're not.

Plaza Caracol, Shopping Center 2nd floor. ☎ *998-883-1395. Main courses: $6.50–$21. AE, MC, V. Open: Daily 11 a.m. to midnight.*

La Habichuela

$$–$$$ Ciudad Cancún   GOURMET SEAFOOD/CARIBBEAN/ MEXICAN

Dine alfresco in a garden setting and enjoy some of downtown Cancún's finest food. Romantic in its setting on a vine-draped patio, La Habichuela boasts tables that are covered in pink-and-white linens and soft music playing in the background. For an all-out culinary adventure, try *habichuela* (string bean) soup; shrimp in any number of sauces, including Jamaican tamarind, tequila, and a ginger-and-mushroom combination; and the Maya coffee with *xtabentun* (a strong, sweet, anise-based liquor). The grilled seafood and steaks are excellent as well, but La Habichuela is a good place to try a Mexican specialty such as *enchiladas suizas (Swiss crepes)* or *tampiqueña*-style beef (thinly sliced, marinated, and grilled). For something totally divine, try the *Cocobichuela,* which is lobster and shrimp in a curry sauce served in a coconut shell and topped with fruit.

Margaritas 25. ☎ *998-884-3158. E-mail:* habichuela@infosel.net.mx. *Free parking. Reservations recommended in high season. Main courses: $10–$32. AE, MC, V. Open: Daily noon to midnight.*

Los Almendros

$$ Ciudad Cancún   YUCATECAN

To steep yourself in Yucatecan cuisine and music, head directly to this large, colorful, air-conditioned restaurant. Regional specialties served here include lime soup, _poc chuc_ (a marinated, barbecue-style pork), chicken or pork _pibil_ (a sweet and spicy barbeque sauce served over shredded meat), and appetizers such as _panuchos_ (soft, fried tortillas with refried beans and either shredded turkey or pork _pibil_). The _combinado Yucateco_ is a sampler of four typically Mexican main courses. Los Almendros is located opposite the bullring.

Av. Bonampak and Sayil. ☎ _998-887-1332. Main courses: $4–$7. AE, MC, V. Open: Daily 11 a.m.–10 p.m._

Lorenzillo's

$$–$$$ Isla Cancún   SEAFOOD

Live lobster is the overwhelming favorite here, and part of the appeal is selecting your dinner out of the giant lobster tank. A dock leads down to the main dining area, overlooking the lagoon and topped by a giant palapa. When the place is packed (which is often), a wharf-side bar handles the overflow. In addition to the lobster — it comes grilled, steamed, or stuffed — good bets are the shrimp stuffed with cheese and wrapped in bacon, the admiral's fillet coated in toasted almonds and a light mustard sauce, or the seafood-stuffed squid. Desserts include the tempting "Martinique": Belgian chocolate with hazelnuts, almonds, and pecans, served with vanilla ice cream. A new sunset pier offers a lighter menu of cold seafood, sandwiches, and salads. There's a festive, friendly atmosphere, and children are very welcome — after all, most of the patrons are wearing bibs! A personal favorite; I never miss a lobster stop here when I'm in Cancún.

Paseo Kukulkán, Km 10.5. ☎ _998-883-1254. Internet:_ www.lorenzillos.com. mx. _Free parking in lot across the street, plus valet parking. Reservations recommended. Main courses: $8–$50. AE, MC, V. Open: Daily noon to midnight._

Mango Tango

$$–$$$ Isla Cancún   INTERNATIONAL

Mango Tango has sizzling floor shows and live reggae music, but its kitchen is the real star. Try the peel-your-own shrimp, Argentine-style grilled meat with _chimichurri_ sauce (sauce with roasted vegetables and a variety of spices), and other tropical specialties. Creole gumbo comes with lobster, shrimp, and squid, and a new coconut-and-mango cake is a fitting finish to the meal. The beauty of dining here is that you can stay and enjoy one of the currently hot nightspots in Cancún.

Paseo Kukulkán Km 14.2, opposite the Ritz-Carlton Hotel. ☎ _998-885-0303. Reservations recommended. Main courses: $10–$16; dinner show $35–$38. AE, MC, V. Open: Daily 2 p.m.–2 a.m._

Dining at sea

One unique way to combine dinner with sightseeing is to board the **Lobster Dinner Cruise** (☎ 998-883-1488). Cruising around the tranquil, turquoise waters of the lagoon, passengers feast on lobster dinners accompanied by wine. The cost is $64.50 per person, and the cruise departs two times daily from the Royal Mayan Marina. A sunset dinner cruise leaves at 4:00 p.m. during winter months and 5:00 p.m. during the summer. A moonlight cruise leaves at 7:30 p.m. during the winter and 8:30 p.m. during the summer.

María Bonita

$$$ Isla Cancún   REGIONAL/MEXICAN/NOUVELLE MEXICAN

Possibly the most "Mexican" of Isla Cancún's dining options, María Bonita combines the music, food, and atmosphere of Mexico's various regions — it's almost like taking a condensed food tour of this vast country! Being that María Bonita is located in a hotel, prices are higher and the flavors are more institutionalized than the traditional Mexican restaurants found in Ciudad Cancún, but the restaurant is still a good choice for those wanting more of the flavors of Mexico — without leaving the Hotel Zone. The restaurant overlooks the water, and the interior is divided by cuisine type. My favorite is *La Cantina Jalisco,* which features an open, colorful Mexican kitchen (with pots and pans on the wall) and tequila bar (with more than 50 different tequilas). For the less adventurous in your party, a few international dishes are thrown in for variety. Trios, marimba, and jarocho music, and the ever-enchanting mariachis serenade the diners. The different peppers used are explained on the front of the menu, and each dish is marked for its heat quotient (from zero to two chiles). The restaurant is to the left of the hotel entrance, and you can enter from the street.

Hotel Camino Real, Punta Cancún. ☎ *998-848-7000, ext. 8060 or 8061. Reservations recommended. Main courses: $25–$31. AE, DC, MC, V. Open: Daily 6:30–11:45 p.m.*

Périco's

$$–$$$ Ciudad Cancún   MEXICAN/SEAFOOD/STEAKS

With colorful murals that almost dance off the walls, a bar area overhung with baskets (and with saddles for bar stools), inviting leather tables and chairs, and waiters dressed like Pancho Villa, there's no wonder why Périco's is always booming and festive. It's arguably the most tourist-friendly spot in Ciudad Cancún. The extensive menu offers well-prepared steak, seafood, and traditional Mexican dishes for moderate rates (except for the lobster), but the food here is less the point than the fun. Périco's is a place not only to eat and drink, but also to let loose and join in the fun. Don't be surprised if everybody drops their forks, dons huge

Mexican sombreros, and snakes around the dining room in a conga dance. You can still have fun whether or not you join in, but Périco's is definitely not the place for that romantic evening alone. There's marimba music from 7:30 to 9:30 p.m. and mariachis from 9:30 p.m. to midnight. Expect a crowd.

Yaxchilán 61. ☎ *998-884-3152. Main courses: $9–$20. AE, MC, V. Open: Daily 1 p.m.–1 a.m.*

Plantation House

$$$$ Isla Cancún CARIBBEAN/FRENCH

Elegant Caribbean fare — styled after the time when it was infused with European influences — is served up in this pale yellow-and-blue clapboard restaurant overlooking Nichupté Lagoon. The decor combines island-style colonial charm with elegant touches of wood and crystal. For starters, try their signature poached shrimp with lemon juice and olive oil or a creamy crabmeat soup. Move on to the main event, which may consist of classic veal Wellington in puff pastry with duck pâté, fish fillet crusted in spices and herbs and topped with a vanilla sauce, or lobster medallions in mango sauce. The service is excellent, but the food is only mediocre, especially considering the price. Flambéed desserts are a specialty, and the Plantation House has one of the most extensive wine lists in town. Plantation House is generally quite crowded, which makes it a bit loud for a truly romantic evening.

Paseo Kukulkán, Km 10.5, Zona Hotelera, 77500, Cancún, Q. Roo. ☎ *998-883-1433, 998-883-2120. Reservations recommended. Main courses: $13–$35. AE, MC, V. Open: Daily 5:00 p.m.–12:30 a.m.*

Rolandi's Pizza

$ Ciudad Cancún ITALIAN

Surprised to find great pizza in Cancún? Don't be — Rolandi's Pizza is an institution in Cancún, and the Rolandi name is synonymous with dining in both Cancún and neighboring Isla Mujeres. At this shaded outdoor sidewalk cafe, you can choose from almost two dozen different wood-oven pizzas and a full selection of spaghetti, calzones, Italian-style chicken and beef, and desserts. There's a full bar list as well. Another Rolandi's Pizza is located in Isla Mujeres at 110 Avenida Hidalgo (☎ 998-877-0430; Open: Monday to Sunday, 11 a.m. to 11 p.m.) and has the same food and prices. Both locations have become standards for dependably good casual fare in Cancún. For a more formal, Italian-dining affair, try the elegant **Casa Rolandi** in Plaza Carocal, Isla Cancún (☎ 988-883-1817).

Cobá 12. ☎ *998-884-4047. Fax: 998-884-3994. Internet: www.rolandi.com. Main courses and pizza: $5–$14; pasta $5–$8. AE, MC, V. Open: Daily 12:30 p.m. to midnight.*

Rosa Mexicana

$$$ Ciudad Cancún MEXICAN HAUTE

Rosa Mexicana is a simply stylish bistro and a top choice for downtown dining. Candlelit tables are set indoors and surrounded by colorful *piñatas* and paper streamers and located on a plant-filled patio in back. The menu features "refined" Mexican specialties. Try the *pollo almendro,* which is chicken covered in a cream sauce sprinkled with ground almonds, or the pork baked in a banana leaf with a sauce of oranges, lime, *chile ancho (smoky flavored chile pepper),* and garlic. The more traditional steak *tampiqueño* is a huge platter that comes with guacamole salad, quesadillas, beans, salad, and rice. Dine to live, romantic Mexican music most nights.

Claveles 4. ☎ *998-884-6313. Fax: 998-884-2371. Reservations recommended for parties of 6 or more. Main courses: $6–$12; lobster $25. AE, MC, V. Open: Daily 5–11 p.m.*

Savio's

$$$ Isla Cancún ITALIAN

Savio's is a great place to stop for a quick meal or coffee, and it's centrally located in the heart of the Hotel Zone. The bar is always crowded with patrons sipping everything from cappuccino to imported beer. Repeat diners look forward to large fresh salads and richly flavored, subtly herbed Italian dishes. The ravioli stuffed with ricotta and spinach is served in a delicious tomato sauce. A stylish place with a black-and-white decor and tile floors, Savio's has two levels and faces Paseo Kukulkán through two stories of awning-shaded windows.

Plaza Caracol. ☎ *and fax: 998-883-2085. Main courses: $8.25–$26. AE, MC, V. Open: Daily 10 a.m. to midnight.*

Stefano's

$$ Ciudad Cancún ITALIAN/PIZZA

Call the food Mexitalian if you will, but it seems to be a winning combination. Stefano's began primarily as a local restaurant, serving Italian food with a few Mexican accents, and is now equally popular with tourists. Among the menu items are ravioli stuffed with *huitlacoche* (a type of mushroom that grows on a cornstalk); rigatoni in tequila sauce; and seafood with chile peppers, nestled proudly alongside the Stefano special pizza, made with fresh tomato, cheese, and pesto. For dessert, ricotta strudel is something out of the ordinary. Stefano's offers lots of different coffees and mixed drinks, plus an expanded wine list.

Bonampak 177. ☎ *998-887-9964. Main courses: $6–$9; pizza $5.75–$9.75. AE, MC, V. Open: Daily noon to 1 a.m.*

Chapter 11

Having Fun On and Off the Beach in Cancún

You're likely to run out of vacation days before you run out of things to do in Cancún. Snorkeling, jet skiing, jungle tours, and visits to ancient Mayan ruins or modern ecological theme parks are among the most popular diversions in this resort that has a little of everything. Beyond Cancún's renowned beaches are over a dozen malls with name-brand retailers and duty-free shops (featuring European goods with better prices than you can find in the United States), plus a seemingly endless supply of nightclubs to revel in.

In addition to Cancún's own attractions, the resort is a convenient distance from the more Mexican-feeling beach towns in **Isla Mujeres, Playa del Carmen,** and **Cozumel.** The **Mayan ruins** at Tulum and Chichén-Itzá, are also close by. All of these diversions are within driving distance for a spectacular day trip.

So what's worth your time? To help you decide, I devote this chapter to giving you an overview of the best beaches in this mecca of white sand and crystalline waters. I also give you the rundown on the area's popular day trips and diversions.

Finding Water Fun for Everyone

Face it: If you're in Cancún, you probably decided to come here based on the vision of powdery, white-sand beaches and translucent, turquoise waters. If you're in search of a beautiful beach, Cancún may be your nirvana. And with the added bonus of the Nichupté Lagoon on the other side of the island, Cancún is packed with ways to make the most of your time in the water.

Basking on a Cancún beach

The big hotels dominate the best stretches of beaches, so you likely have a fine patch of sand at your hotel. All of Mexico's beaches are public property, so technically, you can use the beach of any hotel by accessing it directly from the sand. *Technically* is the key word here. Although this is the law, the reality is that hotel security guards regularly ask non-guests to relocate. You choose if you want to suffer the potential embarrassment of being asked to leave or, if asked, standing your ground — or beach, as it were.

If you're intent on swimming, be careful on beaches fronting the open Caribbean, where the undertow can be quite strong. By contrast, the waters of **Bahía de Mujeres** at the north end of the island are usually calm and ideal for swimming. Get to know Cancún's water-safety pennant system and make sure to check the flag at any beach or hotel before entering the water.

Here's what each flag means:

- ✔ **White:** Excellent
- ✔ **Green:** Normal conditions (safe)
- ✔ **Yellow:** Changeable, uncertain (use caution)
- ✔ **Black or red:** Unsafe (use the swimming pool instead)

In the Caribbean, storms can arrive quickly, and conditions can change from safe to unsafe in a matter of minutes, so be alert: If you see dark clouds heading your way, head to shore and wait until the storm passes.

The public beaches located along the stretch of Cancún Island on the calm, Bahía de Mujeres side include **Playa Linda** (Pretty Beach), **Playa Langosta** (Lobster Beach), **Playa Tortuga** (Turtle Beach), and **Playa Caracol** (Snail Beach). Playa Linda (Km 4) has a shuttle service to Isla Mujeres, as well as a few dive shops and snack bars. Playa Langosta (Km 5) is a protected cove near the Hotel Casa Maya that features a tour-boat pier and a watersports concession, plus some shops and restaurants. Next up is Playa Tortuga (Km 7.5), a popular public beach with changing rooms, public rest rooms, and restaurants. This bit of sand is frequently overrun with families on weekends. The last beach before the island curves toward the Caribbean is Playa Caracol, which stretches for about a mile and passes the Fiesta Americana and Camino Real hotels — a lovely stretch with a few restaurants but no public facilities.

Cancún & Environs

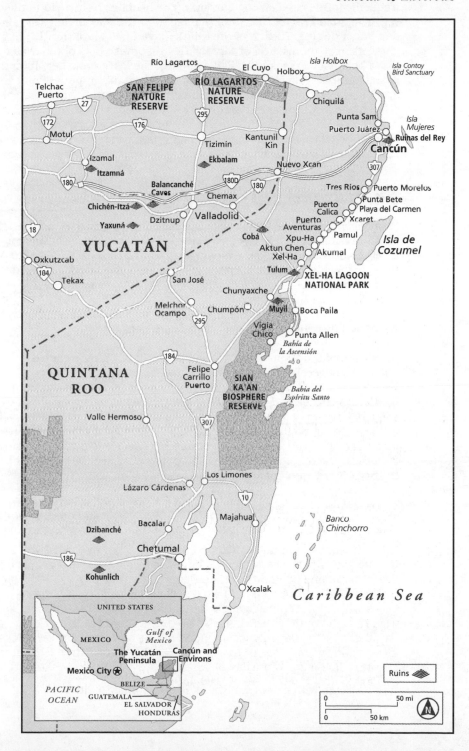

Río Lagartos
El Cuyo
Holbox
Isla Holbox
Isla Contoy
Bird Sanctuary

Telchac
Puerto
SAN FELIPE
NATURE
RESERVE
RÍO LAGARTOS
NATURE
RESERVE
Chiquilá

27

172
176
295

Motul
Tizimín
Kantunil
Kin
Punta Sam
Puerto Juárez
*Isla
Mujeres*

Izamal
Ekbalam
Cancún
Ruinas del Rey

Itzamná
307

Nuevo Xcan

180
180D
180
Tres Ríos
Puerto Morelos

Balancanché
Caves
Chemax
Punta Bete
Playa del Carmen

Chichén-Itzá
Puerto
Calica
Xcaret

Yaxuná
Dzitnup
Valladolid
Puerto
Aventuras
Pamul
*Isla de
Cozumel*

18

YUCATÁN
Cobá
Xpu-Ha

Aktun Chen
Xel-Ha
Akumal

Oxkutzcab
Tulum
XEL-HA LAGOON
NATIONAL PARK

104
Tekax
San José

Chunyaxche

Melchor
Ocampo
Chumpón
Muyil
Boca Paila

295
Vigía
Chico
Punta Allen

*Bahía de
la Ascensión*

184

QUINTANA
ROO
Felipe
Carrillo
Puerto
SIAN
KA'AN
BIOSPHERE
RESERVE
*Bahía del
Espíritu Santo*

Valle Hermoso
307

Los Limones

Lázaro Cárdenas
10

Majahual
*Banco
Chinchorro*

Dzibanché
Bacalar

Chetumal

186

Kohunlich
Xcalak
Caribbean Sea

UNITED STATES

*Gulf of
Mexico*

MEXICO

The Yucatán
Peninsula
Cancún and
Environs

Mexico City

*PACIFIC
OCEAN*
BELIZE
GUATEMALA
EL SALVADOR
HONDURAS

Ruins

0   50 mi
0   50 km

N

The Caribbean side of Cancún faces the open sea, and it's subject to frequent riptides and strong currents. The beaches here include the regally-named **Playa Chac-Mool** (named after the Mayan deity of rain) and **Playa del Rey** (Beach of the King). Playa Chac-Mool (Km 13) has showers, rest rooms, and other facilities that make it as popular as Playa Tortuga on weekends. Playa del Rey, the last public beach on the island before Punta Nizac (see map of the Yucatán's upper Caribbean coast earlier in this chapter), is an unspoiled treasure. This remarkable stretch of sand ends at the entrance to Club Med.

At most beaches, in addition to swimming, you can rent a sailboard and take lessons, ride a parasail, or partake in a variety of other watersports.

Skiing and surfing

Many beachside hotels offer watersports concessions that include the rental of rubber rafts, kayaks, and snorkeling equipment. Outlets for renting **sailboats, Jet Skis, windsurfers,** and **water skis** are located on the calm Nichupté Lagoon. Prices vary and are often negotiable, so check around.

For windsurfing, go to the Playa Tortuga public beach where there's a **windsurfing school** (no phone) with equipment for rent.

A very popular option for getting wet and wild is a **jungle cruise,** offered by several companies. The cruise takes you by Jet Ski or WaveRunner through Cancún's lagoon and mangrove estuaries out into the Caribbean Sea and by a shallow reef. The excursion runs about two and a half hours (you drive your own watercraft) and is priced from $35 to $45, with snorkeling and beverages included. Some of the motorized mini-boats seat you side by side; other crafts seat one person behind the other. The difference? The second person can see the scenery or the back of their companion's head, depending on your choice.

The operators and names of boats offering excursions change often. The popular **Aquaworld** (Paseo Kukulkán, Km 15.2; ☎ **998-885-2288**) calls its trip the Jungle Tour and charges $45 for the 2½-hour excursion, which includes 45 minutes of snorkeling time. They even give you a free snorkel, but their watercrafts have the less-desirable seating configuration of one behind the other. Departures are 9:00 a.m., 12:00 p.m., and 2:30 p.m. daily. To find out what's available when you're there, check with a local travel agent or hotel tour desk; you should find a wide range of options. You can also go to the Playa Linda pier either a day ahead or the day of your intended outing and buy your own tickets for trips on the *Nautibus* or to Isla Mujeres (see information later in this chapter). If you go on the day of your trip, arrive at the pier around 8:45 a.m.; most boats leave by 9:00 or 9:30 a.m.

Exploring the deep blue

Known for its shallow reefs, dazzling colors, and diversity of life, Cancún is one of the best places in the world for beginning **scuba diving.** Punta Nizuc is the northern tip of the **Gran Arrecife Maya (Great Mesoamerican Reef),** the largest reef in the Western Hemisphere and one of the largest in the world. In addition to the sea life present along this reef system, several sunken boats add a variety of dive options. Inland, a series of caverns and wellsprings, known as *cenotes,* are fascinating venues for the more experienced diver. Drift diving is the norm here, with popular dives going to the reefs at **El Garrafón** and the **Cave of the Sleeping Sharks.** For those unfamiliar with the term, drift diving occurs when divers drift with the strong currents in the waters and end up at a point different than where they started. The dive boat follows them. In traditional dives, the divers resurface where they began.

Resort courses that teach the basics of diving — enough to make shallow dives and slowly ease your way into this underwater world of unimaginable beauty — are offered in a variety of hotels. Scuba trips run around $60 for two-tank dives at nearby reefs and $100 and up for locations farther out. **Scuba Cancún** (Paseo Kukulkán, Km 5; ☎ 998-849-7508, 998-849-4736; Internet: www.scubacancun.com.mx), located on the lagoon side, offers a four-hour resort course for $60. In addition to calling or visiting, you can make reservations in the evenings from 7:30 to 10:30 p.m. using the fax line, 998-884-2336. Full certification takes four to five days and costs around $345. Scuba Cancún is open from 8:30 a.m. to 8:00 p.m. and accepts major credit cards.

The largest operator is **Aquaworld,** located across from the Meliá Cancún hotel at Paseo Kukulkán, Km 15.2 (☎ 998-885-2288, 998-848-8300; Internet: www.aquaworld.com.mx). They offer resort courses and diving from a man-made, anchored dive platform, Paradise Island. Aquaworld also has the **Sub See Explorer,** a submarine-style boat with picture windows that hang beneath the surface. The boat doesn't actually submerge — it's more like an updated version of the glass-bottom boat concept — but it does provide non-divers with a look at life beneath the sea. This outfit is open 24 hours a day and accepts all major credit cards.

Scuba Cancún (☎ 998-849-7808, 998-849-4736; E-mail: scuba@cancun.com.mx) also offers diving trips to 20 nearby reefs, including Cuevones at 30 feet, and the open ocean at 30 to 60 feet (offered in good weather only). The average dive is around 35 feet. One-tank dives cost $55, and two-tank dives cost $60.50. Discounts apply if you bring your own equipment. Dives usually start around 9:00 a.m. and return by 2:15 p.m. Snorkeling trips cost $32 and leave every afternoon after 2:00 p.m. for shallow reefs located about a 20-minute boat ride away.

Most of the beaches in Isla are either too rocky or offer no snorkeling opportunities, so Garrafón, or a trip to Isla Contoy are the only real options here. There are few beachfront hotels in Isla, and those that exist, are not located in good snorkeling areas except Casa de los Suenos, which is adjacent to Garrafón. In addition to **snorkeling** at **Garrafón National Park** (see the "Traveling to the Island of Women" section later in this chapter), travel agencies offer an all-day excursion to the natural wildlife habitat of **Isla Contoy** that usually includes time for snorkeling. The island, located an hour and a half past Isla Mujeres, is a major nesting area for birds and a treat for true nature lovers. Only two boats hold permits for excursions to the island. They depart at 9 a.m. and return by 5 p.m. The price of $60 includes drinks and snorkeling equipment.

Reeling in the big one

You can arrange a day of **deep-sea fishing** at one of the numerous piers or travel agencies for around $200 to $360 for four hours, $420 for six hours, and $520 for eight hours for up to four people. Marinas sometimes assist in putting together a group. Charters include a captain, a first mate, bait, gear, and beverages. Rates are lower if you depart from Isla Mujeres or from Cozumel Island, and frankly, the fishing is better closer to these departure points.

Swimming with dolphins

In Cancún, the **Parque Nizuc** (☎ 998-881-3030) marine park offers guests a chance to swim with dolphins and view these wonderful creatures in their dolphin aquarium, Atlántido. It's a fun place for a family to spend the day, with its numerous pools, waterslides, and rides. A new attraction promises the chance to snorkel with manta rays, tropical fish, and tame sharks. Open 10:00 a.m. to 5:30 p.m., the park is located on the southern end of Cancún, between the airport and the Hotel Zone.

La Isla Shopping Center, Blvd. Kukulkán, Km 12.5, also has an **Interactive Aquarium** (☎ 998-883-0413, 998-883-0436, 998-883-5077) with dolphin swims and the chance to feed a shark. Interactive encounters and swims start at $40.

In my opinion, the best option for doing the dolphin thing is found on Isla Mujeres, where you can swim with dolphins at **Dolphin Discovery** (☎ 998-883-0777; Fax: 998-883-0722; Internet: www.dolphindiscovery.com). Each session lasts one hour, with an educational introduction followed by 30 minutes of swim time. The price is $119, and transportation to Isla Mujeres is an additional $15. Advance reservations are required because capacity is limited each day. Assigned swimming times are 9 a.m., 11 a.m., 1 p.m., and 3 p.m., and you must arrive one hour before your scheduled swim time.

Enjoying Land Sports

Even by land, Cancún has its share of winning ways to spend the day. Although golf is a latent developer here, more courses are popping up along the coast south of Cancún. Tennis, however, is tops as a hotel amenity, and courts can be found throughout Cancún. Horseback riding and all-terrain vehicle tours are also great choices for land adventures.

Teeing off

Although the golf options are limited, the most well-known — and well-used — facility is the 18-hole **Club de Golf Cancún** (☎ 998-883-0871; E-mail: poktapok@sybcom.com), also known as the Pok-Ta-Pok Club. Designed by Robert Trent Jones Sr., it's located on the northern leg of the island. Greens fees run $105 per 18 holes. Clubs rent for $25, shoes run $12, and caddies charge $20 per bag. The club is open daily; American Express, MasterCard, and Visa are accepted. The club also has tennis courts.

The **Melía Cancún** (☎ 998-881-1100) offers a nine-hole executive course; the fee is $25, and the club is open daily from 8 a.m. to 4 p.m. American Express, MasterCard, and Visa are accepted.

The most interesting option is at the **Hilton Cancún Golf & Beach Resort** (☎ 998-881-8016; Fax: 998-881-8084). Its championship 18-hole, par-72 course was designed around the Ruinas del Rey (Ruins of the King) archeological site. Greens fees for the public are $110 for 18 holes and $80 for 9 holes; Hilton Cancún guests pay $88 for 18 holes and $66 for 9, which includes a golf cart. Golf clubs and shoes are available for rent as well, and the club is open daily 6 a.m. to 6 p.m.

Not quite up for the full game? There's also the **Mini Golf Palace** (Paseo Kukulkán, Km 14.5; ☎ 998-885-0533), which offers a more compact version of the game for all ages. It's open 11 a.m. to 10 p.m. daily.

Making time for tennis

Many hotels in Cancún offer excellent **tennis** facilities, and many of the courts are lit for night play. Among the best are the facilities at Le Méridian and the Fiesta Americana Coral Beach hotels.

Galloping along

Rancho Loma Bonita (☎ 998-887-5465, 998-887-5423) is Cancún's most popular option for **horseback riding**. Five-hour packages are available for $65. The packages include two hours of riding to caves, *cenotes* (spring-fed, underground caves), lagoons, and Mayan ruins and along the Caribbean coast. A donkey polo game (yes, you get to play!) and some time for relaxing on the beach are also included. The ranch also offers a four-wheeler ride on the same route as the horseback tour for $55. Ranch Loma Bonita is located about 30 minutes south of Cancún. The prices include transportation to the ranch, riding, soft drinks, and lunch, plus a guide and insurance. American Express, MasterCard, and Visa are accepted.

Trailing away

Marina Neptuno (Internet: www.cancunmermaid.com), in Cancún, offers all-terrain-vehicle (ATV) jungle tours priced at $44 per person. The ATV tours travel through the jungles of Cancún and emerge on the beaches of the Riviera Maya. The 2@1/2-hour tour includes equipment, instruction, the services of a tour guide, and bottled water; it departs daily at 9 a.m., 12 p.m., and 3 p.m.

Traveling to the Island of Women

One of the most popular — and in my mind, best — ways to spend the day is to check out a real Mexican beach town across the narrow channel from Cancún. **Isla Mujeres, or "Island of Women,"** located just 10 miles offshore, is one of the most pleasant day trips from Cancún. At one end of the island is **El Garrafón National Underwater Park,** which is excellent for snorkeling and diving. At the other end is a captivating village with small shops, restaurants, and hotels, along with **Playa Norte (North Beach),** the island's best beach.

To get to Isla Mujeres, you have four options:

- The **public ferries** from Puerto Juárez take between 15 and 45 minutes and make frequent trips.

- Traveling by **shuttle boat** from Playa Linda or Playa Tortuga is an hour-long ride. The boats offer irregular service.

- The **watertaxi** is a more expensive but faster option than the public ferry or a shuttle boat. It's located next to the Xcaret terminal.

- Daylong **pleasure-boat trips** to the island leave from the Playa Linda pier.

Pleasure-boat cruises to Isla Mujeres include practically every conceivable type of vessel: Modern motor yachts, catamarans, trimarans, and even old-time sloops — more than 25 boats a day — take swimmers, sun lovers, snorkelers, and shoppers out into the translucent

Isla Mujeres (The Island of Women)

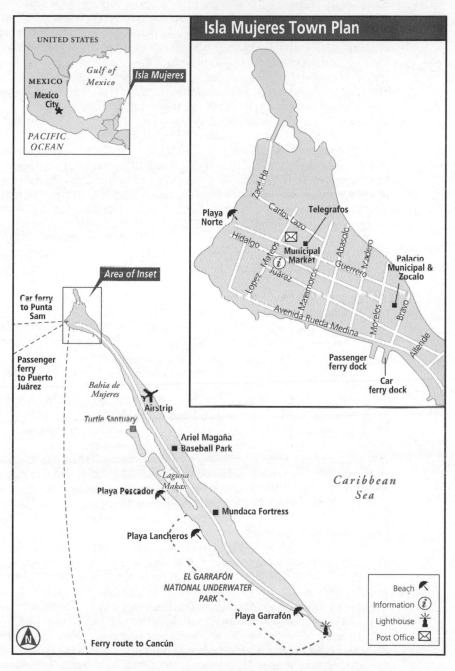

waters. Some tours include a snorkeling stop at Garrafón, lunch on the beach, and a short time for shopping in downtown Isla Mujeres. Most cruises leave at 9:30 or 10:00 a.m., last about five or six hours, and include continental breakfast, lunch, and rental of snorkel gear. Others, particularly the sunset and night cruises, go to beaches away from town for pseudo-pirate shows and include a lobster dinner or Mexican buffet. If you want to actually see Isla Mujeres, go on a morning cruise or go on your own using the public ferry at Puerto Juárez. Prices for the day cruises run around $45 per person.

The inexpensive Puerto Juárez **public ferries** are just a few miles from downtown Cancún, and they give you greater flexibility in planning your day. From Isla Cancún or Cancún City, take either a taxi or the Ruta 8 bus (from Avenida Tulum) to Puerto Juárez. Choose the fast ferry (a 15-minute ride) that costs $3.50 per person over the slower one (a 45-minute ride) that costs $2. Departures are every half-hour from 6:00 a.m. to 8:30 a.m. and then every 15 minutes until 8:30 p.m. Upon arrival, the ferry docks in downtown Isla Mujeres near all the shops, restaurants, hotels, and Norte beach. Take a taxi or rent a golf cart to get to Garrafón Park at the other end of the island. You can stay on the island as long as you like (even overnight) and return by ferry, but be sure to check the time of the last returning ferry — the hours are clearly posted.

The group that runs Xcaret (see the "Xcaret" section later in this chapter) now manages **Garrafón Natural Park,** so it has taken on more of a full-service theme-park atmosphere. A basic entrance fee of $10 entitles you to access the reef, nature trails, and a museum and to use kayaks, inner tubes, life vests, the pool, hammocks, and public facilities and showers. You can rent snorkel gear and lockers for an extra charge. Several restaurants are on-site. An all-inclusive option is available for $36, which adds dining at any of the restaurants, plus unlimited domestic drinks and use of snorkel gear, lockers, and towels. Garrafón also has full dive facilities and gear rentals, plus an expansive gift shop.

Other excursions from Isla Mujeres go to Garrafón **Reefs** in glass-bottom boats, so you can have a near-scuba-diving experience and see many colorful fish. However, the reefs are some distance from the shore, and they're impossible to reach on windy days with choppy seas. Also keep in mind that the reefs have suffered from over-visitation, and their condition is far from pristine.

The glass-bottomed *Nautibus* ($29 adults, $14.50 children ages 6 to 12; ☎ **998-883-3732,** 998-883-2119) has been around for years. The morning and afternoon trips (9:30 a.m., 11:00 a.m., 12:30 p.m., and 2:00 p.m.) take about 1 hour and 20 minutes, including about 50 minutes of transit time back and forth. You travel in a glass-bottom boat from the El Embarcadero pier to the Chitale coral reef and see colorful fish. The **Atlantis Submarine** provides a front-row seat to the underwater action. Departures vary, depending on weather conditions. Atlantis Submarine departs Monday to Saturday every hour from 9 a.m. until 1 p.m. ☎ **987-872-5671;** a one hour and 45 minute tour is $71 per person. You need to take a ferry to Cozumel to catch the submarine. Still other boat excursions visit **Isla Contoy,** a **national bird sanctuary** that's well worth the time. You can call any travel agent or see any hotel tour desk to get a wide selection of tours to Isla Contoy. Prices range from $44 to $65, depending on the length of the trip. If you plan to spend time in Isla Mujeres, the Contoy trip is easier and more pleasurable to take from there.

Touring Ruins or an Eco-Theme Park

One of the best ways to spend a vacation day is by exploring the nearby archeological ruins or one of the new ecological theme parks near Cancún. Historical and natural treasures unlike any you may have encountered before are within easy driving distance. Cancún is a perfect base for day trips to these places that provide a great introduction to Mexico's rich historical past and diverse natural attractions.

The Mayan ruins to the south of Cancún at **Tulum** should be your first goal. Then perhaps, you can check out the *caleta* (cove) of **Xel-Ha** or take the day-trip to **Xcaret.**

Organized day trips are popular and easy to book through any travel agent in town, or you can plan a journey on your own via bus or rental car. **Greenline** (☎ **998-883-4545**) buses offer *paquetes* (packages) to popular nearby destinations. The package to **Chichén-Itzá** departs at 8:30 a.m. and includes the round-trip, air-conditioned bus ride, with video, for the three-hour trip, entry to the ruins, two hours at the ruins, and lunch. The tour returns to Cancún by 7:30 p.m.; cost is $59.

Seeing the archeological sites

There are four great archeological sites within close proximity to Cancún: Tulum, Ruinas del Rey, and Chichén-Itzá.

- ✔ **Tulum:** Summer hours: daily from 8 a.m. to 7 p.m., winter hours: daily from 7 a.m. until 6 p.m. Admission $3.50. Sundays free admission.
- ✔ **Ruinas del Rey:** Daily 8 a.m. until 5 p.m. Admission $2.50
- ✔ **Chichén-Itzá:** Daily 8 a.m. to 5 p.m. Admission $3.50

Touring Tulum

Poised on a rocky hill overlooking the transparent, turquoise Caribbean Sea, ancient **Tulum** is a stunning site — and my personal favorite of all the ruins. It's not the largest or most important of the Mayan ruins in this area, but it's the only one by the sea, which makes it the most visually impressive in my opinion. Intriguing carvings and reliefs decorate the well-preserved structures, which date back to between the 12th and 16th centuries A.D. in the post-classic period.

Tulum Ruins

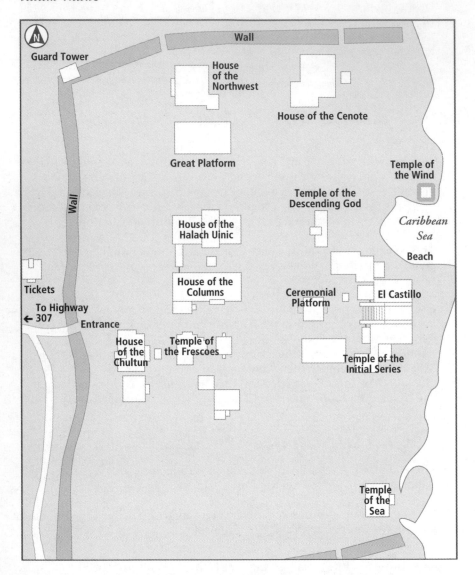

The site is surrounded by a wall on three sides, which explains its name — *tulum* means fence, trench, or wall. Its ancient name is believed to have been *Záma,* a derivative of the Mayan word for "morning" or "dawn," and the sunrise at Tulum is certainly dramatic. The wall is believed to have been constructed after the original buildings to protect the interior religious altars from a growing number of invaders. Although Tulum is considered to have been principally a place of worship, members of the upper classes later took up residence here to take advantage of the protective wall. Between the two most dramatic structures — the castle and the Temple of the Wind — lies Tulum Cove, where you can swim and spend time relaxing on this absolutely magical beach. The cove is a small inlet with a beach of fine, white sand, and it was a point of departure for Mayan trading vessels in ancient times. Entrance to the site without a tour is $2; use of video camera requires a $4 permit. A popular day excursion combines a visit to the ruins at Tulum with the ecological water park Xel-Ha (see the "Xel-Ha" section later in this chapter).

Revealing Ruinas del Rey

Cancún has its own Mayan ruins — **Ruinas del Rey** — a small site that's less impressive than the ruins at Tulum or Chichén-Itzá. Mayan fishermen built this small ceremonial center and settlement very early in the history of Mayan culture and then abandoned it. The site was resettled again near the end of the post-classic period, not long before the arrival of the conquistadors. The platforms of numerous small temples are visible amid the banana plants, papayas, and wildflowers. The Hilton Cancún golf course has been built around the ruins, but there's a separate entrance for sightseers. The ruins are about 13 miles from town, at the southern reaches of the Hotel Zone, close to Punta Nizuc. Look for the Hilton hotel on the left (east) and then the ruins on the right (west). Admission is $4.50 (free on Sundays and holidays); the hours are 8 a.m. to 5 p.m. daily. Call ☎ **998-884-8073** for more information.

Checking out Chichén-Itzá

The fabled pyramids and temples of Chichén-Itzá (no, it doesn't rhyme with "chicken pizza"; the accents are on the last syllables chee *chin* eat-*zah*) are the regions best-know ancient monuments. Walking among these stone platforms, pyramids and ball courts give you an appreciation for this ancient civilization that cannot be had from reading books. The city is built on such scale as to evoke a sense of wonder: To fill the plaza during one of the mass rituals that occurred here a millennium ago would have required an enormous number of celebrants. Even today, with the mass flow of tourist through these plazas, the ruins feel empty

The site occupies four square miles and it takes most of the day to see all the ruins, which are open daily 8 a.m. to 5 p.m. Service areas are open 8 a.m. to 10 p.m. Admission is $8.50, free for children under age 12, and free for all on Sunday and holidays. A permit to use your own video camera costs an additional $4. Chichén-Itzá's sound and light show is worth seeing and is included in the cost of admission. The show is held at 8 p.m. every night and is in Spanish, but headsets are available for rent ($3) in several languages.

Day trips from Cancún can be arranged through your hotel or through a travel agent in the United States (before you go) or in Mexico.

Exploring an eco-theme park

The popularity of the Xcaret and Xel-Ha eco-parks has inspired a growing number of entrepreneurs to ride the wave of interest in ecological and adventure theme parks. Be aware that "theme park" more than "ecological" is the operative part of the phrase. The newer parks of Aktun Chen and Tres Ríos are — so far — less commercial and more focused on nature than their predecessors.

Aktun Chen

This park, consisting of a spectacular 5,000-year-old grotto and an abundance of wildlife, marks the first time that above-the-ground cave systems in the Yucatán have been open to the public. The name means "cave with an underground river inside." The main cave containing three rivers is more than 600 yards long with a magnificent vault. Discreet illumination and easy walking paths make visiting the caves more comfortable, without appearing to alter the caves too much from their natural state. The caves contain thousands of stalactites, stalagmites, and sculpted rock formations, along with a 40-foot-deep *cenote* (an underground, spring-fed cave) with clear blue water.

Aktun Chen was once underwater itself, and fossilized shells and fish embedded in the limestone are visible as you walk along the paths. Caves are an integral part of this region's geography and geology, and knowledgeable guides lead you through the site while providing explanations and offering mini history lessons on the Maya's association with these caves. Tours have no set times — guides are available to take you when you arrive — and groups are kept to a maximum of 20 people.

Nature trails surround the caves throughout the 988-acre park, where spotting deer, spider monkeys, iguanas, and wild turkeys is common. A small, informal restaurant and gift shop are also on-site.

It's easy to travel to Aktun Chen on your own. From Cancún, go south on Highway 307 (the road to Tulum). Just past the turn-off for Akumal, a sign on the right side of the highway indicates the turn-off for Aktun-Chen; from there, it's a 3 kilometer (1.9 mile) drive west along a smooth but unpaved road. Travel time from Cancún is about an hour, and the park is open from 8 a.m. until dark. The entry fee of $12 includes the services of a guide. Call ☎ **998-892-0662,** 998-850-4190 for more information. Or you can visit the park via the Internet at www.aktunchen.com.

Tres Ríos

Tres Ríos — meaning three rivers — is the most "natural" of the area's nature parks. Located on more than 150 acres of land, this park is a true nature reserve that offers guests a beautiful area for kayaking, canoeing, snorkeling, horseback riding, or biking along jungle trails. Essentially, the park is just one big natural spot for participating in these activities. It's definitely less commercial than the other eco-theme parks.

Chichén-Itzá Ruins

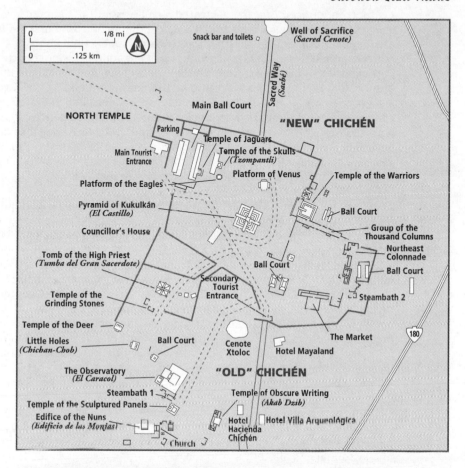

The park is located just 25 minutes south of Cancún. The entrance fee is $19 for adults and $12 for children, which includes canoe trips; the use of bikes, kayaks, and snorkeling equipment; and the use of hammocks and beach chairs after you tire yourself out. Extra charges apply for scuba diving, horseback riding, and extended guided tours through the preserve and its estuary. Tres Ríos also has bathroom facilities, showers, and a convenience store; however, the facilities are much less sophisticated than the area's other, more developed eco-theme parks.

Most Cancún travel agencies sell a half-day "kayak express" tour to Tres Ríos. Priced at $39, the trip includes admission to the park and its activities, round-trip transportation, lunch, and two nonalcoholic drinks. Call ☎ **998-887-4977** in Cancún or visit the park's Web site at www.tres-rios.com for details and reservations. Tres Ríos is open daily 9 a.m. to 5 p.m.

Xcaret

Xcaret (pronounced *ish*-car-et), located 50 miles south of Cancún, is a specially built ecological and archaeological theme park and one of the area's most popular tourist attractions. Xcaret has become almost a reason in itself to visit Cancún. With a ton of attractions — most of them participatory — in one location, it's the closest thing to Disneyland in Mexico. In Cancún, signs advertising Xcaret and folks handing out Xcaret leaflets are everywhere. The park has its own bus terminal in Cancún where buses pick up tourists at regular intervals. Plan to spend a full day here; children love it, and the jungle setting and palm-lined beaches are beautiful. Past the entrance booths (built to resemble small Mayan temples) are pathways that meander around bathing coves, the snorkeling lagoon, and the remains of a group of real Mayan temples.

Xcaret may celebrate Mother Nature, but its builders rearranged quite a bit of her handiwork in completing it. If you're looking for a place to escape the commercialism of Cancún, this may not be it. The park is relatively expensive and may be very crowded, thus diminishing the advertised "natural" experience. Entrance gains you access to swimming beaches, limestone tunnels to snorkel through, marked palm-lined pathways, a wild-bird breeding aviary, horseback riding, scuba diving, a botanical garden and nursery, a sea turtle nursery, a butterfly pavilion, and a tropical aquarium, where visitors can touch underwater creatures such as manta rays, starfish, and octopi. Extra charges apply for some of these activities. One of the park's most popular attractions is the excellent "Dolphinarium," where visitors (on a first-come, first-served basis) can swim with the dolphins for an extra charge of $80.

Oh, but there's more. Xcaret features a replica of the ancient Mayan game, Pok-ta-pok. In this game, six "warriors" bounce around a 9-pound ball with their hips. The Seawalker, a type of watersport designed for non-swimmers, is another attraction. By donning a special suit and helmet with a connected air pump, you can walk on the ocean floor or examine a coral reef in a small bay.

The visitor center has lockers, first-aid assistance, and a gift shop. Visitors aren't allowed to bring in food or drinks, so you're limited to the rather high-priced restaurants on-site. No personal radios are allowed, and you must remove all suntan lotion if you swim in the lagoon to avoid poisoning the lagoon habitat.

The admission price of $39 per person entitles you to use the facilities, boats, life jackets, snorkeling equipment for the underwater tunnel and lagoon, and lounge chairs. Other attractions, such as snorkeling at $22, horseback riding at $39, scuba diving at $45 for certified divers ($65 for a resort course), and the dolphin swim at $80, cost extra. There may be more visitors than equipment (in the case of beach chairs, for example), so bring a beach towel and your own snorkeling gear to be on the safe side.

Travel agencies in Cancún offer day trips to Xcaret that depart at 8 a.m. and return at 6 p.m. The cost is $65 for adults ($45 for children), which includes transportation, admission, and a guide. You can also buy a ticket to the park at the **Xcaret bus terminal** (☎ **998-883-0654,** 998-883-3143), located next to the Fiesta Americana Coral Beach hotel on Cancún Island. The "Xcaret Day and Night" trip includes round-trip transportation from Cancún, a *charreada* festival (where horse riding and roping skills are showcased), lighted pathways to Mayan ruins, dinner, and a folkloric show. The cost is $69 for adults and $45 for children age 6 to 11 (free for kids age 5 and under). Buses leave the terminal at 9:00 and 10:00 a.m. daily, with the "Day and Night" tour returning at 9:30 p.m. The park itself is open Monday to Saturday 8:30 a.m. to 8:00 p.m. Sunday 8:30 a.m. to 5:30 p.m.

Xel-Ha

The sea has carved the Caribbean coast of the Yucatán into hundreds of small *caletas,* or coves, that form the perfect habitat for tropical marine life, both flora and fauna. Many *caletas* along the coast remain undiscovered and pristine, but Xel-Ha, located near Tulum, plays host daily to throngs of snorkelers and scuba divers who come to luxuriate in its warm waters and swim among its brilliant fish. Xel-Ha (shell-*hah*) is a swimmers' paradise with no threat of undertow or pollution. It's a beautiful, completely calm cove that's a perfect place to bring kids for their first snorkeling experience. Experienced snorkelers may be disappointed because the crowds seem to have driven out the living coral and many of the fish here.

The entrance to Xel-Ha (☎ **998-884-9122;** Internet: www.xelha.com.mx) is a half-mile from the main highway. Admission is $19 per adult and $11.50 for children age 5 to 12 (free for children under age 5) and includes use of inner tubes, life vests, and shuttle trains to the river. You can also choose an all-inclusive option for admission, equipment, food, and beverages that runs $43 for adults and $30 for children. The park is open daily 8:30 a.m. to 5:00 p.m., offers free parking with admission, and accepts American Express, MasterCard, and Visa. After you arrive at the 10-acre park, you can rent snorkeling equipment and an underwater camera, but you may also bring your own. Food and beverage service, changing rooms, showers, and other facilities are available. Platforms have been constructed that allow decent sea-life viewing for non-snorkelers.

In addition, the resort offers "snuba," a clever invention that combines snorkeling and scuba. Snuba is a shallow-water diving system that places conventional scuba tanks on secure rafts that float at surface level; the "snuba-diver" breathes normally through a mouthpiece, which is connected to a long air hose attached to the tank above. This setup enables a swimmer to go as deep as 20 feet below the surface and stay down for as long as an hour or more. It's a great transition to scuba, and many divers may even enjoy it more because snuba leaves you remarkably unencumbered by equipment.

When you swim, be careful to observe the "swim here" and "no swimming" signs. The greatest variety of fish can be seen right near the ropes that divide the swimming areas from the non-swimming areas and near any groups of rocks. An interactive dolphin attraction has been added — a 45-minute swim costs $55, and an educational program runs $30. Reservations should be made at least 24 hours in advance for one of the four daily sessions: 9:30 a.m., 12:30 p.m., 2:00 p.m., and 3:15 p.m.

If you're driving, just south of Xel-Ha, turn off on the west side of the highway, so you don't miss the ruins of **ancient Xel-Ha.** You're likely to be the only one there as you walk over limestone rocks and through the tangle of trees, vines, and palms. There's a huge, deep, dark *cenote* to one side, a temple palace with tumbled-down columns, a jaguar group, and a conserved temple group. A covered palapa on one pyramid guards a partially preserved mural. Admission is $2.50.

Xel-Ha is close to the ruins at **Tulum** (check out the "Seeing archeological sites" section earlier in this chapter) and makes a good place for a dip after you finish climbing the Mayan ruins. You can even make the short 8-mile hop north from Tulum to Xel-Ha by public bus. When you get off at the junction for Tulum, ask the restaurant owner when the next buses come by; otherwise, you may have to wait as long as two hours on the highway.

Sightseeing in Cancún

To the right side of the entrance to the Cancún Convention Center is the small **Museo Arqueológico de Cancún** (☎ 998-883-0305), a small but interesting museum with relics from archaeological sites around the state. Admission is $2.00 (free on Sundays and holidays). The museum is open Tuesday to Sunday from 9 a.m. to 7 p.m.

During the winter tourist season, **bullfights** are held every Wednesday at 3:30 p.m. in Cancún's small bullring (☎ 998-884-8372), which is located near the northern end of Paseo Kukulkán opposite the Restaurant Los Almendros (Ave. Bonampak and Sayil). A sport introduced to Mexico by the Spanish viceroys, bullfighting is now as much a part of Mexican culture as tequila. The bullfights usually include four bulls, and the spectacle begins with a folkloric dance exhibition, followed by a performance by the *charros* (Mexico's sombrero-wearing cowboys). You're not likely to see Mexico's best bullfights in Cancún — the real stars are in Mexico City.

Keep in mind that if you go to a bullfight, *you're going to see a bullfight,* so stay away if you're an animal lover or you can't bear the sight of blood. Travel agencies in Cancún sell tickets: $30 for adults, with children admitted free of charge. Seating is by general admission. American Express, MasterCard, and Visa are accepted.

Cancún Area

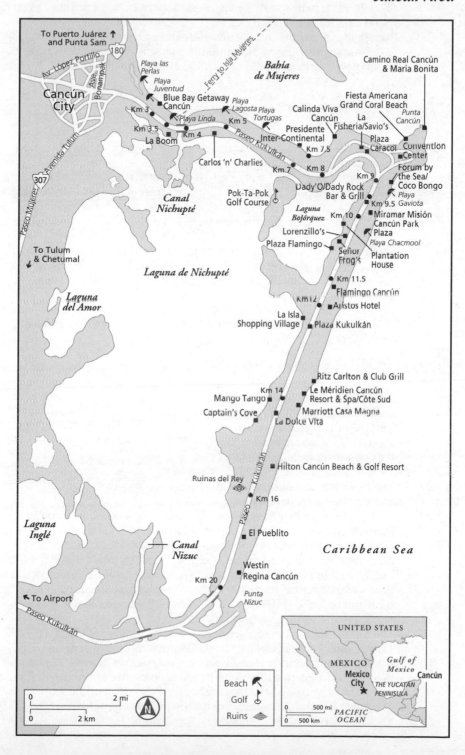

To Puerto Juárez ↑
and Punta Sam
180

Av. López Portillo

Ferry to Isla Mujeres

Bahía de Mujeres

Camino Real Cancún
& Maria Bonita

Playa las Perlas

Playa Juventud

Cancún City

Blue Bay Getaway Cancún

Playa Lagosta

Fiesta Americana
Grand Coral Beach

Punta Cancún

Km 3

Playa Linda

Playa Tortugas

Calinda Viva Cancún

La Fisheria/Savio's

Km 3.5

Km 5

Presidente Inter-Continental

Plaza Caracol

Km 4

Paseo Kukulkán

Km 7.5

Convention Center

La Boom

Carlos 'n' Charlies

Km 7

Km 8

Km 9

Forum by the Sea/
Coco Bongo

Canal Nichupté

Pok-Ta-Pok Golf Course

Dady'O/Dady Rock Bar & Grill

Playa Gaviota

Km 9.5

Av. Bonampak

Ave. Tulum

307

Paseo Mujeres

To Tulum
& Chetumal

Laguna Bojórquez

Km 10

Miramar Misión Cancún Park

Lorenzillo's

Plaza

Plaza Flamingo

Playa Chacmool

Señor Frog's

Plantation House

Laguna de Nichupté

Km 11.5

Flamingo Cancún

Laguna del Amor

Km 12

Aristos Hotel

La Isla Shopping Village

Plaza Kukulkán

Ritz Carlton & Club Grill

Km 14

Le Méridien Cancún Resort & Spa/Côte Sud

Mango Tango

Marriott Casa Magna

Captain's Cove

La Dolce Vita

Hilton Cancún Beach & Golf Resort

Ruinas del Rey

Paseo Kukulkán

Km 16

Laguna Inglé

Canal Nizuc

El Pueblito

Caribbean Sea

Km 20

Westin Regina Cancún

Punta Nizuc

To Airport

Paseo Kukulkán

0   2 mi

0   2 km

N

Beach
Golf
Ruins

UNITED STATES

MEXICO

Gulf of Mexico

Cancún

Mexico City

THE YUCATÁN PENINSULA

PACIFIC OCEAN

0   500 mi
0   500 km

Panoramic **helicopter tours** allow you to see a complete overview of this island paradise and the surrounding areas. Both day and evening flights are available. Tours to the ruins and flights south along the Riviera Maya are also an option. **Heli Data** offers customized tours with hourly rates depending upon the length of flight and time of day. Hotel pickup is provided. For details, call ☎ **998-883-3104.**

Shopping in Cancún

Despite the surrounding natural splendor, shopping has become a favored activity in Cancún, and the place is known throughout Mexico for its diverse array of shops and festive malls catering to large numbers of international tourists. Tourists arriving from the United States may find apparel more expensive in Cancún, but the selection here is much broader than in other Mexican resort.

Numerous duty-free shops offer excellent value on European goods. The largest shop is **UltraFemme** (☎ **998-884-1402,** 998-885-0804), specializing in imported cosmetics, perfumes, and fine jewelry and watches. Its downtown-Cancún location on Avenida Tulum, Supermanzana (intersection) 25, offers lower prices than the locations in Plaza Caracol, Kukulkán Plaza, Plaza Mayafair, and Flamingo Plaza or the store at the international airport.

Handcrafts and other *artesanía* works are more limited and more expensive in Cancún than in other regions of Mexico because they're not produced here, but they are available. Several **open-air crafts markets** are easily visible on Avenida Tulum in Cancún City and near the convention center in the Hotel Zone. One of the biggest markets is **Coral Negro,** located at Paseo Kukulkán, Km 9.5 (☎ **998-883-0758;** Fax: 998-883-0758). It's open daily from 7 a.m. to 11 p.m.

The main venue for shopping in Cancún is the **mall** — not quite as grand as its U.S. counterpart, but close. All of Cancún's malls are air-conditioned, sleek, and sophisticated, with most located on Avenida Kukulkán between Km 7 and Km 12. Everything from fine crystal and silver to designer clothing and decorative objects can be found, along with numerous restaurants and clubs. Stores are generally open daily from 10 a.m. to 10 p.m., with clubs and restaurants remaining open much later. Here's a brief rundown on the malls, running from the northern to the southern end of the island — and some of the shops they contain.

The long-standing **Plaza Caracol** (Ave. Kukulkán, Km 7.5; ☎ **998-883-1038**) holds Cartier jewelry, Guess, Waterford Crystal, Señor Frog clothing, Samsonite luggage, Gucci, and La Fisheria restaurant. It's just before you reach the convention center as you come from downtown Cancún.

The entertainment-oriented **Forum by the Sea** (Ave. Kukulkán, Km 9; ☎ 998-883-4425) has shops including Tommy Hilfiger, Levi's, Diesel,

Swatch, and Harley Davidson, but most people come here for the food and fun. You can choose from Hard Rock Cafe, Coco Bongo, Rainforest Cafe, Sushi-ito, and Santa Fe Beer Factory, plus an extensive food court. It's open 10 a.m. to midnight (bars remain open later).

Planet Hollywood anchors the **Plaza Flamingo** (Ave. Kukulkán, Km 8.5; ☎ 998-883-2945), but branches of Bancrecer, Subway, and La Casa del Habano (for Cuban cigars) are located inside.

Maya Fair Plaza/Centro Comercial Maya Fair, frequently called "Mayfair" (Ave. Kukulkán, Km 10.5; ☎ 998-883-2801), is Cancún's oldest mall and features a lively, bricked center with open-air restaurants and bars, such as Tequila Sunrise, and several stores selling silver, leather, and crafts.

Inside **Plaza Kukulkán** (Ave. Kukulkán, Km 12; ☎ 998-885-2200; Internet: www.kukulcanplaza.com) is a large selection of more than 300 shops, restaurants, and entertainment venues. There's a branch of Banco Serfin; OK Maguey Cantina Grill; a movie theater with U.S. movies; an Internet-access kiosk; Tikal, a shop with Guatemalan textile clothing; several crafts stores; a liquor store; several bathing-suit specialty stores, record and tape outlets; a leather-goods store (including shoes and sandals); and a store specializing in silver from Taxco. In the food court are a number of U.S. franchise restaurants, including Ruth's Chris Steak House, plus a specialty-coffee shop. For entertainment, the plaza has a bowling alley, the Q-Zar laser game pavilion, and a video-game arcade. There's also a large indoor parking garage. The mall is open 10 a.m. to 10 p.m.

The newest and most intriguing mall is the **La Isla Shopping Village** (Paseo Kukulkán, Km 12.5; ☎ 998-883-5025; Internet: www.cancun shoppingmalls.com), an open-air festival mall that looks like a small village, where walkways lined with shops and restaurants crisscross over little canals. The mall also has a "riverwalk" alongside the Nichupté Lagoon and an interactive aquarium and dolphin-swim facility. Shops include Zara clothing, Benetton, Guess, Swatch, H. Stern, Ultra Femme, and the first Warner Brothers Studios store in Mexico. Dining choices include Johnny Rockets, The Food Court (not actually a "food court," but an Anderson's restaurant), and the beautiful Mexican restaurant, La Casa de las Margaritas. There's also a first-run movie theater, a video arcade, and several nightclubs, including Max-O's and Alebrejes. It's located across from the Sheraton, on the lagoon side of the street.

Discovering Cancún after Dark

Ready to party? The nightlife in Cancún is as hot as the sun at noon on a cloudless July day, and clubbing is one of the main attractions of this let-loose town. The current hotspots are centralized in **Forum by the Sea** and **La Isla Village,** but it's not hard to find a party anywhere in town. Hotels also compete for your pesos with happy-hour entertainment and special drink prices as they try to entice visitors and guests from other resorts to pay a visit. (Lobby-bar hopping at sunset is one great way to plan next year's vacation.)

Partying at a club

Clubbing in Cancún can go on each night until the sun rises over that incredibly blue sea. Several of the big hotels have nightclubs — sometimes still called discos here — and others entertain in their lobby bars with live music. On weekends, expect to stand in long lines for the top clubs, pay a cover charge of $10 to $20 per person, and pay $5 to $8 for a drink. Some of the higher-priced clubs include an open bar or live entertainment.

Check out the "Isla Cancún (Hotel Zone) Dining" map in Chapter 10 for club locations.

The **Bar Crawl Tour,** offered by American Express Travel Agency (☎ **998-881-4050;** Fax: 998-884-6942), is a great introduction to the Cancún club scene. It's not as cheesy as it may sound, and it's a great way to check out the top spots without making a major investment in cover charges. For $49, a bus takes you from bar to club to bar to club — generally a range of four to five top choices — where you bypass any lines and spend about an hour at each establishment. Entry to the clubs, one welcome drink at each location, and transportation by air-conditioned bus is included in the fee, allowing you to sample the best of Cancún's nightlife.

What's hot now? As any good clubber knows, popularity can shift like the sands on the beach, but Cancún clubs do seem to have staying power. So take this list as a starting point — extensive research showed me that these were the current hot spots at press time, listed alphabetically:

- ✔ I feel compelled to mention **Christine,** in the Hotel Krystal on the island (☎ **998-883-1793**), because it's been around for years with its signature laser-light shows, infused oxygen, and large video screens. But I mainly mention it to say that hipper clubs have now overtaken it. Christine still maintains a dress code of no shorts or jeans, and it opens at 9:30 p.m. nightly to a largely Mexican-national crowd — and those who still want to believe that disco lives. American Express, MasterCard, and Visa are accepted.

- ✔ **Coco Bongo** in Forum by the Sea (Paseo Kukulkán, Km 9.5; ☎ 998-883-5061; Internet: www.cocobongo.com.mx) continues its reputation as the hottest spot in town. This spot's main appeal is that there's no formal dance floor, so you can dance anywhere you can find the space — that includes on the tables, on the bar, or even on stage with the live band! Coco Bongo can pack in up to 3,000 people — and regularly does. You have to see it to believe it. Despite its capacity, lines are long on weekends and in the high season. The music alternates between Caribbean, salsa, techno, and classics from the 1970s and 1980s. Coco Bongo draws a mixed crowd, but the young and hip dominate.

✔ **Dady'O** (Paseo Kukulkán, Km 9.5; ☎ **998-883-3333;** Internet: www. dady-o.com) is a highly favored rave with frequent, long lines. It opens nightly at 9:30 p.m. and generally charges a cover of $15. **Dady Rock Bar and Grill** (Paseo Kukulkán, Km 9.5; ☎ **998-883-1626**), the offspring of Dady'O, opens early (7:00 p.m.) and goes as long as any other nightspot, offering a new twist on entertainment with a combination of live bands and DJ-orchestrated music. It also features an open bar, full meals, a buffet, and dancing.

✔ **La Boom** (Paseo Kukulkán, Km 3.5; ☎ **998-883-1152;** Fax: 998-883-1458; Internet: www.laboom.com.mx), has two sections: One side is a video bar, and the other is a bilevel disco with cranking music. Both sides are air-conditioned. Each night finds a special deal going on: no cover, free bar, ladies' night, bikini night, and others. Popular with early twenty-somethings, it's open nightly 10:00 p.m. to 6:00 a.m. A sound-and-light show begins at 11:30 p.m. in the disco. The cover varies for the disco and the bar depending on the night — ladies get in free most nights, and men pay covers that vary between $10 and $20 with an open bar.

Numerous restaurants, such as **Carlos 'n Charlie's, Planet Hollywood, Hard Rock Cafe, Señor Frog's, TGI Friday's,** and **Iguana Wana,** double as nighttime party spots offering wild-ish fun at much lower prices than the clubs. Check these out:

✔ **Carlos 'n Charlie's** (Paseo Kukulkán, Km 4.5; ☎ **998-849-4052**) is a reliable place to find both good food and frat-house-type entertainment in the evenings. A dance floor goes along with the live music that starts nightly around 8:30 p.m. A cover charge kicks in if you're not planning to eat. It's open daily 11 a.m. to 2 a.m.

✔ **Hard Rock Cafe,** in Plaza Lagunas Mall and Forum by the Sea (☎ **998-881-8120,** 998-883-2024; Internet: www.hardrock.com), entertains with a live band at 10:30 p.m. every night except Wednesday. At other times, you get lively recorded music to munch by. The menu combines the most popular foods from American and Mexican cultures. It's open daily 11 a.m. to 2 a.m.

✔ **Planet Hollywood** (Flamingo Shopping Center, Paseo Kukulkán, Km 11; ☎ **998-885-3003;** Internet: www.planethollywood.com), is the still-popular brainchild (and one of the last-remaining) of Sylvester Stallone, Bruce Willis, and Arnold Schwarzenegger. It's both a restaurant and a nighttime music/dance spot with megadecibel live music. It's open daily 11 a.m. to 2 a.m. American Express, MasterCard, and Visa are accepted.

Not into the party scene? The most refined and upscale of all Cancún's nightly gathering spots is the **Lobby Lounge** at the **Ritz-Carlton Hotel** (☎ **998-885-0808**). Live dance music and a list of more than 120 premium tequilas for tasting or sipping are the highlights here.

Enjoying a cultural event

Nightly performances of the **Ballet Folklórico de Cancún** (☎ **998-881-0400,** ext. 193 or 194) are held at the Cancún Convention Center. Tickets are sold between 8:00 a.m. and 9:00 p.m. at a booth just inside the convention-center entrance. Dinner is an option to enjoy before the show. Dinner-show guests pay around $48 and arrive at 6:30 p.m. for drinks, which are followed by dinner at 7:00 p.m. and the show at 8:00 p.m. This price includes an open bar, dinner, show, tax, and tip. If you choose to pass on dinner, the cost is only $30 for the show and an open bar — but you need to arrive by 7:30 p.m. American Express, MasterCard, and Visa accepted. Performances take place Tuesday through Saturday.

Several hotels host **Mexican fiesta nights,** which include a buffet dinner and a folkloric dance show; the price, including dinner, ranges from $35 to $50, but you should note that the quality of the performance is likely to be less professional than the show performed at the convention center.

In the Costa Blanca shopping center, **El Mexicano** restaurant (☎ **998-884-4207**) hosts a tropical dinner show every night and also features live music for dancing. The entertainment alternates each night — *mariachis* entertain off and on from 7:00 to 11:00 p.m., and a folkloric show takes place from 8:00 to 9:30 p.m.

You can also get in the party mood at **Mango Tango** (Paseo Kukulkán, Km 14; ☎ **998-885-0303**), a lagoon-side restaurant/dinner-show establishment opposite the Ritz-Carlton Hotel. Diners can choose from two seating levels, one nearer the music and the other overlooking the whole production. The music is loud and varied but mainly features reggae or salsa. The 1-hour-and-20-minute dinner show begins at 8:30 p.m. nightly and costs $40. At 9:30 p.m. live reggae music begins. If you're not dining and come just for the music and drinks, a $10 cover charge applies.

For entertainment that lets tourists and locals mingle, head for the downtown **Parque de las Palapas** (the main park) for *Noches Caribeños* (Caribbean Nights), where live tropical music is provided at no charge for anyone who wants to listen and dance. Performances begin at 7:30 p.m. on Sundays. Sometimes, performances are scheduled for Fridays and Saturdays, but the calendar varies.

Part IV
Cozumel and the Riviera Maya

The 5th Wave   By Rich Tennant

"Did you want to take the Schwinn bicycle dive, the Weber gas grill dive, or the Craftsman riding lawn mower dive?"

In this part . . .

Many travelers who shun the highly stylized, rather Americanized ways of Cancún find other stops in the Yucatán that offer abundant natural pleasures, authentic experiences, and a relaxed charm. These areas are close to Cancún's easy air access, yet miles away in mood and matter.

Cozumel, Playa del Carmen, Tulum, and other sites along the Yucatán coastline boast the lucid waters and white-sand beaches that you find in Cancún, but they add a dash of mystery, history, or simply local color to the equation. With nearby remnants of ancient settlements joining modern enticements, this part of Mexico is gaining the most attention with a bevy of new hotels and attractions to explore.

Chapter 12

Cozumel

● ●

In This Chapter

▶ Cruising Cozumel for the best accommodations

▶ Finding the best places to dine

▶ Discovering sports and other fun in the sun

▶ Adjusting to Cozumel and the lay of the land

● ●

Cozumel was a well-known diving spot before Cancún even existed, and it has ranked for years among the top-five dive destinations in the world. Tall reefs lining the southwest coast create towering walls that offer divers a fairytale landscape to explore.

For non-divers, Cozumel has the beautiful waters of the Caribbean with all the accompanying watersports and seaside activities. In addition to these reasons for visiting, Cozumel definitely has the feel of a small island — roads that don't go very far, lots of mopeds, few buses and trucks, and a certain sense of separation.

Choosing a Location

Cozumel is a large island located across from Playa del Carmen 12 miles off the Yucatan coast. In size, it's 28 miles (45km) long and 11 miles (18km) wide. San Miguel de Cozumel, the only town on the island, occupies only a small portion of the land. Hotels are situated on the coast north and south of the town; the rest of the shore is deserted. The shore is predominantly rocky, but there is a scattering of small, sandy coves that you can have practically all to yourself.

Life here revolves around two major activities: scuba diving and hosting cruise ships as a port of call. Cozumel is far and away the most popular destination along the Yucatán coast for both of these activities. Diving is big because of the fabulous reefs that stretch out along the southwestern coast. Despite the cruise-ship traffic and all the stores that it has spawned, life on the island moves at a relaxed and comfortable pace.

Cozumel's hotels are in three separate locations: along the coast **north** of town, in **town,** and along the coast **south** of town. The hotels in town are the most economical properties.

Staying in town can be both entertaining and convenient, although the hotels in this area tend to be smaller and older. If you choose to stay here, a number of restaurants and nightspots are within easy walking distance. Because Cozumel is so popular with cruise ships, the water-front section of town is wall-to-wall jewelry stores (many more than you would think demand could support) and souvenir shops. However, the waterfront section and the area around the town's main square are as far as most cruise-ship passengers venture into town. Elsewhere, you mainly find offices, restaurants, small hotels, and dive shops.

Because Cozumel is such a big destination for divers, all the large hotels and many of the smaller ones offer dive packages; I don't men-tion this in the reviews later in this chapter, but you should always ask about them. All the large waterfront hotels have dive shops on the premises and a pier, so I don't continually mention these facts in the reviews either. And it's quite okay to stay at one hotel and dive with another operator — any dive boat can pull up to any accessible hotel pier to pick up its customers.

There is one main road on the western side of the island, **Avenida** Raphael **Melgar,** which then becomes the coastal road **Costera Sur** (also called **Carretera a Chankanaab**) to the south and **Carretera Santa Pilar,** or **San Juan,** to the north. All the northern hotels line up in close proximity to each other on the beach side of the road a short distance from town and the airport.

The hotels to the south of town tend to be more spread out and farther from town than the hotels to the north. Some hotels are on the inland side of the road, and some are on the beach side, which makes for a dif-ference in price. The properties farthest away from town are all-inclusive and the beaches along this part of the coast tend to be slightly better than those to the north — as the northern coast is rocky and the south-ern hotels have more of a beach. All of the hotels have swimming pools and all of them can accommodate divers and snorkelers.

The prices I quote for the hotels include the 12% IVA tax. As an alterna-tive to a hotel, you may want to try **Cozumel Vacation Villas and Condos** (Av. 10 Sur no. 124, 77600 Cozumel, Q. Roo; ☎ **800-224-5551** in the U.S., or 987-872-0729, 987-872-1375; E-mail: info@cozumel-villas. com), which offers accommodations by the week. There are also more than half a dozen all-inclusive resorts. I've listed one of them, which offers a good location and a good stretch of coast. Some of the others in the north are less than ideal, and the large ones to the south are far enough away that it becomes a hassle to go into town. You can end up feeling a little like a captive.

Evaluating the Top Accommodations

As far as prices go, I give you rack rates (the maximum that a hotel or resort charges for a room) for two people spending one night in a double room. You can usually do better, especially if you're purchasing a package that includes airfare (see Chapter 6 for tips on avoiding paying rack rates). Prices quoted here include the 12% room tax. Please refer to the Introduction of *Mexico's Beach Resorts For Dummies* for an explanation of the price categories.

All hotels have air-conditioning unless otherwise indicated.

B&B Caribo

$ In town

The American owners of this B&B go out of their way to make you feel right at home. The rates are a good deal for this island because they include air-conditioning, breakfast, and several little extras. Six neatly decorated rooms come with cool tile floors, white furniture, and big bottles of purified drinking water. The six apartments come with small kitchens (minimum stay of one week required). A shared guest kitchen serves the other six rooms. Most rooms have a double bed and a twin bed, but no TVs or phones. There are a number of common rooms, including a television/computer room with e-mail service and a rooftop terrace. Breakfasts are full, and the cooking is good. To find the Caribo from the plaza, walk 6½ blocks inland on Juárez to the smartly painted blue-and-white house on the left.

Av. Juárez No. 799. ☎ 987-872-3195. Internet: www.visit-caribo.com. 12 units. Rack rates: High season $50 double; $60 apartment; low season $40 double; $50 apartment. Rates include full breakfast. AE, MC, V.

El Cozumeleño Beach Resort

$$$$ North of town

An all-inclusive resort, El Cozumeleño is for people who want an active vacation with plenty to do. Attractions include one of the best bits of beach on this stretch of coast, an extravagant pool and sunning area, and a full array of watersports and equipment rentals. As if that isn't enough to keep you busy, just across the road is the new golf course. Recently, the owners have more than doubled the number of rooms in the hotel and added to the amenities. The rooms in the old part are large, much longer than they are wide; rooms in the new part are also large, and their shape allows for a less awkward arrangement of furniture. All rooms have balconies with a great ocean view, attractive decor, large bathrooms, and either a king bed or two double beds. For your libations, they have two restaurants and three bars (including a swim-up bar). There are three pools (including wading pool and a very large pool with a roofed section that provides shade), large whirlpool, tennis court, and nearby golf course that guests can access. On the beach, the resort has an extensive watersports-rental facility. Moped rentals, an ample children's program, a game room, and miniature golf are some of the additional highlights.

Carretera Santa Pilar Km 4. ☎ *800-437-3923 in the U.S. and Canada, or 987-872-0050. Fax: 987-872-0381. Internet:* www.elcozumeleno.com. *252 units. Rack rates: High season $285 double; low season $195–$240 double. All-inclusive. AE, MC, V.*

Flamingo Hotel

$ In town

A small hotel just off Avenida Raphael Melgar, the Flamingo offers three stories of attractive, comfortable rooms around a small, plant-filled inner courtyard. Highlights include an inviting rooftop terrace and a popular alcohol bar/coffee bar. The more expensive second- and third-story rooms have air-conditioning and TVs. All rooms are large and have two double beds, white-tile floors, medium-size bathrooms, and ceiling fans. A penthouse suite comes with a full kitchen and sleeps up to six. The English-speaking staff is helpful and friendly. To find it, walk 3 blocks north on Melgar from the plaza and turn right on Calle 6; the hotel is on the left.

Calle 6 Norte No. 81. ☎ *800-806-1601 in the U.S., or* ☎ *and fax: 987-872-1264. Internet:* www.hotelflamingo.com. *22 units. Rack rates: High season $55–$77 double; low season $36–$45 double. AE, MC, V.*

La Ceiba Beach Hotel

$$$–$$$$ South of town

Located on the beach side of the southbound road, La Ceiba is great for snorkeling and shore diving — a submerged airplane is just offshore. It's a popular hotel with divers — you can tell because the pool area remains uncrowded during the day when the guests are out diving. The rooms, while not outfitted in the latest style, are nicely furnished, large, and comfortable, with most of the beds slightly softer than standard hotel issue (choice of king or two full beds). All rooms have ocean views and balconies. The emphasis here is on watersports, particularly scuba diving, and if this is your passion, be sure to ask about the special dive packages when you call for reservations. Diving is available right from the hotel beach. For those post-dive evenings, choose between two restaurants. (There's also a bar.) Other diversions include a lighted tennis court, a small exercise room with sauna, a whirlpool, and watersports-equipment rentals.

Costera Sur Km 4.5. ☎ *800-435-3240 in the U.S., or 987-872-0844. Fax: 987-872-0065. Internet:* www.dive.cozumel.com. *112 units. Free parking. Rack rates: High season $165–$200 double; low season $122–$140 double. AE, MC, V.*

Cozumel Island

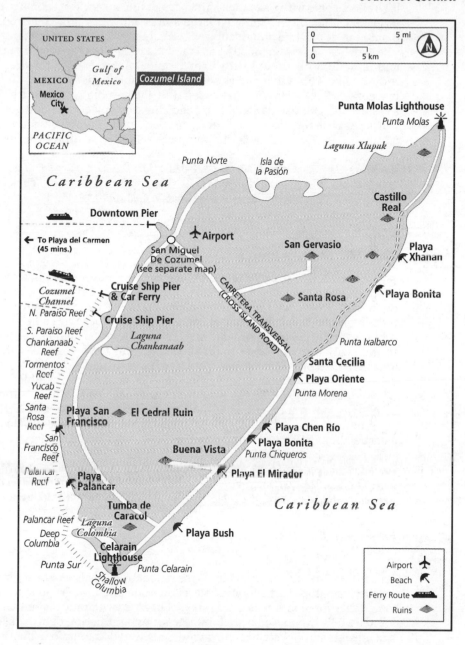

UNITED STATES

Gulf of Mexico

MEXICO

Mexico City

Cozumel Island

PACIFIC OCEAN

0   5 mi
0   5 km

N

Punta Molas Lighthouse
Punta Molas

Laguna Xlapak

Punta Norte

Isla de la Pasión

Caribbean Sea

Castillo Real

Downtown Pier

← To Playa del Carmen (45 mins.)

✈ **Airport**

San Miguel De Cozumel (see separate map)

San Gervasio

Playa Xhanan

Cozumel Channel

Cruise Ship Pier & Car Ferry

N. Paraiso Reef

Cruise Ship Pier

S. Paraiso Reef
Chankanaab Reef

Laguna Chankanaab

Santa Rosa

Playa Bonita

CARRETERA TRANSVERSAL (CROSS-ISLAND ROAD)

Punta Ixalbarco

Tormentos Reef

Yucab Reef

Santa Cecilia

Playa Oriente
Punta Morena

Santa Rosa Reef

Playa San Francisco

El Cedral Ruin

Playa Chen Río

San Francisco Reef

Buena Vista

Playa Bonita
Punta Chiqueros

Palancar Reef

Playa Palancar

Playa El Mirador

Caribbean Sea

Tumba de Caracol

Palancar Reef

Laguna Colombia

Playa Bush

Deep Columbia

Celarain Lighthouse

Punta Sur

Punta Celarain

Shallow Columbia

Airport ✈
Beach ⌁
Ferry Route 🚢
Ruins ◆

Playa Azul

$$$$ North of town

This quiet hotel is perhaps the most relaxing of the island's beachfront properties. It has a small beach with shade palapas that is one of the best on this side of the island. Service is attentive and personal. Almost all the rooms come with balconies and views of the ocean. The rooms in the original section are all suites — large suites with very large bathrooms painted in cool white and decorated with a taste for simplicity (no televisions). The new wing mostly has standard rooms that are comfortable and large and decorated with light tropical colors and furniture. All rooms come with either a king bed or two double beds, and suites offer two convertible single sofas in the separate living-room area. There's also a restaurant, two bars, a small pool, and a nearby golf course that guests can access. On the beach is a watersports-equipment rental pavilion, and a game room with pool table, TV, and videos is located above the lobby.

Carretera San Juan Km 4. ☎ *987-872-0199, 987-872-0043. Fax: 987-872-0110. Internet:*www.playa-azul.com. *50 units. Free parking. Rack rates: High season $210 double, $280 suite; low season $140 double, $180 suite. AE, MC, V.*

Plaza Las Glorias
$$$–$$$$ **South of town**

This all-suite, five-story hotel combines the top-notch amenities of the expensive hotels farther out with the convenience of being 5 blocks from town. For people who must have a beach, this is not the right hotel. (Although don't dismiss it out of hand; this hotel doesn't need a beach. It has a smart, terraced, sunning area above the water and easy access to the sea.) The split-level rooms are large and have separate sitting areas. The decor is decent, though it won't overwhelm you, and the furniture and beds are comfortable. Bed choices include two doubles, two twins, or one king. All rooms face out over the water and have either a balcony or a terrace. Note that the low-season rates make this hotel a good bargain. The dive shop here comes highly recommended. There's a casual dining restaurant and bar, plus a swim-up bar in the large pool.

Av. Rafael Melgar Km 1.5. ☎ *800-342-AMIGO in the U.S. and Canada, or 987-872-2000. Fax: 987-872-1937. Internet:* www.sidek.com.mx. *174 units. Free parking. Rack rates: High season $261 double; low season $137 double. AE, MC, V.*

Presidente Inter-Continental Cozumel
$$$$$ **South of town**

This is Cozumel's finest hotel in terms of location, quality of beachfront, on-site amenities, and service. Palatial in scale and modern in style, the Presidente spreads across a long stretch of coast with only distant hotels for neighbors. Rooms come in four categories — superior, deluxe, deluxe oceanfront, and deluxe beachfront — distributed among four buildings (two to five stories tall). Superior rooms come with a view of the garden; deluxe rooms come with a view of the ocean. Most deluxe and superior rooms are large with large, well-lit bathrooms. Deluxe oceanfront rooms and beachfront rooms are even larger and have spacious balconies or patios. (The main difference is that the beachfronts are at ground level

San Miguel de Cozumel

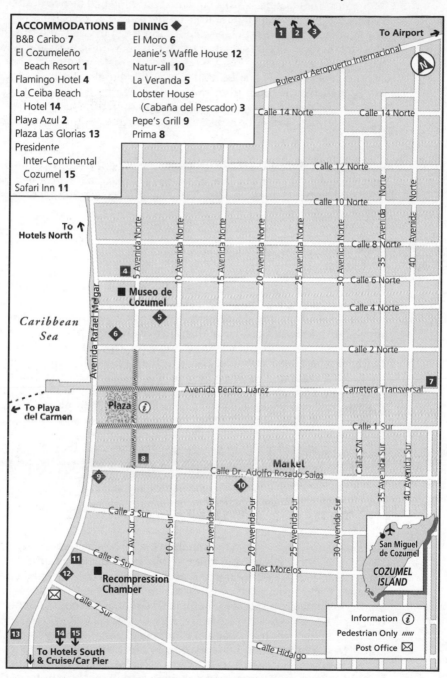

ACCOMMODATIONS ■

B&B Caribo **7**
El Cozumeleño
 Beach Resort **1**
Flamingo Hotel **4**
La Ceiba Beach
 Hotel **14**
Playa Azul **2**
Plaza Las Glorias **13**
Presidente
 Inter-Continental
 Cozumel **15**
Safari Inn **11**

DINING ◆

El Moro **6**
Jeanie's Waffle House **12**
Natur-all **10**
La Veranda **5**
Lobster House
 (Cabaña del Pescador) **3**
Pepe's Grill **9**
Prima **8**

To Airport →

Bulevard Aeropuerto Internacional

Calle 14 Norte Calle 14 Norte

Calle 12 Norte

Calle 10 Norte

To ↑
Hotels North

5 Avenida Norte
10 Avenida Norte
15 Avenida Norte
20 Avenida Norte
25 Avenida Norte
30 Avenida Norte
35 Avenida Norte
40 Avenida Norte

Calle 8 Norte

Calle 6 Norte

■ **Museo de
Cozumel**

Calle 4 Norte

*Caribbean
Sea*

Avenida Rafael Melgar

Calle 2 Norte

Avenida Benito Juárez

Carretera Transversal

← To Playa
del Carmen

Plaza *(i)*

Calle 1 Sur

Calle S/N
35 Avenida Sur
40 Avenida Sur

Market

Calle Dr. Adolfo Rosado Salas

5 Av. Sur
10 Av. Sur
15 Avenida Sur
20 Avenida Sur
25 Avenida Sur
30 Avenida Sur

Calle 3 Sur

Calle 5 Sur

✉ Calle 7 Sur

■ **Recompression
Chamber**

Calles Morelos

San Miguel
de Cozumel

*COZUMEL
ISLAND*

To Hotels South
↓ **& Cruise/Car Pier**

Calle Hidalgo

Information *(i)*
Pedestrian Only ⁄⁄⁄⁄
Post Office ✉

with direct access to the beach and the oceanfronts are on the second floor.) Most rooms come with a choice of one king bed or two double beds and are furnished in an understated, modern style. A long stretch of sandy beach area dotted with palapas and palm trees fronts the entire hotel. This destination features a large pool, plus a wading pool and a water-sports-equipment rental booth. There are two restaurants and a bar, plus 24-hour room service. A special in-room dining option with a serenading trio is available for beachfront rooms. Two lighted tennis courts, a fully equipped gym, and a moped-rental service for getting around the island are also on-site. A children's activities center makes this a good choice for families.

Costera Sur Km 6. ☎ *800-327-0200 in the U.S., or 987-872-0322. Fax: 987-872-1360. Internet:* www.interconti.com. *253 units. Free parking. Rack rates: High season $350–$440 double; low season $280–$350 double. Discounts and packages available. AE, DC, MC, V.*

Safari Inn

$ In town

This budget hotel offers a convenient location for divers: directly above the Aqua Safari Dive Shop and across the street from the shop's pier, which means that you don't have to lug your gear very far. The large rooms have little in the way of furniture aside from beds, but the small bathrooms have good, hot showers. Some rooms could be improved with better lighting, and in some, the air-conditioning is noisy. This hotel becomes a real bargain when four or five people are willing to share a room — some rooms hold a king and two or three twin beds. To find it from the main ferry pier, turn right (south) and walk 3½ blocks on Melgar; the hotel is at the corner of Calle 5 Sur.

Av. Raphael Melgar at Calle 5 Sur. ☎ *987-872-0101. Fax: 987-872-0661. E-mail:* dive@aquasafari.com. *12 units. Rack rates: $39 double. MC, V.*

Settling into Cozumel

Although you can arrive in Cozumel by plane, it's even more common to arrive by ferry after flying into Cancún and making the brief drive down the coast to either Puerto Morelos or Playa del Carmen. It's cheaper, easier, and more convenient. The airport in Cozumel only services smaller aircraft, so you have to connect through Cancún.

If you do arrive by plane, Cozumel's **airport** is immediately inland from downtown. **Transportes Terrestres** provides transportation to all the hotels in air-conditioned sports utility vehicles. Buy your ticket as you exit the terminal. The fare is $4 per person to downtown hotels; it's $7 for hotels along the north shore and $8 and up for hotels along the south shore.

In recent years, the number of international commercial flights in and out of the island has actually decreased while the number of charter flights has increased. You may want to inquire about buying a ticket from one of the travel packagers, such as Funjet or Apple (see Chapter 5 for more information). Some packagers work with a lot of Cozumel's hotels — even some of the small ones in town; others allow you to buy a ticket without making it part of a package. At present, **AeroMexico** flies to and from Atlanta, and Continental flies to and from Houston and Newark. **Aerocozumel,** a Mexicana affiliate, has numerous flights to and from Cancún. **Mexicana** flies from Mexico City (other international flights connect through Mexico City).

If you first receive your **Mexican tourist permit (FMT)** upon arrival into Cozumel, understand that this is an important document, so take good care of it. You're supposed to keep this with you at all times — you may be required to show it if you run into any sort of trouble. You also need to turn it back in upon departure, or you may be unable to leave without a replacement.

Passenger ferries travel to and from Playa del Carmen, and a car/passenger ferry makes the trip to and from Puerto Morelos.

Passenger ferries, run by **Water Jet Service (☎ 987-872-1508,** 987-872-1588) arrive in Cozumel at the Muelle Fiscal dock one block from the town's main square. They make the trip between Cozumel and Playa del Carmen in 45 minutes. The trip costs $7 one-way. The boats are enclosed and air-conditioned and have cushioned seats, bar service, and video entertainment. There are plans to begin running faster ferry boats, which would shorten the trip to about 25 minutes. Departures are almost hourly from 5 a.m. to midnight. In Playa del Carmen, the ferry dock is 1½ blocks from the main square and the bus station. Schedules are subject to change, so you may want to check the departure time at the docks — especially the time of the last returning ferry if that's the one you intend to use. Storage lockers are available at the Cozumel dock for $2 per day.

The car/passenger ferry to Cozumel from Puerto Morelos (20 miles north of Playa del Carmen) takes longer and runs less frequently. If you're considering using a rental car, be aware that you can get a rental on the island. If you must take your car over, the terminal in **Puerto Morelos (☎ 987-871-0008**) is easy to find. The car-ferry schedule is subject to change, so double-check it before arriving in Puerto Morelos. The ferry leaves daily at 5:30 a.m., 10:30 a.m., and 4:00 p.m. The crossing takes approximately two and a half hours. The ferry arrives at **Muelle Internacional** (the **International Pier**, which is just south of town near La Ceiba Hotel). Cargo takes precedence over private cars. Officials suggest that camper drivers stay overnight in the parking lot to be first in line for tickets.

In any case, *plan to arrive at least three hours in advance of the ferry's departure to purchase a ticket and to get in line.* The return trips to Puerto Morelos depart at 8:00 a.m., 1:30 p.m., and 7:00 p.m. daily. Plan on getting in line three hours before departure and double-check the schedule by calling ☎ **987-872-0950.** The fare is $45 per car and driver (more for campers) and $5 per extra passenger. People wanting to go as passengers may find the Playa del Carmen ferry more convenient.

Knowing your way around town

San Miguel is logically planned and very easy to find your way around — somewhat of a rarity in Mexico. The town's main waterfront street is called **Avenida Rafael Melgar** and runs along the western shore of the island. The town is laid out on a grid, with *avenidas* (avenues) running north and south, and *calles* (streets) running east and west. The exception is **Avenida Juárez,** which runs from the passenger-ferry dock through the main square and inland. Juárez divides the town into northern and southern halves.

Heading inland from the dock along Juárez, the avenidas you cross are numbered by fives: Avenida 5, Avenida 10, Avenida 15, and so on. North of Avenida Juárez, *calles* have even numbers: 2 Norte, 4 Norte, 6 Norte, and so on. South of Juárez, *calles* have odd numbers: 1 Sur (also called Adolfo Rosado Salas), 3 Sur, 5 Sur, and so on.

The extension of Avenida Juárez becomes the **Carretera Transversal,** which runs east of the airport and west of the ruins of **San Gervasio** to the deserted eastern coast of the island. North of this highway, there are mostly dirt roads and a scattering of small, badly ruined Mayan sites. A paved road leads to San Gervasio, the principal ruins on the island. After reaching the coast, the highway turns south and follows the coast all the way down to where it meets the road that descends from town along the western shore.

South of the city is **Chankanaab National Park,** centered on the beautiful lagoon of the same name. Beyond Chankanaab are **Playa Palancar** and, offshore, the **Palancar Reef. Punta Celarain** and the lighthouse are at the southern tip of the island.

Getting around town

You can walk to most destinations in town. However, getting to outlying hotels and beaches, including the Chankanaab Lagoon, requires a taxi or rental car.

Car rentals are around $60 per day for an economy-sized car, depending on demand. Avis (☎ **987-872-0099**) and Executive (☎ **987-872-1308**) have counters in the airport. Your hotel tour desk or any local travel agency can arrange rentals, and you can drop the cars off at your hotel.

Moped rentals are a popular alternative on Cozumel. You can find rental mopeds all over the village for a cost of anywhere from $15 to $30 for 24 hours depending upon the season. If you rent a moped, be careful. Riding a moped made a lot more sense when Cozumel had less traffic; now it's a risky activity — motorists have become pushier.

Moped accidents easily rank as the most common cause of injury in Cozumel. Before renting a moped, give it a careful inspection to see that all the gizmos — horn, light, starter, seat, and mirror — are in good shape and be sure to note all damage to the moped on the rental agreement. If the moped vibrates at cruising speed, it's probably due to an unbalanced wheel, and you should return it. Most importantly, read the fine print on the back of the rental agreement, which states that you are not insured, that you are responsible for paying for any damage to the bike (or for the entire bike if it's stolen or demolished), and that you must stay on paved roads. It's illegal to ride a moped without a helmet (subject to a $25 fine).

Taxis remain a good and reasonably priced option unless you plan on doing some major exploring. Here are a few sample fares: island tour, $60; town to southern hotels, $5 to $15; town to northern hotels, $3 to $5; town to Chankanaab, $7. Call ☎ 987-872-0236 for taxi pickup. Fares on the island are fixed with little variation and generally are not open to negotiation. Taxis charge extra for more than two passengers.

Fast Facts: Cozumel

American Express

The local representative is Fiesta Cozumel (Calle 11 No. 598; ☎ 987-872-0725).

Area Code

The telephone area code is **987**. **Note:** This changed from 9 in November 2001.

Banks, ATMs, and Currency Exchange

There are several banks and *casas de cambio* on the island, as well as ATM machines. Most places accept dollars, but you usually get a better deal paying in pesos.

Business Hours

Most offices maintain traditional Mexican hours of operation (9 a.m. to 2 p.m. and 4 to 8 p.m. daily), but shops remain open throughout the day. Offices tend to close on Saturday and Sunday, but shops are open on Saturday, at least, and increasingly offer limited hours of operation on Sunday.

Climate

From October to December strong winds and some rain can prevail all over the Yucatán. In Cozumel, wind conditions in November and December can make diving dangerous. May to September is the rainy season. Temperature during the day in the summer is 80°F to 90°F; in winter 70°F to 75°F.

Diving

If you intend to dive, remember to bring proof of your diver's certification. Underwater currents can be very strong here, and many of the reef drops are quite steep, making them excellent sites for experienced divers but too challenging for novice divers.

Hospital/Recompression Chamber

There are four recompression chambers (*cámaras de recompresión*). Buceo Médico, staffed 24 hours, is on Calle 5 Sur, 1 block off

Avenida Raphael Melgar between Melgar and Avenida 5 Sur (☎ 987-872-2387, 987-872-1430). Another one is the **Hyperbaric Center of Cozumel** (Calle 4 Norte, between avenidas 5 and 10; ☎ 987-872-3070).

Information

The State Tourism Office (☎ and fax: 987-872-7563) is located on the second floor of the Plaza del Sol commercial building, facing the central plaza, and is open Monday to Friday 9 a.m. to 3 p.m. and 6 to 8 p.m.

Internet Access

There are a number of cybercafes on and around the main square. One of the most reliable is **Modutel** (Av. Juárez No. 15, at the intersection with Av. 10). Hours are 10 a.m. to 8 p.m. If you can't find an unoccupied machine at this place or any in the vicinity, you can always go to **Coffee Net,** which is on the north side of the main square. It's larger and keeps longer hours than most, but it's also more expensive.

Police

Dial ☎ 060. Remember that it is very unlikely that you will find an English-speaking operator at the police station.

Post Office

The post office *(correo)* (Av. Rafael Melgar at Calle 7 Sur, at the southern edge of town;

☎ 987-872-0106) is open Monday to Friday 9 a.m. to 6 p.m. and Saturday 9 a.m. to noon.

Taxes

A 15% IVA (value-added tax) on goods and services is charged, and it's generally included in the posted price.

Taxis

Fares on the island are fixed with little variation and generally are not open to negotiation. Taxis charge extra for more than two passengers. Call ☎ 987-872-0236 for taxi pickup.

Telephone

Avoid the phone booths that have signs in English advising you to call home using a special 800 number — these are absolute rip-offs and can cost as much as $20 US per minute. The least expensive way to call is by using a Telmex (LADATEL) pre-paid phone card, available at most pharmacies and mini-supers, using the official Telmex (Lada) public phones. Remember, in Mexico you need to dial 001 prior to a number to reach the United States, and you need to preface long distance calls within Mexico by dialing 01.

Time Zone

Cozumel operates on central standard time, but Mexico's observance of daylight savings time varies somewhat from that in the United States.

Dining in Cozumel

Like many of Mexico's beach resorts, even Cozumel's finest restaurants can be comfortably casual when it comes to dress. Men seldom wear jackets, although ladies are occasionally seen in dressier resort wear. Basically, if you err on the side of casual, you won't go wrong.

For a few good sources of cheap eats beyond the places I list below, consider the following: **Zermatt** (☎ **987-872-1384**), a terrific little bakery, is located on Avenida 5 at Calle 4 Norte. The **Panificadora Cozumel** (Calle 2 Norte, half a block from the waterfront; ☎ **987-872-0058**) is excellent for a do-it-yourself breakfast or picnic supplies. It's open 6 a.m. to 9 p.m. daily.

I arrange the following restaurants alphabetically and note their location and general price category. Please refer to the Introduction of *Mexico's Beach Resorts For Dummies* for an explanation of the price categories. Remember that tips generally run about 15%, and most waitstaff really depend on these gratuities for their income, so be generous if the service warrants.

Please see the "Menu Glossary" in Appendix E for more information on Mexican cuisine.

El Moro
$$ In town   REGIONAL

Crowds flock to El Moro for its good food, service, and prices, but they don't come for the decor, which is orange, orange, orange, Formica, and orange. The restaurant is also located away from everything — a taxi, costing around $1.50 one-way, is a must, costing around $1.50 one way. But all misgivings disappear as soon as you taste something — anything (especially one of the giant, knock-your-socks-off margaritas). The *pollo Ticuleño*, a specialty from the town of Ticul, is a rib-sticking, delicious, layered plate of smooth tomato sauce, mashed potatoes, crispy baked corn tortilla, and batter-fried chicken breast, all topped with shredded cheese and green peas. Besides the regional food, other specialties of Mexico offered by El Moro include enchiladas and seafood prepared many ways, plus grilled steaks, sandwiches, and, of course, nachos. El Moro is 12½ blocks inland from Melgar between calles 2 and 4 Norte.

75 BIS Norte No. 124. ☎ *987-872-3029. Reservations not accepted. Main courses: $5–$12. MC, V. Open: Fri–Wed 1–11 p.m.; closed Thurs.*

Jeanie's Waffle House
$ In town   BREAKFAST/DESSERTS

The specialty here is crisp, light waffles served in a variety of ways, including waffles *ranchero* with eggs and salsa, waffles Benedict with eggs and hollandaise sauce, and waffles with whipped cream and chocolate. Hash browns, homemade breads, and great coffee are other reasons to drop in for breakfast, which is served until 3 p.m.

Av. Raphael Melgar between calles 5 and 7 Sur. ☎ *987-872-4145. Breakfast: $3.25–$6.00. No credit cards. Open: Mon–Sat 6 a.m.–10 p.m.; Sun 6 a.m. to noon.*

La Veranda
$$$$ In town   SEAFOOD/INTERNATIONAL

The perfect place to go if you're getting tired of fried fish or fish with *achiote* sauce (a type of chile paste), or if you just want something different. The highly inventive menu emphasizes tropical ingredients and fuses West Indian and European cooking. Every dish I tried here was delicious and artfully presented. The spiced mussel soup had a delicious broth scented with white wine. The "Veranda mango fish" included a mango sauce that was both light and satisfying. And the "Palancar coconut shrimp" consisted of shrimp boiled in a coconut sauce to which the chef added little bits of raw (not sweet) coconut. The indoor and outdoor dining areas are airy and quite pleasant. You can hear soft jazz and the whirring of ceiling fans in the background. The tables are well separated and attractively set. During high season, the restaurant opens at noon with a lunch menu that includes lighter fare such as baguette sandwiches.

Calle 4 Norte (between av. 5 and 10). ☎ *987-872-4132. Reservations recommended in high season. Main courses: $14–$20. MC, V. Open: Daily noon to midnight (opens at 4:30 p.m. during low season).*

Lobster House (Cabaña del Pescador)
$$$$ North of town   LOBSTER

The thought that most often occurs to me when I eat a prepared lobster dish is that the cook could have simply boiled the lobster to produce a better effect. The owner of this restaurant seems to agree. The only item on the menu is lobster boiled with a hint of spices and served with melted butter accompanied by sides of rice, vegetables, and bread. The price of dinner is determined by the weight of the lobster tail you select with side dishes provided at no charge. Candles and soft lights illuminate the dining rooms. A rustic, tropical-island feel, gardens, fountains, and a small duck pond make the scene inviting and intimate. The owner, Fernando, welcomes you warmly and sends you next door to his brother's excellent Mexican-food restaurant, El Guacamayo, if you must have something other than lobster.

Carretera Santa Pilar Km 4 (across from Playa Azul Hotel). No phone. Main courses: $15–$30, lobsters sold by weight. No credit cards. Open: Daily 6:00–10:30 p.m.

Natur-all
$ In town   FRUIT/SANDWICHES

The sweet smell of fruit greets you as you enter Frutas Selectas, the downstairs grocery store specializing in fresh fruit. Upstairs is this cheery restaurant overlooking the street. A good place to go for light meals, Natur-all offers juices, smoothies, yogurt, veggie sandwiches, a salad bar, baked potatoes with toppings, and pastries.

Calle Rosado Salas No. 352 (between av. 15 and 20 Sur). ☎ *987-872-5560. Breakfast: $1.75–$3.25; salads and sandwiches $1.55–$3.00; fruit and vegetable juices 95¢–$1.55. No credit cards. Open: Wed–Mon 7:00 a.m.–5:00 p.m.; Sun closes at 2:30 p.m.*

Pepe's Grill

$$$ In town   STEAKS/SEAFOOD

The chefs at Pepe's were the first on the island and up and down the mainland coast to popularize grilled food. They seem fascinated with fire; what they don't grill in the kitchen, they flambé at your table. The most popular grilled items are the prime rib, filet mignon (good, quality meat), and lobster. For something out of the ordinary, try the shrimp Bahamas, shrimp flambéed with a little banana and pineapple in a curry sauce with a hint of white wine. Pepe's is a second-story restaurant with one large air-conditioned dining room under a massive beamed ceiling. The lighting is soft, and a guitar trio plays background music. Large windows look out over the town's harbor. The children's menu offers breaded shrimp and broiled chicken. For dessert, Pepe's offers a few more fire-inspired specialties: bananas Foster, crêpes suzette, and café Maya (coffee, vanilla ice cream, and three liquors).

Av. Rafael Melgar at Calle Rosado Salas. ☎ *987-872-0213. Reservations recommended. Main courses: $15–$35; children's menu $6.50. AE, MC, V. Open: Daily 5:00–11:30 p.m.*

Prima

$ In town   NORTHERN ITALIAN

One of the few good Italian restaurants in Mexico. Everything is fresh — the pastas, vegetables, and sourdough pizzas. Owner Albert Domínguez grows most of the vegetables in his local hydroponic garden. The menu changes daily and specializes in northern Italian seafood dishes. It may include shrimp scampi, fettuccine with pesto, or lobster and crab ravioli with cream sauce. The fettuccine Alfredo is wonderful, the salads are crisp, and the steaks are USDA choice. Pizzas are cooked in a wood-burning oven. Desserts include Key lime pie and tiramisu. Dining is upstairs on the breezy terrace.

Calle Rosado Salas No. 109A (corner with Av. 5) ☎ *987-872-4242. Pizzas: $5–$10; pastas $8–$9; steaks $13–$18. AE, MC, V. Open: Daily 4–11 p.m.*

Having Fun On and Off the Beach

One of the advantages of vacationing in Cozumel is that you can indulge in a true island experience and still be just a short hop from mainland Mexico and some of it's remarkable sites. **Playa del Carmen** on the mainland is a convenient 45-minute ferry ride away. Travel agencies on the island can set you up with a tour to see the major ruins on the mainland, such as **Tulum** or **Chichén-Itzá,** or one of the nature parks such as **Xel-Ha** and **Xcaret** (check out Chapter 11).

Cozumel also has its own ruins. (But, honestly, they can't compare with the major cities of the mainland.) During pre-Hispanic times, it's thought that each Mayan woman traveled the 12 miles by boat to the island at least once in her life to worship the goddess of fertility, Ixchel. More than 40 sites containing shrines remain around the island today, and archaeologists still uncover the small dolls that were customarily offered in the fertility ceremony.

For **diving and snorkeling,** it's best to go directly to the shops recommended here. For **island tours, ruins tours** on and off the island, **glass-bottom boat tours, fiesta nights, fishing,** and other activities, go to a travel agency such as **InterMar Cozumel Viajes** (Calle 2 Norte, No. 101-B, between avenidas 5 and 10; ☎ **987-872-1098;** Fax: 987-872-0895; E-mail: intermar@cozumel.com.mx). It's not far from the main plaza.

Combing the beaches

Although most of Cozumel's shoreline is rocky, the island is not without its beach-going highlights. **Playa San Francisco** and, south of it, **Playa Palancar** are ten miles south of the **Chankanaab National Park.** After the beach at Chankanaab Lagoon, these are Cozumel's best beaches. Food (usually overpriced) and equipment rentals are available.

Along both the east and the west coasts are signs advertising this or that beach club. A "beach club" in Cozumel usually means a *palapa* (thatched roof) hut open to the public serving soft drinks, beer, and fried fish. Some of them also rent water gear. The owners of La Ceiba Beach Hotel operate one called **Nachi Cocom** (located on the western side of the island) that's more elaborate than the others. It features a swimming pool, a good restaurant, and watersports-equipment rental. Other beach clubs include **Paradise Cafe** on the southern tip of the island across from Punta Sur Nature Park and **Playa Bonita, Chen Rio,** and **Punta Morena** on the eastern side. Palapa huts are scattered along the coast and do a big business on Sundays when the locals head for the beaches.

Past Playa San Francisco, you eventually come to the southern extreme of the island and the **Punta Sur Nature Park,** which is built around Colombia Lagoon. The park's entrance fee is $7, and you can enjoy the beach, go snorkeling, view some of the flora and fauna of the region, and tour replicas of Mayan structures. This place is quite pleasant when not crowded, but if solitude is what you seek, you may want to try one of the beach clubs (unless it's Sunday).

The road along the **eastern shore** of the island offers views of the sea, the rocky shore, and the pounding surf. Most of the east coast is unsafe for swimming because of the surf. Small beaches occupy the spaces between rocky outgrowths. Halfway up the east coast, the road turns inland and becomes Transversal road (which passes the ruins of San Gervasio) back to town, 9½ miles away.

Exploring the depths

Cozumel is the number-one, *numero uno,* most popular dive destination in the western hemisphere. Don't forget to bring your dive card
and dive log. The dive shops on the island rent scuba gear, but they
won't take you out on the boat until they see some documentation. If
you have a medical condition, bring a letter signed by a doctor stating
that you're cleared to dive. A two-tank, morning dive costs around $60;
some shops are now offering an additional one-tank, afternoon dive for
$9 for folks who took the morning dives. (It's about $25 if you just opt
for the one-tank, afternoon dive.) A lot of divers save some money by
buying a hotel and dive package with or without air transportation and
food. These packages usually include two dives a day with the standard day off at the end.

Diving in San Miguel is different from diving in a lot of places — it's
drift diving, which can be a little disconcerting for novice divers. The
current that sweeps along Cozumel's reefs pulling nutrients into the
reefs and making them as large as they are also dictates how you dive
here. The problem: The current pulls at different speeds at different
depths and in different places. When it's pulling strong, the current can
quickly scatter a dive group. This is why it's important to have a dive
master experienced with the local conditions who can pick the best
place for diving, given the current conditions.

Fortunately, Cozumel has a lot of reefs to choose from. Here are just
a few:

- **Palancar Reef:** Famous for its caves and canyons, plentiful fish,
  and a wide variety of sea coral

- **Santa Rosa Wall:** Monstrous reef famous for its depth, sea life,
  coral, and sponges

- **San Francisco Reef:** Features a shallower drop-off wall than many
  reefs and fascinating sea life

- **Yucab Reef:** Highlights include beautiful coral

Finding a dive shop in town is even easier than finding a jewelry store.
Cozumel is so popular that it has more than 60 dive operators, but two
of them stand out from the crowd. Bill Horn's **Aqua Safari,** on Avenida
Raphael Melgar at Calle 5 Sur (☎ **987-872-0101;** Fax: 987-872-0661) and
in the Hotel Plaza Las Glorias (☎ **987-872-3362,** 987-872-2422), is a
PADI (Professional Association of Diving Instructors) five-star instructor center with full equipment and parts rental and sale. It has its own
pier just across the street. You can visit the Aqua Safari Web site on
the Internet at www.aquasafari.com. **Dive House,** on the main plaza
(☎ **987-872-1953;** Fax: 987-872-0368), offers PADI and NAUI SSI (Scuba
Schools International) instruction. Both shops offer morning, afternoon, and night dives with reliable dive masters.

Underwater Yucatán offers two twists on diving — **cenote diving** and **snorkeling.** On the mainland, the peninsula's underground *cenotes* (say-*noh*-tehs), or sinkholes, which were sacred to the Maya, lead to a vast system of underground caverns. Here, the gently flowing water is so clear that divers appear to be floating on air through the *cenotes* and caves that look just like those on dry land, complete with stalactites and stalagmites.

The experienced cave divers of **Yucatech Expeditions** (☎ and fax: **987-872-5659;** E-mail: yucatech@cozumel.czm.com.mx) offer a trip five times a week. *Cenotes* are 30 to 45 minutes from Playa del Carmen, and a dive in each *cenote* lasts around 45 minutes (divers usually do two or three). Dives are within the daylight zone, about 130 feet into the caverns and no more than 60 feet deep. Company owner Germán Yañez Mendoza inspects diving credentials carefully, and divers must meet his list of requirements before cave diving is permitted. He also offers the equivalent of a resort course in cave diving and a full cave-diving course. For information and prices, call or drop by the office at Avenida 15 No. 144, between Calle 1 Sur and Rosado Salas. There are several other *cenote* dive operators on the mainland who are closer to the *cenotes,* especially in Akumal and near Tulum.

If you're not yet a diver, Cozumel offers a great introduction to the underwater world through **snorkeling.** Anyone who can swim can snorkel. Rental of the snorkel (breathing tube), goggles, and flippers should cost only about $5 for half a day. A three-hour snorkeling trip should cost around $30 and include equipment and soft drinks. One shop that specializes in snorkeling trips is the **Kuzamil Snorkeling Center** (☎ **987-872-4637**) at Calle 1 No. 149 between avenidas 5 and 10. The center also offers an all-day trip that goes to several spots and includes lunch for $55 for adults and $45 for children under 12.

Sailing away

Boat trips are a popular pastime on Cozumel. Some excursions include snorkeling and scuba diving or a stop at a beach with lunch. Various types of tours are offered, including rides in **glass-bottom boats** for around $30. These trips usually go from 9 a.m. to 1 p.m. and include beer and soft drinks. When you sign up for one of these excursions, find out if the boat is likely to be filled with cruise-ship passengers. Boat trips that cater to the cruise-ship crowd can be packed. Tour operators are usually pretty open about this subject, but you may want to double-check. Departures before 10 a.m. are a good bet if you prefer smaller crowds. One rather novel boat trip now being offered is a ride in a submarine from **Atlantis Submarines.** The sub can hold 48 people. It operates almost 2 miles south of town at the Casa del Mar hotel and costs $72 per person. Call ☎ **987-872-5671** or inquire about this underwater voyage at one of the travel agencies in town.

Catching a big one

Any place as renowned for diving as Cozumel has to be good for **fishing** as well, right? The best months for fishing offshore Cozumel are from April to September, when the catch includes blue and white marlin, sailfish, tarpon, swordfish, *dorado,* wahoo, tuna, and red snapper. Fishing excursions costs $450 for six people for the whole day, or $80 to $85 per person for four people for a half day. One travel agency that specializes in fishing (deep-sea and fly fishing) is **Aquarius Travel Fishing** (Calle 3 Sur no. 2, between Avenida Raphael Melgar and Avenida 5; ☎ **987-872-1092;** E-mail: gabdiaz@hotmail.com).

Hitting the links

Cozumel's first golf course — an 18-hole course designed by Jack Nicklaus — recently opened at the Cozumel Country Club. The club is located just north of San Miguel, inland from the hotels along the coast.

Seeing the sights

Companies offer several kinds of tours of the island, but to be frank, the best part of Cozumel isn't on land; it's what's in the water. But, if you're starting to look like a prune from all the time in the water or you want to try something different, travel agencies can book you on a group tour of the island for around $40. Prices may vary a bit depending on whether the tour includes lunch and a stop for snorkeling and swimming at Chankanaab Park. If you're only interested in Chankanaab, you can go by yourself and save money (keep reading, more info is coming up in this section). Taxi drivers charge $60 for four-hour tours of the island, which most people would consider only mildly amusing depending on the personality of the taxi driver.

A four-hour **horseback tour** of the island's interior jungle and some ruins may be up and running, but the last time I was in Cozumel, the tour operator had lost all his animals to some unknown illness. Even in the best of times, this ride can't be called spectacular. Most of the terrain is flat, and the jungle is more scrub-like than the term *jungle* indicates. The same can be said for the "jungle Jeep tours" and the "jungle ATV tours." If you're interested in any of these ho-hum trips, look up the folks at the InterMar Cozumel Viajes travel agency (see the listing at the beginning of the "Having Fun On and Off the Beach" section earlier in this chapter).

Chankanaab National Park is the pride of many of the islanders. *Chankanaab* means "little sea," which refers to a beautiful, land-locked pool connected to the sea through an underground tunnel — a sort of miniature ocean. Snorkeling in this natural aquarium is not permitted, but you can do so at other locations in the park, which also includes a lovely beach for sunbathing. Arrive early to stake out a chair and palapa before the cruise-ship crowd arrives. Likewise, the snorkeling is best before noon. The park has bathrooms, lockers, a gift shop, several snack huts, a restaurant, and snorkeling gear available to rent. You can also swim with dolphins for $120 per person. Call ☎ 987-872-6605 for information and reservations.

Surrounding the lagoon pool is a botanical garden with shady paths. The garden is home to 351 species of tropical and subtropical plants from 22 countries in addition to 451 species of plants from Cozumel. Several Mayan structures have been re-created within the gardens to give visitors an idea of Mayan life in a jungle setting. A small natural history museum is also on the property. Admission to the park costs $10, and it's open daily 8 a.m. to 5 p.m.

When it comes to Cozumel's Mayan remains, getting there is most of the fun — you should do it for the mystique and for the trip, not for the size or scale of the ruins. The buildings, though preserved, were crudely made and wouldn't be much of a tourist attraction if they weren't the island's only cleared and accessible ruins. To get to the ruins of **San Gervasio** (100 B.C. to A.D. 1600), follow the paved transversal road. The well-marked turn-off is about halfway between town and the eastern coast. Stop at the entrance gate and pay the $1 road-use fee. Head straight over the pothole-infested road for about 2 miles until you reach the ruins. Pay the $5 fee to enter; camera permits cost $5 for each still or video camera you want to bring in. A small tourist center at the entrance has cold drinks and snacks for sale.

More significant than beautiful, this site was once an important ceremonial center where the Maya gathered. The important deity here was Ixchel, known as the goddess of weaving, women, childbirth, pilgrims, the moon, and medicine. You won't see any representations of Ixchel at San Gervasio today, but here's a little history: Bruce Hunter, in his *Guide to Ancient Maya Ruins* (University of Oklahoma Press), writes that priests hid behind a large pottery statue of the goddess and became her voice, speaking to pilgrims and answering their petitions. Ixchel was the wife of Itzamná, the sun god and preeminent deity among all Mayan gods.

Tour guides charge $10 for groups of one to six people, but I have a better idea — find a copy of the green booklet *San Gervasio,* sold at local checkout counters and bookstores, and tour the site on your own. Seeing the whole ball of wax takes 30 minutes. Taxi drivers offer a tour to the ruins for about $25; the driver waits for you outside the ruins.

In town, there's a small historical museum, **Museo de la Isla de Cozumel,** on Avenida Raphael Melgar between calles 4 and 6 Norte (☎ 987-872-1475). It's more than just a nice place to spend a rainy hour. The first floor of the museum has an excellent exhibit displaying endangered species in the area, the origin of the island, and its present-day topography and plant and animal life, including an explanation of coral formation. The second-floor galleries feature the history of the town, artifacts from the island's pre-Hispanic sites, and colonial-era relics like cannons, swords, and ship paraphernalia. The museum is open daily from 9 a.m. to 6 p.m. Admission is $3; guided tours in English are free. A rooftop restaurant serves breakfast and lunch.

Shopping

If you like shopping for silver jewelry, you can spend a great deal of time examining the wares of all the jewelers along Melgar who cater to cruise-ship shoppers. Numerous duty-free stores sell items such as perfumes and designer wares. If you're interested in Mexican folk art, a number of stores now display a wide variety of interesting pieces. Check out the following shops, all of which are on Avenida Raphael Melgar (with the exception of Sante Fe):

- **Los Cinco Soles** (☎ 987-872-2040)
- **Indigo** (☎ 987-872-1076)
- **Santa Fe** (no phone), on Rosado Salas no. 58.
- **Talavera** (no phone)

Prices for serapes (cotton ponchos), T-shirts, and other tourist-type goods are less expensive on the side streets off Melgar.

Exploring mainland Mexico from Cozumel

Going to the nearby seaside village of **Playa del Carmen** and the **Xcaret** nature park on your own is as easy as a quick ferry ride from Cozumel. For more details on Playa del Carmen, see Chapter 13. For more information on Xcaret, see Chapter 11. Cozumel travel agencies offer an Xcaret tour that includes the ferry fee, transportation to the park, and the park admission fee for $68. Given what the package includes, this is a reasonable price.

Travel agencies can also arrange day-trips to the fascinating ruins of **Chichén-Itzá** either by air or by bus. The ruins of **Tulum,** overlooking the Caribbean, and Cobá, in a dense jungle setting, are closer to Cozumel, so they cost less to visit. Cobá is a grand city spread out beside a lake within a remote jungle setting. Tulum is smaller, more compact, and right on the beach. Neither has been restored to the same extent as Chichén-Itzá. Trips to Cobá and Tulum begin at 8 a.m. and return around 6 p.m. For more information on these sites, check out Chapter 11.

Enjoying the nightlife

Cozumel is a town frequented by divers and other active visitors who play hard all day and wind down at night. The nightlife scene is generally low-key and peaks in the early evening. The cruise-ship crowd offers an exception to this rule. On Sunday evenings, the place to be is the main square, which usually hosts a free concert and lots of people strolling about and visiting with friends. The nightlife scene is generally low key: people sit in outdoor cafes and enjoy the cool night breezes until the restaurants close. **Carlos 'n Charlie's** (☎ 987-872-0191), **Hard Rock Cafe** (☎ 987-872-5271), and a couple of other clubs are grouped together along Avenida Raphael Melgar on the north side of the main plaza. These spots are among the liveliest and most predictable places in town. **Joe's Lobster Pub** at Avenida 10 and Calle Rosado Salas (no phone) is the most happening place for reggae and salsa music.

Chapter 13

Playa del Carmen and the Riviera Maya

. . . .

In This Chapter

▶ Choosing the right accommodations

▶ Searching for the best grub

▶ Diving into fun

▶ Finding your way around the Riviera Maya

. . . .

The northern half of the **Quintana Roo** Caribbean coast, stretching from Cancún to Tulum, is commonly known as the **Riviera Maya** — for the combination of Mayan remains and a coastline that rivals any "Riviera" in the world in terms of spectacular natural beauty. Quintana Roo is the name of the state that dominates the Yucatán peninsula. A growing number of stylized resort hotels — mostly of the all-inclusive type — and a handful of inexpensive hideaways populate the Riviera Maya. The Riviera Maya is a new marketing term, and is generally considered to cover the area from Cancún south to Tulum, including all the towns along this coast, and offshore Cozumel.

Many travelers become acquainted with Riviera Maya and Playa del Carmen only after an initial stay in Cancún. From Cancún, they often venture out on day trips that take them down the Caribbean coast to Tulum or out to Cozumel to explore the coral reefs.

 If you're more of an explorer than a traveler who prefers the familiar, forego Cancún and start heading down the Riviera Maya for a true Mexico beach experience! This stretch of coastline has hidden coves, white sand beaches and tranquil, tropical waters in abundance.

Deciding Where to Stay

In my opinion, staying in one of the small hotels in **Playa** — as Playa del Carmen is commonly referred to by the locals — is much more fun than staying in one of the growing number of all-inclusive resorts along this coast. Don't hesitate to stay in a place that's not on the beach. Town life here is a big part of the fun, and staying on the beach in Playa has its disadvantages — the noise produced by a couple of the beach-side bars, for one thing. And if you choose accommodations off of the beach, you don't have to worry about not being able to access that perfect strip of sand. Beaches are public property in Mexico, and you can lay out your towel anywhere you like without anyone bothering you. If you really want a quiet room on the beach, consider the Shangri-La Caribe, listed later in this chapter under the "Evaluating the Top Accommodations" section. The Shangri-La is on the outskirts of town far from the bars but within walking distance of downtown ("down-town" is really a small town area — the original town of Playa del Carmen, from where all of the resorts have developed to the north and south). As for the all-inclusive properties along the coast, the **Porto Real** (☎ **987-881-7325;** Internet: www.real.com.mx) has the best loca-tion (for non-golfers). It's on the northern fringe of town.

In Tulum, there are numerous *cabaña* hotels located on the beach that make for great places to stay. Cabaña hotels are generally very rustic in construction, but the amenities can go upscale. Generally, they have no air conditioning, have *palapa* (thatched) roofs, and are mostly open air. There are more than 20 of these, and they run the gamut from provid-ing only the minimal lodging requirements to refined luxury. To get to the hotels on the beach, turn east at the highway intersection, which is well marked and is where the coastal highway intersects with the Tulum road to the beach. One and a half miles ahead, you have to turn either north or south. Most of the cheap *cabañas* are to the north. I want to caution you about staying at one of these hotels; I've heard from several sources that travelers have had their possessions stolen at some of these places. Most of the *cabañas* are located to the south, including some moderately priced places along the road. In the south, the pavement quickly turns to sand, and on both sides of the road, you see thatched-roof structures. You can try your luck at one of the many accommodations located here.

Evaluating the Top Accommodations

As far as prices go, I note rack rates (the maximum that a hotel or resort charges for a room) for two people spending one night in a double room. You can usually do better, especially if you're purchasing a package that includes airfare (go back and read Chapter 6 for tips on avoiding paying rack rates). Prices quoted here include the 17% room tax. Please refer to the Introduction of *Mexico's Beach Resorts For Dummies* for an explanation of the price categories.

Hotels listed here have both air-conditioning and TVs, unless other-wise indicated, and if the review doesn't say anything to the contrary, you can safely assume that you can walk directly out of your hotel and onto the beach.

Playa del Carmen

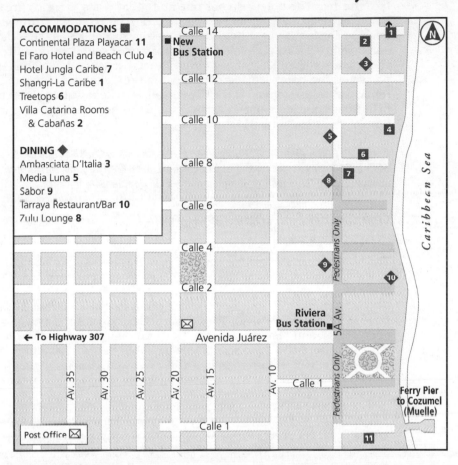

ACCOMMODATIONS ■
Continental Plaza Playacar **11**
El Faro Hotel and Beach Club **4**
Hotel Jungla Caribe **7**
Shangri-La Caribe **1**
Treetops **6**
Villa Catarina Rooms
  & Cabañas **2**

DINING ◆
Ambasciata D'Italia **3**
Media Luna **5**
Sabor **9**
Tarraya Restaurant/Bar **10**
Zulu Lounge **8**

My recommendations in Playa del Carmen and a few options along the rest of the Riviera Maya are all presented in alphabetical order with their exact location designated.

Cabañas Ana y José
$$ Tulum

These cabañas offer a tranquil escape that feels worlds away from the rest of civilization but provide sufficient creature comforts, plus proximity to some of the region's most intriguing attractions. This place started as a restaurant and blossomed into a comfortable inn on a great beach for swimming and sunbathing. All rooms have tile or wood floors, one or two double beds, and patios or balconies. The rock-walled *cabañas* in front (called "oceanfront") are a little larger than the others, but the second-floor "vista del mar" rooms are very attractive and have tall palapa roofs. The standard rooms are much like the others but don't face the sea. The hotel also has one suite that costs extra. There's 24-hour electricity for lights and ceiling fans, but there's no TV. Through the inn, you can rent a car or hook up with a tour to Sian Ka'an (see "Having Fun On and Off the Beach" later in this chapter). Excursions organized by the Friends of Sian Ka'an meet at the hotel's restaurant, which is quite pleasant. The hotel, located 4 miles from the Tulum ruins, can have a rental car waiting for you at the Cancún airport. Reservations are a must in high season, and around Christmas and the New Year, the rates are a little higher than normal high-season prices.

Carretera Punta Allen Km 7, Punta Allen Peninsula. ☎ ***987-887-5470****. Fax: 987-887-5469. Internet:* www.tulumresorts.com*. 15 units. Free parking. Rack rates: High season $100–$125 double; low season $80–$115 double. MC, V.*

Club Akumal Caribe/Hotel Villas Maya Club
$$–$$$ Akumal

The hotel rooms and garden bungalows of this hotel, set along the pristine and tranquil Akumal Bay, are both large and comfortable. The 40 Villas Maya bungalows are simply and comfortably furnished and come with kitchenettes. The 21 rooms in the three-story beachfront hotel are more elaborately furnished. They come with refrigerators, a king or two queen beds, and Mexican accents. Both the bungalows and the rooms have tile floors and good-size bathrooms, but neither have phones or TVs. A large pool on the grounds, a children's activities program (during certain times of the year), two restaurants, and a bar round out the trappings of the Club Akumal Caribe.

Carretera Cancún-Tulum (Hwy. 307) Km 104. ☎ ***800-351-1622*** *in the U.S., 800-343-1440 in Canada, or 915-584-3552 for reservations; 987-875-9012 direct. Internet:* www.hotelakumalcaribe.com*. 70 units. Free parking. Rack rates: High season $120 bungalow, $145 hotel room; low season $95 bungalow, $105 hotel room. Ask for special packages for low season. AE, MC, V. Only cash at the restaurants.*

Continental Plaza Playacar
$$$–$$$$ Playa del Carmen

Located just a block from the *zócalo* (a traditional town plaza in Mexico) is the village's resort hotel that best typifies the term *full-service*. Opened in 1991, the Continental Plaza Playacar set the stage for the mega-hotel growth in this area, but it still remains a top choice of mine due to location — next to the heart of town on a beautiful stretch of beach — and for its facilities. The entrance to this five-story, pale-pink hotel leads you through a wide marble lobby beyond which you see the meandering pool with swim-up bar and the beach. The large, well-furnished rooms all have tile floors, large bathrooms, refrigerators, and balconies with tables and chairs. All but 13 of the rooms have a view of the sea. Suites are even larger and have a wet bar. Bed options include one king or two doubles, and all rooms are very quiet. To find the resort from the ferry pier, turn left when you get off the ferry and follow the road a short distance until you see the Playacar sign. Driving in on the only road into Playa del Carmen from the main coastal highway, turn right at the last street before the main street dead-ends, and the hotel is about 2 blocks ahead. You may want to forego dining at the hotel because the nearby, in-town restaurants are exceptional, but the hotel does have two restaurants on-site, plus a bar. Sporting amenities include the pool, a lighted tennis court, a whirlpool, and extensive watersports equipment. Babysitting services are available, and the light kitchen facilities (coffeemaker, mini-fridge, microwave) make this one of the few family-friendly options in Playa.

Av. Espíritu Santo. ☎ *800-88-CONTI in the U.S., or 987-873-0100. Fax: 987-873-0105. Internet:* www.sidek.com.mx. *180 units. Rack rates: High season $248 double, $310 suite. Ask about off-season rates and special packages. AE, DC, MC, V.*

El Faro Hotel and Beach Club
$$$$ Playa del Carmen

One of the best features of this charming inn is that it rests on an exquisite stretch of prime beachfront in Playa del Carmen. Rooms and suites are spread out on a large property graced by tall palms and manicured gardens fronting 75 meters (about 80 yards) of sandy beachfront. Bordered by cushioned lounges and a palapa bar, a small but stunning pool (heated in winter months) has islands of palms inside of it. The entire property has a cool feel with its white-and-cream stucco exterior. The spacious rooms, most of which are located in two-story buildings, have clay-tile floors, ceiling fans, marble bathrooms, and various bed sizes and combinations. All rooms have a large balcony or terrace. Rates vary according to the dominant view — garden, sea, or beachfront — the size of the room, and the time of year. Also on the property is a functioning lighthouse that serves as the honeymoon suite! A good restaurant is on-site.; Exceptional service and attention to detail throughout the property are also noteworthy.

Calle 10 Norte. ☎ *888-243-7413 from the U.S., or 987-873-0970. Fax: 987-873-0968. Internet:* www.hotelfaro.com. *28 units. Limited free guarded parking. Rack rates: High season $175–$240 double; low season $135–$200 double. Rates include continental breakfast. AE, MC, V.*

Hotel Jungla Caribe
$$ Playa del Carmen

Although not right on the beach, this imaginative property is located right in the heart of all the Avenida 5 action. "La Jungla" has a highly stylized look of neoclassical meets Robinson Crusoe. The character of this hotel fits right in with the quirkiness of the town. Owner Rolf Albrecht envisions space and comfort for guests, so all but eight of the standard rooms are large with gray-and-black marble floors, the occasional Roman column, and large bathrooms. Eight small rooms come without air-conditioning and are priced lower than the rates listed here. Fifteen of the rooms are suites. Catwalks connect the "tower" section of suites to the hotel. There's an attractive pool in the courtyard beneath a giant tree. La Jungla also has its own stylish restaurant and bar, so even if you're not staying here, you can check out the atmosphere.

Av. 5 Norte at Calle 8. ☎ *and fax: **987-873-0650**. Internet:* www.jungla-caribe.com. *25 units. Rack rates: High season $95 double, $110–$135 suite; low season 30% off high-season prices. AE, MC, V.*

La Posada del Capitán Lafitte
$$$ Puerto Morelos

A large sign on the left side of Carretera Cancún-Tulum, fifteen miles from downtown Puerto Morelos, points you in the direction of La Posada del Capitán Lafitte. This lovely seaside retreat on a solitary stretch of sandy beach is located about a mile from the highway down a dirt road. This property allows you to enjoy the feeling of being isolated from the crush of the crowds while still having all the amenities of a relaxing vacation. The numerous bungalows stretch out along a powdery, white beach. The one- and two-story white-stucco bungalows hold one to four rooms. They are smallish but comfortable and feature tile floors; small, tiled bathrooms; two double beds or one king-size bed; and an oceanfront porch. Twenty-nine bungalows have air-conditioning; the rest have fans. There's 24-hour electricity. If you want, coffee can be served as early as 6:30 a.m. in the game room. A dive shop on the premises gets a lot of business from the guests, many of whom are divers. The hotel offers transportation service to and from the Cancún airport for $50 per person (minimum of two passengers). Your room price includes both breakfast and dinner, plus there's a poolside grill and bar. Amenities include a medium-size pool, watersports equipment, and a TV/game room.

Carretera Cancún-Tulum (Hwy. 307) Km 62. ☎ ***800-538-6802** in the U.S. and Canada, or 987-873-0214. Fax: 987-873-0212. Internet:* www.mexicoholiday.com. *62 units. Free guarded parking. Rack rates: High season $210 double; low season $130 double. Rates include breakfast and dinner. MC, V.*

Shangri-La Caribe
$$$–$$$$ Playa del Carmen

This property consists of two-story, thatched bungalows scattered across a wide and beautiful beach. Accommodations come with a patio or terrace (depending upon whether you're on the ground floor or the second floor) complete with the requisite hammock. Most rooms come with two double beds, but a few have a king bed. Windows are screened, and a ceiling fan circulates the breeze. A few of the properties farthest from the sea now have air-conditioning. Prices are higher for the bungalows close to the beach. Though you're close to Playa del Carmen, you get the feeling here of being many comforting miles from civilization. As soon as you enter Playa, look for the road that leads to the hotel — a Volkswagen dealership and a huge sign for the Shangri-La Caribe point the way. One mile of paved road later, you're in paradise. Both breakfast and dinner, served at one of two restaurants or at a grill beside one of the two large pools, is included in your room rate. A whirlpool, watersports equipment, and a full dive shop are also on the premises.

Calle 38 and the beach. ☎ *800-538-6802 in the U.S. or Canada, or 987-873-0611. Fax: 987-873-0500. Internet:* www.shangri-la.com.mx. *107 units. Free guarded parking. Rack rates: High season $200 oceanview double, $240 beachfront double; low season $150 oceanview double, $190 beachfront double. Rates include breakfast and dinner. Book well in advance during high season. AE, MC, V.*

Treetops
$ Playa del Carmen

For the price, the location of Treetops is great: half a block from the beach, half a block from Avenida 5. The rooms at Treetops encircle a patch of preserved jungle that shades the hotel and lends the proper tropical feel. Rooms are large and comfortable and have air-conditioning, fans, refrigerators, and either balconies or patios. Despite their proximity to the town's key action spots, a little bit of distance keeps the rooms quiet. There's also a small pool and bar.

Calle 8 s/n. ☎ *and fax: 987-873-0351. Internet:* www.treetopshotel.com. *17 units. Rack rates: High season $45–$78 double; low season $35–$65 double. Rates include continental breakfast. MC, V.*

Villa Catarina Rooms and Cabañas
$ Playa del Carmen

Hammocks stretch out in front of each of the stylishly rustic rooms and *cabañas* at this property nestled in a grove of palms and fruit trees, just a block from the beach. Each of the clean, well-furnished rooms has one or two double beds on wooden bases with brick or wood floors. Some rooms have a small loft for reading and relaxing; others have palapa roofs or terraces. Furnishings and Mexican folk-art decorations add a great touch that's uncommon for hotels in this price range. Bathrooms are detailed with colorful tiles, and some of the larger rooms have sitting areas. Good cross-ventilation through well-screened windows keeps the rooms relatively cool. Complimentary coffee is available every morning.

Calle Privada Norte between av. 12 and 14. ☎ *987-873-2098. Fax: 987-873-2097. 14 units. High season $55–$75 double; low season $35–$55 double. MC, V.*

Zamas
$$ Tulum

Zamas is a grouping of stylish beach *cabañas* located out on a rocky point on the coast just south of Tulum. Each *cabaña* comes with a small porch area and hammocks, a thatched roof, a large bathroom, and electricity. Mosquito netting hangs over each bed. What the *cabañas* don't have are ceiling fans, which they generally don't need. In this respect, the hotel's location is enviable in that there's almost always a breeze here. Rooms come with a variety of bed combinations and are ranked in three categories: gardenview, oceanview, and beachfront. Note that the rooms also don't have A/C, TV, or phones. The hotel's restaurant is known for having good food.

Carr. Punta Allen, Km. 5. ☎ *800-538-6802 in the U.S. or Canada. E-mail:* zamashotel@slip.net. *16 units. Rack rates: High season $80–$105 double; low season $50–$70 double. MC, V (when paying from the U.S. or Canada only).*

Settling into the Riviera Maya

The name *Riviera Maya* has become the official designation for the entire stretch of coast from just south of Cancún all the way to Tulum and the Sian Ka'an Biosphere Preserve (a large bioreserve where the access is limited to the public). This part of the coast is 130 kilometers (81 miles) long, not including the biosphere. Small towns, a few hideaways, some nature parks, and a growing number of large, all-inclusive resorts dot this stretch of land. A single road, Highway 307, runs along the coast. It's a modern and well-paved road that's easy to drive. From Cancún to Playa del Carmen it's a four-lane divided highway with speed limits up to 110 kph (68 mph). A couple of traffic lights and several reduced-speed zones rear their time-consuming heads around the major turnoffs, but there are no speed bumps.

From Playa to Tulum the road becomes a two-lane highway with wide shoulders and the same speed limits, but more places require you to slow down (still no speed bumps). To drive from the Cancún Airport (on the south side of Cancún) to Tulum takes a little more than an hour and a half.

Knowing where to go

The largest towns on this coast are Puerto Morelos, Playa del Carmen, Puerto Aventuras, Akumal, and Tulum. Hideaways include Punta Bete, Xpu-Ha, Paamul, and Punta Allen. Here's a brief rundown of these areas:

The Riviera Maya

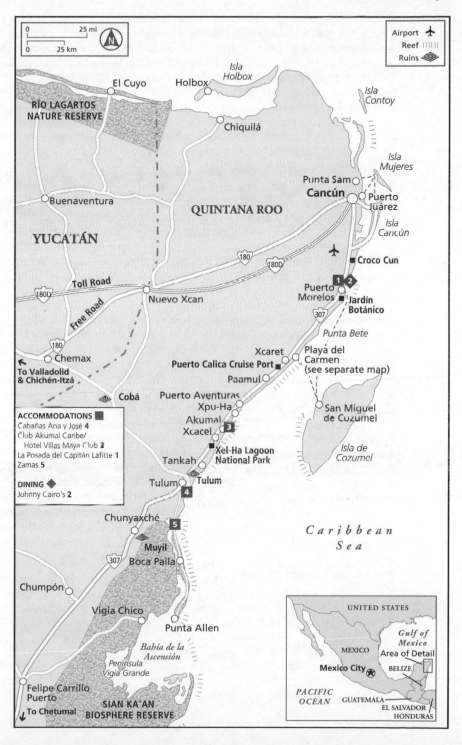

Airport	✈
Reef	‖‖‖‖
Ruins	△

0   25 mi
0   25 km

El Cuyo

RÍO LAGARTOS NATURE RESERVE

Holbox

Isla Holbox

Chiquilá

Isla Contoy

Cancún

Punta Sam

Puerto Juárez

Isla Mujeres

Buenaventura

QUINTANA ROO

Isla Cancún

YUCATÁN

180

180D

Croco Cun

Toll Road

180D

Nuevo Xcan

Free Road

Puerto Morelos

1 **2**

Jardín Botánico

307

Punta Bete

180

Chemax

← To Valladolid & Chichén-Itzá

Xcaret

Puerto Calica Cruise Port

Paamul

Playa del Carmen (see separate map)

Cobá

Puerto Aventuras

Xpu-Ha

San Miguel de Cozumel

ACCOMMODATIONS
Cabañas Ana y José **4**
Club Akumal Caribe/
  Hotel Villas Maya Club **3**
La Posada del Capitán Lafitte **1**
Zamas **5**

DINING
Johnny Cairo's **2**

Akumal

Xcacel

3

Isla de Cozumel

Xel-Ha Lagoon National Park

Tankah

Tulum   **Tulum**

4

Chunyaxché

5

Muyil

307

Boca Paila

Caribbean Sea

Chumpón

Vigia Chico

Punta Allen

Bahía de la Ascensión

Peninsula Vigia Grande

Felipe Carrillo Puerto

↓ To Chetumal

SIAN KA'AN BIOSPHERE RESERVE

UNITED STATES

Gulf of Mexico

Area of Detail

MEXICO

BELIZE

Mexico City ✪

PACIFIC OCEAN

GUATEMALA

EL SALVADOR

HONDURAS

✔ **Puerto Morelos:** Until now, this town located 30 minutes south of Cancún has been a sleepy little village with a few small hotels and rental houses. But developers are throwing up new large hotels as we speak, which should change the whole feel of the town. The coast is sandy and well protected by an offshore reef, which means good snorkeling and diving nearby, but the lack of surf means lots of sea grass and shallow water. If you're looking for good swimming, you should head farther down the coast. If you're looking for a quiet seaside retreat, this location may work for you. Puerto Morelos is perfect for a relaxed vacation of lying about the beach and reading a book (with perhaps the occasional foray into a watersport or two). It's also the place to catch the car ferry to Cozumel.

✔ **Playa del Carmen:** This is the most happening place on the coast with one of the coast's best stretches of beach. Most of the restaurants and nightlife are on or near the Avenida Quinta, Playa's very popular promenade. The town itself has a casual, comfortable simplicity about it. The local architecture has deliberately adopted elements of native building — rustic clapboard walls, thatched roofs, lots of tropical foliage, irregular shapes and angles, and a ramshackle, unplanned look. All of this reflects the toned-down approach to tourism adopted by the locals. Playa attracts a lot of people in their twenties and thirties and travelers looking for a comfortable beach vacation without all-inclusive resorts, timeshares, and other features of modern tourism. Here you find that rare combination of simplicity (in the form of a small town that can easily be crossed on foot) and variety (in terms of the many imaginative and one-of-a-kind restaurants and stores). These aspects of this cosmopolitan village and counter-culture getaway make Playa different from the rest of the coast. A strong European influence has made topless sunbathing (nominally against the law in Mexico) a nonchalantly accepted practice anywhere there's a beach. But Playa is changing. In the last several years, a few large, mainstream resorts have moved in, and a golf course has been constructed. Another reason for considering Playa as a destination: Its location is central to much of the Caribbean coast. From here, it's easy to shoot out to Cozumel on the ferry, take land transportation south to the nature parks and the ruins at Tulum and Cobá, or head north to Cancún.

✔ **Puerto Aventuras:** Sixty-five miles south of Cancún is the large, glitzy development of Puerto Aventuras on Chakalal Bay. This is a marina community with a nine-hole golf course and three expensive hotels, one of these being the **Omni Puerto Aventuras** (☎ 800-THE-OMNI in the U.S., or 987-873-5101) with 30 rooms. Although Puerto Aventuras is almost as large as a city, the population of permanent residents is surprisingly low, and you get the feeling that most of these folks are real estate agents trying to sell you a condo. You may stop here just to see what the place looks like, to swim with dolphins, to eat at a good restaurant, or to see the museum. But I don't think the resort is as interesting a destination as other places along this coast. The museum here is the **Museo CEDAM** (no phone). In Spanish, CEDAM stands for Center for the Study of Aquatic Sports in Mexico. The museum houses exhibits on the history of diving on this coast from pre-Hispanic times to the present. Besides dive-related memorabilia, figures, copper bells, pre-Hispanic pottery found in the *cenotes* of Chichén-Itzá, shell fossils, and the contents of sunken ships are also on display. It's open daily 10 a.m. to 1 p.m. and 2 to 6 p.m. Donations are requested. To make reservations to swim with the dolphins, call **Dolphin Discovery** (☎ **998-883-0779**). A one-hour session costs $125. If you're hungry, Puerto Aventuras has a good restaurant called **Papaya Republic** (☎ **987-873-5029**).

✔ **Akumal:** This small, modern, and ecologically-oriented community is built on the shores of two beautiful bays — Akumal and Half-Moon Bay. This community has been around long enough that it feels more relaxed than other places on the coast that are booming, such as Playa and Tulum, and is the best place along the coast for a family vacation. From the highway, turn off at the sign that reads PLAYA AKUMAL. Don't be confused by other signs reading VILLAS AKUMAL, AKUMAL AVENTURAS, or AKUMAL BEACH RESORT. Less than a half-mile down the road is a white arch. Just before it are a couple of convenience stores and a laundry service. The Club Akumal Caribe/Hotel Villas Maya is to the right just after the arch. If you follow the road to the left and keep to the left, you arrive at the shallow and rocky Half-Moon Bay, lined with two- and three-story condos, and eventually reach Yalku Lagoon. Vacationers can rent most of these condos for a week at a time. A couple of outfits rent condos and villas: Akumal Vacations (☎ **800-448-7137**; Internet: www.akumalvacations.com) and Caribbean Fantasy (☎ **800-523-6618**; Internet: www.caribbfan.com). You don't have to be a guest to enjoy the beach, swim or snorkel, or eat at one of the restaurants. It's a comfortable place to spend the day while on a trip down the coast, but you may consider staying here longer if you're a diver and want to try **technical diving** or **cavern diving.** Two dive shops with PADI-certified instructors are on Akumal Bay. The older shop is the **Akumal Dive Shop** (☎ **987-875-9032;** Internet: www.akumal.com), one of the oldest and best dive shops on the coast. Almost 30 dive sites (from 30 to 80 feet deep) are off-shore. Both Akumal Dive Shop and **Akumal Dive Adventures** (☎ **987-875-9157**), the dive shop at the Vista del Mar hotel on Half-Moon Bay, offer resort courses as well as complete certification.

✔ **Tulum:** The town of Tulum (81 miles from Cancún and close by the ruins of the same name) has a hotel district of about 30 palapa hotels, which stretch down the coast of the Punta Allen peninsula. The town itself, which is growing in popularity, has a half-dozen restaurants and three cybercafes, but no banks or cash machines. A few years ago, Tulum was mainly a destination for backpacker types, but with some of the most beautiful beaches on this coast and many improvements in hotel amenities, it's attracting a greater variety of visitors. Construction is booming, both in the town and along the coast. You can enjoy the beach here in relative solitude and quiet (unless your hotel is busy building additional rooms). Of course, the flip side of peace and quiet is that Tulum doesn't have the variety of restaurants that Playa or Cancún can boast. Tulum and the Punta Allen Peninsula border the northern edge of the Sian Ka'an Biosphere Preserve. The walled Mayan city of Tulum is a large, post-classical site overlooking the Caribbean in dramatic fashion. Tour companies and public buses make the trip regularly from Cancún and Playa del Carmen (get there early to avoid the crowds). Tulum also has wonderful, sandy beaches and no large, resort hotels. It's a perfect spot for those who like to splash around in the water and lie on the beach away from the resort scene.

Getting around the area

By far the easiest way to get to Playa from the Cancún airport is to rent a car, unless your hotel is picking you up. The other possible ways are by taxi ($60) or by bus, which means taking a taxi into Cancún to the bus station. If you're traveling by car, the turn-off to Playa del Carmen from Highway 307 is plainly marked, and you arrive on the town's widest street, Avenida Principal, also known as Avenida Benito Juárez (not that there's a street sign to that effect).

Buses also travel from Cancún to Playa del Carmen and Tulum. Some — but not all — stop in Puerto Morelos. If your destination is the **Puerto Morelos-Cozumel car ferry,** the dock (☎ 987-871-0008) is very easy to find — just keep going south from the main square. You can check out Chapter 12 for details on the car-ferry schedule, but several points bear repeating here: The schedule may change, so double-check it before arriving, and always arrive at least three hours before the ferry's departure to purchase a ticket and get in line. If you're not traveling by car, the best way to get to Cozumel is to take the pedestrian ferry from Playa del Carmen.

If you're traveling by taxi, fares from the Cancún airport are high — about $60 one-way — but taxis are the fastest, most immediate form of travel. *Colectivos* from the Cancún airport can reduce this fee to about $30, but you need to wait for enough people to accumulate to travel together. A service offers shared taxi rides returning to the airport for $14 per person. Check with your hotel or the Caribe Maya restaurant on Avenida 5 at Calle 8 for information and reservations.

The **passenger-ferry dock in Playa del Carmen** is 1½ blocks from the main square and within walking distance of hotels. **Buses** arrive along Avenida Principal, a short distance from hotels, restaurants, and the ferry pier. **Tricycle taxis** are the only vehicles allowed to transport passengers between the bus station and Avenida 5 and the ferry. A number of these efficient taxis meet each bus and ferry and can transport you and your luggage to almost any hotel in town. The new Puerto Calica cruise pier is almost 8 miles south of Playa del Carmen; Playa taxis meet each ship.

Villagers know and use street names, but few street signs exist. The main street, **Avenida Principal,** also known as Avenida Benito Juárez, leads to the *zócalo* (a traditional town plaza in Mexico) from Highway 307. As it does so, it crosses several numbered avenues that run parallel to the beach, all of which are multiples of five. The popular Avenida 5 (also called 5th Avenue), 1 block before the beach, is closed to traffic from the *zócalo* to Calle 6 (and 2 blocks beyond this in the evening). Many restaurants and shops are on this avenue. Almost all the town is north and west of the *zócalo*. Immediately south is the ferry pier and the Continental Plaza Playacar Hotel. This is the southern edge of town; the airstrip and the golf-course development, Playacar, and several resort hotels lie beyond it.

Fast Facts: Playa del Carmen

Area Code

The telephone area code for Playa del Carmen and Tulum is **984. Note:** This changed from 9 in November 2001.

Banks, ATMs, and Currency Exchange

There are several banks in Playa with automated teller machines, along with several money-exchange houses. Many of these offices are located close to the pier and along Avenida 5 at Calle 8. Be aware that there are few ATMs along the Riviera Maya. Your best bet is to handle any banking or money exchange in Playa — the only other ATM along the coast, in Tulum, may be out of service.

Business Hours

Most offices maintain traditional Mexican hours of operation (10 a.m. to 2 p.m. and from 4 p.m. to 8 p.m. daily), but shops remain open throughout the day. Offices tend to close on Saturday and Sunday. Shops are usually open on Saturday but still generally respect the tradition of closing on Sunday.

During peak season, many shops remain open until 9 or even 10 p.m.

Internet Access

In Playa, the speediest connections are at the **Atomic Internet Café** on Calle 8 between avenidas 5 and 10, open daily 9 a.m. to 11 p.m. Playa also has a few other cybercafes. **Cyberia,** at the corner of Calle 4 and Avenida 15, wins the award for best name.

Medical

Dr. E. Medina Peniche speaks English and can be reached around the clock at ☎ 987-873-0134.

Pharmacy

The **Farmacia del Carmen** (☎ 987-873-2330), on Avenida Juárez between avenidas 5 and 10, is open 24 hours.

Post Office

The post office is on Avenida Principal, 3 blocks north of the plaza on the right after the Hotel Playa del Carmen and the launderette.

Taxes

There's a 15% IVA (value-added tax) on goods and services, and it's generally included in the posted price.

Telephone

Avoid the phone booths that have signs in English advising you to call home using a special 800 number — these are absolute rip-offs and can cost as much as $20 US per minute. The least expensive way to call is by using a Telmex (LADATEL) pre-paid phone card, available at most pharmacies and mini-supers, using the official Telmex (Lada) public phones. Remember, in Mexico, you need to dial 001 prior to a number to reach the United States, and you need to preface long-distance calls within Mexico by dialing 01.

Time Zone

The Riviera Maya operates on central standard time, although Mexico's observance of daylight savings time varies somewhat from that in the United States.

Dining Along the Riviera Maya

The following listings include my favorite restaurants in Playa del Carmen as well as one in Puerto Morelos. They're arranged alphabetically, and I note their location and general price category. In Playa, restaurants seem to be constantly opening and closing, but overall, the array of options is impressive, especially for a town as small as Playa. In general, the restaurants are small, fun, and funky — keeping with the spirit of the place. Most restaurants don't take reservations, but don't sweat it. Because of the number of options, getting a table is usually not a problem. Many restaurants also don't accept credit cards, but prices in Playa are much lower than prices in many other beach resorts.

A few restaurants in the town of Tulum have reasonable prices and good food. **Charlie's** (☎ 987-871-2136), my favorite for Mexican food, and **Don Cafeto's** (☎ 987-871-2207) are two safe bets. Both places are on the main street. There's a good, authentic-Italian restaurant called **Il Giardino di Toni e Simone** (☎ 044-987-804-1316, a cellphone; closed Wed) one block off the highway. Look for a large building-supply store called ROCA — the restaurant is on the opposite side of the road one block away. A couple of roadside places that grill chicken and serve it with rice and beans are also in town.

Please refer to the Introduction of *Mexico's Beach Resorts For Dummies* for an explanation of the price categories that I use in the following listings. Remember that tips generally run about 15% and most wait-staff really depend on gratuities for their income, so be generous if the service warrants.

Please see Appendix E for more information on Mexican cuisine.

Ambasciata D'Italia

$$ **Playa del Carmen** NORTHERN ITALIAN

The predominately Italian crowd that fills the tables here is a good sign that the food is authentic and delicious. Entrees cover a range of home-made-pasta and northern-Italian specialties with seafood prominently featured. An admirable selection of wines and exceptional espresso are additional highlights. The ambience is lively and sophisticated.

Av. 5 at Calle 12. ☎ *987-873-0553. Reservations not accepted. Main courses: $8–15. AE, MC, V. Open: Daily 7 p.m. to midnight.*

Johnny Cairo's

$$ **Puerto Morelos** CONTEMPORARY

Operated by a former chef for the Ritz-Carlton in Cancún, this restaurant is meant to be different. The simple menu is divided into two sections: "south of the border" and "north of the border." In both cases, well-known favorites are tweaked a little in one direction or another — thus the label "contemporary." For instance, the fish tacos come topped with finely chopped cabbage and an avocado dressing (which is very good), and the marinade for the *pollo adobado* is done with *guajillo* chiles (a chicken marinaded with a sauce based on the smoky guajillo chiles). You can dine inside, outside on the terrace, or on the beach. The restaurant is especially popular on Sunday afternoons, when it serves up barbecue with all the traditional meats and sides. And every month Johnny Cairo's hosts a full-moon party — the staff moves the entire restaurant down to the beach, builds a bonfire, and cooks up an entirely different menu.

Hacienda Morelos hotel, Av. Rafael E. Melgar. ☎ *998-871-0449. Reservations accepted. Main courses: $5–12. No credit cards. Open: Daily 1–10 p.m.*

Media Luna

$–$$ **Playa del Carmen** VEGETARIAN/SEAFOOD

The owner-chef here has come up with an outstanding and eclectic menu that favors grilled seafood, sautés, and pasta dishes with inventive com-binations of ingredients. Everything I had was quite fresh and prepared beautifully, taking inspiration from various culinary traditions — Italian, Mexican, and Japanese. Keep an eye on the daily specials. The restau-rant also makes sandwiches and salads, black-bean quesadillas, and crêpes. The restaurant is open-air, and the decor is primitive-tropical chic.

Av. 5, between calles 8 and 10. No phone. Main courses: $7–$12; sandwich with a salad $4–$6; breakfast $3–$7. No credit cards. Open: Daily 7:30 a.m.–11:30 p.m.

Sabor
$ Playa del Carmen   BAKERY/HEALTH FOOD

This modest, cheap restaurant is good place to relax and enjoy a bever-age or a snack. The list of available hot and cold drinks includes espresso and cappuccino, hot chocolate, tea, fruit smoothies, and milkshakes. The restaurant also offers some light, vegetarian dishes.

Av. 5 between calles 2 and 4. No phone. Sandwiches: $2.50–$3.50; vegetarian plates $3.00–$5.00; yogurt and granola $1.50–$2.75; pastries $1.00–$1.50. No credit cards. Open: Daily 7 a.m.–11 p.m.

Tarraya Restaurant/Bar
$ Playa del Carmen   SEAFOOD/BREAKFAST

"The restaurant that was born with the town," proclaims the sign outside of this establishment. This is also the restaurant locals recommend as the best for seafood. It's right on the beach, and the water practically laps at the foundations. Because the owners are fishermen, the fish is so fresh that it's practically still wiggling. The wood hut doesn't look like much, but you can have your fish prepared in several ways here. If you haven't tried the Yucatecan specialty *tik-n-xic* fish (named for locally caught fish — like grouper or mahi-mahi — prepared in a spicy barb-cue style sauce), this would be a good place to do so. Tarraya is on the beach opposite the basketball court. It's also now open for breakfast with a set menu that includes hot cakes, French toast, and eggs.

Calle 2 Norte at the beach. ☎ 987-873-2040. Main courses: $4–$7; whole fish $8 per kilo; breakfast is $2.50–$5. No credit cards. Open: Daily 7 a.m.–9 p.m.

Zulu Lounge
$–$$ Playa del Carmen   THAI/VEGETARIAN

This quirky restaurant is a casual and relaxing place to dine on southeast-Asian food. The preparation isn't all that authentic, but it's good. The dec-oration is equal parts tropical palapa, voodoo, and 1950s lounge — amazingly enough, it works! Broken tile-topped tables add a Mexican touch. Asian jazz and techno music underscore the hip ambience. The music gets a little louder in the back room where there are a couple of pool tables and a few rooms with very basic accommodations — bed and common bath — for rent. Most dishes are prepared with your choice of seafood, chicken, beef, or vegetables. Popular dishes include spring rolls, fried rice, and cur-ries. Full bar service and good espresso drinks are available.

Av. 5 between calles 6 and 8. ☎ 987-873-0056. Main courses: $4–$9. MC, V. Open: Daily 5:30–11:30 p.m.

Having Fun On and Off the Beach

Although this is the coastline in Mexico that's undergoing the most rapid development, the Riviera Maya remains an ideal place for more adventurous travelers — those who prefer to explore on their own, pulling into little coves and inland outposts to wander around truly unspoiled, undeveloped nature.

Teeing off and playing tennis

Few of the more-organized sporting activities — like golf and tennis — call this coast home. Your only option for chasing a little white ball and whacking a larger, yellow one is the Playacar Golf Club adjacent to the Continental Plaza Playacar immediately south of Playa del Carmen. It features an 18-hole championship **golf course** (☎ 987-873-0624) designed by Robert Von Hagge. Greens fees are $120 (includes golf cart), caddies charge $20, and club rental costs $20 — the prices include tax. If your hotel is a member of the golf club, greens fees may be reduced to as low as $50. Two **tennis** courts are also available at the club at a rate of $8 per hour.

Going shopping

Playa del Carmen offers the only real opportunity for **shopping** in the area — along its popular Avenida 5. This pedestrian-only street is lined with dozens of small, trendy shops selling imported batik (Balinese-style) clothing, Guatemalan fabric clothing, premium tequilas, Cuban cigars, masks, pottery, hammocks, and a few T-shirts. Throw in a couple of tattoo parlors, and you complete the mix.

Seeing the sights along the coast

The best way to travel this coast is in a rental car. (You can pick up your car at the Cancún airport or visit one of the many rental-car agencies in Playa del Carmen.) Highway 307 runs along the coast. It's a modern and well-paved road that's easy to drive. From Cancún to Playa del Carmen, Highway 307 is a four-lane divided highway with speed limits up to 110 kph (68 mph), but it passes through several towns where you need to slow down. From Playa to Tulum the road becomes a two-lane highway with wide shoulders and the same speed limits, but even more places that require you to slow down pop up. Driving from the Cancún Airport (on the south side of Cancún) to Tulum takes a little more than an hour and a half.

It's an easy one-hour drive from Playa to Tulum. Buses from Playa headed south to Chetumal, the last principal town in Mexico along this coast before Belize, also depart fairly regularly. Most of the buses stop several times along the highway; however, the walk to the coast and your final destination from the highway can be long. Another option is to hire a car and driver; costs run around $10 to $15 per hour, or you can negotiate an all-day rate. Find a driver you like and whose English is good; remember, you may be with him all day.

If you're traveling by car, there are a couple of worthwhile stops along Highway 307 on the way to Puerto Morelos from Cancún. **Croco Cun** (Highway 307 Km 31; ☎ **987-884-4782**), a zoological park where crocodiles are raised, is one of the most interesting attractions in the area. This isn't a zoo in the grand style, but it has interesting exhibits of crocodiles and almost all of the other animal species that have roamed the Yucatán Peninsula. The snake exhibit is fascinating, although it may make you think twice about roaming the jungle. The rattlesnakes and boa constrictors are particularly intimidating, and the tarantulas are downright enormous. Children enjoy the guides' enthusiastic tours, and they become particularly entranced by the spider monkeys and wild pigs. Wear plenty of bug repellent and allow an hour or two for the tour and a bit of time for a cool drink in the restaurant. Croco Cun is open daily from 8:30 a.m. to 5:30 p.m. Admission is $5 (free for children under age 6).

Puerto Morelos attracts people whose recipe for seaside relaxation doesn't include crowds and high prices. **Sub Aqua Explorers** (☎ **987-871-0078;** Fax: 987-871-0027), a good dive shop that also arranges fishing trips, is located on the main square. More than 15 dive sites are nearby, and many are close to shore. A two-tank dive costs around $60, and night dives cost $55. Two hours of fishing costs around $80, and snorkeling excursions run around $5.

From Puerto Morelos, Playa del Carmen is only 20 miles away, but before you get there, you'll pass a couple of places where you can turn in to discover pleasant, undeveloped beaches — at least for now.

The 150-acre **Jardín Botánico Dr. Alfredo Barrera** (no phone), named after a biologist who studied tropical forests, opened in 1990. This park is about a half mile outside of Puerto Morelos along Highway 307. It's a natural, protected showcase for native plants and animals. The hours are Monday to Saturday 9 a.m. to 5 p.m. Admission is $5.50.

The park is divided into six parts: an epiphyte area featuring plants that grow on other plants; Mayan ruins; an ethnographic area (the study of a particular culture or civilization, in this case, the Mayan) with a furnished hut and a typical Mayan garden; a chiclero camp that details the once-thriving *chicle* (chewing gum) industry; a nature park that preserves wild vegetation; and mangroves (large colonies of trees in water). A 3-kilometer (1.9 mile) path winds through the dense jungle of plants and trees. Signs in English and Spanish accompany the plants along the trail. Each sign has the plant's scientific and common name, uses for the plant, and the geographic areas where it's found in the wild. The park is home to about 450 species of plants. The wildlife includes monkeys, but they're not frequently spotted.

About midway between Puerto Morelos and Playa del Carmen is **Tres Ríos,** a nature park similar to Xcaret and Xel-ha. For information, call ☎ **987-887-8077** or visit the park's Web site at www.tres-rios.com. See Chapter 11 for more details on this park.

In Playa, you can arrange to go reef diving through **Tank-Ha Dive Center** (☎ **987-873-0302;** Fax: 987-873-1355; Internet: www.tankha.com). The friendly owner, Alberto Leonard, came to Playa by way of Madrid and now offers cave and *cenote* diving excursions. You can also book his trips at the Hotel Maya Bric and the Royal Albatross. Snorkeling trips cost $25 and include soft drinks and equipment. Two-tank dive trips are $65; resort courses with SSI (Scuba Schools International PADI (Professional Association of Diving) instructors are available for $75.

A succession of commercial nature parks, planned resort communities, and for now anyway, a few rustic beach hideaways and unspoiled coves are located south of Playa del Carmen. The **eco-theme parks** between Playa and Tulum include, in the following order, **Xcaret, Xpu-Ha,** and **Xel-Ha.** The distance from Playa del Carmen to Xel-Ha is 54 kilometers (33 miles). For detailed information on these parks, see Chapter 11.

A lot of *cenotes* are in this region, especially south of Akumal. For **cenote diving,** ask around at the dive shops in Akumal. If you want to snorkel in a *cenote,* **Dos Ojos** is the one that provides the easiest access — you may see the advertisements for this site along the highway. There's also a small nature park, **Aktun Chen,** with a natural cavern located just beyond Xel-Ha.

Two miles beyond Puerto Aventuras is **Xpu-Ha Bay** (sh-poo-*hah*), a wide bay lined by a broad, beautiful, sandy beach that may be the best beach on the entire coast! At one end of the bay is the now-defunct Xpu-Ha eco-park; at the other is the enclosed, all-inclusive **Robinson Club.** The recently opened, all-inclusive **Hotel Copacabana** (☎ **800-562-0197;** Internet: www.hotelcopacabana.com) is located in the middle. The beach is dotted with a few restaurants. On weekends, a lot of people from the surrounding area come to enjoy the beach. To get to the beach, turn off of the highway when you see the Copacabana hotel and take the road that goes along the south side of the hotel. Or you can take the next road, which is labeled X-6.

About 8 miles south of Akumal, just south of the Xel-Ha eco-park, turn-off on the west side of the highway at some simple **Maya ruins** of ancient Xel-Ha. You're likely to be the only one there as you walk over limestone rocks and through the tangle of trees, vines, and palms. There's a huge, deep, dark *cenote* to one side, a temple palace with tumbled-down columns, a jaguar group (group of ruins celebrating the jaguar god), and a conserved temple group (a grouping of temple ruins). A covered palapa on one pyramid guards a partially preserved mural. Admission is $2.50.

For more information about the archaeological sites in the area, including the popular ruins of Tulum, see Chapter 11.

Enjoying the nightlife

It seems like everyone in Playa is out on Avenida 5 or on the square until 10 or 11 p.m. each night. Pleasant strolls, meals and drinks at street-side cafes, shops, and a few bars with live music make up Playa's nightlife. **Cocodrilo's** (no phone), a second-story bar with Latin music (mostly recorded, sometimes live), is on the square. Down by the ferry dock is a **Señor Frog's** (☎ 987-873-0930), which seems a bit out of place in Playa with its patented mix of thumping dance music, gelatin shots, and frat-house antics; it's on the beach at Calle 4. **Captain Tutiz** (no phone) is also on the beach. This cocktail-procurement establishment is designed like a pirate ship and has a large bar area, a dance floor, and live entertainment nightly (though each time I visit, the so-called entertainment shows less and less talent). The beachside bar at the **Blue Parrot** (☎ 987-873-0083) is the most popular hangout in town.

Part V
Puerto Vallarta and the Central Pacific Coast

The 5th Wave   By Rich Tennant

"I know it's a popular American expression, but you just don't say 'Hasta la vista, baby' – to a nun."

In this part . . .

If you're considering basking in Puerto Vallarta's warm hospitality, let me tell you that this area is an excellent choice that offers exquisite surroundings, friendly people, and tons of things to do and see. As a longtime resident of this picturesque town, I share an insider's perspective on getting around and exploring the sights.

Puerto Vallarta boasts a wide variety of places to stay and the most delectable array of dining options of any of Mexico's beach resorts. In the upcoming chapters, I share my recommendations for the best places to stay in the area, and I guide you to the best restaurants — not an easy task considering all the wonderful dining choices Puerto Vallarta offers. Finally, I help you locate the ideal beach along the more than 50 miles of coastline within Banderas Bay.

Chapter 14

The Lowdown on Puerto Vallarta's Hotel Scene

In This Chapter
▶ Getting the scoop on hotel locations
▶ Sizing up Puerto Vallarta's top hotel choices

*P*uerto Vallarta maintains a small-town charm despite offering its visitors a range of sophisticated hotels, great restaurants, a thriving arts community, an active nightlife, and a growing variety of eco-tourism attractions. With its traditional Mexican architecture and gold-sand beaches bordered by jungle-covered mountains, Vallarta is currently the second most visited resort in Mexico (trailing only Cancún).

Most of the luxury hotels and shopping centers have sprung up to the north and south of the original town, allowing Vallarta to grow and become a sizable city of 250,000 without sacrificing its considerable charms. This growth pattern has made it possible for Vallarta to provide visitors with the services and infrastructure of a modern city while retaining the feel of a peaceful Mexican village.

In this chapter, I review the main parts of town, the types of hotel rooms you're likely to find in each place, and the pros and cons of staying in each area. Then I review some of my favorite places to stay in Puerto Vallarta. The selection is so varied that, regardless of your taste or budget, you're sure to find a perfect fit for a satisfying vacation.

Choosing a Location

The part of town you choose to stay in usually impacts your overall vacation experience although everything is relatively close by and getting around is easy and inexpensive. The term *Vallarta* actually encompasses the entire area that borders **Banderas Bay** — a 52-mile stretch of coastline that extends through two Mexican states. My hotel recommendations extend through this entire area as well.

Nuevo Vallarta and the northern coast

Traveling north from the airport (Gustavo Diaz Ordaz International Airport), you first come to **Nuevo Vallarta.** Many people assume Nuevo Vallarta is a section of Puerto Vallarta, but it's really a stand-alone destination located in the state of **Nayarit.** Original plans called for a mega-resort development scheme — complete with marina, golf course, and luxury hotels — but many of the projects remain to be built. Currently, the area is a collection of mostly all-inclusive hotels, located on one of the widest, most attractive beaches on the bay. Two lengthy entrance roads from the highway pass by fields that are great for bird-watching and nearby lagoons that are great for kayaking. Developers have completed a marina, and its once-shallow draft can now accommodate bigger boats. The **Paradise Plaza shopping center** (next to the Paradise Village resort) recently opened, adding a lot to the area in terms of shopping, dining, and services. In addition, two golf courses are slated to open in mid-2002.

Visitors to Nuevo Vallarta usually plan to travel the distance into Puerto Vallarta (about 30 minutes and $15 by cab) for anything other than poolside and beach action — options for dining and other diversions outside of the hotels remain limited. Taxis are available 24 hours a day. A regularly scheduled public-bus service runs between 7 a.m. and 11 p.m. daily and costs about $1.20 for a one-way trip.

Bucerías, a small beachfront village of cobblestone streets, villas, and small hotels, is farther north along Banderas Bay, 12 miles beyond the airport. Past Bucerías, following the curved coastline of Banderas Bay, is **Punta Mita.** Once a truly rustic village of fishermen and bamboo houses, Punta Mita is in the process of developing its own identity as a luxury destination. Five super-exclusive, luxury-boutique resorts, numerous private villas, and three golf courses are in the works. This spot of white-sand beaches and clear waters was once home to an ancient celestial observatory, and you can't imagine a more exquisite setting. Punta Mita is a departure from the other beaches in the area.

Marina Vallarta

If you head south from the airport, the first area you come to is **Marina Vallarta,** a resort city within Puerto Vallarta, located on the immediate right as you come into town from the airport. Guests here feel a world apart from the quaintness of downtown Puerto Vallarta: Marina Vallarta has the most modern luxury hotels of any area in town, plus a huge marina with 450 yacht slips, a golf course, restaurants and bars, a water park, and several shopping plazas.

Because the area began life as a swamp and was later filled in for development, the beaches, with darker sand and seasonal inflows of cobblestones that wash down from the mountains and rivers and wash up on the beaches, are the least desirable in the area. However, the exquisite pools at the oceanfront hotels more than make up for this shortcoming.

The **Marina Vallarta Club de Golf** (☎ **322-221-0073**), an 18-hole golf course designed by Joe Finger, is within walking distance of most of the hotels. The **Mayan Palace Aquapark** (☎ **322-221-1500,** ext. 824) and its inner-tube canal, water slides, pools, and snack-bar facilities is also close to many of the hotels (directly across the street from the Mayan Palace Resort). The park is open to the public from 11 a.m. to 6 p.m. daily. The cost is $15 for adults and $12 for kids.

Although this isn't the area of choice if you're a true beach aficionado, Marina Vallarta is nice for families and for vacationers looking for lots of centralized activity. The complex is attractive and clean, and the public transportation is good. If you choose to travel by taxi, going from the Marina to downtown Puerto Vallarta takes 20 to 30 minutes, which is due to traffic more than distance.

Hotel Zone

The next area you encounter heading south from the airport toward town is known as the **Hotel Zone** because of all the high-rise hotels located side-by-side along the main roadway. Here, the main street running between the airport and town is called Avenida Francisco Medina Ascencio, but it's sometimes referred to as Avenida de las Palmas for the stately palm trees that line the strip of land that divides the road. The tourism boom that Vallarta enjoyed in the mid-1970s gave birth to the hotels that line this road, and most of them have been exceptionally well maintained. All the hotels offer excellent, wide beachfronts with generally tranquil waters for swimming. This area is home to more casual, less expensive hotels that offer a great beach as a bonus.

The long and wide stretch of golden beach fronting the Hotel Zone has smoother sand and more watersports concessions than either Marina Vallarta or downtown. Although many shopping plazas line the main road in front of the hotels, they mostly service the large residential community to the east. The most interesting restaurants and intriguing shops are found downtown or back in the Marina, but from the Hotel Zone, you're only a quick taxi or bus ride away from either of these areas.

El Centro Vallarta

Few beach resorts in Mexico offer what Puerto Vallarta exudes — the feeling that you're actually in Mexico. Staying in the **central downtown** area provides the charm of a traditional village and proximity to a tropical beach. Sophisticated services, all classes and types of restaurants, sizzling nightspots, and enough shops and galleries to tempt even the most-jaded consumers are contained within the cobblestone streets and welcoming atmosphere of the central town.

Cool breezes flow down from the mountains along the Río Cuale (Cuale River), which runs through the center of town. The boardwalk, or *malecón,* that borders the main waterfront street boasts fanciful public sculptures, lively restaurants, shops, bars — and timeshare sales booths. The *malecón* is a magnet for both residents and visitors who walk its length while taking in the ocean breeze, a gorgeous sunset, or a perfect, moonlit night.

Accommodations here may be older, but they're inexpensive and generally well kept; plus they have lots of character. In addition to being able to reach any downtown destination on foot, the neighborhood is as safe as it is charming.

Just south of downtown, the **Playa Los Muertos** area has recently undergone a renaissance. It's now not only a place offering great values in accommodations, dining, and nightlife, but an added plus for the Los Muertos neighborhood is that it also has funky charm, which you can experience in the sidewalk cafes, great restaurants, and casual nightspots. Economically-priced hotels and good-value guesthouses dominate accommodations here. Another bonus for the Los Muertos neighborhood is that most of Vallarta's nightlife activity is now centered in the areas south of the Río Cuale and along Olas Altas Avenue.

The southern shore

Hillsides dotted with private villas and a few large hotels surround the coastal highway. Immediately south of town lies the exclusive residential and rental district of **Conchas Chinas.** La Jolla de Mismaloya resort lies six miles south of town on **Playa Mismaloya** (where *Night of the Iguana* was filmed). No roads service the southern shoreline of Banderas Bay, but three small coastal villages are popular attractions for visitors to Puerto Vallarta: **Las Ánimas, Quimixto,** and **Yelapa,** which are all accessible only by boat. Many visitors mistakenly believe that these villages are islands, but they're actually located along the same coast. Yelapa offers some rustic accommodations in addition to making a great destination for an enjoyable day-trip. There are no accommodations in Las Animas or Quimixto.

Beyond a varied selection of hotels, Puerto Vallarta has many other types of accommodations. Oceanfront or marina-view condominiums and elegant private villas are also available; both options can offer a better value and more ample space for families or small groups. For more information on short-term rentals, check out the Web site at www.virtualvallarta.com, which lists a selection of rental options. Prices start at $99 a night for non-beachfront condos and go up to $1,000 for penthouse condos or private villas. **Vicki Skinner's Doin' it Right in Puerto Vallarta** (☎ **800-936-3646,** 619-297-3642; E-mail: GayPVR@aol.com) is a special service that rents gay-friendly condos and villas for individuals and groups (up to 75 people) and can package private chef and tour services with accommodations.

Puerto Vallarta's Best Accommodations

For each hotel, I include specific rack rates for two people spending one night in a double room during high season (Christmas to Easter) unless otherwise indicated. *Rack rates* simply mean published rates and tend to be the highest rates paid — you can do better, especially if you're purchasing a package that includes airfare (see Chapter 6 for tips on avoiding paying rack rates). Prices quoted here include the 17% room tax. Please refer to the Introduction of *Mexico's Beach Resorts For Dummies* for an explanation of the price categories.

It's not unusual for many hotels to double their normal rates during Christmas and Easter weeks, but low season rates can be anywhere from 20 percent to 60 percent below high season rates. Note that some rates may seem much higher than others, but many of these rates are "all-inclusive" — meaning that your meals and beverages are included in the price of your stay. All-inclusive rates also take into account all tips and taxes and most activities and entertainment.

All hotels listed here have both air-conditioning and TVs, unless otherwise indicated.

Blue Bay Getaway
$$$ Hotel Zone

Blue Bay Getaway is new, conveniently located, and all-inclusive, making it an ideal choice for anyone wanting a completely carefree vacation. Well, anyone over the age of 18 — this hotel caters to adults only. Its location is outstanding, just minutes from town on a wide, beautiful stretch of beach, and I think it offers an exceptional value with all your meals, beverages, activities, and entertainment included in the price of your room. Blue Bay is becoming known for working hard to offer good value for all-inclusive stays — the buffets are varied, and you have the option of dining at an à la carte restaurant.

Three types of rooms are available, but all are decorated in sunny gold and yellow hues with vibrant blue accents. The four-story Coral tower has the best rooms (double superior). Tile floors, small balconies with ocean or mountain views, and bathrooms with showers and tubs are hallmarks of these rooms. The 11-story Arcos tower houses the deluxe and standard rooms. Deluxe rooms in the Arcos tower with private balconies and ocean views are the most spacious. The standard rooms are the least expensive and smaller than the others. They don't have balconies, and the bathrooms have showers but no tubs. These rooms only offer mountain views (through small, curtained windows) but are a great value — you probably won't spend too much time in your room anyway with all the activities the Blue Bay Getaway offers. You have two restaurants to choose from plus a snack bar. For revelry, there's five bars plus nightly entertainment and shows. The large beachfront pool has a non-stop schedule of activities, but if you prefer a little tranquility in the sun, there's also a smaller, quieter pool with a wet bar. A tennis court; spa with sauna, whirlpool tub, and massage service; non-motorized watersports equipment; and bikes round out the offerings. Another bonus of staying here is that you can also enjoy all of the facilities at the Blue Bay Club, located on the southern shore of Puerto Vallarta. Shuttles run between the two resorts every hour. The Blue Bay Club is larger and offers family activities and a disco, but its beach isn't as nice as the Getaway's strip of sand.

Av. Francisco Medina Ascencio Km 1.5, next door to the Sheraton Buganvilias. ☎ *322-223-3600. Fax: 322-223-3601. Internet:* www.bluebayresorts.com. *358 units. Ample free parking. Rack rates: High season $115–$130 per person double; low season $80–$95 per person double. Rates are all-inclusive. Adults only. AE, MC, V.*

Camino Real

$$$$ South Shore/Conchas Chinas

The original luxury hotel in Puerto Vallarta, the Camino Real has retained its place as a premier property despite newer arrivals. It unquestionably has the nicest beach of any Vallarta hotel — soft, white sand and a private cove. On the beach, numerous shade palapas are available, along with a chair, towels, and food and beverage service. Both the nature of the geography, as well as the physical boundaries set it apart from other properties — with a lush mountain backdrop, the Camino Real retains the exclusivity that made it popular from the beginning — yet it's only a five- to ten-minute ride to town. The hotel consists of two buildings: the 250-room main hotel, which curves gently as it traces the shape of the Playa Las Estacas, and a newer, 11-story Camino Real Club tower, also facing the beach and ocean. An ample pool with an in-pool bar fronts the main building and faces the beach. Standard rooms in the main building are large. Some of the rooms have sliding doors that open onto the beach, and others have balconies. The standard rooms in the tower at the Royal Beach Club feature balconies with whirlpool tubs. All rooms are decorated in the signature vibrant colors of Camino Real hotels. New owners have scheduled this hotel for some major renovations and upgrades in the coming year, though it's still remarkably well-maintained. For libations and sustenance, the property has four restaurants and a lobby bar that specializes in a wide selection of premium tequilas. Two lighted, grass tennis courts and a small fitness room with weights are also on-site.

Carretera Barra de Navidad Km 3.5, Playa Las Estacas. ☎ *800-722-6466 in the U.S. and Canada, or 322-221-5000. Fax: 322-221-6000. Internet:* www.caminoreal.com. *337 units. Free secured parking. Rack rates: High season $180–$200 double, $500–$1,000 suite; low season $135–$150 double, $400–$880 suite. AE, DC, MC, V.*

Puerto Vallarta Hotel Zone Accommodations

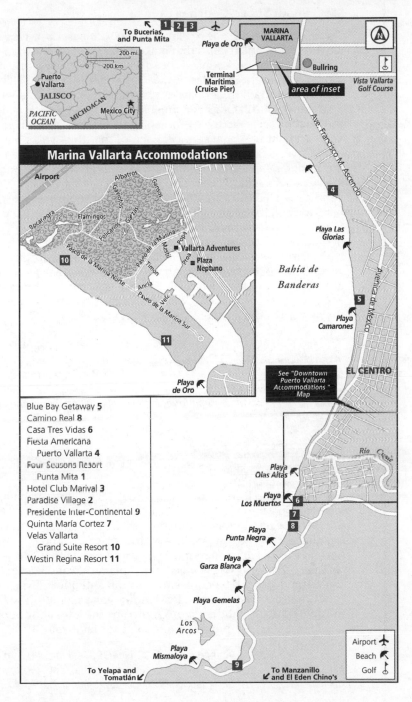

Marina Vallarta Accommodations

Blue Bay Getaway **5**
Camino Real **8**
Casa Tres Vidas **6**
Fiesta Americana
   Puerto Vallarta **4**
Four Seasons Resort
   Punta Mita **1**
Hotel Club Marival **3**
Paradise Village **2**
Presidente Inter-Continental **9**
Quinta María Cortez **7**
Velas Vallarta
   Grand Suite Resort **10**
Westin Regina Resort **11**

Casa Tres Vidas

$$$ South Shore/Conchas Chinas

Terraced down a hillside to Playa Conchas Chinas, Casa Tres Vidas is actually three individual villas that make a great — and affordable — place to stay for families or groups of friends. Set on a stunning private cove, Tres Vidas provides the experience of having your own private villa — complete with service staff. Under new ownership since 2000, Tres Vidas has been upgraded in furnishings and amenities, and it's an outstanding value for the location (close to town), sweeping panoramic views from every room, and excellent personal service. Each of the three villas has at least two levels, over 5,000 square feet of mostly-open living area, a private swimming pool, a heated whirlpool, and air-conditioned bedrooms. (Because the layout is so open, the rest of the rooms don't have A/C.) The Villa Alta penthouse villa has three bedrooms, plus a rooftop deck with pool and bar. Vida Sol, the center villa, has an 18-foot-high domed living room with fireplace and features graceful arches and columns. Although it has three bedrooms, it can sleep ten — two of bedrooms each have two king-size beds. Directly on the ocean, Vida Mar is a four-bedroom villa that can accommodate eight guests. An added bonus is that gourmet meals are prepared in your villa twice a day — you only pay for the cost of the food, and you choose the menu. Casa Tres Vidas is now owned and managed by the owners of the adjacent Quinta Maria Cortez.

Sagitario 134, below the Conchas Chinas Mercado. ☎ *888-640-8100 or 801-531-8100 in the U.S., or 322-221-5317. Fax: 322-221-53-27. Internet:* www.casatresvidas. com. *3 villas. Very limited street parking available. Rack rates: High season: Villa Alta $510, Villa Sol $485, Villa Mar $510. Low season: Villa Alta $375, Villa Sol $350, Villa Mar $375. Prices are per night for complete villa, full services, and two meals prepared. AE, MC, V.*

Fiesta Americana Puerto Vallarta

$$$ Hotel Zone

The Fiesta Americana's towering, three-story, thatched-palapa lobby is a landmark in the Hotel Zone, but this hotel is even more well-known for its excellent beach and friendly service. The nine-story, terracotta-colored building embraces a large plaza with a large pool and bar area facing the beach. Marble-trimmed rooms in neutral tones with pastel accents come with carved headboards and comfortable rattan and wicker furniture. All rooms have private balconies with ocean and pool views. In addition to the three restaurants, the Fiesta Americana has a lobby bar with live music nightly. A children's program and the excellent pool and beach facilities make this hotel a great choice for families.

Av. Francisco Medina Ascencio Km 2.5. ☎ *800-FIESTA-1 in the U.S., or 322-224-2010. Fax: 322-224-2108. Internet:* www.fiestaamericana.com. *291 units. Limited free parking. Rack rates: High season $180 double; low season $120–$160 double. AE, DC, MC, V.*

Downtown Puerto Vallarta Accommodations

Hotel Molino de Agua **2**
Hotel Playa Los Arcos **3**
Los Cuatro Vientos **1**

Four Seasons Resort Punta Mita

$$$$$ **Punta Mita**

The Four Seasons Resort has brought a new standard of luxury to Mexico. This boutique hotel artfully combines seclusion and pampered service with a welcoming sense of comfort. The 113 rooms and 27 suites are in three-story *casitas* (little houses), which surround the main building where the lobby, cultural center, restaurants, and pool are located. The stretch of beach fronting the resort is the only white-sand beach in the bay. Every guestroom offers views of the ocean from a large terrace or balcony. Most suites also offer a private plunge pool, as well as a separate sitting room. Room interiors are typically Four Seasons — plush and spacious with a king or two double beds, a seating area, and an oversized bathroom with a deep soaking tub, a separate glass-enclosed shower, and a dual-vanity sink. This is the place to go to completely get away from it all, but remember that you're at least 45 minutes from Puerto Vallarta's activities. For most guests, this isn't a problem — the

Four Seasons is so relaxing and comfortable that it's hard to think of any-place else. The centerpiece of the resort is the 18-hole (with an optional 19th hole of play on a natural island) Jack Nicklaus signature golf course. The course has ocean views from every hole, and eight holes border the ocean. A full-service spa, complete tennis center, and watersports center round out the activities. In addition to the two restaurants, there's a golf clubhouse, a lobby bar, and 24-hour room service. The heated infinity pool (a type of pool that has the edge that seems to disappear into the horizon) is surrounded by private cabanas, and waiters come by every so often to offer chilled towels or a spritz of water. A notable attraction is the cultural center — a library-style environment with free Internet access and a menu of entertaining lectures on Mexican culture, including a popular tequila tasting! The Kids for All Seasons activities program is hands-down the best place for children to enjoy their vacation as much as you will.

Bahía de Banderas, Nay. 63734. ☎ 800-332-3442, 322-291-6000. Fax: 322-291-6060. Internet: www.fourseasons.com. *140 units. Valet parking. Rack rates: High season $360–$527 double, $680–$900 suite; low season $280–$360 double, $480–$650 suite. AE, DC, MC, V.*

Hotel Club Marival
$$$ **Nuevo Vallarta**

This all-inclusive hotel, located almost by itself at the northernmost end of Nuevo Vallarta, is a refreshing choice compared to the mega-resorts that tend to dominate all-inclusive-vacation options. The broad, sandy beach is one of the real assets here — it stretches over 500 yards. There's also an extensive activities program, including fun for children. This Mediterranean-style property is relatively small, but it offers a large variety of rooms ranging from standard rooms with no balconies to large master suites with whirlpools. Choose from among four restaurants, plus seven bars, for your dining and drinking desires. The hotel has three pools and a whirlpool for adults, plus two pools for children and four lighted tennis courts. If you're coming from the Puerto Vallarta airport, Club Marival is the first resort to your right on Cocoteros Avenue when you enter Nuevo Vallarta from the second entrance.

Paseo de los Cocoteros y Blvd. Nuevo Vallarta s/n. ☎ 322-297-0100. Fax: 322-297-0160. Internet: www.clubmarival.com. *504 units. Rack rates: High season $123 per person double, low season $115 per person double. Rates are all-inclusive. Ask about seasonal specials. AE, MC, V.*

Hotel Molino de Agua
$$ **Centro**

With an unrivaled location adjacent to both the Río Cuale and the ocean, this hotel is a mix of stone and stucco-walled bungalows and small beach-front buildings spread out among winding walkways and lush tropical gardens. If you want a place that's more intimate than a standard hotel, in a location that's more immersed in town activities, this is the best choice. It's located immediately past the Río Cuale — after crossing the southbound bridge, the hotel is on your right. Although the hotel is centrally located on a main street, open spaces, big trees, birds, and lyrical fountains lend tranquility to the space. The individual bungalows are located in the gardens between the entrance and the ocean — make sure to request one away from the front of the property where street noise can keep you up at night. The bungalows are well maintained, and the simple furnishings include a bed, wooden desk and chair, Mexican tile floors, beamed ceilings, and beautifully tiled bathrooms. Wicker rocking chairs grace their private patios. Rooms and suites in the small, two- and three-story buildings on the beach have double beds and private terraces. There are no TVs or telephones in any of the rooms. In addition to an oceanside pool, a second pool with a whirlpool is adjacent to the Lion's Court restaurant and bar.

Ignacio L. Vallarta 130, just over the southbound bridge on the right side. ☎ *322-222-1957. Fax: 322-222-6056. Internet:* www.molinodeagua.com. *58 units including bungalows and suites. Free secured parking. Rack rates: High season $92 garden bungalows, $128–$150 oceanfront rooms and suites; low season $58 bungalows, $83–$95 rooms and suites. AE, MC, V.*

Hotel Playa Los Arcos
$–$$ Centro

An excellent value and always popular, this hotel is a personal favorite of mine. Its stellar location in the heart of Playa Los Muertos is central to the Olas Altas sidewalk-cafe action and close to downtown. The four-story structure is U shaped, facing the ocean, with a small swimming pool in the courtyard. Rooms with private balconies overlook the pool, and the ten suites have ocean views. Five of the suites have kitchenettes. The standard rooms are small but pleasantly decorated with carved wooden furniture painted pale pink, and they're immaculate. A palapa beachside bar with occasional live entertainment, a gourmet coffee shop, and the popular Maximilian's gourmet restaurant are on the premises. The hotel is located 7 blocks south of the river.

Olas Altas 380. ☎ *800-648-2403 in the U.S., or 322-222-1583. Fax: 322-222-2418. Internet:* www.playalosarcos.com. *175 units. Limited street parking available. Rack rates: High season $92–$120 double, $150 suite; low season $65 double, $95 suite. AE, MC, V.*

Los Cuatro Vientos
$ Centro

Solo women travelers, as well as groups of women traveling together, favor this quiet, secluded inn. Located in the center of downtown on a hillside overlooking Banderas Bay, it features rooms built around a small, central patio and pool where the cozy Chez Elena restaurant opens for service in the evenings. The cheerful, spotless, colorful rooms have fans, small tiled bathrooms, brick ceilings, red-tile floors, and glass-louvered windows. Each room is decorated with simple Mexican furnishings, folk art, and antiques. The rooftop, with a panoramic view of the city, is great for sunning and is among the best places in the city for sunset drinks. Continental breakfast is served in the restaurant for guests only from 7 to 11 a.m. The hotel also offers occasional weeklong "Women's Getaway" packages several times a year that include cultural discussions and recreational activities.

Matamoros 520. ☎ 322-222-0161. Fax: 322-222-2831. Internet: www.cuatro vientos.com. *14 units. Very limited street parking available. Rack rates: High season $80 double, $130 suite; low season $55 double, $69 suite. (Suite rates include up to 4 people.) All rates include continental breakfast. MC, V.*

Paradise Village
$$$$ Nuevo Vallarta

This resort truly lives up to its name. It feels more like a self-contained village than a resort and is indeed a paradise bordering one of the most stunning stretches of broad, sandy beach in the bay. Paradise Village offers a full array of guest services, ranging from an on-site disco to a full-service European spa and health club. Styled in a Mayan-influenced design, the collection of pyramid-shaped buildings houses all-suite accommodations in studio, one-bedroom, and two-bedroom configurations. All the suites are well designed and feature muted color schemes, sitting areas, and kitchenettes — making them ideal for families or groups of friends. The Mayan theme extends to both oceanfront pools with mythical creatures forming water slides and waterfalls. The exceptional spa is reason enough to book a vacation here. Services include treatments, hydrotherapy, massage (including massage on the beach), and fitness and yoga classes. Special spa packages are always available, and they can include a full fitness evaluation if you're up for it. Four tennis courts, a lap pool, a basketball court, beach volleyball courts, and a watersports center complement the spa and fitness center. In addition to the two full-service restaurants, beachfront snack bars and special theme nights add to the dining options. The kid's club and petting zoo are especially popular with families.

*Paseo de los Cocoteros 001. ☎ 800-995-5714, 322-226-6770. Fax: 322-226-6713. Internet: www.*paradisevillage.com. *Free covered parking. 490 units. Rack rates: High season $182–$350 double; low season $140–$280 double. AE, DC, MC, V.*

Presidente Inter-Continental
$$$$ South Shore

The most upscale all-inclusive hotel in the area, this property is the ideal place for those travelers who really want to get away from everything and keep decision-making to a minimum. Presidente Inter-Continental is also a top choice for honeymooners looking for a little romantic seclusion.

Backed by a jungle mountain landscape and fronted by a beautiful golden sand beach, the 11-story building is draped in colorful, flowering bougainvillea. Meals, drinks, and sports are included here — a convenient necessity because this welcoming hotel is 20 minutes south of Puerto Vallarta and secluded from the activity of town. Deluxe rooms all have large furnished balconies with ocean views, tile floors, white wood furnishings, and muted colored textiles. Marble tub/shower-combination bathrooms are extra large with separate vanity areas. The 19 suites have in-room whirlpools. A large mosaic pool with swim-up bar is on a terrace overlooking the beach, adjacent to the grass tennis court and small fitness room. Guests aren't limited to buffet dining. They can order a la carte from two restaurants and enjoy premium drinks at their choice of bars. There's also a year-round kid's club.

Carretera Barra de Navidad Km 8.5. ☎ *800-327-0200, 322-228-0507. Fax: 322-228-0609. Internet:* www.basshotels.com. *120 units. Limited free parking. Rack rates: High season $330–$350 double; low season $260–$300 double. Rates are all-inclusive. AE, DC, MC, V.*

Quinta María Cortez

$$$–$$$$ South Shore/Conchas Chinas

An eclectic, sophisticated, and imaginative B&B on the beach, this is Puerto Vallarta's most original place to stay — and one of Mexico's most memorable inns. Seven large suites, uniquely decorated in antiques, whimsical curios, and original art, all feature a private bathroom, and most include a kitchenette and balcony. Sunny terraces, a small pool, and a central gathering area with fireplace and palapa-topped dining area (where an excellent full breakfast is served) occupy different levels of this seven-story house. A rooftop terrace offers yet another alternative for taking in the sun and is among the very best sunset-watching spots in town. Quinta María is located on a beautiful cove on Playa Conchas Chinas where the rocks sitting just offshore form tranquil tide pools. This B&B wins my highest recommendation, but admittedly, it's not for everyone. Air-conditioned areas are limited due to the open nature of the suites and common areas, but then, the openness is a large part of the allure. Vacationers who love Quinta María find themselves charmed by this remarkable place and consistently gracious service return year after year. Not appropriate for children.

Sagitario 132, Playa Conchas Chinas. ☎ *888-640-8100 or 801-536-5850 in the U.S., or 322-221-5317. Fax: 322-221-5327. Internet:* www.quinta-maria.com. *E-mail:* qmc@travel-zone.com. *7 units. Very limited street parking available. Rack rates: High season $150–$250 double; low season $100–$185 double. Rates include breakfast. AE, MC, V.*

Velas Vallarta Grand Suite Resort

$$$–$$$$ Marina Vallarta

The beachfront Velas Vallarta is an excellent choice for families because each suite offers a full-size, fully equipped kitchen, ample living and dining areas, separate bedroom(s), and a large balcony with seating. The apartments are tastefully decorated with light wood furnishings, cool terrazzo floors, bright fabrics, and marble tub/shower-combination bathrooms. This property is actually part hotel and part full-ownership condominium, which means each suite is the size of a true residential unit offering the feeling of a home away from home. The suites all have partial ocean views, and they face onto a central area where three free-form swimming pools, complete with bridges and waterfalls, meander through tropical gardens. A full range of services — including restaurants, mini-market, deli, tennis courts, spa, and boutiques — means you'd never need to leave the place if you didn't want to. The Marina Vallarta Golf Club is across the street, and special packages are available to Velas guests.

Paseo de la Marina 485. ☎ *800-659-8477 in the U.S. and Canada, or 322-221-0091. Fax: 322-221-0755. Internet:* www.velasvallarta.com. *361 units. Free indoor parking. Rack rates: High season $220 double, $300–$540 suite; low season $150 double, $220–$380 suite. AE, DC, MC, V.*

Westin Regina Resort

$$$–$$$$ **Marina Vallarta**

The service standard of Westin hotels combined with the stunning architecture and vibrant colors of this resort make it a Puerto Vallarta favorite — ideal for almost any traveler or type of vacation. Although the grounds are large — over 21 acres with 850 feet of beachfront — the warm service and gracious hospitality always reminds me of an intimate resort. The central free-form pool with hundreds of tall palms surrounding it is spectacular. You may find hammocks strung between the palms closest to the beach where there's also a wooden playground for kids. Rooms are contemporary in style and brightly colored in textured fabrics. They feature oversized wood furnishings, tile floors, original art, tub/shower-combination bathrooms, and in-room safes. Balconies have panoramic views. Two floors of rooms are designated as the Royal Beach Club and come with special VIP services and amenities. The fitness center here is one of the most modern, well-equipped facilities of its kind in Vallarta, and three grass tennis courts are available for day or night play. Guests enjoy play privileges at the Marina Vallarta Golf Club and a kid's club takes care of the activities for younger travelers. Of the two restaurants, the beachside Garibaldi is known as the best seafood restaurant in the Marina Vallarta area.

Paseo de la Marina Sur 205. ☎ *800-228-3000 in the U.S., or 322-221-1100. Fax: 322-221-1121. Internet:* www.westinpv.com. *280 units. Free parking. Rack rates: High season $195–$295 double, $415–$520 suite; low season $160–170 double, $335–$420 suite. AE, DC, MC, V.*

Chapter 15

Settling into Puerto Vallarta

● ●

In This Chapter

▶ Knowing what to expect when you arrive

▶ Finding your way around town

▶ Discovering helpful information and resources

● ●

*F*rom the moment you arrive, you're likely to settle into Puerto Vallarta's welcoming ways. In this chapter, I take you from the plane, through the airport, and to your hotel, helping you quickly get your bearings in this easy-to-navigate town. I also provide tips on everything from taxis to Internet access. You've got insider information here — Puerto Vallarta has been my home for the past ten years!

Arriving in Puerto Vallarta

Puerto Vallarta's airport is easy to get through, so you can reach the sun-soaked days waiting outside in no time. Recently recognized as the friendliest international city by a leading travel magazine, Puerto Vallarta is a pleasure. The people here are genuinely welcoming and proud to share their town with visitors. They strive to make your stay as pleasant as possible. Visitors usually get a taste of Puerto Vallarta's hospitality right from the start — you should find both immigration and customs to be brief, generally easy procedures.

Navigating passport control and customs

After you deplane, you go through a jetway and wind your way down some stairs into the immigration-clearance area, or a bus may take you directly to immigration from your plane. When you reach immigration, an officer will ask you to show your passport and your completed tourist card, the **FMT** (see Chapter 7 for all the FMT details).

Your FMT is an important document, so take good care of it. You're supposed to keep the FMT with you at all times because you may be required to show it should you run into any sort of trouble. You also need to turn it back in upon departure, or you may be unable to leave without replacing it.

Next up is the baggage claim area. Here, porters stand by to help with your bags, and they're well worth the price of the tip — about a dollar a bag. After you collect your luggage, you pass through another checkpoint. Something that looks like a traffic light awaits you here. You press a button, and if the light turns green, you're free to go. If it turns red, you need to open each of your bags for a quick search. It's Mexico's random search procedure for customs. If you have an unusually large bag, or an excessive amount of luggage, you may be searched regardless of the traffic-light outcome.

Just past the traffic light, a bustling crowd of people waiting for fellow passengers, transportation representatives, and taxi drivers promoting their services greet you. If you're part of a package tour that includes ground transportation to your hotel, start looking for your rep here. Generally he or she will be carrying a sign with your name or the name of your tour company on it.

Salespeople hustling timeshares hang out at the airport, but they come on to you like they're available to help you find a hotel or transportation. Unless you want to get into a lengthy conversation, head straight for the blue and orange booths marked "Taxi" to purchase your set-price tickets to your hotel.

Getting to your hotel

The airport (PVR) is close to the north end of town near the Marina Vallarta, about six miles from downtown. **Transportes Terrestres** minivans and **Aeromovil** taxis make the trip from the airport to all the hotel areas. Costs for both options are determined by zones — clearly posted at the respective ticket booths. Fares start at $8 for a ride to Marina Vallarta and go up to $25 for a trip to the south-shore hotels. **Airport taxis** are federally licensed taxis that operate exclusively to provide transportation from the airport. Their fares are almost three times as high as city (yellow) taxis. A trip from the airport to downtown Puerto Vallarta costs $12, whereas a return trip using a city taxi costs only $4.50. Yellow cabs are restricted from picking up passengers leaving the airport.

However, if you don't have too much baggage, you can walk across the highway via the new overpass. Yellow cabs are lined up on the other side and ready to take you anywhere your heart desires for a third of the price of the airport cabs.

Getting Around Puerto Vallarta

Puerto Vallarta is very easy to get around. Essentially, one main road stretches from the airport in both directions around the bay. It changes names a few times along the way. Puerto Vallarta has followed this central roadway as it has grown along the beach to the north and south. Linking the airport to downtown, the road is called **Avenida Francisco Medina Ascencio** (sometimes still referred to by its previous name, Avenida de las Palmas). Along this main thoroughfare are many luxury hotels (in the area called the **Zona Hotelera,** or **Hotel Zone**), plus several shopping centers with casual restaurants.

As you come into the central downtown area, known as *El Centro,* this road becomes **Paseo Díaz Ordaz,** which runs north to south through the town. The seaside promenade, called the *malecón,* which borders Paseo Díaz Ordaz, is frequently used as a reference point for giving directions. This section of downtown marked off by the *malecón* is the original town and sometimes referred to as *Viejo Vallarta* — the cultural and civic heart of Puerto Vallarta. City hall, the waterfront, the open-air Los Arcos Theater, the landmark Our Lady of Guadalupe church, and scores of restaurants, galleries, and shops all call this area home.

From the waterfront, the town stretches back into the hills a half-dozen blocks. The areas bordering the **Río Cuale** (Cuale River) are the oldest parts of town — and home to Gringo Gulch, named for the dozens of U.S. expatriates that made their homes here in the late 1950s.

The area immediately south of the river, called **Olas Altas** after its main street (and sometimes **Los Muertos** after the beach of the same name), is now home to a growing selection of sidewalk cafes, fine restaurants, espresso bars, and hip nightclubs (many with live music).

From the center of town, nearly everything both north and south of the river is within walking distance. **Bridges** on Insurgentes (northbound traffic) and Ignacio L. Vallarta (southbound traffic) link the two sections of town.

Taking a taxi

Taxi travel is the preferred way for getting around Puerto Vallarta. Away from the airport, taxis are plentiful and relatively inexpensive. Most trips from downtown to the northern Zona Hotelera and Marina Vallarta cost between $3.50 and $5.00; a trip between Marina Vallarta and Playa Mismaloya to the south costs $8.00. Rates are charged by zone and are generally posted in the lobbies of hotels. Taxis can also be hired by the hour or day for longer trips when you prefer to leave the driving to someone else. Rates run between $10 and $12 per hour with discounts available for full-day rates — consider this as an alternative to renting a car.

I do have a word to the wise about taxis: Beware of restaurant recommendations offered by taxi drivers — many drivers receive a commission from restaurants where they discharge passengers. Be especially wary if a driver tries to talk you out of a restaurant you've already selected and to one of his own personal "favorites."

Catching a bus

Another option — combining cheap, easy transportation with some local color — is Puerto Vallarta's city buses. They run from the airport through the Zona Hotelera along Calle Morelos (1 block inland from the *malecón*), across the Río Cuale, and inland on Vallarta, looping back through the downtown hotel and restaurant districts on Insurgentes and several other downtown streets. To get to the northern Zona Hotelera strip from old Puerto Vallarta, take the Zona Hoteles, Ixtapa, or Las Juntas bus. These buses in the Zona Hotelera follow the same route and may also post the names of hotels they pass such as Krystal, Fiesta Americana, Sheraton, and others. Buses marked "Marina Vallarta" travel inside the Marina Vallarta area and stop at the major hotels. City buses, which cost about 30¢, can service just about all your transportation needs frequently and inexpensively.

Buses generally run from 6 a.m. to 11p.m., and it's rare to wait more than a few minutes for one. An additional bus route travels south every 10 to 15 minutes to either Playa Mismaloya or Boca de Tomatlán (the last point on the southern shore of the bay that can be reached by land — the destination is indicated in the front window) from Plaza Lázaro Cárdenas, a few blocks south of the river at Cárdenas and Suárez, and along Basilio Badillo, between Piño Suárez and Insurgentes.

Buses in Vallarta tend to be rather aggressive, and some even sport names — "Terminator," "Rambo," and "Tornado" are three of my favorites. Don't tempt fate by assuming that these buses stop for pedestrians. Although Vallarta is an extremely low-crime city, bus accidents are frequent — and frequently fatal.

Renting a car

Rental cars are available at the airport and through travel agencies, but unless you're planning a distant side trip, don't bother. Car rentals are expensive, averaging $60 per day, and parking around town is difficult.

If you see a sign for a $10 Jeep rental or $20 car rental, be aware that it's a lure to get people to attend timeshare presentations. Unless you're interested in a timeshare, stopping to inquire is a waste of your time.

Cruising around

The cruise-ship pier or *muelle,* also called Terminal Marítima, is where **excursion boats** to Yelapa, Las Ánimas, Quimixto, and the Marietas Islands depart. It's north of town near the airport and just an inexpensive taxi or bus ride away. Just take any bus marked "Ixtapa," "Las Juntas," "Pitillal," or "Aurora" and tell the driver to let you off at the Terminal Marítima. *Note:* Odd though it may seem, you have to pay a 50¢ fee to access the pier where the tour boats are docked.

Water taxis offering direct transportation to Yelapa, Las Ánimas, and Quimixto leave at 10:30 and 11:00 a.m. from the pier at Playa Los Muertos (south of downtown) on Rodolfo Rodríguez next to the Hotel Marsol. Another water taxi departs at 11 a.m. from the beachfront pier at the northern edge of the *malecón*. A round-trip ticket to Yelapa (the farthest point) costs $12. Return trips usually depart between 3 and 4 p.m., but confirm the pickup time with your water-taxi captain. Other water taxis depart from Boca de Tomatlán, located about 30 minutes south of town by public bus. These Boca de Tomatlán water taxis are a better option than those at Playa Los Muertos if you want more flexible departure and return times from the southern beaches. Generally, they leave on the hour for the southern shore destinations, or more frequently if there's heavy traffic. The price is about $10 round-trip with rates clearly posted on a sign on the beach. You can hire a private, boat taxi for between $35 and $50 (depending on your destination), which allows you to choose your own return time. The boats take up to eight people for that price, so people often band together at the beach to hire one.

Fast Facts: Puerto Vallarta

American Express

The local office (Morelos 660, at the corner of Abasolo; ☎ 01-800-333-3211 in Mexico, or 322-223-2955) is open Monday to Friday 9 a.m. to 6 p.m. and Saturday 9 a.m. to 1 p.m. This location offers excellent, efficient, travel-agency services in addition to offering currency-exchange and traveler's checks services.

Area Code

The telephone area code is **322. Note:** The area code changed from 3 in November 2001. The area code for Nuevo Vallarta and the northern areas is **329.**

Babysitters

Most of the larger hotels can easily arrange babysitters, but many speak limited English. Rates range from $3 to $8 per hour.

Banks, ATMs, and Currency Exchange

Banks are located throughout downtown and in the other prime shopping areas of Vallarta. Most banks are open Monday to Friday 9 a.m. to 5 p.m. with partial hours on Saturday. ATMs can be found throughout Vallarta, including the central plaza downtown. They're increasingly becoming the most favorable way to exchange currency because they offer bank rates plus 24-hour, self-service convenience. Money exchange houses *(casas de cambio)* are also located throughout town and offer longer hours than the banks with only slightly lower exchange rates.

Business Hours

Most offices maintain traditional Mexican hours of operation (9 a.m. to 2 p.m. and 4 p.m. to 8 p.m., daily), but shops remain open throughout the day. Offices tend to be closed on Saturday and Sunday, but shops are open on Saturday, at least, and increasingly offer limited hours of operation on Sunday. During peak season, many shops and galleries remain open as late as 10 p.m.

Climate

It's warm all year with tropical temperatures; however, evenings and early mornings in the winter months can turn quite cool. Summers are sunny, but an increase in humidity during the rainy season, between May and October, is the norm. Rains come almost every afternoon in June and July. These usually brief but strong showers are just enough to cool off the air for evening activities. September is the month in which heat and humidity are the least comfortable and rains are the heaviest.

Consular Agents

Both the U.S. and Canadian consulates maintain offices here in the building on the southern border of the central plaza (note the U.S. and Canadian flags). The **U.S. Consular Agency** office (☎ 322-222-0069; Fax: 322-223-0074; both available 24 hours a day for emergencies) is open Monday to Friday 10 a.m. to 2 p.m. The **Canadian Consulate** (☎ 322-222-5398, 322-223-0858; 24-hour emergency line 01-800-706-2900) is open Monday to Friday 9 a.m. to 5 p.m.

Emergencies

Police emergency (☎ 060); **local police** (☎ 322-221-2588, 322-221-0759); **intensive care ambulance** (☎ 322-225-0386; **Note:** English-speaking assistance is not always available at this number); **Red Cross** (☎ 322-222-1533).

Hospitals

Ameri-Med Urgent Care (☎ 322-221-0023; Fax: 322-221-0026; Internet: www.amerimed-hospitals.com) offers health-care service 24 hours a day that meets U.S. standards and is located at the entrance to Marina Vallarta in the Neptune Plaza. In addition to excellent diagnostic capabilities, it also has emergency facilities and helicopters to evacuate patients to the United States. The new **San Javier Marina Hospital** (☎ 322-226-1010) also offers U.S.-standards health-care service that's available 24 hours. It's located on the main highway across from the cruise-ship terminal (Terminal Marítima).

Information

The **Municipal Tourism Office** (Juárez and Independencia; ☎ 322-223-2500, ext. 230, ask for the Tourism Office) is in a corner of the white Presidencia Municipal building (city hall) on the northwest end of the main square. In addition to offering a listing of current events and a collection of promotional brochures for local activities and services, these folks can also assist you with specific questions — an English-speaking person is usually on staff. This is also the office of the tourist police. It's open Monday to Friday 9 a.m. to 8 p.m. During low season, the office has been known to close for lunch between 1 and 3 p.m. or 2 and 4 p.m.

The **State Tourism Office** (Plaza Marina L 144, 2nd floor; ☎ 322-221-2676, 322-221-2677, 322-221-2678) also offers promotional brochures and can assist you with specific questions about Puerto Vallarta and other points within the state of Jalisco including Guadalajara, the Costa Alegre, and the town of Tequila. It's open Monday to Friday 9 a.m. to 7 p.m. and Saturday 9 a.m. to 1 p.m.

Internet Access

Puerto Vallarta is probably the best-connected destination in Mexico as far as the Internet goes. Of the numerous cyber-cafes around town, one of the most popular is **The Net House** (Ignacio L. Vallarta 232, two blocks past the southbound bridge; ☎ 322-222-6953; E-mail: info@ vallartacafes.com). It's open daily 7 a.m. to 2 a.m. Rates are $4 per hour, and there are 21 computers with fast connections and English keyboards. **Café Net** (Olas Altas 250, at the corner of Basilio Badillo; ☎ 322-222-0092) has become a social hub. Rates run $2 for 30 minutes. Complete computer services, a full bar, and food service are also available. It's open daily 8 a.m. to 2 a.m. Some hotels also offer e-mail kiosks in their lobbies, but this is a more expensive option than the Net cafes.

Maps

One of the best around is the free American Express map, usually found at the tourist information offices and the local American Express office. Other free maps of the area are available at the Municipal Tourism Office, on the southeast corner of city hall (the corner nearest to the Our Lady of Guadalupe church).

Newspapers/Magazines

Vallarta Today, a daily English-language newspaper (☎ 322-225-3323, 322-224-2829), is a good source for local information and upcoming events. The quarterly city magazine, *Vallarta Lifestyles* (☎ 322-221-0106), is also very popular. It has lots of helpful information and good colored maps of all the major tourist areas. Both publications are available for sale at area newsstands and hotel gift shops although you can also find them distributed for free at local businesses. The weekly *P.V. Tribune* (☎ 322-223-0585) is distributed free throughout town and offers an objective local viewpoint.

Pharmacy

CMQ Farmacia (Basilio Badillo 365; ☎ 322-222-1330) is open 24 hours and can also deliver to your hotel free of charge with a minimum purchase of $10. **Farmacia Guadalajara** (Emiliano Zapata 232; ☎ 322-224-1811) is also open 24 hours a day.

Police

The policemen in white, safari-style uniforms with white pith helmets belong to a special corps of English-speaking police established to assist tourists. For the main police department, call ☎ 322-221-2588 or 322-221-0759.

Post Office

The post office *(correo)* (Mina 188; ☎ 322-222-1888) is open Monday to Friday 9:00 a.m. to 6:30 p.m. and Saturday 9:00 a.m. to 1:00 p.m.

Safety

Puerto Vallarta enjoys a very low crime rate. Public transportation is perfectly safe to use, and tourist police (dressed in white safari uniforms with white hats) are available to answer questions, give directions, and offer assistance. Most crimes or encounters with the police are linked to using or purchasing drugs, so simply don't do it. **Note:** The tourist police are making a more frequent habit of conducting random personal searches for drugs. Although some questions have arisen about their right to do this, the best course of action is to comply if they want to frisk you — objecting may result in a free tour of the local jail. Report any unusual incidents to the local consular office.

Special Events

Each November, **Fiestas del Mar** (SeaFest) is celebrated with the Gourmet Dining Festival, a cultural festival, art exhibitions, tennis tournaments, regattas, and more. Dates vary, so call the Tourism Board (☎ 888-384-6822 from the U.S.) for dates and a schedule.

From December 1 through December 12, the **Festival of the Virgin of Guadalupe** — Mexico's patron saint — is celebrated in one of the most authentic displays of culture and community in Mexico. Each business, neighborhood, association, and group makes a pilgrimage (called *peregrinaciones*) to the Church of Our Lady of Guadalupe where offerings are exchanged for a brief blessing by the priest. These processions, especially those offered by hotels, often include floats, Aztec dancers, and mariachis, and fireworks usually follow. Hotels frequently invite guests to participate in the walk to the church. It's an event not to be missed.

Taxes

There's a 15% value-added tax (IVA) on goods and services, and it's generally included in the posted price.

Taxis

Taxis are plentiful and relatively inexpensive. Most trips from downtown to the northern Zona Hotelera and Marina Vallarta cost between $3.50 and $5; trips between Marina Vallarta and Mismaloya Beach to the south costs $8. Rates are charged by zone and are generally posted in the lobbies of hotels. Taxis can also be hired by the hour or day for longer trips when you prefer to leave the driving to someone else. Rates run between $10 and $12 per hour with discounts available for full-day rates

Telephone

Avoid the phone booths that have signs in English advising you to call home using a special 800 number — these are absolute rip-offs and can cost as much as $20 US per minute. The least expensive way to call is by using a Telmex (LADATEL) pre-paid phone card, available at most pharmacies and mini-supers, using the official Telmex (Lada) public phones. In, Mexico you need to dial 001 prior to a number to reach the United States and you need to preface long distance calls within Mexico by dialing 01.

Time Zone

Puerto Vallarta operates on central standard time, but Mexico's observance of daylight savings time varies somewhat from that in the United States.

Chapter 16

Dining in Puerto Vallarta

• •

In This Chapter

▶ Discovering Puerto Vallarta's best restaurants

▶ Finding a restaurant with true Mexican ambiance

▶ Dining on the boardwalk and in the jungle

• •

*P*uerto Vallarta has the most exceptional dining scene of any resort town in Mexico. Over 250 restaurants serve cuisines from around the world in addition to fresh seafood and regional dishes. Chefs from France, Switzerland, Germany, Italy, and Argentina have come for visits and then stayed on to open restaurants of their own. In celebration of the diversity of dining experiences available, Vallarta's culinary community hosts a 2-week-long Gourmet Dining Festival each November.

Nonetheless, dining is not limited to high-end options — there are plenty of small, family-owned restaurants, local Mexican kitchens, and vegetarian cafes. Vallarta also has its share of imported, food-and-fun chains: Hard Rock Cafe, Planet Hollywood, Outback Steakhouse, and even Hooters. I won't bother to review these restaurants because the consistency and decor are so familiar. Resist the temptation to go with what you know. Trust me — the locally owned restaurants offer both the best food and the best value.

Contrary to conventional travel wisdom, most of the best restaurants in the Marina Vallarta area are actually located in the hotels. Especially notable are **Andrea,** at Velas Vallarta, for fine Italian cuisine, and **Garibaldi,** on the beachfront of the Westin Regina Resort, for exceptional seafood. (See Chapter 14 for more information on these resorts.) Other choices are found along the boardwalk bordering the marina yacht harbor.

The best inexpensive local spots are found downtown. The long-standing favorite spot for light meals and fresh fruit drinks is the tiny **Tutifruti** (Morelos 552; ☎ **322-222-1068**), which is open Monday through Saturday 8 a.m. to 8 p.m. A favorite for inexpensive grub is **Archi's** (Morelos 799 at Pípila, behind Carlos O'Brian's; ☎ **322-222-4383**), which serves only (great) chargrilled hamburgers, chicken burgers, fish-filet burgers, hot dogs, and homemade fries in a surfer-inspired atmosphere. Archi's is perfect for late-night munchies — open 11 a.m. to 1 a.m. Tuesday to Sunday — but remember to bring cash because credit cards aren't accepted. An inexpensive, bountiful, and delicious vegetarian lunch buffet is a daily hit at **Planeta Vegetariano** (Iturbide 270, just down the street from the main church; ☎ **322-223-3073**). The buffet is offered from 11 a.m. to 5:30 p.m. and costs $4.50. Like Archi's, credit cards are taboo here too. À la carte dinners are served 6 to 10 p.m. Planeta Vegetariano is closed on Sundays.

The most condensed restaurant area, "Zona Romántica," is south of the Cuale River. The street, Basilio Badillo, is even nicknamed "Restaurant Row." A second main dining drag has emerged along Calle Olas Altas where you can find all varieties of foods and price categories. The wide sidewalks are lined with cafes and espresso bars, which are generally open 7 a.m. to midnight.

As in many of Mexico's beach resorts, even the finest restaurants in town can be comfortably casual when it comes to dress. Men seldom wear jackets, although ladies are frequently seen in dressy resort wear — basically, everything goes. Remember that dinner tends to take on the dual nature of Puerto Vallarta — many tourists dine at earlier hours, but locals are apt to just be thinking about dinner at 9 p.m., so many restaurants stay open late.

Vallarta on the whole is a very child-friendly place, and families are welcome to bring their children almost anywhere. If your young ones are particular to more American tastes, standards like McDonald's, Burger King, and Hard Rock Cafe — good choices — are here, but you may also want to try one of their Mexican counterparts — Carlos O'Brian's or Papaya 3, both located downtown.

All the restaurants I include in the following listings are arranged alphabetically with their location and general price category noted. Please refer to the Introduction of *Mexico's Beach Resorts For Dummies* for an explanation of the price categories. Remember that tips generally run about 15%, and most wait-staff really depend on these for their income, so be generous if the service warrants.

Please see the "Menu Glossary" in Appendix E for more information on Mexican cuisine.

Puerto Vallarta's Best Restaurants

Unless it is the height of high seasons, reservations are generally not necessary — especially with the number and range of excellent restaurants in Vallarta. I've noted reservation information for the few exceptions that tend to be very busy.

Marina Vallarta Dining

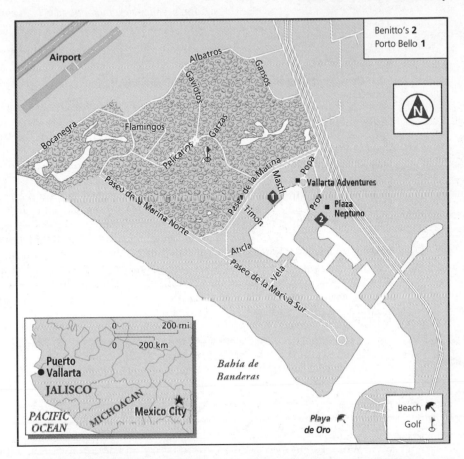

Benitto's **2**
Porto Bello **1**

Airport
Albatros
Gaviotas
Gansos
Bocanegra
Flamingos
Pelicanos
Garzas
Paseo de la Marina Norte
Paseo de la Marina
Timón
Mastil
Popa
Proa
Vallarta Adventures
Plaza Neptuno
Ancla
Vela
Paseo de la Marina Sur

0   200 mi
0   200 km

Puerto Vallarta
JALISCO
MICHOACAN
PACIFIC OCEAN
Mexico City

Bahía de Banderas

Playa de Oro

Beach
Golf

Adobe Café
$$$ Centro/Restaurant Row   INTERNATIONAL

Adobe Café offers a stylish atmosphere and innovative cuisine based on traditional Mexican specialties. A Santa Fe-style decor with rustic wood accents provides a serene backdrop, and tables are comfortably large — perfect for enjoying a leisurely meal. Waiters possess that ideal skill of being attentive without being intrusive. The menu features imaginative dishes, including grilled jumbo shrimp battered in coconut and served with homemade apple sauce, penne pasta with Italian sausage in a creamy tequila sauce, and tenderloin of beef stuffed with *huitlacoche* (wild mushroom that grows on a corn stalk; it is black in color with a very delicate flavor) in a cheese sauce — to name just a few specialties. The enclosed, air-conditioned atmosphere eliminates the street noise that's prevalent at many in-town restaurants, which makes Adobe a serene setting — ideal for a romantic evening. It's located opposite Los Pibes restaurant on the Calle de los Cafés, or Restaurant Row.

Basilio Badillo 252, corner with Ignacio L. Vallarta. ☎ ***322-222-6720**, 322-223-1925. Internet:* www.adobecafe.com.mx. *Reservations recommended in high season. Main courses: $11–$19. MC, V. Open: Wed–Mon 6–11 p.m. Closed Aug–Sept.*

Archie's Wok

$$ Centro/Zona Romántica   ASIAN/SEAFOOD

Since 1986, Archie's has been legendary in Puerto Vallarta for serving original cuisine influenced by the intriguing flavors of Thailand, China, and the Philippines. Archie was Hollywood director John Huston's private chef during the years Huston spent in the area. Today, Archie's wife Cindy continues his legacy. Their Thai mai tai and other tropical drinks are made from only fresh fruit and juices. The drinks are a good way to kick off a meal here as are the Filipino spring rolls, which are consistently crispy and delicious. The popular Singapore fish fillet features lightly battered fillet strips in a sweet-and-sour sauce, and the Thai garlic shrimp are prepared with fresh garlic, ginger, cilantro, and black pepper. Vegetarians have plenty of options, including the broccoli, tofu, mushroom, and cashew stir-fry in a black bean and sherry sauce. Finish things off with the signature Spice Islands coffee or a slice of lime cheese pie. Live classical music sets the atmosphere in Archie's Oriental garden Thursday to Saturday from 8 to 11 p.m.

Francisco Rodríguez 130, ½ block from the Los Muertos pier. ☎ *322-222-0411. E-mail:* awok@pvnet.com.mx. *Main courses: $6–$12. AE, MC, V. Open: Mon–Sat 2–11 p.m. Closed Sept–Oct.*

Benitto's

$ Marina Vallarta   CAFÉ

Wow! What a sandwich! Benitto's food is reason enough to come, but this tiny yet terrific cafe (located inside the Plaza Neptuno) also offers an original array of sauces and very personable — albeit slow — service. Popular with locals for light breakfasts, filling lunches, or even fondue and wine in the evenings, Benitto's is the best place in town to find pastrami, corned beef, or other traditional (gringo!) sandwich fare, all served on your choice of gourmet bread. Draft beer and wine are available as are Benitto's specialty infused waters.

Inside Plaza Neptuno, Francisco Medina Ascencio by Marina Vallarta. ☎ *322-209-0287. Main courses: $2.50–$7.00; breakfast $2.00–$5.00. No credit cards. Open: Daily 8 a.m.–11 p.m.*

Café des Artistes

$$$$ Centro   FRENCH/INTERNATIONAL

If you want one over-the-top dining experience in Puerto Vallarta, Café des Artistes is the hands-down choice. Creative in its menu and innovative

Downtown Puerto Vallarta Dining

Adobe Café **12**
Archi's **3**
Archie's Wok **16**
Café des Artistes **6**
Café Maximilian **15**
Café San Angel **14**
de Santos **2**
Fajita Republic **13**
La Bodeguita del Medio **1**
La Dolce Vita **5**

La Palapa **17**
Las Palomas **7**
Los Pibes **11**
Planeta Vegetariano **9**
Red Cabbage Café
  (El Repollo Rojo) **18**
Rito's Baci **4**
Trio **10**
Tutifruti **8**

in design, the dinner-only restaurant rivals those in any major metropolitan city for its culinary sophistication. Located in a restored house
that resembles a castle, the interior combines murals, lush fabrics, and
an array of original works of art. The Nobel Prize-winning Mexican nov-
elist Carlos Fuentes wrote of this restaurant, "At Café des Artistes, there
is no dish that is not a work of art, nor a work of art that does not feed
the spirit." Of the three distinct dining areas, my favorite is the terraced
garden, open only during the winter and spring. (Be sure to request it
when making a reservation.) The remaining choices include a street-side
balcony and the various interior dining rooms. Despite the attention
given to the decorative setting, the real star here is the food — the award-
winning chef and owner, Thierry Blouet, is both a member of the French
Academie Culinaire and a Maitre Cuisinier de France (and to think, he
never took one cooking class in France!). The menu draws heavily on
Chef Blouet's French training, yet uses regional specialty ingredients. A
few of the noteworthy entrees include shrimp sautéed with mushrooms,

guajillo chili (a dry mild-flavored chile pepper that makes a dark red sauce) and *raicilla* (an alcoholic drink, similar to mezcal that comes from the single destillation of a plant called lechiguilla that is from the area that surrounds the bay) sauce, and the renowned roasted duck glazed with honey, soy, ginger, and lime sauce, and served with a pumpkin risotto. And speaking of pumpkin, don't miss the signature starter, pumpkin and prawn soup served from a carved gourd. The only downside here is that Café des Artistes is easily the most expensive meal in town, but it's worth the splurge.

Guadalupe Sanchez 740, at Leona Vicario. ☎ *322-222-3228/29/30. Main courses: $9–$24. AE, MC, V. Open: Daily 6–11:30 p.m.*

Café Maximilian
$$$ **Centro/Zona Romántica   INTERNATIONAL**

Café Maximilian is the prime place to go if you want to combine exceptional food with great people-watching. This bistro-style cafe has a casually elegant atmosphere with a genuinely European feel to it. Austrian-born owner Andreas Rupprechter is always on hand to ensure that the service is as impeccable as the food is delicious. Indoor, air-conditioned dining is at cozy tables dressed in crisp white linens; sidewalk tables are larger and great for groups of friends. The cuisine merges old-world European preparations with regional, fresh ingredients. My personal favorite is the filet of trout with almonds and a creamy beet sauce, served on a bed of spinach. I like it so much that I've never tried any other dish, although friends tell me the mustard chicken with mashed potatoes is excellent, and the braised baby lamb with rosemary and poblano peppers is simply divine. Maximilian also offers northern-European classics like *rahmschnitzel* (sauteed pork loin and homemade noodles in a creamy mushroom sauce). Desserts are especially tempting, as are the gourmet coffees — Maximilian has its own Austrian cafe and pastry shop next door. It's located at the intersection of calles Basilio Badillo and Olas Altas, in front of the Playa los Arcos Hotel.

Olas Altas 380, on the sidewalk level of the Playa Los Arcos Hotel. ☎ *322-223-0760. Reservations recommended in high season. Main courses: $7–$18. AE, MC, V. Open: Mon–Sat 6–11 p.m.*

Café San Angel
$ **Centro/Zona Romántica   CAFÉ**

A comfortable, classic, sidewalk cafe, Café San Angel has become a local gathering place from sunrise to sunset. For breakfast, choose between a burrito stuffed with eggs and chorizo sausage, a three-egg Western omelet, crèpes filled with mushrooms, or a tropical fruit plate. Deli sandwiches, crèpes, and pastries round out the small but ample menu. The cafe also has exceptional fruit smoothies (like the Yelapa — a blend of mango, banana, and orange juice) and perfectly made espresso drinks. Note that the service is reliably slow and frequently frustrating, so choose this place if time is on your side. Bar service and Internet access are also available.

Olas Altas 449, corner of Francisco Rodríguez. ☎ 322-223-2160. Main courses: $3.50–$6.00; breakfast $3.50–$5.00. Open: Daily 8 a.m. to midnight.

de Santos
$$ Centro   MEDITERRANEAN

From the moment it opened two years ago, de Santos quickly became the hot spot in town for late-night dining and bar action. Although the dining aspect initially didn't live up to the atmosphere and music, it does now. The fare is Mediterranean-inspired; the best bets include lightly breaded calamari, seafood casserole, lobster ravioli, and excellent thin-crust pizzas. Good bets are the nightly specials — always the most creative offerings on the menu. The cool, refined interior, with exposed brick walls, crisp white-clothed tables, and lots of votive candles, feels more urban than resort, and the joint boasts the most sophisticated sound system in town — including its own DJ who spins vinyl to match the mood of the crowd. It probably helps that one of the partners is also a member of Mana, the chart-topping, wildly popular Latin group. Prices are extremely reasonable for the quality and overall experience of an evening here. Start with dinner — then stay on and enjoy the most favored bar in town.

Morelos 771, between Pipila and Leona Vicario. ☎ 322-223-3052. Main courses: $5–$15; wine and mixed drinks $3–$5. AE, MC, V. Open: Dinner 5 p.m.–1 a.m.; bar open until 4 a.m. on weekends.

El Repollo Rojo (Red Cabbage Café)
$ Centro   MEXICAN

This tiny, hard-to-find cafe is worth the effort — a visit here rewards you with exceptional, traditional Mexican cuisine and a whimsical crash course in the contemporary culture of Mexico. The small room is covered wall to wall and table to table with photographs, paintings, movie posters, and news clippings about the cultural icons of Mexico. The Mexican painter Frida Kahlo figures prominently in the decor, and there's a special menu that duplicates dishes she and husband Diego Rivera prepared for guests. Specialties from all over Mexico are featured, including the divine *chiles en nogada* (*poblano chiles* stuffed with ground beef, pine nuts, and raisins, topped with a sweet cream sauce and served cold), an intricate chicken *mole* from Puebla, and the hearty *carne en su jugo* (steak in its juice). Red Cabbage Café is not the place for an intimate conversation however — the poor acoustics cause everyone's conversations to blend together, although generally what you're hearing from adjacent tables are raves about the food.

Calle Rivera del Río 204 A, across from the Río Cuale. ☎ 322-223-0411. Main courses: $3–$10. No credit cards. Open: Daily 5–11 p.m.

Fajita Republic

$$ Centro/Restaurant Row   MEXICAN/SEAFOOD/STEAKS

Fajita Republic has hit on a winning recipe: delicious food, ample portions, welcoming atmosphere, and low prices. The restaurant is casual, fun, and festive in atmosphere and situated in a garden of mango and palm trees with a view of the passing action on the bordering street. The specialty is, of course, fajitas, grilled to perfection in every variety: steak, chicken, shrimp, combo, and vegetarian. All come with a generous tray of salsas and toppings. This tropical grill also serves sumptuous BBQ ribs, Mexican *molcajetes* (dishes served in these stone bowls traditionally used in Mexico for grinding and pureeing) with incredibly tender strips of marinated beef fillet, and grilled shrimp. Starters include fresh guacamole served in a giant spoon and the ever-popular Mayan cheese sticks (cheese, breaded and deep-fried). Try a "Fajita Rita Mango Margarita" — or one of the other spirited temptations — served in oversized mugs or by the pitcher.

Vallarta's jungle dining

Want to get wild while you dine? One of the unique attractions of Puerto Vallarta is its "jungle restaurants," located to the south of town toward Mismaloya. Each restaurant offers open-air dining in a tropical setting by the sea or beside a mountain river. A stop for swimming and lunch at one of these places is included in many of the "jungle" or "tropical" tours.

If you travel on your own, a taxi is the best transportation because all the jungle restaurants are located quite a distance from the main highway. Taxis are usually waiting for return patrons.

Just past Boca de Tomatlán, at Highway 200 Km 20, is **Chico's Paradise** (☎ **322-222-0747**, 322-223-0413; E-mail: chicos@prodigy.net), offers spectacular views of massive rocks and the surrounding jungle and mountains. Natural pools and waterfalls for swimming are located here, plus a small *mercado* (market) selling pricey trinkets. The menu features excellent seafood (the seafood platter for two is excellent — lobster, clam, giant shrimp, crab, and fish fillet) as well as Mexican dishes. The quality is quite good, and the portions are generous, although prices are higher than in town — remember, you're paying for the setting. Chico's is open daily from 9 a.m. to 7 p.m.

The newest and most recommendable of the jungle restaurants is **El Nogalito** (☎ and fax: **322-221-5225**). Located beside a clear jungle stream, this exceptionally clean, beautifully landscaped ranch serves lunch, beverages, and snacks on a shady terrace in a very relaxing atmosphere. Several hiking routes also depart from the grounds. El Nogalito's guides point out the native plants, birds, and wildlife of the area. To get to El Nogalito, take a taxi or travel to Punta Negra, just about 5 miles (8km) south of downtown Puerto Vallarta. A well-marked sign points to Calzada del Cedro, a dirt road leading to the ranch. El Nogalito is much closer to town than the other jungle restaurants and is open daily from noon to 5:30 p.m.

Pino Suárez 321, corner of Basilio Badillo, 1 block north of Olas Altas. ☎ *322-222-3131. Main courses: $9–$17. MC, V. Open: Daily 4–11 p.m.*

La Bodeguita del Medio

$$$ Centro   CUBAN

This genuine Cuban restaurant and bar is a local favorite for its casual energy, terrific live Cuban music, and the *mojitos* — a stiff rum-based drink with fresh mint and lime juice. The food is as authentic as the

atmosphere. Black beans and rice, a variety of styles of plantains, and delicious seafood casseroles are but a few of the offerings. La Bodeguita del Medio, a branch of the original Bodeguita in Havana (reportedly Hemingway's favorite restaurant there), opened in 1942, and if you can't get to that one, the Vallarta version has successfully imported the essence. (Plus, there's a small souvenir shop with Cuban cigars, rum, and other items for sale.) The downstairs dining area has large wooden windows that open up to the *malecón* street action, and the upstairs offers terrific views of the bay. The walls throughout this restaurant are decorated with old photographs and the scrawled signatures of the many patrons who have beaten a path here — if you can, find a spot and add yours!

Malecón (at Allende). ☎ *322-223-1585. Main courses: $5–$19. AE, MC, V. Open: Daily 11:30 a.m.–3:00 a.m.*

La Dolce Vita

$$ Centro   ITALIAN

This popular eatery combines good food, a casually upbeat atmosphere, attentive service, and great entertainment. Overlooking the *malecón,* La Dolce Vita offers excellent views and prime people-watching through its oversized windows and second-floor balcony. Despite its choice location and superb food, prices remain more than reasonable. Owned by an engaging group of Italian friends, the food is authentic in preparation and flavor, from the thin-crust, brick-oven pizzas to savory homemade pastas — my favorite is the "Braccio de Fiero," topped with spinach, black olives, and fresh tomatoes. Sultry jazz by the house band The Sweet Life plays Thursday and Friday evenings.

Paseo Díaz Ordaz 674. ☎ *322-222-3852. Main courses: $5.00–$15.00; wine and mixed drinks $2.00–$3.60. AE, MC, V. Open: Mon–Sat noon to 2 a.m.; Sun 6 p.m.–1 a.m.*

La Palapa

$$$ Centro/Zona Romántica   SEAFOOD/MEXICAN

This colorfully decorated, open-air, *palapa*-roofed (thatched umbrella) restaurant on the beach is a decades-old local favorite, yet recent improvements have taken it to a higher level. Enjoy a tropical breakfast by the sea, lunch on the beach, cocktails at sunset, or a romantic dinner — at night the staff sets cloth-covered tables in the sand. For lunch and dinner, seafood is the specialty. Featured dishes include macadamia and coconut shrimp in a litchi-fruit sauce and pan-seared scallops over a mussel risotto, served with mango chutney. The fresh catch is listed on a chalkboard and is served in much thicker portions than at most local restaurants — simply sumptuous, and prepared to your preference. La Palapa's location in the heart of Playa Los Muertos makes it an exceptional place to either start or end the day; I favor it for breakfast or, even better, for a late-night, sweet temptation and specialty coffee enjoyed while watching the moon over the bay with the sand at my feet. A particular favorite is their all-you-can-enjoy Sunday brunch, which entitles you to a spot on popular Playa Los Muertos for the day! There are acoustic guitars and vocals nightly from 8 to 11 p.m., frequently performed by the very talented owner Alberto himself.

Pulpito 103. ☎ *322-222-5225. Reservations recommended for dinner in high season. Main courses: $7.00–$25.00; salads or sandwiches $5.00–$10.00; breakfast $2.50–$7.00. AE, MC, V. Open: Daily 8 a.m.–11 p.m.*

Las Palomas

$ Centro MEXICAN

One of Puerto Vallarta's first restaurants, this is the power-breakfast place of choice for local movers and shakers — and a generally popular hangout for everyone else throughout the day. Authentic in atmosphere and menu, Las Palomas is one of Puerto Vallarta's few genuine Mexican restaurants and has an atmosphere of a gracious home. Breakfast is the best value. The staff pours mugs of steaming coffee spiced with cinnamon as soon as you're seated. Try the classic *huevos rancheros* (fried eggs served on a soft fried corn tortilla and topped with red sauce — spicy or mild) or *chilaquiles* (tortilla strips, fried and topped with a red or green spicy sauce, cream, cheese, and fried eggs). Lunch and dinner offer other traditional Mexican specialties plus a selection of stuffed crèpes. This best place for checking out the *malecón* and watching the sun set while sipping an icy margarita is in the spacious bar or upstairs terrace.

Paseo Díaz Ordaz 594. ☎ *322-222-3675. Main courses: $6.00–$18.00; breakfast $3.50–$7.00; lunch $5.00–$12.00. AE, MC, V. Open: Daily 8 a.m.–11 p.m.*

Los Pibes

$$$$ Centro/Restaurant Row (& Marina Vallarta) ARGENTINIAN/ STEAKS

You won't find a better steak anywhere in Vallarta — or many other places. Los Pibes offers signature thick cuts, exceptional quality, and a variety of preparations. Argentinean Cristina Juhas opened this restaurant in 1994 for her *pibes* (children), and the rave reviews have grown over the years. You select your steak from a tray of fresh meat (portions are huge, all imported from the U.S.). While the steak is being prepared, try one of the wonderful *empanadas,* pastry filled with meat or corn and cheese, or savor an order of *alubias* (marinated beans served with bread). The homemade sausage is also delicious, and you won't find a better *chimichurri* sauce (made of garlic, parsley, mint, onion, and olive oil). In addition to beef, Los Pibes has an ample selection of salads, side dishes, chicken, and pastas, as well as an excellent wine list. This slice of Argentina is on Basilio Badillo across from Adobe Café. A second location, equally delicious, is located on the Marina Vallarta *malecón* (☎ 322-221-0669).

Basilio Badillo 261. ☎ 322-223-1557. Reservations recommended in high season. Main courses: $12–$22. AE, MC, V. Open: Wed–Mon 2 p.m.–2 a.m.

Porto Bello

$$$ **Marina Vallarta   ITALIAN**

One of the first restaurants in the marina, Porto Bello remains a favorite. It features authentically flavorful Italian dishes in a casual atmosphere overlooking the marina and exceptional service. For starters, the fried calamari is delicately seasoned, and the grilled vegetable antipasto can easily serve as a full meal. Signature dishes include Fusilli Porto Bello prepared with black olives, artichokes, lemon juice, olive oil, and basil, and veal scaloppine with a creamy white-wine sauce, mushrooms, and shrimp. Most people prefer seating on the gazebo-like patio overlooking the boats in the marina. Indoor dining is air-conditioned, and occasionally, live music fills the air in the evenings.

Marina Sol, Local 7 (Marina Vallarta malecón). ☎ 322-221-0003. Main courses: $4–$14. AE, MC, V. Open: Daily noon to 11 p.m.

Rito's Baci

$ **Centro   ITALIAN**

If the food wasn't a reason to come here (and it definitely is), then Rito himself and his gentle, devoted way of caring for every detail of this cozy *trattoria* would be the draw. His grandfather emigrated from Italy, so the recipes and traditions of Italian food come naturally to him. His passion for food is obvious as he describes the specialties, which include lasagna (vegetarian, *verde,* or meat filled); ravioli stuffed with spinach and ricotta cheese; spaghetti with garlic, anchovy, and lemon zest; and a side of homemade Italian sausage. Everything, in fact, is made by hand from fresh ingredients. Pizza lovers favor the Piedmonte, with that famous sausage and mushrooms, and the Horacio, a cheeseless pizza with tomatoes, oregano, and basil. Sandwiches come hot or cold and are a two-handed operation. Rito's is located 1½ blocks off the *malecón* on Josefa O. de Domínguez next to Galeria A.L.

Domínguez 181, between Morelos and Juárez. ☎ 322-222-6448. Pasta $6.50–$9.50; salads and sandwiches $2.00–$5.60; pizzas $13.00–$14.50. MC, V. Open: Daily 1:00–11:30 p.m.

Trio

$$–$$$ Centro   INTERNATIONAL

Trio is the current darling of Vallarta restaurants. Diners are beating a path to this modest but stylish cafe because chef/owner Bernhard Güth's undeniable passion for food is exhibited in each dish. Güth has combined local ingredients with his impressive culinary experience; the result is memorable entrees such as San Blas shrimp in a fennel-tomato vinaigrette served over broiled Nopal cactus, ricotta ravioli with sun-dried tomatoes, and chile-roasted red-snapper filet served over ratatouille and lime cilantro sauce — but these dishes may not be on the menu when you arrive because Trio is a constantly changing work of art! Trio is noted for its perfect melding of Mexican and Mediterranean flavors. What's great about this place, besides everything I've already mentioned, is that despite a sophisticated menu, the atmosphere is always comfortable and welcoming — Bernhard is regularly seen chatting with guests at the end of an evening. A rooftop bar area makes for a comfortable wait for a table or a great spot to enjoy an after-dinner coffee. A real treat!

Guerrero 264. ☎ *322-222-2196. Reservations recommended. Main courses: $6.50–$19. Lunch available in high season only. AE, MC, V. Open: Mon–Sat noon to 4 p.m.; dinner daily 6 p.m. to midnight.*

Chapter 17

Having Fun On and Off the Beach in Puerto Vallarta

In This Chapter

▶ Hitting the beaches Puerto Vallarta style

▶ Enjoying Puerto Vallarta's best sports on land and by sea

▶ Seeing the sights like a tour professional

▶ Dancing until dawn, and maybe even later

Decisions, decisions . . . With so many fun-filled options competing for your time, choosing among them should be the biggest problem you encounter on a Vallarta vacation. Besides a bevy of beautiful beaches — some secluded coves, other outrageous in their people-watching potential — dry land also offers intriguing and entertaining possibilities.

In this chapter, I give you an overview of the best beaches tucked into the 26 miles of coastline surrounding Bahía de Banderas and the best ways to get to each. I also reveal the most interesting sights in town and a few cool activities to try.

Vallarta is gaining recognition as a veritable treasure chest for eco-tourism. A number of tours permit you to explore the culture or nature of the area — while having a sunny-good time in the process. I cover these excursions as well.

Hitting the Beaches

For years, beaches were Puerto Vallarta's main attraction. Although visitors today explore more of the surrounding geography, the golden sands and cobalt waters are still a powerful draw. The coast of Bahía de Banderas is over 50 miles with 26 miles of beaches ranging from action-packed party spots to secluded coves accessible only by boat.

Puerto Vallarta Area

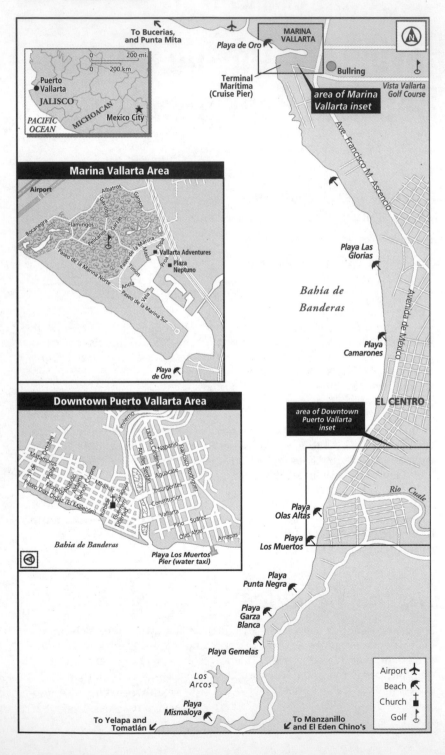

To Bucerias, and Punta Mita

Playa de Oro

MARINA VALLARTA

area of Marina Vallarta inset

Terminal Marítima (Cruise Pier)

Bullring

Vista Vallarta Golf Course

200 mi
0
200 km
0

Puerto Vallarta

JALISCO

PACIFIC OCEAN

MICHOACAN

Mexico City

Marina Vallarta Area

Airport

Albatros

Gaviotas

Garzas

Bocanegra

Flamingos

Pelicanos

Garzas

Paseo de la Marina Norte

Paseo de la Marina

Popa

Masti

Proa

Timón

Ancla

Paseo de la Marina Sur

Paseo de Vela

Vallarta Adventures

Plaza Neptuno

Playa de Oro

Playa Las Glorias

Bahía de Banderas

Playa Camarones

Ave. Francisco M. Ascencio

Avenida de México

EL CENTRO

area of Downtown Puerto Vallarta inset

Downtown Puerto Vallarta Area

Cumbre

Matamoros

Aldama

Abasolo

Peru

Invierno

Lazaro Cardenas

Napapito

Francisco Rodriguez

Aguacate

Insurgentes

Constitución

Vallarta

Pino Suárez

Olas Altas

Amapas

Aquiles Serdán

Miramar

Iturbide

Zaragoza

Guerrero

Libertad

Morelos

Zaragoza

Paseo Díaz Ordaz (El Malecón)

Bahía de Banderas

Playa Los Muertos Pier (water taxi)

Río Cuale

Playa Olas Altas

Playa Los Muertos

Playa Punta Negra

Playa Garza Blanca

Playa Gemelas

Los Arcos

Playa Mismaloya

To Yelapa and Tomatlán

To Manzanillo and El Eden Chino's

Airport ✈

Beach

Church ■

Golf

Northern beaches

The entire northern coastline from Punta Mita to Bucerías is a succession of sandy coves alternating with rocky inlets. For years, the beaches to the north, with their long, clean breaks, have been the favored locale for surfers.

Public transportation to any of the north-shore beaches is easy and inexpensive. Buses and minivans marked "Bucerías" or "Punta Mita" stop at the bus stop in front of the airport gas station. You can ask your driver to let you off at any of the beaches listed above. Buses generally run every 20 minutes from 6 a.m. to 11 p.m., but check with your hotel concierge for current schedules. For the return trip, simply flag a bus down. The cost is less than $2 each way. That price will get you all the way to Punta Mita.

As you travel south on highway 200A from Punta Mita, the first public beach you come to is **Playa Anclote** — a broad, sandy beach with protected swimming areas and a few great *palapa* (thatched roof) restaurants. The water is gentle and shallow for quite a distance out, and boats regularly anchor offshore and take dinghies in for a fresh fish lunch. Of the restaurants, El Anclote and El Dorado are the favorites, and they both have beach chairs available for your post-margarita nap in the sun.

You can also hire a *panga* (small motorized boat) at Playa Anclote from the fisherman's cooperative on the beach and have the captain take you to the **Marietas Islands** just offshore. These uninhabited islands are a great place for bird-watching, diving, snorkeling, or just exploring. Blue-footed booby birds (no joke) can be spotted all along the islands' rocky coast, and giant mantas, sea turtles, and colorful tropical fish swim among the coral cliffs. The islands are honeycombed with caves and hidden beaches — including the stunning Playa de Amor (beach of love) that only appears at low tide. You enter a shallow passageway to access this semi-circular stretch of sand. There's also a cave 40-feet below the surface with an air pocket where divers can dispose of their regulators and have an underwater conversation! Humpback whales congregate around these islands during the winter months, and *pangas* can be rented for a do-it-yourself whale-watching excursion. Trips cost about $20 per hour. You can also visit these islands aboard one of the numerous day cruises that depart from the cruise-ship terminal in Puerto Vallarta.

The **Villa Vera Beach Club,** located 6.9 miles south of El Anclote and 18.1 miles north of Puerto Vallarta, is a great place to spend a day — all the facilities and amenities of a pampering, private club are available at a daily cost of $13.50 for adults and $9 for children. Two crystalline pools — one with a wet bar for adults only — showers, towel service, an exceptional stretch of beach, and a full-service restaurant and bar make this patch of sand a favorite of mine for an indulgent beach day. My friends with kids think it's one of the best places around to spend a day in the sun with the little ones. In addition to the kid-friendly main swimming pool, a full playground with water slides and a tropical bird show are always a hit with the youngsters.

One mile south of Villa Vera is the rustic, natural setting of **Playa Destiladeras.** It has talc-smooth sand and a couple of thatched-roof restaurants, making for a quick but meaningful getaway from town. **Playa Piedra Blanca** and **Playa Manzanillo** are beaches similar in style and spirit located just before the curve in the bay, past the small town of La Cruz de Huanacaxtle.

The small coastal town of **Bucerías,** with its broad, smooth-sand beaches, has caught on as a great day-trip. Come here from Puerto Vallarta to enjoy the long, wide, and uncrowded beach, along with the fresh seafood served at the beachfront restaurants or at one of the great cafes. One of the top choices is **Karen's Place** on the beach at the Costa Dorada, Calle Lazaro Cardenas (☎ 329-298-1499). Open Tuesdays through Sundays from 9 a.m. to 10 p.m., it caters to American tastes and has a super Sunday brunch served from 9 a.m. to 3 p.m. Sunday is also street-market day in town, but in keeping with the casual pace of Bucerías, the market doesn't get going until noon or so. The **Coral Reef Surf Shop** (Heroe de Nacozari 114 F; ☎ 329-298-0261) offers a great selection of surfboards and gear for sale. It also features surfboard and boogie-board rentals, surf lessons, ATV tours, and other adventure tours to surrounding areas.

The gold-sand **beaches of Nuevo Vallarta** are the main reason people choose to stay in Nuevo Vallarta hotels. If you want to check the beaches out for yourself, spend a day at the **Etc. Beach Club** (Paseo de los Cocoteros 38; ☎ 322-297-0174). This casual beach club has a volleyball net, showers, restroom facilities, and food and drink service on the beach (both day and night). Public transportation is okay to get to Nuevo Vallarta, since it is the most economic way to get there in relative comfort — the buses are fairly new and some even have A/C. Taxis are a bit expensive — $13.50 one way, but they are a faster, more convenient way to get to Nuevo Vallarta. To get here from Puerto Vallarta, take the second entrance to Nuevo Vallarta and turn right on Paseo de los Cocoteros; it's past the Vista Bahia hotel. Nuevo Vallarta is south of Bucerías and technically you could say that it also falls on the northern coastline.

The club is open daily during the winter from 11:00 a.m. to 10:30 p.m. and from 11:00 a.m. to 7:00 p.m. in the summer. Bring cash for food and drink purchases — credit cards aren't accepted.

Central and town beaches

In Chapter 14, I caution you that the beaches at **Marina Vallarta,** with darker sand and seasonal inflows of stones, are the least desirable in the area. If you're a traveler whose priority is the beauty of the beach, you'll want to venture to areas other than Marina Vallarta. Though it has its charms, the beaches are not one of them.

The **Hotel Zone** beach runs for three miles from just beyond the cruise-ship terminal to the north to just south of the *malecón* (boardwalk). The names of the beaches change along the way, from Playa de Oro to Playa Camarones, but most people just refer to the hotel property that the beaches front.

It's a wide, clean, and generally uncrowded stretch of sand, but the shore does drop steeply just offshore. This is the best place to rent watersports equipment, especially Jet Skis and sailboards.

As you reach the central town, you may notice that relatively few people choose to swim along the central stretch of sand running from the start of the *malecón* to the Río Cuale, because it's more of a commercial area, and there are no services for chairs or beverages on the sand, although it's a popular place for parasailing.

Playa Los Muertos (also known as Playa Olas Altas or Playa del Sol) begins just south of the Río Cuale and is hands-down the most popular town beach. The water can be rough here, but the wide beach is home to a large array of *palapa* restaurants with food, beverage, and beach-chair service. The two most popular spots to grab some grub are the adjacent El Dorado and La Palapa, both of which are located at the end of Calle Pulpito. On the southern end of this beach is a section known as "Blue Chairs" — the most popular gay beach. Vendors stroll the length of Los Muertos, and beach volleyball, parasailing, and Jet Skis are all popular pastimes.

Playa Mismaloya is in a magnificent, sheltered cove about 6 miles south of town along Highway 200. The water here is clear and beautiful and ideal for snorkeling off the beach. Entrance to the public beach is just to the left of the **La Jolla de Mismaloya Resort and Spa (☎ 226-0660).** Colorful *palapa* restaurants dot the small beach, and you can rent beach chairs for sunbathing. You can also stake out a table under a *palapa* for the day. Using a restaurant's table and *palapa* is a recipro-cal arrangement — the restaurant provides a comfortable place to hang out, and you buy your drinks, snacks, and lunch there. The 1960s Elizabeth Taylor and Richard Burton movie, *Night of the Iguana,* was filmed at Mismaloya. La Jolla de Mismaloya has a restaurant, **La Noche de la Iguana Set Restaurant (☎ 226-0660),** on the restored film set that's open daily noon to 11 p.m. The movie runs continuously in **John Huston's Bar and Grill** (serving drinks and light snacks 11 a.m. to 6 p.m.) located below the La Noche de la Iguana.

Three miles past Mismaloya is **Boca de Tomatlán,** which is similar in setup to Mismaloya but without a large resort looming in the backdrop. Both Mismaloya and Boca de Tomatlán are accessible by public buses that depart from Lázaro Cárdenas Park, at the corner of Basilio Badillo and Insurgentes, every 15 minutes from 5:30 a.m. to 10:00 p.m. and cost just 50¢. La Boca is the end of the bus line and the point at which the highway turns inland.

South-shore beaches

Boca de Tomatlán is also the jumping-off point for the south-shore beaches of **Las Ánimas, Quimixto,** and **Yelapa,** all of which are accessible only by boat. In addition to having the ambiance of a south-seas cove, each location offers intriguing hikes to jungle waterfalls and plays host to restaurants that front a wide beach. Las Animas is my favorite of the three spots. The beach has the most tranquil waters for swimming and two rocky headlands for protection. Quimixto's palm-fringed crescent of sand takes a back seat to hiking and horseback rides to the waterfall. Although the waterfall rages impressively from August to January, as the dry winter season progresses, you're likely to be less than blown away.

Yelapa, located on a beautiful sheltered cove, is the most remote location of these three beaches. Once a haven for those looking to escape the confines of society — or equally as likely, the law — it became a popular haven for long-term, expatriate visitors and artists due to its seclusion, natural beauty, and simplicity of life. Yelapa, which has only solar-powered electricity, also offers a few primitive accommodations, beachside restaurants, and hikes to one of two jungle waterfalls. Although the mellow attitude still prevails, yoga is rapidly becoming the preferred way to reach an altered state of mind here.

For more information on these beaches see Chapter 15.

Finding Water Fun For Everyone

In my opinion, you haven't experienced Puerto Vallarta unless you've been to the bay — on a boat, under the water, or playing along the shoreline. Bahía de Banderas is as deep as the surrounding mountains are high, and with the wealth of sea life found here, you're as likely to spot whales or dolphins as you are to see other tour boats. The view of town from the bay is simply stunning. And, when it comes to having fun in the water, your biggest challenge will be deciding what to do first.

Cruising Puerto Vallarta

Puerto Vallarta offers a number of different boat trips, including sunset cruises and trips for snorkeling, swimming, and diving. Most of the excursions generally travel one of two routes: to the **Marietas Islands,** which are about a 30- to 45-minute boat ride off the northern shore of Bahía de Banderas, or to **Yelapa, Las Ánimas,** or **Quimixto** along the southern shore.

All of the trips to the southern beaches make a stop at **Los Arcos,** an island rock formation south of Puerto Vallarta, for snorkeling. Don't base your opinion of underwater Puerto Vallarta on this location though. Dozens of tour boats dump large numbers of snorkelers overboard at the same time each day, and the fish have figured out that these are the times *not* to be there. Los Arcos is, however, an excellent site for night diving.

When comparing all the boat cruises, note that some include lunch and most provide music and an open bar on board. Most boats leave around 9:30 a.m., stop for 45 minutes of snorkeling, arrive at the beach destination around noon for a 2½ hour stay, and return around 3 p.m. At Quimixto and Yelapa, visitors can take a half-hour hike to a jungle waterfall or rent a horse for the trip. Prices range from $20 for a sunset cruise or a trip (with open bar) to one of the beaches to $70 for an all-day outing with open bar and meals.

Here are some great choices for a boat cruise:

- ✔ One boat, the *Marigalante* (☎ 322 223-0309), is an exact replica of Columbus's ship the *Santa Maria* that was built in honor of the 500-year anniversary of his voyage to the Americas. It offers a daytime "pirate's cruise" complete with picnic barbecue and treasure hunt and a sunset dinner cruise with folkloric dance and fireworks. The day tour is $55 per person, and the sunset dinner cruise is $70 per person.

- ✔ My choice for the best day-trip is an excursion to **Caletas,** the cove where John Huston (the director of such movie classics as *The Maltese Falcon, The Treasure of Sierra Madre,* and *Annie*) made his home for years. **Vallarta Adventures** (☎ 322-297-1212; Internet: www.vallarta-adventures.com) holds the exclusive lease on this private cove and has done an excellent job of restoring Huston's former home, adding exceptional day-spa facilities, and landscaping the beach, which is wonderful for snorkeling. The quality facilities, combined with the relative privacy that this day-trip offers at $65 per person, has made it one of the most popular excursions. Vallarta Adventures also offers an evening cruise that comes complete with dinner and a spectacular contemporary dance show, "Rhythms of the Night."

✔ **Whale-watching tours** are becoming more popular each year because spotting humpback whales is almost a certainty from mid-November (sometimes a few weeks later) through March. For centuries, these majestic whales have migrated to Bahía de Banderas (called Humpback Bay in the 1600s) to reproduce and bear calves. **Open Air Expeditions** (Guerrero 339; ☎ and fax: **322-222-3310;** E-mail: openair@vivamexico.com) is the noted, local, whale-watching authority. These folks offer ecologically oriented tours (for up to 12 people) in small, specially designed, soft boats that allow for better observation from a level that is closer to water and the sound of their engine is less disturbing to the whales than the engines of the larger boats. The twice-daily, $65 tours (8:30 am and 1:30 p.m.) last 4 hours and include a healthful snack and T-shirt.

Vallarta Adventures (☎ **322-297-1212**) offers whale-watching photo excursions in small boats for $70. The trip includes a predeparture briefing on whale behaviors. This company also features whale watching on its tours to the Marietas Islands. For $60 you get lunch, time at a private beach, and an ambiance that is more festive than educational while traveling aboard the large catamaran boats.

Skiing and surfing

Watersports — including water-skiing, parasailing, and windsurfing — are available at many beaches along the Bahía de Banderas. The best-known spot for watersports-equipment rental is **Club Bananas Water Sports Center,** which is located on the beachfront of the Las Palmas Hotel (Avenida Francisco Medina Ascencio Km 2.5, Hotel Zone; ☎ **322-224-0650;** ask for the Water Sports Center). WaveRunners, banana boats, and water-skiing equipment are available for hourly, half-day, or full-day rentals. You can also find rental equipment at Playa Los Muertos in between La Palapa and El Dorado restaurants.

Exploring the deep blue

Although Puerto Vallarta lacks the crystal-clear waters of Cancún and other Caribbean coastal venues, it's still a great dive site. The reefs are much smaller than those is Caribbean destinations, however, the abundance of marine life is spectacular. You can see an abundance of sea life, including giant mantas, sea turtles, dolphins, and tropical fish. During the winter months, you're also apt to hear the beautiful underwater songs of humpback whales as you dive. Underwater enthusiasts from beginners to experts can arrange scuba diving with the following folks:

✔ **Vallarta Adventures** (☎ 322-297-1212; Internet: www.vallarta-adventures.com) is a five-star PADI dive center that offers instructional programs ranging from the resort-course level to instructor certification. Dives take place at Los Arcos, a company-owned site at Caletas Cove, Quimixto Coves, the Marietas Islands, and the offshore El Morro and Chimo reefs.

✔ **Chico's Dive Shop** (Díaz Ordaz 772–5, near Carlos O'Brian's; ☎ 322-222-1895; Internet: www.chicos-diveshop.com) offers similar dive trips and is also a PADI five-star dive center. Chico's is open daily 8 a.m. to 10 p.m. and has branches at the Marriott, Vidafel, Villa del Palmar, Camino Real, Paradise Village, and Playa Los Arcos hotels.

Sailing away

Put some wind in your sails and experience the bay in the most natural of ways:

✔ **Sail Vallarta** (Club de Tenis Puesta del Sol, Local 7-B, Marina Vallarta; ☎ 322-221-0096; E-mail: sail@pnet.puerto.not.mx) offers several different sailboats for hire. A group day-sail, including crew, use of snorkeling equipment, drinks, food, and music, plus a stop at a beach for swimming and lunch, costs $82. Most trips include a crew, but you can make arrangements to sail yourself or on a smaller boat. Prices vary for full boat charters depending on the vessel and amount of time you want to spend on the water.

✔ **Vallarta Adventures** (☎ 322-297-1212; Internet: www.vallarta-adventures.com) also offers two beautiful sailboats for charter and small group sails (up to 12 people for day or evening sails). The service is superb, as is the quality of the food and beverages served on board. And the Vallarta Adventures boats are known for being the sailboats most frequently under sail — many of the other sailing charters prefer to simply motor around the bay.

Reeling in the big one

You can arrange a fishing trip through travel agencies or through the **Cooperativa de Pescadores** (Fishing Cooperative; ☎ 322-222-1202, 322-224-7886) on the *malecón* north of the Río Cuale, next door to the Rosita Hotel. Fishing charters cost $180 to $350 a day for four to eight people; price varies with the size of the boat. Although the posted price at the fishing cooperative is the same as what you'd find through travel agencies, you may be able to negotiate a lower price at the cooperative. Bring cash — the cooperative doesn't accept credit cards. It's open

Monday to Saturday from 7 a.m. to 10 p.m., but make arrangements a day in advance. You can also arrange fishing trips at the Marina Vallarta docks or by calling **Fishing with Carolina** (☎ **322-224-7250,** or cellular (044) 322-292-2953; E-mail: fishingwithcarolina@hotmail.com), which features a 30-foot Uniflite Sportsfisher fully equipped with an English-speaking crew. Fishing trips generally include equipment and bait, but drinks, snacks, and lunch are optional, so check to see what the price includes.

Swimming with dolphins

Ever been kissed by a dolphin? Take advantage of a unique and absolutely memorable opportunity to swim with Pacific bottlenose dolphins in a clear lagoon or oceanarium. **Dolphin Adventure** (☎ **322-297-1212;** Internet: www.vallarta-adventures.com) operates an interactive dolphin-research facility — considered the finest in Latin America — that allows a limited number of people to swim with the dolphins Monday through Saturday at scheduled times. Cost for the swim is $170, and advance reservations are required — they're generally sold out at least a week in advance. You may prefer the **Dolphin Encounter** ($75) at the same facility, which allows you to touch and learn about these dolphins in smaller pools, so you're ensured up-close and personal time with these fascinating creatures — it's also a better choice for children. Dolphin Adventures has two facilities — one in the lagoon of Nuevo Vallarta, and a newer, more expansive oceanarium-style facility on Av. Las Palmas No. 39-A., which also serves as the headquarters of Vallarta Adventures. The oceanarium gets my highest recommendation. The experience leaves you with an indescribable sensation, and it's a joy to see these dolphins — they're well cared for, happy, and spirited. After a few swims with these dolphins, I now consider them to be my friends, and they even remember me — that's how it seems to me anyway. The program is about education and interaction, not entertainment or amusement, and I especially recommend it for children 10 and older.

Enjoying Land Sports

What's great about Puerto Vallarta is that many of the best things to do on land here are free. Vallarta is a town of simple pleasures — walking along the *malécon* at sunset, catching a concert at the open-air theater across from the central plaza, strolling through the impressive Our Lady of Guadalupe church, or wandering into any of the dozens of local art galleries.

In addition to these laid-back diversions, Puerto Vallarta is a virtual playground for activities ranging from mountain biking to golf. Eco-friendly tours can take you into the tropical jungle or to remote mountain villages. I'll bet that you can find more things to do here than you have days in which to do them.

Teeing off

Puerto Vallarta is rapidly positioning itself to rival Los Cabos as the golf capital of Mexico. Three new courses opened in the last two years, and two more are scheduled to open in the coming year.

A set of fairways and greens that's been around for awhile is the Joe Finger-designed course at the **Marina Vallarta Golf Club** (☎ 322-221-0073), an 18-hole, par-74, private course that winds through the Marina Vallarta peninsula and provides great ocean views. It's for members only, but most of the luxury hotels in Puerto Vallarta have memberships that their guests can use. A bar, restaurant, and pro shop are on the premises, and a golf pro is around to offer his services. The greens fees are $125 in high season and $85 during low season. (These rates may vary depending on the type of membership your hotel has.) Fees include golf cart, range balls, and tax. Caddies charge $5 to $10. Club rentals, lessons, and special packages are also available.

North of town in the state of Nayarit, about 10 miles beyond Puerto Vallarta, is the public, 18-hole, par-72 **Los Flamingos Club de Golf** (☎ 329-296-5006), the oldest course in town. It features beautiful jungle vegetation and has just undergone a facelift. The club is open 7 a.m. to 5 p.m. daily and has a snack bar (but no restaurant) and full pro shop. The greens fee is $60; add $34 for the use of a golf cart, $12 for a caddy, and $22 for club rental. A free shuttle service is available from downtown Puerto Vallarta; call for pickup times and locations.

The new Jack Nicklaus Signature course at the **Four Seasons Punta Mita** (☎ 322-291-6000; Fax: 322-291-6060) is breathtaking as well as challenging. It has eight ocean-facing holes, but you can see the ocean from every hole on the course. Its hallmark is Hole 3B, the "Tail of the Whale," with a long drive to a green located on a natural island — the only natural-island green in the Americas. It requires an amphibious golf cart to take you to the green when the tide is high, and the management has thoughtfully added an alternative-play hole for times when the ocean or tides are not accommodating. The course is open only to guests of the Four Seasons resort or to members of other golf clubs with a letter of introduction from their pro. A few other Vallarta-area hotels also have guest privileges — ask your concierge. Greens fees for non-guests of the Four Seasons are $175. Cart rental is an extra charge of $25, and club rental (Calloway) is $45. Golf lessons are also available.

Two additional Jack Nicklaus Signature-design courses recently opened at **Vista Vallarta** (☎ 322-290-0030). It's located in the foothills of the Sierra Madre behind the bullring in Puerto Vallarta. A round of golf at Vista Vallarta costs just $125 per person, including cart.

Taking time for tennis

A lot of hotels in Puerto Vallarta offer excellent **tennis** facilities, many with clay courts, and there's also a full-service public tennis club. The **Continental Plaza Tennis Club** (☎ 322-224-0123), located at the Continental Plaza hotel in the Hotel Zone, offers indoor and outdoor courts (including a clay court), a full pro shop, lessons, clinics, and partner match-ups.

Trailing away

One of the best ways to get some exercise, and see some great local sites in the process, is to take a mountain bike tour with **Bike Mex** (Calle Guerrero 361; ☎ 322-223-1834; Internet: www.bikemex.com). Bike Mex offers expert **guided biking and hiking tours** up the Río Cuale canyon and to outlying areas. The popular Río Cuale bike trip costs $42 for 4 hours and includes bike, helmet, gloves, insurance, water, lunch, and an English-speaking guide. Trips take off at either 9 a.m. or 2 p.m., but starting times are flexible; make arrangements a day ahead.

And . . . did I say Yelapa is accessible only by boat? For anyone serious about their biking, I've traveled with Bike Mex on its all-day, advanced-level bike trip to this magical cove, and it's great. You and your fellow riders depart at 7:30 a.m. in a van and travel to your starting point in the town of El Tuito. The 33-mile ride includes 18½ miles of climbs to a peak elevation of 3,600 feet. The journey covers switchbacks, fire roads, single tracks, awesome climbs, and steep downhills before ending up at a beachfront *palapa* restaurant in Yelapa. You have the option of staying the night in Yelapa or returning that afternoon by small boat. This tour costs $150, takes 4 to 6 hours, and includes all the bike gear, drinks, lunch, boat and land transportation, guide, and *ample* encouragement.

Other bicycle trips, such as those along the beachfront of Punta Mita, are also available. Guided **hiking tours** are available along the same routes. The prices start at $30 and vary depending on the route.

Saddling up

You can arrange guided **horseback rides** through travel agents or directly through one of the local ranches. **Rancho Palma Real** (Carretera Vallarta-Tepic 4766; ☎ 322-221-2120) offers by far the nicest horseback riding tour in the area. The horses are in excellent health and condition, plus you get an added tour of local farms on your way to the ranch. The office is 5 minutes north of the airport, and the ranch is in Las Palmas, approximately 40 minutes northeast of Vallarta. Breakfast and lunch are included with the $45 fee.

Rancho El Charro (Avenida Francisco Villa 895; ☎ **322-224-0114**; Internet: www.ranchoelcharro.com) and **Rancho Ojo de Agua** (Cerrada de Cardenal 227; ☎ and fax: **322-224-0607**) also offer high-quality tours. Both of these ranches are about a 10-minute taxi ride north of downtown toward the Sierra Madre foothills. The morning and sunset rides last 3 hours and take you up into the mountains overlooking the ocean and town. The cost is $30. They also have their own comfortable base camp for serious riders who want to stay out overnight.

Enjoying an eco-tour

The **Sierra Madre Expedition** is an excellent tour offered by **Vallarta Adventures** (☎ **322-297-1212**; Internet: www.vallarta-adventures.com). This daily excursion travels in special Mercedes all-terrain vehicles through jungle trails north of Puerto Vallarta, stopping at a small town and in a forest for a brief nature walk. The tour winds up on a pristine secluded beach for lunch and swimming. The $65 outing is worthwhile because it takes tourists on exclusive trails through scenery that would otherwise be off-limits.

In addition to their seasonal whale-watching excursions, **Open Air Expeditions** (☎ and fax: **322-222-3310**; E-mail: openair@vivamexico.com) offers other nature-oriented trips, including **bird-watching** outings and **ocean kayaking** sessions in Punta Mita. The tours at **Ecotours de México** (Ignacio L. Vallarta 243; ☎ and fax: **322-222-6606**) include seasonal trips (August to November) to a **turtle preservation camp** where you can witness baby olive ridley turtles hatch.

Tukari Tours travel agency specializes in ecological and culturally oriented tours. These folks can arrange bird-watching trips to the fertile birding grounds near **San Blas** (three to four hours north of Puerto Vallarta in the state of Nayarit), shopping trips to **Tlaquepaque and Tonalá** (six hours inland near Guadalajara), or a day-trip to **Rancho Altamira** (a 50-acre, hilltop, working ranch) for a barbecue lunch and horseback riding followed by a stroll through **El Tuito,** a small colonial-era village nearby. They can also arrange an unforgettable morning at **Terra Noble Art and Healing Center** (☎ **322-223-3530**, 322-223-3531), a mountaintop day spa and center for the arts where participants can get a massage or treatment, work in clay and paint, and have lunch in a heavenly setting overlooking the bay.

Sightseeing in Puerto Vallarta

Puerto Vallarta, itself, is a sight to see — cobblestone streets lined with tiny shops, rows of windows edged with curling wrought iron, and vistas of red-tile roofs set against the sea. Start with a walk up and down the *malecón,* the boardwalk that borders the main seaside street.

One of the great pleasures of strolling Puerto Vallarta's *malecón* is taking in the fanciful sculptures that line this seaside promenade. Among the notable works on display is *Nostalgia,* located across from Carlos O'Brian's restaurant. Created by Ramiz Barquett, this sculpture depicts a couple sharing a romantic moment while gazing out on the bay. Farther south is the sculpture group at the *Rotonda del Mar,* locally known as *Fantasy by the Sea.* It's an array of sculpture "chairs" by renowned Mexican artist Alejandro Colunga. This wildly creative series — one chair is topped by a large octopus head, another bench has two giant ears for backrests — seems to always draw a crowd. Closer to the main square is the *Boy on the Seahorse* sculpture, an image that has come to represent this resort town. Photo ops abound — don't miss the fountain across from the main square; its three bronze dolphins seem ready to leap right into the bay.

Across the street from the fountain is the **palacio municipal** (city hall), located on the main square (next to the tourism office). Besides housing the local government, the building has a large Manuel Lepe mural painted inside its stairwell. Nearby, up Calle Independencia, sits the **Parrish of Nuestra Señora de Guadalupe church** (Hidalgo 370; ☎ 322-222-1326), topped with its curious crown held in place by angels — a replica of the one worn by Empress Carlota during her brief time in Mexico as Emperor Maximilian's wife. On the church steps, women sell religious mementos, and across the narrow street, vendors sell native herbs for curing common ailments. Services in English are held Sundays at 10:00 a.m. Regular parish hours are from 7:00 a.m. until 9:30 or 10:00 p.m. daily.

Three blocks south of the church, head east on Calle Libertad, lined with small shops and pretty second-story windows, to the **municipal market** by the river. After exploring the market, cross the bridge to the island in the river; sometimes a painter is at work on island's banks. Walk down the center of the island toward the sea, and you come to the tiny **Museo Río Cuale** (no phone), which has a small but impressive permanent exhibit of pre-Columbian figurines. It's open Monday to Saturday 10 a.m. to 4 p.m. Admission is free.

Retrace your steps back to the market and Libertad and follow Calle Miramar to the brightly colored steps up to Calle Zaragoza. Midway up the steps is a magnificent view over rooftops to the sea, plus a cute cafe, **Graffiti** (no phone), where you can break for a cappuccino and a snack. There are close to 100 steps, but you walk leisurely to climb them and coming down is a breeze, the idea is to experience the streets of Vallarta and the feel of this place that was built on the side of the mountain. Up Zaragoza to the right 1 block is the famous **pink arched bridge** that once connected Richard Burton and Elizabeth Taylor's houses. This area, known as **"Gringo Gulch,"** is where many Americans have houses.

You can also tour the **Taylor-Burton villas** (Casa Kimberley; Calle Zaragoza 445; ☎ 322-222-1336). Tours of the two houses once owned by Elizabeth Taylor and Richard Burton cost $6. Just ring the bell between 10 a.m. and 6 p.m., and if the manager is available, he'll take you through the estate.

You can get a peek at some of the other villas in Vallarta every Wednesday and Thursday (from late November through Easter) on the **International Friendship Club** private-home tours (☎ 322-222-5466). You get to view four private villas in town for a donation of $25 per person with proceeds benefiting local charities. Tour arrangements begin at 10 a.m. at the Hotel Molino de Agua (Avenida Ignacio L. Vallarta 130, adjacent to the southbound bridge over the Río Cuale) where you can buy breakfast while you wait for the group to gather. Arrive early because this tour sells out quickly! The tour departs at 11 a.m. and lasts approximately 2½ hours.

There's a new, spirited tour in town — the **Don Porfidio Tequila Distillery Tour** (☎ 322-221-2543, 322-221-2545) at Porfidio's facility just 10 minutes north of town. For an entry fee of $10, you can see how agave plants are juiced, fermented, distilled into tequila, and bottled for shipping. Entrance to the facility is also available through **Celebrity Tours** (☎ 322-221-1909). The entry fee includes a glass of Porfidio, which is reputed to be one of Mexico's finest tequilas, but in reality, it's a blend of other premium tequilas with exceptional packaging and marketing. It doesn't quite compare to a visit to the actual tequila fields and traditional tequila-making haciendas, but if your time is limited, this is an interesting glimpse at the tequila-making process.

Hotel travel desks and travel agencies can book you on the ever-popular **Tropical Tour** or **Jungle Tour** ($21 each), a basic orientation to the area. These tours are really expanded city tours that include a drive through the workers' village of Pitillal, the affluent neighborhood of Conchas Chinas, the cathedral, the market, the Taylor-Burton houses, and lunch at a jungle restaurant. Any stop for shopping usually means the driver picks up commission for what you buy.

Shopping Puerto Vallarta

What makes shopping in Puerto Vallarta so great is that it's generally concentrated in small, eclectic, and independent shops rather than impersonal malls. You can find excellent-quality **folk art,** original **clothing** designs, and fine **home accessories** at great prices. Vallarta is known for having the most diverse and impressive selection of **contemporary Mexican fine art** available outside Mexico City. If you want the more typical Mexico resort shopping experience, don't worry — you can still find plenty of tacky T-shirts and the ever-present **silver jewelry.**

The best shopping is concentrated in a few key areas: central downtown, the Marina Vallarta *malecón,* the popular *mercados,* and on the beach — where the merchandise comes to you. Some of the more attractive shops are found 1 to 2 blocks in **back of the *malecón.*** Although still home to a few interesting shops, the marina boardwalk *(marina malecón)* is dominated by real estate companies, timeshare vendors, restaurants, and boating services. Start at the intersection of Corona and Morelos streets — interesting shops are found in all directions from here. **Marina Vallarta** does offer two shopping plazas (Plaza Marina and Neptuno Plaza, both on the main highway coming from the airport into town) but both have a limited selection of shops.

Puerto Vallarta's **municipal market** is just north of the Río Cuale where Libertad and A. Rodríguez meet. The *mercado* sells clothes, jewelry, serapes, shawls, leather accessories and suitcases, papier-mâché parrots, stuffed frogs and armadillos, and of course, T-shirts. Be sure to do some comparison-shopping and definitely bargain before buying. The market is open daily 9 a.m. to 7 p.m. Up the *mercado* stairs, a **food market** serves inexpensive Mexican meals — for more adventurous diners, it's probably the best value and most authentic dining experience in Vallarta. An **outdoor market** can be found along Río Cuale Island, between the two bridges. Vendors sell crafts, gifts, folk art, and clothing.

Along any public beach, walking **vendors** approach tourists and try to sell merchandise ranging from silver jewelry to rugs, T-shirts to masks. "Almost free!" they call out in seemingly relentless efforts to attract your attention. If you're too relaxed to think of shopping in town, this can be an entertaining alternative for picking up a few souvenirs. (Remember that bargaining is expected.) The most reputable beach vendors are concentrated at Playa Los Muertos in front of the El Dorado and La Palapa restaurants (on the beach near Calle Pulpito).

However, you need to be aware that much of the silver sold on the beach is actually alpaca, a lesser-quality silver metal (even though many pieces are still stamped with the designation "9.25," supposedly indicating that it's true silver). The prices for and quality of silver on the beach are much lower than they are elsewhere. If you're looking for a more lasting piece of jewelry, you're better off shopping in a true silver shop.

In most of the better-quality shops and galleries, shipping, packing, and delivery services to Puerto Vallarta hotels are available, and some also ship to your home address.

Clothing

Here are some of recommend shops and galleries:

✔ Vallarta's only true department store is **LANS** (Juárez 867, ☎ 322-223-2829), which also has a new location in the Hotel Zone in front of the Gigante shopping center (☎ **322-225-4242**). LANS offers a wide selection of name-brand clothing, accessories, footwear, cosmetics, and home furnishings.

✔ Elegant, European-style fashions and made-to-order clothing are the specialties of the **Adriana Gangoiti** (☎ 322-221-2343) boutique and designer studio, found on the Marina Vallarta boardwalk in Marina las Palmas II. It's open Monday to Saturday 10 a.m. to 2 p.m. and 6 to 10 p.m.

✔ **Laura López Labra Designs** (Basilio Badillo 324; ☎ **322-222-3074**) just may have the most comfortable clothing you've ever worn. LLL is renowned for her trademark, all-white (or natural) designs in 100% cotton or lace. Laura's fine gauze fabrics float through her designs of seductive skirts, romantic dresses, blouses, beachwear, and baby dolls. Men's offerings include cotton drawstring pants and lightweight shirts. It's open Monday to Saturday 10 a.m. to 2 p.m. and 5 to 9 p.m.

Contemporary art

Known for sustaining one of the stronger art communities in Latin America, Puerto Vallarta has an impressive selection of fine galleries featuring quality, original works of art. Here are some that are worth a visit:

✔ **Galería AL (Arte Latinoamericano)** (Josefa Ortiz Dominguez 155; ☎ and fax: **322-222-4406**) showcases contemporary works created by young, primarily Latin-American artists, as well as Vallarta favorite Marta Gilbert. It's open Monday to Saturday 10 a.m. to 9 p.m.

✔ **Galería Dante** (Basilio Badillo 269; ☎ **322-222-2477**; E-mail: dante@pvnet.com.mx) showcases contemporary sculptures and classical reproductions of Italian, Greek, and Art Deco bronzes — all set against a backdrop of gardens and fountains in a former private villa. Located on the "calle de los cafés," the gallery is open daily during the winter 10 a.m. to 5 p.m.

✔ Since opening in 1987, **Galería Pacífico** (Aldama 174, 2nd floor, 1½ blocks inland from the fantasy sculptures on the *malecón;* ☎ **322-222-1982;** Internet: www.artmexico.com) has been considered one of the finest galleries in Mexico. The gallery has a wide selection of sculptures and paintings by midrange masters and up-and-comers on display. During high season, it's open Monday to Saturday 10 a.m. to 9 p.m. and Sundays by appointment.

Huichol Indian art: What it is and where to buy it

Puerto Vallarta offers the best selection of Huichol art in Mexico. Descendants of the Aztecs, the Huichol Indians are one of the last remaining indigenous cultures in the world that has remained true to its ancient traditions, customs, language, and habitat. The Huichol live in adobe structures in the mountains north and east of Puerto Vallarta. Due to the decreasing fertility of the land surrounding their villages, they have come to depend more on the sale of their artwork for sustenance.

Huichol art has always been cloaked in a veil of mysticism — probably one of the reasons this form of *artesanía* (handcrafts) is so sought after by serious collectors. Huichol art is characterized by colorful, symbolic yarn "paintings," inspired by visions experienced during spiritual ceremonies. In these ceremonies, artists ingest peyote, a hallucinogenic cactus, which induces brightly colored visions; these are considered to be messages from their ancestors. The symbolic and mythological imagery seen in these visions is reflected in the art, which encompasses not only yarn paintings but fascinating masks and bowls decorated with tiny colored beads.

The Huichol might be geographically isolated, but they have business savvy and have adapted their art to meet consumer demand — original Huichol art, therefore, is not necessarily traditional. Designs depicting iguanas, jaguars, sea turtles, frogs, eclipses, and eggs are a result of popular demand. For more traditional works, look for pieces that depict deer, scorpions, wolves, or snakes.

Huichol Indians may also be seen on the streets of Vallarta — they are easy to spot, dressed in white clothing embroidered with colorful designs. A number of fine galleries that sell Huichol pieces are located in downtown Puerto Vallarta (see "Decorative and folk art" and "Crafts and gifts" later in this chapter). A notable place for learning more about the Huicholes is **Huichol Collection,** Morelos 490, across from the sea-horse statue on the *malecón* (☎ 322-223-2141). Not only does this shop offer an extensive selection of Huichol art in all price ranges, but it also has a replica of a Huichol adobe hut, informational displays explaining more about their fascinating way of life and beliefs, and usually a Huichol Indian at work creating art.

Huichol art falls into two main categories: yarn paintings and beaded pieces. All other items you might find in Huichol art galleries are either ceremonial objects or items used in their everyday lives.

Yarn paintings are made on a wood base covered with wax that is meticulously overlaid with colored yarn. Designs represent the magical vision of the underworld, and each symbol gives meaning to the piece. Paintings made with wool yarn are more authentic than those made with acrylic; however, acrylic yarn paintings are usually brighter and have more detail because the threads are thinner. It is normal to find empty spaces where the wax base shows. Usually the artist starts with a central motif and works around it, but it's common to have several independent motifs that, when combined, take on a different meaning. A painting with many small designs tells a more complicated story than one with only one design and fill-work on the background. Look for the story of the piece on the back of the painting. Most Huichol artists will write in pencil in Huichol and Spanish.

Beaded pieces are made on carved wooden shapes depicting different animals, wooden eggs, or small bowls made from gourds. The pieces are covered with wax and tiny *chaquira* beads are applied one by one to form different designs. Usually the beaded designs represent animals; plants; the elements of fire, water, or air; and certain symbols that give a special meaning to the whole. Deer, snakes, wolves, and scorpions are traditional elements; other figures such as iguanas, frogs, and any animals not indigenous to Huichol territory are incorporated by popular demand. Beadwork with many small designs that do not exactly fit into one another is more time consuming and has a more complex symbolic meaning. This kind of work has empty spaces where the wax shows.

✔ **Galería Rosas Blancas** (Juárez 523; ☎ 322-222-1168) features contemporary painters from throughout Mexico. The downstairs courtyard exhibition space showcases a featured artist, and the upstairs offers a sampling of the artists that regularly exhibit here. A shop next door sells art supplies and books on Mexican art in English and Spanish. Rosas Blancas is open Monday to Saturday 9 a.m. to 9 p.m.

✔ One of Vallarta's first galleries, **Galería Uno** (Morelos 561 at Corona; ☎ 322-222-0908), features an excellent selection of contemporary paintings by Latin-American artists, plus a variety of posters and prints. Set in a classic adobe building with an open courtyard, it's also a casual, *salón*-style gathering place for friends of owner Jan Lavender. The gallery is open Monday to Saturday 10 a.m. to 9 p.m.

✔ **Arte de las Americas** (☎ 322-221-1985) at Marina Vallarta (between La Taberna and the Yacht Club) is an arm of the Galeri Uno; it exhibits some of the same artists but has a decidedly more abstract orientation. Business hours are Monday to Saturday 10 a.m. to 10 p.m.

Crafts and gifts

Check out these choices for finding crafts and gifts:

✔ Opened in 1953, **Alfarería Tlaquepaque** (Avenida México 1100; ☎ 322-223-2121) is Vallarta's original source for Mexican ceramics and decorative crafts — all at excellent prices. Talavera pottery and dishware, colored glassware, birdcages, baskets, and wood furniture are just a few of the many items found in this warehouse-style store. The hours are Monday to Sunday 9 a.m. to 9 p.m.

✔ A collection of ethnic and contemporary gifts can be found at **El Vuelo** (Morelos 684, ½ block from American Express; ☎ 322-222-1822) including world music (the Cuban music recordings are outstanding), books, woven fabrics, jewelry, and decorative objects for the home. The shop is open Monday to Saturday 10 a.m. to 10 p.m.

✔ Flickering candles glowing from within colored-glass holders welcome you into **Safari Accents** (Olas Altas 224, Local 4; ☎ 322-223-2660), a highly original shop overflowing with creative gifts, one-of-a-kind furnishings, and reproductions of paintings by Frida Kahlo and Botero. It's open 10 a.m. to 11 p.m. daily.

Decorative and folk art

Find some one-of-a-kind pieces at these unique shops:

✔ Religious figurative pieces, antique *retablos* (painted scenes on tin backgrounds depicting the granting of a miracle), artistic jewelry, and beeswax candles in grand sizes all come together in **Azul Siempre Azul** (Ignacio L. Vallarta 228, just across the southbound bridge, across from Club Roxy; ☎ 322-223-0060), a tiny store brimming with captivating treasures. It's open Monday to Saturday 10 a.m. to 2 p.m. and 5 to 10 p.m. and Sunday 5 to 10 p.m.

✔ Fine antiques and decorative objects for the home, including unique furniture, religious-themed items (including *retablos*), glassware, and pewter, can be found at **La Tienda** (Rodolfo Gómez 122, near Los Muertos Beach; ☎ 322-222-1535) and at a second, smaller location at Basilio Badillo 276 (☎ 322-223-0692). Both locations are open Monday to Saturday 10 a.m. to 2 p.m. and 4 to 8 p.m.

✔ **Lucy's CuCu Cabaña and Zoo** (Basilio Badillo 295; no phone) has one of the most entertaining, eclectic, and memorable collections of Mexican folk art — about 70 percent of which is animal-themed. Items include metal sculptures, Oaxacan wooden animals, *retablos* (commemorations of miracles), and fine Talavera ceramics. Five percent of all sales go to benefit the Puerto Vallarta Animal Protection Association, organized by the shop's owners. The shop is open Monday to Saturday 10 a.m. to 10 p.m., but it's closed May 15 to October 15.

✔ **Querubines** (Juárez 501 A, on the corner with Galeana behind Planet Hollywood; ☎ 322-223-1727) is my personal favorite for the finest-quality artisanal works from throughout Mexico, including exceptional artistic silver jewelry, embroidered and hand-woven clothing, bolts of loomed fabrics, tin mirrors and lamps, glassware, pewter frames and trays, high-quality wool rugs, straw bags, and Panama hats. It's open Monday to Sunday 10 a.m. to 9 p.m.

Jewelry and accessories

Jewelry and other accessories can be found at the following:

- ✔ **Mosaiqe** (Basilio Badillo 277; ☎ 322-223-3183) is a potpourri of global treasures. The shop features extensive selection of silk, cotton, and cashmere pareos and shawls, plus resort bags, jewelry, and home decor items. It's open daily 10 a.m. to 7 p.m.

- ✔ At **Viva** (Basilio Badillo 274; ☎ 322-222-4078), both the shop and the jewelry are stunning. You enter through a long corridor lined with displays showcasing exquisite jewelry from 72 international designers. The main room has a large, glass, pyramid-shaped skylight as its roof, and more memorable jewelry displays surround comfy couches. Viva also features the largest selection of authentic French espadrilles and ballet slippers in Latin America. It's open daily 10 a.m. to 10 p.m.

Tequila and cigars

Looking for quality tequila and cigars? Check out these shops.

- ✔ **La Casa del Habano** (Aldama 174; ☎ 322-223-2758) is a fine tobacco shop with certified-quality cigars from Cuba, Mexico, and the Dominican Republic, along with humidors, cutters, elegant lighters, and other smoking accessories. It's open Monday to Saturday 10 a.m. to 10 p.m.

- ✔ At **La Casa del Tequila** (Morelos 589; ☎ 322-222-2000) you can find an extensive selection of premium tequilas, plus information and tastings to help guide you to an informed selection. In the back, a garden patio has a bar for enjoying espresso drinks and tequila drinks. Business hours are Monday to Friday 9:30 a.m. to 11:00 p.m.

Embarking on a Side Trip

If you haven't heard about **San Sebastián** yet, it probably won't be long until you do — its remote location and historic appeal have made it the media's new darling destination in Mexico. Originally discovered in the late 1500s and settled in 1603, the town peaked as a center of mining operations, swelling to a population of over 30,000, by the mid-1800s. Today, with roughly 600 year-round residents, San Sebastián retains all the charm of a village locked in time. Highlights include an old church, a coffee plantation, an underground tunnel system — and not a T-shirt shop to be found. San Sebastián is about 100 miles from Puerto Vallarta.

Vallarta Adventure's **San Sebastián Air Adventure** is a great introduction to this town. A 15-minute flight aboard a 14-seat, turbo-prop Cessna Caravan takes you into the heart of the Sierra Madre before settling in San Sebastián. The plane is equipped with raised wings, which allows you to admire — and photograph — the mountain scenery below. The plane arrives on a gravel landing strip in San Sebastián for a half-day tour — it's more like an informal stroll through town and a chance to talk with the more colorful personalities of the area — and each day is different. The package costs $125 and includes the flight, a walking tour of the town (including a stop at the old Hacienda Jalisco, an inn, located in a historic building, once used as the headquarters of a silver mining company — a favored getaway of John Huston, Elizabeth Taylor, Richard Burton, and their friends), and brunch in town. Reserve your space by calling ☎ 322-297-1212 or e-mail Vallarta Adventure's at info@vallarta-adventures.com.

Pacific Travel (☎ 322-225-2270) offers a **Jeep tour** to San Sebastián for $65 (up to four people per Jeep including a guide). You can choose to drive along steep, narrow, rocky mountain roads or leave that part of the adventure to your guide. This tour departs at 9 a.m. and returns at 5 p.m.

If you'd like to stay over night, you have two options. The first is the very basic **El Pabellon de San Sebastián,** which has nine rooms facing the town square. Don't expect extras here, but the rates run $12.00 per double or $7.50 for singles. Reservations are handled through the town's central phone lines — you call and leave a message or send a fax, and hopefully, the hotel will receive it. On any given day, either of the following can serve as the phone and fax line: ☎ 322-297-0200 or 322-0333. A more secure method of contacting the hotel is e-mail at ssb@pvnet.com.mx. Except on holidays, there's generally room at this inn, but bring cash — credit cards aren't accepted.

A more enjoyable option is the stately **Hacienda Jalisco** (make your reservations through the town telephones listed in the preceding paragraph or via e-mail at ssb@pvnet.com.mx), built in 1850 and once the center of mining operations in this old mining town. Located near the airstrip (a 15-minute walk from town), the beautifully landscaped, rambling old hacienda has walls that seem to whisper tales of its past. If proprietor Bud Acord is feeling social, his stories usually outshine any the hacienda has to tell. He's welcomed John Huston, Liz Taylor, Richard Burton, Peter O'Toole, and a cast of local characters as his guests.

The extra-clean rooms have wood floors, rustic furnishings and antiques, and working fireplaces; some are decorated with pre-Columbian reproductions. The ample bathrooms are beautifully tiled and have skylights. Hammocks grace the upstairs terrace. A sort-of museum on the lower level attests to the celebrity guests and prior importance the hacienda has enjoyed over the years. Because of its remote location, all meals are included. Rates are $120 per couple per night including meals; alcoholic beverages are extra. Group rates are available and discounts may be possible for longer stays. No credit cards are accepted.

Anyone for a shot of tequila? I'm talking about taking a picture of the town — although you can also sample the beverage of the same name on this side trip. **Vallarta Adventures** (☎ **322-297-1212**; E-mail: info@vallarta-adventures.com) offers a half-day trip (187.5 miles/ 300 km) that takes you to the classic town of **Tequila,** where you visit one of the original haciendas and tequila fields. It's just a comfortable 35-minute flight aboard a private, 16-passenger plane to the town of Tequila. This is the only region in the world where this legendary spirit is distilled, much like the exclusive Champagne region in France. The visit centers around Herradura Tequila's impressive 18th-century **Hacienda San Jose** where you learn about the myth and the tradition of producing tequila from the stately plants that line the hillsides of this town — an experience comparable to California's winery tours. The tour departs every Thursday at 1:00 p.m. from the Aerotron private airport (adjacent to the PV International Airport) and returns to Puerto Vallarta by 8 p.m. The cost is $255, which includes all air and ground transportation, tours, lunch, and beverages.

Yelapa, the same south-shore beach I discuss earlier in this chapter, is also a great overnight escape. It's a cove straight out of a tropical fantasy and only a 45-minute trip by boat from Puerto Vallarta. Yelapa has no electricity or cars and just installed its first paved (pedestrian-only) road last year. (The cove remains accessible only by boat.) Yelapa's tranquility, natural beauty, and seclusion have made it a popular home for hippies, hipsters, artists, writers, and a few expatriates (looking to escape the stress of the rest of the world or, perhaps, the law). Yes, it's a seemingly strange cast of characters, but you're unlikely to ever meet a stranger here — Yelapa remains casual and friendly.

To get to Yelapa, take an excursion boat or an inexpensive water taxi. You can spend an enjoyable day in this wonderful spot, but I recommend a longer stay — it provides a completely different perspective of the place.

When you're in Yelapa, you can lie in the sun, swim, snorkel, eat fresh, grilled seafood at a beachfront restaurant, or sample the local moonshine, *raicilla*. The beach vendors specialize in the most amazing pies I've ever tasted (coconut, lemon, or chocolate), and the way pie ladies walk the beach while balancing the pie plates on their heads is equally amazing. Vendors sell crocheted swimsuits too. You can also tour this tiny town or hike up a river to see one of two waterfalls. The waterfall closest to town is about a 30-minute walk from the beach.

If you use a local guide, agree on a price before you start out. Horseback riding, guided bird-watching excursions, fishing trips, and paragliding are also available.

For overnight accommodations, local residents frequently rent out rooms, or you can check out the rustic **Hotel Lagunita** (☎ 01-329-298-0554;; Internet: www.hotel-lagunita.com www.lalagunita.com.mx). With 27 cabañas (all with private a bathroom), a saltwater pool, massage services, and an amiable restaurant/bar, this is the most accommodating place for most visitors — although you may need to bring your own towel because they're known to be in short supply. Also, note that the hotel only has a few hours of power daily. Rates generally run $55 to $70 per night, but they vary depending on the cabaña and the time of year. Hotel Lagunita accepts American Express, MasterCard, and Visa with a 10% surcharge. This location has become quite popular for yoga students and other groups.

If you stay over on a Wednesday or Saturday night during winter months, don't miss the regular dance at the **Yelapa Yacht Club** (no phone). Typically tongue-in-cheek for Yelapa, the "yacht club" consists of a cement dance floor and a disco ball, but the DJ spins a great range of tunes ranging from Glenn Miller to 'N Sync and attracting all ages and types of musical aficionados to the dance. Dinner is a bonus — the food may be the best anywhere in the bay. The menu changes depending on what's fresh. Ask for directions; it's located in the main village on the beach.

Discovering Puerto Vallarta after Dark

Puerto Vallarta's spirited nightlife reflects the town's dual nature: part resort, part colonial Mexican town. In the past few years, Vallarta's nightlife has seen an expansion of live music, especially in clubs along Calle Ignacio L. Vallarta (the extension of the main southbound road) after it crosses the Río Cuale. A live blues club, a sports bar, live mariachi music, a gay dance club, a steamy-hot live salsa dance club, and the obligatory **Señor Frogs** are along one 3-block stretch of the road. Walk from place to place and take in a bit of it all!

The *malecón,* which used to be lined with restaurants, is now known more for its selection of dance clubs and a few more-relaxed club options, all of which look out over the ocean. You can walk along the broad walkway by the water's edge and check out the action at the various clubs, which extend from the Cuban-themed **La Bodeguita del Medio** on the north end to **Hooters** just off the central plaza.

Marina Vallarta has its own array of clubs with a more upscale, indoor, and air-conditioned atmosphere. South of the Río Cuale, the **Olas Altas zone** literally buzzes with action pouring out of its wide selection of small cafes and martini bars. In this zone, there's also an active gay and lesbian club scene.

Taking in a cultural event

As in most Mexican beach resorts, Vallarta has a limited selection of cultural nightlife beyond the **Mexican fiesta,** but as a growing center for the visual arts in Mexico, Vallarta is more diverse than most. Popular events include the winter season of art-exhibition openings. Puerto Vallarta's gallery community comes together to present almost weekly **art walks** where new exhibits are presented, featured artists are in attendance, and complimentary cocktails are served. These social events alternate between the galleries along the Marina Vallarta *malecón* and the galleries in the central downtown area. Check listings in the daily English-language newspaper, *Vallarta Today,* upon arrival to see what may be on the schedule during your stay.

Celebrating a fiesta

Major hotels in Puerto Vallarta feature frequent fiestas for tourists — an open-bar, a Mexican buffet dinner, and live-entertainment extrava-ganzas. Some of the fiestas are fairly authentic and serve as good intro-ductions for first-time travelers to Mexico; others can be a bit cheesy. Shows are usually held outdoors but move indoors when necessary.

The **Krystal Vallarta (☎ 322-224-1041)** hosts one of the best fiesta nights on Tuesdays and Saturdays at 7 p.m. These things are difficult to quantify, but Krystal's program is probably less tacky than most of its hotel counterparts. The charge is $47, and major credit cards are accepted.

My personal favorite of the nocturnal fiestas is **Rhythms of the Night,** which combines a sunset boat cruise to the cove of Caletas with an evening of dining and entertainment under the stars at John Huston's former home. The smooth, fast Vallarta Adventure catamaran takes you to the site, providing entertainment along the way until you're greeted at the dock by tiki torches and native drummers. There's no electricity here — you dine by the light of the multitude of candles, the stars, and the moon. The buffet dinner is delicious — steak, seafood, and generous vegetarian options, accompanied by wine. Everything is first class. The show, set to the music of native bamboo flutes and gui-tars, showcases indigenous dances in a contemporary style. The boat departs from the Terminal Marítima at 6 p.m. and returns by 11 p.m. To reserve a spot, contact **Vallarta Adventures (☎ 322-297-1212;** Internet: www.vallarta-adventures.com). The cost is $75 and includes the boat cruise, dinner, open bar, and entertainment. Major credit cards are accepted.

Enjoying the club and music scene

Some of Vallarta's best bets for nightlife are actually found in popular restaurants — combining food and fun. Other options are one of the many clubs featuring live music. Whatever your final selection is, one thing is for sure — Vallarta offers something for everyone, and there's rarely a quiet night in town.

Restaurants/bars

Although it may be the most chic dining spot in Vallarta, **de Santos** (Morelos 771; ☎ **322-223-3052**) is better known for the urban, hip crowd that the bar draws. The atmosphere really rocks after midnight on weekends. One of the owners is a member of the super-hot Latin rock group Mana who uses Vallarta as a home base for writing new songs. As the hour grows later, the music volume increases and the lights dim. The in-house DJ spins Euro, techno, and house music to match the mood of the crowd, which varies in age from their 20s on up, but shares a common denominator of cool style. It's open daily 5 p.m. to 2 a.m. (5 a.m. on weekends). An added bonus: no cover.

Vallarta's original nightspot is **Carlos O'Brian's** (Paseo Díaz Ordaz 786, along the *malecón* at Pípila; ☎ **322-222-1444,** 322-222-4065), once considered the only place you'd think of going for an evening of revelry. Although the competition is stiffer nowadays, COB's still packs them in — especially the 20-something set. Late at night, the scene resembles a college party. It's open daily noon to 2 a.m.

Kit Kat Club (Pulpito 120, Playas Los Muertos; ☎ **322-223-0093**) is swank, sleek, and reminiscent of a New York, high-style club, but don't be fooled — the club also has a terrific sense of humor. In the golden glow of candlelight, you can lounge around in cushy, leopard-patterned chairs or cream-colored, overstuffed chaise-lounges listening to swinging tunes while sipping on a martini. The place is not only very hip, but it also serves good food with especially tasty appetizers — that can double as light meals — and scrumptious desserts. Michael, the owner, describes his lounge and cafe as cool, crazy, wild, jazzy, and sexy. I agree. It's open daily 11 a.m. to 2 a.m.

A Mexican classic gone contemporary is **La Cantina** (Morelos 709, downtown; ☎ **322-222-1734**). *Cantinas* have been a centuries-old tradition in Mexico, and this one has retained the fundamentals while updating the concept to a hip club. Cantinas serve little complimentary plates of food as your table continues to order drinks. The grub is served here from 1 p.m. to 5 p.m. and may include *carne con chile* (meat in a chile sauce), soup of the day, or quesadillas. In the evenings, enjoy a romantic, clubby atmosphere with recorded music alternating between sultry boleros and the hottest in Mexican rock at levels that still permit conversation. If you require more stimulation, board games are available to play in one of the brightly colored, smaller rooms or on the larger open-air patio. La Cantina is open Sunday to Wednesday noon to 2 a.m. and Thursday to Saturday noon to 4 a.m. No cover, also no credit cards.

Live music

Currently the most popular live-music club in Vallarta, **Club Roxy,** (Ignacio L. Vallarta 217; ☎ **322-223-2402**) features a hot house band, led by club owner Pico, that plays a mix of reggae, blues, rock, and anything by Santana. Live music jams between 10 p.m. and 2 a.m. Monday to Saturday nights. It's located south of the river between Madero and Cárdenas, and it's open nightly 6 p.m. to 2 a.m. There's no cover.

El Faro Lighthouse Bar (☎ **322-221-0541,** 322-221-0542) is a circular cocktail lounge at the top of the Marina Vallarta lighthouse and, it's one of Vallarta's most romantic nightspots. Live or recorded jazz plays, and conversation is manageable. Drop by at twilight for the magnificent panoramic views. It's open daily 5 p.m. to 2 a.m. with no cover.

Mariachi Loco (Lázaro Cárdenas 254, at Ignacio Vallarta; ☎ **322-223-2205**) is a live and lively mariachi club that also features singers belting out boleros and ranchero classics. The mariachi show begins at 9 p.m. — the mariachis stroll and play as guests join in impromptu singing — and by 10 p.m., things really get going. After midnight, the mariachis play for pay, which is around $3.50 for each song. The kitchen serves Mexican food until 1 a.m. The club itself is open daily 1 p.m. to 4 a.m.

Dance clubs and discos

A few of Vallarta's clubs or discos charge admission, but generally you just pay for drinks — $3 for a margarita, $2 for a beer, and more for whiskey and mixed drinks. Keep an eye out for the discount passes frequently available in hotels, restaurants, and other tourist spots. Most clubs are open daily 10 p.m. to 4 a.m.

Proving that disco is alive and well, **Christine** (☎ **322-224-0202**) is a dazzling club that still draws a crowd with an opening laser-light show, pumped-in dry ice and oxygen, flashing lights, and a dozen large-screen video panels. The sound system is truly amazing, and the mix of music can get almost anyone dancing. This spot is open nightly 10 p.m. to 4 a.m.; the light show begins at 11 p.m. No shorts (for men), tennis shoes, or thongs are permitted. It's part of the Krystal Vallarta Hotel, north of downtown, and is very visible off Avenida Francisco Medina Ascencio. Cover varies depending on the night from $0 to $15, and major credit cards are accepted.

Emporium by Collage (Calle Proa s/n, Marina Vallarta; ☎ **322-221-0505,** 322-221-0861) is a multilevel monster of nighttime entertainment that features a pool hall, video arcade, bowling alley, and the always-packed disco bar (with frequent live entertainment). Open daily 10 a.m. to 6 a.m., the club is easily visible from the main highway, just past the entrance to Marina Vallarta, and it's very popular with a young and mainly local crowd.

The **J&B Salsa Club** (Avenida Francisco Medina Ascencio Km 2.5, Hotel Zone; ☎ 322-224-4616) is the locally-popular place to go for dancing to Latin music — from salsa to samba, the dancing here is hot! The club features live bands on Fridays, Saturdays, and holidays. It's open from 9 p.m. to 6 a.m. with a $5 cover.

The sheer size of **Señor Frogs** (Ignacio L. Vallarta and Venustiano Carranza; ☎ 322-222-5171, 322-222-5177), an outpost of the famed Carlos 'n Charlie's chain, may be daunting, but it still fills up with partiers and rocks until the early morning hours. Those cute waiters remain a signature of the chain, and one never knows when they'll assemble on stage and call on a bevy of beauties to join them in a tequila-drinking contest. Occasionally, live bands appear. Although mainly popular with the 20s set, all ages find it fun. There's food service, but it's better known for its dance-club atmosphere. It's open from noon to 4 a.m.

A visit to the **Zoo** (Paseo Díaz Ordaz 630, the *malecón;* ☎ 322-222-4945) gives you a chance to be an animal and get wild in the night — this joint even has cages to dance in if you're feeling really unleashed. The Zoo has a terrific sound system and a great variety of dance music including techno, reggae, and rap. Every hour is a happy hour here with two-for-one drinks. The club is open 11:30 a.m. until the wee hours of the morn, and cover is usually free to $5.

Sports bar/adult club

With a multitude of TVs and enough sports memorabilia to start a mini-museum, **Micky's No Name Café** (Morelos 460 at Mina, the *malecón;* ☎ 322-223-2508) is a great venue for catching your favorite game. They play all NBA, NHL, NFL, and MLB games and pay-per-view sporting events. Mickey's also serves great BBQ ribs and imported steaks from the United States. It's open daily 11 a.m. to midnight.

Q'eros (Avenida Francisco Medina Ascencio in front of Plaza Genovesa; ☎ 322-222-4367; sorry, no Web site) is the most popular of a number of adult nightclubs that feature exotic dancers, private shows, and stripteases. Q'eros is open nightly 9 p.m. to 6 a.m. and has a $5 cover.

Gay and lesbian clubs

Vallarta is home to a vibrant gay community and a wide variety of clubs and nightlife options including special bay cruises and evening excursions to nearby ranches. The free *Southside PV Guide* (Amapas 325; ☎ 322-222-2517; E-mail: pvguide@hotmail.com) specializes in gay-friendly listings.

Club Paco Paco (Ignacio L. Vallarta 278; ☎ 322-222-1899; Internet: www.pacopaco.com) is a combination disco, cantina, and rooftop bar that also hosts a spectacular "Trasvesty" transvestite show every

Friday, Saturday, and Sunday night at 1:30 a.m. The club is open noon to 6 a.m. daily and is air-conditioned. **Paco's Ranch,** around the corner at Venustiano Carranza 239, has nightly specials including Western Night on Tuesdays and Leather Night on Thursdays. A nightly "Ranch Hand's Show" is performed at 9:00 p.m., 12:30 a.m., and 3:00 a.m. This club, which can be accessed from Club Paco Paco, is open 8 p.m. to 6 a.m. The cover of $6 applies to both clubs and includes a drink.

Los Balcones (Juárez 182; ☎ **322-222-4671**), one of the original gay clubs in town, is a bi-level space with several dance floors and an excellent sound system. It earned a few chuckles when it was listed as one of the most romantic spots in Vallarta by *Brides* magazine. This air-conditioned club is open 9 p.m. to 4 a.m. and posts nightly specials including exotic male dancers.

Part VI
Ixtapa and Zihuatanejo

The 5th Wave   By Rich Tennant

"Well, if you're not drinking tequila with your breakfast burrito, then why is your cereal bowl rimmed in salt."

In this part . . .

Think of a vacation here as getting two destinations (and the best of both worlds) for the price of one: The side-by-side beach resorts of Ixtapa and Zihuatanejo may share a common geography, but they couldn't be more different in character. Ixtapa has a modern infrastructure, tons of services, and luxury hotels. Zihuatanejo — or Zihua to the locals — is the quintessential Mexican beach village.

The only thing that some visitors may find lacking is the nightlife, which is rather subdued in both towns — especially compared to other more developed resorts like Acapulco, Los Cabos, and Puerto Vallarta. But, if you're looking for laid-back evenings of good conversation and cocktails in the moonlight, the absent party crowd may be a plus.

Chapter 18

The Lowdown on the Ixtapa and Zihuatanejo Hotel Scene

In This Chapter

▶ Sizing up the hotel locations

▶ Checking out top hotel choices in Ixtapa and Zihuatanejo

Think of a vacation to this slice of Mexico as cashing in a two-for-one coupon and getting the best of both worlds: The side-by-side beach resorts of **Ixtapa** and **Zihuatanejo** may share a common geography, but they couldn't be more different in character. Ixtapa boasts a modern infrastructure, a wide array of services, and luxury hotels. Zihuatanejo — or Zihua to the locals — is the quintessential Mexican beach village and offers lower-priced rooms and one-of-a-kind inns. If you're the type of traveler who prefers comforts reminiscent of home, opt for Ixtapa and take advantage of well-appointed rooms in a setting of tropical beauty. You can easily and quickly make the four-mile trip into Zihuatanejo for a sampling of life in this *pueblo* by the sea. But, if you prefer a more rustic retreat with real personality, consider settling in Zihuatanejo. Its funky charm has attracted a community of Swiss and Italian immigrants, adding an air of sophistication to the laid-back village life.

With a backdrop of palm-covered hills and the Pacific Ocean waters serving as a foreground, you can enjoy a full range of activities and diversions here — scuba diving, deep-sea fishing, bay cruises to remote beaches, and golf are among the favorites. The one exception is the nightlife, which is rather subdued in both towns, especially compared to other more-developed resorts like Acapulco, Los Cabos, and Puerto Vallarta.

As a dual destination, Ixtapa and Zihuatanejo is the ideal choice for the traveler looking for a little bit of everything, from resort-styled indulgence to unpretentious good times.

These two resorts are more welcoming to couples and adults than they are to families. A number of places are off-limits to children under 16 — something of a rarity in Mexico.

Zihua is a relaxed, down-to-earth paradise, and it's also known for its collection of unique hillside boutique hotels, which cater to an international crowd looking for pampered luxury and individualized style. Terrific bargains also exist and still offer character, cleanliness, and safety — if not the full range of amenities. Of all of the resorts in Mexico, Ixtapa-Zihuatanejo has the best selection of one-of-a-kind places to stay.

Choosing Your Location

Because the ambiance is so different between these two sister towns, choosing the right place to stay makes a big difference in your overall vacation experience — though the ride between the two is an easy one.

Ixtapa, as I note earlier in the chapter, is the more modern, made-for-tourism town. Developed by the Mexican government in the 1970s as a complement to Zihua's fetching charms, Ixtapa places a bevy of conveniences at your disposal: shopping centers, sleek eateries, golf courses, and high-rise hotels. Almost everything is accessible by walking or is an inexpensive cab ride away.

Each of the Ixtapa hotels listed in this chapter (with the exception of Las Brisas) lies along the wide, attractive Playa Palmar and is largely self-contained — with shops, bars, restaurants, and water fun on-site — meaning you never need to leave the resort's property if you don't want to. The main difference between Ixtapa and Zihuatanejo is that while Ixtapa hotels offer every conceivable comfort and convenience, they lack the charm and originality of Zihua accommodations. Also you need to remember that Ixtapa hotels, on the whole, are priced much higher.

If you choose the traditional appeal of **Zihuatanejo,** you still need to narrow down your preference in terms of staying in the central town or on one of Zihua's neighboring beaches. In either case, Zihua is small, friendly, colorful, and full of Mexico's authentic charms.

The places to stay in town — known as *el centro* — are generally small and inexpensive with the exception of Puerto Mio (which isn't technically located downtown anyway, so forget about the whole "exception" thing). Many establishments offer bare-bones accommodations without air-conditioning and are subject to local street noise, but they're clean, priced right, and within easy walking distance of plenty of places to eat and shop. Note that none of the *centro* Zihua hotels are situated directly on the beach, and only Puerto Mio has an ocean view.

Also worth knowing is that the term "bungalow" is loosely defined in Zihuatanejo, just as it is elsewhere in Mexico. Thus, a bungalow may be an individual unit with a kitchen and bedroom, or it may be a mere bedroom. It may also be like a hotel, located in a two-story building with multiple units with or without kitchens. The "bungalow" may be cozy or rustic, with or without a patio or balcony.

Two lovely beaches and a couple of Mexico's most notable small hotels are just east of *centro* Zihuatanejo. **Playa Madera** and **Playa La Ropa,** separated from each other by only a craggy shoreline, are both accessible by road. Prices here tend to be higher than those in town, but the value is much better, and people tend to find that the beautiful and tranquil setting is worth the extra cost. The area is rich with charm and a stellar selection of sand for anyone who truly treasures a great beach. The only drawback to this area is that dining is limited to *palapa* (thatched roof) beach restaurants or the on-site restaurants at the hotels, and there's essentially no shopping or nightlife to speak of. That means hopping in a taxi to town for any diversions other than beach-related fun and limited dining. The town is just 5 to 20 minutes away depending on whether you walk or take a taxi, which costs about $2.

Ixtapa's and Zihuatanejo's Best Accommodations

As far as prices go, I note rack rates (the maximum that a hotel or resort charges for a room) for two people spending one night in a double room. You can usually do better, especially if you're purchasing a package that includes airfare. Expect to pay more — up to double the rack-rate prices — if you're planning a visit during Christmas or Easter weeks. Prices quoted here include the 17 percent room tax. Please refer to the Introduction of *Mexico's Beach Resorts For Dummies* for an explanation of the price categories.

As I mention earlier in this chapter, Ixtapa-Zihuatanejo tends to not be very kid friendly, so if you plan on bringing the whole family, including the little ones, please pay special attention to the "Kid Friendly" icons highlighting the best choices. Unless otherwise indicated, all hotels have air-conditioning.

Apartamentos Amueblados Valle
$ **Zihuatanejo Centro**

These accommodations are actually apartments, but you can rent them by the day or week, meaning you can enjoy a well-furnished apartment for the price of an inexpensive hotel room. This property is a great choice for friends traveling together on a budget. Five one-bedroom apartments accommodate up to three people; the three two-bedroom apartments can fit four comfortably. Request an apartment that doesn't face the street; they're less noisy. Each apartment is different, but all are clean and airy with ceiling fans, private balconies, and kitchenettes, but no air-conditioning. Maid service is provided daily, and there's a paperback-book exchange in the office. Reserve well in advance during high season.

Vincente Guerrero 14, about two blocks in from the waterfront between Ejido and N. Bravo. ☎ *755-554-2084. Fax: 755-554-3220. 8 units. Rack rates: High season $60 1-bedroom apartment, $90 2-bedroom apartment; low season $40 1-bedroom apartment, $60 2-bedroom apartment. Ask for special rates during low season and for prolonged stays. No credit cards.*

Barceló Ixtapa
$$$ Ixtapa

A grand, 12-story resort hotel (formerly the Sheraton), Barceló Ixtapa is one of the best choices in the area for families. A modern, well-equipped resort, Barceló boasts handsomely furnished public areas and tropical gardens surrounding a large pool, which has a swim-up bar and a separate section for children. Most rooms have balconies with views of either the ocean or the mountains, and non-smoking and handicapped-accessible rooms are available. You never need to leave this hotel if you choose not to — with four restaurants plus room service, a nightclub, a lobby bar, and the area's most popular Mexican fiesta (held weekly) with a sumptuous buffet and live entertainment outdoors, the Barceló Ixtapa lacks for nothing. If you choose to spend all of your time here, be sure to take advantage of the optional, all-inclusive pricing rates. Four tennis courts and a fitness room are available for the actively inclined. For all the Barceló offers on-site, it may be the best value in Ixtapa.

Boulevar Ixtapa s/n, at the southeastern end of Playa del Palmar. ☎ *800-325-3535 in the U.S. and Canada, or 755-553-1858. Fax: 755-553-2438. Internet:* www. barcelo.com. *331 units. Free parking. Rack rates: High season $170 double all-inclusive, $85 double with breakfast only; low season $130 double all-inclusive. AE, DC, MC, V.*

Bungalows Ley
$$ Zihuatanejo Beaches/Playa Madera

Located on a small complex on Playa Madera, Bungalows Ley is another great option for friends traveling together. No two suites are the same here. If you're traveling with a group, you may want to book the most expensive suite (called Club Madera), which comes with a rooftop terrace with tiled hot tub, outdoor bar and grill, and a spectacular view. All the rooms are immaculate; the simplest layouts are studios with one bed and a kitchen in the same room. All rooms have terraces or balconies just above the beach, and all are decorated in Miami South Beach ice cream colors. Bathrooms, however, tend to be small and dark. Clients praise the management and the service. To find the property, follow Calle Eva S. de López Matéos to the right up a slight hill; the hotel is on the left.

Calle Eva S. de López Matéos s/n. ☎ *755-554-4087. Fax: 755-554-4563. 8 units. Rack rates: $76 double with A/C; $117 for 2-bedroom suite with kitchen for up to 4 persons or $170 for up to 6 persons. AE, MC, V.*

Zihuatanejo and Ixtapa Area Accommodations

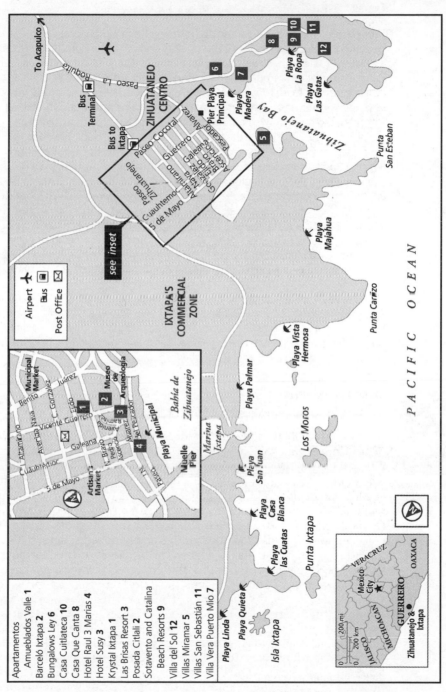

Apartamentos
Amueblados Valle 1
Barceló Ixtapa 2
Bungalows Ley 6
Casa Cuitlateca 10
Casa Que Canta 8
Hotel Raul 3 Marias 4
Hotel Susy 3
Krystal Ixtapa 1
Las Brisas Resort 3
Posada Citlali 2
Sotavento and Catalina
  Beach Resorts 9
Villa del Sol 5
Villas Miramar 5
Villas San Sebastián 11
Villa Vera Puerto Mio 7

Casa Cuitlateca

$$$$$ Zihuatanejo Beaches/Playa La Ropa

The perfect place for a romantic holiday, Casa Cuitlateca is an exclusive bed and breakfast and one of the unique inns that has made Playa la Ropa a standout. Done in the architectural style that has made Zihua famous, Casa Cuitlateca has *palapa* roofs and earthy colors and is built into the hillside across from Playa La Ropa. Each room offers a stunning view. Two smaller rooms have their own private terrace and a small sitting area. There's also a suite with a large terrace, and a second suite with no view but a very nice sitting area and small private garden. The bar is on the first level behind the pool and serves cocktails to the public from 4:30 to 8 p.m. Guests can help themselves to soft drinks and beers on the honor system when the bar is closed. The small pool, like everything else here, is beautifully designed. Each room is carefully decorated with handcrafts and textiles from all over Mexico. On the top level of the two suites, there's a sundeck and a hot tub for all guests. From the entrance to the property, you climb a steep staircase of 150 steps. The driveway is also very steep, and there's parking for six cars. The parking lot connects to the house through a hanging bridge. Playa La Ropa is just a short walk away.

Calle Playa La Ropa, a short walk in from La Ropa beach. ☎ *877-541-1234 or 406-252-2834 from the U.S., or 755-554-2448. Fax: 406-252-4692. Internet:* www.casa cuitlateca.com. *E-mail:* casacuitlateca@cdnet.com.mx. *4 units. Rack rates: $425 double, $50 each extra person. Rates include round-trip transfers to the airport and breakfast. AE, MC, V. No children under 15.*

Casa Que Canta

$$$$$ Zihuatanejo Beaches/Playa La Ropa

Another striking inn, and another ideal choice for a romantic getaway is "The House that Sings," located on a mountainside overlooking Zihuatanejo Bay. Designed with striking molded-adobe architecture, Casa Que Canta was the first of a rustic-chic style of architecture now known as Mexican Pacific. All the rooms are individually decorated in unusual, painted, Michoacán furniture; antiques; and stretched-leather *equipales* (a traditional Mexican chair characterized by the round-design and sturdy construction), with hand-loomed fabrics and handsome, natural-tile floors used throughout. All units have large, beautifully furnished terraces with bay views. Hammocks under the thatched-roof terraces, supported by rough-hewn *vigas* (wooden beams), are perfectly placed for watching yachts sail in and out of the harbor. The four categories of rooms are all spacious: three terrace suites, four deluxe suites, nine grand suites, and two private-pool suites. Rooms meander up and down the hillside, and while no one staircase is terribly long, you should know that Casa Que Canta doesn't have elevators. Technically, the hotel is not on Playa La Ropa (or any beach) but on the road leading there. The closest stretch of beach (the very beginning of Playa La Ropa) is down a steep hill. Casa Que Canta has a small restaurant-bar on a shaded terrace, a small pool on the main terrace, and a second, saltwater pool on the bottom level.

Little extras like laundry, room service, and complimentary soft drinks and beer in your mini-fridge are present to pamper you.

Camino Escénico a la Playa La Ropa. ☎ **888-523-5050** _in the U.S., 755-555-7000, 755-555-5730, or 755-554-6529. Fax: 755-554-7900. Internet:_ www.lacasaque canta.com.mx. _24 suites. Rack rates: High season $330–$680; low season $290–$320 double. AE, MC, V. No children under 16._

Hotel Raul 3 Marias
$ Zihuatanejo Centro

Although it's a small, basic hotel with strictly functional rooms, the Raul is very clean and known for its friendly guest services. Nine rooms have a balcony overlooking the street, and the small office offers telephone and fax service to guests. Downstairs is the landmark Zihuatanejo seafood restaurant, Garrobos, which is open for lunch and dinner. The hotel also offers deep-sea fishing and diving charters.

Juan Alvarez 52, between 5 de Mayo and Cuautemoc streets. ☎ **755-554-6706.** _E-mail:_ garroboscrew@cdnet.com.mx. _17 units. Rack rates: High season $42 double; variable prices in low season. AE, MC, V._

Hotel Susy
$ Zihuatanejo Centro

Consistently clean with lots of plants along a shaded walkway set back from the street, this two-story hotel offers small rooms with fans (no air-conditioning) and louvered-glass windows with screens. Hotel Susy is a good choice if you're looking for a central location, a cheap price, and a comfortable, simple place to stay. Request an upper-floor room and enjoy a balcony that overlooks the street. To get here, face away from the water at the basketball court on the _malecón_ (boardwalk), turn right, and walk two blocks; the hotel is on your left at the corner of Guerrero.

Juan Álvarez 3 at Guerrero. ☎ **755-554-2339.** _18 units. Rack rates: High season $30 per person, per room; low season $25 double. MC, V._

Krystal Ixtapa
$$$$ Ixtapa

Welcoming, exceptional service is what the Krystal chain of hotels is known for in Mexico, and the Ixtapa version is no exception. In fact, many of the staff members have been with the hotel for all of its 20-some years of operation and are on hand to greet returning guests. The Krystal is probably the best hotel in the area for families because it has a playground and a special kid's club activities program. Each spacious and nicely furnished room has a balcony with an ocean view, game table, and tile bathroom. Master suites have large, furnished, triangular-shaped balconies that overlook the spacious grounds and the large pool, which has a special kid's section as well as a waterfall and waterslide. A tennis court, racquetball court, and a small gym are also on-site. Note that some rates include a daily breakfast buffet — a great deal if you make the buffet your main meal of the day. Krystal Ixtapa has five restaurants to choose from, including the evenings-only Bogart's, plus room service. Also important to note is that the center of Ixtapa nightlife is found here, at Krystal's famed Christine Disco.

Boulevar Ixtapa s/n, at the northwestern end of Playa del Palmar. ☎ *800-231-9860 in the U.S., or 755-553-0333. Fax: 755-553-0216. 255 units. Internet:* www.krystal.com. *Free parking. Rack rates: High season $190 double, $250 suite; low season $170 double, $225 suite. 2 children under 12 stay free in parents' room. Ask for special packages. AE, DC, MC, V.*

Las Brisas Resort
$$$$$ Ixtapa

Set above the high-rise hotels of Ixtapa on its own rocky promontory, Las Brisas (formerly the Westin Brisas) is clearly the most stunning of Ixtapa's hotels and the hotel most noted for gracious service. The austere but luxurious public areas, all in stone and stucco, are bathed in sweeping breezes and an air of exclusivity. A minimalist luxury also characterizes the rooms, which have Mexican-tile floors and private, plant-decked patios with hammocks and lounges. All rooms face the hotel's cove and private beach, Vista Hermosa. Although this beach is true to its name (beautiful view), it's dangerous for swimming. The six master suites come with private pools, the 16th floor is reserved for nonsmokers, and three rooms on the 18th floor are equipped for travelers with disabilities. Like many of Ixtapa's hotels, Las Brisas is so complete that you may never feel the urge to leave — choose from among five restaurants, room service, and three bars including a lobby bar with live trio music at sunset. Three swimming pools (including one for children) connected to one another by waterfalls, lighted tennis courts (with a pro available on request), and a fitness center with massage services round out the offerings.

Boulevar Ixtapa s/n. ☎ *800-228-3000 in the U.S., or 755-553-2121. Fax: 755-553-1091. 423 units. Free parking. Rack rates: High season $280 deluxe, $310 Royal Beach Club; low season $175 deluxe, $202 Royal Beach Club. AE, DC, MC, V.*

Posada Citlali
$ Zihuatanejo Centro

A pleasant, three-story hotel, Posada Citlali is a major bargain. Although the rooms are small, they're spotless, and they border a very pleasant plant-filled courtyard decked out with comfortable rockers and chairs. Bottled water is in help-yourself containers on the patio, and fans are found in all rooms (there's no air-conditioning). Although you may hear the children heading for the nearby school in the morning, the location avoids most of the evening noise and sounds of traffic, making Posada Citlali a peaceful retreat in *el centro*. The stairway to the top two floors is narrow and steep.

Vicente Guerrero 3, near the corner of Alvarez. ☎ *755-554-2043. 19 units. Rack rates: $35 double. No credit cards.*

Sotavento and Catalina Beach Resorts
$$ Zihuatanejo Beaches/Playa La Ropa

Perched on a hill above the beach, these small side-by-side resorts are for people who want to relax near the ocean in a simple, lovely setting without being bothered by televisions or closed up in air-conditioned rooms. A throwback to the style of the 1970s, when Zihua was first being discovered by an international jet set, the Catalina consists of a collection of bungalows tucked away in tropical gardens. The Sotavento is made up of two multi-story buildings set apart from the bungalows. Between the two, quite a variety of rooms are available to choose from — ask to see a few different rooms to find something that suits you. My favorites are the doubles on the upper floors of the Sotavento, which are about three times the size of a normal double room. The furnishings in all of the rooms are simple but comfortable, and all have ocean-view terraces that are half-sheltered and half-open with chaises for basking in the sun and hammocks for enjoying the shade. Screened windows filter the ocean breezes, and ceiling fans keep the rooms airy even when the breeze is absent (remember — there's no air-conditioning). One curious feature of the Sotavento is that the floors are always slightly slanted in one direction or another — by design of the owner.

The bungalows in the Catalina are more decoratively furnished with Mexican-tile floors, wrought iron furniture, and folk artwork. Some come with ocean-view terraces. A restaurant; a small lobby bar; and a pool with whirlpool server both the Sotavento and Catalina. The resorts are built into the side of a hill and are not for people who dislike climbing stairs. Take the highway south of Zihuatanejo about a mile, turn right at the hotels' sign, and follow the road.

Playa La Ropa. ☎ *755-554-2032. Fax. 755-554-2975. Internet.* www.giya.com. *E-mail.* cat@cdnet.com.mx. *126 units. 85 units. Rack rates: $58–$95 standard room, $65–$120 bungalow or terrace suite, $95 small-terrace double. AE, DC, MC, V.*

Villa del Sol
$$$$$ Zihuatanejo Beaches/Playa La Ropa

Villa del Sol is an exquisite inn known as much for its unequivocal attention to luxurious detail as for its exacting German owner, Helmut Leins, who is almost always present to ensure the quality of his guests' stay. Villa del Sol is a haven of tranquility that caters to guests looking for complete privacy and serenity. Each room is a harmony of magnificent design. The spacious, split-level suites have one or two bedrooms, plus a living area and a large terrace, some of which have a private mini-pool. King-size beds are draped in white netting, and comfy lounges and hammocks beckon to you at siesta time. Standard rooms are smaller, and they don't have TVs or telephones, but they're still artfully appointed with artistic Mexican details. Nine beachfront suites have recently been added, but I still prefer the original rooms. No two are alike. Suites have CD players and private fax machines. Villa del Sol is one of only two hotels in Mexico to meet the demanding standards of the French Relais and Châteaux, and it's also a member of the "Small Luxury Hotels of the World." No children under 14 are allowed during high season, and a "no children" and "no excess noise" sentiment prevails in general. Travelers who relish a more typically-welcoming Mexican ambiance may find a stay here less enjoyable. The hotel sits on a private, 600-foot-long, palm-shaded beach and also has three pools (including one 60-foot lap pool), two tennis courts, and massage service. After you work up an appetite, enjoy an outstanding gourmet meal at the open-air, beachfront restaurant-bar or room service in your sumptuous surroundings. The rooms are stocked with deluxe amenities, and the hotel offers every service expected at a five-star resort.

Playa la Ropa. ☎ *755-554-2239, 755-554-3239. Fax: 755-554-2758. Internet:* www. hotelvilladelsol.com. *E-mail:* hotel@villasol.com.mx. *45 individually designed rooms and suites. Rack rates: High season $270–$1000 double; low season $160–$800 double. Meal plan, including breakfast and dinner, for $60 per person per day is mandatory during the high season. AE, MC, V.*

Villa Vera Puerto Mio
$$$$$ **Zihuatanejo Centro**

This idyllic inn is located on 25 acres of beautifully landscaped grounds apart from the rest of the hotels in Zihuatanejo. Technically not in *el centro,* Villa Vera Puerto Mio is on the furthest end of the bay, almost directly across from Playa Las Gatas. All rooms are artfully decorated with handcrafted details from around Mexico, and all enjoy beautiful views of either Zihuatanejo's bay or the Pacific Ocean. The rooms are divided into three main areas: Casa de Mar, the cliffside mansion closer to the main entrance where most of the rooms are located; the Peninsula, located on the tip of the bay; and a more secluded area with two deluxe suites. (These two suites have no TVs to disturb the tranquility.) Three other suites, located between Casa de Mar and the Peninsula, have recently been added and have private pools. The upper-level suite is the largest in size. One of the hallmarks of Villa Vera Puerto Mio is its seclusion — the location sets the hotel apart, and the small beach below is private by virtue of the fact that it can only be reached through the hotel. The hotel has two restaurants, plus a small marina with a sailboat that's available for charters. Children under 16 are welcome only during the summer.

Paseo del Morro 5. ☎ *and fax: 755-553-8165. Internet:* www.puertomio.com.mx. *22 rooms and suites. Rack rates: High season $225–$275 double, $425–$475 villa suite; low season prices drop by $25 per room. AE, MC, V.*

Villas Miramar

$$ Zihuatanejo Beaches/Playa Madera

A lovely hotel with beautiful gardens, Villas Miramar offers a welcoming atmosphere, attention to detail, and superb cleanliness. For the price, you may expect less, but the rooms are colorful and well equipped, and some have kitchenettes. Several of the suites are built around a shady patio that doubles as a restaurant, which serves a basic menu for breakfast, lunch, and dinner. Suites across the street face a swimming pool and have private balconies and sea views. A new terrace with a view to the bay was added last year and has a bar that features a daily happy hour from 5 to 7 p.m. Of all the more budget-priced accommodations around, Villas Miramar is the most welcoming to children. To find Villas Miramar, follow the road leading south out of town toward Playa La Ropa, take the first right after the traffic circle, and then hang a left on Adelita.

Calle Adelita, Lote 78. ☎ *755-554-2106, 755-554-3350. Fax: 755-554-2149. Internet:* www.villasmiramarzihua.com. *E-mail:* villasm@prodigy.net.mx. *18 units. Free enclosed parking. Rack rates: High season $95 suite for 1 or 2 or $100 with ocean view, $130 2-bedroom suite; low season $60 suite for 1 or 2 or $70 with ocean view, $90 2-bedroom suite. AE, MC, V.*

Villas San Sebastián

$$ Zihuatanejo Beaches/Playa La Ropa

A nine-villa complex nestled on the mountainside above Playa La Ropa, Villas San Sebastián offers great views of Zihuatanejo's bay and an indulgent sense of seclusion. The villas, all with beautiful ocean views, are surrounded by tropical vegetation and border a central swimming-pool area. Each comes complete with kitchenette and its own spacious, private terrace. The personalized service is one reason these villas come so highly recommended; owner Luis Valle, whose family dates back decades in the community, is always available to help guests with any questions or needs.

Boulevar Escénico, across from the Dolphins Fountain. ☎ *755-554-2084. Fax: 755-554-3220. 9 units. Rack rates: High season $155 1-bedroom, $190 2-bedroom; low season $105 1-bedroom, $155 2-bedroom. No credit cards.*

Chapter 19

Settling into Ixtapa and Zihuatanejo

. . . .

In This Chapter

▶ Knowing what to expect when you arrive

▶ Finding your way around

▶ Discovering helpful information and resources

. . . .

*O*ne of the pleasures of a vacation in Ixtapa-Zihuatanejo is how easy it is to find your way around. The airport is a breeze to navigate, and the towns are just as simple to figure out; both are basically oriented around one main road each.

In this chapter, I cover the basics of getting around the towns, and I provide you with tips on everything from exchanging money to Internet access. Truly, Ixtapa-Zihuatanejo is a place for complete relaxation, and it almost seems like the towns have trivialized the everyday details of life to make everything just a little bit easier.

Arriving in Ixtapa-Zihuatanejo

Your arrival at the Ixtapa-Zihuatanejo airport is likely to set the tone for your trip here — arrivals are usually easy, uncomplicated, and hassle free. But the airport lacks any real source of tourist information or currency exchange, so you're on your own until you reach town.

In recent years, the airport has been in a more-or-less constant state of renovation, but it's a generally simple building to navigate. When you exit the plane, head down the portable stairway to the tarmac and walk to the airport building.

The climate change is likely to be intense upon your arrival especially if you're heading here during the winter months. Remember to wear layered clothes so you're not unbearably hot when you get off the plane.

Navigating passport control and customs

Your task upon entering the airport is to clear immigration. At the immigration booth, an officer will ask you to show your passport and your completed tourist card, the **FMT** (see Chapter 7 for all the FMT details).

Your FMT is an important document, so take good care of it. You're supposed to keep the FMT with you at all times because you may be required to show it should you run into any sort of trouble. You also need to turn it back in upon departure, or you may be unable to leave without replacing it.

After you pass through immigration, you go through glass doors to the baggage claim area — essentially one carousel, so it should be simple enough to find your bags. Here, porters stand by to help with your bags, and they're well worth the price of the tip — about a dollar a bag. After you collect your luggage, you pass through another checkpoint. Something that looks like a traffic light awaits you here. You press a button, and if the light turns green, you're free to go. If it turns red, you need to open each of your bags for a quick search. It's Mexico's random search procedure for customs. If you have an unusually large bag, or an excessive amount of luggage, you may be searched regardless of the traffic-light outcome.

Finally, you pass through a second set of sliding glass doors that open to the general airport-arrival area. This is where you find transportation to your hotel. Booths sell tickets for *colectivos* (shared van service) and private taxis. The fares for both are based on distance (see the following "Getting to your hotel" section). Taxis are always around, but *colectivos* only gather for the larger flights. Clear, well-marked signs indicate the way to the taxis.

Getting to your hotel

The **Ixtapa-Zihuatanejo airport** is 7 miles from Zihuatanejo and 8 miles from Ixtapa. Taxi fares into town range from $12 to $19.

The least expense way to make the trip to either town is by using the *colectivos* (collective minivans), by the company **Transportes Terrestres.** For transportation to any of the hotels in Zihuatanejo or Ixtapa, or to Club Med, purchase a ticket at the booth located just outside the baggage-claim area. Cost depends on distance, but fares generally run between $3 and $6.

Several **car-rental agencies** also have booths in the airport. These companies include **Dollar** (☎ **800-800-4000** in the U.S.; Internet: www. dollar.com) and **Hertz** (☎ **800-654-3131** in the U.S., or 755-554-2590, 755-554-2952; Internet: www.hertz.com).

Getting Around Ixtapa-Zihuatanejo

Zihuatanejo is both a fishing village, in the traditional sense of the term, and a resort town. The town spreads out around the beautiful Bay of Zihuatanejo, which is framed by the downtown to the north and a beautiful, long beach and the Sierra foothills to the east. The heart of Zihuatanejo is the waterfront walkway, **Paseo del Pescador** (also called the *malecón*), bordering the Playa Municipal.

One aspect of Zihua that I enjoy most is that the town centerpiece isn't a plaza, as it is in most Mexican villages, but a **basketball court,** which fronts the beach. It's a useful point of reference for directions. The main thoroughfare for cars is **Juan Álvarez,** a block behind the *malecón*. The town has designated several sections of the main streets as the *zona peatonal* (pedestrian zone blocked off to cars). The *zona peatonal* follows a zigzag pattern, and to me, it seems to block parts of streets haphazardly.

A cement-and-sand walkway, lit at night, runs from the downtown-Zihuatanejo *malecón* along the water to **Playa Madera (Wood Beach)** making it easy to walk between these two points. Access to **Playa La Ropa** (Clothing Beach) is via the main road, **Camino a Playa La Ropa.** Playa La Ropa and **Playa Las Gatas** (Cats Beach) are connected only by boat. La Ropa and Playa Madera are connected by car (the rocks between the two beaches are dangerous). All of these beaches are described in detail Chapter 21.

Highway 200 connects Zihua to **Ixtapa,** which is located four miles to the northwest. The 18-hole **Ixtapa Golf Club** marks the beginning of the inland side of Ixtapa. Tall hotels line Ixtapa's wide beach, **Playa Palmar** (Palm Grove Beach), against a backdrop of palm groves and mountains. The main street, **Boulevar Ixtapa,** provides access to the beach. A large expanse of small shopping plazas (many of the shops are air-conditioned) and restaurants lie on the opposite the beach. At the far end of Boulevar Ixtapa, **Marina Ixtapa** has excellent restaurants, private yacht slips, and an 18-hole **golf course.** Condominiums and private homes surround the marina and golf course, with exclusive residential communities in the hillsides past the marina en route to **Playa Quieta** (Still Beach) and **Playa Linda** (Lovely Beach). Ixtapa also has a great paved bicycle track that begins at the marina and continues around the Marina Ixtapa Golf Course and on towards Playa Linda.

Getting around the two resorts is easy — **taxis** are the preferred form of transportation. Rates are reasonable, but from midnight to 5 a.m., they increase by 50 percent. The average fare between Ixtapa and central Zihuatanejo is $4; a trip from Playa La Ropa (just east of Zihuatanejo) to downtown Zihuatanejo is about $2; and it costs approximately $1.50 to get from one end of the Ixtapa Hotel Zone to the other.

A **mini bus** goes back and forth between Zihuatanejo and Ixtapa every 15 or 20 minutes from 5 a.m. to 11 p.m. daily, but it's generally very hot and crowded with commuting workers. In Zihuatanejo, it stops near the corner of Morelos-Paseo Zihuatanejo and Juárez, about three blocks north of the market. In Ixtapa, it makes numerous stops along Boulevar Ixtapa.

The highway leading from Zihuatanejo to Ixtapa is now a broad, four-lane highway, which makes driving between the towns easier and faster than ever. Street signs are becoming more common in Zihuatanejo, and good signs now lead you in and out of both towns. However, both locations have an area called the **Zona Hotelera** (Hotel Zone), so if you're trying to reach Ixtapa's Hotel Zone (the area alongside Bulevar Ixtapa), signs in Zihuatanejo pointing to that village's own Hotel Zone (the area alongside Playa Madera and Playa La Ropa) may confuse you.

Fast Facts: Ixtapa and Zihuatanejo

American Express

The main office (☎ 755-553-0853; Fax: 755-553-1206) is in the commercial promenade of the Krystal Ixtapa Hotel. It's open Monday to Saturday 9 a.m. to 6 p.m.

Area Code

The telephone area code is **755**. **Note:** The area code changed from 7 in November 2001.

Babysitters

Most of the larger hotels in Ixtapa can arrange babysitters, but many speak limited English. Rates range from $3 to $8 per hour. Babysitting services may be more difficult to come by in Zihuatanejo because the more upscale places tend to discourage children and the smaller ones simply may not have the resources.

Banks, ATMs, and Currency Exchange

Ixtapa's banks include Bancomer, located in the La Puerta shopping center. The most centrally located Zihuatanejo bank is Banamex, located on Cuauhtémoc 4. Banks change money during normal business hours, which are now generally 9 a.m. to 6 p.m. Monday to Friday and Saturday 9 a.m. to 1 p.m. Automated teller machines and *casas de cambio* (currency exchange booths) are available during these and other hours, and they generally have the best rates. Most establishments accept U.S. dollars as readily as pesos but at reduced exchange rates, so you're better off using local currency whenever possible. The airport has a currency exchange booth, so upon arrival, it is recommended to exchange just enough to pay for your cab fare and have a bit of cash to move around until you make it to a bank.

Business Hours

Most offices maintain traditional Mexican hours of operation (10 a.m. to 2 p.m. and 4 p.m. to 8 p.m. daily), but shops remain open throughout the day. Offices tend to be closed on Saturday and Sunday, but shops are open on Saturday, at least, and increasingly offer limited hours of operation on Sunday.

Climate

Although the climate is always quite warm, summer is particularly hot and humid, but sea breezes and brief showers temper the heat. September is the peak of the tropical rainy season, and showers are concentrated in the late afternoons.

Consular Agency

There is a Consular Agency in Zihuatanejo (☎ 755-553- 2100; fax 755-557-1106).

Emergencies

Police (☎ 755-554-2040, 755-554-3837); **fire department** (☎ 755-554-7351); **Red Cross** (☎ 755-554-2009).

Hospitals

Medica Ixtapa (Plaza Tulares 13; ☎ 755-553-0280) provides doctors who speak English and French. The larger hotels in Ixtapa have a doctor either on premises or on-call. In Zihuatanejo, try the **Clinica Maciel** (Calle de la Palma 12; ☎ 755-554-2380). Its staff also includes a reliable dentist.

Information

The **State Tourism Office** (☎ 888-248-7037 from the U.S., or ☎ and fax: 755-553-1967, 755-553-1968) is in the **La Puerta** shopping center in Ixtapa across from the Presidente Inter-Continental Hotel. It's open Monday to Friday 8:00 a.m. to 8:30 p.m. This location is mainly a self-service office where you can collect brochures; the staff is less helpful than in other offices in Mexico.

The **Zihuatanejo Tourism Office Module** is on the main square by the basketball court at Álvarez. It's open Monday to Friday 9 a.m. to 8 p.m. and serves basic, tourist-information purposes.

Note: According to recent regulations, the very few time-share sales booths that exist in both towns must be clearly marked with the names of the businesses and can't display signs claiming to be tourist-information centers.

Internet Access

Several cybercafes are located in the Los Patios Shopping Center in Ixtapa. **Comunicación Mundial** is in Local 105 (the number of the commercial shopping center). Go to the back of the shopping center and take the stairs to the second level; Comunicación Mundial is to your right. You can find many Internet cafes in Ixtapa, and the average fee is $3 per hour.

Maps

One of the best around is the free American Express map, usually found at the tourist information offices and hotel concierge desks.

Pharmacy

Farmacias Coyuca are open 24 hours a day and deliver. The Ixtapa branch doesn't have a phone number; in Zihuatanejo call ☎ 755-554-5390.

Post Office

The post office for both towns (☎ 755-554-2192) is in the SCT building (called Edificio SCT) behind El Cacahuate. It's open Monday to Friday 8 a.m. to 3 p.m. and Saturday 9 a.m. to 1 p.m.

Safety

Generally speaking, both Ixtapa or Zihuatanejo are quite safe, and you should feel very comfortable walking around here — even at night.

The one main safety warning applies to travelers who elect to drive: Motorists planning to follow Highway 200 northwest up the coast from Ixtapa or Zihuatanejo toward Lázaro Cárdenas and Manzanillo should be aware of reports of car and bus hijackings on that route, especially around Playa Azul. Bus holdups are more common than car holdups. Before heading in that direction, ask locals, the police or the tourism office about the status of the route. Don't drive at night. According to tourism officials, police and military patrols of the highway have increased recently, and the number of incidents has dropped dramatically.

As is the case anywhere, tourists are vulnerable to thieves. This is especially true when shopping in a market, lying on the beach, wearing jewelry, or visibly carrying a camera, purse, or bulging wallet.

Taxes

There's a 15% value-added tax (IVA) on goods and services, and it's generally included in the posted price.

Taxis

Always establish the price of a ride with the driver before starting out. Taxi rates are reasonable, but from midnight to 5 a.m., rates increase by 50%. The average fare between Ixtapa and Zihuatanejo is $3.

Telephones

Avoid the phone booths that have signs in English advising you to call home using a special 800 number — these are absolute rip-offs and can cost as much as $20 US per minute. The least expensive way to call is by using a Telmex (LADATEL) pre-paid phone card, available at most pharmacies and mini-supers, using the official Telmex (Lada) public phones. In, Mexico you need to dial 001 prior to a number to reach the United States, and you need to preface long distance calls within Mexico by dialing 01.

Time Zone

Ixtapa and Zihuatanejo operate on central standard time, but Mexico's observance of daylight savings time varies somewhat from that in the United States.

Chapter 20

Dining in Ixtapa and Zihuatanejo

. . . .

In This Chapter

▶ Discovering the best restaurants in Ixtapa and Zihuatanejo

▶ Uncovering a number of bargains

. . . .

ining destinations in this area are divided as neatly as the accommodations: More modern, stylized places can be found in Ixtapa, and eateries with more local color (and flavor) tend to be located in neighboring Zihuatanejo. Although the majority of the best-known restaurants in Ixtapa are found inside the grounds of the larger hotels, Zihua's top spots are small, mostly family-owned treasures. The restaurants on Zihuatanejo's Playa Madera and Playa La Ropa run the gamut from *palapa* (umbrella) topped seafood shacks to elegant, upscale bistros.

Zihuatanejo's **central market,** located on Avenida Benito Juárez (about five blocks inland from the waterfront), is a perfect place for cheap and tasty food at breakfast and lunch before the market activity winds down in the afternoon. Look for what's hot and fresh. The market area is one of the best places on this coast for shopping and people watching.

Two excellent **bakeries** in Zihua — smaller Mexican towns are known for their fresh pastries and *bolillos* (freshly baked, crusty mini-loaves) — are also noteworthy. Try **El Buen Gusto** (Guerrero 4, a half a block inland from the museum; ☎ 755-554-3231), which is open daily 7:30 a.m. to 10:00 p.m. and sells banana bread, French bread, doughnuts, and cakes. For more fresh-baked bread aroma, head for **Panadería Francesa** (González 15, between Cuauhtémoc and Guerrero; ☎ 755-554-2742) — open daily 7 a.m. to 9 p.m. You can buy sweet pastries or grab a long baguette or loaf of whole-wheat bread to munch on with picnic supplies.

From sunset to dinner, cocktails are the highlight of the nocturnal action here, and although these towns may be lacking in nightclub action, they do offer a varied and excellent selection of restaurants. Seafood is the star, of course, but the preparations vary wildly, and in other cuisines, the influences of the European expatriate community are evident.

Mexico's 15 percent value-added tax (IVA) is added into most restaurant bills, but the tip is not, and the wait-staff in Mexico depends on tips for the majority of their income — the usual tip here is 15 percent.

Ixtapa and Zihuatanejo's Best Restaurants

I list all of the following restaurants alphabetically with references to price and location. Please refer to the Introduction of *Mexico's Beach Resorts For Dummies* for an explanation of the price categories.

Because restaurants price shrimp and lobster so much higher than other entrees, I note the price ranges exclusive of these dishes unless they make up the major part of the menu. And, unless otherwise specified, reservations are either not accepted or not necessary.

Please see Appendix E for more information on Mexican cuisine.

Beccofino
$$$ Ixtapa   NORTHERN ITALIAN

Beccofino is a standout not only in Ixtapa but also in all of Mexico. Owner Ángelo Rolly Pavia serves up the flavorful northern-Italian specialties he grew up enjoying. The breezy location is under a covered slip overlooking the yachts of the marina. The menu is strong on pasta. Ravioli, a house specialty, comes stuffed with the freshest of seafood, whether swordfish or shrimp. The garlic bread is terrific, and the wine list is extensive with an impressive selection of imported wines to choose from. It's a popular place, and the restaurant tends to be loud when crowded, which is often. Beccofino is increasingly becoming a popular breakfast spot.

Marina Ixtapa, near the lighthouse. ☎ 755-553-1770. Main courses: $12–$25; breakfast $4–$6. AE, MC, V. Open: Daily 9:30 a.m. to midnight.

Casa Puntarenas
$ Zihuatanejo Centro   MEXICAN/SEAFOOD

A modest spot with a tin roof and nine wooden tables, Puntarenas is one of the best places in town for fried whole fish served with toasted *bolillos* (crusty, white-bread mini-loaves), sliced tomatoes, onions, and avocado. The place is renowned for *chile rellenos,* served mild and stuffed with plenty of cheese, and the pork chops, in my opinion, are divinely inspired. Although it may appear a little too rustic for less experienced travelers to Mexico, Casa Puntarenas is very clean, and the food is known for its freshness. To get to Puntarenas from the pier, turn left on Álvarez and cross the footbridge on your left. Turn right after you cross the bridge; the restaurant is on your left.

Zihuatanejo and Ixtapa Area Dining

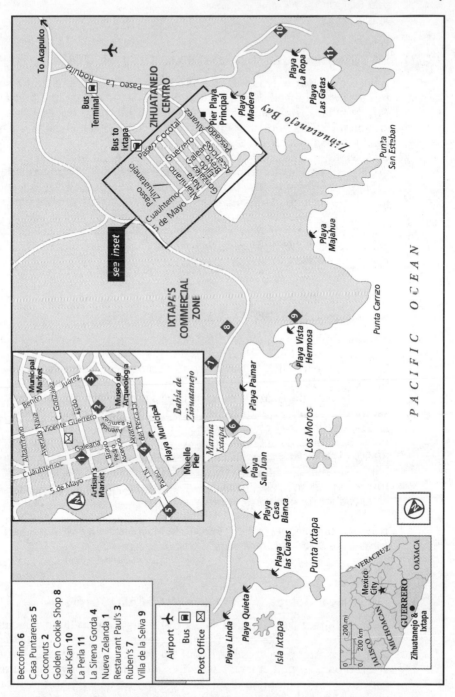

Beccofino **6**
Casa Puntarenas **5**
Coconuts **2**
Golden Cookie Shop **8**
Kau-Kan **10**
La Perla **11**
La Sirena Gorda **4**
Nueva Zelanda **1**
Restaurant Paul's **3**
Ruben's **7**
Villa de la Selva **9**

Airport ✈
Bus ⊞
Post Office ⊠

Calle Noria s/n. No phone. Main courses: $3.50–$7.00. No credit cards. Open: Daily 6:30–9:00 p.m.

Coconuts

$$$ Zihuatanejo Centro   INTERNATIONAL/SEAFOOD

What a find! Not only is the food innovative and delicious, but also the restaurant is housed in a historic building — the oldest in Zihuatanejo. This popular restaurant set in a tropical garden was the former weigh-in station for Zihua's coconut industry in the late 1800s. Fresh is the operative word on this creative, seafood-heavy menu. Chef Patricia Cummings checks the market daily for the freshest of foods and uses only top-quality ingredients to prepare dishes like seafood pâté and Grilled Fillet of Snapper Coconuts. The bananas flambé has earned a loyal following of its own — with good reason. Expect friendly, efficient service here.

Augustín Ramírez 1, at Vicente Guerrero. ☎ 755-554-2518, 755-554-7980. Main courses: $9–$25. AE, MC, V. Open: Daily 6 p.m.–11 p.m. during high season. Closed during rainy season.

Golden Cookie Shop

$$ Ixtapa   PASTRIES/INTERNATIONAL

Although the name is misleading — they sell more than cookies here — Golden Cookie's fresh baked goods beg for a detour, and the coffee menu is the most extensive in town — and includes iced-espresso drinks for those sultry Ixtapa days. Although the prices are high for the area, the breakfasts are particularly noteworthy as are the deli sandwiches. Large sandwiches, made with fresh soft bread, come with a choice of sliced deli meats, like smoked ham. Chicken curry is among the other specialty items, and the Golden Cookie folks serve up a hearty German buffet every Friday evening at 7 p.m. To get to the shop, walk to the rear of the Los Patios shopping center as you face Mac's Prime Rib; walk up the stairs, turn left, and the restaurant is on the right. An air-conditioned area, reserved for nonsmokers, is new.

Los Patios shopping center. ☎ 755-553-0310. Main courses: $6–$8; breakfast $4–$6; sandwiches $4–$6. No credit cards. Open: Daily 8 a.m.–3 p.m.

Kau-Kan

$$$ Playa La Ropa   NUEVA COCINA/SEAFOOD]

Open architecture, stunning views of the bay, and refined cuisine are among the hallmarks of this popular restaurant. Head Chef Ricardo Rodriguez supervises every detail of this operation from the ultra-smooth background music that invites after-dinner conversation to the spectacular presentation of all the dishes. The baked potato with baby lobster and the mahi-mahi carpaccio are two of my favorites, but I recommend you consider the daily specials — Ricardo always gets the freshest seafood available and prepares it with great care. For dessert, the pecan and chocolate cake served with a dark chocolate sauce is simply delicious. A casual spot during the day, Kau-Kan turns elegantly understated at night under the glow of candles. During high season, reservations are essential. Located on the road to Playa La Ropa, the restaurant is on the right hand side of the road past the first curve coming from downtown.

Camino a Playa La Ropa. ☎ 755-554-8446. Reservations recommended during high season. Main courses: $8–$25. AE, MC, V. Open: Daily 1:00–11:30 p.m.

La Perla
$ Playa La Ropa   SEAFOOD

Along Playa La Ropa, you can find any number of casual, *palapa*-style restaurants, but La Perla, with its tables under the trees and a thatched roof, is the most popular. Although it's known more as a tradition than for the food or service, somehow, this long stretch of pale sand and groups of wooden chairs under *palapas* (thatched roof umbrellas) have made a charming combination. Some diners joke that getting a waiter's attention at La Perla can be so hard that, if you get take-out food from a competitor and bring it here to eat, they won't even notice. Still, La Perla is considered the best spot around for tanning and socializing and serves a whopper of a *gringo* (American) breakfast. Lunches are lighter — *cerviche* (fresh fish cocktail made with finely cubed raw fish that is marinated with lime, vinegar and spices) are the specialty. In the evening, casual dinners and cold *cervezas* (beers) are accompanied by satellite-dish-delivered sports. La Perla is located near the southern end of Playa La Ropa. Take the right fork in the road; a sign is in the parking lot. The kitchen doesn't open until 10 a.m. but the restaurant is open at 9 a.m. for customers who arrive early to get the best spots on the beach!

Playa La Ropa. ☎ 755-554-2700. Main courses $6.00–$11.00; breakfast $2.50–$5.00. AE, MC, V. Open: Daily 9 a.m.–10 p.m.; breakfast served 10 a.m. to noon.

La Sirena Gorda
$ Zihuatanejo Centro   MEXICAN

Head to La Sirena Gorda (the chubby mermaid) for one of the most popular breakfasts in town. Choose from a variety of eggs and omelets, hotcakes with bacon, or fruit with granola and yogurt. The house specialty is seafood tacos — fish in a variety of sauces plus lobster — but I consider these selections overpriced at $3 for the fish and $20 for the lobster. To me, a taco is a taco is a taco, but they did earn rave reviews in *Bon Appétit* a few years back. Instead, I recommend something from the short list of daily specials such as blackened red snapper, steak, or fish kebabs. The food is excellent and patrons enjoy the casual sidewalk-cafe atmosphere. To get here from the basketball court, face the water and walk to the right along the *Paseo;* La Sirena Gorda is on your right just before the town pier.

Paseo del Pescador. ☎ *755-554-2687. Main courses: $3–$6; breakfast $2–$4. MC, V. Open: Thurs–Tues 7 a.m.–10 p.m.*

Nueva Zelanda
$ **Zihuatanejo Centro   MEXICAN**

Rich cappuccinos sprinkled with cinnamon, fresh fruit *liquados* (milk-shakes), and pancakes with real maple syrup draw patrons to this open-air snack shop. The mainstays of the menu are tortas and enchiladas, and everything is offered with friendly, efficient service. Dine indoors and watch your food get prepared in the spotless open kitchen, or choose a seat at one of the sidewalk tables for a pleasant people-watching session. Nueva Zelanda is easily found by walking three blocks inland from the waterfront on Cuauhtémoc; the restaurant is on your right. A second location (☎ **755-553-0838**) is located in Ixtapa in the back section of the Los Patios shopping center.

Cuauhtémoc 23 at Ejido. ☎ *755-554-2340. Main courses: Tortas $2.50–$3.50; enchi-ladas $2.50–$4.00; fruit-and-milk liquados $1.80; cappuccino $1.50. No credit cards. Open: Daily 8 a.m.–10 p.m.*

Restaurant Paul's
$$$ **Zihuatanejo Centro   INTERNATIONAL/SEAFOOD**

Neither the ambiance nor the service quite live up to the food, but that's okay — what really matters is that you enjoy an exceptional meal here. From thick and juicy pork chops and duck breast to vegetarian main courses, such as pasta with fresh artichoke hearts and sun-dried toma-toes, Chef Paul's offerings are consistent and delicious continental cui-sine. I'm sure that this is the only place in town that serves fresh artichokes as an appetizer, and the fish fillet here comes covered with a smooth, delicately flavored shrimp-and-dill sauce. No reservations are accepted, so expect a wait if you plan to dine after 7 p.m. Paul's is on Benito Juárez, half a block from the Bancomer and Serfin banks. Taxi drivers all know how to get here.

Benito Juárez s/n. ☎ *755-554-6528. Main courses: $9–$25. MC, V. Open: Mon–Sat noon to 2 a.m.*

Ruben's
$ **Ixtapa   BURGERS/VEGETABLES**

If time in Ixtapa also means a vacation from decision making, then this is the spot for you. The choices are easy — you can order either a big, juicy burger made from top-sirloin beef grilled over mesquite or a foil-wrapped packet of baked potatoes, chayote, zucchini, or sweet corn. Ice cream, plus beer and soda fill out the menu, which is posted on the wall by the kitchen. The place is kind of a do-it-yourself affair: Guests snare a waitress and order, grab their own drinks from the cooler, and tally their own tabs. But because of the ever-present crowds, it can still be a slow process. For years, Ruben's was a popular fixture in the Playa Madera neighborhood, but it moved to two locations in Ixtapa. The food remains as dependable as ever, even if the locale has expanded and spiffed up a bit.

Flamboyant shopping center, next to Bancomer. Also on Boulevar Ixtapa across from the Radisson. ☎ *755-554-4617. Main courses: Burgers $2.50–$3.50; vegetables $1.50; ice cream $1. No credit cards. Open: Daily 6–11 p.m.*

Villa de la Selva

$$$$ Ixtapa   MEXICAN/CONTINENTAL

Once the summer home of one-time president Luis Echevarria, this exquisite restaurant is set into the edge of a cliff overlooking the sea. Elegant and romantic, it offers diners the most spectacular sea-and-sunset view in Ixtapa. Candlelit tables are arranged on three terraces; try to come early in hopes of getting one of the best vistas — my favorite is the lower terrace. The cuisine is delicious, artfully appointed, and classically rich: *Filet Villa de la Selva* is red snapper topped with shrimp and hollandaise sauce. The cold avocado soup or hot lobster bisque make a good beginning; finish with chocolate mousse or bananas Singapore. The restaurant is just above Las Brisas resort, overlooking Vista Hermosa beach.

Paseo de la Roca. ☎ *755-553-0362. Reservations recommended during high season. Main courses: $15–$35. AE, MC, V. Open: Daily 6–11 p.m.*

Chapter 21

Having Fun On and Off the Beach in Ixtapa and Zihuatanejo

*W*hile you're in Ixtapa-Zihuatanejo, life isn't just a beach; it's a choice of beaches! From rocky coves to smooth stretches of golden sand, this chapter gives you the rundown on all the key beaches in the area and highlights the beaches that are best for watersports and safest for swimming so that you can choose the patch of sand that's perfect for you. If you're looking for adventure beyond the sea, I have some recommendations for you too — along with tips on the best shopping and nightlife.

It's worth noting that all beaches in Zihuatanejo are safe for swimming because undertow is rarely a problem, and the municipal beach is protected from the main surge of the Pacific. Beaches in Ixtapa are more dangerous for swimming because of frequent undertow problems, so keep an eye on the safety flags posted in front of the hotel beaches.

Hitting the Beaches

Here's the skinny on the area's beaches, traveling from the beaches northwest of Ixtapa to those south of Zihuatanejo. Even if you fall in love at first sight with the stretch of sand immediately in front of your hotel, explore a bit to see what other beauties are out there.

Playa Linda and **Playa Quieta** are about as far out as you're likely to travel to find a beach in this area. Playa Linda, about eight miles north of Ixtapa (about ten minutes by taxi), is the departure point for the inexpensive water taxis that ferry passengers to Isla Ixtapa. It's also the primary out-of-town beach, a long stretch of flat sand with watersports equipment and horse rentals. Along with a collection of small stands selling trinkets, the La Palapa restaurant makes a good place to spend the afternoon. Playa Linda faces the open ocean but also lies near a freshwater estuary that's home to birds, iguanas, and the occasional alligator — visible through a safety fence. Club Med and Qualton Club have largely claimed neighboring Playa Quieta directly across from Isla Ixtapa. The beach at Playa Quieta is beautiful, but unless you are staying at any of those resorts you won't find shade, drinks, or any sort of beach club facilities. If you are not staying on Playa Quieta, skip it. The other beaches are just as beautiful and a lot easier to get to.

Some notable beaches, along with clear water, snorkeling, and a few nature trails, are out on **Isla Ixtapa.** Four small beaches are found on the island, the busiest of which is **Playa Cuachalatate,** named for a native tree. It's the arrival point for the ferryboats and has a selection of palapa-topped restaurants. **Playa Varadero,** with calm clear waters that make it a favorite for snorkeling, is along a paved walkway to the right of Playa Cuachalatate. Group tours here usually include lunch at El Marlin restaurant. El Marlin is one of several restaurants on the island, but it's not appreciably better than the others, so feel confident in making your way on your own.

Continue to the right along the same path past Playa Varadero and you come to **Playa Coral,** which true to name, offers the most varied groupings of underwater coral in the area — it's excellent for snorkeling. The most isolated of the beaches is **Playa Carey** — to the left of the Playa Cuachalatate dock. It doesn't have any facilities but makes a great spot for a picnic. (Be sure to take your trash with you as you leave — no containers are available here for disposal.)

Boats leave the dock at Playa Linda for Isla Ixtapa every 10 minutes between 11:30 a.m. and 5:00 p.m., so you can depart and return at your own pace. The round-trip boat ride is $2.50 and takes anywhere from 20 to 35 minutes (depending on the boat and the boat's captain). Along the way, you pass dramatic rock formations, and you can see **Los Morros de Los Pericos islands** in the distance where a great variety of birds nest on its rocky points jutting out into the blue Pacific. When you reach Isla Ixtapa, you can find snorkeling, diving, and other watersports gear available for rent. Be sure to catch the last water taxi back at 5 p.m., but double-check that time upon arrival on the island.

Around the Punta Ixtapa peninsula lies **Playa Las Cuatas,** a pretty beach and cove a few miles north of Ixtapa. It has heavy surf and a strong undertow, so I don't recommend it for swimming.

Ixtapa and Zihuatanejo Area

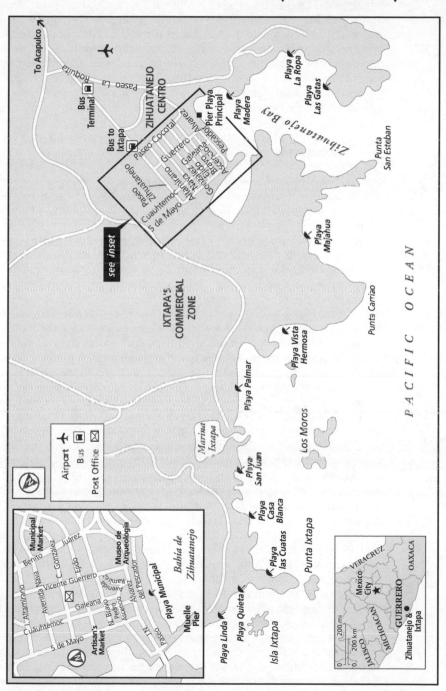

To Acapulco ↗

✈

Paseo La Roquita

Bus Terminal

Bus to Ixtapa

ZIHUATANEJO CENTRO

Paseo Cocotal

Guerrero
Ejido
Galeana
González
N. Bravo
Ascencio
Alvarez
Altamirano

Paseo Zihuatanejo

Cuauhtémoc

5 de Mayo

Pescador

Pier Playa Principal

Playa Madera

Playa La Ropa

Playa Las Gatas

Zihuatanejo Bay

Punta San Esteban

see inset

IXTAPA'S COMMERCIAL ZONE

Playa Majahua

Playa Vista Hermosa

Punta Carrizo

PACIFIC OCEAN

Playa Palmar

Los Moros

Marina Ixtapa

Playa San Juan

Airport ✈
Bus ◼
Post Office ⊠

Playa Casa Blanca

Playa las Cuatas

Punta Ixtapa

Municipal Market

Benito Juárez

C. González

Vicente Guerrero

Museo de Arqueología

Bahía de Zihuatanejo

Altamirano
Avenida Nava
Cuauhtémoc
Pedro Ascencio
N. Bravo
Galeana
Avenida Ramira Alvarez
Paseo del Pescador

Playa Municipal

Muelle Pier

5 de Mayo

Artisan's Market

Playa Quieta

Playa Linda

Isla Ixtapa

VERACRUZ
OAXACA
Mexico City ★
JALISCO
MICHOACÁN
GUERRERO
Zihuatanejo & Ixtapa ●

0   200 mi
0   200 km

Ixtapa's main beach, **Playa Palmar,** is a lovely white-sand arc on the edge of the Hotel Zone. Almost 3 miles long, this beach features dramatic rock formations by the sea. The surf here can be rough; use caution and don't swim when a red flag is posted. Several of the nicest beaches in the area are essentially closed to the public — resort developments rope them off exclusively for their guests. Although by law all Mexican beaches are open to the public, it's a common practice for hotels to create artificial barriers (such as rocks or dunes) to preclude entrance to their beaches.

Next up is lovely **Playa Vista Hermosa,** framed by striking rock formations and bordered by the Las Brisas Hotel high on the hill.

 Although very attractive for sunbathing or a stroll, this patch of sand is also known for its heavy surf and strong undertow, so use extreme caution if swimming or snorkeling here.

 The Zihuatanejo town beach, **Playa Municipal,** is still used by local fishermen to pull their colorful boats up onto the sand — a fine photo-op. The small shops and restaurants lining the waterfront here are great for people-watching and absorbing the flavor of daily village life.

Just east of Playa Municipal lies **Playa Madera**, which is accessible by following a lighted concrete and sand walkway that cuts through the rocks for about 100 yards from the Paseo de Pescador. The beach itself is open to the Pacific surf but is generally peaceful. A number of attractive budget lodgings overlook this area from the hillside, and beachside restaurants line the shore.

South of Playa Madera is Zihuatanejo's largest and most beautiful beach, **Playa La Ropa,** a long sweep of sand with a great view of the sunset. Some lovely, small hotels and restaurants nestle into the hills; palm groves edge the shoreline. Although it's also open to the Pacific, waves are usually gentle. A taxi from town costs $2. The name "Playa La Ropa," *ropa* means clothing, comes from an old tale of a *galeón* that sunk during a big storm. The silk clothing that boat was carrying back from the Philippines all washed ashore on this beach — hence the name.

 The nicest beach for swimming and the best beach for children is the secluded **Playa Las Gatas**. Speckled with minute seashells, this delicate ribbon of sand can be seen across the bay from Playa La Ropa and Zihuatanejo. The small coral reef just offshore is a nice spot for snorkeling and diving, and a few small dive shops on the beach rent gear. The waters at Las Gatas are exceptionally clear and there's no undertow or big waves, which is due in large part to a rock wall surrounding the beach that turns the waters into a virtual wading pool. The pre-Hispanic emperor Calzonzin, who chose this beach as his private playground over 500 years ago, constructed the wall. Open-air seafood restaurants on the beach make it an appealing lunch spot. (Two of the restaurants are now open for dinner as well.) Small, shaded *pangas* (small boats) make the voyage to Las Gatas from the Zihuatanejo town pier, a 10-minute trip; the captains can take you across whenever you want between 8 a.m. and 4 p.m.; evening ferries are less predictable, so check for the current schedule. A round-trip fare generally runs about $2.50.

Finding Water Fun For Everyone

The beaches here are so appealing because the waters are crystal clear and obviously free of pollution and over-fishing. Snorkel, dive, cast a line, or take a dip — it's a slice of heaven. And there are other ways to enjoy splashing around . . . or cruising above the deep blue.

Skiing and surfing

Stands with **sailboats, windsurfers,** and other **watersports equipment** available for rent are located at numerous points along Playa La Ropa and Playa Las Gatas in Zihuatanejo, Playa Palmar in Ixtapa, and even on Isla Ixtapa. You can **parasail** (about $20 for a 15-minute ride) at La Ropa and Palmar. **Kayaks** are available for rent at the **Zihuatanejo Scuba Center** (Cuauhtémoc 3; ☎ and fax: **755-554-2147;** Internet: www.dive mexico.com), hotels in Ixtapa, and some watersports operations on Playa La Ropa. A few places also have **WaveRunners,** which rent for about $30 per half-hour.

Exploring the deep blue

These clear waters just beg to be explored! Water visibility frequently is more than 100 feet, especially from December through May when the temperature is usually also comfortably warm. Over 30 deep-dive sites wait to be explored. You're likely to see an abundance of sea life — as well as the possibility of spotting an old anchor or other artifacts from the days of the Spanish conquistadors.

Arrange your **scuba-diving trip** through the **Zihuatanejo Scuba Center** (Cuauhtémoc 3; ☎ and fax: **755-554-2147;** Internet: www.divemexico. com). Fees start at around $70 for two dives including all equipment and lunch. Marine biologist and dive instructor Juan Barnard speaks excellent English and is known as a very fun guide. He's very knowledgeable about the area, which has excellent dive sites, including walls and caves, for all experience levels. Certification courses are available, and the dive-guide-to-diver ratio is an outstanding one-to-three. Note that the nearest decompression chamber is in Acapulco.

Advance reservations for dives are advised during Christmas and Easter.

The diving here is great, but you can also enjoy many of the underwater sites without going to such depths. **Snorkeling** is best at Zihuatanejo's Playa Las Gatas, Isla Ixtapa's Playa Varadero, and Playa Vista Hermosa in front of the Las Brisas hotel. Equipment rentals are available at all locations and range from $5 to $15 a day.

Reeling in the big one

Looking for the big one? Billfish — notably blue and black marlin and Pacific sailfish — are found in the waters off Zihuatanejo. And, when you catch the big one, release it. It may sting a bit, but this conservation effort is increasingly popular in Mexico, and I encourage it. You can arrange **fishing trips** with the **boat cooperative** (☎ 755-554-2056) at the Zihuatanejo town pier. Excursions cost $140 to $300 per trip depending on boat size, trip length, and other factors. Most trips last about 6 hours; no credit cards are accepted. The price includes 10 soft drinks and 10 beers, bait, and fishing gear. Lunch is on your own.

You pay more for a trip arranged through a local travel agency; the least expensive trips are on small launches called *pangas* — most have shade. Outfits offer both small-game and deep-sea fishing. The fishing here is adequate, but it's not on par with that of Mazatlán or Baja.

You can also arrange trips that combine fishing with a visit to the nearly deserted ocean beaches that extend for miles along the coast north and south of the towns of Zihua and Ixtapa. Zihuatanejo. Sam Lushinsky at **Ixtapa Sportfishing Charters** (19 Depue Lane, Stroudsburg, PA 18360; ☎ 570-688-9466; Fax: 570-688-9554; Internet: www.ixtapasport fishing.com; E-mail: ixtsptf@epix.net) is a noted fishing outfitter.

Boating and fishing expeditions from the new **Marina Ixtapa,** a bit north of the Ixtapa Hotel Zone, can also be arranged. As a rule, everything available in or through the marina is more expensive, in addition to being more "Americanized."

Tipping the captain 10 percent to 15 percent of the total price of your charter is customary, depending on the quality of the service. Give the money to the captain, and he'll split it with the mates.

Cruising Ixtapa-Zihuatanejo

The area's most popular boat trip is probably the voyage to **Isla Ixtapa** for snorkeling and lunch at the El Marlin restaurant, one of several on the island. You can book this outing as a tour through any local travel agency or your hotel tour desk, or you can head out on your own from Playa Linda, which allows you to follow your own schedule. (Check out the "Hitting the Beaches" section earlier in this chapter for more info on getting to Isla Ixtapa from Playa Linda.)

Local travel agencies can also arrange day-trips to **Los Morros de Los Pericos** islands for **bird-watching**, though it's less expensive to rent a boat with a guide at Playa Linda. These islands are located offshore from off shore from Playa Palmar; however, you must leave from Playa Linda as no boats depart from Playa Palmar.

Day cruises and **sunset cruises** on the trimaran (a catamaran with an extra hull) *TriStar* can be arranged through **Yates del Sol** (☎ 755-554-2694, 755-554-8270) or through any travel agent (with no difference in price). Both day and sunset cruises depart from the Zihuatanejo town pier at Puerto Mío.

The day cruise sails to Playa Manzanillo, where you have time for swimming, snorkeling, and shell collecting. On the return trip, the boat anchors off Playa La Ropa. The price of $59 includes lunch, an open bar, and round-trip transportation from your hotel. Snorkeling gear is $5 extra. There's also an all-day trip to Isla Ixtapa on this very comfortable and rarely crowded yacht that begins at 10 a.m., costs $49, and includes an open bar and lunch. The sunset cruise, generally running from 5:00 p.m. to 7:30 p.m., costs $39 and includes an open bar and snacks. Because schedules and special trips vary, call for current information.

Enjoying Land Sports

Ixtapa and Zihuatanejo offer plenty of popular land sports for vacationers. In this section, I cover golf, tennis, and horseback riding. If you're looking for an activity I don't list here, be sure to consult the concierge at your hotel or resort for more information.

Teeing off

Ixtapa has two locations where you can tee off. One spot is the **Club de Golf Ixtapa Palma Real** (☎ 755-553-1062, 755-553-1163), located in front of the Barceló Hotel at the entrance to Ixtapa's Hotel Zone as you arrive from Zihuatanejo. Its 18-hole course was designed by Robert Trent Jones, Jr., and much of the land here is protected as a wildlife preserve, so you may see flamingos or cranes near the lagoon at the 15th hole. Greens fees are $64; caddies cost an additional $16 for 18 holes or $11 for 9 holes. Electric carts are $25, and clubs are $20. Tee times begin at 7 a.m., but the club doesn't take reservations. (AE, MC, V are accepted.) Another option is the **Marina Ixtapa Golf Course** (☎ 755-553-1410; Fax: 755-553-0825), which was designed by Robert von Hagge and features 18 challenging holes. It's located at the opposite end of Hotel Zone from the Palma Real — the courses kind of form two bookends. The greens fees are $102; carts, caddies, and clubs are $20 each. The first foursome tees off at 7 a.m. Call for reservations 24 hours in advance. (AE, MC, V are accepted.)

Taking time for tennis

If you want to work on your **tennis** game in Ixtapa, both the **Club de Golf Ixtapa** (☎ **755-553-1062,** 755-553-1163) and the **Marina Ixtapa Golf Course** (☎ **755-553-1410;** Fax: 755-553-0825) have lighted public courts and equipment available for rent. Fees are $10 per hour during the day and $12 per hour at night. Call for reservations. In addition, the **Dorado Pacífico** and most of the better hotels on the Playa Palmar have courts. Although priority play is given to guests, most hotel courts are also open to the public.

Galloping along

For **horseback riding, Rancho Playa Linda** (☎ **044-755-557-0222** cellular) offers guided trail rides from the Playa Linda beach (about 8 miles north of Ixtapa). Guided rides begin at 8:30, 9:45, and 11:00 a.m. and 3:00, 4:00, and 5:00 p.m. The early morning ride is the coolest, and it's a beautiful way to start a day; the 5:00 p.m. trip offers a view of the sunset. Groups of three or more riders can arrange their own tour, which is especially nice a little later in the evening around sunset (though you need mosquito repellent). Riders can chose to ride along the beach to the mouth of the river and then follow the river back through coconut plantations, or they can hug the beach for the whole ride (which usually lasts between an hour and an hour and a half). The fee is around $25, cash only. Travel agencies in either town can arrange your trip but do charge a bit more for transportation. Reservations are suggested in the high season. Another good place to go horseback riding is in **Playa Larga.** There's a ranch on the first exit coming from Zihuatanejo on Hwy. 200 going south (no phone, but you can't miss it — it's the first corral to the right as you drive towards the beach). The horses are in excellent shape, and the fee is $25 for 45 minutes.

Sightseeing in Ixtapa-Zihuatanejo

One of the most enjoyable things to do here doesn't even cost a peso — stroll along Zihuatanejo's **Paseo del Pescador** and take in the local life. Fishing boats bob in the waters, gulls circle overhead, and the basketball court is constantly used.

The **Museo de Arqueología de la Costa Grande,** which traces the history of the area from Acapulco to Ixtapa-Zihuatanejo from pre-Hispanic times through the colonial era, is at the east end of the Paseo near Guerrero road. Most of the museum's pottery and stone artifacts provide evidence of extensive trade between the peoples of this area and far-off cultures and regions, including the Toltec and Teotihuacán cultures near Mexico City, the Olmec culture on both the Pacific and Gulf coasts, and areas along the northern Pacific coast. This museum easily merits the half-hour or less it takes to stroll through; information signs are in Spanish, but an accompanying brochure is available in English. Admission is $1 and it's open Tuesday to Sunday from 10 a.m. to 6 p.m.

Shopping in Ixtapa-Zihuatanejo

Shopping is not especially memorable in Ixtapa — T-shirts and Mexican crafts make up most of the offerings. Several of the town's numerous plazas have air-conditioned shops that carry resort wear — as well as the requisite T-shirts and silver jewelry. All of these shops are within the same area on Boulevar Ixtapa, across from the beachside hotels, and most are open 9 a.m. to 2 p.m. and 4 to 9 p.m. including Sunday.

Zihuatanejo, like other resorts in Mexico, also has its quota of T-shirt and souvenir shops, but it's becoming a better place to buy Mexican crafts, folk art, and jewelry. The **artisan's market** on Calle Cinco de Mayo is a good place to start your shopping before moving on to specialty shops. A **municipal market** is located on Avenida Benito Juárez (about five blocks inland from the waterfront, sprawling over several blocks), but most of the vendors offer the same things — *huaraches* (Mexican-style sandals made of hard leather), hammocks, and baskets — with little variety. Numerous small shops spread inland from the waterfront some three or four blocks and are well worth exploring.

Shops are generally open Monday to Saturday 10 a.m. to 2 p.m. and 4 to 8 p.m.; many of the better shops close on Sunday, but some smaller souvenir stands stay open, although the hours vary.

I recommend the following shops:

- ✔ If you find your wardrobe isn't weathering the heat very well, **Boutique D'Xochitl** (Ejido at Cuauhtémoc; ☎ 755-554-2131) is the place to find crinkle-cotton clothing that's perfect for tropical climates.

- ✔ The small **Casa Marina** (Paseo del Pescador 9, along the waterfront heading in the direction of Álvarez near Cinco de Mayo; ☎ 755-554-2373) complex houses four shops, each specializing in handcrafted wares from all over Mexico including handsome rugs, textiles, masks, colorful woodcarvings, and silver jewelry. Café Marina, the small coffee shop in the complex, has shelves and shelves of used paperback books in several languages for sale.

- ✔ **Coco Cabaña Collectibles** (Guerrero and Álvarez, next to Coconuts Restaurant; ☎ 755-554-2518) is filled with carefully selected crafts and folk art, including fine Oaxacan woodcarvings, from all across the country. Owner Pat Cummings once ran a gallery in New York, and the inventory reveals her discriminating eye.

Taking a Side Trip

Take a daylong tour of the surrounding countryside — you'll visit a fishing village, coconut and mango plantations, and the **Barra de Potosí Lagoon,** located 14 miles south of Zihuatanejo and known for its tropical birds. Known as the **Countryside Tour,** this package is available through local travel agencies for $55 to $70. The tour typically lasts 5½ hours and includes lunch and time for swimming. Because Barra de Potosí is very small without much to see or do, this tour is really a day at a remote beach, but the lush tropical landscapes and the kayak rides through the mangroves are enjoyable. The beach is generally crowded around noon with people from the tour buses, but it's tranquil at other times. If you don't want to participate in an organized tour, a roundtrip taxi to Barra de Potosí costs about $50. Or you can take a second-class bus from the main bus station in Zihua for about $1 — the half-hour trip is likely to leave you sweaty, but you can save a bundle. The bus station, *Central de Autobuses,* is about a mile from the center of town on Paseo Zihuatanejo at Paseo la Boquita, opposite the Pemex station and IMSS hospital.

For another option, try the **off-the-beaten-track tours,** organized by Alex León Pineda, the friendly and knowledgeable owner of **Fw4 Tours** (Los Patios Center Blvd. Ixtapa s/n, Ixtapa; ☎ 755-553-1442; Fax: 755-553-2014). His countryside tour ($48) goes to coconut and banana plantations, small villages of palm-thatch huts inhabited by traditional brick makers, and to the beach at La Saladita where fishermen and visitors together prepare a lunch of fresh lobster, *dorado (mahi-mahi),* or snapper. His tour to **Petatlán** and the **Laguna de San Valentín** is also very popular at $58. Highlights include visits to a small museum, the local market, and the town church. A stop at Laguna (lagoon) de San Valentín is next, followed by lunch on a small island. Major credit cards are accepted with a surcharge.

Twenty miles northwest of Ixtapa, the tiny fishing hamlet of **Troncones,** with its long beaches, has become a favorite escape for visitors to Ixtapa and Zihuatanejo — when that pace of life becomes too hectic. Troncones is so remote that only a few people have phones. Strolling the empty beach, swimming in the sea, and hiking in the jungle and to nearby caves is about the extent of the action. When you've built up and appetite, satisfy it with fresh seafood at one of the fisherman-shack restaurants.

No public buses serve this area, so you must join a tour or hire a taxi to take you to Troncones. For about $30, the taxi driver can take you to the area and return at the hour you request to bring you back to town. Some travel agencies have day trips here for about $25, which usually include lunch; it's cheaper, but less flexible than a taxi.

If you're only spending the day in Troncones, you can use the restaurant **El Burro Borracho** (☎ 755-553-2800) as your headquarters and have the taxi return for you there. This casual beachfront establishment is not your ordinary beach-shack restaurant. Owned by a former chef from San Francisco, it offers fish, shrimp, and lobster as well as steak and grilled meat. Try the shrimp tacos for a uniquely-Troncones treat. Wash the tasty grub down with a frosty margarita, an iced cappuccino, a glass of wine, or a cold beer. Remember that El Burro Borracho doesn't accept credit cards, and it's open daily from 8 a.m. to 9 p.m.

Discovering Ixtapa and Zihuatanejo After Dark

With an exception or two, Zihuatanejo nightlife dies down around 11 p.m. or midnight. For a decent selection of clubs, discos, hotel fiestas, and special events, head for Ixtapa. Just keep in mind that shuttle-bus service ends at 11 p.m., and a taxi ride back to Zihuatanejo after midnight costs 50% more than the regular price. During low season (after Easter and before Christmas), club hours vary. Some places are open only on weekends, and others are closed completely. In Zihuatanejo, the most popular hangout for local residents and expatriates is **Paccolo.** It's the one place where you can find a lively crowd of locals almost every night.

Many of the Ixtapa hotels hold Mexican fiestas and other special events that include dinner, drinks, live music, and entertainment for a fixed price (generally $33). The **Barceló Ixtapa** (☎ 755-553-1858) hosts the most popular fiesta, held each Wednesday night. Call for reservations or book your seats through your hotel's travel agency.

Many discos and dance clubs in Zihua and Ixtapa stay open until the last customers leave, so closing hours depend upon the revelers.

Most discos have a ladies night at least once a week — admission and drinks are free for women, making it easy for men to buy them a drink.

The Anderson chain of festive restaurants are a standard in Mexican nightlife, and Ixtapa has two of them. **Carlos 'n Charlie's** (Boulevar Ixtapa, just north of the Best Western Posada Real; ☎ 755-553-0085) runs knee-deep in nostalgia, bric-a-brac, silly sayings, and photos from the Mexican Revolution. This restaurant-nightclub boasts a party ambiance and good food. The eclectic menu includes iguana in season (with antacids and aspirin on the house). Out back by the beach is an open-air section (partly shaded) with a raised wooden platform for "pier-dancing" at night. The recorded rock-and-roll mixes with sounds of the ocean surf. The restaurant is open daily from 10 a.m. to midnight; pier dancing is held nightly from 9 p.m. to 3 a.m. The second tried-but-true Mexican nightspot from the Anderson lineup is **Señor Frog's** (Boulevar Ixtapa, in the La Puerta Center; ☎ 755-553-2282), which features several dining sections and a warehouse-like bar with raised dance floors. The rock-and-roll playing from large speakers sometimes prompts even dinner patrons to shimmy by their tables between courses. The restaurant is open daily 6 p.m. to midnight; the bar is open until 3 a.m.

Of all of the clubs in Ixtapa, **Christine** (Boulevar Ixtapa, in the Hotel Krystal; ☎ 755-553-0456) is both the best known and the glitziest. A throwback to the days of disco, Christine is famous for its midnight light show, which features classical music played on a mega sound system. A semicircle of tables arranged in tiers overlooks the dance floor. No tennis shoes, sandals, or shorts are allowed, and reservations are advised during high season. It's open nightly during high season from 10 p.m. to the wee hours of the mornin' (off-season hours vary). Cover varies depending on the day of the week from free to $20, and all major credit cards are accepted.

Ixtapa's newest and most progressive nocturnal option is **Liquid** (☎ 755-553-1725), located behind D'Rafaello restaurant in the Las Fuentes Shopping Center. A chill-out club in the true European tradition, Liquid opens at 1 a.m., plays the most progressive of electronica tunes, and stays open until 6 a.m. or so, although after you're inside, you'll never know a new day has dawned. With a cover charge ranging from free to $10, a very young, very hip crowd has claimed Liquid for its own.

Part VII
Acapulco

AFTER SAILING AROUND ACAPULCO BAY, RON AND DARLENE HEAD FOR THE INTERESTING GROTTOS OF NOSE CAY

In this part . . .

1t's a beach resort . . . and it's a big glittering city. The largest and most decadent of the Mexican beach resorts, Acapulco can be daunting at first glance.

With its 24-hour, nonstop action, Acapulco can overwhelm first-time visitors. But have no fear — I'm here for you. In this part, I help you choose your accommodations, and I share my insights on the best places to dine — from simply delectable fish-taco stands to cliff-side gourmet restaurants with views of Acapulco Bay's dazzling night-lights, I've got you covered. Nightlife? You can't visit Acapulco without sampling this part of the action. The Acapulco club scene remains *the* super-hot attraction of this grande dame of Mexico's beach resorts.

Chapter 22

The Lowdown on Acapulco's Hotel Scene

Acapulco was the first Mexican beach town to attract tourism to its golden sands, warm waters, and sunny days. Since the late 1930s, this beach resort has welcomed visitors from around the world, and at one time, it rivaled Rio as the playground of the elite and famous. Today, Acapulco offers one of the widest ranges of hotel choices among Mexican beach resorts — something for every taste and budget.

Because Acapulco's heyday occurred somewhere between 1950 and 1970, many of the hotels are notably dated; however, others have been kept up admirably and offer a funky, kind of retro charm. To me, the single most striking feature of Acapulco is the view of the twinkling lights of the bay at night — an impressive sight that tends to draw you into its nocturnal energy. The best views are from the hilltop hotels and the resorts on the bay's southern border, but any of the high-rise locations along Playa Condesa also offer prime views.

Choosing a Location

During my first encounter with Acapulco, I dismissed it as an outdated resort — a tired and ill-kempt relic most appropriate for those who enjoy a carnival-type atmosphere and sleeping all day to prepare for nights that last until sunrise. But my opinion was colored by where I was staying — in the heart of the rowdiest beach-bar action — which didn't suit my mood at the time. As I grew to know Acapulco and became acquainted with her other sides, it didn't take long for me to succumb to this diva's unique charms. Acapulco's energy is tireless (if occasionally tawdry), and her appeal lies somewhere between that of Las Vegas and Palm Beach. I feel strongly that your decision about where to stay plays a huge role in determining how happy you'll be with your Acapulco vacation.

Although Acapulco is an expansive city of several million residents, most visitors only come in contact with the area directly bordering Acapulco Bay and its beaches, which is easy to navigate and can be divided into three main areas. There's really no need to explore further — and you're not likely to have enough time to take in all of the sights, activities, and options for dining and nightlife in these areas during a typical one-week stay anyway.

Running from north to south, the first principal area is **Old Acapulco,** the historic section with a true downtown and plenty of budget accommodations.

Old Acapulco — the original heart of this grand dame of Mexico's beach resorts — has a great selection of basic, inexpensive hotels and lots of local color. Travelers familiar with Acapulco — or comfortable with travel in Mexico — tend to prefer this area. Numerous budget hotels dot the streets fanning out from the *zócalo* (Acapulco's official and original central plaza). These accommodations are among the best values in Acapulco but generally offer only the most basic of comforts.

Next comes the **Costera Hotel Zone.** The mid-range, high-rise hotels — lined up side by side, looking much like Miami Beach — are concentrated along this golden stretch of Condesa beach. The area is easy to navigate and offers lots of options for shopping, dining, and nightlife, so it's the best choice for first-time visitors.

If you're looking to spoil yourself, the hotels in the southern neighborhoods and up in the hillsides overlooking the bay are your best bets. The hillside neighborhood bordering the curve of the southern edge of Acapulco Bay is **Las Brisas,** the elegant address in town and home of Acapulco's exclusive villas and lusher hotels. Encompassing the Las Brisas area, south of Acapulco Bay, as you travel toward the airport, are the neighborhoods of Punta Diamante and Revolcadero Beach, which fronts the Pacific Ocean. This is where the most expensive and luxurious resorts are found, complete with golf courses.

However, this area is several miles from the heart of Acapulco; anytime you want to travel into the Hotel Zone to enjoy its restaurants, shopping malls, or nightclubs, you're looking at a round-trip taxi fare of anywhere from $12 to $20.

Acapulco's Best Accommodations

Each hotel listing includes specific rack rates for two people spending one night in a double room during high season (Christmas to Easter), unless otherwise indicated. Rack rates simply mean published rates and tend to be the highest rate paid — you can do better, especially if you're purchasing a package that includes airfare (see Chapter 6 for tips on avoiding paying rack rates). Please refer to the Introduction of *Mexico's Beach Resorts For Dummies* for an explanation of the price categories.

It's not unusual for many hotels to double their normal rates during Christmas and Easter weeks, but low-season rates can be anywhere from 20 percent to 60 percent below high-season rates. Note that some rates may seem much higher than others — until you realize that they are "all inclusive" — meaning that your meals and beverages are included in the price of your stay. These rates also include all tips, taxes, and most activities and entertainment.

All hotels have air conditioning unless otherwise indicated.

Camino Real Acapulco Diamante

$$$$$ Punta Diamante/Puerto Marqués

I love this hotel — it's an oasis of tranquility in the middle of Acapulco's non-stop energy. This relaxing, self-contained resort is an ideal choice for families or for travelers who already know Acapulco and don't care to explore much. If swimming in the ocean is a priority, this is your best bet in the area — it's located on the clean and safe-for-swimming Playa Marqués, but you do miss out on the compelling views of Acapulco Bay. In terms of contemporary decor, services, and amenities, I consider this to be Acapulco's finest hotel. The Camino Real is tucked in a secluded, 81-acre location — part of the enormous Acapulco Diamante project. From Carretera Escénica, you wind down a handsome brick road to the site of the hotel overlooking Puerto Marqués Bay. The spacious rooms have balconies or terraces, small sitting areas, marble floors, a safe-deposit box in the closet, and comfortable, classic furnishings. A bonus, in my opinion: The Camino Real offers 24-hour room service with a terrific menu at very reasonable prices — competitive with area restaurants after you figure in the cost of a round-trip taxi ride. The property also offers special amenities for children including the kid's "Mischief Club" and a children's pool. For adults, a small health club, spa, and tennis court are on-site.

Carretera Escénica Km 14 and Baja Catita 18. ☎ **744-435-1010.** *Fax: 744-435-1020. Internet:* www.caminoreal.com/acapulco. *146 rooms. Complimentary parking. Rack rates: High season $300 double, $410 master suite (includes American breakfast); low-season and midweek discounts available. AE, MC, V.*

Acapulco Bay Area Accommodations

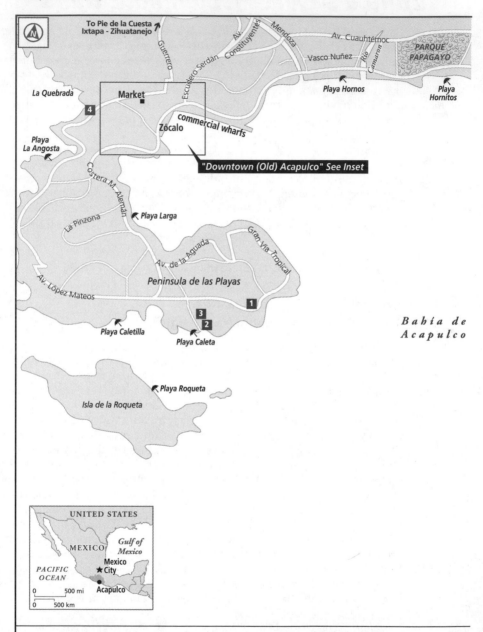

Camino Real Acapulco Diamante **11**	Hotel Sands **5**
Costa Linda Hotel **3**	Hyatt Regency Acapulco **9**
Elcano Hotel **8**	Las Brisas **10**
Fiesta Americana Condesa Acapulco **6**	Los Flamingos Hotel **1**
Grand Meigas Acapulco Resort **2**	Plaza Las Glorias/El Mirador **4**
Hotel Misión **12**	Villa Vera Hotel & Racquet Club **7**

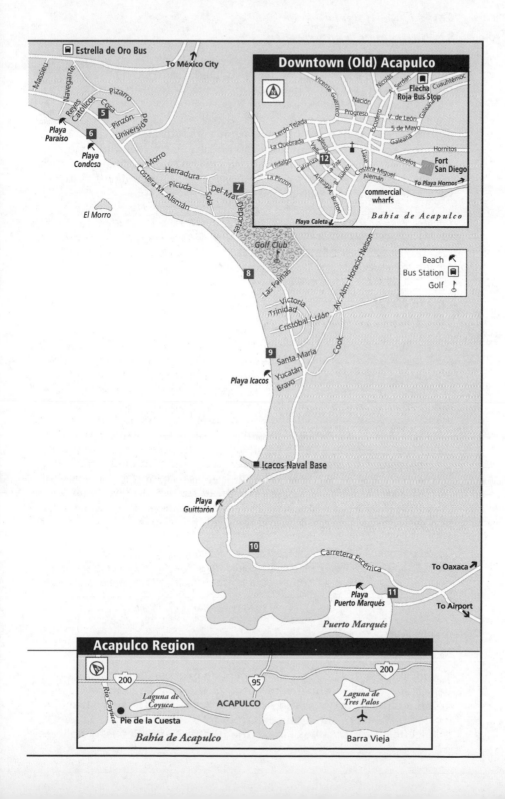

Estrella de Oro Bus

To México City

Massieu
Navegante
Reyes Católicos
Pizarro
Cosa
Pinzón
Universidad

5

6

Playa
Paraíso

Playa
Condesa

Morro

Herradura

Picuda

Sola

Del Mar

Costera M. Alamán

Deportes

El Morro

7

Golf Club

8

Las Palmas

Victoria

Trinidad

Cristóbal Colón

Av. Alm. Horacio Nelson

Cook

9

Santa María

Yucatán

Bravo

Playa Icacos

Icacos Naval Base

Playa
Guittarón

10

Carretera Escénica

To Oaxaca

11

Playa
Puerto Marqués

To Airport

Puerto Marqués

Downtown (Old) Acapulco

Vicente Guerrero

Nicolás

A. Serdén

Cuauhtémoc

Flecha
Roja Bus Stop

Nación

Progreso

Escudero

V. de León

5 de Mayo

Galeana

Lerdo Tejada

La Quebrada

Iglesia

Valle

La Paz

I. Hidalgo

Carranza

La Pinzón

Altengua

Baston

Juárez

Llave

Costera Miguel
Alemán

Morelos

Hornitos

Fort
San Diego

To Playa Hornos

commercial
wharfs

12

Playa Caleta

Bahía de Acapulco

Beach

Bus Station

Golf

Acapulco Region

200

95

200

Río Coyuca

Laguna de
Coyuca

ACAPULCO

Laguna de
Tres Palos

Pie de la Cuesta

Bahía de Acapulco

Barra Vieja

Costa Linda Hotel

$ **Playa Caleta /Old Acapulco**

Budget-minded American and Mexican couples are drawn to the clean, sunny, and well-kept rooms of the Costa Linda, one of the best values in the area. Caleta Beach is just a one-block walk from the property. All rooms have a mini-fridge, and some have a small kitchenette, making it a good choice for longer stays or for those who want to save vacation dollars by preparing a few of their own meals. Although the Costa Linda is cozy, it's situated adjacent to one of the busier streets in Old Acapulco, so traffic noise can be bothersome. Rooms surround a small pool with lounge chairs and tropical plants. Choose an upstairs room for more privacy. A tennis court is also available.

Costera Miguel Alemán 1008, just above the entrance to Caleta Beach pier. ☎ *744-482-5277, 744-482-2549. Fax: 744-483-4017. 44 units. Free parking. Rack rates: High season $60 double; low season $35 double. Two children under 8 stay free in parents' room. MC, V.*

Elcano Hotel

$$$ **Costera Hotel Zone**

An Acapulco classic and a personal favorite of mine, the Elcano is known for its prime location near the convention center on a broad stretch of golden-sand beach. The retro-style, turquoise-and-white lobby, and beachfront pool area are the closest you can get to a South Beach Miami atmosphere in Acapulco, and its popular open-air restaurant adds to the lively waterfront scene. On the whole, the Elcano reminds me of a set from a classic Elvis-in-Acapulco movie — you almost expect to see the King among the tanned beach regulars here. The hotel's reputation is further enhanced by its exceptional service. The continually upgraded rooms, featuring classic navy-and-white accents, are bright and very comfortable, and most offer ample oceanfront balconies. This is an ideal place if you attend a convention in Acapulco or want the optimal location between hillside nightlife and the Costera beach zone.

Costera Miguel Alemán 75, just west of the convention center. ☎ *800-972-2162 in the U.S., or 744-484-1950. Fax: 744-484-2230. Internet:* http://hotel-elcano. com. *180 units. Rack rates: $132 studio and standard room, $155 junior suite, $213 master suite. AE, DC, MC, V.*

Fiesta Americana Condesa Acapulco

$$ **Costera Hotel Zone**

The location of this hotel — in the absolute heart of Playa Condesa — is perfect for travelers who don't want to miss a beat and look to be right in the middle of the casual beach-bar action. The 18-story structure, located just east of and up the hill from the Glorieta Diana (a landmark traffic circle with a statue of Diana the Huntress — which is a duplicate of the one in Mexico City — at its center), towers above Playa Condesa. The unremarkable but comfortable rooms tend to be loud (depending on the crowd) — music from the pool wafts up into the rooms. All rooms have a private terrace or balcony with an ocean view. In addition to a beachfront pool, an adults-only hilltop, swimming pool offers one of the finest views of Acapulco in the city, plus the hotel has a smaller children's pool and a sundeck.

Costera Miguel Alemán 97. ☎ *800-FIESTA1 in the U.S., or 744-484-2355. Fax: 744-484-1828. Internet:* www.fiestamericana.com. *500 units. Free private parking. Rack rates: High season $112–$150 double; low season $93–$124 double. Ask about "Fiesta Break" packages, which include meals. AE, DC, MC, V.*

Grand Meigas Acapulco Resort
$$$ Playa Caleta /Old Acapulco

If you prefer the authentic feel of a Mexican holiday with all its boisterous, family-friendly, and spirited charms, then the Meigas is a great choice. It's also a great value. The rooms at this all-inclusive property are simple — stark even — but the hotel itself is usually plenty populated and teeming with activity. This high quality, 9-floor resort is built into a cliff on the Caleta peninsula and located adjacent to one of the liveliest beaches in Old Acapulco. Successions of stepped terraces are home to tropical gardens, restaurants, and pools — both saltwater and freshwater. A private beach and boat dock is located down a brief flight of stairs. Rooms surround a central plant-filled courtyard topped by a glass ceiling, and all rooms have large terraces with ocean views, although some layouts lack separation from the neighboring terrace. As is traditional in all-inclusive resorts, meals and drinks are available at almost any hour, and the resort has a changing agenda of theme nights and evening entertainment.

Cerro San Martín 325, just east of Caleta Beach. ☎ *744-483-9940, 744-483-9140. Fax: 744-483-9125. E-mail:* meigaca@pordigy.net.mx. *255 units. Rack rates: High season $82–$120 per person, all-inclusive; low season $50–$80 per person, all-inclusive. Room-only prices are sometimes available upon request. AE, DC, MC, V.*

Hotel Misión
$ Old Acapulco (Downtown)

If this courtyard hotel reminds you of an old monastery, it may be because the original structure is over a century old — truly and authentically "Old Acapulco"! Rooms are located in the L-shaped building that borders a plant-filled, brick courtyard shaded by two enormous mango trees. The hotel's location, on a narrow street surrounded by tiny shops, lends a distinctly different atmosphere to an Acapulco holiday here. You're in the center of town life just two blocks inland from the Costera, fishermen's wharf, *zócalo,* and la Quebrada — the site of the famous cliff divers. Playa Caleta is about a half-mile away. The rooms have colonial touches, such as colorful tile and wrought iron, and come simply furnished with a fan (no air conditioning here) and one or two beds with good mattresses. Unfortunately, the promised hot water is not reliable — request a cold-water-only room and receive a discount. Breakfast is served on the patio.

Felipe Valle 12, between La Paz and Hidalgo. ☎ *744-482-3643. Fax: 744-482-2076. 27 units. Rack Rates: $50 double. No credit cards.*

Hotel Sands
$ Costera Hotel Zone

Comfortable and unpretentious, the Hotel Sands is a great option for budget-minded travelers. The hotel's location on the inland side of the Costera translates to greatly reduced prices, and the fact that it's about a block off the main highway means it's far enough away from all the traffic noise to make your nights peaceful. Still, the Hotel Sands is close enough — walking distance — to the lively Costera Hotel Zone. From the street, you enter the hotel lobby through a stand of umbrella palms and an attractive garden restaurant — one that offers terrific, authentic Mexican food at rock-bottom prices. Rooms are light and airy in the style of a good, modern motel and have basic furnishings, wall-to-wall carpeting, and a terrace or balcony. The bungalow units are located across the street — all have kitchenettes. Two swimming pools (one for adults only), a kid's playground, a volleyball court, and complimentary coffee served in the lobby round out the features.

Costera Miguel Alemán 178, across from the Acapulco Plaza Hotel. ☎ *744-484-2260. Fax: 744-484-1053. Internet:* www.sands.com.mx. *93 units. Limited free parking. Rack rates: $58 standard room, $47 bungalow (all year except Christmas, Easter, and other major Mexican holidays). AE, MC, V.*

Hyatt Regency Acapulco
$$$ Costera Hotel Zone

The Hyatt is one of the largest and most modern hotels in Acapulco and about as sophisticated as they come here — which is still less sophisticated that most other resorts. It's a good choice for couples looking for a romantic break or for folks attending conventions. (It's close to the convention center.) Two large, free-form pools meander through tropical gardens on the broad, golden-sand beachfront. The sleek lobby has an inviting sitting area and bar that hosts live music every evening and boasts the largest selection of tequilas in Acapulco. All rooms are large with sizable balconies overlooking the pool and ocean. Regency Club guests receive special amenities (***Note:*** Children aren't allowed in Regency Club rooms). Kitchenettes are available in some rooms for an extra charge. Three outdoor tennis courts lit for night play and access to a nearby gym are included in with your stay making this hotel a good choice for travelers who prefer their vacations a little on the active side. The Hyatt Acapulco caters to a large Jewish clientele and offers a full-service kosher restaurant, an on-premise synagogue, and a special Sabbath elevator.

Costera Miguel Alemán 1. ☎ *800-233-1234 in the U.S. and Canada, 01-800-005-0000 in Mexico, or 744-469-1234. Fax: 744-484-3087. Internet:* www.hyattacapulco. com.mx. *645 units. Rack rates: High season $165 double, $175 Regency Club; low season $140 double, $150 Regency Club. AE, DC, MC, V.*

Las Brisas
$$$$$ Las Brisas

With its hilltop views, terrace pools, and 24-hour, pampering service, the pink-themed Las Brisas hotel is the quintessential Acapulco experience for many Acapulco veterans. A local landmark, Las Brisas is known for its tiered, pink-stucco facade and the 175 pink Jeeps rented exclusively to Las Brisas guests. If you stay here, you better like pink because the color scheme extends to practically everything. Las Brisas is also known for inspiring romance and is best enjoyed by couples indulging in time together — alone. Although the marble-floored rooms with mostly built-in furnishings are simple, they are each like separate villas and offer the most spectacular panoramic views of Acapulco Bay from the private balconies and terraces. Each room also has a private (or semi-private) swimming pool. (Altogether, Las Brisas boasts 250 swimming pools.) The more spacious Regency Club rooms are located at the apex of the property and offer the best views. You stay at Las Brisas more for the panache and setting than for the amenities. TVs are a recent addition, but they feature volume control so you don't disturb other guests. Early each morning, continental breakfast arrives in a discreet cubbyhole, so your coffee is ready when you are. Although the property isn't located on the beach, Las Brisas offers courtesy shuttle service to its own private beach club located 5 minutes away on the southwestern tip of Acapulco Bay. Here, freshwater and saltwater pools, plus a large restaurant and bar — though still not much of a real beach — compete for your attention. Five tennis courts, daily activities, and access to a nearby gym round out the action. A mandatory service charge takes care of the shuttle service from the hillside rooms to the lobby and all other service tips. The hotel is located on the southern edge of the bay overlooking the road to the airport and close to the hottest nightclubs in town.

Carretera Escénica 5255. ☎ *800-228-3000 in the U.S., or 744-469-6900. Fax: 744-446-5332. 263 units. Rack rates: High season $450 shared pool, $550 private pool, $650 Royal Beach Club; low season $230 shared pool, $345 private pool, $380 Royal Beach Club. $20 per day service charge extra (in lieu of all tips) plus 17% tax. Rates include continental breakfast. AE, DC, MC, V.*

Los Flamingos Hotel
$$ Old Acapulco

What a find! I fell in love with Los Flamingos as soon as I saw it — who wouldn't? — with its funky charm that transports you back to the days when there was a Hollywood jet set and Acapulco was their playground. Perched on a cliff 500 feet above Acapulco Bay, this hotel was frequented by such old Hollywood stars as John Wayne, Cary Grant, Johnny Weissmuller, Fred McMurray, Errol Flynn, Red Skelton, Roy Rogers, and a host of others. In fact, the stars liked the Flamingos so much that at one point they bought it and converted it into a private club. Though it enjoys a colorful history, it's in excellent shape and exceptionally clean. Los Flamingos offers visitors a totally different perspective of Acapulco because it maintains all the charm of that grand era gone by. Photos of movie stars grace the lobby, especially those of Wayne, Grant, and Weissmuller — who constructed the large "Tarzan Suite" (also known as the "Round House") as his part-time residence. All rooms have dramatic ocean views with either a large balcony or terrace, but most of them are not air-conditioned (those that are also have TVs). Still, the constant sea breeze is cool enough. Rooms are colorful with mosaic-tile tables and mirrors and brightly painted walls. A small pool is the popular gathering point during the day; the large bar is the place to be in the evening. I don't recommend this hotel for small children though — the same dramatic setting that produces such spectacular views can also inspire a constant state of panic for parents. A weekly *pozole* (a special stew made from hominy, served with shredded pork or chicken and an assortment of toppings) party makes Thursdays especially popular. Live music performed by a Mexican band that was probably around in the era of Wayne — note the seashell-pink bass — accompanies the festivities. Even if you don't stay here, plan to come for a margarita at sunset and a walk along the dramatic lookout point — not for the faint of heart!

Av. López Matéos s/n. ☎ 744-482-0690. Fax: 744-483-9806. 40 rooms. Rack rates: High season $80 double, $110 with A/C, $100 junior suite; low season $62 double, $88 with A/C, $80 junior suite. AE, MC, V.

Plaza Las Glorias/El Mirador
$$ Old Acapulco

The best part about staying here is watching those amazing Acapulco cliff divers every day and evening from the comfort of your room. It's an unforgettable sight and a real adrenaline rush. The hotel is built in a horseshoe shape at the apex of la Quebrada, the famous cove where the cliff divers perform. Rooms lack a little in the way of upkeep but offer a choice of double or queen-size beds, small kitchenette areas with mini-fridges and coffee makers, and large bathrooms with marble counters. Most have a separate living room, some have a whirlpool tub, and all feature colorful, Saltillo-tile accents and other Mexican decorative touches. Be sure to ask for a room with a balcony or ocean view. The restaurant and bar also offer great views of the cliff-diving shows and are popular with tourists from other hotels during the evening performances. Logically, the beach here is a steep jump down the cliff, but the resort does offer an alternative in the form of a saltwater pool as well as two freshwater pools. A protected cove with good snorkeling is located nearby.

Quebrada 74. ☎ *800-342-AMIGO in the U.S., or 744-483-1221, or 744-484-0909 for reservations. Fax: 744-482-4564. 132 units. Limited parking on street. Rack rates: High season $120 double; low season $98 double; suites with whirlpool year-round $140. An extra charge of $10 applies if you use the kitchenette. AE, MC, V.*

Villa Vera Hotel and Racquet Club

$$$$$ Costera Hotel Zone

Another "address of distinction" in Acapulco is the legendary Villa Vera, which is ideal for a romantic getaway. A smaller inn with a decidedly clubby feel to it, this property started off as a private home with adjacent villas serving as accommodations for houseguests. After a while, it became popular with stars such as Liz Taylor, who married Mike Todd here. Richard M. and Pat Nixon celebrated their 25th wedding anniversary here, and it also served as the set for much of Elvis's film, *Fun in Acapulco.* The hotel is located on a hill above the Costera Hotel Zone and offers the closest experience to Acapulco villa life that you can find in a public property. Starwood Hotels has taken over management of Villa Vera and made significant renovations and upgrades in facilities that have returned it to a standard of excellence — in the style of today's more popular boutique-style hotels. Rooms are large, airy, and more sophisticated in decor than most others in Acapulco. Villa Vera offers the very finest spa facilities in the area as well as two clay tennis courts, two lighted racquetball courts, and a small gym. The total of 14 pools includes 8 private pools for the six villas and two houses. Most of the other rooms share pools, except for standard, least expensive rooms, which have the use of the large public pool located across from the restaurant.

Lomas del Mar 35 (from the Costera, take Av. de los Deportes inland and go left on Av. Prado, which curves right and turns into Av. Lomas del Mar). ☎ *800-710-9300 inside Mexico, or 744-484-0334, 744-484-0335. Fax: 744-484-7479. E-mail:* hotel_villavera_aca@clubregina.com. *69 rooms including suites, villas, and 2 houses. Rack rates: High season $190 studio, $195–$260 double, $315–$350 suite, $380 villa, $1095 Casa Teddy for 4 people, $1,210 Casa Julio for 6 people; Low-season rates around 10 percent less than high season. AE, MC, V.*

Chapter 23

Settling into Acapulco

● ●

In This Chapter

▶ Knowing the scene before you arrive

▶ Finding transportation around town

▶ Reading up on all kinds of useful resources and tips

● ●

Though most beach resorts have "relaxing" written all over them, Acapulco offers visitors nonstop, 24-hours-a-day energy. With so much to do, you won't want to loose a minute figuring out the details, so this chapter guides you through the fundamentals of settling into Acapulco. I help you get your bearings upon arrival at Acapulco's bustling airport, get settled into your hotel, and gain confidence in finding your way around the area. Finally, I give you tips on everything from currency exchanges to Internet access to finding the cheapest — and most entertaining — ways to get around town.

Arriving in Acapulco

No matter the time of year or where you're coming from, the first thing you're likely to notice about Acapulco when you depart the plane is the sizzling climate. The heat is tangible here, but most travelers quickly become adjusted. Both immigration and customs are brief, generally easy procedures. Mexico's second most important industry is tourism, so the country's aim is to be as welcoming as possible.

Navigating passport control and customs

The immigration clearance area is generally a lengthy walk from the plane's jetway and down a flight of stairs. When you reach immigration, an officer will ask you to show your passport and your completed tourist card, the **FMT** (see Chapter 7 for all the FMT details).

Your FMT is an important document, so take good care of it. You're supposed to keep the FMT with you at all times because you may be required to show it should you run into any sort of trouble. You also need to turn it back in upon departure, or you may be unable to leave without replacing it.

Next up is the baggage claim area. Here, porters stand by to help with your bags, and they're well worth the price of the tip — about a dollar a bag. After you collect your luggage, you pass through another check-point. Something that looks like a traffic light awaits you here. You press a button, and if the light turns green, you're free to go. If it turns red, you need to open each of your bags for a quick search. It's Mexico's random search procedure for customs. If you have an unusually large bag, or an excessive amount of luggage, you may be searched regardless of the traffic-light outcome.

Getting to your hotel

The airport (ACA) is 14 miles southeast of town — over the hills east of Acapulco Bay. Private taxis are the fastest option to get to downtown Acapulco. A taxi ride runs from $15 to $50 depending on your destination.

 The major rental-car agencies all have booths at the airport, but I advise against getting a car unless you determine you really want one — they tend to be very expensive and generally more troublesome than convenient.

 Transportes Terrestres has desks at the front of the airport (just as you exit the baggage-claim area) where you can buy tickets for minivan *colectivo* (shared minivan) transportation into town for $5 to $10 — rates are preset and based on the distance to your hotel. Return service to the airport must be reserved through your hotel. Taxis to the airport tend to be much less expensive (about half the price) than taxis from the airport because the taxis that pick you up at the airport are federally chartered cars with exclusive rights to airport transportation — and the associated steep fares.

Getting Around Acapulco

Acapulco stretches for more than four miles around the huge bay. The most popular tourist areas are divided roughly into three sections: **Acapulco Viejo (Old Acapulco);** the **Costera Hotel Zone,** which follows the main boulevard, Costera Miguel Alemán (or just "the Costera"); and **the southern shore,** whose exclusive neighborhoods border the scenic highway (Carretera Escénica) between the airport and the International Center.

Street names and numbers in Acapulco can be confusing and hard to find — many streets either aren't well marked or change names unexpectedly. Fortunately, there's seldom a reason to be far from the Costera, so it's hard to get lost. But remember that street numbers on the Costera don't follow a logical order, so you can't assume that similar numbers are necessarily close together.

Taking a taxi

Taxis, which are more plentiful than tacos in Acapulco (and practically as inexpensive if you're traveling in the downtown area only), are the best way to get around here.

Significant differences in prices for different types of taxis are common, so always establish the price with the driver before starting out. Hotel taxis may charge three times the rate of a taxi hailed on the street, and nighttime taxi rides cost extra, too. Taxis are also more expensive if you're staying in the Puente Diamante neighborhood, south of Las Brisas, which includes Puerto Marqués — these are on the southern highway, between town and the airport. The minimum fare is $1.50 per ride for a roving VW bug-style taxi in town. The fare from Puerto Marqués costs $8 to the Hotel Zone and $10 into downtown. *Sitio* taxis are nicer cars, but they're also more expensive — $3 minimum fare.

Acapulco-taxi fashion demands that drivers decorate their cars with flashy, Las Vegas-style neon lights — the more colorful and pulsating, the better. It almost appears to be a local competition. And there's no extra charge for the added embellishments. These decked-out rides are especially popular in Old Acapulco.

Catching a bus

Buses are another great option for traveling along the Costera — they're easy to use and inexpensive. Two kinds of buses run along this main drag: pastel, color-coded buses and regular "school buses." The difference is in the price: New, air-conditioned, color-coded, tourist buses (Aca Tur Bus) cost 35¢; old buses cost 3¢. Covered bus stops, with handy maps on the walls showing bus routes to major sights and hotels, are located all along the Costera. If you want to go downtown from the Costera, take the bus marked "Centro" or "Zócalo;" to get to the southeast side (the Acapulco Diamante area), take a bus marked "Base" (pronounced *bah*-say). Buses traveling these popular routes come along at least every ten minutes. Buses also head out to more distant destinations such as **Puerto Marqués** to the east (marked "Puerto Marqués-Basa") and **Pie de la Cuesta** to the northwest (marked "Zócalo-Pie de la Cuesta"). Be sure to verify the time and place of the last bus back if you hop on along one of these routes.

Renting a car

Rental cars are available at the airport and at hotel desks along the Costera, but I wouldn't recommend one — they're expensive, and parking is hard to find. Unless you plan on exploring outlying areas, you're better off taking taxis or using the easy and inexpensive public buses. Besides, it's much easier to leave the driving to someone else.

Fast Facts: Acapulco

American Express

The main office (Costera Alemán 1628, in the Gran Plaza shopping center; ☎ 744-469-1100) is open Monday to Saturday 10 a.m. to 7 p.m.

Area Code

The telephone area code is **744. Note:** The area code changed from 7 in November 2001.

Babysitters

Most of the larger hotels can easily arrange for babysitters, but many speak limited English. Rates range from $3 to $8 per hour with an additional charge of about $3 for a taxi if you stay out past 10 p.m.

Banks, ATMs, and Currency Exchange

Numerous banks are located along the Costera and are open Monday to Friday 9 a.m. to 6 p.m. and Saturday 10:00 a.m. to 1:30 p.m. Banks, and their automated teller machines, generally have the best rates. *Casas de cambio* (currency exchange booths) along the street may have better exchange rates than hotels, and they're open late. Most establishments accept U.S. dollars as readily as pesos but at reduced exchange rates, so you're better off using local currency whenever possible.

Climate

Acapulco boasts sunshine 360 days a year and an average daytime temperature of 80°F (27°C). Humidity varies. Acapulco receives approximately 59 inches of rain per year — June through October is the rainy season, although July and August are relatively dry. Tropical showers are brief and usually occur at night.

Consular Agents

The **U.S. Consular Agency** office is at the Hotel Club del Sol on Costera Alemán at Reyes Católicos (☎ 744-481-1699, 744-469-0556), across from the Hotel Acapulco Plaza. The office is open Monday to Friday 10 a.m. to 2 p.m. The **Canadian Consulate** (Centro Comercial Marbella, Local 23; ☎ 01-800-706-2900 toll-free emergency number inside Mexico, or 744-484-1305) is open Monday to Friday 9 a.m. to 5 p.m.

Hospitals

Hospital Magallanes (Avenida Wilfrido Massieu 2, on the corner with Colon, one block from the Costera; ☎ 744-485-6194, 744-485-6096) has an English-speaking staff and doctors. Another option is **Hospital Pacífico** (Calle Fraile y Nao 4; ☎ 744-487-7180, 744-487-7161).

Information

The **State of Guerrero Tourism Office** (☎ and fax: 744-484-4583, 744-484-4416) operates the **Procuraduría del Turista** on the street level in front of the International Center, a convention center set back from Avenida Alemán. (It's down a lengthy walkway with fountains.) The office offers maps and information about the city and state as well as police assistance for tourists; it's open daily 9 a.m. to 10 p.m.

Internet Access

Cyber-café (Costera Miguel Alemán 93, in the Torres Gemelas building; ☎ 744-484-7010, 744-484-4828, ask for the cyber-cafe extension) is open daily 10 a.m. to 8 p.m. The charge for 30 minutes of online access is just $2.

Maps

One of the best around is the free American Express map, usually found at tourist information offices and hotel concierge desks. Sanborn's or Wal-Mart may also have more detailed maps for sale.

Newspapers/Magazines

The larger Costera hotels generally carry a good selection of English-language newspapers (like *USA Today*) and magazines in their gift shops as well as the English-language *Mexico City News.* You can also find English-language paperbacks and magazines at **Sanborn's** department stores (Costera Miguel Alemán 209, downtown across from the ship docks, ☎ 744-484-4413; Costera Miguel Alemán 1226, in the Estrella Condo Tower, ☎ 744-484-4465, and Costera Miguel Alemán 163, at the Hotel Calinda, ☎ 744-481-2426).

Pharmacy

One of the largest drugstores in town is **Farmacia Daisy** (☎ 744-484-7664, 744-484-5950). The **Sam's Club** and **Wal-Mart** (open 24 hours), are both located on the Costera, have pharmacy services and lower prices on medicines.

Police

Policemen in white and light blue uniforms belong to a special corps of English-speaking police established to assist tourists. For the main police department, call ☎ 744-485-0650.

Post Office

The central post office *(correo)* is located next door to Sears (close to the Fideicomiso office). Other branches are located in the Estrella de Oro bus station on Cuauhtémoc, inland from the Acapulco Qualton Hotel, and on the Costera near Caleta Beach.

Safety

Riptides claim a few lives every year, so pay close attention to warning flags posted on Acapulco beaches. Red or black flags mean stay out of the water, yellow flags signify caution, and white or green flags mean it's safe to swim.

As is the case anywhere, tourists are vulnerable to thieves. This is especially true when shopping in a market, lying on the beach, wearing jewelry, or visibly carrying a camera, purse, or bulging wallet.

Taxes

There's a 15 percent value-added tax (IVA) on goods and services, and it's generally included in the posted price.

Taxis

Always establish the price of a trip with the driver before starting out. Hotel taxis charge more than a taxi hailed on the street, and nighttime taxi rides cost extra, too. The minimum fare is $1.50 per ride for a roving VW bug-style taxi in town. The fare from Puerto Marqués costs $8 to the Hotel Zone and $10 into downtown. *Sitio* taxis are nicer cars, but they're also more expensive — $3 minimum fare.

Telephone

Phone numbers seem to change frequently in Acapulco — the most reliable source for telephone numbers is the **Procuraduría del Turista** (☎ 744-484-4583) where an exceptionally friendly staff can help you locate what you need. Avoid the phone booths that have signs in English advising you to call home using a special 800 number — these are absolute rip-offs and can cost as much as $20 US per minute. The least expensive way to call is by using a Telmex pre-paid phone card, available at most pharmacies and mini-supers, using the official Telmex (Lada) public phones. In, Mexico you need to dial 001 prior to a number to reach the United States and you need to preface long distance calls within Mexico by dialing 01.

Time Zone

Acapulco operates on central standard time, but Mexico's observance of daylight savings time varies somewhat from that in the United States.

Chapter 24

Dining in Acapulco

• •

In This Chapter

▶ Discovering Acapulco's best restaurants

▶ Finding the best Mexican cuisine in Acapulco

• •

*B*eing the cosmopolitan city that it is, Acapulco offers world-class international cuisine, much of it served in the romantic restaurants located along the southern coast. The quintessential Acapulco dining experience is sitting at a candlelit table with a view of the glittering bay spread out before you. If, however, you're looking for simple, good food or an authentic, local dining experience, you're best off checking out the scene in Old Acapulco. Being a beach town, Acapulco restaurants serve up a ton of fresh seafood. My personal Acapulco favorites include a small place that specializes in fish tacos and one that has what must be the world's most delectable mussels.

Despite the growing profusion of American-influenced chain restaurants, resist the temptation to go with what you know — trust me, the locally owned restaurants offer the best food and best value.

And, although most of Mexico's beach resorts fall on the casual side when it comes to dress, Acapulco goes against the trend, especially for the ladies. Feel free to go all out with your sexy resort wear when dining here. Also note that dinner tends to be a late affair. Most Acapulco regulars wouldn't think of dining before 10 p.m. so that they finish up just in time to hit the clubs, which open at midnight.

You can find American standards like McDonald's, Tony Roma's, Burger King, and Hard Rock Cafe — good choices if you're traveling with kids — but you may also want to try the Mexican alternatives of Carlos 'n Charlie's and 100% Natural, both located along the Costera.

If you're visiting Acapulco on a Thursday, indulge in the local custom of eating *pozole,* a bowl of white hominy and meat in a broth garnished with sliced radishes, shredded lettuce, onions, oregano, and lime. The truly traditional version is served with pork, but a newer chicken version has also become a standard. You can also find green *pozole,* which is made by adding a paste of roasted pumpkin seeds to the traditional *pozole* base giving the broth its green color. For a uniquely Acapulco experience, enjoy your Thursday *pozole* at the cliff-side restaurant of the Las Flamingos Hotel.

Acapulco's Best Restaurants

All the restaurants I include here are arranged alphabetically with their location and general price category noted. Remember that tips generally run about 15 percent, and most wait-staff really depend on tips for their income, so be generous if the service warrants. See the Introduction of *Mexico's Beach Resorts For Dummies* for an explanation of the price categories.

Please see Appendix E for more information on Mexican cuisine.

100% Natural
$ Costera   MEXICAN/HEALTH FOOD

Healthful versions of Mexican standards are the specialty at this clean, breezy, plant-filled restaurant, located on the second level of the shopping center across from the Acapulco Plaza Hotel. (There are five other branches in Acapulco including another one further east on the Costera.) Especially notable are the fruit *liquidos,* blended fresh fruit and your choice of purified water or milk. Yogurt shakes, steamed vegetables, and cheese enchiladas are alternatives to their yummy sandwiches served on whole grain breads. If you've over-indulged the night before, this is the place to get yourself back on track. It's also a great place for families.

Costera Miguel Alemán 200, across from the Acapulco Plaza Hotel. ☎ *744-485-3982. Sandwiches: $2.50–$4.00; other food items $2.00–$7.00. No credit cards. Open: Daily 24 hours.*

Casa Nova
$$$$ Las Brisas   GOURMET ITALIAN

This long-standing favorite of Mexico City's elite is easily one of Acapulco's top spots for a romantic evening and one of the cliff-side restaurants noted for its food as much as for its view. Enjoy an elegant meal and a fabulous view of glittering Acapulco Bay at this restaurant located east of town on the scenic highway just before the entrance to the Las Brisas hotel. You can dine in one of several elegantly appointed dining rooms awash in marble and stunning murals or outdoors on the terrace that features a dramatic view. The crowd here is generally decked out in fashionable resort attire, and the peak dining hour is 10 p.m.

Notable dishes include veal scaloppini and seafood ravioli, and the service is as impeccable as the presentation. A changing tourist menu offers a sampling of the best selections for a fixed price. There's also an ample selection of reasonably priced national and imported wines as well as live piano music nightly.

Carretera Escénica 5256. ☎ *744-484-6815/19. Reservations required. Main courses: $15–$32; $30 fixed-price 4-course meal. AE, MC, V. Open: Daily 7:00–11:30 p.m.*

El Amigo Miguel
$ Old Acapulco   MEXICAN/SEAFOOD

The ever-present crowd of locals is a sure sign that El Amigo Miguel, 3 blocks west of the *zócalo,* is a standout among Acapulco seafood restaurants — you can easily pay more elsewhere and not eat better. Impeccably fresh seafood reigns here, and the large, open-air dining room is usually brimming with seafood lovers. When it overflows, head to a second branch with the exact same menu across the street. Dining at El Amigo Miguel is a casual way to enjoy the best of the bay's bounty. Try the delicious *camarones borrachos* (drunken shrimp) in a sauce made with beer, applesauce, ketchup, mustard, and bits of fresh bacon — the ingredients may not sound great when listed individually, but trust me, this stuff is heaven. The *filete Miguel* is red-snapper fillet stuffed with seafood and covered in a wonderful *chipotle*-pepper sauce. *Mojo de ajo* (grilled shrimp with garlic) and whole red snapper are also served at their classic best.

Juárez 31, at Azueta. ☎ *744-483-6981. Main courses: $2.70–$12.00. AE, MC, V. Open: Daily 10 a.m.–11 p.m.*

El Cabrito
$ Costera   NORTHERN MEXICAN

A hacienda-inspired facade marks the entrance to this popular joint located in the heart of the Costera. El Cabrito is known for its authentic and well-prepared Northern Mexican cuisine. Although the decor appears to shout out "tourist trap," this restaurant enjoys a strong reputation among Mexican nationals as well. Among the specialties are *cabrito al pastor* (roasted goat), *charro* beans (a dish made with pinto beans), Oaxaca-style *molé* (a complex sauce that uses a variety of ingredients ranging from chocolate to chiles — there are red, yellow, green, and black molés), and *burritos de machaca.*

Costera Miguel Alemán 1480, on the ocean side of the Costera opposite of Hard Rock Cafe. ☎ *744-484-7711. Main courses: $2–$8. AE, MC, V. Open: Mon–Sat 2 p.m.–1 a.m.; Sun 2–11 p.m.*

Acapulco Bay Area Dining

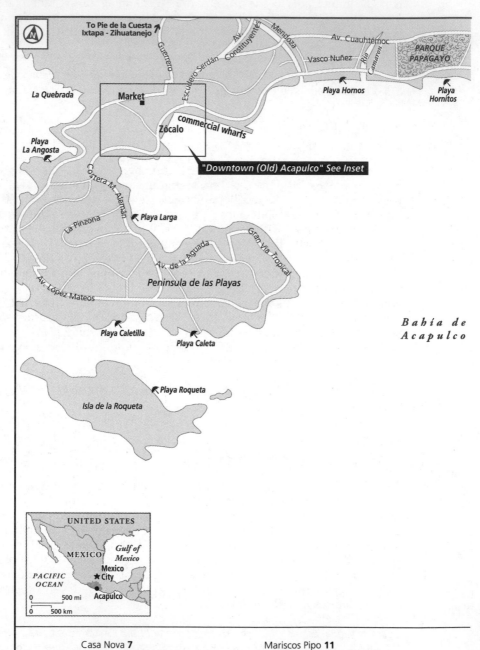

To Pie de la Cuesta
Ixtapa - Zihuatanejo

PARQUE
PAPAGAYO

Av. Cuauhtémoc

Vasco Nuñez

Av. Constituyentes

Av. Mendoza

Guerrero

Escudero Serdán

Río Camarón

Playa Hornos

Playa
Hornitos

La Quebrada

Market

Zócalo

commercial wharfs

"Downtown (Old) Acapulco" See Inset

Playa
La Angosta

Costera M. Alemán

La Pinzona

Playa Larga

Av. de la Aguada

Gran Vía Tropical

Av. López Mateos

Península de las Playas

*Bahía de
Acapulco*

Playa Caletilla

Playa Caleta

Playa Roqueta

Isla de la Roqueta

UNITED STATES

MEXICO

*Gulf of
Mexico*

PACIFIC
OCEAN

Mexico
★ City

0   500 mi

0   500 km

Acapulco

Casa Nova **7**	Mariscos Pipo **11**
El Amigo Miguel **12**	Mezzanotte Acapulco **8**
El Cabrito **6**	Mi Parri Pollo **10**
El Olvido **1**	100% Natural **3**
Ika Tako **4**	Spicey **9**
La Petite Belgique **2**	Su Casa/La Margarita **5**

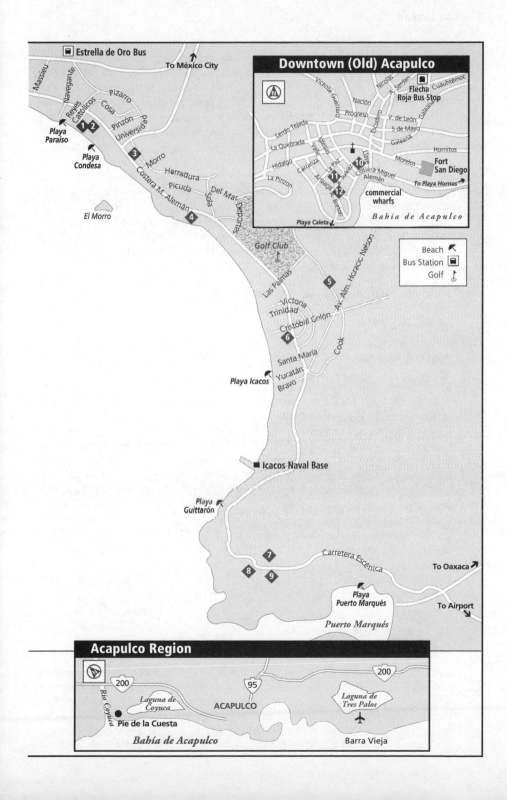

Estrella de Oro Bus

To México City

Massieu

Navegante

Reyes Católicos

Pizarro

Cosa

Pinzón

Universidad

Playa Paraíso

Playa Condesa

Morro

Costera M. Alemán

Herradura

Picuda

Del Mar

Sola

Deportes

El Morro

Downtown (Old) Acapulco

Vicente Guerrero

Nicolás

A. Serdán

Cuauhtémoc

Nación

Flecha Roja Bus Stop

Escudero

Progreso

V. de León

5 de Mayo

Lerdo Tejada

La Quebrada

Iglesias

Valle

Carranza

La Paz

Juárez

Galeana

Hornitos

Morelos

Fort San Diego

Hidalgo

Arteaga

Costera Miguel Alemán

To Playa Hornos

La Pinzón

Bravo

commercial wharfs

Playa Caleta

Bahía de Acapulco

Beach

Bus Station

Golf

Golf Club

Las Palmas

Victoria

Trinidad

Cristóbal Colón

Av. Alm. Hcracic Nelson

Cook

Santa María

Yucatán

Bravo

Playa Icacos

Icacos Naval Base

Playa Guittarón

Carretera Escénica

To Oaxaca

Playa Puerto Marqués

To Airport

Puerto Marqués

Acapulco Region

200

95

200

ACAPULCO

Río Coyuca

Laguna de Coyuca

Laguna de Tres Palos

Pie de la Cuesta

Bahía de Acapulco

Barra Vieja

El Olvido
$$$$ Costera MEXICANA

This stylish restaurant tucked in a shopping mall gives you all the glittering bay-view ambiance of the posh Las Brisas restaurants without the taxi ride from the Costera hotels. The menu is one of the most sophisticated in the city. Each dish is a delight in both presentation and taste — truly some of the finest "new-style" Mexican cuisine in the country. Start with one of the 12 house-specialty drinks such as Olvido — made with tequila, rum, Cointreau, tomato juice, and lime juice. Soups include a delicious cold melon and a thick, black bean and sausage. Among the innovative entrees are quail with honey and *pasilla chiles* and thick sea bass with a mild sauce of cilantro and avocado. For dessert, try the chocolate fondue or the *guanabana* (a tropical fruit) mousse in a rich *zapote negro* (black-colored tropical fruit) sauce. El Olvido is in the same shopping center as La Petite Belgique on Diana Circle. Aca Joe clothing store fronts the plaza. Walk into the passage to the right of Aca Joe and head left; it's in the back.

Plaza Marbella, at the Diana Glorieta (Circle). ☎ *744-481-0203, 744-481-0256, 744-481-0214, 744-481-0240. Reservations recommended. Main courses: $11–$29. AE, DC, MC, V. Open: Daily 6 p.m.–2 a.m.*

Ika Tako
$ Costera SEAFOOD/TACOS

This is my favorite place to eat in Acapulco, and I never miss it when I'm in town. Perhaps I have simple tastes, but these fresh fish, shrimp, and seafood tacos served in combinations that include grilled pineapple, fresh spinach, grated cheese, garlic, and bacon are addictive. Unlike most inexpensive eateries, the setting here is lovely — a handful of tables overlook tropical trees and the bay below. The lighting may be a bit bright, the atmosphere occasionally hectic, and the service dependably slow, but the tacos are delectable. You can also get beer, wine, soft drinks, and a dessert of the day. This restaurant is located along the Costera, next to Beto's lobster restaurant. A second branch of Ika Tako sits across from the Hyatt Regency hotel, but it lacks the atmosphere of this location.

Costera Miguel Alemán 99. No phone. Main courses: $2.50–$5.00. No credit cards. Open: Daily 6 p.m.–5 a.m.

La Petite Belgique
$$$ Costera SEAFOOD/NORTHERN EUROPEAN

La Petite Belgique is a real treasure — you're not likely to find a finer meal in town — although the atmosphere is charmingly dated. This intimate and exceptional restaurant is known principally to locals. Although the dining room overlooks Acapulco Bay, the view is dominated by an adjacent parking lot. But never mind that — your attention is focused on the plates in front of you. The menu boasts an impressive selection of pâtés, continental classics, and fresh fish, but I'm hooked on the fresh mussels that are flown in daily from a mussel farm in Baja California that's also owned by the proprietor. The huge pot of perfectly steamed mussels I enjoyed here could possibly be one of the top-five dining experiences of my life. Great espresso drinks, cordials, and sumptuous sweets — there's a full French bakery on site — provide a fitting close to a truly special dinner. The restaurant is in the shopping center fronted by the Aca Joe clothing store on Diana Circle. Walk into the passage to the right of Aca Joe; it's in the back.

Plaza Marbella, at the Diana Glorieta (Circle). ☎ *744-484-7725. Fax: 744-484-0776. Reservations recommended. Main courses: $8.50–$21.00. AE, MC, V. Open: Daily 5 p.m. to midnight (or until the last customer is satisfied).*

Mariscos Pipo
$ Old Acapulco   SEAFOOD

Check out the photographs of Old Acapulco on the walls while relaxing in this airy dining room decorated with hanging nets, fish, glass buoys, and shell lanterns. The English-language menu lists a wide array of seafood, including *ceviche*, lobster, octopus, crayfish, and baby-shark quesadillas. This local favorite is two blocks west of the *zócalo* on Breton, just off the Costera. Another branch (☎ **744-484-0165**), open daily 1:00 to 9:30 p.m., is at Costera Miguel Alemán and Canadá, across from the convention center.

Almirante Breton 3. ☎ *744-482-2237. Main courses: $2–$10 (though lobster will be a bit more). AE, MC, V. Open: Daily noon to 8 p.m.*

Mezzanotte Acapulco
$$$$ Las Brisas   ITALIAN/FRENCH/MEXICAN

Mezzanotte, a current hot spot in Acapulco dining, offers a contemporary blending of classic cuisines in a lively atmosphere that borders on being a little too noisy at times. The view of the bay is outstanding, but the food quality is inconsistent. Dress up a bit for dining here. Mezzanotte is in the La Vista complex near the Las Brisas hotel.

Plaza La Vista, Carretera Escénica, adjacent to Pepe's Piano Bar parking lot. ☎ *744-484-7874, 744-446-5727, 744-446-5728. Reservations required. Main courses: $20–$30. AE, MC, V. Open: Daily 6:30 p.m. to midnight; closed Sun during the low season.*

Mi Parri Pollo
$ Old Acapulco   MEXICAN/INTERNATIONAL

Umbrella-covered tables on one of the coolest and shadiest sections of the *zócalo* comprise this tiny and typically Mexican restaurant. It's especially popular for breakfast with specials that include a great fresh-fruit salad with mango, pineapple, and cantaloupe and coffee refills. Other specials include fish burgers, *tortas,* a special rotisserie-grilled chicken, and steak *Milanesa.* Fruit drinks, including fresh mango juice, come in schooner-size glasses. To find the restaurant, enter the *zócalo* from the Costera and walk toward the kiosk. On the right, about midway into the *zócalo,* is a wide, shady passageway that leads onto Avenida Jesus Carranza and the umbrella-covered tables under the shady tree.

Jesus Carranza 2B, Zócalo. ☎ *744-483-7427. Breakfast: $1.50–$2.50; sandwiches $1.00–$2.00; fresh-fruit drinks $1.25; daily specials $2.00–$4.00. No credit cards. Open: Daily 7 a.m.–11 p.m.*

Spicey
$$$$ **Las Brisas   CREATIVE CUISINE**

Of all the cliff-side restaurants, this one gets my vote for consistently delicious food, stellar views, and charming service. Diners can enjoy the air-conditioned indoor dining room or — better — the completely open rooftop terrace with a sweeping view of the bay. To begin, try the Shrimp Spicey in a fresh coconut batter with an orange marmalade and mustard sauce. Among the main courses, the grilled veal chop in pineapple and papaya chutney is a winner, as is the beef tenderloin prepared Thai- or Santa Fe-style or blackened. The *chiles rellenos* in mango sauce wins raves. An exceptional selection of premium tequilas for sipping is another highlight. Attire is resort dressy.

Carretera Escénica, next to Kookaburas. ☎ *744-446-6003, 744-446-5991. Reservations recommended on weekends. Valet parking available. Main courses: $15–$30. AE, DC, MC, V. Open: Daily 7:00–11:30 p.m.*

Su Casa/La Margarita
$$ **Costera Zone (Inland)   INTERNATIONAL**

A comfortable setting, terrific food, and moderate prices are what you get at Su Casa. Owners Shelly and Ángel Herrera created this pleasant and breezy open-air restaurant on the patio of their hillside home overlooking the city. Both are experts in the kitchen and stay on hand nightly to greet guests on the patio. The menu changes often, so each time you go there's something new to try. But some items are standard — shrimp *a la patrona* in garlic; grilled fish, steak, and chicken; and flaming *fillet al Madrazo,* a delightful brochette marinated in tropical juices. Most entrees come garnished with cooked banana or pineapple. The margaritas are big and delicious. Su Casa is the hot-pink building on the hillside above the convention center.

Av. Anahuac 110, up the hill from the convention center. ☎ *744-484-4350, 744-484-1261. Fax: 744-484-0803. Reservations recommended. Main courses: $8–$18. MC, V. Open: Daily 6 p.m. to midnight.*

Chapter 25

Having Fun On and Off the Beach in Acapulco

Acapulco's beaches are not all created equal, and knowing that sun and sand are a key part of any vacation here, I use this chapter to guide you to the areas that are best for watersports and safest for swimming, and I throw in a few out-of-the-way finds.

In and out of the water, Acapulco features a wealth of things to do and see, so I point out the top attractions. Though the town is lacking in true cultural options, I've found a few hidden gems that I reveal in this chapter.

And then there's the nightlife! Oh the nightlife! I wrap this chapter up with a guide of the top clubs in town, giving you a rundown of the typical crowd and type of action you're likely to encounter in each location. This info can help you pick a spot that best meets your tastes — without having to cough up a bunch of cover charges just to find the right scene.

Hitting the Beaches

Acapulco Bay is a stunning sight — night or day — that practically cries out in temptation. But, before I dive into the best beaches, I have a few words of wisdom I need to mention:

Acapulco Bay Area

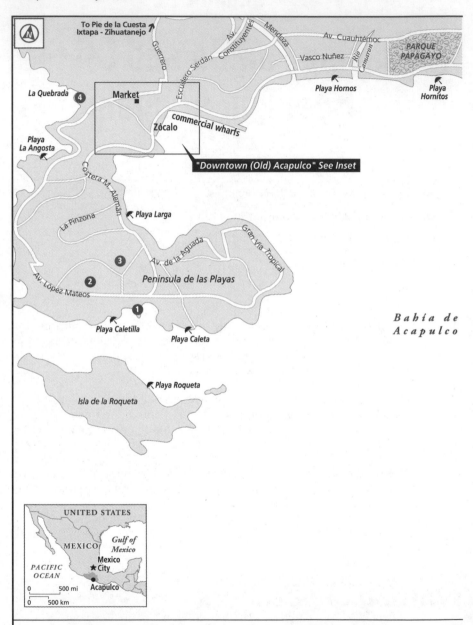

To Pie de la Cuesta
Ixtapa - Zihuatanejo

PARQUE PAPAGAYO

Av. Cuauhtémoc
Mendoza
Constituyentes
Escudero Serdán
Vasco Nuñez
Río Camarón

La Quebrada ④
Market ■
Zócalo
commercial wharfs

Playa Hornos
Playa Hornitos

Playa
La Angosta

"Downtown (Old) Acapulco" See Inset

Costera M. Alemán

La Pinzona

↖ Playa Larga

Av. de la Aguada
Gran Via Tropical

③
②
Av. López Mateos

Peninsula de las Playas

①
↖ Playa Caletilla
↖ Playa Caleta

Bahía de Acapulco

↖ Playa Roqueta

Isla de la Roqueta

UNITED STATES

MEXICO
Gulf of Mexico
★ Mexico City
PACIFIC OCEAN
Acapulco ●

0   500 mi
0   500 km

Cathedral Nuestra Señora de la Soledad **7**	Jai-Alai Frontón Stadium **3**
Centro Acapulco (Convention Center) **5**	Mágico Mundo Marino **1**
Centro Internacional de Convivencia Infantil **6**	Plaza de Toros **2**
Cliff Divers **4**	Zócalo/Plaza Álvarez **8**
Fort San Diego/Museo Histórico de Acapulco **9**	

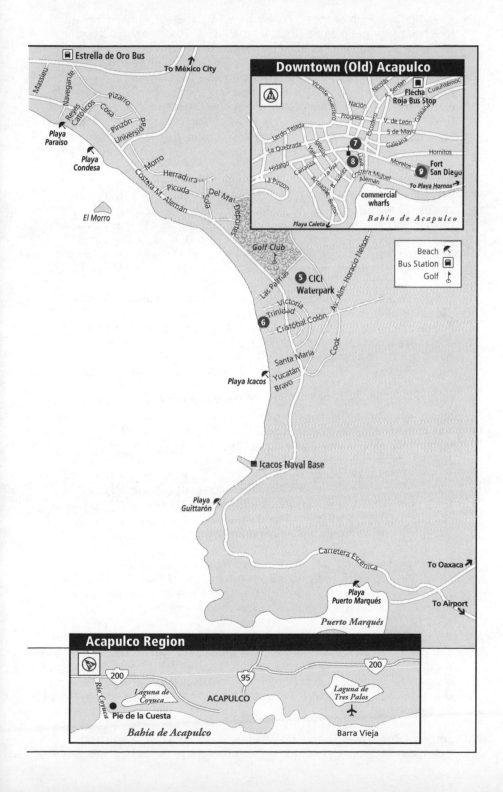

Estrella de Oro Bus

To México City

Playa Paraíso

Playa Condesa

Massieu

Reyes Católicos

Navegante

Pizarro

Cosa

Pinzón

Universida

Morro

Herradura

Picuda

Del Mar

Costera M. Alemán

Sola

El Morro

Golf Club

Las Palmas

Victoria

Trinidad

Cristóbal Colón

Santa María

Yucatán

Bravo

Playa Icacos

Icacos Naval Base

Playa Guittarón

Carretera Escénica

To Oaxaca

Playa Puerto Marqués

Puerto Marqués

To Airport

Downtown (Old) Acapulco

Vicente Guerrero

Nicolás

A. Serdán

Cuauhtémoc

Flecha Roja Bus Stop

Nación

Escudero

V. de León

5 de Mayo

Galeana

Morelos

Galeana

Hornitos

Fort San Diego

To Playa Hornos

Progreso

Lerdo Tejada

La Quebrada

Hidalgo

La Pinzón

Valle

Iglesias

a Paz

Carranza

Aldama

R. Juárez

Arteaga

Bruto

Costera Miguel Alemán

commercial wharfs

Bahía de Acapulco

Playa Caleta

Av. Alm. Horacio Nelson

Cook

5 CICI Waterpark

6

7

8

9

Beach

Bus Station

Golf

Acapulco Region

200

95

200

Río Coyuca

Laguna de Coyuca

ACAPULCO

Laguna de Tres Palos

Pie de la Cuesta

Bahía de Acapulco

Barra Vieja

Acapulco's golden beaches, cobalt-blue bay, and sun-soaked climate lured so many people here that, by the late 1970s, Acapulco became a victim of its own success. Beaches began to lose their luster as waves of garbage and pollution started coming in with the tides. As the numbers of visitors sharply declined, authorities took notice, and over the past decade, the city has gone to great lengths (and great expense) to clean up the waters of its beautiful bay. Despite the notable success of these efforts, I believe it still pays to be cautious in some areas. (This is an active, industrial port.) You may also notice the fleet of more than 20 power-sweeper boats that skim the top of the bay each morning to remove any debris or oil film or. . . .

The tides in the area can also be treacherous, especially in the open ocean north and south of Acapulco Bay. Each year, at least one or two unwary swimmers drown in the area because of deadly riptides and undertow, so heed any posted warnings — red or black flags mean stay out of the water altogether, and yellow warns you to exercise caution. The safest swimming is in either Acapulco Bay or Puerto Marqués Bay.

I'm glad I got that off of my chest; now I can tell you about the best places to play. In the old days, the downtown beaches were the focal point of Acapulco, but today, the resort developments stretch along the entire length of the shore. The beaches and coves tucked into Acapulco Bay go by as many as 50 different names, but I just focus on the best as I note the most popular beaches from west to east.

Located 8 miles west of Acapulco Bay is **Pie de la Cuesta.** Traveling by taxi or car (this is the one day you might consider renting) is the best way to reach this beach because it is much faster than taking the bus. However, buses run regularly along the Costera, leaving every 5 or 10 minutes. A taxi costs about $18. The water here is too rough for swimming, but it's a great spot for checking out big waves and the spectacular sunset — especially over *coco locos* (drinks served in a fresh coconut with the top whacked off) at one of the rustic beachfront restaurants hung with hammocks. The area is known for excellent bird-watching and the surrounding coconut plantations.

Heading on the road northwest, beyond the bay, along the Pacific coastline, you come to **Coyuca Lagoon** on your right. *Colectivo* boat tours — or small boats that band together a group of people to comprise a tour — of the lagoon are offered for about $8.

Back toward Acapulco, around the area near La Quebrada (where the cliff divers perform), is **Playa la Angosta,** a small, sheltered, and often-deserted cove. If you're staying in Old Acapulco, this beach is great not only for it's location, but it's much less crowded than public beaches in Old Acapulco and dramatic in its setting — though generally too rough for swimming.

South of downtown on the Peninsula de las Playas lie **Caleta** and **Caletilla** — the image I hold in my mind of these sister beaches is one of bright colors, lots of laughter, kids, and an almost carnival-like atmosphere. A small outcropping of land that contains an aquarium and water park, **Mágico Mundo Marino** (open daily 9 a.m. to 7 p.m.), separates the two beaches. In this area, you find thatched-roofed restaurants, watersports equipment for rent, and brightly painted boats that ferry passengers to Isla Roqueta. You can also rent beach chairs and umbrellas for the day. Mexican families favor these beaches because they're close to several inexpensive hotels. In the late afternoon, fishermen pull their colorful boats up on the sand; you can buy the fresh catch of the day and, occasionally, oysters on the half shell.

Speaking of **Roqueta Island,** it has two small beaches amidst a hilly, forested terrain. **Playa Marin** is the more deserted of the two. **Playa Roqueta** has thatched-roof restaurants where you can enjoy a snack and a cold beer or rent snorkeling equipment. The island also has a small zoo of exotic animals kept in pitifully small cages — I kindly ask you to boycott it in the hope that these poor creatures will one day be released. You can get here via one of the *panga* boats (small, open-air fishing boats) departing from Caletilla Beach. The ferries cost about $3 round trip and depart about every 20 minutes from 10 a.m. to 6 p.m. daily.

You need to remember the name of **Playa Manzanillo** if you're planning to set out on a pleasure-boat excursion — including chartered fishing trips. This is where they dock. It's located just south of the *zócalo.*

East of the *zócalo,* the major beaches are **Hornos** (near Papagayo Park and sometimes referred to as Playa Papagayo), **Hornitos, Condesa,** and **Icacos,** which merge one into the other. Icacos is the beach just beyond the Hyatt Hotel. Of the four beaches, it's closest to the naval base (La Base), which is directly opposite the bay from the *zócalo.* All of these strips of sand are wide, and the surf is gentle, but I remain cautious about swimming along this interior curve of Acapulco Bay — based on my concerns about water cleanliness. Of these beaches, Condesa is the liveliest with watersports equipment for rent and a regular crowd of beach babes of both sexes.

As you travel around the bay, down the Costera to the Scenic Highway (Carretera Escénica), and past the legendary Las Brisas hotel, the road continues to **Playa Marqués,** located in the small, clean, and separate bay of **Puerto Marqués.** It's my top choice for beach swimming in Acapulco, and one key reason for staying at the Camino Real (see Chapter 22). The water is calm, and the bay is sheltered, meaning the water quality here is much better than in Acapulco Bay, and it's a great place for water-skiing — rentals are generally available. A row of palapa-topped, beachfront restaurants draws a sizable crowd every weekend, so arrive early, or better yet, come during a weekday.

Past the bay lies **Playa Revolcadero,** a magnificent wide stretch of beach on the open ocean where many of Acapulco's grandest resorts are found — including the Acapulco Princess, Mayan Palace, and Pierre Marqués. About 4 miles further south lies **Barra Vieja,** a lovely, wide beach with firm sand (ideal for running on the beach) — but also strong waves. **Tres Palos Lagoon,** a fascinating freshwater jungle lagoon, is nearby. You can hire a boat for about $12 to take you around these wetlands found at the east end of the fishing village that adjoins Barra Vieja.

Finding Water Fun For Everyone

It seems like you can find more ways to have fun in Acapulco in the water than out of it — after all, this resort grew up around the bay. Whether it's plowing through the surf on a Jet Ski or diving below the surface, if you can do it in the water, you can find it in Acapulco!

Skiing and surfing

Acapulco watersports tend to lean toward the motorized variety — the louder the engine, the better the fun. In Acapulco's heyday, images of bronzed, muscled water-skiers were commonplace, and today, this sport remains as popular during the day as dancing is at night. An hour of water-skiing can cost as little as $35 or as much as $65. Boats and rental equipment are available at Playa Caletilla, Puerto Marqués Bay, and Coyuca Lagoon. You can also check out the **Club de Esquis** (Costera Miguel Alemán 100; ☎ 744-482-2034); water-skiing rates run $40 per hour here.

Concessions for other watersports equipment are found on the beaches fronting the Costera hotels — most notably the Qualton Club, Acapulco Plaza, Fiesta Americana, and Hyatt hotels. Banana boats ($3 per person for about 15 minutes), parasail rides (about $15 for the longest ten minutes of your life), and Jet Skis ($50 per hour) are usually available. Although these concessions are also available on Caletilla Beach and Coyuca Lagoon near Pie de la Cuesta, the equipment tends to be in better shape along the Costera hotel beaches.

The mother of all motorized watersports in Acapulco is, without a doubt, the **Shotover Jet.** These 12-person, soft-sided boats careen down the otherwise tranquil Papagayo River propelled by 8-liter, V-8 engines. You travel at speeds of 40 to 50 miles per hour and make 360-degree turns, so the ride is a thrill. Book these trips directly through the Shotover Jet office (Costera Miguel Alemán 121, in front of the Continental Plaza Hotel; ☎ 744-484-1154). Tickets cost $44 for adults and $22 for children and include round-trip transportation from this departure point to the river.

It's a 4-hour excursion, door-to-door. And be sure to bring a change of dry clothes — you will get wet on this trip.

Exploring the deep blue

Scuba diving is not as brilliant in Acapulco as it is in other parts of Mexico (the previous problems with pollution have resulted in fewer fish and less sea life), so it may disappoint. But, as an avid diver, I always say that there's no such thing as a bad dive. For novice divers, or those needing a refresher course, you can expect to pay $30 for an hour and a half of instruction if you book directly with an instructor on Playa Caleta. Two of the dive operators I recommend are **Divers de Mexico** (Costera Miguel Alemán 100; ☎ 744-482-1398) and **Nautilus** (Costera Miguel Alemán 450; ☎ 744-483-1108). Typical prices are about $55 for equipment, a dive guide, and a boat for three hours. The best snorkeling sites are off **Roqueta Island.** You can rent gear at a concession on the island, or you can take one of the regularly scheduled snorkeling trips from Playa Caleta to the island, which costs about $20 for two hours, including equipment.

Reeling in the big one

For deep-sea fishing excursions, go to the pale-pink building housing the fishing-boat cooperative **Pesca Deportiva** opposite the *zócalo* or book a day in advance (☎ 744-482-1099). Charter fishing trips run from $150 to $200 for up to four people for six hours, tackle and bait included. Credit cards are accepted, and ice, drinks, lunch, and a fishing license (about $10) are extra. Generally, boats leave at 8 a.m. and return by 3 p.m. and travel anywhere from 3 to 10 miles offshore. Sailfish, marlin, and tuna are popular catches. If you book through a travel agent or hotel, fishing trips start at around $200 to $280 for four people, and again, fishing license, food, and drinks cost extra.

If you're into planning ahead, consider booking with either of these reliable sport-fishing outfitters: **Ixtapa Sportfishing Charters** (19 Depue Land, Stroudsburg, PA 18360; ☎ 570-688-9466; Fax: 570-688-9554; Internet: www.ixtapasportfishing.com/acapulco; E-mail: ixtsptf@epix.net) and **Fish-R-Us** (Costera Miguel Alemán 100; ☎ 877-3-FISH-R-US in the U.S., or 744-482-8282; Internet: www.fish-r-us.com.mx; E-mail: reservationsacatravel@fish-r-us.com.mx). Their boats range in size from 40- to 48-foot custom cruisers and are priced from $275 to $520 for up to eight people, including crew, tackle, and taxes.

Finding family fun

One of the best options for family fun is the **CICI water park** (Centro Internacional de Convivencia Infantil; Costera Miguel Alemán at Colón; ☎ 744-484-8033). Located just east of the convention center, the park has swimming pools with waves, water slides, water toboggans, and sea-life shows. The park is open daily 10:00 a.m. to 6:00 p.m. with dolphin shows (in Spanish) taking place at noon, 2:30, and 5:00 p.m. The dolphin swim program, which includes 30 minutes of introduction and 30 minutes of swim time, is one I can't recommend because this park tends to overwork its dolphins. CICI is an amusement park, and it's not representative of the more caring and sensitive dolphin-swim facilities found in Cancún and Puerto Vallarta. CICI also has a snack bar and restrooms. General admission is $5; children under 2 are admitted free.

Cruising Acapulco shores

Although a booze cruise may not technically qualify as a watersport (even though it requires extensive repetitions of the one-arm cocktail curl), I'll go out on a limb. Because the activity takes place on the water, it counts in my book. A booze cruise is one of the most popular ways to spend a day — or evening — in Acapulco, and the options are numerous. Choose from yachts, catamarans, and trimarans (single- and double-deckers) to take in the sun (and a few beverages) and enjoy expansive views of the bay. Cruises run morning, afternoon, and evening, and some offer buffets, open bars, and live music; others just have snacks, selected drinks, and taped music. You'll notice a difference in prices, too, which can range from $15 to $50. Your hotel's tour desk or any Acapulco travel agency can explain the current options, as well as provide brochures or recommendations.

Having said that, one cruise still stands out — the **Aca Tiki** (☎ **744-484-6140,** 744-484-6786) with its heart-shaped strand of red lights visible from the boat's tall masts. The moonlight cruise, known as the "love boat," has live music, dancing, snacks, and an open bar each evening from 10:30 p.m. to 1:00 a.m. Aca Tiki also offers sunset cruises with departure times based on the time of sunset. Both cruises leave from the *malecón* across from the central plaza downtown and cost $15 each.

Enjoying Land Sports

Acapulco has a number of ways to spend the day on land. From golf to tennis to horseback riding, you're sure to find an activity — or two — to suit your interests.

Teeing off

If you aim to hit the links during your stay, the best **golf** is found at the courses in the Playa Revelcadero Beach. Both the **Acapulco Princess** (☎ **744-469-1000**) and **Pierre Marques** (☎ **744-466-1000**) hotels have top-notch courses. The Princess's course is a rather narrow, level, Ted Robinson design. The Marques course, redesigned by Robert Trent Jones, Sr., in 1972 for the World Cup Golf Tournament, is longer and more challenging. A round of 18 holes at either course costs $63 for guests and $84 for non-guests; American Express, Visa, and MasterCard are accepted. Tee-times begin at 7:35 a.m., and reservations should be made a day in advance. Club rental is available, and costs an extra $21. The **Mayan Palace Golf Club** (Geranios 22; ☎ **744-466-1924**), designed by Latin American golf great Pedro Guericia, lies further east. Greens fees are $75, and caddies are available for an additional $15.

The main public course in town is the **Club de Golf Acapulco** (☎ **744-484-0781**), located off the Costera next to the convention center. You can play 9 holes for $35 and 18 holes for $55 with equipment renting for $12. There are no carts, but caddies are available for about $10. To tell you the truth, the course is not very well maintained.

Taking time for tennis

Tennis is vastly more popular in Acapulco than golf, and getting a game up is a fairly easy process. There are several public tennis clubs — court time averages about $11 an hour. One option is the **Club de Golf Acapulco** (☎ **744-484-0781**), which is open daily 7 a.m. to 9 p.m. Outdoor courts cost $15 an hour during the day and $22 per hour at night; the indoor courts costs $25. Rackets rent for $4, and a set of balls will set you back $2. Many of the hotels along the Costera have tennis facilities for their guests.

Galloping along

If you're not entirely comfortable swimming in Acapulco Bay, then try **horseback riding** along the beach. Independent operators stroll the Hotel Zone beachfront offering rides for about $20 to $40 for one to two hours. Horses for riding are also commonly found on the beach in front of the Acapulco Princess Hotel. There's no phone; you have to go directly to one of the beaches to make arrangements.

Experiencing Acapulco's Front Row Attractions

Traditionally called *Fiesta Brava,* **bullfights** are held during Acapulco's winter season at a ring up the hill from Playa Caletilla. Tickets purchased through travel agencies cost around $35 and usually include transportation to and from your hotel. The festivities begin at 5:30 p.m. each Sunday from December to March. Although bullfights in Acapulco tend to feature better matadors than those in other Mexican resort towns, you're still seeing amateur or up-and-coming matadors rather than the real pros — they practice this sport in Mexico City.

The Basque sport of **jai alai** is amazing to watch, and Acapulco has a great spot from which to view this game (on the Costera, across from the Hyatt Regency). The competition is similar to handball, but it's played with a *fronton* — a narrow, woven scoop. The players move the ball around the court at lightening speed. A big part of the fun is betting on the games, which you can do at the adjacent sports book that also takes bets on numerous other sports. Admission to jai alai is around $10.

The must-see spectacle in Acapulco is the renowned **cliff divers.** High divers perform at **La Quebrada** each day at 12:30, 7:30, 8:30, 9:30, and 10:30 p.m. for a $1.25 admission. From a spotlighted ledge on the cliffs, divers (holding torches for the final performance) plunge into the roaring surf 130 feet below — after wisely praying at a small shrine nearby. To the applause of the crowd, divers climb up the rocks and accept congratulations and cash tips from onlookers. This is the essential Acapulco experience, and no visit here is complete without watching these death-defying divers — this goes for jaded travelers as well.

The public areas have great views, but arrive early because all performances quickly fill up. Another option is to watch from the lobby bar and restaurant terraces of the **Hotel Plaza Las Glorias/El Mirador** (☎ 744-483-1155). At the bar, you have to pay a $9.50 cover charge, which includes two drinks. Reservations are recommended during the high season. The best way to reach La Quebrada is by taxi. It's located uphill from Avenida Lopez, 3 blocks west of the *zócalo*.

Sightseeing in Acapulco

Acapulco is best known for its beaches and bay, and sadly, few visitors bother to explore its traditional downtown area. But a trip to the shady *zócalo* (also called Plaza Álvarez) is an experience that offers a true glimpse of local life and color. Inexpensive cafes and shops border the plaza, and the **Cathedral Nuestra Señora de la Soledad** — with its blue, onion-shaped domes and Byzantine towers — is at the north end. Though reminiscent of a Russian Orthodox church, the structure was originally built as a movie set and then later adapted for use as a house of worship. Take a taxi up to the top of the hill from the main plaza and follow the signs leading to **El Mirador** (lookout point) for an unparalleled view of Acapulco.

Of all the exclusive villas and homes in Acapulco, one stands far apart from the others. Though not as elegantly impressive as the villas of Las Brisas, the **home of Dolores Olmedo** in Acapulco's traditional downtown area is a veritable work of art. In 1956, the renowned Mexican artist Diego Rivera covered its outside wall with a mural of colorful mosaic tiles, shells, and stones. The work is unique, and one of the last he created. Rivera, considered one of Mexico's greatest artists, has been credited with being one of the founders of the 20th-century

Mexican-muralist movement. The Olmeda mural, which took him 18 months to complete, features Aztec deities such as Quetzalcoatl and Tepezcuincle, the Aztec dog. Rivera and Olmeda were lifelong friends, and Rivera lived in this house for the last two years of his life during which time he also covered the interior with murals. However, because this home is not a museum, you have to settle for enjoying the exterior masterpiece. The house is located a few blocks behind the Casablanca Hotel, a short cab ride from the central plaza, at Calle Cerro de la Pinzona 6. Have the driver wait while you look around because there's not much traffic and it's a steep climb back to the plaza.

Acapulco wasn't always a beach resort. Originally, it was an important port for the Spanish Empire, and because of the rich trade that took place here, the city was subject to frequent pirate attacks. In 1616, the **Fuerte de San Diego** was constructed to help protect Acapulco. Today, this fort is home to the **Museo Histórico de Acapulco** (Acapulco Historical Museum). It contains exhibits that tell the story of Acapulco from its roles as a port in the conquest of the Americas, as a center for local Catholic conversion campaigns, and as a key site for trade with the Orient. The fort you see today was rebuilt after a large earthquake damaged the original structure in 1776, and it just benefited from another renovation in 2000. To reach the fort, follow Costera Miguel Alemán from the Hotel Zone toward Old Acapulco and the *zócalo;* the fort is on a hill on the right. The museum is open Tuesday to Sunday from 10 a.m. to 5 p.m. The museum was just redone in 2002, and now has exceptional bilingual exhibitions, and excellent air-conditioning. The $2 admission is waived on Sunday.

Sightseeing on the water isn't limited to the ferryboats that take travelers to Roqueta Island. Old, wooden glass-bottom boats circle the bay, and you can look down at a few fish and watch a diver or two swim down to the underwater sanctuary of the **Virgin of Guadalupe,** patron saint of Mexico. The statue of the Virgin — created by sculptor Costillo Diaz — was placed at its submerged location in 1959 in memory of a group of divers who lost their lives at the spot. You can purchase tickets (for approximately $3) at any loading boat or from the information booth on Playa Caletilla at a discount (☎ 744-482-2389).

Shopping in Acapulco

Shopping, like attractions in Acapulco, tends to favor the popular over the cultural — you're more likely to find a sexy swimsuit than a true artistic treasure here. Yet, Acapulco does have a few interesting shops. The best are found at the **Mercado Parazal** (often called the **Mercado de Artesanías**) on Calle Velázquez de León near Cinco de Mayo in the downtown *zócalo* area. (When you see Sanborn's, turn right and walk behind it for several blocks; ask for directions if you need to.) It's a collection of covered stalls selling unique curios from around the country including silver, embroidered cotton clothing, rugs, pottery, and papier-mâché.

Markets like this are made for bargaining, and the shopkeepers here test both your negotiating skills and your patience — they start with a steep price and then drag it down little by little. The more time you play their game, the better price you pay. As always, acting uninterested often brings down prices in a hurry. The market is open daily 9 a.m. to 6 p.m.

For a well-known department store with fixed prices, try **Artesanías Finas de Acapulco** (☎ **744-484-8039**), called AFA-ACA for short. Tour guides bring groups to this mammoth, air-conditioned place where the merchandise includes a mix of mass-produced, tacky junk along with some fairly good folk art among the clothes, marble-top furniture, saddles, luggage, jewelry, pottery, papier-mâché, and more. The store is open Monday to Saturday 9 a.m. to 6 p.m. and Sunday 9 a.m. to 2 p.m. To find it, go east on the Costera until you see the Hotel Romano Days Inn on the seaward side. Then take a right on Avenida Horacio Nelson; on the right, half a block up is the AFA-ACA.

What Acapulco does offer in abundance are stores selling resort wear, casual clothing, and the ever-present T-shirt. The Costera is crowded with shops and boutiques like these including some brand-name locations like Tommy Hilfiger that often have much lower prices than their stateside counterparts. If you find a sale, you can find incredible bargains.

For the serious shopper, Acapulco even has a few malls. One of the nicest, air-conditioned shopping centers on the Costera is **Plaza Bahía** (Costera Miguel Alemán 125; ☎ **744-485-6939,** 744-485-6992), which has four stories of shops, movie theaters, small fast-food restaurants, and a bowling alley. The center is located just west of the Costa Club Hotel. The bowling alley, **Bol Bahía** (☎ **744-485-0970,** 744-485-7464), is open Monday to Saturday noon to 1:30 a.m. and Sundays 10 a.m. to midnight. Another popular shopping strip is the **Plaza Condesa,** adjacent to the Fiesta Americana Condesa, with shops that include Guess, Izod, and Bronce Swimwear. **Olvida Plaza,** near the restaurant of the same name, has Tommy Hilfiger and Aca Joe.

Sanborn's is the hands-down standard in department stores in Mexico and offers an array of staples including cosmetics, drugstore items, electronics, music, clothing, books, and magazines. There are three branches in Acapulco:

✔ Downtown at Costera Miguel Alemán 209, across from the boat docks (☎ **744-484-4413**)

✔ Costera Miguel Alemán 1226 at the Condo Estrella Tower, close to the convention center (☎ **744-484-4465**)

✔ Costera Miguel Alemán 163 at the Hotel Calinda (☎ **744-481-2426**)

Acapulco also has a Sam's Club and a Wal-Mart located on the inland side of the main highway just prior to its ascent to Las Brisas.

Taking a Side Trip

The nearby colonial town of **Taxco** (*tahs*-ko) is known worldwide for its silver, but when you arrive, you may see that the town's geography and architecture are equally precious. Taxco sits at nearly 5,000 feet on a hill among hills, and almost any point in the city offers fantastic views.

The center of town is the tiny **Plaza Borda,** shaded by perfectly manicured Indian laurel trees. On one side is the imposing twin-towered, pink-stone **Santa Prisca Church;** whitewashed, red-tile buildings housing the famous silver shops and a restaurant or two line the other sides. Beside the church, deep in a crevice of the mountain, is the **wholesale silver market** — absolutely the best place to begin your silver shopping, to get an idea of prices for more standard designs. You'll be amazed at the low prices. Buying just one piece is perfectly acceptable, though buying in bulk can lower the per-piece price. One of the beauties of Taxco is that its brick-paved and cobblestone streets are completely asymmetrical, zigzagging up and down the hillsides. The plaza buzzes with vendors of everything from hammocks and cotton candy to bark paintings and balloons.

The tiny, one-man factories that line the cobbled streets all the way up into the hills supply most of Taxco's silverwork. Your success at finding bargains depends somewhat on how much you know about the quality and price of silver, but Taxco's quantity and variety of silver can't be matched anywhere else in the country.

It takes about four hours by bus to travel between Acapulco and Taxco, but the resulting bargains in exquisite silver and jewelry are well worth the trip — you won't be disappointed. You can get your fill of silver and an idea of what Taxco is like by spending an afternoon here, but this picturesque town has a lot more to offer than just the Plaza Borda and the shops surrounding it. Stay overnight and give yourself time to wander the steep cobblestone streets and discover the little plazas, fine churches, and of course, the abundance of silversmith shops. If Acapulco is all you've seen during your vacation, a visit here will make you feel that, at last, you're in "Mexico."

The best way to travel to Taxco from Acapulco is through one of the numerous day-trip charters that you can easily arrange at your hotel's tour desk or a local travel agent. Most excursions leave around 6:30 a.m. and return at 9:00 p.m. for a cost of about $60. You can also venture on your own — but I'd strongly recommend taking a bus over renting a car because the bus drivers know the route and much of the trip is along narrow, curvaceous roads through steep mountains.

Exploring Taxco

Shopping for jewelry and other items is the major pastime for tourists. Prices for silver jewelry at Taxco's more than 300 shops are about the best in the world, and everything is available, from $1 trinkets to artistic pieces costing hundreds of dollars.

In addition, Taxco is the home of some of Mexico's finest stone sculptors and is also a good place to buy masks. However, beware of so-called "antiques" — there are virtually no real ones for sale.

Taxco also offers cultural attractions. **Santa Prisca y San Sebastián Church** (Plaza Borda, ☎ 762-622-0184; open daily 6:30 a.m.–8 p.m.; free admission) is Taxco's centerpiece parish church; Completed in 1758 after eight years of labor, it's one of Mexico's most impressive baroque churches.

Stroll along Ruíz de Alarcón and look for the **Humboldt House/Museo Virreynal de Taxco** (the street behind the Casa Borda) where the renowned German scientist and explorer Baron Alexander von Humboldt (1769–1859) spent a night in 1803. The museum houses eighteenth-century memorabilia pertinent to Taxco. (Calle Juan Ruíz de Alarcón 12, ☎ 762-622-5501; admission $1.75, $1.15 for students and teachers with ID; open: Tues–Sat 10 a.m.–6:30 p.m.; Sun 9 a.m.–3:30 p.m.)

The Silver Museum, operated by a local silversmith, is a relatively recent addition to Taxco. After entering the building next to Santa Prisca (upstairs is Sr. Costilla's restaurant), look for a sign on the left; the museum is downstairs. It's not a traditional public museum; nevertheless, it does the much-needed job of describing the history of silver in Mexico and Taxco, as well as displaying some historic and contemporary award-winning pieces. Time spent here seeing quality silver work will make you a more discerning shopper in Taxco's silver shops. (Plaza Borda, ☎ 762-622-0658; admission $1.50 adults, $1 children; open daily 10 a.m.–5:30 p.m.)

A plaque in Spanish explains that most of the collection of pre-Columbian art displayed at the **Museo de Taxco Guillermo Spratling**, as well as the funds for the museum, came from William Spratling. You'd expect this to be a silver museum, but it's not. The entrance floor of this museum and the one above display a good collection of pre-Columbian statues and implements in clay, stone, and jade. The lower floor has changing exhibits. To find the museum, turn right out of the Santa Prisca Church and right again at the corner; continue down the street, veer right, then immediately left. It will be facing you. (Calle Porfirio A. Delgado 1, ☎ 762-622-1660; admission $3.35 adults, free for children under 13; free admission Sun. Tues–Sat 9 a.m.–6 p.m.; Sun 9 a.m.–3 p.m.)

Staying a night

Taxco is an overnight visitor's dream: charming and picturesque, with a respectable selection of pleasant, well-kept hotels. Hotel prices tend to rise at holiday times (especially Easter week). The following are some suggestions in case you decide to spend a night or two.

The Hacienda del Solar comprises several Mexican-style cottages, all on a beautifully landscaped hilltop with magnificent views of the surrounding valleys and the town. The decor is slightly different in each cottage, but most contain lots of beautiful handcrafts, red-tile floors, and bathrooms with handmade tiles. Several rooms have vaulted tile ceilings and private terraces with panoramic views. (Paraje del Solar s/n [Apdo. Postal 96], 40200 Taxco, Gro., ☎ and fax **762-622-0323**; $130 double; $130–$150 jr. or deluxe suite)

Hotel Los Arcos occupies a converted 1620 monastery. The handsome inner patio is bedecked with Puebla pottery and has a lively restaurant area, all around a central fountain. (Juan Ruíz de Alarcón 4, 40200 Taxco, Gro., ☎ **762-622-1836**; fax 762-622-7982; $39 double)

The **Rancho Taxco Victoria** clings to the hillside above town, with stunning views from its flower-covered verandas. It exudes the charm of old-fashioned Mexico. The comfortable furnishings, though slightly run-down, evoke the hotel's 1940s heyday. Even if you don't stay here, come for a drink in the comfortable bar and living room, or sit on the terrace to take in the fabulous view. (Carlos J. Nibbi 5 and 7 [Apdo. Postal 83], 40200 Taxco, Gro., ☎ **762-622-0004**; fax 762-622-0010; $62 standard double, $89 deluxe double; $100 jr. suite)

The **Santa Prisca** is one of the older and nicer hotels in town. Rooms are small but comfortable, with standard bathrooms (showers only), tile floors, wood beams, and a colonial atmosphere. There is a reading area in an upstairs salon overlooking Taxco, as well as a lush patio with fountains. (Cenaobscuras 1, 40200 Taxco, Gro., ☎ **762-622-0080** or 762-622-0980; fax 762-622-2938; $46 double; $52 superior; $64 suite)

Each room at the delightful **Posada de los Castillo** is simply but beautifully appointed with handsome carved doors and furniture; bathrooms have either tubs or showers. (Juan Ruíz de Alarcón 7, 40200 Taxco. Gro., ☎ and fax **762-622-1396**; $33 double).

Dining in Taxco

Taxco gets a lot of day-trippers from the capital and Acapulco, most of whom choose to dine close to the Plaza Borda. Prices in this area are high for what you get. Just a few streets back, you'll find some excellent, simple restaurants.

Toni's (in the Hotel Monte Taxco; ☎ 762-622-1300) is an intimate, classic restaurant (albeit a tad expensive) enclosed in a huge, cone-shaped *palapa* with a panoramic view of the city. The menu, mainly shrimp or beef, is limited, but the food is superior. Try tender, juicy prime roast beef, which comes with Yorkshire pudding, creamed spinach, and baked potato. Lobster is sometimes available. To reach Toni's, it's best to take a taxi. Note that it's open for dinner only.

In a more moderate price range is **Cielito Lindo** (Plaza Borda 14; ☎ 762-622-0603) is probably the most popular place on the plaza for lunch. The menu is ample — there's something for every taste — but the best choices are the classic Mexican dishes. You can get anything from soup to roast chicken, enchiladas, tacos, steak, and dessert, as well as frosty margaritas.

The spectacular view of the city from **La Ventana de Taxco** (in the Hacienda del Solar hotel, Paraje del Solar s/n; ☎ 762-622-0323) makes it one of the best places to dine in Taxco. The food — standard Italian fare — is also quite good, if not predictable. The pasta dishes are the most recommendable. Lasagna is a big favorite, and Sicilian steak is also popular.

Another favorite is **Sotavento Restaurant Bar Galería** (Juárez 8, next to City Hall; no phone) offers many Italian specialties — try deliciously fresh spinach salad and large pepper steak for a hearty meal; or Spaghetti Barbara, with poblano peppers and avocado, for a vegetarian meal. To find this place from the Plaza Borda, walk downhill beside the Hotel Agua Escondida, then follow the street as it bears left (don't go right on Juan Ruíz de Alarcón) about a block. The restaurant is on the left just after the street bends left.

An inexpensive alternative is **Restaurante Ethel** (Plazuela San Juan 14; ☎ 762-622-0788). This family-run place is opposite the Hotel Santa Prisca, 1 block from the Plaza Borda. It has colorful cloths on the tables and a tidy, homey atmosphere. The hearty daily *comida corrida* consists of soup or pasta, meat (perhaps a small steak), dessert, and good coffee.

Discovering Taxco after dark

Paco's (no phone) is the most popular place overlooking the square for cocktails, conversation, and people-watching, all of which continue until midnight daily. Taxco's version of a disco, **Windows,** is high up the mountain in the **Hotel Monte Taxco** (☎ 762-622-1300). The whole city is on view, and music runs the gamut from the hit parade to hard rock. For a cover of $6.70, you can dance away Saturday night from 10 p.m. to 3 a.m.

Completely different in tone is **Berta's** (no phone), next to the Santa Prisca Church. Opened in 1930 by a lady named Berta, who made her fame on a drink of the same name (tequila, soda, lime, and honey), it's the traditional gathering place of the local gentry and more than a few tourists. Spurs and old swords decorate the walls, and a saddle is casually slung over the banister on the stairs leading to the second-floor room, where tin masks leer from the walls. A Berta (the drink, of course) costs about $2; rum, the same. It's open daily from 11 a.m. to around 10 p.m.

National drinks (not beer) are two-for-one nightly between 6 and 8 p.m. at the terrace bar of the **Hotel Rancho Taxco Victoria** (☎ 762-622-0004), where you can also drink in the fabulous view.

Discovering Acapulco after Dark

If there's anything Acapulco is more famous for than its beaches, it's the nightlife. Even if you feel that your "clubbing" days are behind you — trust me — give it a try. The views from the hillside clubs are among the best in town, and it's an equally fascinating scene inside. As is typical with clubs, the names and crowds change with the seasons, and places don't remain "hot" forever, but the ones I list below tend to always be in the upper end of popularity. In addition, here are some general tips:

Every club seems to have a cover charge of around $20 in high season and $10 in low season; drinks can cost anywhere from $3 to $10. Women can count on paying less or entering for free. Don't even think about going out to one of the hillside discos before 11 p.m., and don't expect much action until after midnight. The party goes on until 4 or 5 a.m. — and occasionally until 8 a.m. On weekends, the live dance shows — bordering on performance art — are well worth the lack of sleep.

Many discos periodically waive their cover charge or offer some other promotion to attract customers. Another popular option is to have a higher cover charge but an open bar. Look for promotional materials displayed in hotel reception areas, at travel desks or concierge booths, and in local publications. You may also be hit up with promotions for nightclubs as you take in the sun at the local beaches.

Acapulco has essentially two different club scenes: the strip of beach bars along the Costera Hotel Zone and the glitzier club scene in the hillsides near Las Brisas.

The younger crowd seems to prefer a little fresh air with their nightlife and favor the growing number of open-air, oceanfront dance clubs along Costera Miguel Alemán. These establishments are concentrated between the Fiesta Americana and Continental Plaza hotels; tend to feature techno, house, or alternative rock; and are an earlier and more casual option for nightlife. Faves include the jammin' **DiscoBeach** (☎ 744-484-7064), **El Sombrero** (you'll know it when you see it), **Tabu,** and the pirate-themed **Barbaroja.** These places generally offer an open bar with cover charge (around $10). Women frequently drink for free or with a lesser charge. (Men may pay more, but then, the young and tanned beach babes are here. So who's complaining?) And if you're brave enough — or inebriated enough — there's even a **bungee jump** (Costera Miguel Alemán 107; ☎ **744-484-7529**) in the midst of the beach bar zone.

Of the more traditional clubs, here's my alphabetical rundown of the current scene including some uniquely entertaining options:

✔ Exterior reflection pools and flaming torches mark the entrance to **Alebrijes** (Costera Miguel Alemán 3308, across the street from the Hyatt Regency Acapulco; ☎ **744-484-5902**). Inside, booths and round tables with a seating capacity of 1,200 surround the vast dance floor — the disco doubles as a venue for concerts and live performances by some of Mexico's most notable singers. A Mexican crowd in their mid-twenties are the regulars here, but the crowd may vary with featured performers. Alebrijes is open nightly 11 p.m. to 5 a.m. Cover (including open bar) for women is $5 to $19; for men it's $5 to $25. On Mondays, the open bar is for tequila drinks only.

✔ A long-time favorite in Acapulco is **Baby-O's** (Costera Miguel Alemán, across the street from the Hotel Romano Days Inn; ☎ **744-484-7474**), which has kept current and maintained its place among the top clubs. The mid- to late-twenties crowd dances to everything from swing to hip-hop to rock 'n' roll on the small dance floor surrounded by several tiers of tables and sculpted, cave-like walls. Drinks are more moderately priced than in most Acapulco clubs and cost $2.50 to $5.00. Baby-O's is open 10:30 p.m. to 5:00 a.m. Cover for women is $5 to $10; for men, it's $10 to $15. Both covers include two national drinks.

✔ Venture into the stylish chrome-and-neon extravaganza that is **Enigma** (Carretera Escénica; ☎ **744-484-7154,** 744-484-7164) for a true Acapulco-nightlife experience. Perched on the side of the mountain between Los Rancheros Restaurant and La Vista Shopping Center, the club is easy to spot with its neon and laser lights pulsating in the night. The plush, dim interior dazzles patrons with a sunken dance floor and a panoramic view of the lights of Acapulco Bay. The club also has a more intimate piano bar upstairs overlooking the disco, which draws a more mature and moneyed crowd. Downstairs, the club alternates between pumping in mood smoke and fresh oxygen to keep you dancing. The door attendants wear tuxedos indicating that they encourage a more sophisticated dress — tight and slinky is the norm for ladies; no shorts for gentlemen. The club opens nightly at 10:30 p.m. Fireworks rock the usually full house at 3 a.m., which is when a stylized dance performance takes place on weekends in the style of Euro clubs. During peak season, you should call to find out if reservations are needed. Cover varies but is around $15 to $20, and all major credit cards are accepted.

✔ **Palladium** (Carretera Escénica; ☎ 744-481-0330) is just down the road from Enigma, but it lacks both the style and the classy clientele of the neighboring club. A younger, rowdier crowd enjoys the equally fabulous views and the dancing platforms set in the large glass windows overlooking the bay.

✔ Billing itself as "the cathedral of salsa," **Salon Q** (Costera Miguel Alemán 3117; ☎ 744-481-0114) is known as the place to get down to the Latin rhythms when in Acapulco. Frequently, management raises the cover and features impersonators doing their thing as the top Latin American musical acts. Cover runs from $10 to $15.

✔ One of my more memorable Acapulco evenings was spent with friends enjoying the "talent" at **Tequila's Le Club** (Calle Urdaneta 20; ☎ 744-485-8623). Female-impersonator shows used to be considered fun for the whole family in old Acapulco — and this club is a throwback to those times. The early show features international (English lip-syncing) "ladies," and the later show stars Mexican drag divas. Cover is $13 Tuesdays and Thursdays and $25 on Mondays, Wednesdays, and Fridays. Those prices include two national drinks.

✔ Across the street from Enigma is **Zucca** (Carretera Escénica 28, in the La Vista Shopping Center; ☎ 744-484-6727, 744-484-6764), which offers up yet another fantastic bay view. It claims to cater to a slightly more mature crowd — stating that only those over 25 are admitted — but seems to bend the rules, especially for younger ladies. Zucca is particularly popular with the moneyed Mexico City set. Periodically during the evening, the club projects a laser show across the bay. The dress code prohibits shorts, jeans, T-shirts, or sandals. The club is open nightly 10:30 p.m. to 2:30 a.m., but it stays open later (until 4 a.m.) on weekends or when the crowd demands it. The cover charge, which ranges from $10 to $15, is occasionally waived, at least until a sufficient crowd builds.

Besides nightclubs, you've got other options. The **Gran Noche Mexicana** combines a performance by the Acapulco Ballet Folklórico with one by Los Voladores from Papantla. One of the few options to experience some authentic Mexican culture in town, it's held in the plaza of the convention center every Monday, Wednesday, and Friday night at 7 p.m. With dinner and an open bar, the show costs $50; general admission (including three drinks) is $30. Call for reservations (☎ 744-484-7046) or consult a local travel agency. Many major hotels also host Mexican fiestas and other theme nights that include dinner and entertainment.

Part VIII

Huatulco and the Southern Pacific Coast

The 5th Wave   By Rich Tennant

SHELLING ON MEXICO'S SOUTHERN PACIFIC COAST

© RICHTENNANT

"Oooo! Back up Robert. There must be a half dozen Lightening Whelks here."

In this part . . .

The southern beach resorts of Huatulco and Puerto Escondido are Mexico's purest eco-tourism beach resorts. Unspoiled nature and a laid-back sentiment combine to offer up the uninterrupted experience of Mexico's pure, natural splendor. Puerto Escondido is a little-known paradise of exceptional values and unique, independent accommodations. Neighboring Huatulco puts on a bit of a different face as it combines indulgent hotels and modern facilities with pristine beaches and jungle landscapes.

In the following chapters, I take you through these lesser-known treasures among Mexico's beach resorts and help you uncover their unique and worthwhile charms.

Chapter 26

Bahías de Huatulco

· ·

· ·

*L*ocated in the state of Oaxaca (wah-*hah*-cah), Huatulco's nine bays encompass 36 beaches and countless inlets and coves. The resort as a whole is a staged development project by the Mexican government's tourism development arm (FONATUR) that aims to cover 52,000 acres of land with over 40,000 acres remaining as ecological preserves. Huatulco has not grown as rapidly as Cancún, the previous planned-development resort, meaning plenty of undeveloped stretches of pure white sands and isolated coves are still around to enjoy.

Huatulco has increasingly become known for its eco-tourism attractions — including river rafting, rappelling, and jungle hiking. It's not a destination for travelers who care a lot about shopping, nightlife, or even dining because its options for these pursuits are fewer than other beach resorts in Mexico. However, if you're especially drawn to snorkeling, diving, boat cruises to virgin bays, and simple relaxation, you may quickly find that Huatulco fits the bill perfectly.

In this chapter, I describe the layout of Huatulco and explain some of the best hotels to stay at. I also take you from the plane, through the airport, and to your hotel, helping you quickly get your bearings in this easy-to-navigate resort situated along successive bays. I also offer tips on everything from transportation to dining out to enjoying the best of the numerous natural treasures of this pristine part of Mexico.

Choosing a Location

Unspoiled nature can be an idyllic retreat from the stress of daily life — and for some people, it's even more attractive when viewed from a luxury-hotel balcony. Huatulco is for vacationers who want to enjoy the beauty of nature during the day and then retreat to well-appointed comfort by night. Slow-paced and still relatively undiscovered, the hotels located among the nine bays of Huatulco enjoy the most modern infrastructure of any resort destination along Mexico's Pacific coast.

The area is distinctly divided into three sections: **Santa Cruz, Crucecita,** and **Tangolunda Bay.** In the next few sections, I review these three main parts of Huatulco and the types of hotel rooms you're likely to find in each. Then, I run down a selection of my favorite places to stay. Huatulco offers enough variety in accommodations that you're sure to find something to satisfy your vacation expectations regardless of your taste or budget.

The main differences between locations here can be simply summarized: Tangolunda Bay hotels are the newest, most deluxe properties in the area offering full-service pampering. Hotels in Santa Cruz are older, simpler in style, and lower in price. The village of Crucecita by far offers the best value, but you must take a shuttle to the beach. Although you certainly may find that the part of town you stay in impacts your overall experience, you should note that everything is relatively close by, and getting around is both easy and inexpensive.

Moderate- and budget-priced hotels in Santa Cruz and Crucecita are generally higher in price compared to similar hotels in other Mexican beach resorts. The luxury beach hotels in Tangolunda Bay have rates comparable to similar properties in other destinations, especially when part of a package that includes airfare. The trend here is toward all-inclusive resorts, which in Huatulco are an especially good option given the lack of memorable dining and nightlife options around town. Hotels that aren't oceanfront generally have an arrangement with one of the beach clubs at Santa Cruz or Chahué Bay and provide shuttle service to the beach. Low-season rates refer to the months of August through November only.

Evaluating the Top Accommodations

As far as prices go, I note rack rates (the maximum that a hotel or resort charges for a room) for two people spending one night in a double room. You can usually do better, especially if you're purchasing a package that includes airfare (go back and read Chapter 6 for tips on avoiding paying rack rates). Prices quoted here include the 17 percent room tax. Note that some rates may seem much higher than others — until you realize that they're "all inclusive" — meaning that your meals and beverages are included in the price of your stay. These rates also include all tips, taxes, and most activities and entertainment. Please refer to the Introduction of *Mexico's Beach Resorts For Dummies* for an explanation of the price categories.

All hotels have air-conditioning unless otherwise indicated.

Bahías de Huatulco

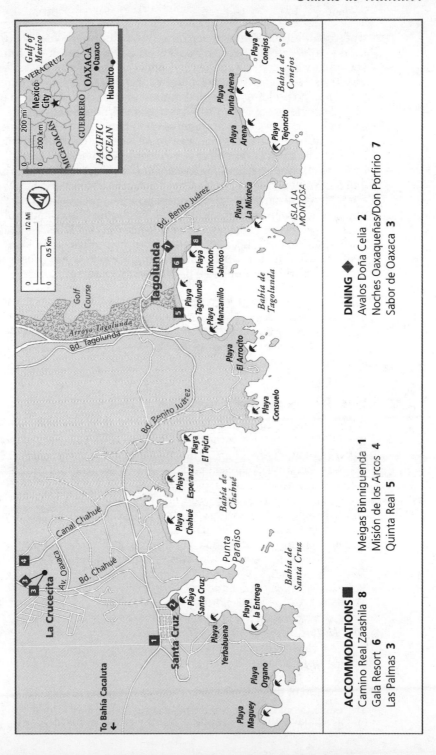

ACCOMMODATIONS ■
Camino Real Zaashila **8**
Gala Resort **6**
Las Palmas **3**

Meigas Binniguenda **1**
Misión de los Arcos **4**
Quinta Real **5**

DINING ◆
Avalos Doña Celia **2**
Noches Oaxaqueñas/Don Porfirio **7**
Sabor de Oaxaca **3**

Camino Real Zaashila
$$$$$ **Tangolunda Bay**

One of the original hotels in Tangolunda Bay — and my top choice here — the Camino Real is located on a wide stretch of sandy beach secluded from other beaches by small rock outcroppings. With calm water, it's perfect for swimming and snorkeling and ideal for families. The white-stucco building is Mediterranean in style and washed in colors on the ocean side, looking a little like a scene from the Greek isles. Rooms on the lower levels — 41 of them — each have their own sizable dipping pools. All rooms are large and have an oceanview balcony or terrace, marble tub/shower-combination bathrooms, wicker furnishings, and decors with bold colors. The main pool is a freeform design that spans 400 feet of beach with chaises built into the shallow edges. Well-manicured, tropical gardens surround the pool and the guestrooms. You have your choice of three restaurants here, including Chez Binni, noted for its excellent regional Oaxacan cuisine (featuring pork dishes and *moles*), plus room service and a lobby bar with live music. A full watersports center is also on its exceptional stretch of beach. Other pluses include a large outdoor whirlpool and a lighted tennis court.

Bulevar Benito Juárez No. 5. ☎ *800-722-6466 in the U.S., or 958-581-0460. Fax: 958-581-0461. Internet:* www.caminoreal.com/zaashila. *120 rooms, 10 suites. Rack rates: High season $210 double, $263 Camino Real Club; low season $170 double, $252 Camino Real Club. AE, DC, MC, V.*

Gala Resort
$$$ **Tangolunda Bay**

With all meals, drinks, entertainment, tips, and a slew of activities included in the price of admission, the Gala is a value-packed experience. It caters to adults of all ages (married and single) who enjoy both activity and relaxation. An excellent kids' activities program probably makes it the best option in the area for families. Rooms have tile floors and Oaxacan wood trim, large tub/shower-combination bathrooms, and ample balconies — all with views of Tangolunda Bay. Three restaurants serve both buffet and à la carte meals, and the Gala has changing theme nights. A large, free-form pool, a complete beachfront watersports center, four lighted tennis courts, and a full gym are on-hand to keep you active.

Bulevar Benito Juárez s/n. Located north of the Sheraton, south of Quinta Real. ☎ *958-581-0000. Fax: 958-581-0220. 290 units. Rack rates: Year-round rates $150 single, $250 double for two people, $100 per extra adult, $51 per child 7–11, $76 per child 12–15. Children under 7 stay free in parents' room. AE, MC, V.*

Las Palmas
$ **Crucecita**

The central location and accommodating staff are an added benefit to the clean, bright, but very basic rooms at Las Palmas. Located half a block from the main plaza in the town of Crucecita, the hotel is also connected to the popular El Sabor de Oaxaca restaurant (see the "Dining in Huatulco" section later in this chapter), which offers room service to guests. Rooms have tile floors, cotton textured bedspreads, tile showers, and cable TV.

Av. Guamuchil 206. ☎ *958-587-0060. Fax: 958-587-0057. Internet:* http:// hotels.baysofhuatulco.com.mx/laspalmas/index.html. *25 units. Free parking. Rack rates: High season $35 double; low season $24 double. AE, MC, V.*

Meigas Binniguenda
$$ Santa Cruz

This property was Huatulco's first hotel, and it retains the Mexican charm and comfort that originally made it memorable. A recent addition has more than doubled the hotel's size. Rooms have Mexican-tile floors, artisan-crafted bedspreads, and colonial-style furniture; French doors open onto tiny wrought-iron balconies overlooking the main street of Juárez or the pool and gardens. The newer rooms have more modern teak furnishings and are generally much nicer — request this section. A nice shady area surrounds the hotel's small pool in back of the lobby. The hotel is away from the marina at the far end of Juárez, only a few blocks from the water. These folks offer free transportation every hour to the beach club at Santa Cruz Bay.

Bulevar Santa Cruz 201. ☎ *958-587-0077, 958-587-0078. Fax: 958-587-0284. E-mail:* binniguenda@huatulco.net.mx. *165 units. Rack rates: High season $100 per person (all-inclusive), $90 double (room only); low season $65 per person (all-inclusive), $50 double (room only). AE, MC, V.*

Misión de los Arcos
$$ Crucecita

This new hotel located just a block from the central plaza has a similar style to the elegant Quinta Real — at a fraction of the cost. The hotel is completely white and accented with an abundance of greenery (no flowering plants), which gives it a very fresh, clean, and inviting feel. Rooms, washed in white with cream and beige bed coverings and upholstery, have the same ambiance. Built-in desks, French windows, and minimal but interesting decorative accents give this budget hotel a real sense of style. A cafe with Internet access (open 7:30 a.m. to 11:30 p.m.) is at the entrance level. Guests can enjoy the services of an adjacent restaurant. The hotel expects to add a swimming pool this year. At present, guests have the use of a beach club, to which the hotel provides a complimentary shuttle. The hotel is cater-corner from La Crucecita's central plaza — close to all the shops and restaurants.

Gardenia 902. ☎ *958-587-0165. Fax 958-587-1135. E-mail:* losarcos@huatulco. net.mx. *13 rooms. Rack rates: High season $59 without A/C, $70 with A/C, $76 suite; low season $30 without A/C, $35 with A/C, $40 suite. AE, MC, V.*

Quinta Real
$$$$$ Tangolunda Bay

The most romantic of Huatulco's hotels, the Quinta Real is known for its understated elegance and cool, efficient service. Double Moorish domes mark this relaxed hotel that has a richly appointed cream-and-white decor. The Quinta Real cascades down a hillside — from the welcoming reception area to the luxurious beach club below. The small groupings of suites are built into the sloping hill down to Tangolunda Bay and offer spectacular views of the ocean and golf course. (Rooms on the eastern edge of the resort sit above the highway and have some traffic noise.) Interiors are elegant and comfortable with stylish Mexican furniture, wood-beamed ceilings, marble tub/shower-combination bathrooms with whirlpool tubs, and original works of art. Telescopes grace many of the suites. Balconies have overstuffed seating areas and floors of stone inlay. Selected suites have private pools of their own. One restaurant serves breakfast and dinner, and the beach club poolside-casual restaurant is open for lunch. The beach club has two pools — one for children — as well as showers and *palapas* on the beach with chair and towel service. The elegant, library-style bar offers up a stunning view and makes a great place for a drink even if you're not staying here. The Quinta Real is perfect for weddings, honeymoons, or small corporate retreats.

*Bulevar Benito Juárez No. 2. ☎ **888-561-2817** in the U.S., or 958-581-0428, 958-581-0430. Fax: 958-581-0429. 28 units. Rack rates: High season $250 Master Suite, $320 Grand Class Suite, $420 with private pool; low season $180 Master Suite, $220 Grand Class Suite, $250 with private pool. AE, DC, MC, V.*

Settling into Huatulco

In Huatulco, it's easy to get into the swing of things. From the small airport, the ride into town along well-paved roads is quick. You're likely to encounter exceptional graciousness and a truly warm welcome from everyone from taxi drivers to bellhops.

Arriving in Huatulco by air

Huatulco's international airport (HUX) (☎ **958-581-9004,** 958-581-9017) is located about 12 miles northwest of the Spanish Bahías. As you deplane, you go down some stairs onto the tarmac and take a brief walk into the terminal — important to know if you're planning on carrying on any heavy luggage. After you're inside the small terminal, you reach the immigration clearance area. At the immigration booth, an officer will ask you to show your passport and your completed tourist card, the **FMT** (see Chapter 7 for all the FMT details).

Your FMT is an important document, so take good care of it. You're supposed to keep the FMT with you at all times because you may be required to show it should you run into any sort of trouble. You also need to turn it back in upon departure, or you may be unable to leave without replacing it.

Next, grab your baggage from the baggage-claims carousel. If needed, porters are available to help with your bags for a tip of about a dollar a bag. After you collect your luggage, you pass through another check-point. Something that looks like a traffic light awaits you here. You press a button, and if the light turns green, you're free to go. If it turns red, you need to open each of your bags for a quick search. It's Mexico's random search procedure for customs. If you have an unusually large bag, or an excessive amount of luggage, you may be searched regardless of the traffic-light outcome.

With your bags, exit the terminal where taxis and other transportation services are waiting.

Getting from the airport to your hotel

From the airport, private **taxis** charge $10 to the town of Crucecita, $12 to Santa Cruz Bay, and $25 to Tangolunda Bay. **Transportes Terrestres** *colectivo* (shared) minibus fares range from $6 to $10 per person.

When returning to airport, make sure to specifically ask for a taxi unless you have a lot of luggage. Taxis to the airport run $10, but unless you request one, companies send a sport-utility vehicle, which costs $25 for the same trip.

Because this beach destination is so spread out and has excellent roads, you may want to consider a rental car (at least for a day or two for a bit of exploring). The bays are spread out, and having a car allows you to see more of them, and explore a bit on your own. Also, taxis are pricey, so if you plan on dining in Crucecita it makes sense to have a car — and the roads are modern, well-paved and nice. If you opt for a rental, consider either picking up your car upon arrival or returning it as you depart. **Budget** (☎ **800-322-9976** in U.S., or 958-587-0010, 958-581-9000) and **Advantage** (☎ **958-587-1379**) have offices at the airport that are open when flights arrive. Daily rates run around $56 for a Volkswagen sedan, $79 for a Nissan Sentra or Geo Tracker, and $100 for a Jeep Wrangler. **Dollar** has rental offices at the Royal and Barceló hotels and downtown, and offers one-way drop service if you're traveling on to Puerto Escondido.

Knowing your way around town

Bahías de Huatulco includes all nine bays of this resort area. The town of Santa María de Huatulco, the original settlement in this area, is 17 miles inland. **Santa Cruz Huatulco,** usually just called Santa Cruz, was the first area on the coast to be developed. It has a central plaza with a bandstand kiosk that has been converted into a cafe serving regionally grown coffee. Santa Cruz also has an artisan's market on the edge of the plaza that borders the main road, a few hotels and restaurants, and a marina from which bay tours and fishing trips set sail. **Juárez** is Santa Cruz's main street. It's about four blocks long in all and anchored at one end by the Hotel Castillo Huatulco and at the other by the Meigas Binniguenda hotel. Opposite the Hotel Castillo is the marina, and beyond the marina are restaurants housed in new, colonial-style buildings facing the beach. The area's banks are on Juárez. It's impossible to get lost; you can take in almost everything at a glance.

A mile and a half inland from Santa Cruz is **Crucecita,** a planned city that sprang up in 1985 centered on a lovely grassy plaza edged with flowering hedges. Crucecita is the residential area for the resorts. Neighborhoods of new stucco homes are mixed with small apartment complexes. The town has evolved into a lovely, traditional town where you can find the area's best — and most reasonably priced — restaurants, plus some shopping and several clean, less-expensive hotels.

Tangolunda Bay, three miles east of Crucecita, is the focal point of bay development. Over time, half the bays should have resorts. For now, Tangolunda has an 18-hole golf course, the Club Med, and the Quinta Real, Barceló Huatulco, Royal, Casa del Mar, and Camino Real Zaashila hotels, among others. Small strip centers with a few restaurants occupy each end of Tangolunda Bay. **Chahué Bay,** between Tangolunda and Santa Cruz, is a small bay with a marina under construction as well as houses and two new hotels.

It's too far to walk between any of the three destinations of Crucecita, Santa Cruz, and Tangolunda, but **taxis** are inexpensive and readily available. The fare between Santa Cruz and Tangolunda is roughly $2; between Santa Cruz and Crucecita, $1.50; and between Crucecita and Tangolunda, $2.50.

Minibus service between towns costs 50¢. In Santa Cruz, catch the bus across the street from Castillo Huatulco; in Tangolunda, it stops in front of the Grand Pacific; and in Crucecita, the bus stop is cater-corner from the Hotel Grifer.

Fast Facts: Huatulco

Area Code
The telephone area code is **958. Note:** The area code changed from 9 in November 2001.

Babysitters
Most of the larger hotels can easily arrange babysitters, but many speak limited English. Rates range from $3 to $8 per hour.

Banks, ATMs, and Currency Exchange

All three areas have banks, including the main Mexican banks Banamex and Bancomer, with automated teller machines. Banks change money during business hours, which are 9 a.m. to 5 p.m. Monday to Friday and 9 a.m. to 1 p.m. on Saturdays. Banks are located along Calle Juárez in Santa Cruz and surround the central plaza in Crucecita.

Business Hours

Most offices maintain traditional Mexican hours of operation (10 a.m. to 2 p.m. and 4 p.m. to 8 p.m., daily), but shops remain open throughout the day. Offices tend to be closed on Saturday and Sunday, but shops are open on Saturday, at least, and increasingly offer limited hours of operation on Sunday.

Emergencies

Police emergency (☎ 060); **local police** (☎ 958-587-0815); **transit police** (☎ 958-587-0192); and **Red Cross** (Blvd. Chahué 110; ☎ 958-587-1188).

Hospitals

The **Centro Medica Huatulco** (Flamboyant 205, La Crucecita; ☎ 958-587-0104, 958-587-0435) is very modern and clean and has English-speaking doctors. Dr. Ricardo Carrillo (☎ 958-587-0687, 958-587-0600) speaks English.

Information

The **State Tourism Office** (Oficina del Turismo; ☎ 958-587-1542; Fax: 958-587-1541; E-mail: sedetur6@oaxaca-travel. gob.mx) has an information module in Tangolunda Bay near the Grand Pacific hotel. The **Huatulco Convention and Visitor's Bureau** (☎ 958-587-1037; E-mail: info@ baysofhuatulco.com) is located in the Plaza San Miguel in Santa Cruz at the corner of Santa Cruz and Monte Albán. It's open Monday to Friday 9 a.m. to 6 p.m. and Saturdays 10 a.m. to 2 p.m. The folks here offer very friendly, helpful service.

Internet Access

Two Internet cafes are located in La Crucecita. One is on the ground-floor level of the **Hotel Plaza Conejo** (Ave. Guamuchil 208, across from the main plaza; ☎ 958-587-0054, 958-587-0009; E-mail: conejo3@ mexico.com). The other is **Portico's** (Gardenia 902; ☎ 958-587-0165).

Maps

One of the best around is the free American Express map, usually found at the tourist information offices and the local tourism office.

Pharmacy

Farmacia del Carmen (☎ 958-587-0878), one of the largest drugstores in Crucecita, is located just off the central plaza. **Farmacia La Clinica** (☎ 958-587-0591) is located at Sabalí 1602 in Crucecita and offers both 24-hour service and home/hotel delivery.

Post Office

The post office at Blvd. Chahué 100, Sector R (☎ 958-587-0551) is open Monday to Friday 9 a.m. to 3 p.m. and Saturdays 9 a.m. to 1 p.m.

Safety

Huatulco enjoys a very low crime rate. Most crime or encounters with the police are linked to pickpocket thefts, so use common sense and never leave your belongings unattended at the beach.

Taxes

A 15 percent IVA (value-added tax) on goods and services is charged, and it's generally included in the posted price.

Taxis

In Crucecita, a taxi stand is opposite the Hotel Grifer and another is on the Plaza Principal. Taxis are readily available in Santa Cruz and Tangolunda through your hotel. The fare between Santa Cruz and Tangolunda is roughly $2.00; between Santa Cruz and Crucecita, $1.50; and between Crucecita and Tangolunda, $2.50. You can also rent taxis by the hour (about $10 per hour) or for the day if you want to explore of the area.

Telephone

Avoid the phone booths that have signs in English advising you to call home using a special 800 number — these are absolute rip-offs and can cost as much as $20 US per minute. The least expensive way to call is by using a Telmex (LADATEL) pre-paid phone card, available at most pharmacies and mini-supers, using the official Telmex (Lada) public phones. Remember, in Mexico you need to dial 001 prior to a number to reach the United States, and you need to preface long distance calls within Mexico by dialing 01.

Time Zone

Huatulco operates on central standard time, but Mexico's observance of daylight savings time varies somewhat from that in the United States.

Dining in Huatulco

Contrary to conventional travel wisdom, many of the better restaurants in the Tangolunda Bay area — or from a practical standpoint, most of the restaurants period — are located in the hotels. Outside the hotels, the best choices are in Crucecita and on the beach in Santa Cruz.

Like many of Mexico's beach resorts, even the finest restaurants in town can be comfortably casual when it comes to dress. Men seldom wear jackets, although ladies are frequently seen in dressy resort wear — basically, everything goes.

I list the following restaurants alphabetically and note their location and general price category. Remember that tips generally run about 15%, and most wait-staff really depend on these for their income, so be generous if the service warrants. Please refer to the Introduction of *Mexico's Beach Resorts For Dummies* for an explanation of the price categories.

Please see Appendix E for more information on Mexican cuisine.

Avalos Doña Celia
$ **Santa Cruz Bay   SEAFOOD**

For years, Doña Celia, an original Huatulco resident, chose to stay in business in the same area where she started her little thatch-roofed restaurant. Now, she's in a new building at the end of Santa Cruz's beach serving the same good eats. Among her specialties are *filete empapelado,* a foil-wrapped fish baked with tomato, onion, and cilantro, and *filete almendrado,* a fish fillet covered with hotcake batter, beer, and almonds. The *ceviche* is terrific (one order is plenty for two) as is the *platillo a la huatulqueño* (shrimp and young octopus fried in olive oil with chile and onion and served over white rice). The ambiance is basic, but the food is the reason for its popularity. If you dine here during the day, beach chairs and shade are available, so you can make your own "beach club" away from your hotel in this more traditional and accessible part of Huatulco.

Santa Cruz Bay. Located at the end of Santa Cruz Beach. ☎ 958-587-0128. Seafood prices: $4–$25; breakfast $2.50–$3.50. No credit cards. Open: Daily 8:30 a.m.– 11:00 p.m.

Noches Oaxaqueñas/Don Porfirio
$$$ Tangolunda Bay   SEAFOOD/OAXACAN

At this restaurant, the colorful, traditional folkloric dances of Oaxaca are performed in an open-air courtyard reminiscent of an old hacienda despite being located in a modern strip mall. The dancers clearly enjoy performing this traditional ballet under the direction of owner Celicia Flores Ramirez (wife of Don Willo Porfirio, a locally renowned restaurateur). For dinner, I recommend the *plato Oaxaqueño,* a generous, flavorful sampling of traditional Oaxacan fare including a tamale, sope, Oaxacan cheese, a grilled fillet, a pork enchilada, and a chile relleno for $10. Other house specialties include shrimp with mezcal and spaghetti marinara with seafood. Meat lovers can enjoy American-style cuts of beef or a juicy *arrachera* (skirt steak). Groups are welcome.

Bulevar Benito Juárez s/n, across from Royal Maeva. ☎ 958-581-0001. Show: $15; dinner and drinks available á la carte. Main courses: $15–$20. AE, MC, V. Open: Fri–Sun 8:30–10:00 p.m.

Sabor de Oaxaca
$$ Crucecita   OAXACAN

Sabor de Oaxaca is the best place in the area to enjoy authentic and richly flavorful Oaxacan food, which is among the best of traditional Mexican cuisine. This restaurant is a local favorite that also meets the quality standards of tourists. The "Mixed Grill for Two" — with *chorizo* (a zesty Mexican sausage), Oaxacan beef fillet, tender pork-tenderloin, and pork ribs — is among the most popular items, and the "Oaxacan Special for Two" — a generous sampling of the best of the menu with tamales, Oaxacan cheese, pork mole, and more — is a can't-miss selection. Generous breakfasts are just $2.22 and include eggs, bacon, ham, beans, toast, and fresh orange juice. The colorful decor and lively music create a nice ambiance, and special group events are happily arranged.

Av. Guamuchil 206. ☎ 958-587-0060. Main courses: $1.50–$16.00. AE, MC, V. Open: Daily 7 a.m. to midnight.

Having Fun On and Off the Beach

Attractions around Huatulco concentrate on the nine bays in the area and their related watersports, and the number of eco-tours and interesting side-trips into the surrounding mountains is growing. Huatulco is truly a nature-lover's paradise offering travelers inclined toward more adventurous activities everything from rafting to rappelling.

Hitting Huatulco's best beaches

Huatulco's major attraction is its coastline — that magnificent stretch of pristine bays bordered by an odd blend of cactus and jungle vegetation that runs right to the water's edge. The only way to really grasp its beauty is by taking a cruise of the bays, stopping at **Organo Bay** or **Maguey Bay** for a dip in the crystal-clear water and a fish lunch at one of the *palapa* restaurants on the beach.

As far as the more accessible, local beaches go, a section of the beach at **Santa Cruz** (away from the small boats), an inviting spot to soak in the sun, is the location of the beach clubs that guests of non-oceanfront hotels use. Several restaurants are also on this beach, and you can find *palapa* umbrellas down to the water's edge.

The most popular beach club along this stretch of sand is **Tipsy's** (☎ **958-587-0576**), which offers full beach-bar and restaurant service, lounge chairs, towel service, and showers. All kinds of watersports equipment are available for rent here including kayaks ($9 per hour), snorkeling equipment, catamarans, Jet Skis ($40 per hour), and banana boats — plus there's water-skiing ($95 for 10 classes). Tipsy's is open daily 10 a.m. to 7 p.m., but credit cards aren't accepted.

For about $10 one way, *pangas* (small boats) from the marina in Santa Cruz ferry passengers to **Playa La Entrega,** also in Santa Cruz Bay. A row of *palapa* restaurants, all with beach chairs out front, greet you at La Entrega. Find an empty *palapa,* call it home for the day, and in return, use that restaurant for your refreshment needs. A snorkel-equipment-rental booth is about midway down the beach, and there's some fairly good snorkeling on the end away from where the boats arrive.

Between Santa Cruz and Tangolunda bays is **Chahué Bay.** A beach club here has *palapas,* beach volleyball, and refreshments for an entrance fee of about $2. However, a strong undertow makes this a dangerous place for swimming.

Tangolunda Bay beach, fronting the best hotels, is wide and beautiful. Theoretically, all beaches in Mexico are public; however, if you're not a guest at a Tangolunda Bay hotel, you may have difficulty entering a hotel to get to the beach.

Cruising Huatulco

The most popular way to tour Huatulco's bays is to jump on a boat, such as the *Tequila,* and join one of the organized day-long bay cruises complete with guide, drinks, and on-board entertainment. Any travel agency can easily arrange these tours, which cost about $25 per person with an extra charge of $4 for snorkeling equipment rental and lunch. Another, more romantic option is the *Luna Azul,* a 44-foot sailboat that offers bay tours and sunset sails. Call ☎ **958-587-0945** for reservations.

If you prefer to venture out on your own, arrange your own bay tour by going to the **boat-owners' cooperative** in the red-and-yellow tin shack at the entrance to the marina. Prices are posted there, and you can buy tickets for sightseeing, snorkeling, or fishing. Besides La Entrega Beach, other more distant beaches are noted for good offshore snorkeling, plus they also have *palapa* restaurants and other facilities. These strips of sand include **Maguey** and **San Agustín.** Just remember that several of these beaches are completely undeveloped and pristine, so you need to bring your own provisions. Boatmen at the cooperative can arrange return pick-up at an appointed time. Prices run about $10 for one to ten people to La Entrega and $30 for a trip to Maguey and Organo bays. The most distant bay is **San Agustinillo,** and that all-day trip runs $60 in a private *panga* (small boat).

In Crucecita, **Shuatur Tours** (Plaza Oaxaca, Local No. 20; ☎ and fax: **958-587-0734**) offers bay tours as well as tours to Puerto Ángel, Puerto Escondido, and associated beaches. This outfit also has an eco-tour on the Río Copalita (a 7-hour trip) and an all-day tour to the coffee plantations located in the mountains above Huatulco.

Doing the eco-tour thing

Both the popularity and number of eco-tours are growing throughout the bays of Huatulco. **Huatulco Outfitters** (☎ **958-581-0315**) specializes in river-rafting expeditions down the Río Copalita. The mountain areas surrounding Río Copalita are home to other natural treasures worth exploring including the **Copalitilla Cascades.** Located 30 kilometers (18.5 miles) north of Tangolunda at 400 meters (1,300 feet) above sea level, this group of waterfalls — averaging heights of 20 to 25 meters (65 to 80 feet) — form natural whirlpools and clear pools for swimming. The area is also popular for horseback riding and rappelling.

Taking time for tennis or golf

For the more traditional sportsmen and sportswomen, the 18-hole, par-72 **Tangolunda Golf Course** (☎ **958-581-0037**) is adjacent to Tangolunda Bay and has tennis courts as well. The greens fee is $37 and carts cost about the same. Tennis courts are also available at the **Barceló** hotel (☎ **958-581-0055**).

Brewing up some fun

The Huatulco region of Mexico is known for its rich *pluma* coffee, grown in the mountainous areas surrounding Huatulco. Centuries-old plantations, most of which continue to use traditional methods, grow and harvest coffee beans. The majority of the plantations are located around the mouth of the Río Copalita in small towns, including Pluma Hidalgo, Santa María de Huatulco, and Xanica, located roughly an hour to an hour and a half from Tangolunda Bay. Both day tours and overnight stays from Huatulco are available to select coffee plantations.

Café Huatulco (☎ 958-587-0339) is a unique project developed by the area's coffee producers' association to bring awareness to the region's coffee and to offer an unusual excursion for tourist. Two Café Huatulco shops sell whole-bean, regional coffee and serve coffee and espresso beverages. One is located in a kiosk in the central plaza of Santa Cruz, and the other is in the Plaza Esmerelda shopping center in Tangolunda Bay. The association can arrange coffee tastings for groups of six or more and overnight stays at the coffee plantations for travelers who are really serious about their coffee.

Sightseeing and shopping

A day in Crucecita can be enjoyable. Just off the central plaza is the **Iglesía de Guadalupe** with its large mural of Mexico's patron saint gracing the entire ceiling of the chapel. The image of the Virgin is set against a deep-blue, night sky, which includes 52 stars — a modern interpretation of the original cloak of Juan Diego.

You can **dine** in Crucecita for a fraction of the price of dining in Tangolunda Bay and get the added benefit of some local color. Considering that **shopping** in Huatulco is generally limited, and unmemorable, the bays' best choices are in Crucecita — in the shops that surround the central plaza. The stores tend to stay open late and offer a good selection of regional goods and typical, tourist take-homes including *artesania,* silver jewelry, Cuban cigars, and tequila.

You can also check out the **Crucecita Market** (open from 10 a.m. to 8 p.m.) on Guamuchil, half a block from the plaza in Crucecita, and the Plaza Oaxaca, adjacent to the central plaza. This small shopping center has several clothing shops including **Poco Loco Club/Coconut's Boutique** (☎ 958-587-0279) for casual sportswear; **Mic Mac** (☎ 958-587-0565), featuring beachwear and souvenirs; and **Sideout** (☎ 958-587-0254) for active wear. **Coconuts** (☎ 958-587-0057) has English-language magazines, books, and music. A small, free trolley is available to take visitors on a short tour of the town. Hop on at the central plaza.

The other main option for shopping is the **Santa Cruz Market** (open 10 a.m. to 8 p.m.), located by the marina in Santa Cruz. Among all of the typical souvenirs, you may want to search out regional specialties that include Oaxacan embroidered blouses and dresses and *barro negro,* a pottery made from a dark clay found exclusively in the Oaxaca region. Several shopping centers in Tangolunda Bay offer a selection of crafts and Oaxacan goods but are pricier than the markets.

The most worthwhile sightseeing excursion in the area is the daylong trip to **Oaxaca City** and **Monte Albán.** The tour includes round-trip airfare on Aerocaribe, lunch, admission to the archaeological sight of Monte Alban, and a tour of the architectural highlights of Oaxaca City — all for $100. Contact any travel agency or the **Aerocaribe** office (☎ **958-587-1220**) for more information.

Enjoying the nightlife

There's a very limited selection of dance clubs around Huatulco — meaning that's where everyone goes. The local branch of the popular Mexican club **Magic Circus** (☎ **958-587-0017**), in Santa Cruz, is the area's most popular disco. It's open from 9 p.m. until the last dance is danced. **Poison** (☎ **958-587-0971**) is the top late-night spot with open-air dancing on the Santa Cruz beachfront. Located next to the Marina Hotel on the beach, it's open until 5 a.m. playing techno, house, and rock. Across the channel, **Tipsy's** (see the "Hitting Huatulco's best beaches" section earlier in this chapter) extends its daytime popularity by staying open until 5 a.m. on weekend nights with dancing under the stars.

Chapter 27

Puerto Escondido

● ●

In This Chapter

▶ Finding a place to stay

▶ Dining in Puerto Escondido

▶ Hitting the beach and checking out turtles

▶ Getting the lay of the land in Puerto Escondido

● ●

Although it may be best known as Mexico's top surf break, I feel Puerto Escondido has a much broader appeal — it simply offers the very best all-around value of any beach resort in Mexico. What's the attraction? Consider this: stellar beaches, friendly locals, and terrific and inexpensive dining, places to stay, and nightlife — plus a notable absence of beach vendors and time-share salespeople and an abundance of English speakers. If you're traveling with children, Puerto Escondido may not be the perfect fit — it's really a better choice for younger or more adventurous travelers.

In this chapter, I cover the best of Puerto Escondido — where to stay and dine and where to find the best adventures. I also offer tips on everything from transportation to where to find the best nightlife.

Evaluating the Top Accommodations

The town of Puerto Escondido is very small — all of the hotels are in or bordering the town. The main pedestrians-only zone is known locally as the *Adoquin* after the hexagonal-shaped, interlocking bricks used in its paving. The hotels along Playa Zicatela really cater to surfers.

As far as prices go, I note rack rates (the maximum that a hotel or resort charges for a room) for two people spending one night in a double room. You can usually do better, especially if you're purchasing a package that includes airfare (go back and read Chapter 6 for tips on avoiding paying rack rates). Prices quoted here include the 17 percent room tax. Please refer to the Introduction of *Mexico's Beach Resorts For Dummies* for an explanation of the price categories.

The hotels that I list here have both air-conditioning and TVs, unless otherwise indicated, and if the review doesn't say anything to the contrary, you can safely assume that you can walk directly out of your hotel and onto the beach.

Best Western Posada Real
$$–$$$ Playa Bacocho

Set on top of a cliff overlooking the beach just west of town, this property is the area's best choice for family travelers. The clean but smallish standard rooms are less enticing than the hotel grounds, which include an expanse of manicured lawn that is one of the most popular places in town for a sunset cocktail. A big plus here is the hotel's Coco's Beach Club — a half-mile stretch of soft-sand beach, a large swimming pool, a kid's playground, and a bar with swing-style chairs and occasional live music. A shuttle service (or a lengthy walk down a set of stairs) takes you to the beach club, which is also open to the public ($2.50 cover for non-guests). The hotel is located only five minutes from the airport and about the same distance from Puerto Escondido's Tourist Zone — you must take a taxi to get to town. In addition to Coco's, the hotel has two restaurants and a lobby bar plus two swimming pools — one is a wading pool for children — tennis courts, and a putting green. It's the most traditional (hotel-chain style) hotel I recommend in Puerto Escondido.

Av. Benito Juárez 1. ☎ *800-528-1234 in the U.S., or 954-582-0133, 954-582-0237. Fax: 954-582-0192. 100 rooms. Rack rates: High season $130 double; low season $85 double. AE, DC, MC, V.*

Bungalows and Cabañas Acuario
$ Playa Zicatela

Facing Playa Zicatela, this surfer's sanctuary offers clean, cheap accommodations plus an on-site gym, surf shop, vegetarian restaurant, and Internet cafe. The two-story hotel and the bungalows surround a pool shaded by great palms. Rooms are small and basic, but bungalows offer fundamental kitchen facilities. The *cabañas* are more open and have hammocks. Parking, public telephones, money-exchange facilities, a pharmacy, and the vegetarian restaurant are located in the adjoining commercial area. The well-equipped gym costs an extra $1 per day or $15 per month.

Calle del Morro s/n. ☎ *954-582-0357, 954-582-1026. 40 units. Rack rates: High season $25 double, $30 double with A/C, $40 bungalow (no A/C); low season $22 double, $27 double with A/C, $35 bungalow (but you can often negotiate a better deal after you're there). No credit cards.*

Puerto Escondido

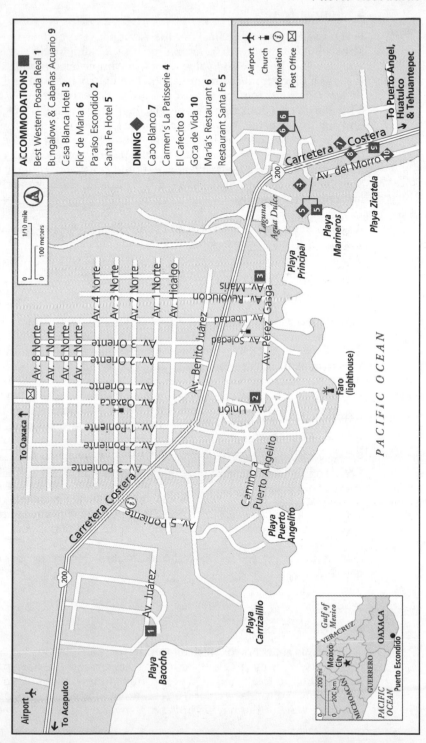

ACCOMMODATIONS ■
Best Western Posada Real **1**
Bungalows & Cabañas Acuario **9**
Casa Blanca Hotel **3**
Flor de María **6**
Paraíso Escondido **2**
Santa Fe Hotel **5**

DINING ◆
Cabo Blanco **7**
Carmen's La Patisserie **4**
El Cafecito **8**
Goza de Vida **10**
María's Restaurant **6**
Restaurant Santa Fe **5**

✈ Airport ✝■ Church ⓘ Information ⊠ Post Office

To Puerto Angel,
Huatulco
& Tehuantepec

Carretera Costera
Av. del Morro

Laguna
Agua Dulce

Playa Zicatela

Playa
Marineros

Playa
Principal

Av. Marís
Av. Revolución

Av. 4 Norte
Av. 3 Norte
Av. 2 Norte
Av. 1 Norte
Av. Hidalgo

Av. Liberad
Av. Pérez Gasga

Av. 8 Norte
Av. 7 Norte
Av. 6 Norte
Av. 5 Norte

Av. Benito Juárez

Av. Soledad

Av. 2 Oriente
Av. 3 Oriente
Av. 1 Oriente
Av. Oaxaca

Av. Unión

Faro
(lighthouse)

Av. 1 Poniente
Av. 2 Poniente
Av. 3 Poniente

PACIFIC OCEAN

⊠
To Oaxaca →

Carretera Costera
Av. 5 Poniente

Camino a
Puerto Angelito

Playa
Puerto
Angelito

Av. Juárez

Playa
Carrizalillo

Playa
Bacocho

✈ Airport
↓ To Acapulco

1/10 mile
100 meters

Gulf of
Mexico

VERACRUZ

México
City ★

MICHOACÁN

GUERRERO

OAXACA

PACIFIC
OCEAN

Puerto Escondido

200 mi
200 km

Casa Blanca Hotel
$ **Tourist Zone**

If you want to be in the heart of the Adoquin (the pedestrian-oriented street that is paved with "adoquin" or interlocking bricks), this hotel is your best bet for excellent value and clean, ample accommodations; plus it's just a block from the main beach. The courtyard pool and adjacent *palapa* (umbrella roof) restaurant is a great place to hide away and enjoy a margarita or a book from the hotel's exchange rack. The bright, clean, and simply furnished rooms offer a choice of bed combinations, but all have at least two beds and a fan. Some rooms have both air-conditioning and a mini-fridge. The best rooms have a balcony overlooking the action in the street below, but light sleepers should consider a room in the back. Some rooms can sleep up to five ($60). This is an excellent and economical choice for families.

Av. Pérez Gasga 905. ☎ **954-582-0168.** *21 units. Rack rates: year-round $45 double with A/C, $26 double without A/C. MC, V.*

Flor de María
$ **Playa Marinero**

Though not right on the beach, this hotel is a real find and very popular with older travelers. Canadians María and Lino Francato own this cheery, three-story hotel facing the ocean, which you can see from the rooftop. The structure is built around a garden courtyard, and each room is colorfully decorated with beautiful, realistic still lifes and landscapes painted by Lino. Two rooms have windows with a view; the rest face into the courtyard. All have double beds with orthopedic mattresses and small safes. The roof, in addition to the great view, has a small pool, a shaded hammock terrace, and an open-air bar (open 5 to 9 p.m. during high season) with a TV that receives American channels. All in all, the roof is a great sunset spot. I highly recommend the first-floor restaurant (see the "Puerto Escondido's Best Places to Dine" section later in this chapter). Ask about off-season discounts for long-term stays. The hotel is a third of a mile from the center of town and 200 feet up a sandy road from Playa Marinero on an unnamed street at the eastern end of the beach.

Playa Marinero. ☎ *and fax:* **954-582-0536.** *24 units. Rack rates: Year-round $35 double. MC, V.*

Paraíso Escondido
$$ **Tourist Zone**

The curious collection of Mexican folk art, masks, religious art, and paintings on the walls make this eclectic inn an exercise in Mexican magic realism in addition to a tranquil place to stay. An inviting pool, surrounded by gardens, Adirondack chairs, a restaurant, and a fountain, has a commanding view of the bay — but it's a several block walk to the main public beach in town. Each room has one double and one twin bed, a built-in desk, and a cozy balcony or terrace with French doors. Each has a slightly different decorative accent, and all are very clean. The suites, added in 2000, have a much more deluxe decor than the rooms and feature recessed lighting, desks set into bay windows with French-paned windows, living areas, and large private balconies. The penthouse suite has its own whirlpool tub and kitchenette plus a tile chessboard inlaid in the floor and murals adorning the walls — it's the owners' former apartment. Limited free parking is available in front of the hotel.

Calle Union 10. ☎ **954-582-0444.** *20 rooms, 5 suites. Rack rates: year-round $75 double, $150 suite. No credit cards.*

Santa Fe Hotel
$–$$ Playa Zicatela

If Puerto Escondido is the best beach value in Mexico, then the Santa Fe is without a doubt one of the best hotel values in Mexico — and a personal, all-around favorite of mine. It's got a winning combination of unique Spanish-colonial style, a welcoming staff, and clean, comfortable rooms. The hotel has grown up over the years alongside the surfers who came to Puerto in the 1960s and 1970s — and nostalgically return today. It's located a half a mile southeast of the town center, off Highway 200, at the curve in the road where playas Marinero and Zicatela join — a prime sunset-watching spot. The three-story, hacienda-style buildings have clay-tiled stairs, archways, and blooming vines surrounding the two courtyard swimming pools. The ample but simply stylish rooms feature large tile bathrooms, colonial furnishings, handwoven fabrics, Guerrero pottery lamps, and TVs with local channels only. Most rooms have a balcony or terrace — ocean views on upper floors. Bungalows are next to the hotel, and each has a living room, kitchen, and bedroom with two double beds. The Santa Fe Restaurant is one of the best on the southern Pacific coast.

Calle del Morro s/n. ☎ **954-582-0170,** *954-582-0266. Fax: 954-582-0260. E-mail:* info@hotelsantafe.com.mx. *59 rooms, 2 suites, 8 bungalows. Free parking. Rack rates: High season $95.50 double, $120.00 bungalow; low season $56.00 double, $100.00 bungalow. AE, MC, V.*

Settling into Puerto Escondido

Puerto Escondido's very small **airport** (PXM) is about two and a half miles north of the center of town near Playa Bacocho. A trip on the collective **minibus** to your hotel is $2.25 per person. **Aerotransportes Terrestres** sells *colectivo* tickets to the airport through **Rodimar Travel** (☎ **954-582-1551;** Fax: 954-582-0737) on Pérez Gasga Street (the pedestrian-only zone) next to Hotel Casa Blanca. The minibus can pick you up at your hotel.

Flying directly into Puerto Escondido can sometimes be a challenge. I find it generally easier (and less expensive) to fly into the Huatulco airport via scheduled or charter flights. An airport taxi costs $75 between Huatulco and Puerto Escondido. If you can find a local taxi, rather than the government-chartered cabs, you can reduce this fare by about 50%, including the payment of a $5 mandatory airport exit tax. Frequent bus service also travels between the two destinations. **Budget Car Rental** has cars available for one-way travel to Puerto Escondido with an added drop charge of about $10. See a representative at the Huatulco airport location (☎ 954-587-0010). In Puerto Escondido, Budget is located at the entrance to Playa Bacocho (☎ 954-582-0312). By car, the trip from Huatulco to Puerto Escondido takes just under two hours. Because the roads are unlit and frequently curvy and travel through a mountainous zone, you should only plan on traveling during daylight hours.

Knowing your way around town

Looking out on the Bahía Principal and its beach, to your left is the eastern end of the bay consisting of a small beach, **Playa Marinero,** followed by rocks jutting into the sea. Beyond this is **Playa Zicatela,** unmistakably the main surfing beach. Playa Zicatela has really come into its own as the most popular area for visitors with restaurants, bungalows, surf shops, and hotels located well back from the shoreline. The western side of the bay, to your right, is about a mile long with a lighthouse and low green hills descending to meet a long stretch of fine sand. Beaches on this end aren't quite as accessible by land as those to the east, but hotels are overcoming this difficulty by constructing beach clubs accessed by steep private roads and Jeep shuttles.

The town of Puerto Escondido has roughly an east-west orientation with the long Playa Zicatela turning sharply southeast. Residential areas behind (east of) Playa Zicatela tend to have unpaved streets; the older town (with paved streets) is north of the Carretera Costera (Highway 200). The streets are numbered — Avenida Oaxaca serves as the dividing line between east *(oriente)* and west *(poniente),* and Avenida Hidalgo acts as the divider between north *(norte)* and south *(sur).*

North of Zicatela is the old town, through which Avenida Pérez Gasga makes a loop. Part of this loop is a paved, pedestrians-only zone, known as the *Adoquin.* Hotels, shops, restaurants, bars, travel agencies, and other services are all conveniently located here. In the morning, taxis, delivery trucks, and private vehicles are allowed to drive here, but at noon it's closed off to all but foot traffic.

Avenida Pérez Gasga angles down from the highway at the east end of the Adoquin; on the west, where the Adoquin terminates, it climbs in a wide northward curve to cross the highway, after which it becomes Avenida Oaxaca.

The beaches — Playa Principal in the center of town and Marinero and Zicatela southeast of the town center — are interconnected. It's easy to walk from one to the other crossing behind the separating rocks. Puerto Ángelito, Carrizalillo, and Bacocho beaches are west of town and can be reached by road or water. Playa Bacocho hosts the few more-expensive hotels located in Puerto Escondido.

Getting around Puerto Escondido

Almost everything is within walking distance of the Adoquin. **Taxis** are inexpensive when traveling around town; call ☎ **954-582-0990** for service. You can rent mountain bikes, motorcycles, and cars at **Arrendadora Express** (Avenida Pérez Gasga 605-F; ☎ **954-582-1355**) on your right just as you enter the Adoquin on the east. Bike rentals run about $5 per day and $15 per week.

Hiring a boat is easy, but it's possible to walk beside the sea from Playa Principal to the tiny beach of Puerto Ángelito though it's a bit of a hike.

Fast Facts: Puerto Escondido

Area Code

The telephone area code is **954. Note:** The area code changed from 9 in November 2001.

Banks, ATMs, and Currency Exchange

Banamex, Bancomer, Bancrear, and Banco Bital all have branches in town, and all change money during business hours; each bank's hours vary, but you can generally find one of the above open Monday to Saturday 8 a.m. to 7 p.m. ATMs and currency-exchange offices are also located throughout town.

Business Hours

Most offices maintain traditional Mexican hours of operation (10 a.m. to 2 p.m. and from 4 p.m. to 8 p.m. daily), but shops remain open throughout the day. Offices tend to close on Saturday and Sunday. Shops are usually open on Saturday but still generally respect the tradition of closing on Sunday.

Hospitals

Try **Unidad Medico-Quirurgica del Sur** (Avenida Oaxaca 113; ☎ 954-582-1288), which offers 24-hour emergency services and has an English-speaking staff and doctors.

Information

The **State Tourist Office, SEDETUR** (☎ 954-582-0175), is about a half mile from the airport at the corner of Carretera Costera and Bulevar Benito Juárez. It's open Monday to Friday 9 a.m. to 5 p.m. and Saturday 10 a.m. to 1 p.m. A kiosk at the airport is open for incoming flights during high season, and another, near the west end of the paved Tourist Zone, is open Monday to Saturday 9 a.m. to 1 p.m.

Internet Access

An excellent cybercafe is on the second floor of La Tigre Azul (☎ 954-582-1871) on the Adoquin. It charges $2 per half hour or

$4 per hour for Internet access; hours are Monday to Friday 11 a.m. to 11 p.m. and Saturday to Sunday from 3 to 11 p.m. **Cyber-café** is a small, extremely busy Internet service at the entrance to the Bungalows and Cabañas Acuario (Calle de Morro s/n; ☎ 954-582-0357, ask for the cybercafe). It's open daily 8 a.m. until 9 p.m. The rate to get online is $1.50 for 15 minutes, $3 for a half hour, or $5 per hour. But this joint had painfully slow, older computers when I was last there.

Pharmacy

Farmacia de Mas Ahorro, on Primera Norte corner and Segunda Poniente (☎ 954-582-1911), is open 24 hours a day.

Post Office

The post office is on Avenida Oaxaca at the corner of Avenida 7 Norte (☎ 954-582-0959). It's open Monday to Friday 8 a.m. to 4 p.m. and Saturday 8 a.m. to 1 p.m.

Safety

Depending on who you talk to, you need to be wary of potential beach muggings, primarily at night. However, the hope is that the new public lighting at Playa Principal and Playa Zicatela goes a long way in preventing these incidents. Local residents say most incidents happen after tourists overindulge and then go for a midnight stroll along the beach. Puerto Escondido is so casual that it's easy to let your guard down, but don't carry valuables and use common sense and normal precautions. Also, respect the power of the magnificent waves here. Drownings occur all too frequently.

Taxes

A 15 percent IVA value added tax (IVA) is charged on goods and services, and it's generally included in the posted price.

Taxis

Taxis are easy to find around town. They're also inexpensive, generally costing $1 to $3 for various parts of town; call ☎ 954-582-0990 for service.

Telephone

Numerous businesses offer long-distance telephone service. Many of these establishments are along the Adoquin, and several offer credit-card convenience.

Avoid the phone booths that have signs in English advising you to call home using a special 800 number — these are absolute rip-offs and can cost as much as $20 US per minute. The least expensive way to call is by using a Telmex (LADATEL) pre-paid phone card, available at most pharmacies and mini-supers, using the official Telmex (Lada) public phones. Remember, in Mexico, you need to dial 001 prior to a number to reach the United States, and you need to preface long-distance calls within Mexico by dialing 01.

Time Zone

Puerto Escondido operates on central standard time, although Mexico's observance of daylight savings time varies somewhat from that in the United States.

Dining in Puerto Escondido

I find dining in Puerto Escondido an absolute pleasure. The food is excellent — generous portions display innovative flavorings at some of the lowest prices I've ever seen anywhere. The atmosphere is exceedingly casual — but don't let that throw you. I've enjoyed some very memorable meals in these funky settings, starting with the mango éclairs at **El Cafecito.** In fact, Puerto Escondido is even more casual than Mexico's other beach resorts — no need to even think about bringing dressy attire or jackets. Personally, I think that Playa Zicatela has the highest concentration of great eats.

All the restaurants I include in the listings below are arranged alphabetically with their location and general price category noted. Remember that tips generally run about 15%, and most wait-staff really depend on these for their income, so be generous if the service warrants.

In addition to the places I list below, the *palapa* restaurants on Playa Zicatela are a Puerto Escondido tradition for early-morning surfer breakfasts or casual dining and drinks by the sea at night. One of the most popular *palapa* restaurants is **Los Tíos,** offering very economical prices and surfer-sized portions. After dinner, enjoy homemade Italian ice cream from **Gelateria Giardino** (Calle Morro at Zicatela Beach, and on the Adoquin at Pes Gasga 609; ☎ 954-582-2243).

Cabo Blanco
$ **Playa Zicatela   INTERNATIONAL**

"Where Legends are Born" is the logo at this beachfront restaurant, and the local crowd craves Gary's special sauces that top his grilled fish, shrimp, steaks, and ribs. Favorites include his dill-Dijon mustard, wine-fennel, and Thai-curry sauces. But you can't count on these sauces always being on the menu because Gary buys what's fresh and then goes from there. An added bonus is that Cabo Blanco turns into a hot bar on Playa Zicatela with live music each Thursday and Saturday after 11 p.m. Gary's wife Roxana and an all-female team of bartenders keeps the crowd well served and well behaved.

Calle del Morro s/n. ☎ 954-582-0337. Main courses: $4–$10. V. Open: Daily Dec–May 6 p.m.–2 a.m. Closed June–Nov.

Carmen's La Patisserie
$ **Playa Marinero   FRENCH PASTRY/SANDWICHES/COFFEE**

This tiny, excellent cafe/bakery has a steady and loyal clientele. Carmen's baked goods are unforgettable and go quickly, so arrive early for the best selection. La Patisserie is across the street from the Hotel Flor de María.

Playa Marinero. No phone. Pastries: 50¢–$1.25; sandwiches $1.75–$2.25. No credit cards. Open: Mon–Sat 7 a.m.–3 p.m.; Sun 7 a.m. to noon.

El Cafecito
$ **Playa Zicatela   FRENCH PASTRY/SEAFOOD/VEGETARIAN/COFFEE**

Carmen's second shop, with a motto of "Big waves, strong coffee!" opened a few years ago on Playa Zicatela. Featuring all the attractions of

Carmen's La Patisserie, El Cafecito is now also open for lunch and dinner. This restaurant actually spans two facing corners; the northern corner is set up more for coffee or a light snack with oceanfront bistro-style seating. The southern corner offers a more relaxed setting with wicker chairs and Oaxacan cloth-topped tables set under a *palapa* roof. Giant shrimp dinners are priced under $5, and the creative, daily specials are always a sure bet. An oversized mug of cappuccino is $1.00, a fresh and filling fruit smoothie goes for $1.50, and her mango éclairs — I'd pay any price — are a steal at $1.00.

Calle del Morro s/n. No phone. Main courses: $1.75–$4.75; pastries 50¢–$1.25. No credit cards. Open: Wed–Mon 6 a.m.–10 p.m.

Gota de Vida
$ **Playa Zicatela   VEGETARIAN/COFFEE**

This popular vegetarian restaurant, located just in front of the Bungalows Acuario, is generally packed — it's known for healthy food, ample portions, and low prices. Under a *palapa* roof and facing Playa Zicatela, Gota de Vida offers an extensive menu that includes fruit smoothies, espresso drinks, herbal teas, and a complete juice bar. These folks make their own tempeh, tofu, pasta, and whole grain bread. Creative vegetarian offerings are based on Mexican favorites like chiles rellenos, cheese enchiladas, and bean tostadas. Fresh seafood is also featured.

Calle del Morro s/n. No phone. Main courses: $1.50–$4.50. No credit cards. Open: Daily 10 a.m.–11 p.m.

María's Restaurant
$ **Playa Marinero   INTERNATIONAL**

This first-floor, open-air, hotel dining room near the beach is popular with the locals. The menu changes daily and features specials such as María Francato's fresh homemade pasta dishes. María's is a third of a mile from the center of town and 200 feet up a sandy road from Playa Marinero on an unnamed street at the eastern end of the beach.

Hotel Flor de María. ☎ 954-582-0536. Main courses: $3.00–$5.00; breakfast $2.50. No credit cards. Open: Daily 8:00–11:30 a.m., noon to 2 p.m., and 6–10 p.m.

Restaurant Santa Fe
$$ **Playa Zicatela   INTERNATIONAL**

The atmosphere here is classic and casual with great views of the sunset and Playa Zicatela. Big pots of palms are scattered around, and fresh flowers grace the tables — all beneath a lofty *palapa* roof. The shrimp dishes are a bargain relative to the rest of the world, but at $15, they're a little higher-priced than in the rest of the town's eateries. Perfectly grilled tuna, served with homemade french-fried potatoes and whole-grain bread, is an incredible meal deal for under $7. A *nopale* (cactus leaf) salad on the side ($2) is a perfect complement. Vegetarian dishes are reasonably priced and creatively adapted from traditional Mexican and Italian dishes. A favorite is the house specialty, chiles rellenos. The bar offers an excellent selection of tequilas.

Hotel Santa Fe, Calle del Morro s/n. ☎ **954-582-0170.** *Main courses: $5.00–$15.00; breakfast $2.50–$6.00; AE, MC, V. Open: Daily 7 a.m.–11 p.m.*

Having Fun On and Off the Beach

Playa Principal is the main beach in town where small boats are available for fishing and tour services. Playa Principal and the adjacent **Playa Marinero** are the best swimming beaches. Beach chairs and sun shades rent for about $2, a charge which may be waived if you order food or drinks from the restaurants that offer them.

Playa Zicatela, a world-class surf spot, adjoins Playa Marinero about a mile and a half from Puerto Escondido's town center and extends to the southeast for several miles. Due to the size and strength of the waves here, it's not a swimming beach, and only experienced surfers should attempt to ride Zicatela's powerful waves. A surfing competition is held each August, and Fiesta Puerto Escondido, held for at least three days each November, also celebrates Puerto Escondido's renowned waves. (The tourism office can supply exact dates and details.) Beginning surfers often start out at Playa Marinero before graduating to Zicatela's awesome waves.

New, stadium-style lighting has recently been installed in both of these beach areas in an attempt to crack down on nocturnal beach muggings. The lights have diminished the appeal of the Playa Principal restaurants — you look into bright lights rather than at the nighttime sea now. Lifeguard service has recently been added to Playa Zicatela.

Barter with one of the fishermen on the main beach for a ride to **Playa Manzanillo** and **Puerto Ángelito,** two beaches separated by a rocky outcropping (the best way to get here is by boat). Here, and at other small coves just west of town, swimming is safe and the overall atmosphere is calmer than it is in town. You can also find *palapas,* hammock rentals, and snorkeling equipment — the clear blue water is perfect for snorkeling. Enjoy fresh fish, tamales, and other Mexican dishes cooked right at the beach by local entrepreneurs. Puerto Ángelito is also accessible by a dirt road that's a short distance from town, so it tends to be busier.

Playa Bacocho is on a shallow cove farther to the northwest and is best reached by taxi or boat rather than walking. It's also the location of Coco's Beach Club at the Posada Real Hotel. It's open to the public for a cover charge of $2.50, which gains you access to the pools, food and beverage service, and facilities.

Embarking on an excursion

Ana's Eco Tours, located in Un Tigre Azul, an art gallery and Internet cafe on the Adoquin (☎ **954-582-1871,** 954-582-2001; E-mail: ana@anas ecotours.com), is an exceptional provider of ecologically oriented tour services. "Ana" Marquez was born in the small, nearby, mountain village of Jamiltepec and has an intimate knowledge of the customs, people, and flora and fauna of the area. She and her expert guides lead small groups on both eco-adventures and cultural explorations.

Tours into the surrounding mountains include a five-hour horseback excursion up to the jungle region of the Chatino **healing hot springs** and a trip to **Nopala,** a Chatino mountain village, and a neighboring coffee plantation. An all-day trip to **Jamiltepec** (a small, traditional regional Indian community called a Mixtex village) offers the opportunity to experience day-to-day life in an authentic village. The visit includes stops at a market, the church, the cemetery, and the homes of local artisans.

Turismo Rodimar Travel Agency (☎ **954-582-0734;** Fax: 954-582-0737), on the landward side of the Adoquin, is an excellent source of information and can arrange all types of tours and travel. It's open daily 8 a.m. to 10 p.m. Manager Gaudencio Díaz speaks English and can arrange individualized tours or more standard ones such as **Michael Malone's Hidden Voyages Ecotours.** Malone, a Canadian ornithologist, takes you on a dawn or sunset trip to **Manialtepec Lagoon,** a bird-filled mangrove lagoon about 12 miles northwest of Puerto Escondido. The cost is $32 and includes a stop on a secluded beach for a swim.

One of the most popular all-day tours offered by both companies is a trip to **Chacahua Lagoon National Park,** about 42 miles west of Puerto, at a cost of $35 with Rodimar or $25 with Ana's. These excursions are true eco-tours — small groups treading lightly. You visit a beautiful sandy spit of beach and the lagoon, which has an incredible array of birds and flowers including black orchids. Locals provide fresh barbecued fish on the beach. If you know Spanish and get information from the tourism office, it's possible to stay overnight under a small *palapa,* but bring plenty of insect repellent.

An interesting and slightly out-of-the-ordinary excursion is **Aventura Submarina,** located "on the strip" (Playa Zicatela, Calle del Morro s/n, in the Acuario building near the Cafecito; ☎ **954-582-2353**). Jorge, who speaks fluent English and is a certified scuba instructor, guides individuals and small groups of qualified divers along the Coco trench just offshore. The price is $55 for a two-tank dive or $35 for a one-tank dive. This outfit offers a refresher course at no extra charge. Jorge also arranges surface activities such as deep-sea fishing, surfing, and trips to lesser-known yet nearby swimming beaches. If you want to write ahead, contact Jorge at Aventura Submarina, Apdo. Postal 159, Puerto Escondido, 71980 Oaxaca.

Fishermen keep their colorful *pangas* (small boats) on the beach beside the Adoquin. A **fisherman's tour** around the coastline in a *panga* costs about $35, but a ride to Zicatela or Puerto Ángelito beaches is only $5. Most hotels offer or gladly arrange tours to meet your needs.

The beaches around Puerto Escondido and Puerto Ángel (located between Huatulco and Puerto Escondido) are important **turtle nesting grounds** for the endangered ridley sea turtle. During the summer months, tourists can sometimes see the turtles laying eggs or observe the hatchlings trekking to the sea. **Playa Escobilla** near Puerto Escondido and **Playa Barra de la Cruz** near Puerto Ángel seem to be the favored nesting grounds of this species.

In 1991, the Mexican government established the Centro Mexicano la Tortuga, known locally as the **Turtle Museum,** for the study and life enhancement of the turtle. Examples of all species of marine turtles living in Mexico are on view, plus six species of freshwater turtles and two species of land turtles. The center is located on **Playa Mazunte** near the town of the same name. Hours are 10:00 a.m. to 4:30 p.m. Tuesday to Saturday and Sunday 10:00 a.m. to 2:00 p.m.; entry is $2.50.

Mazunte is also home to a unique shop that sells naturally produced shampoos, bath oils, and other personal-care products. All the products are made and packaged by the local community as part of a project to replace the income lost from turtle poaching. The products are excellent in quality, and purchasing them goes a long way in ensuring the cessation of turtle poaching in the community. Buses go to Mazunte from Puerto Ángel about every half-hour, and a taxi ride is around $4.50. You can fit this trip in with a visit to Playa Zipolite Beach, the next one closer to Puerto Ángel.

Planning a side trip to Puerto Ángel and Playa Zipolite

Fifty miles southeast of Puerto Escondido and 30 miles northwest of the bays of Huatulco is the tiny fishing port of **Puerto Ángel.** Puerto Ángel, with its beautiful beaches, unpaved streets, and budget hotels, is popular with the international backpacking set and travelers seeking an inexpensive and restful vacation. Its small bay and several inlets offer peaceful swimming and good snorkeling. The village follows a slow and simple way of life: Fishermen leave very early in the morning and return with their catch by late forenoon.

The golden sands and peaceful village life of Puerto Ángel are the reasons you should visit. **Playa Principal,** the main beach, lies between the Mexican navy base and the pier that's home to the local fishing fleet. Near the pier, fishermen pull their colorful boats on the beach and unload their catch in the late morning while trucks wait to haul it off to processing plants in Veracruz. The rest of the beach seems light years away from the world of work and purpose. Except on Mexican holidays, it's relatively deserted.

Playa Panteón is the main swimming and snorkeling beach. "Cemetery Beach," ominous as that sounds, is about a 15-minute walk from the center of town. Just walk straight through town on the main street that skirts the beach. The *panteón* (cemetery), which is also worth a visit with its brightly colored tombstones backed by equally brilliant blooming vines, is on the right.

In Playa Panteón, some of the *palapa* restaurants and a few of the hotels rent snorkeling and scuba gear and can arrange boat trips, but they all tend to be rather expensive. Check the quality and the condition of the gear — particularly scuba gear — that you rent.

Playa Zipolite and its village are 3.7 miles down a paved road from Puerto Ángel. Taxis charge around $1.00 to $1.50 (taxis are relatively inexpensive here), or you can catch a *colectivo* on the main street in the town center and share the cost.

Zipolite is well known as a good surf break and nude beach. Although public nudity (including topless sunbathing) is technically against the law throughout Mexico, it's allowed here — one of only a handful of beaches in Mexico to share the designation. This sort of open-mindedness has attracted an increasing number of young European travelers. Most sunbathers concentrate beyond a large rock outcropping at the far end of the beach. Police occasionally patrol the area, but they're much more intent on searching for drug users than harassing au natural sunbathers. Spots to tie up a hammock and a few *palapa* restaurants where you can grab a light lunch and a cold beer dot the beach.

In Zipolite, as in the rest of Mexico, the purchase, sale, or use of drugs is definitely against the law, no matter what the local custom may be (and their use is relatively customary here). Because the ocean currents are quite strong (Natch! That's why the surf is so good!), a number of drownings have occurred over the years — so, know your limits.

If you're traveling here by car, you arrive via Highway 200 from the north or south. Take coastal Highway 175 inland to Puerto Ángel. The road is well marked with signs leading to Puerto Ángel. From either Huatulco or Puerto Escondido, the trip should take about an hour.

Taxis are a readily available to take you to Puerto Ángel, Zipolite Beach, the Huatulco airport, or Puerto Escondido for a reasonable price.

Shopping in Puerto Escondido

The Adoquin sports a row of tourist shops selling straw hats, postcards, and Puerto Escondido T-shirts, and a few excellent shops feature Guatemalan, Oaxacan, and Balinese clothing and art. You can also get a tattoo or rent surfboards and bodyboards here. Pharmacies and mini-markets for basic necessities are interspersed among the shops, hotels, restaurants, and bars.

The largest of these mini-marts is **Oh! Mar** (Avenida Pérez Gasga 502; ☎ 954-582-0286), which not only sells anything you'd need for a day at the beach but also sells phone (LADATEL) cards, stamps, and Cuban cigars. Plus, the store has a mail drop box and arranges fishing tours.

During high season, businesses and shops are generally open all day, but during low season, they close between 2 p.m. and 5 p.m. Some highlights along the Adoquin include:

- ✔ **Casa di Bambole** (Avenida Pérez Gasga 707; ☎ 954-582-1331) sells high-quality clothing, bags, and jewelry from Guatemala and Chiapas.

- ✔ **La Luna** (Avenida Pérez Gasga s/n; no phone) has a selection of jewelry, Batik surf wear, and Balinese art.

- ✔ The name of **1000 Hamacas** (Avenida Pérez Gasga s/n; no phone) says it all. Custom-made hammocks in all colors — it's the favored way to take a siesta here — can double as your bedding if you're staying in one of the numerous surfer hangouts on Playa Zicatela.

- ✔ **Central Surf** shops are located on the Adoquin (☎ 954-582-0568) as well as on Playa Zicatela (Calle Morro s/n; ☎ 954-582-2285). The stores rent and sell surfboards and related gear and offer surf lessons.

- ✔ **Un Tigre Azul** (Avenida Pérez Gasga s/n; ☎ 954-582-1871) is the only true art gallery in town. It features quality works of art and a cafe-bar, plus Internet services upstairs.

- ✔ Also of interest is **Bazaar Santa Fe** (Hotel Santa Fe lobby, on Playa Zicatela, Calle del Morro s/n; ☎ 954-582-0170), which sells antiques including vintage Oaxacan embroidered clothing, jewelry, and religious artifacts.

- ✔ **Bikini Brazil** (Calle del Morro s/n; no phone) has the hottest bikinis under the sun imported from Brazil, the land of the tanga.

- ✔ Just in front of the Rockaway Resort on Playa Zicatela, a 24-hour **mini-super** (no phone) sells the basic necessities: beer, suntan lotion, and basic food supplies.

Enjoying the nightlife

As hot as the daytime surf action is in Puerto Escondido, the nocturnal offerings offer some stiff competition that can make catching those first morning waves somewhat of a challenge.

Sunset-watching is a ritual to plan your day around, and good lookout points abound here. Watch the surfers at Zicatela and catch up on local gossip at **La Galera** (Calle del Morro s/n; ☎ 958-582-0432), upstairs on the third floor of the Arco Iris hotel. La Galera has a nightly happy hour (with live music during high season) from 5 to 7 p.m. For other great sunset spots, head to the **Hotel Santa Fe** at the junction of playas Zicatela and Marinero or the rooftop bar of **Hotel Flor de María.** For a more tranquil, romantic setting, take a cab or walk half an hour or so west to the **Hotel Posada Real.** The hotel's cliff-top lawn is a perfect sunset perch. You can also climb down the cliff (or take the Real's shuttle bus) to Coco's on the beach below.

Puerto Escondido is beginning to develop a more cultural side to its nightlife. At **The Library,** located on the main street of Playa Zicatela (a few blocks past the Santa Fe hotel), you can play chess or backgammon, browse through the selection of books for sale, take a Spanish class, or just enjoy an espresso or a drink from the bar.

Further down the street at the far southern end of Calle Morro, **Surf Papaya** restaurant has an upstairs art gallery that also features occasional children's theatre. A **Cine Club,** at the Rinconada movie theatre, features new releases in air-conditioned comfort. Movies are shown Friday, Saturday, and Sunday nights at 7:30 p.m. A free shuttle runs from El Cafecito on Playa Zicatela each Saturday and Sunday at 7:00 p.m. Call ☎ 954-582-1723 for current movie listings.

When it comes to bars and clubs, Puerto has a nightlife that satisfies anyone dedicated to late nights and good music. Along the Adoquin, here are some spots that may lure you in:

- ✔ **Son y la Rumba** is home to live jazz featuring its house band with Andria Garcia playing each night 8 to 11 p.m. with a $1 cover. It's located beneath the El Tigre Azul, on the western end of the Adoquin.

- ✔ **Tequila Sunrise,** a two-story, open, and spacious disco overlooking the beach, plays Latino, reggae, *cumbia,* tropical, and salsa music. It's a half a block from the Adoquin on Avenida Marina Nacional. A small cover charge generally applies — about $1 or $2.

- ✔ The **Bucanero Bar and Grill** has a good-sized bar and outdoor patio fronting Playa Principal.

- ✔ **Bar Fly, The Blue Iguana,** and **Rayos X** cater to a younger surf crowd with alternative and techno tunes.

✔ **Montezuma's Revenge** has live bands usually playing contemporary Latin American music.

✔ **El Tubo** is an open-air, beachside disco just west of Restaurant Alicia on the Adoquin.

Out on Zicatela, don't miss **Cabo Blanco** (see the "Dining in Puerto Escondido" section earlier in this chapter), where local musicians get together and jam Thursdays and Saturdays during high season. **Split Coco,** just a few doors down, has live music on Tuesdays and Fridays and TV sports on other nights. It has one of the most popular happy hours on the beach and serves barbecue as well.

Most nightspots are open until 3 a.m. or until the customers leave.

Part IX
Los Cabos and Southern Baja

The 5th Wave   By Rich Tennant

"All I know is what the swim-up bartender told me. Wearing these should improve our game by 25 percent."

In this part . . .

Cabo San Lucas, San José del Cabo, and the stretch of coastline that connects them, known as the Corridor, are collectively known as Los Cabos (The Capes). They're located at the tip of Mexico's Baja peninsula. "The end of the line," "the last resort," and "no man's land" are all terms used in the past to describe Mexico's remote but diverse Baja Sur, an exquisite setting that artfully blends desert landscapes with vibrant seascapes. With five championship golf courses open for play, golf has overtaken sport fishing as the main draw here. Other activities you can find in Cabos to keep you busy are sea kayaking, whale-watching, diving, surfing, and hiking.

In the next four chapters, I explain the differences between the three distinct parts of Los Cabos and their unique attractions. I also clue you in on the best places to stay and dine, great things to do, and the craziest spots for nighttime diversion.

Chapter 28

The Lowdown on the Hotel Scene in Los Cabos

*P*art of the attraction of the towns of Los Cabos seems to be the feeling that they are an extension of Southern California's brand of American style — luxury accommodations, golf courses, shopping, franchise restaurants, and a spirited nightlife. **Cabo San Lucas** has retained its boisterous, party-town traditions, and **San José del Cabo** still has the appearance and ambiance of a quaint Mexican town, though it has become gentrified in recent years.

Eighteen miles of smooth highway, known as **the Corridor,** lie between the two Cabos. Along this stretch of pavement, major new resorts, including some of the world's finest golf courses and residential communities, have sprung up.

And the area's signature natural beauty continues to beckon: Dozens of pristine coves and inlets with a wealth of marine life just offshore greet visitors.

The Los Cabos area has earned a deserved reputation for being much higher priced than other Mexican resorts. Although a boom in new hotel construction has occurred, these new properties have all been luxury resorts — solidifying Los Cabos' higher average room prices, not adjusting prices downward with the added supply of rooms. The other factor driving up prices here is that compared to mainland Mexico, little agriculture activity takes place in Baja; most foodstuffs (and other daily required items) must be shipped into the area. U.S. dollars are the preferred currency here, and it's not uncommon to see price listings in dollars rather than pesos.

In this chapter, I review the two main towns, the Corridor between them, and the types of hotel rooms you're likely to find in each as well as the pros and cons of staying in each area. Then, I run down a selection of my favorite places to stay in Los Cabos. The accommodations options are so varied here that no matter your taste or budget, you're sure to find the perfect fit for a satisfying vacation.

Choosing a Location

Los Cabos is actually three destinations in one — the traditional town of San José, the rowdy, party town of Cabo San Lucas, and the luxury-lined corridor between the two. Where you stay impacts your overall experience, although you can move around from one location to another — for a price. My hotel recommendations extend through this entire area.

San José del Cabo, located closest to the airport, has pastel cottages and flowering trees lining its narrow street, retaining the air of a provincial Mexican town. Originally founded in 1730 by Jesuit missionaries, it's the seat of the Los Cabos government and the center of the region's business community. The main square, adorned with a wrought-iron bandstand and shaded benches, faces the cathedral, which was built on the site of an early mission.

San José is becoming increasingly sophisticated. A collection of noteworthy cafes, art galleries, and intriguing small inns adds a newly refined flavor to the central downtown area. Still, San José is the best choice for travelers who want to travel to this paradoxical Mexican landscape but still be aware that they're in Mexico. Most of the hotels I list here are found in the town — meaning away from the beaches of San José — but not so far away that it's an inconvenience.

The Corridor between the towns of San José del Cabo and Cabo San Lucas contains some of Mexico's most lavish resorts designed as self-contained dream getaways. Most growth in this area is occurring along the Corridor, which has already become a major international locale for championship golf. The three major resort areas are Palmilla, Cabo Real, and Cabo del Sol. Each location is a self-enclosed community with golf courses, elegant hotels, and million-dollar homes.

If you plan to explore the region while staying at a Corridor hotel, you should rent a car for at least a day or two for easier access; cars are available at the hotels. Even if you're not staying here, the beaches and dining options are worth the visit. All of the hotels along the Corridor qualify as "very expensive" selections. Golf and fishing packages are available at most resorts.

The hundreds of luxury hotel rooms along the Corridor to the north of Cabo San Lucas have transformed the very essence of this formerly rustic and rowdy outpost. Although it still retains a boisterous nightlife that runs counter to the pampered services that surround it, Cabo San Lucas is no longer the simple town John Steinbeck wrote about and enjoyed. Once legendary for the big-game fish that lurk beneath the deep blue sea, Cabo San Lucas now draws more people for its nearby fairways and greens — and the world-class golf played on them. Today, it caters to a traveler getting away for a long weekend or indulgent stay of sport and relaxation. Cabo San Lucas has become Mexico's most elite resort destination.

Travelers here enjoy a growing roster of adventure-oriented activities, and playtime doesn't end when the sun goes down. The nightlife here is as hot as the desert in July and oddly casual, having grown up away from the higher-end hotels. It remains the raucous, playful party scene that helped put Cabo on the map. A collection of popular restaurants and bars, spread along Cabo's main street, stay open and active until the morning's first fishing charters head out to sea. Despite the growth in diversions, Cabo remains more or less a "one stoplight" town with most everything located along the main strip within easy walking distance.

Budget accommodations are scarce in Cabo San Lucas, but a growing number of small inns and B&Bs, with several notable ones, have opened in the past few years. Because most of the larger hotels are well maintained, and packages are available through travel agents, I focus on the smaller, more unique accommodations available in Cabo San Lucas.

Best Accommodations in Las Cabos

There's more demand than supply for hotel rooms in the Corridor, so prices tend to be higher than equivalent accommodations in other parts of Mexico. San José has only a handful of budget hotels, so it's best to call ahead for reservations if you want economical accommodations. A new trend throughout the region is toward smaller inns, or bed-and-breakfasts, offering stylish accommodations in town. The beachfront Hotel Zone in San José often offers package deals that bring room rates down to the moderate range, especially during summer months. Check with your travel agent.

For each hotel, I include specific rack rates for two people spending one night in a double room during high season (Christmas to Easter), unless otherwise indicated. Keep in mind that summer rates are about 20 percent less. Rack rates simply mean published rates, and tend to be the highest rate paid — you can do better, especially if you're purchasing a package that includes airfare (go back and read Chapter 6 for tips on avoiding paying rack rates). Please refer to the Introduction of *Mexico's Beach Resorts For Dummies* for an explanation of the price categories.

It's not unusual for many hotels to double their normal rates during Christmas and Easter weeks. Note that some rates may seem much higher than others — until you realize that they are "all inclusive" — meaning that your meals and beverages are included in the price of your stay. This rate also includes all tips and taxes and most activities and entertainment.

All hotels I list here have both air-conditioning and TVs, unless otherwise indicated, and if the review doesn't say anything to the contrary, you can safely assume that you can walk directly out of your hotel and onto the beach.

The Bungalows
$$ Cabo San Lucas

The Bungalows is one of the most special places to stay in Los Cabos. Each "bungalow" is a charming retreat decorated with authentic Mexican furnishings. Terra-cotta tiles, hand-painted sinks, wooded chests, blown glass, and other creative touches make you feel as if you're a guest at a friend's home rather than in a hotel. Each room has a mini-kitchenette, a private bath, purified water, a TV with VCR, and designer bedding. The varied bungalows, which include eight one-bedrooms, two one-bedroom deluxe, and six two-bedroom, surround a lovely heated pool with cushioned lounges and tropical gardens — but the nearest beach is a few miles away. Fountains and flowers are found throughout the grounds, and a brick-paved breakfast nook serves a complete gourmet breakfast daily including fresh-ground coffee and fresh juices. The breakfast nook is also where guests become friends and share travel tips and experiences. Under owner Steve's warm and welcoming management, this is Cabo's most spacious and comfortable full-service inn with exceptionally helpful service. A 100% smoke-free environment, the property is located 5 blocks from downtown Cabo.

Miguel A. Herrera s/n, in front of Lienzo Charro. ☎ and fax: 624-143-5035, 624-143-0585. Internet: www.cabobungalows.com. *16 units. Street parking available. Rack rates: $90 double, $100–$110 suites. Rates include complimentary breakfast. Ask for summer promotions. AE.*

Cabo Inn
$ Cabo San Lucas

This three-story hotel on a quiet street is a real find, and it keeps getting better. The Cabo Inn is a rare combination of low rates, extra-friendly management, and great, funky style — not to mention extra clean — but you are about a mile to the nearest public beach. Rooms are basic and very small — this inn was a bordello in a prior life. All rooms have upgraded furnishings and those on the lower level also have mini-refrigerators. Muted desert colors add a spark of personality, and rooms come with either two twin beds or one queen bed. The rooms surround a courtyard where you

San José del Cabo Accommodations

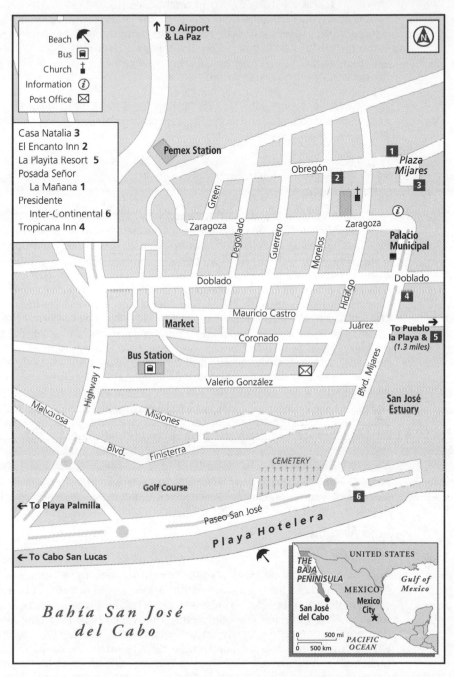

Beach
Bus
Church
Information
Post Office

Casa Natalia **3**
El Encanto Inn **2**
La Playita Resort **5**
Posada Señor
    La Mañana **1**
Presidente
    Inter-Continental **6**
Tropicana Inn **4**

To Airport
& La Paz

Pemex Station

Obregón

1 Plaza
Mijares
2
3

Green

Zaragoza

Degollado

Guerrero

Morelos

Zaragoza

Palacio
Municipal

Doblado

Doblado

Hidalgo

4

Mauricio Castro

Market

Juárez

To Pueblo
la Playa & **5**
(1.3 miles)

Coronado

Highway 1

Bus Station

Blvd. Mijares

Valerio González

San José
Estuary

Malvarosa

Misiones

Blvd.   Finisterra

CEMETERY

Golf Course

To Playa Palmilla

6

Paseo San José

P l a y a   H o t e l e r a

To Cabo San Lucas

*Bahía San José
del Cabo*

THE
BAJA
PENINSULA

UNITED STATES

Gulf of
Mexico

MEXICO

San José
del Cabo

Mexico
City

0   500 mi

0   500 km

PACIFIC
OCEAN

can enjoy satellite TV, a barbecue grill, and free coffee. The third floor has a rooftop terrace with *palapa* and a small swimming pool. Also on this floor is Juan's Love Palace, also known as the honeymoon suite. It's a colorful, *palapa*-topped, open-air room with hanging *tapetes* (woven palm mats) for additional privacy. The hotel is just 2 blocks from downtown and the marina. A lively restaurant next door can deliver pitchers of margaritas and dinner to your room.

20 de Noviembre and Leona Vicario. ☎ *and fax:* **624-143-0819.** *Internet:* www. mexonline.com/caboinn.htm. *20 units. Street parking available. Rack rates: $58 double. No credit cards.*

Casa del Mar
$$$$$ **Corridor**

A little-known treasure, this intimate resort is one of the best values along the Corridor, and it's one of my top recommendations for honeymooners. The hacienda-style building offers guests luxury accommodations complemented by an on-site spa. Located within the Cabo Real development, it's conveniently located by the 18-hole championship Cabo Real golf course. Gentle waterfalls lead to the adults-only pool area with hot tub, and a flowered path takes you further along to the wide, sandy stretch of beach with a clear surf break. The Casa del Mar even has a "quiet area" on the lawn for those looking for a siesta. Guest rooms have a clean, bright feel to them with white marble floors, light wicker furnishings, separate sitting areas, and large hot tubs, plus separate showers on the raised bathroom level. Balconies have oversized chairs and views of the ocean beyond the pool. It's a romantic hotel for couples known for its welcoming, personalized service. In addition to golf, two lighted Astroturf tennis courts, the full-service Avanti Spa, and a small but well-equipped workout room round out the offerings.

Hwy. 1 Km 19.5. ☎ **800-221-8808** *in the U.S., or 624-144-0030. Fax: 624-144-0034. Internet:* www.mexonline.com/casamar.htm. *56 units. Rack rates: High season $396 double, $477 suite; low season $220 double, $275 suite. AE, MC, V.*

Casa Natalia
$$$$ **San José**

This property may be Mexico's most exquisite boutique hotel. Owners Nathalie and Loic have transformed a former residence into a beautiful combination of palms, waterfalls, and flowers that mirrors the beauty of the land. The inn itself is a completely renovated historic home, which now combines modern architecture with traditional Mexican touches. Each of the rooms has a name that reflects the decor such as Conchas (seashells), Azul (blue), or Talavera (ceramics); all have sliding glass doors that open onto small private terraces with hammocks and chairs, shaded by bougainvillea and bamboo. The two spa suites each have a private terrace with a hot tub and hammock. Thirty-nine tall California

Cabo San Lucas Accommodations

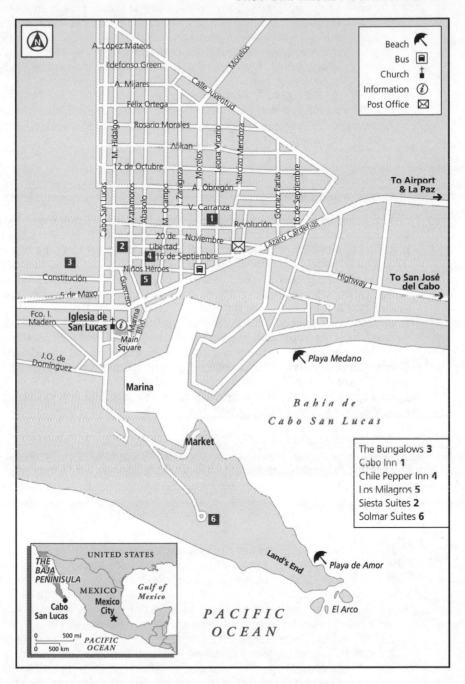

Beach ☂
Bus 🚌
Church ✝
Information ⓘ
Post Office ✉

A. López Mateos
Ildefonso Green
A. Mijares
Félix Ortega
Rosario Morales
Alikan
12 de Octubre
M. Hidalgo
Calle Juventud
Morelos
A. Morelos
Leona Vicario
Narcizo Mendoza
Gómez Farías
16 de Septiembre
Cabo San Lucas
Matamoros
Abasolo
M. Ocampo
I. Zaragoza
A. Obregón
V. Carranza
Revolución
20 de Noviembre
Libertad
16 de Septiembre
Niños Héroes
Constitución
5 de Mayo
Guerrero
To Airport & La Paz
Lázaro Cárdenas
Highway 1
To San José del Cabo

Fco. I. Madero
Iglesia de San Lucas
Marina Blvd
Main Square
J.O. de Domínguez
Marina
Market

Playa Medano

Bahía de
Cabo San Lucas

The Bungalows **3**
Cabo Inn **1**
Chile Pepper Inn **4**
Los Milagros **5**
Siesta Suites **2**
Solmar Suites **6**

Land's End
Playa de Amor

PACIFIC
OCEAN

El Arco

UNITED STATES
THE BAJA PENÍNISULA
MEXICO
Cabo San Lucas
Mexico City
Gulf of Mexico
PACIFIC OCEAN
0   500 mi
0   500 km

palms surround a small courtyard pool; the terraces face this view. The inn, however, is several miles from the nearest public beach. In its favor, Casa Natalia offers its guests privacy, style, and romance, and it only welcomes children 13 and older. One of the highlights of being here is being so close to the exceptional gourmet restaurant (see Chapter 30). It's in the heart of the Boulevard Mijares action, just off of the central plaza.

Blvd. Mijares 4. ☎ ***888-277-3814*** *in the U.S., or 624-142-5100. Fax: 624-142-5110. Internet:* www.casanatalia.com. *16 units including 2 spa suites. Rack rates: high season $220 standard, $345 spa suite; low season $180 standard, $295 spa suite. AE, MC, V.*

Chile Pepper Inn
$ Cabo San Lucas

This bright-yellow, stucco building contains simple but very tasteful rooms surrounding a common courtyard. One of the best values in town, Chile Pepper is for travelers who only need a room for sleeping but want that room to be clean, stylish, and well-appointed. Light wood furnishings are of the hand-carved, rustic variety so popular in Mexico. Palm mats line the floors, and muslin curtains cover the windows that open onto the courtyard. The beds have top-quality orthopedic mattresses and colorful, cotton designer bedding. The bathrooms, although small, are decorated in painted tiles with Talavera sinks. Individual air-conditioning units are new and quiet, the in-room phones offer free local calls, and DirecTV has a large variety of U.S. channels. The one suite has two queen beds in an L-shaped room. The inn is located 4 blocks from the Hard Rock Cafe on a quiet street, but it's still close to Cabo's nightlife action and about 3 miles from Cabo's main public beach.

16 de Septiembre and Abasolo. ☎ *and fax:* ***624-143-0510,*** *624-143-8611. Internet:* www.chilepepperinn.com. *9 units including 1 master suite. Street parking available. Rack rates: $59 double, $85 suite. AE, MC, V.*

El Encanto Inn
$–$$ San José

Located on a quiet street in the historic downtown district, this charming, small inn borders a grassy courtyard with a fountain, offering a very relaxing alternative to busy beachfront hotels. Rooms are all attractively decorated — each is unique — with rustic wood and contemporary iron furniture. The nice-sized bathrooms have colorful tile accents. Rooms have two double beds, and suites have king-size beds and an added sitting room. El Encanto's welcoming owners, Cliff and Blanca, can also help arrange fishing packages, as well as golf and diving outings. Blanca is a lifelong resident of San José, so she's a great resource for information and dining tips. This inn is best for couples or singles looking for a peaceful place from which to explore historic San José. Continental breakfast is included with room rates. It's located between Obregón and Comonfort, half a block from the church.

The Corridor Accommodations

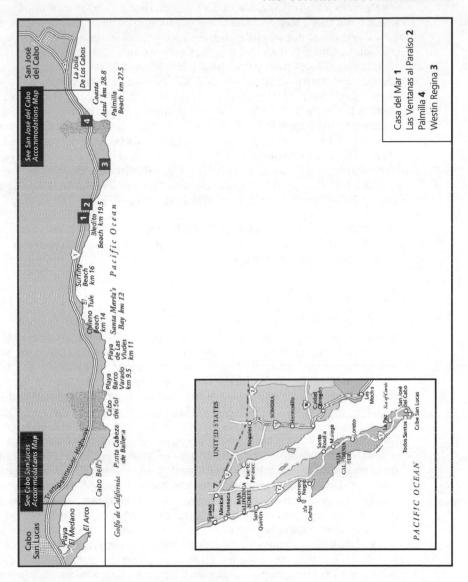

Morelos 17. ☎ *624-142-0388*. *Internet:* www.bajaquest.com/elencantoinn/. *19 units. Limited street parking available. Rack rates: $69 double, $99 suite. Breakfast included. MC, V.*

La Playita Resort

$ **San José**

Distancing itself from even the slow pace of San José, this older yet impeccably clean and friendly courtyard hotel is ideal for fishermen and those looking for something removed from a traditional hotel vacation. It's the only hotel on San José's only beach that's safe for swimming. Just steps from the water and the lineup of fishing *pangas* (small boats), the two stories of sunlit rooms frame a patio with a swimming pool just large enough to allow you to swim laps. Each room is spacious and features high ceilings, high-quality (but basic) furnishings, screened windows, and nicely tiled bathrooms, plus cable TV. Two large suites on the second floor have small refrigerators. If you catch the big one, there's a fish freezer for storage. Services include coffee every morning and golf-cart shuttles to the beach. Next door, the hotel's La Playita Restaurant is open from noon. to 10 p.m. and serves up a great mix of seafood and standard favorites, plus occasional live jazz or tropical music. To find the hotel from Boulevard Mijares, follow the sign pointing to "Pueblo la Playa," taking a dirt road for about 2 miles to the beach. The hotel is on the left facing the water and at the edge of the tiny village of Pueblo la Playa.

Pueblo la Playa. ☎ *888-288-8137 in the U.S., or 624-142-4166. Internet:* www. laplayitahotel.com. *26 units. Free parking. Rack rates: High season $75 double; low season $65 double. MC, V.*

Las Ventanas al Paraíso

$$$$$ Corridor

Mexico's most renowned luxury hotel, Las Ventanas consistently offers luxury accommodations and attention to detail. The architecture, with adobe structures and rough-hewn wood accents, provides a soothing complement to the desert landscape. The only burst of color comes from the dazzling *ventanas* (windows) of pebbled rainbow glass — handmade by regional artisans — that reflect the changing positions of the sun. Richly furnished, Mediterranean-style rooms are large (starting at 1,000 square feet) and appointed with every conceivable amenity, from wood-burning fireplaces to computerized telescopes for stargazing or whale-watching from your own room. Fresh flowers and glasses of tequila welcome each guest, and room standards include satellite TVs with VCRs, stereos with CD players, and dual-line phones. Larger suites offer pampering extras like rooftop terraces, sunken hot tubs on a private patio, or personal pools. The Spa is among the best in Mexico — particularly notable is its Sea and Stars nighttime massage for two, a relaxing aromatherapy massage with two therapists that takes place on the rooftop terrace of your private suite. With a staff that outnumbers guests by four to one, this is the place for travelers who want (and can afford) to be seriously spoiled. The ocean-view gourmet restaurant has an impressive wine cellar and an adjoining terrace bar with live classical music. A seaside casual-dining grill and a fresh-juice bar are also on the property. Guests enjoy access to the adjoining championship Cabo Real golf course. And Las Ventanas has its own sportfishing boats and luxury yachts for charter.

Hwy. 1 Km 19.5. ☎ *888-525-0483 in the U.S., or 624-144-0300. Fax: 624-144-0301. Internet:* www.rosewood-hotels.com. *61 suites. Complimentary valet parking. Rack rates: $550 double with partial ocean view, $675 double with full ocean view,*

$775 split-level suite with rooftop terrace. Special spa and golf packages available, as are inclusive meal plans. AE, DC, MC, V.

Los Milagros
$$ Cabo San Lucas

The elegant, white, two-level buildings that contain the 11 suites and rooms of Los Milagros (The Miracles) border either a grassy garden area or small pool. Rooms are each different, but all are decorated with contemporary iron beds with straw headboards, buff-colored tile floors, and artistic details — but no TVs. Some units have kitchenettes, and the master suite has a sunken tub. E-mail, fax, and telephone services are available through the office only, and coffee service takes place in the mornings on the patio. In the evenings, the garden is lit with candles, and classical music plays. Request a room in one of the back buildings because conversational noise is less intrusive. Los Milagros is located just a block and a half from the Giggling Marlin and Cabo Wabo nightclubs and a couple of miles from Cabo's main public beach.

*Matamoros 116. ☎ and fax: **624-143-4566**. Internet:* www.gotocabo.com/milagros.html. *11 units. Limited street parking. Rack rates: $75 double; ask for summer discounts, group rates, and long-term discounts. No credit cards.*

Palmilla
$$$$$ Corridor

One of the most comfortably luxurious hotels in Mexico, the Palmilla is the grand dame of Los Cabos resorts. Though it's the oldest property along the Corridor, constant upgrades mean that the rooms and facilities surpass even the newest luxury resorts built in the area. The feeling here is one of classic resort-style comfort. The Palmilla has become renowned as a location for destination weddings and anniversary celebrations with a renewal of vows; ceremonies take place in its small, signature chapel that graces a sloped hillside. Perched on a clifftop above the sea (with beach access), the resort is a series of white buildings with red-tile roofs, towering palms, and flowering bougainvillea. Talavera vases, carved dressers and headboards, heavy-weave drapes and spreads, and bathrooms walled in hand-painted tiles give the rooms a colonial-Mexico feeling. Private balconies have extra comfortable, overstuffed chairs. TVs have built-in VCRs, and a wide selection of movies is available at the concierge office. Standard amenities include fresh juice, coffee, and croissants delivered after your wake-up call. A restaurant and the popular Neptuno Bar, known for both its views and margaritas, are on site. The pool has a swim-up bar. Across the highway, the resort's own championship golf course, designed by Jack Nicklaus, is available for guests, and the Palmilla also has two lighted tennis courts, a small fitness center, a croquet court, two volleyball courts, and horseback riding facilities. The hotel automatically adds a 15 percent service charge to all rates, which is included in the rates I quote.

Hwy. 1 Km 27.5. ☎ ***800-637-2226*** *in the U.S., or 624-144-5000. Fax: 624-144-5100. Internet:* www.palmillaresort.com. *114 units. Rack rates: High season $450 double, $690 and up for suites and villas; low season $230–$260 double, $435 and up for suites and villas. AE, MC, V.*

Posada Señor La Mañana
$ San José

This comfortable two-story guest house, set in a grove of tropical fruit trees, offers basic rooms with tile floors and funky furniture and an abundance of hammocks strewn about the property. Younger travelers and the backpack set are the mainstays here. Guests have cooking privileges in a large, fully equipped common kitchen set beside two palapas. Ask about discounts and weekly rates. It's next to the Casa de la Cultura, behind the main square in San José. A small swimming pool is on-site, but you're about 3 miles from the beach here.

Obregón 1. ☎ *and fax:* ***624-142-1372***. *E-mail:* sr_manana@1cabonet.net.mx. *18 units. Rack rates: $30–$45 double. No credit cards.*

Presidente Inter-Continental
$$$$$ San José

The Presidente, set on a long stretch of beach next to the Estero San José, is San José's most upscale all-inclusive property and an ideal choice for anyone wanting to simply stay put on a lovely stretch of beach and have their every need attended to. Low-rise, Mediterranean-style buildings frame the beach and San José's largest swimming pool, which has a swim-up bar. If possible, select a ground-floor oceanfront room because the lower level offers spacious terraces as an alternative to a tiny balcony on upper-level units. The rooms have satellite TVs and large bathrooms; suites include a separate sitting area. The all-inclusive nature of this resort makes it a good choice for vacationers who want to principally stay in one place; it's also popular with families. In addition to the three restaurants and a garden cafe, theme-night buffet dinners take place a few nights per week. The roster of activities and facilities includes golf clinics, tennis, a small gym, bicycle rentals, and horseback riding. For a fee, the hotel also offers a twice-daily shuttle to Cabo San Lucas.

Blvd. Mijares s/n, at the very end of the road abutting the estuary. ☎ ***800-327-0200*** *in the U.S., or 624-142-0211. Fax: 624-142-0232. 240 units. Rack rates: $442 double standard room, $470 double oceanfront room. Rates include all meals, beverages, and many sports. AE, DC, MC, V.*

Siesta Suites
$ Cabo San Lucas

Reservations are a must at this immaculate, small inn popular with return visitors to Cabo. (It's especially popular with fishermen.) The very basic rooms have white tile floors and white walls, kitchenettes with seating areas, refrigerators, and sinks. The mattresses are firm, and the bathrooms are large and sparkling clean. Rooms on the fourth floor have two queen beds each. The accommodating proprietors offer free movies and VCRs, a barbecue pit and outdoor patio table on the second floor, and a comfortable lobby with TV. They can also arrange fishing trips. Weekly and monthly rates are available. The hotel is 1½ blocks from the marina, where parking is available.

Zapata at Hidalgo. ☎ *and fax: **624-143-2773**. E-mail:* siesta@1cabonet. net.mx. *20 suites (15 with kitchenette). Rack rates: $55 double. No credit cards.*

Solmar Suites
$$$$ Cabo San Lucas

Set against sandstone cliffs at the very tip of the Baja Peninsula, the Solmar is beloved by travelers seeking seclusion, comfort, and easy access to Cabo's diversions. The beach here is spectacular, though not for swimming. Suites are located in two-story, white-stucco buildings along the edge of the broad beachfront and have either a king or two double beds, satellite TVs, separate seating areas, and private balconies or patios on the sand. Guests gather by the pool and on the beach at sunset and all day long during the winter whale migration. With one of the best sportfishing fleets in Los Cabos, including the deluxe *Solmar V*, used for long-range diving, fishing, and whale-watching expeditions, the Solmar is especially popular with fishing enthusiasts. Every Saturday, Solmar hosts a popular Mexican fiesta. Advance reservations are necessary almost year-round. A small time-share complex adjoins the Solmar; some units are available for nightly stays. Rates below include the hotel's mandatory 10% service charge.

Av. Solmar 1, past the Marina. ☎ ***624-143-3535**. Fax: 624-143-0410. Internet:* www. solmar.com. *(Reservations: P.O. Box 383, Pacific Palisades, CA 90272;* ☎ ***800- 344-3349**, 310-459-9861; Fax: 310-454-1686.) 194 units. Rack rates: $165–$433 suite. AE, MC, V.*

Tropicana Inn
$$ San José

This small, colonial-style inn has been a long-standing favorite in San José and welcomes many repeat visitors. The Tropicana is considered "gringo central" in San José and caters to American tastes in a very traditional Mexican setting. Set just behind (and adjacent to) the Tropicana Bar and Grill, it frames a plant-filled courtyard with a graceful arcade bordering the rooms and inviting swimming pool. Each nicely furnished, medium-size room in the L-shaped building (which has a two- and a three-story wing) comes with tile floors, two double beds, a window looking out on the courtyard, a brightly tiled bathroom with shower, and a coffee pot. Each morning, the staff sets out freshly brewed coffee, delicious sweet rolls, and fresh fruit for hotel guests. You can order room service until 11 p.m. from the adjacent Tropicana Bar and Grill (owned by the hotel). The inn is located behind the restaurant, a block south of the town square, and about a mile and a half from the nearest beach.

Blvd. Mijares 30. ☎ ***624-142-0907,** 624-142-1580. Fax: 624-142-1590. 38 units. Free limited parking in back. Rack rates: High season $85 double; low season $70 double. AE, MC, V*

Westin Regina
$$$$$ Corridor

Architecturally dramatic, the Westin Regina sits at the end of a long, paved road atop a seaside cliff. Vivid terra-cotta, yellow, and pink walls rise against a landscape of sandstone, cacti, and palms with fountains and gardens lining the long pathways from the lobby to the rooms. Electric carts carry guests and their luggage through the vast property. The rooms are gorgeous and feature both air-conditioning and ceiling fans, private balconies, satellite TVs, and walk-in showers separate from the bathtubs. This property is probably the best choice among my selections for families vacationing along the Corridor because of the wealth of activities available for children (plus babysitting). With six restaurants and two bars, you may never need to leave the resort. For golfers, both the Palmilla and Cabo Real golf courses are nearby, and the Westin also has two tennis courts, 7 pools, 2 children's pools, a beach club, and complete fitness center with massage services.

Hwy. 1 Km 22.5. ☎ ***800-228-3000** in the U.S., or 624-142-9000. Fax: 624-142-9010. 295 units. Rack rates: $308 double with partial ocean view, $347 double with full ocean view. Rates drop 20% in low season. AE, DC, MC, V.*

Chapter 29

Settling into Los Cabos

● ●

In This Chapter

▶ Knowing what to expect when you arrive

▶ Getting the lowdown on the layout

▶ Discovering helpful information and resources

● ●

*E*ven though Los Cabos may feel like an extension of Southern California in spirit, it's still a foreign country, so a few things are important to know and keep in mind. Still, if you're a first time traveler to Mexico, you'll immediately feel comfortable — English appears to be more accepted than Spanish in terms of languages, and U.S. dollars are the widely accepted currency.

In this chapter, I take you from the plane, through the airport and to your hotel, helping you quickly get your bearings in this easy-to-navigate area. I continue on with tips on everything from where to find a babysitter to how to save a buck or two on transportation.

Arriving in Los Cabos by Air

Los Cabos International Airport is small and easy to make your way through. It's located closest to San José del Cabo. From this town, continue down a long, well-paved stretch of highway known as the Corridor until you reach the proverbial "end of the line" — Cabo San Lucas and it's rowdy charms. From the very beginning of your Cabo experience, everything should be smooth sailing — you'll find both immigration and customs to be brief, generally easy procedures.

Navigating passport control and customs

When you arrive, you walk right from your plane straight into the immigration clearance area. Here, an officer will ask you to show your passport and your completed tourist card, the **FMT** (see Chapter 7 for all the FMT details).

Your FMT is an important document, so take good care of it. You're supposed to keep the FMT with you at all times because you may be required to show it should you run into any sort of trouble. You also need to turn it back in upon departure, or you may be unable to leave without replacing it.

Next up is the baggage claim area. Here, porters stand by to help with your bags, and they're well worth the price of the tip — about a dollar a bag. After you collect your luggage, you pass through another check-point. Something that looks like a traffic light awaits you here. You press a button, and if the light turns green, you're free to go. If it turns red, you need to open each of your bags for a quick search. It's Mexico's random search procedure for customs. If you have an unusually large bag, or an excessive amount of luggage, you may be searched regardless of the traffic-light outcome.

While you're waiting for your bags, you may notice the corral-like area with lots of people waving you over. No, they're not exceptionally friendly locals; they're timeshare salespeople — hot to offer you a deal on a rental car, transportation to your hotel, or some other ploy in exchange for a generally aggressive sales pitch. Trust me — settle in first and then decide if a timeshare presentation is something that should be included in your vacation agenda.

Just past the baggage claim are the real rental car booths, taxi stands, and other transportation options. If you're part of a package tour that includes ground transportation to your hotel, this is where you look for your representative — generally carrying a sign with your name or the name of your tour company on it.

Getting to your hotel

The one airport that serves both Cabos and the connecting Corridor is 7½ miles northwest of San José del Cabo and 22 miles northeast of Cabo San Lucas. Public transportation here is minimal — but improving — and taxis are expensive. This is one Mexican beach resort where I find having a rental car for even part of your stay can not only be practical but may even save you some green if you plan on explor-ing the area even a little bit. The main road connecting the two Cabos is a modern, well-paved stretch of road, and driving here is easy — it's hard to get lost, and parking, though a challenge in the heart of the two towns, isn't impossible.

Renting a car

Advance reservations aren't always necessary, and don't be afraid of requesting a better price than the first one a representative quotes — bargaining sometimes works. You can, however, generally get a much better rate by booking your car in advance through a company's U.S.

toll-free number. Before signing on, be sure you understand the total price after insurance and taxes are added. Rates can run between $40 and $75 per day with insurance costing an extra $10 per day. The major car-rental agencies all have counters at the airport open during flight arrivals. Major car rental services include:

- ✔ **Avis** (☎ **800-331-1212** in the U.S., or 624-146-0201; Internet: www. avis.com; E-mail: avissjd@avis.com.mx; Open: 7 a.m. to 9 p.m.)

- ✔ **Budget** (☎ **800-527-0700** in the U.S., or 624-143-4190; Internet: https://rent.drivebudget.com; Open: 8 a.m. to 7 p.m.)

- ✔ **Hertz** (☎ **800-654-3131** in the U.S., or 624-142-0375; Internet: www.hertz.com; Open: 8 a.m. to 8 p.m.)

- ✔ **National** (☎ **800-328-4567** in the U.S., or 624-142-2424; Internet: www.nationalcar.com; Open: 8 a.m. to 8 p.m.)

One of the best and most economical local car-rental agencies is **Advantage Rent-A-Car** (Lázaro Cárdenas, between Leona Vicario and Morelos, downtown Cabo; ☎ **624-143-0909**; Fax: 624-143-0466; E-mail: advantage@1cabonet.com.mx). Volkswagen sedans rent for $48 per day, and weekly rates include one free day. The collision damage waiver adds $14 per day to the rental price. If you pick up the car downtown, you can return it to the airport at no extra charge.

If you decide to rent a car, picking it up at the airport may be a good idea because doing so saves you the airport to hotel transportation expense. You won't have to drive to the airport to return it either — most of the car companies have pick-up service at your hotel or local offices within both towns. Conversely, if you prefer to settle in first, plan your car rental for the last part of your vacation. The agency can deliver the car to your hotel, and then you can return it to the airport prior to departing (but allow as much as an extra 30 minutes for checking it in).

Hiring transportation

If you do opt to let someone else do the driving, buy a ticket inside the airport for a *colectivo* (shared minivan) or a taxi. *Colectivo* fares run about $7 to San José, about $10 to hotels along the Corridor, and $12 to Cabo for up to eight passengers, and they're only available from the airport. A private taxi can be shared by up to four people and costs about $12 to San José and about $60 to Cabo San Lucas.

Getting Around Los Cabos

You exit the airport onto Mexican Highway 1, also known as the Transpeninsular Highway. The first main town you come to is San José del Cabo. The highway continues west to the shore and then curves and heads south for about the next 20 miles, after which point you reach Cabo San Lucas. In the center of Cabo, Highway 1 turns into Lázaro Cárdenas.

If you're staying in San José del Cabo, turn off Highway 1 on Zaragoza, the main street leading from the highway into town; Paseo San José runs parallel to the beach and is the principal boulevard of this hotel zone. The mile-long Boulevard is the main street in San José with restaurants, shops, banks, and other services. San José has two principal zones: downtown, where sophisticated inns as well as traditional budget hotels are located, and the hotel zone along the beach. Note that no local bus service runs between downtown San José and the beach; a taxi is the only means of getting between the two places.

The road that connects San José del Cabo to Cabo San Lucas is the centerpiece of resort growth. Known as the Corridor, this stretch of four well-paved lanes offers cliff-top vistas but still has no nighttime lighting. The area's most deluxe resorts and renowned golf courses are found here, along with a collection of dramatic beaches and coves.

The small town of Cabo San Lucas, edged by foothills and desert mountains to the west and south, grew up around the harbor of Cabo San Lucas Bay and spreads out to the north and west. The main street leading into town from the airport and San José del Cabo is Lázaro Cárdenas; as Cárdenas nears the harbor, Marina Boulevard branches off from it and becomes the main artery that curves around the waterfront. Lázaro Cárdenas, the main street into town from Highway 1, splits off to the right and then loops back around a shady plaza, turning into Marina Boulevard, which runs along the waterfront. Most of the shops, restaurants, and nightlife in Cabo are all located within this loop.

Touring around town

TourCabos (Paseo San José, in the Plaza Los Cabos, across from the Fiesta Inn on the *malécon* [boardwalk]; ☎ **624-142-0982;** Fax: 624-142-2050) offers a day tour to Cabo San Lucas for around $35. The tour leaves at 9 a.m. and returns around 4 p.m.

Many of the Corridor hotels offer some sort of shuttle service into the two towns, usually for a $10 charge, but the hotels have to disguise it as a "tour" due to the strength of the taxi union here.

Taking a bike ride is a great way to tour around the towns. Bicycles rent for $3 an hour and $15 a day from **Baja Bicycle Club** (☎ **624-142-2828**) at the Brisa del Mar Trailer Park on the highway just south of town. Ask about special offers; the Baja Club also has surfboard, bodyboard, and snorkel-equipment rentals. The shop is open daily from 9:30 a.m. to 8:00 p.m.

Taking a taxi

Taxis may be easy to find, but in keeping with the high cost of everything else, they're expensive within Cabo. Expect to pay about $15 or $25 for a taxi between Cabo and the Corridor hotels, and about $30 if you're going all the way to San José.

Whenever you take a taxi, establish the price before setting out. You should also check with your hotel to see the average rates to and from different areas.

Considering a car rental

Because more than 20 miles separate the two Cabos and numerous attractions in between, you should consider renting a car even if it's only for a day. Transportation by taxi is expensive here, and if you're at all interested in exploring, a rental car is your most economical option. Each of the two towns has its own distinctive character and attractions, so make the most of this two-for-one resort.

See "Renting a car" earlier in this chapter for car-rental information.

Fast Facts: Los Cabos

American Express

The representative in San José is **TourCabos** (☎ 624-142-4040). In Cabo, the office is located in the **Pueblo Bonito Hotel** in Playa Medano (☎ 624-143-2787).

Area Code

The local telephone prefix is **624.** Calls between Cabo San Lucas, San José del Cabo, and northern Corridor hotels are toll calls, so you must use the area code.

Beach Safety

Before swimming in the open water here, it's important to check whether the conditions are safe. Undertows and large waves are common. In Cabo, **Playa Medano** (close to the marina and town) is the principal beach that's safe for swimming; it has several lively beachfront restaurant-bars. It's also easy to find watersports equipment for rent here. The Hotel Melia Cabo San Lucas, on Playa

Medano, has a roped-off swimming area to protect swimmers from Jet Skis and boats. **Note:** Colored flags signaling the safety of swimming conditions aren't generally used in Cabo, and neither are lifeguards.

Babysitters

Most of the larger hotels can easily arrange for babysitters, but many speak limited English. Rates range from $4 to $10 per hour.

Banks, ATMs, and Currency Exchange

Banks exchange currency during normal business hours, generally Monday through Friday from 9 a.m. to 6 p.m. and Saturday from 10 a.m. to 2 p.m. Currency-exchange booths, found all along Cabo's main tourist areas, aren't as competitive, but they're more convenient. ATMs are widely available and even more convenient, and they dispense pesos — and in some cases dollars — at bank-exchange rates.

Business Hours

Most offices maintain traditional Mexican hours of operation (10 a.m. to 2 p.m. and 4 p.m. to 8 p.m. daily), but shops remain open throughout the day. Offices tend to be closed on Saturday and Sunday, but shops are open on Saturday, at least, and increasingly offer limited hours of operation on Sunday.

Climate

It's warm all year; however, evenings and early mornings in the winter months can turn quite cool. Summers can be very hot, but tropical rainstorms may cool the afternoons.

Emergencies

You can try **060,** but generally, no one answers. The local city-hall number is ☎ 624-142-0361.

Hospitals

In Cabo, **Baja Medico** (Camino de la Plaza s/n, on the corner with Pedegral; ☎ 624-143-0127, 624-143-0175) has a 24-hour walk-in clinic. Most of the larger hotels have a doctor on-call.

Information

In San José, the **city tourist information office** (☎ 624-142-0465) is in the old post-office building on Zaragoza at Mijares. It offers maps, free local publications, and other basic information about the area. It's open Monday through Friday from 8 a.m. to 3 p.m.

The **Secretary of Tourism** (Medano, between Hidalgo and Guerrero; ☎ 624-142-0446; Fax: 624-142-0260) functions as the information office in Cabo San Lucas. The English-language **Note:** The many visitor-information booths along the street are actually time-share sales booths, and their staffs aim to pitch a visit to their resort in exchange for discounted tours, rental cars, or other giveaways.

Internet Access

In San José, **Cabo Online** (Malvarrosa and Gobernadora; ☎ 624-142-2905; Internet: www.caboonline.com) is open Monday through Friday 9 a.m. to 2 p.m. and 4 to 6 p.m. and Saturday 9 a.m. to 2 p.m. The cost is $2 for 15 minutes or $3 for 30 minutes. **Trazzo Internet,** located a block from the central plaza at the intersection of Zaragoza and Morelos, charges $2.50 for 30 minutes or less of high-speed access.

Access in Cabo San Lucas is available at **Dr. Z's Internet Café & Bar** (Lázaro Cárdenas 7, Edificio Posada, across from the Pemex gas station; ☎ 624-143-5390). Access costs $5 for 15 minutes, $7 for 30 minutes, or $8 for an hour. It's open 9 a.m. to 6 p.m. Monday through Saturday.

Maps

One of the best around is the free American Express map, usually found at the tourist information offices and the hotel concierge desks.

Newspapers/Magazines

The English-language **Los Cabos Guide, Los Cabos News, Cabo Life, Baja Sun,** and the irreverent and extremely entertaining **Gringo Gazette** are distributed free at most hotels and shops and have up-to-date information on new restaurants and clubs.

You can find the best selection of English-languages books and magazines, as well as books on Baja, at **Libros** (Plaza Bonita Mall, Moreles and Lázaro Cárdenas, Cabo; ☎ 624-143-3171). It's visible from the street.

Pharmacy

In San José, **Farmacia ISSTE** (Carretera Transpeninsular Km 34, Plaza California; ☎ 624-142-2645) and **Farmacia Plaza Dorada** (Carretera Transpeninsular Km 29, Plaza Dorada; ☎ 624-142-0140) are the two major pharmacies in the area.

A long-standing drugstore in Cabo San Lucas, with a wide selection of toiletries as well as medicines, is **Farmacia Aramburo** (Cárdenas at Zaragoza, Plaza Aramburo; no phone). It's open daily from 7 a.m. to 9 p.m. Also try **Farmacia Faro Viejo** (Cárdenas and Hidalgo 4;☎ 624-143-3655), open daily from 9 a.m. to 9 p.m.

Police

In San José, call ☎ 624-142-0361; in Cabo San Lucas, the number is ☎ 624-143-3977.

Post Office

In San José, the *correo* on Boulevard Mijares 1924 at Valerio González (☎ 624-142-0911) is open Monday through Friday 8 a.m. to 4 p.m. and Saturday 9 a.m. to 1 p.m.

The correo (☎ 624-143-0048) in Cabo San Lucas is at Cárdenas and Francisco Villa on the highway to San José del Cabo, east of the bar El Squid Roe. It's open Monday through Friday 9 a.m. to 1 p.m. and 3 to 6 p.m. and Saturday from 9 a.m. to noon.

Special Events

The feast of the patron saint of San José del Cabo is celebrated on March 19 with a fair, music, dancing, feasts, horse races, and cockfights. October 12 is the festival of the patron saint of Todos Santos, a town about 65 miles north. October 18 is the feast of the patron saint of Cabo San Lucas, celebrated with a fair, feasts, music, dancing, and other special events.

Taxes

There's a 15 percent value-added tax (IVA) on goods and services, and it's generally included in the posted price.

Taxis

Taxis are plentiful but relatively expensive. Trips between the two towns average $30; trips between hotels along the Corridor average $15. Rides within San José cost around $3, but rides within Cabo cost between $5 and $10.

Telephone

Avoid the phone booths that have signs in English advising you to call home using a special 800 number — these are absolute rip-offs and can cost as much as $20 US per minute. The least expensive way to call is by using a Telmex (LADATEL) pre-paid phone card, available at most pharmacies and mini-supers, using the official Telmex (Lada) public phones. In, Mexico you need to dial 001 prior to a number to reach the United States, and you need to preface long-distance calls within Mexico by dialing 01.

Time Zone

Los Cabos operates on mountain standard time, but Mexico's observance of daylight savings time varies somewhat from that in the United States.

Chapter 30

Dining in Los Cabos

● ●

In This Chapter

▶ Discovering the best of Los Cabos

▶ Dining with the locals

● ●

*P*aying a lot for mediocre food isn't uncommon in Los Cabo, so try to get a couple of unbiased recommendations before settling in for a meal. If people are only drinking and not dining, take that as a clue because many seemingly popular places are long on party atmosphere but short on food quality. Prices (and subsequently so does the quality) decrease the farther you walk inland from the waterfront.

Besides the restaurants mentioned in this chapter, dozens of good, clean taco stands and taco restaurants dot the downtown area. To find additional, good restaurants explore Hidalgo and Cárdenas and the Marina at the Plaza Bonita. North-of-the-border tastes have heavily influenced Cabo's dining scene. The usual suspects (U.S. franchise chains like KFC, Subway, Pizza Hut, and a host of others) are everywhere downtown. Note that many restaurants automatically add the tip to the bill.

Cabo is a very casual town, and shorts and jeans are accepted everywhere except the most upscale of resort restaurants, but dressier resort wear is still acceptable too. Despite the relaxed atmosphere, prices here are generally higher than you find in comparable restaurants in the United States or other parts of Mexico. This situation is due to the necessity of importing many ingredients from the mainland. Cabo has also imported some customs of "upper" California — it's becoming more common to have segregated non-smoking areas in restaurants here due to the demand by visitors.

With several exceptional choices and culinary offerings more representative of Mexico, San José is becoming known as the preferred dining town. Prices also tend to be more reasonable. If you're staying along the Corridor, remember to figure in transportation costs when calculating the price of your meal — you may just decide to dine at your hotel, which is likely to have a top-notch chef anyway. Cabo has the most restaurant offerings, but sad to say, few are truly spectacular.

When it comes to welcoming young ones at restaurants, Los Cabos is more like the United States than Mexico — less than enthusiastic, except at the more traditional establishments and casual hotel restaurants. If your children are particular to American tastes, you can go with the standards like McDonald's, Burger King, and Hard Rock Cafe — all good choices. But you may also want to try the Mexican alternatives of Carlos O'Brian's or Squid Roe, which seem to be fun at any age — and if you dine early, the atmosphere is less raucous.

The Best Restaurants in Los Cabos

I arrange the following restaurants by location and alphabetically and note their general price category. Remember that tips generally run about 15%, and most wait-staff really depend on these for their income, so be generous if the service warrants. Please refer to the Introduction of *Mexico's Beach Resorts For Dummies* for an explanation of the price categories.

Please see the "Menu Glossary" in Appendix E for more information on Mexican cuisine.

Damiana
$$$$ San José   SEAFOOD/MEXICAN

For one of the area's finest Mexican meals, this casually elegant restaurant in an 18th-century hacienda is a great bet. The 150-year-old colonial home is decorated in the colors of a Mexican sunset: walls painted a deep orange, and tables and chairs clad in bright rose, lavender, and orange cloth. Mariachis play nightly from 8 to 9 p.m. (mid-December through March) in the tropical courtyard where candles flicker under the trees and flowering vines. For an appetizer, try the mushrooms diablo — a moderately zesty dish of mushrooms with garlic and guajillo chiles. For a main course, the ranchero shrimp in cactus sauce or grilled lobster tail are flavorful choices. You can also enjoy brunch almost until the dinner hour. The interior dining room is nice, but the courtyard is the most romantic dining spot in San José. It's located on the east side of the town plaza.

San José town plaza. ☎ *624-142-0499, 624-142-2899. Fax: 624-142-3027. E-mail: damiana@1cabonet.com.mx. Reservations recommended during Christmas and Easter holidays. Main courses: $30.00–$40.00; lunch $7.50–$20.00. AE, MC, V. Open: Daily 11:00 a.m.–10:30 p.m.*

San José del Cabo Dining

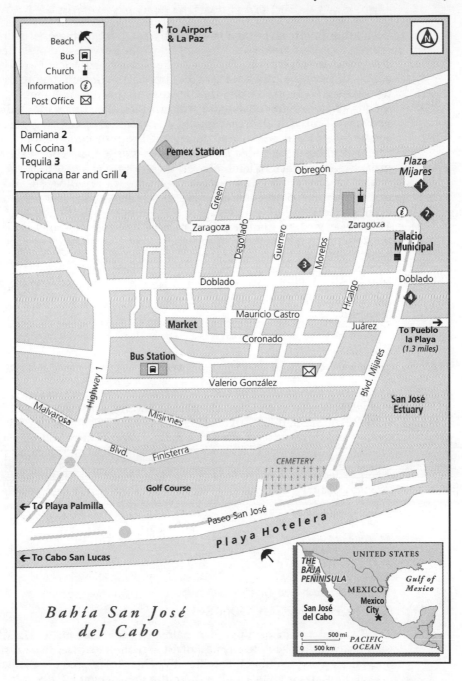

Beach ☂
Bus ⊡
Church ✝
Information ⓘ
Post Office ✉

Damiana **2**
Mi Cocina **1**
Tequila **3**
Tropicana Bar and Grill **4**

To Airport
& La Paz

Pemex Station

Obregón

Plaza
Mijares
1

2

Green

Zaragoza

Degollado

Guerrero

Morelos

Zaragoza

ⓘ

Palacio
Municipal

3

Hidalgo

Doblado

Doblado

Mauricio Castro

Juárez

4

Market

Coronado

To Pueblo
la Playa
(1.3 miles)

Bus Station

✉

Blvd. Mijares

San José
Estuary

Valerio González

Highway 1

Malvarosa

Misiones

Blvd.

Finisterra

CEMETERY

To Playa Palmilla

Golf Course

Paseo San José

Playa Hotelera

To Cabo San Lucas

*Bahía San José
del Cabo*

☂

UNITED STATES

THE
BAJA
PENINSULA

MEXICO

Gulf of
Mexico

San José
del Cabo

Mexico
City ★

0   500 mi
0   500 km

PACIFIC
OCEAN

Mi Cocina

$$$$ **San José** **NUEVELLE MEXICAN/EURO CUISINE**

Without a doubt, Mi Cocina is currently the best dining choice in the entire Los Cabos area. From the setting to the service, a dinner here is sure to be unforgettable. The plant-filled courtyard, with its towering palms and exposed brick walls, accommodates alfresco dining. But it's not just the romantic setting that makes this restaurant special — the food is creative and consistently superb. Notable starters include the *patoludo* — cured duck breast served on organic greens with grapes and apples — and the *vol-u-vent* puff pastry filled with shrimp, scallops, mushrooms, and basil *beurre blanc*. Among the favorite main courses are the provençal-style rack of lamb served on a potato cake with onion marmalade and the jumbo shrimp sautéed with rosemary, olive oil, and sundried tomatoes. Save room for dessert; choices range from chocolate éclairs to fresh-fruit-filled meringue discs topped with Chantilly cream. The full-service palapa bar offers an excellent selection of wines, premium tequilas, and single-malt scotches, as well as an extensive array of specialty drinks.

Blvd. Mijares, inside Casa Natalia. ☎ ***624-142-5100****. Main courses: $15–$20. AE, MC, V. Open: Daily 7:00 a.m.–4:00 p.m. to hotel guests only and 6:30–11:00 p.m. to the public.*

Tequila

$$$–$$$$ **San José** **MEXICAN/ASIAN**

The contemporary Mexican cuisine with a light and flavorful touch is the star attraction here, although the garden setting, with rustic leather and twine furniture and lanterns scattered among palms and giant mango trees, is also lovely. Start with a heavenly version of the traditional *chiles en nogada* stuffed with couscous, raisins, and papaya and seasoned with cinnamon. Grilled tuna with ginger sauce arrives perfectly seared; the whole-grain bread is fresh and hot. Jazz and attentive service complement the fine meal. An added touch: Cuban cigars and an excellent selection of tequilas are available.

M. Doblando s/n. ☎ ***624-142-1155****. Main courses: $10–$45. AE. Open: Daily 11:00 a.m.–3:00 p.m. and 6:00–10:30 p.m.*

Tropicana Bar and Grill

$$$ **San José** **SEAFOOD/MEAT**

The Tropicana remains a popular mainstay, especially for tourists. The bar has a steady clientele day and night and often features live music or special sporting events on satellite TV. The dining area is in a garden (candlelit in the evening) with a tiled mural at one end. Cafe-style sidewalk dining is also available, but a twirling, brightly lit dessert display makes this option a little less romantic. The menu is too extensive to lay

Cabo San Lucas Dining

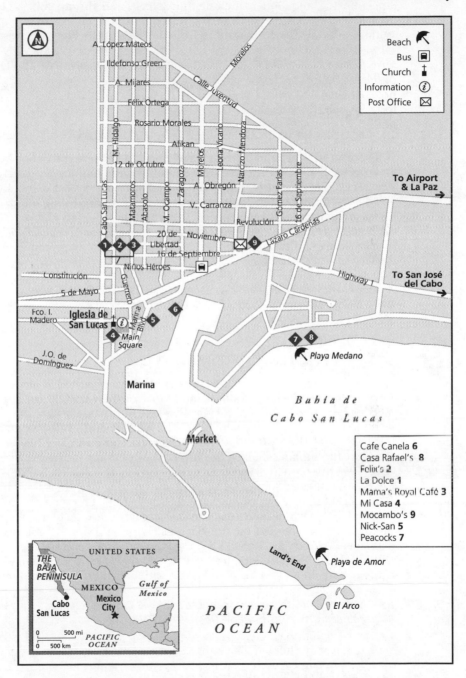

Beach
Bus
Church
Information
Post Office

A. López Mateos
Ildefonso Green
A. Mijares
Félix Ortega
Rosario Morales
Afikan
12 de Octubre
A. Obregón
V. Carranza
Revolución

Morelos
Calle Juventud
Leona Vicario
Narcizo Mendoza
Gómez Farías
16 de Septiembre

M. Hidalgo
Cabo San Lucas
Matamoros
Abasolo
M. Ocampo
I. Zaragoza
Morelos

To Airport
& La Paz

20 de
Libertad
16 de Septiembre

Niños Héroes

Lázaro Cárdenas

Highway 1

To San José
del Cabo

Constitución
5 de Mayo

Guerrero

Fco. I.
Madero

Iglesia de
San Lucas

Marina Blvd

Main
Square

J.O. de
Domínguez

Marina

Playa Medano

*Bahía de
Cabo San Lucas*

Market

Cafe Canela **6**
Casa Rafael's **8**
Felix's **2**
La Dolce **1**
Mama's Royal Café **3**
Mi Casa **4**
Mocambo's **9**
Nick-San **5**
Peacocks **7**

Land's End

Playa de Amor

El Arco

*PACIFIC
OCEAN*

UNITED STATES

*THE
BAJA
PENINISULA*

MEXICO

*Gulf of
Mexico*

Cabo
San Lucas

Mexico
City

500 mi
500 km

*PACIFIC
OCEAN*

claim to any specialty; it aims to please everyone. All meats and cheeses are imported, and dinners include thick steaks and shrimp fajitas. *Paella* (a saffron-flavored rice dish with chicken, seafood, and sausage) is the Sunday special. The restaurant is 1 block south of the Plaza Mijares.

Blvd. Mijares 30. ☎ *624-142-1580. Main courses: $8–$20; breakfast $4–$6. AE, MC, V. Open: Daily 6 a.m.–11 p.m.*

Cafe Canela

$ Cabo San Lucas   COFFEE/PASTRY/LIGHT MEALS

This cozy, tasty cafe and bistro is a welcome addition to the Cabo Marina boardwalk. Espresso drinks or fruit smoothies and muffins are good eye-openers for early risers. Enjoy a light meal or a tropical drink either inside or on the bustling waterfront terrace. The appealing menu also offers breakfast egg wraps, salads (for example, curried chicken salad with fresh fruit), sandwiches (such as blue-cheese quesadillas with smoked tuna and mango), and pastas — all reasonably priced. Full bar service is also available.

Marina boardwalk, below Plaza Las Glorias hotel. ☎ *624-143-3435. Main courses: $4.00–$9.00; coffee $1.75–$3.50. AE, MC, V. Open: Daily 7:00 a.m.–4:30 p.m.*

Casa Rafael's

$$$$ Cabo San Lucas   INTERNATIONAL

Although I consider it overpriced, Casa Rafael's is regarded as among the most romantic places in Cabo. Dine in one of the candlelit rooms and alcoves (air-conditioned) of this large house or outside beside the small swimming pool. Piano music plays in the background while you enjoy a leisurely meal; the staff times the courses so you don't feel rushed. To start, try the sublime smoked dorado paté or perhaps the hearts of palm with a raspberry vinaigrette dressing. House specialties include the Chicken Parmesan Sonia and scampi with pasta. The steaks are black Angus beef imported from the United States; the lamb comes from New England. The rich desserts may make you wish you'd seen them first before stuffing yourself on the entrees. Wine and aperitif menus are extensive. To find Casa Rafael's, follow Hacienda Road toward the ocean; when you top the hill, look left. Turn left when you see the rosy-pink château with an arched front and patio with caged birds and a fountain.

Calle Medano and Camino el Pescador. ☎ *624-143-0739. Reservations suggested. Main courses: $19–$52. AE, MC, V. Open: Daily 6–10 p.m.*

Felix's

$$ Cabo San Lucas   MEXICAN

This colorful, friendly, family-run place has grown up since opening in 1958 from just serving tacos to offering a full array of tasty Mexican and seafood dishes — among the best eats in Cabo. Everything is fresh and

The Corridor Dining

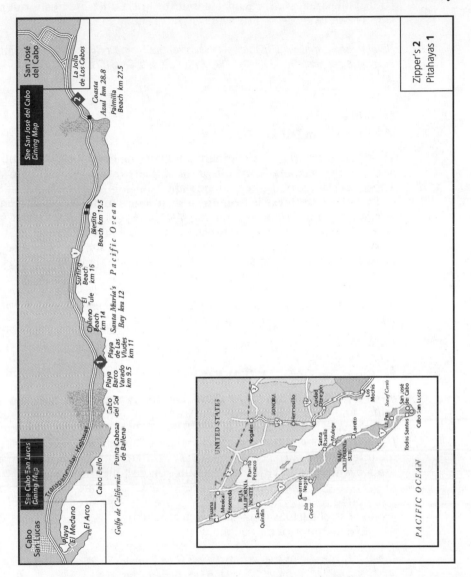

homemade including the corn tortillas and the numerous and varied salsas — more than 30! — served from the salsa bar. Fish tacos made with fresh dorado are superb, as are any of the shrimp dishes — the honey-mustard shrimp are especially tasty. Don't leave without someone at your table sampling Felix's original recipe for Mexican bouillabaisse, a rich stew of shrimp, crab, sea bass, scallops, Italian sausage, and savory seasonings. Mexican specialties include *carne asada* (beef cooked on a grill with a *chile verde* — green chile — sauce) and chimichangas. A year back, Felix's combined space with the family's other Cabo dining institution,

Mama Royal's, and now offers a casual-dining area and outdoor shaded patio. Full bar service is available, but the specialties are fresh-fruit margaritas and daiquiris — just $2.50 each.

Hidalgo and Zapata s/n, in the same location as Mama's Royal Café (its name for breakfast service). ☎ *624-143-4290. Main courses: $8–$15. MC, V. Open: Mon–Sat 3–10 p.m.*

La Dolce

$$$ Cabo San Lucas   ITALIAN

This Cabo restaurant, with authentic Italian thin-crust, brick-oven pizzas and other specialties, is the offspring of Puerto Vallarta's La Dolce Vita. The food is some of the best in the Baja Peninsula, and the fact that 80% of La Dolce's business is from local customers underscores the point. Partner Stefano (a dead-ringer for Michaelangelo's *David,* albeit with pants) keeps the service attentive and welcoming and ensures that the food meets the high standards it's known for. The simple menu also features sumptuous pastas and calzones, plus great salads. This spot is the best late-night dining option.

M. Hidalgo and Zapata s/n. ☎ *624-143-4122. Main courses: $8–$14. No credit cards. Open: Mon–Sat 6 p.m. to midnight. Closed Sept.*

Mama's Royal Café

$ Cabo San Lucas   BREAKFAST

What a great place to start the day! The shady patio with cloth-covered tables and the bright and inviting interior dining room are both comfortable. And the food is just as appetizing. Effrain and Pedro preside over this dining mecca featuring well-prepared breakfast selections that include grilled sausage; French toast stuffed with cream cheese and topped with pecans, strawberries, and orange liqueur; several variations of eggs Benedict; home fries; fruit crêpes; and traditional breakfasts; plus free coffee refills. The orange juice is freshly squeezed, and a regular group of strolling musicians usually gets your morning off to a lively start with live marimba or mariachi music.

Hidalgo at Zapata. ☎ *624-143-4290. Breakfast special: $2.50; breakfast à la carte $2.50–$10.00. MC, V. Open: Wed–Mon 7:30 a.m.–1:00 p.m.*

Mi Casa

$$$ Cabo San Lucas   MEXICAN/NOUVELLE MEXICAN

The building's vivid, cobalt-blue facade is your first clue that this place celebrates Mexico; the menu confirms that impression. Mi Casa is one of Cabo's most renowned gourmet Mexican restaurants, although it's equally noted for its inconsistency. Traditional specialties, such as *manchamanteles* (literally interpreted as "tablecloth stainers," it's a stew of meat and vegetables), *cochinita pibil* (a local pork dish), and *chiles en nogada* (chile peppers stuffed with a mixture of meat, nuts and fruit) are everyday menu staples. Fresh fish is prepared with delicious seasonings from recipes found throughout Mexico. Especially pleasant at night, the restaurant's tables, scattered around a large patio, are set with colorful cloths, traditional pottery, and glassware. It's across from the main plaza.

Calle Cabo San Lucas at Madero. ☎ 624-143-1933. Reservations recommended. Main courses: $15–$25. AE, MC, V. Open: High season Mon–Sat noon to 10:30 p.m.; low season Mon–Sat 5–10 p.m.

Mocambo's
$$ Cabo San Lucas   SEAFOOD

The newer location of this long-standing Cabo favorite isn't very inspirational — it's basically a large cement building — but somebody obviously likes the food. The place is always packed, generally with local diners tired of high prices and small portions. Ocean-fresh seafood is the order of the day here, and the specialty platter can easily satisfy the healthy appetites of four people. The restaurant is a block and a half inland from Lázaro Cárdenas.

Leona Vicario and 20 de Noviembre. ☎ 624-143-6070. Main courses: $5–$23. No credit cards. Open: Daily 1:30 a.m.–10:00 p.m.

Nick-San
$$$ Cabo San Lucas   JAPANESE/SUSHI

Exceptional Japanese cuisine and sushi are the specialties in this air-conditioned restaurant with a clean, minimalist decor. A rosewood sushi bar with royal blue tiled accents invites diners to watch the master sushi chef at work. An exhibition kitchen behind the sushi chef demonstrates why this place has been honored with a special award for cleanliness.

Blvd. Marina, Plaza de la Danza. ☎ 624-143-4484. Reservations recommended. Main courses: $12–$25; sushi $3.50 and up. MC, V. Open: Tues–Sun 11:30 a.m.–10:30 p.m.

Peacocks
$$$$ Cabo San Lucas   INTERNATIONAL

One of Cabo's most exclusive patio-dining establishments, Peacocks emphasizes creatively prepared fresh seafood. Start off with the house paté or a salad of feta cheese with cucumber, tomato, and onion. For the main course, try one of the pastas — linguini with grilled chicken and sun-dried tomatoes is one of my favorites. Heartier entrees include steaks, shrimp, and lamb, all prepared several ways.

Paseo del Pescador s/n, corner of Melia Hotel. ☎ 624-143-1858. Reservations recommended. Main courses: $15–$30. AE, MC, V. Open: Daily 6:00–10:30 p.m.

Pitahayas

$$$$ Corridor   PACIFIC RIM

Pitahayas' beachfront setting in the Hacienda del Mar resort offers gourmet dining under a grand palapa or on open-air terraces under a starlit sky. Master chef Volker Romeike has assembled a creative — if not slightly pretentious — menu that blends Pacific Rim cuisine with Mexican native herbs and seasonings. Notable sauces include mango, black bean, and curry. The rotisserie-barbecued duck is a house specialty, along with anything done over a mesquite grill or in a wok — all prepared in an impressive exhibition kitchen. A dessert pizza with fresh fruit, chocolate, and marzipan makes a fitting finish to a stunning meal. Pitahayas also boasts the largest wine cellar in Los Cabos with vintages from around the world housed in an underground *cava*. Formal resort attire is requested, and reservations are an absolute must during high season.

Hacienda del Mar, Hwy. 1 Km 10, Cabo del Sol. ☎ *624-145-8010. Reservations required during high season. Main courses: $12–$30. AE, MC, V. Open: Daily 7–11 p.m.*

Zipper's

$$ Corridor   BURGERS/MEXICAN/SEAFOOD

Enjoy a hearty, American-style lunch served seaside at this popular, casual hangout. Sitting at the far south end of the beach heading toward Cabo San Lucas and fronting the best surfing waters, Zipper's has become popular with gringos in search of American food and TV sports. Burgers have that back-home flavor — order one with a side of spicy curly fries. Steaks, lobster, beer-batter shrimp, deli sandwiches, and Mexican combination plates round out the menu, which is printed with dollar prices.

Playa Costa Azul, just south of San José. No phone. Main courses: $7–$18; burgers and sandwiches $7–$10. No credit cards. Open: Daily 8 a.m.–10 p.m.

Chapter 31

Having Fun On and Off the Beach in Los Cabos

In This Chapter

▶ Checking out the beach scene

▶ Landing the big one and shooting a low score

▶ Visiting La Paz and Todos Santos

▶ Saddling up to the bar

Geographically, Baja California is set apart from mainland Mexico, which greatly contributes to its unique culture and personality, as well as to its many attractions and diversions. Volcanic activity created the craggy desertscape populated mainly by forests of cardón cactus, spiky Joshua trees, and spindly ocotillo bushes that you see today. Hard to believe such a formidable landscape could become home to a vacation haven, but it has. Today, Los Cabos offers visitors a ton of options for fun in the sun — eco-tours, golfing, sport fishing, diving, and whale-watching, to name a few — amidst beautiful settings and posh resorts.

In this chapter, I give you an overview of the best beaches tucked into the miles of coastline between the two Cabos (and in the neighboring areas). I point out the most interesting sights in these twin towns, and I also offer a rundown of the best ways to spend an active day — or night — here.

Hitting the Beaches

The beaches of Los Cabos are stunning — cobalt-blue waters set against a backdrop of rugged desert terrain. The countless inlets and small coves in the Sea of Cortez have made Cabos a popular destination for ocean kayaking, and the abundant sea life attracts both divers and sport fishermen. And as for the beaches here, you can choose from dozens of tranquil coves or opt to take on the long stretches of challenging surf breaks. One after another, these beautiful patches of sand hug the shoreline between the two Cabos.

Beach aficionados who want to explore the beautiful coves and beaches along the 22-mile coast between the two Cabos should consider renting a car for a day or so. Rental cars cost $40 to $75 per day and up. (Check out Chapter 29 for all the details on renting a car in Cabo.) Frequent bus service between San José del Cabo and Cabo San Lucas also makes it possible to take in the pleasures of both towns.

Cabo's northern beaches

The relaxed pace of San José del Cabo makes it an ideal place to unwind and absorb authentic Mexican flavor while enjoying a stretch of sand.

The nearest beach to San José that's safe for swimming is **Pueblo la Playa** (also called La Playita), located about 2 miles east of town. From Boulevard Mijares, turn east at the small "Pueblo la Playa" sign and follow the dusty, dirt road through cane fields and palms to a small village and beautiful beach where local fishermen pull their *pangas* (skiffs) ashore. The La Playita Resort and its adjacent restaurant (see the hotel listings in Chapter 28) offer the only formal sustenance on the beach. You should also note that there are no shade *palapas*.

The beach that forms the southern border of San José is a broad stretch of sand, but because hotels front most of it, hotel guests are the primary beachgoers here — it can be a hassle for non-guests to access the beach.

Corridor beaches

Traveling from San José to Cabo San Lucas, the first beach along the Corridor is **Playa Costa Azul** (Highway 1 Km 28–29) where Zipper's restaurant is located (see Chapter 30). It's a long stretch of sand next to the Mykonos and La Jolla condo developments. Most of the year, Costa Azul has a gentle, but regular, surf break; however, from late summer to early fall, a southwest swell brings consistent wave action with some truly exceptional surf conditions.

Bird-watching

Between Pueblo la Playa and San José's Presidente Inter-Continental Hotel lies the **Estero San José,** an estuary and protected ecological reserve with at least 270 species of birds. A small cultural center (☎ 624-142-1504) at the edge of the water features occasional exhibitions and educational programs. A footpath leads you further into the estuary for one heck of a bird-watching experience.

Los Cabos

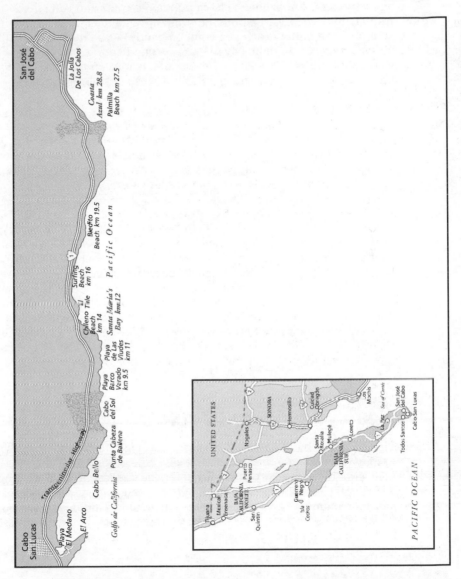

Playa Palmilla, with its beautiful rock formations, is the nearest swimming beach after you've set off down the Corridor. It's located 5 miles west of Playa Costa Azul near the Spanish-colonial-style Hotel Palmilla — an elegant place to stay or dine. To reach Playa Palmilla, take a taxi to the road that leads to the Hotel Palmilla grounds. Then take the left fork in the road (without entering the hotel grounds) and follow the signs to Pepe's restaurant on the beach.

Playa Chileno is the largest and most popular of the public beaches along the corridor, and it has both public restrooms and showers — a rarity in Mexico. A watersports-equipment rental facility located at the southern end of the beach can come in handy — the rocky headlands at both ends of this small bay offer some good snorkeling. Nearby **Playa Santa María** has less in the way of facilities and shade, but it's better for snorkeling and diving. Both of these beaches are noted for their abundance of marine life.

The remains of the Japanese tuna boat *Inari Maru* make **Playa Barco Varado** (Shipwreck Beach, Highway 1 Km 9–10) noteworthy and provide the beach with its name. The boat became stranded on the rocky shoals in 1966. It's now one of the main dive sites in the area. The hull and other wreckage lie 6.5 to 85 feet underwater.

In addition to Playa Palmilla, the beaches of Chileno and Santa María are generally safe for swimming — but always be careful. The other beaches along the Corridor should not be considered safe. Experienced snorkelers may want to check them out, but other visitors should go for the view only. Always check at a hotel or travel agency for directions and swimming conditions. Although a few travel agencies run snorkeling tours to some of these beaches, there's no public transportation. If you want to explore these beaches on your own, your only option is to rent a car. To find these beaches, follow the blue-and-white signs along Highway 1. The signs are sometimes labeled "Acesso a Playa," but more often, they simply bear the international symbol for a swimmer or a snorkeler.

Cabo's southern beaches

The main beach in Cabo San Lucas is a curving sweep of sand known as Playa **Medano** and located on the east side of the bay. The swimming conditions here are generally safe. You can also rent snorkeling gear, boats, WaveRunners, kayaks, pedal boats, and windsurf boards and score some windsurfing lessons. The people-watching at Medano Beach is as hot as the action — take your pick from the many outdoor restaurants along the shore and settle in for a cold one.

Finding Water Fun for Everyone

It began with the stories of John Steinbeck and continued with the tall tales of the early sport fishermen who came here in the 1940s and '50s. With over 3,000 estimated species of fish in the waters offshore Baja California and the title of undisputed bill-fishing capital in the world, Los Cabos enjoyed early fame among visitors who wanted to reel in the big one. In the years that followed, travelers to Los Cabos have discovered an even greater number of ways to revel in the treasures of this deep, blue sea.

Cruising Los Cabos

Whether by day or in the fading light of the sunset, numerous cruises are available to take you around Land's End — the famed tip of Baja California — to enjoy this truly stunning sight. Boats depart from Cabo San Lucas. The cruise prices and offerings vary but usually include music, an open bar, and snacks for between $30 and $45 per person. Variables include the type of boat, duration of the cruise, and amenities.

The sunset cruise on the 42-foot catamaran *Pez Gato* (☎ 624-143-3797, 624-143-2458; E-mail: pezgato@1cabonet..com.mx) is always a favorite. The excursion departs from the Plaza las Glorias Hotel dock at 5 p.m. This 2-hour cruise costs $35 and includes margaritas, beer, and sodas. Similar boats also leave from the Plaza las Glorias Hotel dock and from the marina. Almost any travel agency or hotel tour desk can make the arrangements for you, or you can call **Xplora Adventours** (in the Sierra Madre store on the plaza, Boulevard Mijares at Zaragoza, San José; ☎ **624-142-9000,** ext. 8316). Xplora handles all the tour providers in the area and can give you the unbiased lowdown on which one will meet your individual needs.

Another great way to see the aquatic sights is aboard one of the **glass-bottom boats.** These boats leave from the Cabo San Lucas marina every 45 minutes between 9 a.m. and 4 p.m. daily. The cost is about $10 for an hour tour past sea lions and pelicans to see the famous El Arco (Rock Arch) at Land's End where the Pacific Ocean and the Sea of Cortez meet. Most boats make a brief stop at Playa de Amor or drop you off if you ask; you can use your ticket to catch a later boat back. (Be sure to check what time the last boat departs.)

When the gray whales migrate to the Los Cabos area between January and March, **whale-watching cruises** aren't to be missed. In San José, fishermen at Pueblo la Playa take small groups out to see the whales; a 4-hour trip runs about $45 per person. Another option is **Cabo Travel Advisors** (Plaza José Green, Local 6-C, San José; ☎ 624-142-4444), which arranges whale-watching adventures for groups of four or more people; the 2½-hour trip costs $45 per person and includes snacks and beverages.

Sport-fishing boats, glass-bottom boats, and cruise catamarans also offer whale-watching trips at prices ranging from $35 to $60 for a half-day trip. You can also spot the whales from shore; good whale-watching spots include the beach by the Solmar Suites hotel on the Pacific and the beaches and cliffs along the Corridor.

The ultimate whale excursion is an all-day trip to Magdalena Bay, a 1-hour plane ride away. In a small skiff, you get close enough to touch the whales. The cost for the trip, including air transportation, is $380.

Preferring a paddleboat

Fully guided, ecologically oriented **sea kayaking tours** are available through **Cabo Travel Advisors** (Plaza José Green, Local 6-C, San José; ☎ 624-142-4444). The tour runs from 8:30 to 11:30 a.m. and includes breakfast and beverages for a price of $55. No previous experience is necessary — guides provide complete instructions at the start of the tour. Kayaks are the most popular and practical way to explore the pristine coves that dot this shoreline.

Further south in Cabo, you can't beat kayaking around the El Arco (Rock Arch) formation. It's $40 for a morning kayak trip or $60 to see the spectacular sight at sunset.

Catching a wave

When summer hurricanes spin off the southern end of the peninsula, they send huge surf northward to beaches like **Zippers, Punta Gorda,** and **Old Man's.** People have compared Zippers (near the Brisa del Mar Trailer Park and the Costa Azul surf shop outside San José del Cabo) with places like Pipeline on the North Shore of Oahu. That may be a bit of an exaggeration, but this area does feature great waves nonetheless.

Playa Costa Azul (Highway 1 Km 29, just south of San José) is the most popular surfing beach in the area. A few bungalows are available for rent here, and surfers can camp on the beach. You can rent surfboards and surf racks for your rental car by the day here. Spectators can watch the action from the highway lookout point at the top of the hill south of Costa Azul.

You can find good surfing from March through November all along the beaches west of Cabo, and **Playa Chileno,** near the Cabo San Lucas Hotel east of town, has a famous right break. Other good surfing beaches along the corridor are **Acapulquito, El Tule,** and **La Bocana.**

The Pacific Coast has yet to face the onslaught of development that has rapidly changed the landscape to the east. An hour-long drive up the coast to the little towns of Pescadero and Todos Santos can be a great surf journey. There are a couple good point breaks near here. You can reach **Playa San Pedrito** via the dirt road that begins 7.4 kilometers (4.5 miles) south of the Todos Santos town limits. Follow the "San Pedrito Campground" signs. The point is very rocky and sharp, but it's a wonderful wave at the right swell direction and tide (northwest swell, rising tide). Further down the road is **Playa los Cerritos,** located 12.8 kilometers (8 miles) south of Todos Santos. Cerritos is a lovely beach with a surfable point break off a big headland.

Exploring the deep blue

Diving in Los Cabos is so special because of the abundance of marine life, which includes giant mantas, sea turtles, dolphins, and tropical fish. You can choose between diving the coral reefs at the southern tip of the cape region or one of the shipwrecks in the area. April through November is the best time to dive, but diving is most crowed from October to mid-January — it's important to make reservations in advance if you're planning to dive then. During the winter months, you're also likely to hear the moving, tonal songs of the humpback whales as you dive. Note that during the winter months, the water here can be quite cold, so a wet suit is necessary — even for most snorkelers.

Several companies offer snorkeling; a 2-hour cruise to sites around El Arco costs $30, and a 4-hour trip to Santa Maria costs $55. Both prices include gear rental. Certain beaches, such as Playa de Amor, Santa María, Chileno, and Barco Varado, have snorkeling gear for rent at the beach; it's generally priced between $10 and $15.

For scuba diving, contact **Amigos del Mar** (☎ 800-344-3349 in the U.S., or 624-143-0505; Fax: 213-545-1622 in the U.S., or 624-143-0887; www.amigosdelmar.com), located at the marina in Cabo San Lucas. Diving specialist Ricardo Sevilla has all the answers to your Cabo diving answers. Dives are made along the wall of a canyon in San Lucas Bay where you can see the "sandfalls" that even Jacques Cousteau couldn't figure out — no one knows its source or cause. Amigos del Mar also has scuba trips to Santa María Beach and places farther away including the Gordo Banks and Cabo Pulmo. Dive prices start at $40 for a one-tank dive and $660 for two tanks. Trips to the coral outcropping at Cabo Pulmo start at $125. Located two hours from Cabo San Lucas, Cabo Pulmo is rated for beginners and up. Gordo Banks, for advanced divers, is an underwater mountain about 5 miles offshore with a black-coral bottom and schools of game fish and manta rays at a rate of $120 for a two-tank dive. Resort courses cost $100 per person and open-water certification costs around $450.

In addition to Amigos del Mar in Cabo San Lucas, snorkeling and scuba trips can also be arranged through **Xplora Adventours** (☎ 624-142-9000, ext. 8316) and Cabo Travel Advisors (☎ 624-142-4444) — both in San José.

Reeling in the big one

Superb sport fishing put Cabo San Lucas on the map, and many travelers still come here with the dream of dropping a line and waiting for the big one. The fishing really lives up to its reputation — bringing in a 100-pound marlin is considered routine. Angling is good all year, though the catch varies with the season. Here's the fishing lineup by time of year and the most prevalent fish:

✔ **January-April:** Yellowtail

✔ **May-December:** Yellowfin tuna

✔ **June-November:** Sailfish and wahoo

✔ **July-December:** Black and blue marlin

✔ **All year:** Striped marlin

For most cruises and excursions, try to make fishing reservations at least a day in advance; keep in mind that some trips require a minimum number of people. You can arrange your fishing trip through a travel agency or directly at one of the fishing-fleet offices at the far south end of the marina in Cabo San Lucas.

The marina is located on the south side of the harbor. You can easily find fleet operators with offices near the docks. To choose a boat, take a stroll around the marina and talk with the captains — you may arrive at an economical deal. Try **ABY Charters** (☎ **624-143-0831**, 624-143-0874) or the **Picante/Blue Water Sport-fishing Fleet** (☎ **624-143-2474**). Both companies have booths located at the sport-fishing dock at the far south end of the marina.

The going rate for a day on a fully equipped cruiser with captain and guide (many of the larger hotels, like the Solmar, have their own fleets) starts at around $700 for up to four people. For deluxe trips with everything included aboard a 40-foot boat, you should budget $1,250.

The *panga* **fleets** offer the best deals. Pair up with another angler and charter a *panga,* a 22-foot skiff used by local fishermen, at Playa la Puebla, in San José. Several *panga* fleets offer up to 6-hour sport-fishing trips, usually from held from 6 a.m. to noon, for $25 per hour (with a 3-hour minimum). You can split the cost with one or two other people. For information, contact the fisherman's cooperative in Pueblo la Playa, or you can call **Victor's Aquatics** (☎ **949-496-0960** in the U.S., or 624-142-1092; Fax: 624-142-1093) at the Hotel Posada Real. Victor's also has its own fishing fleet with both pangas ($165 for 6 hours) and cruisers ($380 to $495). Outfitters supply the boat and tackle, and the client buys the bait, drinks, and snacks.

You need daily fishing permits in Cabos, but your captain can take care of the details. Daily permits range from $4 to $10, and annual permits are also available. Check with your outfitter when you make your reservation to determine how they handle permits.

Catch and release is strongly encouraged in Los Cabos. Anglers reel in their fish, which are tagged and released unharmed into the sea.

Anglers get a certificate that documents the catch, and they leave Los Cabos with the knowledge that plenty of billfish will still be in the sea when they return.

Enjoying Land Sports

The rugged terrain of Baja and the cape region once kept people out of the area. Now it seems to be a main lure, attracting travelers in search of an active vacation and true interaction with nature. If you prefer your nature somewhat on the tame side, you may find your game on one of Cabo's many famed golf courses. In fact, golf has overtaken sport fishing in popularity in Cabo.

Teeing off

Los Cabos has become Mexico's golf mecca. The master plan for golf in Los Cabos calls for 207 total holes in the future. The fees I list in this section are for 18 holes of play, including golf cart, water, club service, and tax, during high season. Summer rates are about 25% lower, and many hotels offer special golf packages. I list the courses in geographical order, starting in San José, heading down along the Corridor, and ending in Cabo San Lucas (for specifics on the playability of the various courses, see the "Lowdown on golfing in Cabo" sidebar in this chapter):

✔ As with many things in Los Cabos, visitors find that the most economical way to enjoy this sport is to play in San José. Greens fees at the nine-hole **Club Campo de Golf San José** (Paseo Finisterra, across from the Howard Johnson Hotel; ☎ 624-142-0900, 624-142-0905) are just $45 for nine holes or $75 for 18 holes with carts costing an extra $30. The course is open daily from 7 a.m. to 4 p.m., and club guests can also use the swimming pool.

✔ The 27-hole course at the **Palmilla Golf Club** (Palmilla resort, the Corridor; ☎ 800-386-2465 in the U.S., or 624-144-5250) was the first Jack Nicklaus signature layout in Mexico. The course was built in 1992 on 900 acres of dramatic oceanfront and desert. The 27-hole course offers you a choice between two back-nine options. Greens fees are $214.50.

✔ Just a few miles down the road from the Palmilla is another Jack Nicklaus signature course, the 18-hole Ocean Course at **Cabo del Sol** (Cabo del Sol resort, the Corridor; ☎ 800-386-2465 in the U.S., or 624-145-8200). The 7,100-yard course is known for its challenging final three holes. Although Palmilla is currently a semiprivate club, most Corridor hotels have membership benefits. Greens fees are $208 to $228.

✔ The 18-hole, 6,945-yard course at **Cabo Real** (Melia Cabo Real resort, the Corridor; ☎ 624-144-0232) was designed by Robert Trent Jones, Jr., and features holes that sit high on mesas overlooking the Sea of Cortez. Fees run $190 for 18 holes.

✔ The **El Dorado Golf Course** (Melia Cabo Real resort, next to the Westin Regina hotel, the Corridor; ☎ 624-144-5451) is a Jack Nicklaus signature course. The course is open daily from 7 a.m. until dusk. Eighteen holes are $225. After 2 p.m., a twilight special offers a round for $150. Carts are included; caddies are available for $40.

✔ Located in Cabo San Lucas, the **Cabo San Lucas Country Club** (501 Palo Blanco; ☎ 800-854-2314 in the U.S., or 624-143-4653; Fax: 624-143-5809) features an 18-hole course designed by Roy Dye. The entire course overlooks the juncture of the Pacific Ocean and Sea of Cortez, including the famous Land's End rocks. The layout includes the 607-yard, par-five 7th hole — the longest hole in Mexico. Greens fees are $176 and a twilight game is $121.

The golf offerings in Los Cabos continue to expand — another five courses are currently under various phases of construction. All courses generally offer 50 percent off their rates if you play after 2:00 or 2:30 p.m. Actually, this is a great time to play because the temperatures are cooler and play is generally faster. Course fees are high in Cabo — generally over $200 per round, but these courses are truly world class and worth the world-class price to play them.

Lowdown on golfing in Cabo

In golf, it's not always how you play the course, but how the course plays you. Los Cabos is now considered one of the world's finest golf destinations, which means some of the courses can be pretty challenging. It's important to pick a course that matches your abilities, so a challenge doesn't become a frustration. Los Cabos has an ample and intriguing variety of courses for golfers of all levels.

Beyond the selection, quality, and beauty of the courses in Los Cabos, a key reason so many golfers choose to play here is the very reliable weather. The courses highlighted in this chapter compare to the great ones in Palm Springs and Scottsdale with the added beauty of the ocean views, as well as the wider variety of desert cacti and flowering plants.

✔ **Cabo del Sol:** A Jack Nicklaus signature course, its dramatic, finishing, oceanside holes have earned it the nickname "the Pebble Beach of Baja." Compared to the Palmilla course (also by Nicklaus), this layout is much more difficult with less room for error. Seven of the holes are set along the water. This is very challenging target golf with numerous forced carries — even from the red tees. The signature hole here is 17, which runs by the water. Don't be fooled by the wide and welcoming 1st hole.

✔ **Cabo Real:** This Robert Trent Jones, Jr., course is known for its holes along the Sea of Cortez that sit high on mesas overlooking the sea; exceptional among these holes is the frequently photographed 12th hole. Jones designed the course to test low handicappers, but multiple tees make it enjoyable for average players as well. The par-72 layout is 6,945 yards long and was designed with professional tournament play in mind. The most famous hole is the 14th, which sits right on the beach near the Melia Cabo Real resort.

✔ **Cabo San Lucas Country Club:** Different designers in the Dye family designed the front and back nine here, so the course plays like two different courses. Characteristic of Roy Dye-designed courses, it has deep waste bunkers, subtle terracing-up hillsides, and holes built into the natural desert terrain. The most challenging hole is the extremely long, 607-yard, par-five 7th around a lake; it's the longest hole in Mexico. The course is designed to offer a variety of play options, from a short course played on front tees to a super-long course with numerous bunkers and hazards.

✔ **El Dorado Golf Course:** Another Jack Nicklaus signature course located at Melia Cabo Real, El Dorado is a links-style course in the Scottish tradition. The layout is challenging — 7 holes border the Sea of Cortez and 12 are carved out of two pristine canyons. The ocean isn't the only water you see on this course — manmade lakes are also a part of the scenery. El Dorado bills itself as the "Pebble Beach of Baja" — but then again, so does Cabo del Sol — you decide.

✔ **Palmilla Golf Club:** The original Cabo course is now a 27-hole course. You must play the Arroyo (the original front nine) for your first nine holes, and then you choose between Mountain (the name given to the original back nine) and Ocean Nine (the new holes — although these newer holes lie closer to the water, only one of them has a true ocean view) for your back nine. If you play this course only once, choose the Mountain back nine — it offers better ocean views. The views at the mountaintop clubhouse are also pretty spectacular. The eventual plan is for this course to be exclusive to guests of the Palmilla Hotel and residents of the adjacent real estate development. It's beautiful, playable, and well maintained, and views of desert mountains and the cobalt ocean without any interfering construction are featured throughout. It's one of a handful of places in the world where a golfer can play by water, mountain, and desert views surrounded by flowering vegetation. Bermuda short-cut grass makes putting fast, and the signature hole is the Mountain 5 hole; you hit over a canyon and then down to the greens below over a forced carry. This is target golf, and as a Jack Nicklaus course, the layout was constructed with strategy in mind.

✔ **Querencia:** The newest course to open in Los Cabos is Querencia (1 Querencia Blvd., ☎ **624-145-6670**; Internet: www.loscabosquerencia.com), a Tom Fazio-designed course. However, it's a strictly private club with play limited to property owners and golf club members (no provision for resort guests).

Making time for tennis

You can play tennis at the two courts of the **Club Campo de Golf Los Cabos** (Paseo Finisterra No. 1; ☎ **624-142-0905**) for $10 an hour during the day or $20 an hour at night. (Club guests can also use the swimming pool.) Tennis is also available at the **Hotel Palmilla** (two lighted courts) and the **Presidente Inter-Continental** (two lighted courts). See Chapter 28 for more info on these properties.

Taking Adventure and Nature Tours

Expeditions on all-terrain vehicles (ATVs) to the Cabo Falso lighthouse and La Candelaria (an Indian pueblo in the mountains) are among the most popular of the adventure tours available is Los Cabos. These excursions are a great way to explore the land, and they're available through most travel agencies. The 3-hour tour to Cabo Falso includes a stop at the beach, a look at some sea-turtle nests (without disturbing them) and the remains of a 1912 shipwreck, a ride over 500-foot sand dunes, and a visit to the lighthouse. Guided tours cost around $45 per person on a single vehicle or $60 for two people riding on one ATV. You can also rent ATVs for $35 for 3 hours. Ask your hotel concierge for more information.

La Candelaria is an isolated Indian village in the mountains 25 miles north of Cabo San Lucas. As described in *National Geographic,* the old pueblo is known for the white and black witchcraft still practiced here. An underground river that emerges at the pueblo provides water for the lush landscape of palms, mango trees, and bamboo. The return trip of the tour travels down a steep canyon, along a beach (giving you time to swim), and past giant-sea-turtle nesting grounds. Departing at 9 a.m., the La Candelaria tour costs around $80 per person or $100 for two on the same ATV.

A variety of land- and water-based adventure and nature tours are available through **Tio Sports** (☎ **624-143-3399;** Internet: www.tio sports.com) including the popular ATV tours to Cabo Falso and Candelaria and parasailing at $40 single or $70 tandem.

Xplora Adventours (☎ **624-142-9000,** ext. 8316) is a great contact for a complete rundown of what's available. They offer all the tours from all the local companies rather than working with only a select few. Xplora has tour desks in the Westin Regina hotel, the Sierra Madre stores in San José and on Lázaro Cárdenas in Cabo San Lucas, and at the Cabo Wabo Beach Club at Medano Beach in Cabo.

Sightseeing in Los Cabos

Sports and partying are Cabo's main attractions, but you can find a few — very few is a better description — cultural and historical points of interest. In San José, the Spanish missionary Nicolás Tamaral established the stone **Iglesia de San Lucas** (Church of San Lucas; Calle Cabo San Lucas, close to the main plaza) in 1730. According to local lore, the

Pericúe Indians reportedly resisted Tamaral's demands that they practice monogamy and eventually killed the missionary. Buildings on the streets facing the main plaza in San José are gradually being renovated to house restaurants and shops, and the picturesque neighborhood promises to have the strongest Mexican ambiance of any place in town.

Shopping in Los Cabos

San José has the better shopping of the two towns when it comes to higher quality items, but if you're after a beer-themed T-shirt, Cabo San Lucas can't be topped. In San José, a growing selection of unique shops, hip boutiques, and collections of fine Mexican *artesanía* (handcrafts) are clustered around Boulevard Mijares and Zaragoza, the main street. The municipal market on Mauricio Castro and Green has edibles and utilitarian wares.

In Cabo San Lucas, a popular shopping stop for tourists is the open-air market at Plaza Papagayo on Boulevard Marina opposite the entrance to Pueblo Bonito. The market mainly has trinkets and traditional souvenirs — little in the way of real craftwork. Be sure to bargain. Most shops in Cabo are on or within a block or two of Boulevard Marina and the plaza.

Unless otherwise noted, these shops that follow are in San José del Cabo.

Clothing

Escape (Plaza Florentine, on Zaragoza, across from the cathedral in; no phone) features designer and casual sportswear and accessories including designer jeans, leather bags, belts, and a trendy selection of sunglasses. An interior-decor shop by the same name next door has a small cafe and espresso bar in the connecting courtyard.

Contemporary art

San José has a growing number of art galleries — mainly artist studios open to the public — and the town's creative ambience is blossoming. The most notable gallery is **Galeria Wentworth Porter** (Avenida Obregón 20; ☎ **624-142-3141**), which features a selection of original fine art along with prints and art cards by local artists. As the name implies, the work of locally popular artist Dennis Wentworth Porter figures prominently. The gallery is open Monday through Saturday 10 a.m. to 5 p.m.

In the Medano Beach area, the handsome **Galería Gattamelata** (Hacienda Road; ☎ 624-143-1166) specializes in antiques and colonial-style furniture. It's open daily from 9 a.m. to 8 p.m.

Crafts and gifts

Copal (Plaza Mijares; ☎ 624-142-3070) features traditional and contemporary Mexican artesanía and silver jewelry in a former residence tastefully converted into a contemporary shop. You can shop here daily from 9:00 a.m. to 10:30 p.m.

Cuca's Blanket Factory (Cárdenas at Matamoros; no phone) is an open-air stand that sells the standard, Mexican, cotton and woolen blankets with an added attraction — you can design your own blanket and have it ready the next day. The stand is open daily from 9 a.m. to 9 p.m.

Nature-inspired gifts, books, and collectibles with a conservationist theme can be found at **Sierra Madre** (plaza at Zaragoza; ☎ 624-142-3537). Xplora Adventours also has a location inside the shop. The shop is open daily 9 a.m. to 10 p.m.

Decorative and folk art

Arte, Diseño y Decoración (ADD) (Zaragoza at Hidalgo, San José; ☎ 624-142-2777) sells creative home accessories and furnishings, mostly made of rustic wood, pewter, and Talavera ceramics, and offers shipping services back home for travelers who shop too much and can't carry it all.

Casa Maya (Calle Morelos,; ☎ and fax: 624-143-3197) has unusual decorative items for the home at excellent prices. Tin lamps, colored glass, and rustic wood furnishings are just of few of the wares. Casa Maya is open Monday through Saturday from 9 a.m. to 7 p.m.

El Callejon (Vicente Guerrero s/n, between Cárdenas and Madero; ☎ 624-143-1139; Fax: 624-143-3188) may just be the most eclectic shop in Cabo San Lucas. It features antiques, unique gifts, paintings, and home furnishings. Local artists make most of the one-of-a-kind items. It's open Monday through Saturday from 10 a.m. to 8 p.m.

Walls of wooden masks and carved religious statues are the draw at **Rostros de México** (Cárdenas at Matamoros; ☎ 624-143-0558), a Cabo San Lucas gallery whose name means "Faces of Mexico." It's open Monday through Saturday 10 a.m. to 7 p.m. and Sunday 10 a.m. to 2 p.m. No credit cards are accepted.

Other stores

The Plaza Bonita Shopping Center (Blvd. Marina at Cárdenas) is among the best in the area. This large terra-cotta-colored plaza on the edge of the Cabo San Lucas marina has been around since 1990, and it finally has a group of successful businesses. **Libros** (☎ 624-143-3171), at the front of the mall, is a bookstore with English-language novels and magazines and a good selection of books on Baja. A branch of **Dos Lunas** (☎ 624-143-1969) sells colorful casual sportswear. **Cartes** (☎ 624-143-1770) is filled with hand-painted ceramic vases and dishes, pewter frames, carved furniture, and hand-woven textiles. Most shops in the plaza are open daily from 9 a.m. to 9 p.m.

One of the spiffiest (but commercial) shops in Los Cabos is **Mamma Eli's** (Calle Cabo San Lucas, west of the plaza at Madero; ☎ 624-143-1616), a three-level store packed with folk art, crafts, clothing, and furniture. It's open Tuesday through Sunday from 9 a.m. to 2 p.m. and 4 to 7 p.m.

Embarking on a Side Trip

You can book a day-trip to the city of **La Paz** through a travel agency or through **Cabo Travel Advisors** (☎ 624-142-4444) for around $55, which includes beverages and a tour of the countryside along the way. The tours usually stop at the weaving shop of Fortunato Silva who spins his own cotton and weaves it into wonderfully textured rugs and textiles. Cabo Travel Advisors also offers a day trip to **Todos Santos** for $60 — a guided walking tour of the Cathedral Mission, a museum, the Hotel California, and various artists' homes.

A few years back, Todos Santos became known as "Bohemian Baja." It found its way on the travel agendas of folks looking for the latest, the trendiest, and the hippest of artist outposts — and in the plans of travelers who were simply weary of the L.A.-ization of Cabo San Lucas. In no time, Todos Santos blossomed as a true gem of a place that seems to foster the creative spirit while retaining its pervasive beauty and lovely heritage that held the original attraction.

The art and artistry created here now — from the culinary plate to the canvas — cares less about commercial appeal than quality, and in doing so, it becomes more of a draw. Not to be overlooked are the attendant arts of agriculture, masonry, and weavings created by some of the town's original residents. From the superb meals at **Café Santa Fe** to an afternoon spent browsing the numerous shops and galleries, Todos Santos is intriguing to its core.

For me — and I suspect for many others — a meal at the **Café Santa Fe** (Calle Centenario 4; ☎ 624-145-0340) is reason enough to visit Todos Santos. Much of the attention the town has received in recent years can be directly attributed to this outstanding cafe, and it continues to live up to its lofty reputation. Owners Ezio and Paula Colombo refurbished a large stucco house across from the plaza, creating an exhibition kitchen, several dining rooms, and a lovely courtyard adjacent to a garden of hibiscus, bougainvillea, papaya trees, and herbs.

The excellent Northern Italian cuisine emphasizes local produce and seafood. Try the homemade ravioli stuffed with spinach and ricotta in a Gorgonzola sauce or the ravioli with lobster and shrimp accompanied by one of their organic salads. Simply put, a meal here is likely to be one of the best you experience anywhere at any price. In high season, the wait for a table at lunch can last quite a while. Everything is prepared fresh when ordered, and reservations are recommended. Main courses run between $10 and $15. The restaurant is open Wednesday through Monday from noon to 9 p.m., but it's closed September 29 to October 18.

A more casual option, and a magical place to kick off a day in Todos Santos, is the garden setting of the **Caffé Todos Santos** (Calle Centenario 33, across from the Todos Santos Inn; ☎ 624-145-0300). Among the espresso drinks served here is the bowl-sized café latte that should be enjoyed with a freshly baked croissant or one of the cafe's signature cinnamon buns. Lunch or a light meal may include a frittata or a fish filet wrapped in banana leaves with coconut milk. Main courses average $3 to $6, and the cafe is open Tuesday through Sunday from 7 a.m. to 9 p.m. and Monday from 7 a.m. to 2 p.m.

At least half a dozen galleries are in town including the noted **Galería de Todos Santos** (Topete and Legaspi; ☎ 624-145-0040), which features a changing collection of works by regional artists. The **Galería Santa Fe** (Centenario, across from the plaza; ☎ 624-145-0340) holds an eclectic collection of truly original and creative Mexican folk art and *artesanía* treasures and "shrines" — kid-sized chairs decorated in bottle caps, Virgin of Guadalupe images, and more. Galería Santa Fe is open Wednesday to Monday from 10 a.m. to 5 p.m.

El Tecolote Libros (Hidalgo and Juárez; ☎ 624-145-0295), though tiny, gets my vote for the best bookstore in Mexico due to its exceptional selection of Latin American literature, poetry, children's books, and reference books centering on Mexico. English- and Spanish-language books, both new and used, are sold here along with maps, magazines, cards, and art supplies.

Casual visitors can easily explore Todos Santos in a day, but a few tranquil inns welcome charmed guests who want to stay a little longer. A day's visit can be arranged through tour companies in Los Cabos or done on your own with a rental car.

Discovering Los Cabos after Dark

San José's nightlife is nonexistent outside of the restaurant and hotel bars. The bars at Casa Natalia and Tropicana — the former catering to sophisticated romantics and the latter to those in search of rowdier good times — are particularly notable. On some weekends, Tropicana even brings in a live Cuban band for dancing. Several of the larger hotels along the beach have Mexican fiestas and other weekly theme nights that include a buffet (usually all-you-can-eat), drinks, live music, and entertainment for $25 to $35 per person. A large disco on Boulevard Mijares seems to be under different ownership each year — it was closed at press time but had a "re-opening soon" sign on the door. Travelers intent on finding real nightlife should look to Cabo San Lucas.

In fact, Cabo San Lucas is the undisputed nightlife capital of Baja and a contender for the title within all of resort Mexico. After-dark fun is centered around the party ambience and camaraderie found in the casual bars and restaurants on Boulevard Marina and those facing the marina, rather than around a flashy disco scene. You can easily find a happy hour with live music and a place to dance or a Mexican fiesta with mariachis.

To enjoy live music in a more sedate setting, check out the **Sancho Panza Wine Bar and Bistro** (see the description later in the chapter) and the new **Jazz on the Rocks** (Zaragoza and Niños Heroes; ☎ 624-143-8999), a restaurant and live jazz bar. Both locations offer classic jazz in a club-style atmosphere that accommodates conversations.

Enjoining a theme night

Some of the larger hotels have weekly fiesta nights, Italian nights, and other buffet-plus-entertainment theme nights that can be fun and a good buy. Check with travel agencies and the following hotels: the **Solmar** (☎ 624-143-3535), the **Finisterra** (☎ 624-143-0000), the **Hacienda** (☎ 624-143-0123), and the **Melia San Lucas** (☎ 624-143-0420). Prices generally range from $16 (drinks, tax, and tips are extra) to $35 (everything is covered including an open bar with national drinks).

Watching a sunset

At twilight, check out Land's End — where the Sea of Cortez meets the Pacific Ocean — and watch the sun sink into the Pacific. The **Whale Watcher's Bar** (Hotel Finisterra; ☎ 624-143-3333) is considered Los Cabo's premier place for sunset-watching. Its location at Land's End offers a truly world-class view of the setting sun. The high terrace offers vistas of both sea and beach as well as magical glimpses of whales from January to March. "Whale margaritas" cost $4, and beers will set you back $3. The bar is open daily from 10 a.m. to 11 p.m.

Hanging out and happy hours

If you shop around, you can usually find an *hora alegre* (happy hour) somewhere in town between noon and 7 p.m. On my last visit, the most popular places to drink and carouse until all hours were the Giggling Marlin and El Squid Roe.

El Squid Roe (Boulevard Marina, opposite Plaza Bonita; ☎ 624-143-0655) is one of the late Carlos Anderson's inspirations, and it still attracts wild, fun-loving crowds of all ages. This two-story bar features nostalgic decor and eclectic food that's far better than you'd expect from such a party place. As fashionable as blue jeans, El Squid Roe is a place to see and see what can be seen — women's tops are known to be discarded with regularity here as the tabletop dancing moves into high gear. A patio out back serves as a place to dance when the tables, chairs, and bar spots have all been taken. It's open daily from noon to 2 a.m.

Live music alternates with recorded tunes at the **Giggling Marlin** (Cárdenas at Zaragoza, across from the marina; ☎ 624-143-0606) to get the happy patrons dancing — and occasionally jumping up to dance on the tables and bar. A contraption of winches, ropes, and pulleys above a mattress provides entertainment as couples literally string each other up by the heels — just like a captured marlin. The food is only fair here; stick with nachos and drinks. It's open daily 8 a.m. to 1 a.m. Beer is $1.75 to $2.50; margaritas cost $4 to $6. Drinks are half-price during happy "hour," which in the tradition of excess that Cabo adores, lasts for four hours — 2 to 6 p.m.

Latitude 22+ (Cárdenas s/n; ☎ 624-143-1516) is a semi-seedy restaurant/bar that never closes. License plates, signs, sports caps, and a 959-pound blue marlin are the backdrop for U.S. sports events that play on six TVs scattered among pool tables, dart boards, and assorted games. The kitchen offers dishes from hamburgers to chicken-fried steak, or you can have breakfast any time. Latitude 22+ is 1 block north of the town's only traffic light.

Finally, an alternative to beer bars! **Sancho Panza Wine Bar and Bistro** (Plaza Las Glorias boardwalk, next to the lighthouse; ☎ 624-143-3212) combines a gourmet-food market with a wine bar that features live jazz music plus an intriguing menu of nuevo-Latino cuisine. The place has a cozy neighborhood feeling. Tourists and locals take advantage of the selection of more than 150 wines, plus espresso drinks. During high season, reservations are needed.

The best Web sites for Los Cabos and Baja

All About Cabo (www.allaboutcabo.com) features a weekly fishing report, live golf cam, and information on hotels, restaurants, golf courses, and more.

Baja Travel Guide (http://bajatravel.com) provides a good overview of activities and how to get around, but its extensive Yellow Pages are the most useful part of the site. The site can help you with tours, ground transportation, and outdoor excursions before you go.

Visit Cabo (www.visitcabo.com) is the official site of the Los Cabos Tourism Board. The site has plenty of details about things to do and current news and a lodging and dining guide. You can also book your reservations online for select hotels.

The **Tropicana Bar and Grill** (Mijares 30, San José; ☎ 624-142-0907) is definitely the most popular place in San José. Patrons hang out in leather barrel chairs at the large bar where, during the day, they tune in to American sports events on the big-screen TV. Come evening, guitarists play Mexican *boleros* and other traditional music from 6 to 11 p.m. After 9 p.m. on some nights, a band plays Americanized rock and pop for those inclined to dance. The Tropicana is open daily from 7 a.m. to 1 a.m. Drinks go for $3 and up.

Going dancing

Owned by Sammy Hagar (formerly of Van Halen) and his Mexican and American partners, the **Cabo Wabo Cantina** (Vicente Guerrero at Cárdenas; ☎ 624-143-1188) packs in youthful crowds — especially when rumors fly that a surprise appearance by a vacationing musician is imminent. Rock bands from the United States, Mexico, Europe, and Australia perform live frequently on the well-equipped stage. When live music is absent, a disco-type sound system plays mostly rock but some alternative and techno music as well. Overstuffed furniture frames the dance floor. For snacks, the Taco-Wabo, just outside the club's entrance, stays up late too. The cantina is open from 11 a.m. to 4 a.m.

Lively and tropical in theme and spirit, **Kokomo** (CSL - Blvd. Marina at the Main Corner Overlooking the Marina; ☎ 624-143-0600) is a happening dance club. Kokomo serves lunch and dinner, but the drinks are better than the food. A happy hour features two-for-one drinks daily from 4 to 6 p.m. Grab a table along the oversized windows looking out over Marina Boulevard for your people-watching enjoyment. It's open daily from 7 a.m. to 3 a.m.

Part X
The Part of Tens

In this part . . .

I give you the ten most common myths and misconceptions about Mexico. For instance, if you think all Mexican food is fiery hot, keep reading. And, speaking of Mexican food, I share my top-ten picks for the most deliciously Mexican dishes. I also pass along my top-ten quintessential Mexican moments — those places and experiences that you can only find in this magical, charismatic culture. Finally, I have a warning list for all honeymooners that will help ensure your trip is a breeze.

Chapter 32

Top Ten Mexican Moments

Want to watch the sun sink into the horizon from the deck of a sailboat while balmy breezes swirl around you? Do you know the truly proper way to drink tequila? Care to be amazed by watching men leap into a narrow, rocky passage of surging ocean from a ledge 130 feet above the surface of the water?

Along with all the classic, beach-going fun you can have in a Mexico beach resort, several singular experiences exist that you can only have here in grand ol' Mexico. These events become the unforgettable moments that make traveling to another country, another land, a unique experience.

Enjoying a Mexican Fiesta

Mexican fiestas, colorful celebrations of Mexican food, dance, and fun, are mainstays among the entertainment options at Mexican beach resorts. Though the varieties of a *fiesta mexicana* can range from the cheesy to the sublime, it's generally a party that begins with a shot of tequila and an ample buffet, goes on to take you through presentations of different regional dances, and ends in a display of fireworks. Viva Mexico!

Setting Sail at Sunset

Virtually every Mexican beach resort offers some variation of the sunset sail, which is, in my opinion, the very best way to experience a Mexican beach resort. In Acapulco, Ixtapa, Huatulco, and Puerto Vallarta, these trips tend to be romantic bay cruises — with plenty of libations. In Cancún, try a replica pirate cruise with a lobster dinner; in Los Cabos, make that sail at sunset around the famous El Arco (the Arch) at the end of the Baja Peninsula past Lovers Beach. No matter where you set sail from, an excursion at sunset provides memories that can make a vacation.

Mixing It Up with Mariachi Music

From the first impressive note of the trombone, to the last strum of the guitar, mariachi music is synonymous with Mexico. Mariachi music is played on the streets and in restaurants by strolling musicians often dressed to the nines in charro outfits and sombreros.

Sipping on Margaritas at Sunset

Actually, feel free to pick your poison, but a cocktail at sunset is the quintessential Mexican beach vacation experience. This plan works best when you're on the Pacific coast so that you can watch the sun sink into the horizon; however, it doesn't really seem to dampen the spirits to sip at sunset on the East coast either!

Strolling the Malecón or Plaza

Call it a cheap thrill, but in most of Mexico's beach resorts, one of the best experiences is absolutely free — just stroll along the seaside walkway in Puerto Vallarta or Zihuatanejo or sit in the plaza in Cabo San Lucas or Acapulco. You're certain to be both charmed and entertained by the parade of local life. And while you're at it, splurge on classic fare sold by vendors — I'm talking corn on the cob and a colorful swirl of cotton candy.

Feasting on Fresh Fish Under a Palapa

Eating fresh fish — or, more specifically, grilled, fresh fish on a plate served under a *palapa* (a thatched umbrella) by the ocean's edge and accompanied by a cold *cerveza* and a balmy sea breeze — is an experience. I promise — you've never tasted anything more delicious.

Looking for Whales in Baja or Puerto Vallarta

It's a thrill to watch the majestic — and enormous — whales leap out of the water, splash their tail, or corral in their young. Each winter, whales migrate to Mexico's Pacific shores. You can find the greatest concentration of whales in Baja California and in Banderas Bay, just offshore Puerto Vallarta. Ecologically sensitive whale-watching tours are becoming a favored Mexico-vacation experience.

Watching Cliff Divers in Acapulco

The only place in the world to see this sight is in Acapulco — bikini-clad men dive from a rocky cliff into the roaring surf of a narrow crevice 130 feet below. Why? Because they can . . . and because you keep watching them do it! Don't miss this sight when in Acapulco.

Visiting Tulum

Although Tulum is not the largest or most important Mayan ruin, it's the only one by the sea, which makes it the most visually impressive in my humble opinion. Ancient Tulum is a stunning site — and my personal favorite of all the ruins — poised on a rocky hill overlooking the transparent, turquoise Caribbean Sea. You can't visually sum up Mexico's combination of exquisite beaches and a centuries-old culture more aptly.

Drinking Tequila — Properly

Tequila is a drink to be appreciated and sipped — not slammed down in a shot, its flavor masked by salt and lime. If you need to do that, you're drinking the wrong tequila. Insist on only 100% blue agave tequila — the mark of a pure, quality tequila — and then learn to appreciate the subtleties and nuances of this tasteful beverage.

Chapter 33

Top Ten Myths and Misconceptions About Mexico

. . . .

In This Chapter

▶ Getting the geography straight

▶ Dissecting the stereotypical preconceptions

▶ Solving food and drink misconceptions

. . . .

*I*f you've never visited Mexico, you may have some preconceptions about what you're likely to find here. Perhaps you think that the geography — apart from the beaches — is an arid landscape with a uniformly hot climate. Or you may think that you should only drink tequila as a shot — doused with lime and salt.

This chapter explains some of the most common misconceptions about this vast country and its rich culture. Read on — and the next time someone starts talking about how you can't drink the water in Mexico, you can set them straight!

Mexico Is a Desert, and It's Hot Everywhere

Not true: The geography of Mexico includes pine forests, and occasional snowfalls hit some of the country's higher elevations. Most of the beach resorts covered in this book, however, do enjoy sultry climates, but it's always wise to bring along a sweater or light jacket for cool evenings, especially during winter months.

Mexico Is the Land of Sombreros and Siestas

The common image of a Mexican napping under his sombrero exists in some minds, but this stereotype is mostly made of myth. Today, Mexico is a mix of contemporary business professionals and traditional agrarian populations. The afternoon break — between 2 and 4 p.m. — is still a wonderful tradition, but rather than being a time for *siesta,* it's the time when families come together for their main meal of the day. The more familiar you become with Mexico, the more you find that the people are overwhelmingly hard working, hospitable, and honest.

Mexico's Beaches Are All the Same

With over 125,000 miles of coastline bordering this geographically diverse country, Mexico's beaches are as varied as they can possibly be. From the flat, white sand and translucent turquoise waters of the Caribbean coast to the jungle-draped mountains that descend to rocky coves along the Pacific coast, Mexico offers the ideal beach for everyone. Farther west from the Pacific coast, the striking combo of desert and sea makes Baja California one of the most memorable sights in the world.

There Are No Drinking or Drug Laws

When on vacation, many travelers tend to let loose — and some tend to overindulge. Because of the welcoming and casual nature of Mexico, many visitors believe that the sale of alcoholic beverages — or illegal drugs — is unregulated. This belief is simply not true. The legal drinking age in Mexico is 18, and technically, you're not allowed to drink openly in public. However, if you're not acting intoxicated, you can generally enjoy a beer or even a cocktail while you stroll around town. As with most things in Mexico, it's not so much what you do but how you do it. Although you can drink on public beaches, you can't be inebriated in public, so once again, beware of how much you drink and how well you can handle your alcohol intake. White-clad police patrolling Mexico's beaches are a common sight.

With regard to drugs, I want to get straight to the point: They're illegal, and carrying even a small amount of marijuana can earn you a very unpleasant trip to jail. So keep your trip free of undesired encounters with the law and don't carry, buy, or use any kind of drugs. Remember that Mexican law states that you're guilty until proven innocent.

If in Trouble, Pay a Mordida

The concept of paying off someone for a favor or to overlook a transgression is as clichéd as the image of the sleeping Mexican under his *sombrero*. Although the idea of paying a *mordida,* or "bite," may have been rooted in truth for a long time, in Mexico's new political era, an active campaign is underway to keep dishonesty to a minimum and to clean house of corrupt public servants. Many old-school traffic cops will still take a bribe when offered; however, officers belonging to the new generation of federal policemen are tested for honesty, and the penalties for corrupt behavior are severe — as are the penalties for those civilians inducing corruption by offering bribes to police officers. My suggestion is don't offer a "tip" or *mordida* to ease your way out of trouble; the best course of action is to just act politely and see what the problem is.

All Mexican Food Is Spicy

Not all Mexican food is spicy — although Mexican food does include some of the most intriguingly flavored foods I've ever enjoyed. Although it's likely that spicy sauces may always be in the vicinity of the food you're served, the truth is that many delicious Mexican dishes don't include chile peppers among their ingredients.

Don't Drink the Water

In the past, visitors often returned home from Mexico with stomach illnesses, but this type of vacation souvenir is a rarity today. Massive investments in an improved infrastructure and a general increase in standards of cleanliness and hygiene have practically wiped out the problem. However, it's easy to play it safe and drink bottled water. And ice served in tourist establishments is purified.

A Jeep Rental Is Really $10 a Day

One of the most common lures a timeshare salesperson uses is the "Rent a Jeep for $10 per day" enticement. Sure, it's true that the Jeep is only $10 but only after you spend up to half a day listening to an often high-pressured sales pitch. You decide — what's your vacation time really worth? And always remember: *If it looks too good to be true. . . .*

It's Okay to Go Everywhere Wearing Just Your Swimsuit

Although you may be in a seaside resort, keep in mind that it's also a home and place of business for many Mexicans. It's fine to wear swim trunks or a pareo skirt wrapped around your bikini while you're on your way to the beach, but I recommend that you put on a shirt or a sundress when you plan to explore the town or when you take a tour that involves riding around in a bus. You can still go casual, but Mexicans frown upon tourists who can't tell the difference between beach and town — especially true when it comes to going into any church wearing inappropriate clothing. If you want to blend in, just take a few minutes to see what the locals wear around town. Usually, walking shorts and T-shirts are fine everywhere. One more thing: Topless sunbathing is neither customary nor legal in Mexico — avoid problems with the law and keep your top on.

Mexicans Who Don't Speak English Are Hard of Hearing

Or at least it appears that many tourists buy into this statement. It's as if some travelers believe that a native Spanish-speaker will somehow get over his or her inability to understand English if the English-speaking individual talks really loudly into the Spanish-speaker's face. The truth is that many Mexicans understand at least some English, especially in popular tourist areas. Try this (I guarantee it will work): Instead of panicking and starting to yell in order to get your point across, ask nicely for help, and an English-speaking local will come to assist you. Another thing to keep in mind is that should you voice any negative comments about Mexico or Mexicans, don't assume that no one around you can understand your comments — you may find yourself in a rather embarrassing situation.

Chapter 34

Top Ten Most Deliciously Mexican Dishes

. . . .

In This Chapter

▶ Knowing your Mexican meals and sauces

▶ Indulging in uniquely Mexican beverages

. . . .

Some like it hot . . . and then there's Mexican food! But true Mexican cuisine is noted more for its unique way of combining flavors — chocolate and chiles, sweet and hot — than for its fire appeal.

This chapter explains some of the most flavorful and traditional Mexican dishes that you're likely to see on a menu here — go ahead and be adventurous! Let your taste buds have a vacation from the foods you know and explore the favored flavors of Mexico.

Pescado Sarandeado or Pescado en Talla

You're in a Mexican beach resort, so you're almost certain to indulge in the fresh fish and seafood. One of the most traditional and tasty ways to prepare fish is *sarandeado* (the term used along the beaches of Puerto Vallarta) or *en talla* (as they refer to this dish in Acapulco and Huatulco). The fish is prepared by marinating it in a sauce of Worcestershire, lime, mild red-pepper paste, and other seasonings that vary slightly depending of the region. The fish is then cooked slowly over a wood fire. The Mexican-Caribbean variation of this fish is called *tikik-chik* or *tikin-chik,* and it includes a regional *achiote* — annatto seed — paste in the marinade.

Mole

Mole is a rich sauce that's often considered Mexico's most important culinary contribution. A thick, deeply colored sauce, mole comes in hues of green, red, yellow, and even black. Mole blends the flavors of fresh and dried peppers, nuts, and — depending on the area — fruits or chocolate. Mole is traditionally served with chicken but is sometimes found accompanying fish and pork. It truly reflects the spirit of Mexico — the ingredients are a combination of both European and pre-Hispanic elements. The final taste varies according to the individual cook. If I had to compare it with something, curry would be the closest association.

Tamales

Tamales in Mexico are quite different from the ones typically found in the United States, which tend to be compact and greasy. In Mexico, these tasty bundles of corn dough are fluffy and come in a variety of fillings ranging from spicy to sweet. One popular variety is *rajas con queso,* a filling of poblano pepper strips and cheese. Other possibilities are *rojos* (red) or *verdes* (green) tamales filled with shredded chicken or pork — the names refer to the type of sauce included. Sweet tamales may come filled with cinnamon and raisins, stewed mangos, or pineapple. On the southern-Pacific coast, tamales come wrapped in banana leaves and have a heavier consistency. Traditional *Oaxaqueño* (from Oaxaca) tamales are filled with mole and chicken and wrapped in palm leaves.

Tacos al Pastor

Tacos al pastor are only for the more adventurous travelers — you may have heard about the dangers of eating tacos on the street, but this is truly a Mexican specialty. *Tacos al pastor* are made from shanks of marinated pork, which are skewered and slowly cooked on a vertical charcoal grill. The traditional ones are served with a chunk of fresh pineapple, diced onion, and cilantro. I recommend you enjoy them at a small taco restaurant rather than a street stall.

Pozole

A traditional dish from the coastal states of Jalisco, Colima, and Guerrero, *pozole* represents the blending of the pre-Hispanic Mexican culture and European influences. It's a soup-like dish made with hominy and pork, but nowadays many places make it with chicken. You can find red, green, and white versions of *pozole,* depending on the area, and garnishes include shredded lettuce or cabbage.

Chilaquiles

One of the most traditional and satisfying breakfast dishes in Mexico is *chilaquiles,* fried tortilla strips cooked in a mild or spicy red or green sauce. They're usually served with a fried egg or shredded chicken and topped with fresh cream, chopped onions, and shredded, white cheese.

Ceviche

Ceviche is one of Mexico's more traditional ways to enjoy fish and seafood. *Ceviche* is usually made of fish, but it may also be made from seafood including shrimp, octopus, crab, and even conch. The fresh fish — or seafood — is marinated in lime and vinegar and mixed with chopped tomatoes, onions, and depending of the region, cucumbers and carrots.

Pescadillas

Pescadillas, flour tortillas filled with melted cheese and fresh grilled fish, are truly succulent. Most places serve them with a mild tomato sauce.

Liquados

Not quite a meal, yet much more than a beverage, *liquados* are blended drinks of fresh fruit, ice, and either water or milk. Popular flavors include mango, banana, pineapple, or watermelon. You can also make up your own combination of tropical fruit flavors!

Café de Olla

The popularity and tradition of drinking coffee is nothing new to Mexico, so to experience a taste of the past try the traditional Mexican version called *café de olla.* The espresso-strength coffee is prepared in an earthenware pot. It's spiced with cinnamon, cloves, and raw brown sugar. It's certain to wake you up!

Chapter 35

Top Ten Mistakes Honeymooners Make

• •

In This Chapter

▶ Avoiding common honeymoon gaffes

▶ Preventing a crisis on your honeymoon

• •

*O*kay, if you're planning your honeymoon, I assume that you are marrying Mr./Ms. Right. After that, here's the countdown on the most common-yet-moronic ways couples mess up their honeymoon. Fortunately, all these goofs are preventable.

Leaving too Soon after the Wedding

Saturday night reception? Sunday morning 8 a.m. flight to Acapulco? Puh-leeeease! You wear yourself out before you even start your honeymoon with a schedule like that. Solution: Wait a day or two before departing on your honeymoon.

Booking the Bride's Airline Tickets under Her Married Name

Airline check-in personnel and immigration officials verify that the name of the person on the airline ticket matches the name on the passport or other identification. Solution: Book the tickets under the bride's maiden name.

Not Booking an Oceanview-or-Better Room

Sure you want to save money. But odds are that you'll be grievously disappointed if you end up facing the garbage dumpster instead of sea-forever blue water. Even if you don't think that you're going to spend a lot of time in your room, you'll be sorry if it isn't special. Solution: Check around for the best deal that gives you at least a peek at paradise.

Not Booking a King-Size Bed

Double doubles just don't cut it romantically. Solution: Make sure that the king-size set-up is confirmed in writing.

Not Packing Contraceptives in Check-In Luggage

When airlines lose your bags, even for 24 hours, it's bad not having your favorite pair of shorts. But it's dismal to get short shrift in the bedroom department. Solution: Keep contraceptives in your carry-on bags, along with other honeymoon necessities, like a bathing suit.

Not Telling Everyone You're Honeymooners

Airline personnel, hotel front-desk clerks, and even supercilious maitre d's generally go out of their way to be helpful to newlyweds. (Besides, with those virginally shiny gold rings and eyes locked on each other, you're not fooling many people anyway.) Why not get the best? Solution: When you're making reservations, be sure to mention it's your honeymoon.

Counting on Renting a Car if You're under 25

The car's reserved, you have your confirmation number, and you're relying on having your own wheels to get around. But many car rental companies only rent to people over age 25. Solution: If you are under 25, double-check the agency's rental policy.

Not Budgeting Beforehand

Talking about money isn't romantic. Arguing about it after your new spouse blows $500 on a near-life-size carving of a dolphin is worse. Solution: Before you go away, set up a tentative budget and decide where you plan to splurge: shopping, dinners out, golfing, and so on.

Trying to Do too Much

No time for a room-service breakfast because you're booked into that 9 a.m. snorkel trip? Unable to linger in that marvelous corner cafe because you scheduled a massage? Women and Men Who Love To Do Too Much often try to cram in too many activities. Solution: Leave plenty of free time in your itinerary so that you can relax and enjoy what you see.

Not Making Sure that Your New Rings Fit

You don't want to spend the first day of your honeymoon vacation mourning the loss of your new gold bands, which slipped off in the water. (Cold makes fingers shrink, remember.) Solution: If it doesn't fit, don't swim in it until you can get it properly sized.

Appendix A

Quick Concierge

• •

Abbreviations

Common address abbreviations include *Apdo.* (post office box), *Av.* or *Ave.* (*avenida;* avenue), *Blvd.* (*boulevard*), *c/* (*calle;* street), *Calz.* (*calzada;* boulevard), *Dept.* (apartments), and *s/n* (*sin numero* or without a number).

The "C" on faucets stands for *caliente* (hot), and "F" stands for *fría* (cold). "PB" (*planta baja*) means ground floor, and most buildings count the next floor up as the first floor (1).

American Express

All major resort destinations have local American Express representatives. For a detailed list of all representatives, visit the AmEx Web site at www.american express.com/mexico/. For credit card and traveler's checks information call ☎ 800-504-0400 toll-free inside Mexico. The local offices in the beach resorts covered in this guide are Acapulco (Costera Miguel Alemán 1628, Centro Comercial La Gran Plaza; ☎ 744-691-1122), Cancún (Av. Tulum 408; ☎ 998-884-6942), Puerto Vallarta (Morelos 660; ☎ 322-223-2955), Ixtapa-Zihuatanejo (Blvd. Ixtapa. Hotel Cristal; ☎ 755-553-0853), Huatulco (Av. Carrizal 704, La Crucecita; ☎ 958-587-0811), Cabo San Lucas (Plaza Bonita Mall, Local 48e/49e; ☎ 624-143-5766), and San José del Cabo (Plaza La Misión, Local 1-b, Blvd. Mijares/Paseo Finisterra; ☎ 624-142-1336).

ATMs

Automated teller machines are widely avail-able in all major resort towns, with fewer to be found in the smaller destinations. They're a great option to get cash at an excellent exchange rate. To find the closest ATM, visit the Web sites for the most popular networks: Plus (www.visa.com/pd/atm) and Cirrus (www.mastercard.com/atm). (See Chapter 6 for further details.)

Business Hours

In general, businesses in resort destinations are open daily between 9 a.m. and 8 p.m.; although many close between 2 and 4 p.m. Smaller businesses also tend to close on Sundays. The larger resort destinations have extended business hours — many shops stay open until 10 p.m. Bank hours are Monday to Friday 8:30 or 9:00 a.m. to anywhere between 3:00 and 7:00 p.m. Increasingly, banks are offering Saturday hours in at least one branch for at least a half-day, usually from 10 a.m. until 2 p.m.

Credit Cards

Most stores, restaurants, and hotels accept credit cards. However, smaller destinations like Puerto Escondido, where telephone lines are not always available to process the authorization for the charge, may not be so credit-card friendly. Same goes for smaller, family-run shops and restaurants. You can withdraw cash from your credit card at most ATMs, but make sure that you know your PIN and you've cleared the card for foreign with-drawals with your bank. For credit-card emergencies, call the following numbers: **American Express** ☎ 001-880-221-7282, **MasterCard** ☎ 001-880-307-7309, and **Visa**

☎ 001-880-336-8472. These numbers connect you to the U.S. toll-free numbers to report lost or stolen credit cards; however, the call is not toll free from Mexico.

Currency

The currency in Mexico is the Mexican peso. Paper currency comes in denominations of 20, 50, 100, 200, and 500 pesos. Coins come in denominations of 1, 2, 5, 10, 20, and 50 centavos (100 centavos equal 1 peso). The currency-exchange rate is about nine pesos to one U.S. dollar.

Customs

All travelers to Mexico are required to present proof of citizenship, such as an original birth certificate with a raised seal, a valid passport, or naturalization papers, and need to have a Mexican tourist card (FMT), which is free of charge and can be attained through travel agencies and airlines and at all boarder-crossing points going into Mexico. For more information, see Part II.

Doctors/Dentists

Every embassy and consulate can recommend local doctors and dentists with good training and modern equipment; some of the doctors and dentists even speak English. See the list of embassies and consulates under the "Embassies/Consulates," section later in this appendix. Hotels with a large foreign clientele can often recommend English-speaking doctors as well. Most first-class hotels in Mexico's resort areas have a doctor on call.

Drug Laws

To be blunt, don't use or possess illegal drugs in Mexico. Mexican officials have no tolerance for drug users, and jail is their solution. If you go to jail, there's very little hope of getting out until the sentence (usually a long one) is completed or heavy fines or bribes are paid. Remember, in Mexico, the legal system assumes you're guilty until proven innocent. (**Note:** It isn't uncommon to be befriended by a fellow user, only to be turned in by that "friend," who has collected a bounty.) Bring prescription drugs in their original containers. If possible, pack a copy of the original prescription with the generic name of the drug.

U.S. Customs officials are also on the lookout for diet drugs that are sold in Mexico but illegal in the United States. Possession of these could land you in a U.S. jail. If you buy antibiotics over the counter (which you can do in Mexico) — say, for a sinus infection — and still have some left, you probably won't be hassled by U.S. Customs.

Electricity

The electrical system in Mexico is 110 volts AC (60 cycles), as it is in the United States and Canada. But in reality, it may cycle more slowly and overheat your appliances. To compensate, select a medium or low speed for hair dryers. Many older hotels still have electrical outlets for flat, two-prong plugs; you'll need an adapter for any modern electrical apparatus that has three prongs or an enlarged end on one of the two prongs. Many first-class and deluxe hotels have the three-holed outlets (*trifásicos* in Spanish). Hotels that don't may have adapters to loan, but to be sure, it's always better to carry your own.

Embassies/Consulates

Embassies and consulates can provide valuable lists of doctors and lawyers, as well as regulations concerning marriages in Mexico. Contrary to popular belief, your embassy cannot get you out of a Mexican jail, provide postal or banking services, or fly you home when you run out of money. However, consular officers can provide you with advice on most matters and problems. Most countries have a representative embassy in Mexico City and many have consular offices or representatives in the provinces.

The embassy of the **United States** is in Mexico City (Paseo de la Reforma 305; ☎ 5-5209-9100). It's hours are Monday to Friday 8:30 a.m. to 5:30 p.m. You can visit the embassy's Web site at www.usembassy-mexico.gov for a list of street addresses for the U.S. consulates inside Mexico. U.S. consular agencies are located in Acapulco (☎ 744-481-1699, 744-484-0300, 744-469-0556), Cabo San Lucas (☎ 624-143-3566), Cancún (☎ 998-883-0272), Cozumel (☎ 987-872-4574), Ixtapa (☎ 755-553-1108), and Puerto Vallarta (☎ 322-222-0069).

The embassy of **Australia** is in Mexico City at Rubén Darío 55, Polanco (☎ 5-5531-5225; Fax: 5-5531-9552). It's open Monday to Friday 9 a.m. to 1 p.m.

The Embassy of **Canada** is also in Mexico City (Schiller 529, in Polanco; ☎ 5-5724-7900). It's open Monday through Friday 9 a.m. to 1 p.m. and 2 to 5 p.m. (At other times the name of a duty officer is posted on the embassy door.) Visit their Web site at www.canada.org.mx for a complete list of the addresses of the consular agencies in Mexico. In Acapulco, the Canadian consulate is located in Centro Comercial Marbolla, Local 23, Prolongación Farallón s/n (☎ 744-484-1305; E-mail: acapulco@canada.org.mx). And here's some additional contact info for Cancún (☎ 998-883-3360; E-mail: cancun@canada.org.mx), Puerto Vallarta (☎ 322-222-5398; E-mail: vallarta@canada.org.mx), and San José del Cabo (☎ 624-142-4333; E-mail: loscabos@canada.org.mx).

The embassy of **New Zealand** in Mexico City is at José Luis Lagrange 103, 10th floor, Col. Los Morales Polanco (☎ 5-5281-5486; Fax: 5-5281-5212; E-mail: kiwimexico@compuserve.com.mx).

The Embassy of the **United Kingdom** is at Río Lerma 71, Col. Cuauhtemoc (☎ 5-5207-2089, 5-5207-7672) in Mexico City. The embassy's Web site, which you can visit at www.embajadabritanica.com.mx, has an updated list of honorary consuls in Mexico. There are honorary British consuls in Acapulco (☎ 744-484-1735), Cancún (☎ 998-881-0100), and Huatulco (☎ 958-587-1742) — leave a message.

The Embassy of **Ireland** is located in Mexico City on Blvd. Cerrada Avila Camacho 76, 3rd floor, Col. Lomas de Chapultepec (☎ 5-5520-5803).

The embassy of **South Africa** is also in Mexico City on Andres Bello, 109th floor, Col. Polanco (☎ 5-5282-9260).

Emergencies

In case of emergency, always contact your embassy or consulate. For police emergencies, you must dial ☎ **060** — this will connect you to the local police department. Remember that in most cases the person answering the phone doesn't speak English. The 24-hour tourist help line from Mexico City is ☎ 800-903-9200 or 5-5250-0151. A tourist legal assistance office *(Procuraduría del Turista)* is located in Mexico City (☎ 5-5625-8153, 5-5625-8154). Although the phones are frequently busy, they do offer 24-hour service, and an English-speaking person is always available.

Health

No special immunizations are required. As is often true when traveling anywhere in the world, intestinal problems are the most common afflictions experienced by travelers. Drink only bottled water and stay away from uncooked foods, especially fruits and vegetables. Antibiotics and antidiarrheal medications are readily available in all drugstores. Contact your embassy or consulate for a list of accredited doctors in the area.

Hotlines

The Mexico Hotline (☎ 800-44-MEXICO) is an excellent source for general information; you can request brochures on the country and get answers to the most commonly asked questions. While in Mexico, contact the 24-hour tourist help line, Infotur, (☎ 800-903-9200) for information regarding hotels, restaurants, tourist attractions, hospitals with English-speaking staff, and so on.

Information

The best source of information is the tourist help line Infotur (☎ 800-909-9200); however, it's important that you have a general idea of the information you're requesting — the approximate name of the hotel or restaurant, the name or subject matter of the museum, and so on. You can also find telephone-number information inside Mexico by dialing ☎ 040; however, it's very common to find that the telephone numbers are not listed under the known name of the establishment. A reminder: Very few information operators speak English.

Internet Access

In large cities and resort areas, a growing number of five-star hotels offer business centers with Internet access. You'll also find cybercafes in destinations that are popular with expatriates and business travelers. Even in remote spots, Internet access is very common now — it's often their best way of communicating with the outside world. Note that many Internet service providers will automatically cut off your Internet connection after a specified period of time (say, 10 minutes) because telephone lines are at a premium. Some Telmex offices also have free-access Internet kiosks in their reception areas. If you plan to check your e-mail while in Mexico, it's a good idea to register for a Web-based e-mail address, such as those from Hotmail or Yahoo!.

Language

The official language in Mexico is Spanish, but you'll find that a fair number of Mexicans who live and work in resort areas speak some English. Mexicans are very patient when it comes to foreigners trying to speak Spanish. See Appendix D for commonly used terms in Spanish.

Legal Aid

International Legal Defense Counsel (111 S. 15th St., 24th floor, Packard Building, Philadelphia, PA 19102; ☎ 215-977-9982) is a law firm specializing in legal difficulties of Americans abroad. Also, see the "Embassies/Consulates" and "Emergencies," sections earlier in this appendix.

Liquor Laws

The legal drinking age in Mexico is 18; however, it's extremely rare that anyone is asked for identification or denied purchase. Grocery stores sell everything from beer and wine to national and imported liquors. You can buy liquor 24 hours a day, but during major elections and a few official holidays, dry laws often are enacted as long as 24 hours beforehand. The laws apply to foreign tourists as well as local residents, even though it's not uncommon to find a few hotels and nightclubs that manage to obtain special permits to sell alcohol. Mexico doesn't have any "open container" laws for transporting alcohol in cars, but authorities are beginning to target drunk drivers more aggressively. It's a good idea to drive defensively.

Drinking in the street is not legal, but many tourists do it. Use your better judgment and try to avoid carrying on while sporting beer bottles and cans — you're not only exposing yourself to the eyes of the authorities, but public intoxication is considered tacky behavior by most Mexicans. If you're getting too drunk, don't drink in the street because you're more likely to get stopped by the police. As is the custom in Mexico, it's not so much what you do, it's how you do it.

Mail

Postage for a postcard or letter is 59¢, and the item may arrive at its destination anywhere between one to six weeks after you send it off. A registered letter costs $1.90 Sending a package can be quite expensive — the Mexican postal service charges $8.00 per kilo (2.20 pounds) — and is unreliable — it takes between two and six weeks, if it arrives at all. Packages are frequently lost within the Mexican postal system, although the situation has improved in recent years. Federal Express, DHL, UPS, or any other reputable, international-mail service is the recommended option for a package or important letter.

Newspapers/Magazines

The English-language newspaper, the *News,* is published in Mexico City and distributed nationally. The publication carries world news and commentaries, plus a calendar of the day's events, including concerts, art shows, and plays. Newspaper kiosks in larger Mexican cities carry a selection of English-language magazines. Most resort towns have their own local publications in English, which provide helpful hints and fun reading tailored to tourists and foreigners who have made their homes in the different resort destinations around Mexico. In Puerto Vallarta, the *Vallarta Today* and *PV Tribune* are two of these newspapers — the former is a daily publication, and the latter is published weekly. In Los Cabos, you can find a wealth of information in the *Los Cabos Guide, Los Cabos News, Cabo Life, Baja Sun,* and the irreverent and extremely entertaining *Gringo Gazette.*

Pets

Taking a pet into Mexico is easy but requires a little pre-planning. For travelers coming from the United States and Canada, your pet's health needs to be checked within 30 days before arrival in Mexico. Most veterinarians in major cities have the appropriate paperwork — an official health certificate, to be presented to Mexican Customs officials, which ensures the pet is up-to-date on its vaccinations. When you and your pet return from Mexico, U.S. Customs officials will require the same type of paperwork. If your stay extends beyond the 30-day time frame of your U.S.-issued certificate, you need to get an updated certificate of health issued by a veterinarian in Mexico that also states the condition of your pet and the status of its vaccinations. To find out about any last-minute changes in requirements, consult a Mexican-government tourist office.

Pharmacies

Farmacias will sell you just about anything you want, with or without a prescription. Most pharmacies are open Monday to Saturday 8 a.m. to 8 p.m. Generally, one or two 24-hour pharmacies are located in the major resort areas. Pharmacies take turns staying open during off-hours, so if you're in a smaller town and you need to buy medicine after normal hours, ask for the *farmacia de turno* (pharmacist on duty).

Police

It's quite common to find that the majority of police forces in tourist areas are very protective of international visitors. Several cities, including Cancún, Puerto Vallarta, and Acapulco, have gone so far as to set up a special corps of English-speaking tourist police to assist with directions, guidance, and more. In case of a police emergency, dial ☎ **060** to contact the local police department, keeping in mind that, unless you're dealing with tourist police, the force is very unlikely to speak English.

Restrooms

Public restrooms are usually more of an adventure than a service — you can never tell whether they'll be clean or toilet paper will be available. You can usually resort to using the restroom in a restaurant.

Safety

Most resort areas in Mexico are very safe; however, it's better to be prepared than sorry. A few points to keep in mind: Before you leave home, prepare for the theft or loss of your travel documents by making two photo-copies of them. Keep each copy and the orig-inal documents in separate places. Lock your passport and valuables in the hotel safety-deposit box. Keep credit-card company phone numbers and the numbers of traveler's checks somewhere other than your purse or wallet. Don't dress or behave in a conspicu-ous manner. When visiting crowded places, be aware of your wallet or purse at all times. Leave your best jewelry at home — who wants jewelry tan lines anyway?

Taxes

Most of Mexico has a 15 percent value-added tax (IVA) on goods and services, and it's supposed to be included in the posted price. This tax is 10 percent in Cancún, Cozumel, and Los Cabos. Mexico charges all visitors an entry tax of $15, which is usually included in the price of your plane ticket. Mexico also imposes an exit tax of around $18 on every foreigner leaving the country, which again, is usually included in the price of airline tickets.

Telephone/Fax

In November 2001, telephone area codes were changed. Now, all telephone numbers in Mexico are seven digits plus a three-digit area code, except for Mexico City, Guadalajara, and Monterrey where local calls require that you dial the last eight digits of the published phone number. Many fax numbers are also regular telephone numbers — you have to ask whoever answers your call for the fax tone. *("Me da tono de fax, por favor.")* Cellular phones are very popular for small businesses in resort areas and smaller com-munities. To dial a cellular number inside the same area code, dial 044 and then the number — depending on the area, you may need to dial the last seven digits or the seven digits plus the three digit area code. To dial the cellular phone from anywhere else in Mexico, first dial 01, and then the ten-digit number, including the area code. To dial any number inside Mexico from the United States, just dial 011-52 plus the ten-digit number.

The country code for Mexico is 52. To call home from Mexico, dial 00 plus the country code you're calling and then the area code and phone number. To call the United States and Canada, you need to dial 001 plus the area code and the number. The country code for the United Kingdom is 44; the country code for New Zealand is 64, and the country code for Australia 61.

To call operator assistance for calls inside Mexico, dial 020; for operator assistance for international calls, dial 090. Both numbers provide assistance for person-to-person and collect calls.

Time Zone

Central standard time prevails throughout most of Mexico. The west-coast states of Sonora, Sinaloa, and parts of Nayarit are on mountain standard time. The state of Baja California Norte is on Pacific time, but Baja California Sur is on mountain time. Most of Mexico observes daylight savings time, but the time change lasts for a shorter period of time than it does in the rest of the world. Mexico doesn't spring forward until June, and the country falls back in early October. This time-change pattern has created a lot of political arguments, and the guidelines may change again.

Tipping

Most service employees in Mexico count on tips for the majority of their income — especially true for bellboys and waiters. Bellboys should receive the equivalent of 50¢ to $1US per bag; waiters generally receive 10 percent to 20 percent depending on the level of service. In Mexico, it's not customary to tip taxi drivers, unless you hire them by the hour, or they provide guide or other special services. Don't use U.S. coins to tip.

Water

Most hotels have decanters or bottles of purified water in the rooms, and the better hotels have purified water from regular taps or special taps marked *agua purificada.* Some hotels will charge for in-room bottled water. Virtually any hotel, restaurant, or bar will bring you purified water if you specifically request it, but they'll usually charge you for it. Bottled, purified water is sold widely at drugstores and grocery stores. Some popular brands are Santa María, Ciel, and Bonafont. Evian and other imported brands are also widely available.

Appendix B

Toll-Free Numbers and Web Sites

- -

Airlines Serving Select Mexican Destinations

Aeromexico
☎ 800-237-6639
www.aeromexico.com
Acapulco, Cancún, Huatulco, Los Cabos,
Ixtapa, Puerto Vallarta, Zihuatanejo

Air Canada
☎ 888-247-2262
www.aircanada.ca
Puerto Vallarta

Alaska Airlines
☎ 800-426-0333
www.alaskaair.com
Los Cabos, Cancún, Puerto Vallarta

American Airlines
☎ 800-433-7300
www.im.aa.com
Acapulco, Cancún, Cozumel, Los Cabos,
Puerto Vallarta

American Trans Air
☎ 800-225-2995
www.ata.com
Cancún, Puerto Vallarta

America West Airlines
☎ 800-235-9292
www.americawest.com
Acapulco, Los Cabos, Puerto Vallarta

British Airways
☎ 800-247-9297
☎ 0845-77-333-77 in Britain

www.british-airways.com
Flights from London to Cancún

Continental Airlines
☎ 800-525-0280
www.continental.com
Acapulco, Cancún, Cozumel, Los Cabos,
Puerto Vallarta

Delta Air Lines
☎ 800-221-1212
www.delta.com
Cancún, Cozumel

Serviced through Aeromexico: Acapulco, Huatulco, Ixtapa, Los Cabos, Puerto Vallarta, Zihuatanejo

Mexicana
☎ 800-531-7921
www.mexicana.com
Acapulco, Cancún, Cozumel, Huatulco,
Ixtapa, Los Cabos, Puerto Vallarta,
Zihuatanejo

Northwest Airlines
☎ 800-225-2525
www.nwa.com
Seasonal flights to: Acapulco, Cancún,
Cozumel, Los Cabos, Puerto Vallarta

US Airways
☎ 800-428-4322
www.usairways.com
Cancún, Cozumel

Major Car-Rental Agencies

Advantage
☎ 800-777-5500
www.advantagerentacar.com
Cancún, Huatulco, Los Cabos, Puerto
Vallarta

Alamo
☎ 800-327-9633
www.goalamo.com
Acapulco, Cancún, Cozumel, Los Cabos,
Puerto Vallarta

Auto Europe
☎ 800-223-5555
www.autoeurope.com
Cancún

Avis
☎ 800-331-1212 in the continental U.S.
☎ 800-TRY-AVIS in Canada
www.avis.com
Acapulco, Cancún, Cozumel, Los Cabos,
Puerto Vallarta

Budget
☎ 800-527-0700
www.budgetrentacar.com
Acapulco, Cancún, Cozumel, Huatulco, Los
Cabos, Puerto Escondido, Puerto Vallarta

Dollar
☎ 800-800-4000
www.dollar.com
Cancún, Ixtapa, Los Cabos, Puerto Vallarta,
Zihuatanejo

Hertz
☎ 800-654-3131
www.hertz.com
Acapulco, Cancún, Cozumel, Ixtapa, Los
Cabos, Puerto Vallarta, Zihuatanejo

National
☎ 800-CAR-RENT
www.nationalcar.com
Acapulco, Cancún, Cozumel, Los Cabos,
Puerto Vallarta

Payless
☎ 800-PAYLESS
www.paylesscarrental.com
Cancún, Los Cabos

Thrifty
☎ 800-367-2277
www.thrifty.com
Cancún, Los Cabos, Puerto Vallarta

Major and Select Local Hotel and Motel Chains

Best Western
☎ 800-528-1234
www.bestwestern.com
Acapulco, Cancún, Los Cabos, Puerto
Escondido, Puerto Vallarta

Blue Bay Getaway
☎ 800-BLUE-BAY
www.bluebayresorts.com
Cancún, Puerto Vallarta

Camino Real
☎ 800-722-6466
www.caminoreal.com
Acapulco, Cancún, Huatulco, Puerto Vallarta

Days Inn
☎ 800-325-2525
www.daysinn.com
Cozumel

Fiesta Americana
☎ 800-FIESTA-1
www.fiestaamericana.com
Acapulco, Cancún, Los Cabos, Puerto Vallarta

Hilton Hotels
☎ 800-HILTONS
www.hilton.com
Cancún, Los Cabos

Holiday Inn
☎ 800-HOLIDAY
www.basshotels.com
Cancún, Puerto Vallarta

Hyatt Hotels and Resorts
☎ 800-228-9000
www.hyatt.com
Acapulco, Cancún

Inter-Continental Hotels and Resorts
☎ 888-567-8725
www.interconti.com
Cancún, Cozumel, Los Cabos, Puerto Vallarta

Le Méridien Hotel
☎ 800-543-4300
www.lemeridien-hotels.com
Cancún

Marriott Hotels
☎ 800-228-9290
www.marriott.com
Cancún, Puerto Vallarta

Plaza Las Glorias
☎ 800-342-AMIGO
Acapulco, Cozumel, Los Cabos, Puerto Vallarta

Quinta Real
☎ 888-561-2817
www.quintareal.com
Acapulco, Huatulco

Radisson Hotels International
☎ 800-333-3333
www.radisson.com
Acapulco

Ritz-Carlton Hotel
☎ 800-241-3333
www.ritzcarlton.com
Cancún

Sheraton Hotels and Resorts
☎ 800-325-3535
www.sheraton.com
Cancún, Los Cabos, Puerto Vallarta

Velas Vallarta Grand Suite Resort
☎ 800-659-8477
www.velasvallarta.com
Nuevo Vallarta, Puerto Vallarta

Westin Hotels and Resorts
☎ 800-937-8461
www.westin.com
Cancún, Los Cabos, Puerto Vallarta

Appendix C

Where to Get More Information

• •

*T*he following tourist boards and embassies provide valuable information regarding traveling in Mexico, including information on entry requirements and customs allowances.

Mexico Tourism Boards (www.visitmexico.com)

There are several offices in major North American cities, in addition to the main office in Mexico City (☎ 55-5203-1103). The toll-free information number is ☎ 800-44-MEXICO.

Locations in the United States: Chicago, IL (300 N. Michigan, 4th floor, Chicago, IL, 60601; ☎ 312-606-9252), Houston, TX (4507 San Jacinto, Suite 308, Houston, TX, 77074; ☎ 713-772-2581 ext.105), Los Angeles, CA (2401 W. 6th Street, Los Angeles, CA, 90057; ☎ 213-351-2069; Fax: 213-351-2074), Miami, FL (1200 NW 78th St., Miami, FL, 33126; ☎ 305-718-4095), New York, NY (21 E. 63rd St., 2nd Floor, New York, NY, 10021; ☎ 212-821-0304), and the Mexican Embassy Tourism Delegate in Washington D.C. (1911 Pennsylvania Ave., Washington, DC 20005; ☎ 202-728-1750). Locations in Canada: Montreal (1 Place Ville-Marie, Suite 1931, Montreal, QUEB, H3B 2C3; ☎ 514-871-1052), Toronto (2 Bloor St. W., Suite 1502, Toronto, ON, M4W 3E2; ☎ 416-925-0704), and Vancouver (999 W. Hastings, Suite 1110, Vancouver, BC, V6C 2W2; ☎ 604-669-2845). Embassy office: 1500-45 O'Connor St., Ottawa, ON, K1P 1A4 (☎ 613-233-8988; Fax: 613-235-9123).

U.S. State Department

Travel information from the U.S. State Department and the Overseas Citizens Services division (☎ 202-647-5225) offers a consular information sheet on Mexico that contains a compilation of safety, medical, driving, and general travel information gleaned from reports by official U.S. State Department offices in Mexico. In addition to calling, you can request the consular information sheet by fax at ☎ 202-647-3000. The State Department is also on the Internet: Check out http://travel.state.gov/mexico.html for the consular information sheet on Mexico; http://travel.state.gov/travel_warnings.html for other consular information sheets and travel warnings; and http://travel.state.gov/tips_mexico.html for the State Department's *Tips for Travelers to Mexico*.

24-hour Tourist Help Line

Dial ☎ 800-903-9200 toll-free inside Mexico, and you can get information from English-speaking operators as to where to go for medical assistance and other types of assistance. It's also a great source for general tourism information. You can always find helpful operators who will try to get the information that you need. To call this office from the United States, dial ☎ 800-482-9832.

Centers for Disease Control Hotline (www.cdc.gov/travel)

A source for medical information for travelers to Mexico and elsewhere. Dial. The Centers for Disease Control (CDC) Web site, www.cdc.gov/, provides detailed information on health issues for specific countries, or you can call the CDC at ☎ 800-311-3435 or 404-639-3534. For travelers to Mexico and Central America, the number with recorded messages about specific health issues related to this region is ☎ 877-FYI-TRIP. The toll-free fax number for requesting information is ☎ 888-232-3299.

Embassies and Consulates provide valuable lists of doctors and lawyers, as well as regulations concerning travel in Mexico.

The main **Embassy of the United States** is in Mexico City, Paseo de la Reforma 305, ☎ 55-5209-9100. Visit www.usembassy-mexico.gov for a list of all the street addresses of the U.S. consulates inside Mexico. There are U.S. consular agencies in Acapulco ☎ 744-481-1699, 744-484-0300 or 744-469-0556; Cabo San Lucas ☎ 624-143-3566; Cancún ☎ 998-883-0272; Cozumel ☎ 987-872-4574; Ixtapa ☎ 755-553-1108 and Puerto Vallarta ☎ 322-222-0069.

The **Embassy of Canada** is in Mexico City, Schiller 529, in Polanco ☎ 55-5724-7900. Visit their Web site at www.canada.org.mx for a complete listing of the addresses of the consular agencies in Mexico. Acapulco, Centro Comercial Marbella, Local 23, Prolongación Farallón S/N, ☎ 744-484-1305; E-mail: acapulco@canada.org.mx. Cancún ☎ 998-883-3360; E-mail: cancun@canada.org.mx, Puerto Vallarta ☎ 322-222-5398; E-mail: vallarta@canada.org.mx, and San José del Cabo ☎ 624-142-4333; E-mail: loscabos@canada.org.mx.

Local **tourist information offices** offer all kinds of information to travelers, including brochures, maps, and destination-specific magazines and posters. If you want them to mail information to you, allow four to six weeks for the mail to reach you.

Cancún Convention and Visitors Bureau (Ave. COBA Esq. Ave. Nader S.M.5, Cancún, Quintana Roo, Mexico 77500; ☎ 998-884-8073, 998-884-6531, 998-884-3438; Internet: www.gocancun.com). Calling their U.S. toll-free number, ☎ 800-CANCUN-8, is the easiest and quickest way to get a free Cancún vacation planner.

Isla Mujeres Tourism Office (Av. Rueda Medina 130, Isla Mujeres, Quintano Roo, Mexico, C.P. 77400) across from the main pier between Immigration and Customs; ☎ 998-877-0767; E-mail: infoisla@prodigy.net.mx).

City of Puerto Vallarta Tourism Office (Independencia 123, Puerto Vallarta, Jalisco, 48300, on one side of the city-hall building; ☎ 322-223-2500, ext. 230, ask for the tourism office).

State of Jalisco Tourism Office in Puerto Vallarta (Centro Comercial Plaza Marina Locales 144–146, Marina Vallarta, Puerto Vallarta, Jalisco, 48321, next to La Explosiva; ☎ 322-221-2676, 322-221-2677, 322-221-2678).

Puerto Vallarta Tourism Board and Convention and Visitors Bureau (Local 18 Planta Baja, Zona Comercial Continental Plaza, Puerto Vallarta, Jalisco, 48310; ☎ 888-384-6822 toll-free from the U.S., or 322-224-1175; Fax: 322-224-0915; Internet: www.visitpuertovallarta.com; E-mail: info@visitpuertovallarta.com).

Ixtapa Tourism Office or Subsecretaría de Fomento Turístico (Centro Comercial La Puerta, Locales 2, 3, 8–9, Ixtapa, Guerrero, 408880; ☎ 755-553-1967, 755-553-1968).

Zihuatanejo Tourism Office or Dirección de Turismo Municipal (located in the city-hall building in Zihuatanejo; ☎ 755-554-4455, ask for the tourism office; Internet: www.ixtapa-zihuatanejo-ocv.com; E-mail: presidencia@ixtapa-zihuatanejo.com). The Web site was under construction at the time this book was published, but it claims to be the only official Web site for Ixtapa-Zihuatanejo.

Acapulco's State of Guerrero Tourism Office (Costera Miguel Aleman 4455, Centro Internacional Acapulco, Acapulco, Guerrero, located on the Costera side of the convention center; ☎ 744-484-4583, 744-484-4416; Internet: www.acapulco.gob.mx; E-mail: sefotur@yahoo.com, procurador2000@yahoo.com). The Web site is being updated and was available in Spanish only when I last checked.

Huatulcos State Tourism Office (Blvd. Benito Juarez s/n Bahía de Tangolunda, Bahías de Huatulco, Oaxaca, 70989; ☎ 958-581-0176, 958-581-0177; Internet: http://oaxaca.oaxaca.gob.mx/sedetur; E-mail: sedetur6@oaxaca.gob.mx). The Web site offers information about the whole state of Oaxaca, including some information on Huatulco; however, the information is in Spanish and not very consumer oriented.

Huatulco Convention and Visitors Bureau (Blvd. Santa Cruz s/n local 1B, Bahía de Santa Cruz, Bahías de Huatulco, Oaxaca, 70989; ☎ 958-587-1037; Internet: www.baysofhuatulco.com; E-mail: info@baysof huatulco.com.mx, ocvhuatulco@prodigy.net.mx). The Web site is being updated.

Puerto Escondido State Tourism Office (SEDETUR, Blvd. Benito Juarez s/n, Puerto Escondido, Oaxaca, 71980; ☎ 954-582-0175).

Los Cabos Tourism Office (Bolivar Maureceo Casro, Edificio del Gobierno de la Estado; Madero between Hidalgo and Guerrero, Cabo San Lucas, BCS; ☎ 624-142-3310; Internet: www.visitcabo.com). You can try to call them for information, and who knows, someone may even be there to answer the phone; however, you're better off visiting their Web site.

Following is a list of several Web sites where you will be able to find updated information about Mexico and traveling to the most popular beach resorts; however, keep in mind that most of the companies that these Web sites recommend received this lofty status by paying some sort of advertising fee.

The **Mexico Ministry of Tourism** official Web site (www.mexico-travel. com) offers ample information (15,000 pages worth) about Mexico. However, the pages are slow to load and the information is a little outdated.

The Mexico Tourism Promotion Council developed another official site (www.visitmexico.com) with more current information on the different destinations in Mexico. Again, the pages are slow to load, but the navigation is a lot easier. The site features sections for travelers divided by region; a good search engine usually takes you to the information you're looking for.

For low-impact travel planning, visit the **Eco Travels in Mexico** section of the award-winning Web site www.planeta.com. You can find up-to-date information on reliable eco-tour operators in Mexico. This site also offers an excellent source to find banks and telephone services. Planeta.com is one of the best sources for current information because it's updated monthly.

The electronic version of **Connect Magazine** (www.mexconnect.com) offers a wealth of information and is the ideal site to begin a more in-depth, online exploration about when and where to visit Mexico. The site offers a great index where you can find everything from out-of-the-way adventures to Mexico's history to recommended accommodations.

Cancun South (www.cancunsouth.com) is a great site for independent travelers looking to explore the Riviera Maya. The site is easy to navigate and offers a wealth of information specific to the area.

Cozumel.net (www.cozumel.net) provides detailed information about the island's life. In my opinion, this site has the most reliable information about Cozumel — it even lists ferry schedules in the "About Cozumel" section.

Two good sites feature information on Los Cabos: **Baja Travel Guide** (www.bajatravel.com) and **All about Cabo** (www.allaboutcabo.com). Personally, I prefer the factual and less flashy presentation of the Baja Travel Guide site; however, if you want to learn a bit more about activities like golf and fishing and get an up-to-date beach forecast, All About Cabo is the site to visit.

Following is a selection of Web sites that can help you with all the important stuff related to your Mexican beach resort vacation — figuring out where to get cash, how to ask for a cold beer, where to go to send an e-mail to your friends back home, how to find really great deals, and so on.

Foreign Languages for Travelers (www.travlang.com)

Learn basic terms in more than 70 languages and click on any underlined phrase to hear what it sounds like. **Note:** Free audio software and speakers are required.

Intellicast (www.intellicast.com)

Weather forecasts for all 50 United States and cities around the world. **Note:** Temperatures are in Celsius for many international destinations.

Mapquest (www.mapquest.com)

Choose a specific address or destination, and in seconds, get a map and detailed directions.

Universal Currency Converter (www.xe.net/ucc/)

See what your dollar or pound is worth in more than 100 other countries.

Visa ATM Locator (www.visa.com) or MasterCard ATM Locator (www.mastercard.com)

Find ATMs in hundreds of cities in the U.S. and around the world.

Travel Secrets (www.travelsecrets.com)

This is one of the best compilations around. The site offers advice and tips on how to find the lowest prices for airlines, hotels, and cruises, and it also provides a listing of links for airfare deals, airlines, booking engines, discount travel, resources, hotels, and travel magazines.

Appendix D

Glossary of Spanish Words and Phrases

• •

Most Mexicans are very patient with foreigners who try to speak their language. And your trip can be much easier and more enjoyable if you know a few basic Spanish phrases.

In this glossary, I include a few lists of simple words and phrases for expressing basic needs.

English-Spanish Phrases

English	Spanish	Pronunciation
Good day (Good morning)	**Buenos días**	*bway*-nohss *dee*-ahss
Good evening/afternoon	**Buenas tardes**	*bway*-nahss *tar*-days
Good night	**Buenas noches**	*bway*-nahss *noh*-chase
How are you?	**¿Cómo está?**	*koh*-moh ess-*tah?*
Very well	**Muy bien**	mwee byen
Thank you	**Gracias**	*grah*-see-ahss
You're welcome	**De nada**	day *nah*-dah
Good-bye	**Adiós**	ah-*dee-ohss*
Please	**Por favor**	pohr fah-*vohr*
Yes	**Sí**	see
No	**No**	noh
Excuse me	**Disculpe**	dees-*kool*-peh
Give me	**Déme**	*day*-may

(continued)

English-Spanish Phrases *(continued)*

English	Spanish	Pronunciation
Where is...?	¿Dónde est*...?	*dohn*-day ess-*tah?*
the station	la estación	lah ess-tah-*seown*
a hotel	un hotel	oon oh-*tel*
a gas station	una gasolinera	*oon*-uh gah-so-lee-*nay*-rah
a restaurant	un restaurante	oon res-tow-*rahn*-tay
the toilet	el baño	el *bahn*-yoh
a good doctor	un buen médico	oon bwayn *may*-dee-co
the road to...	el camino...	el cah-*mee*-noh ah/
To the right	A la derecha	ah lah day-*reh*-chuh
To the left	A la izquierda	ah lah ees-ky-*ehr*-thah
Straight ahead	Derecho	day-*reh*-cho
I would like	Quisiera	key-see-*ehr*-ah
I want	Quiero	*kyehr*-oh
to eat	comer	ko-*mayr*
a room	una habitación	*oon*-nuh ha-bee-tah-*seeown*
Do you have...?	¿Tiene usted...?	tyah-nay oos-*ted?*
a book	un libro	oon *lee*-bro
a dictionary	un diccionario	oon deek-see-on-*ar*-ee-oh
How much is it?	¿Cuánto cuesta?	*kwahn*-to *kwess*-tah?
When?	¿Cuándo?	*kwahn*-doh?
What?	¿Qué?	kay?
There is (Is there ...?)	(¿)Hay?	eye?
What is there?	¿Qué hay?	kay eye?
Yesterday	Ayer	ah-*yer*
Today	Hoy	oy
Tomorrow	Mañana	mahn-*yahn*-ah
Good	Bueno	*bway*-no
Bad	Malo	*mah*-lo

English	Spanish	Pronunciation
Better (best)	**Mejor**	meh-*hor*
More	**Más**	mahs
Less	**Menos**	*may*-noss
No smoking	**Se prohibe fumar**	say pro-*ee*-bay foo-*mahr*
Postcard	**Tarjeta postal**	tar-*heh*-ta pohs-*tahl*
Insect repellent	**Repelente contra insectos**	reh-peh-*lehn*-te *cohn*-trah een-*sehk*-tos

More Useful Phrases

English	Spanish	Pronunciation
Do you speak English?	**¿Habla usted inglés?**	*ah*-blah oo-*sted* een-*glays?*
Is there anyone here who speaks English?	**¿Hay alguien aquí que hable inglés?**	eye *ahl*-gyen ah-*key* kay *ah*-blay een-*glays?*
I speak a little Spanish.	**Hablo un poco de español.**	*ah*-blow oon *poh*-koh day ess-pah-*nyol*
I don't understand Spanish very well.	**No entiendo español muy bien.**	noh ehn-tee-*ehn*-do ess-pah-*nyol* moo-ee bee-ayn
The meal is good.	**Me gusta la comida.**	may *goo*-sta lah koh-*mee*-dah
What time is it?	**¿Qué hora es?**	kay *oar*-ah ess?
May I see your menu?	**¿Puedo ver el menu?**	*puay*-tho veyr el may-*noo*?
The check, please.	**La cuenta, por favor.**	lah *quayn*-tah pohr fa-*vorh*
What do I owe you?	**¿Cuánto le debo?**	*kwahn*-toh leh *day*-boh?
What did you say?	**¿Mande?** (formal)	*mahn*-day?
	¿Cómo dijo? (informal)	*koh*-moh dee-ho?
I want (to see)	**Quiero (ver)**	key-*yehr*-oh vehr
a room	**un cuarto** or **una habitación**	oon *kwar*-toh *or* oon-nah ah-bee-tah-*see-on*
for two persons	**para dos personas**	*pahr*-ah doss pehr-*sohn*-as
with (without) bathroom	**con (sin) baño**	kohn (seen) *bah*-nyoh

(continued)

More Useful Phrases *(continued)*

English	Spanish	Pronunciation
We are staying here only	**Nos quedamos aquí solamente**	nohs kay-*dahm*-ohss ah-*key* sohl-ah-*mayn*-tay
one night	**una noche**	oon-ah *noh*-chay
one week	**una semana**	oon-ah say-*mahn*-ah
We are leaving	**Partimos or Salimos**	pahr-*tee*-mohss; sah-*lee*-mohss
tomorrow	**mañana**	mahn-*nyan*-ah
Do you accept...?	**¿Acepta usted...?**	ah-*sayp*-tah oo-*sted*
...traveler's checks?	**... el cheques de viajero?**	*chay* kays day bee-ah-*hehr*-oh
...credit cards	**...tarjetas de crédito**	tar-*hay*-tahs day *kray*-dee-toh
Is there a Laundromat?	**¿Hay una lavandería?**	eye *oon*-ah lah-*vahn*-day-*ree*-ah
Is...near here?	**Es...cerca de aquí?**	*sehr*-ka day ah-*key*
Please send these clothes to the laundry	**Hágame el favor de mandar esta ropa a la lavandería.**	*ah*-ga-may el fah-*vhor* day mahn-*dahr ays*- tah *rho*-pah a lah lah- *vahn*-day-*ree*-ah

Numbers

1	**uno** (*ooh*-noh)
2	**dos** (dohs)
3	**tres** (trayss)
4	**cuatro** (*kwah*-troh)
5	**cinco** (*seen*-koh)
6	**seis** (sayss)
7	**siete** (*syeh*-tay)
8	**ocho** (*oh*-choh)
9	**nueve** (*nway*-bay)
10	**diez** (dee-ess)

11	**once** (*ohn*-say)
12	**doce** (*doh*-say)
13	**trece** (*tray*-say)
14	**catorce** (kah-*tor*-say)
15	**quince** (*keen*-say)
16	**dieciseis** (de-*ess*-ee-sayss)
17	**diecisiete** (de-*ess*-ee-*syeh*-tay)
18	**dieciocho** (dee-*ess*-ee-*oh*-choh)
19	**diecinueve** (dee-*ess*-ee-*nway*-bay)
20	**veinte** (*bayn*-tay)
21	**veinteuno** (*bayn*-tay-*ooh*-noh)
30	**treinta** (*trayn*-tah)
40	**cuarenta** (kwah-*ren*-tah)
50	**cincuenta** (seen-*kwen*-tah)
60	**sesenta** (say-*sen*-tah)
70	**setenta** (say-*ten*-tah)
80	**ochenta** (oh-*chen*-tah)
90	**noventa** (noh-*ben*-tah)
100	**cien** (see-*en*)
200	**doscientos** (*dos*-se-en-tos)
500	**quinientos** (keen-ee-*ehn*-tos)
1,000	**mil** (meal)

Transportation Terms

English	Spanish	Pronunciation
Airport	**Aeropuerto**	ah-ay-row-*por*-tow
Arrival gates	**Llegadas**	yay-*gah*-dahs
Departure gate	**Puerta de embarque**	*por*-tow day em-*bark*- kay
Baggage	**Equipajes**	eh-key-*pah*-hays

(continued)

Transportation Terms *(continued)*

English	Spanish	Pronunciation
Baggage-claim area	**Recibo de equipajes**	ray-see-boh day eh-key-*pah*-hay
First class	**Primera**	pree-*mehr*-oh
Second class	**Segunda**	say-*goon*-dah
Flight	**Vuelo**	bw*ay*-low
Nonstop	**Directo**	dee-*reck*-toh
	Sin escala	seen ess-*kah*-lah
Rental car	**Arrendadora de autos**	ah-rain-da-dow-rah day autos
Bus	**Autobús**	ow-toh-*boos*
Bus or truck	**Camión**	ka-mee-*ohn*
Intercity	**Foraneo**	fohr-ah-*nay*-oh
Lane	**Carril**	kah-*rreal*
Luggage storage area	**Guarda equipaje**	gwar-dah eh-key-*pah*-hay
Originates at this station	**Local**	loh-*kahl*
Originates elsewhere	**De paso**	day *pah*-soh
Stops if seats available	**Para si hay lugares**	pah-rah-see-aye-loo-gahr-ays
Waiting room	**Sala de espera**	*saw*-lah day ess-*pehr*-ah
Ticket window	**Taquilla**	tah-*key*-lah
Toilets	**Sanitarios**	sahn-ee-tahr-*ee*-oss

Appendix E

Authentic Mexican Cuisine

• •

*A*uthentic Mexican food differs quite dramatically from what is frequently served up in the United States under that name. For many travelers, Mexico will be new and exciting culinary territory. Even grizzled veterans will be pleasantly surprised by the wide variation in specialties and traditions offered from region to region.

Despite regional differences, it's possible to make some generalizations. Mexican food usually isn't pepper-hot when it arrives at the table (though many dishes must have a certain amount of spiciness, and some home cooking can be very spicy, depending on a family's or chef's tastes). The piquant flavor is added with chiles and sauces after the food is served; you'll never see a table in Mexico without one or both of these condiments. Mexicans don't drown their cooking in cheese and sour cream (which is the case in many Tex-Mex restaurants), and they use a great variety of ingredients. But the basis of Mexican food is simple — tortillas, beans, chiles, squash, and tomatoes — the same as it was centuries ago, before the Europeans arrived.

Knowing the Basic Dishes

Traditional **tortillas** are made from corn that has been cooked in water and lime, and then ground into *masa* (a grainy dough), patted and pressed into thin cakes, and cooked on a hot griddle known as a *comal.* In many households, the tortilla takes the place of fork and spoon; Mexicans merely tear them into wedge-shaped pieces, which they use to scoop up their food. Restaurants often serve bread rather than tortillas because it's easier, but you can always ask for tortillas. A more recent invention from northern Mexico is the flour tortilla, which is seen less frequently in the rest of Mexico.

Dishes made with tortillas

The tortilla is the basis of several Mexican dishes, but the most famous of these is the **enchilada.** The original name for this dish would have been *tortilla enchilada,* which simply means a tortilla dipped in a chile sauce. In a similar manner, there's the *entomatada* (tortilla dipped in a tomato sauce) and the *enfrijolada* (tortilla dipped in a bean sauce). The enchilada began as a very simple dish: A tortilla is dipped in chile sauce (usually with ancho chile) and then into very hot oil, and then is quickly folded or rolled on a plate and sprinkled with chopped onions and a little *queso cotija* (crumbly white cheese) and served with a few fried potatoes and carrots. You can get this basic enchilada in food stands across the country. I love them, and if you come across them in your travels, give them a try. In restaurants, you get the more elaborate enchilada, with different fillings of cheese, chicken, pork, or even seafood, and sometimes in a casserole.

A **taco** is anything folded or rolled into a tortilla, and sometimes a double tortilla. The tortilla can be served either soft or fried. *Flautas* and *quesadillas* are species of tacos. For Mexicans, the taco is the quintessential fast food, and the taco stand (*taquería*) — a ubiquitous sight — is a great place to get a filling meal. See the section "Eating Out: Restaurants, *Taquerías,* and Tipping," later in this section for information on taquerías.

All about beans

An invisible "bean line" divides Mexico: It starts at the Gulf Coast in the southern part of the state of Tamaulipas and moves inland through the eastern quarter of San Luis Potosí and most of the state of Hidalgo, and then goes straight through Mexico City and Morelos and into Guerrero, where it curves slightly westward to the Pacific. To the north and west of this line, the pink bean known as the *flor de mayo* is the staple food; to the south and east, the standard is the black bean.

In private households, beans are served at least once a day and, among the working class and peasantry, with every meal, if the family can afford it. Mexicans almost always prepare beans with a minimum of condiments — usually just a little onion and garlic and perhaps a pinch of herbs. Beans are meant to be a contrast to the heavily spiced dishes. Sometimes they are served at the end of a meal with a little Mexican-style sour cream.

Mexicans often fry leftover beans and serve them on the side as *frijoles refritos*. "Refritos" is usually translated as refried, but this is a misnomer — the beans are fried only once. The prefix "re" actually means "well" (as in thoroughly), and what Mexicans actually mean is the beans are well fried.

Getting to know tamales

You make a *tamal* by mixing corn *masa* with a little lard, adding one of several fillings — such as meats flavored with chiles (or no filling at all) — then wrapping it in a corn husk or in the leaf of a banana or other plant, and finally steaming it. Every region in Mexico has its own traditional way of making *tamales*. In some places, a single *tamal* can be big enough to feed a family, while in others they are barely 3 inches long and an inch thick.

Understanding the chile pepper

Many kinds of chile peppers exist, and Mexicans call each of them by one name when they're fresh and another when they're dried. Some are blazing hot with only a mild flavor; some are mild but have a rich, complex flavor. They can be pickled, smoked, stuffed, stewed, chopped, and used in an endless variety of dishes.

Eating Out: Restaurants, Taquerias, and Tipping

First of all, I feel compelled to debunk the prevailing myth that the cheapest place to eat in Mexico is in the market. Actually, this is almost never the case. You can usually find better food at a better price without going more than 2 blocks out of your way. Why? Food stalls in the marketplace pay high rents, they have a near-captive clientele of market vendors and truckers, and they get a lot of business from many Mexicans for whom eating in the market is a traditional way of confirming their culture.

On the other side of the spectrum, avoid eating at those inviting sidewalk restaurants that you see beneath the stone archways that border the main plazas. These places usually cater to tourists and don't need to count on getting any return business. But they are great for getting a coffee or beer.

In most nonresort towns, there are always one or two restaurants (sometimes it's a coffee shop) that are social centers for a large group of established patrons. These establishments over time become virtual institutions, and change comes very slowly to them. The food is usually good standard fare, cooked as it was 20 years ago; the decor is simple. The patrons have known each other and the staff for years, and the *charla* (banter), gestures, and greetings are friendly, open, and unaffected. If you're curious about Mexican culture, these places are fun to eat in and observe the goings-on.

During your trip, you're going to see many *taquerías* (**taco stands**). These are generally small places with a counter or a few tables set around the cooking area; you get to see exactly how they make their tacos before deciding whether to order. Most tacos come with a little chopped onion and cilantro, but not tomato and lettuce. Find one that seems popular with the locals and where the cook performs with *brio* (a good sign of pride in the product). Sometimes there will be a woman making the tortillas right there (or working the *masa* into *gorditas, sopes,* or *panuchos* if these are also served). You will never see men doing this — this is perhaps the strictest gender division in Mexican society. Men do all other cooking and kitchen tasks, and work with already-made tortillas, but they will never be found working *masa.*

For the main meal of the day, many restaurants offer a multicourse blue-plate special called **comida corrida** or **menú del día.** This is the most inexpensive way to get a full dinner. In Mexico, you need to ask for your check; it is generally considered inhospitable to present a check to someone who hasn't requested it. If you're in a hurry to get somewhere, ask for the check when your food arrives.

Tips are about the same as in the United States. You'll sometimes find a 15 percent **value-added tax** on restaurant meals, which shows up on the bill as "IVA." This is a boon to arithmetically challenged tippers, saving them from undue exertion.

To summon the waiter, wave or raise your hand, but don't motion with your index finger, which is a demeaning gesture that may even cause the waiter to ignore you. Or if it's the check you want, you can motion to the waiter from across the room using the universal pretend-like-you're-writing gesture.

Most restaurants do not have **nonsmoking sections;** when they do, I mention it in the reviews. But Mexico's wonderful climate allows for many open-air restaurants, usually set inside a courtyard of a colonial house, or in rooms with tall ceilings and plenty of open windows.

Drinking in Mexico

All over Mexico you'll find shops selling *jugos* (**juices**) and *liquados* (**smoothies**) made from several kinds of tropical fruit. They're excellent and refreshing; while traveling, I take full advantage of them. You'll also come across *aguas frescas* — water flavored with hibiscus, melon, tamarind, or lime. Soft drinks come in more flavors than in any other country I know. Pepsi and Coca-Cola taste the way they did in the United States years ago, before the makers started adding corn syrup. The coffee is generally good, and **hot chocolate** is a traditional drink, as is *atole* — a hot, corn-based beverage that can be sweet or bitter.

Of course, Mexico has a proud and lucrative **beer**-brewing tradition. A lesser-known brewed beverage is *pulque,* a pre-Hispanic drink: the fermented juice of a few species of maguey or agave. Mostly you find it for sale in *pulquerías* in central Mexico. It is an acquired taste, and not every gringo acquires it. **Mezcal** and **tequila** also come from the agave.

Tequila is a variety of mezcal produced from the *A. tequilana* species of agave in and around the area of Tequila, in the state of Jalisco. Mezcal comes from various parts of Mexico and from different varieties of agave. The distilling process is usually much less sophisticated than that of tequila, and, with its stronger smell and taste, mezcal is much more easily detected on the drinker's breath. In some places such as Oaxaca, it comes with a worm in the bottle; you are supposed to eat the worm after polishing off the mezcal. But for those teetotalers out there who are interested in just the worm, I have good news — you can find these worms for sale in Mexican markets when in season.

Glossary of Spanish Menu Terms

The following is a list of common menu items and a description for each to take some of the guesswork out of ordering meals on your vacation.

Achiote — Small, red seed of the *annatto* tree.

Agua fresca — Fruit-flavored water, usually watermelon or cantaloupe where ingredients such as lemon and hibiscus flower are added.

Antojito — Typical Mexican supper foods, usually made with *masa* or tortilla*s* and contain a filling or topping such as sausage, cheese, beans, and onions; includes such things as *tacos, tostadas, sopes,* and *garnachas* (thick tortillas).

Atole — A thick, lightly sweet, hot drink made with finely ground corn and usually flavored with vanilla, pecan, or chocolate.

Botana — An appetizer.

Buñuelos — Round, thin, deep-fried, crispy fritters dipped in sugar.

Carnitas — Pork that's been deep-cooked (not fried) in lard, then simmered, and then served with corn tortillas for tacos.

Ceviche — Fresh, raw seafood marinated in fresh lime juice, garnished with chopped tomatoes, onions, chiles, and sometimes cilantro, and served with crispy, fried, whole-corn tortillas or crackers.

Chayote — A type of spiny pear-shaped squash boiled and served as an accompaniment to meat dishes.

Chiles en nogada — Poblano peppers stuffed with a mixture of ground pork and chicken, spices, fruits, raisins, and almonds, fried in a light batter, and covered in a walnut-and-cream sauce.

Chiles rellenos — Usually poblano peppers stuffed with cheese or spicy ground meat with raisins, rolled in a batter, and fried.

Churro — Tube-shaped, bread-like fritter, dipped in sugar and sometimes filled with *cajeta* (caramel) or chocolate.

Enchilada — A tortilla dipped in a sauce and usually filled with chicken or white cheese; sometimes topped with mole sauce *(enchiladas rojas or de mole),* tomato sauce and sour cream *(enchiladas suizas* — Swiss enchiladas), a green sauce *(enchiladas verdes),* or onions, sour cream, and guacamole *(enchiladas potosinas).*

Escabeche — A lightly pickled sauce used in Yucatecán chicken stew.

Frijoles charros — Beans flavored with beer; a northern Mexican specialty.

Frijoles refritos — Pinto beans mashed and cooked with lard.

Gorditas — Thickish fried-corn tortillas, slit and stuffed with choice of cheese, beans, beef, and chicken; served with or without lettuce, tomato, and onion garnish.

Gusanos de maguey — Maguey worms, considered a delicacy; delicious when deep-fried to a crisp and served with corn tortillas for tacos.

Horchata — Lightly sweetened, refreshing drink made of ground rice or melon seeds, and ground almonds. Also know as *agua de arroz* in certain destinations on the Pacific Coast, such as Puerto Vallarta and Ixtapa.

Huevos Mexicanos — Scrambled eggs with chopped onions, hot peppers, and tomatoes.

Huevos rancheros — Fried eggs on top of a fried corn tortilla covered in a spicy or mild tomato sauce.

Huitlacoche — Sometimes spelled "cuitlacoche." A mushroom-flavored black fungus that appears on corn in the rainy season; considered a delicacy.

Machaca — Shredded, dried beef scrambled with eggs or in a mild red sauce; a specialty of northern Mexico.

Masa — Ground corn soaked in lime used as the basis for tamales, corn tortillas, and soups.

Menudo — Stew made with the lining of the cow's stomach. It can be served in a red or white broth. A traditional hangover cure.

Pan dulce — Lightly sweetened bread in many configurations, usually served at breakfast or bought in any bakery.

Pibil — Pit-baked pork or chicken in a sauce of tomato, onion, mild red pepper, cilantro, and vinegar.

Pipián — A sauce made with ground pumpkin seeds, nuts, and mild peppers.

Poc chuc — Slices of pork with onion marinated in a tangy, sour, orange sauce and charcoal-broiled; a Yucatecán specialty.

Pozole — Pork or chicken broth with hominy and shredded pork or chicken. The traditional recipe calls for the pork's head, but now it's commonly prepared with chicken or pork loin. Pozole is served red in Jalisco and white in Guerrero. Thursdays are the traditional day to eat pozole in Acapulco and Ixtapa.

Quesadilla — Corn or flour tortillas stuffed with melted white cheese and lightly fried.

Queso relleno — "Stuffed cheese;" a mild yellow cheese stuffed with minced meat and spices; a Yucatecán specialty.

Rompope — Delicious Mexican eggnog, invented in Puebla, made with eggs, vanilla, sugar, and rum.

Salsa verde — A cooked sauce using the green tomatillo puréed with spicy or mild hot peppers, onions, garlic, and cilantro; on tables countrywide.

Sopa de lima — A tangy soup made with chicken broth and accented with fresh lime; popular in Yucatán.

Sopa de Tortilla — A traditional chicken broth–based soup, seasoned with chilies, tomatoes, onion, and garlic, with crispy fried strips of corn tortillas.

Sope — Pronounced "*soh*-pay;" an *antojito* similar to a *garnacha* (a thick tortilla), except spread with refried beans and topped with crumbled cheese and onions.

Tacos al pastor — Thin slices of flavored pork roasted on a revolving cylinder dripping with onion slices and the juice of fresh pineapple slices. Served in small corn tortillas, topped with chopped onion and cilantro.

Tamal — Incorrectly called a "tamale" (*tamal* singular; *tamales* plural). A meat or sweet filling rolled with fresh *masa*, wrapped in a corn husk or banana leaf, and then steamed; many varieties and sizes throughout the country.

Torta — A sandwich, usually on *bolillo* bread, typically comprising sliced avocado, onions, and tomatoes with a choice of meat and often cheese.

Tostadas — Crispy, fried corn tortillas topped with meat, onions, lettuce, tomatoes, cheese, avocados, and sometimes sour cream.

Making Dollars and Sense of It

Expense	Daily cost	x	Number of days	=	Total
Airfare					
Local transportation					
Car rental					
Lodging (with tax)					
Parking					
Breakfast					
Lunch					
Dinner					
Snacks					
Entertainment					
Babysitting					
Attractions					
Gifts & souvenirs					
Tips					
Other					
Grand Total					

Fare Game: Choosing an Airline

When looking for the best airfare, you should cover all your bases — 1) consult a trusted travel agent; 2) contact the airline directly, via the airline's toll-free number and/or Web site; 3) check out one of the travel-planning Web sites, such as www.frommers.com.

Travel Agency_____ Phone_____

    Agent's Name_____ Quoted fare_____

Airline 1_____ Quoted fare_____

    Toll-free number/Internet_____

Airline 2_____ Quoted fare_____

    Toll-free number/Internet_____

Web site 1_____ Quoted fare_____

Web site 2_____ Quoted fare_____

Departure Schedule & Flight Information

Airline_____ Flight #_____ Confirmation #_____

Departs_____ Date_____ Time_____ a.m./p.m.

Arrives_____ Date_____ Time_____ a.m./p.m.

Connecting Flight (if any)

Amount of time between flights_____ hours/mins

Airline_____ Flight #_____ Confirmation #_____

Departs_____ Date_____ Time_____ a.m./p.m.

Arrives_____ Date_____ Time_____ a.m./p.m.

Return Trip Schedule & Flight Information

Airline_____ Flight #_____ Confirmation #_____

Departs_____ Date_____ Time_____ a.m./p.m.

Arrives_____ Date_____ Time_____ a.m./p.m.

Connecting Flight (if any)

Amount of time between flights_____ hours/mins

Airline_____ Flight #_____ Confirmation #_____

Departs_____ Date_____ Time_____ a.m./p.m.

Arrives_____ Date_____ Time_____ a.m./p.m.

Sweet Dreams: Choosing Your Hotel

Make a list of all the hotels where you'd like to stay and then check online and call the local and toll-free numbers to get the best price. You should also check with a travel agent, who may be able to get you a better rate.

Hotel & page	Location	Internet	Tel. (local)	Tel. (Toll-free)	Quoted rate

Hotel Checklist

Here's a checklist of things to inquire about when booking your room, depending on your needs and preferences.

- ❑ Smoking/smoke-free room
- ❑ Noise (if you prefer a quiet room, ask about proximity to elevator, bar/restaurant, pool, meeting facilities, renovations, and street)
- ❑ View
- ❑ Facilities for children (crib, roll-away cot, babysitting services)
- ❑ Facilities for travelers with disabilities
- ❑ Number and size of bed(s) (king, queen, double/full-size)
- ❑ Is breakfast included? (buffet, continental, or sit-down?)
- ❑ In-room amenities (hair dryer, iron/board, minibar, etc.)
- ❑ Other_____

Menus & Venues

Enter the restaurants where you'd most like to dine. Then use the worksheet below to plan your itinerary.

Name	Address/Phone	Cuisine/Price

Places to Go, People to See, Things to Do

Enter the attractions you would most like to see and decide how they'll fit into your schedule. Next, use the "Going My Way" worksheets that follow to sketch out your itinerary.

Attraction/activity	Page	Amount of time you expect to spend there	Best day and time to go

Going "My" Way

Day 1

Hotel_____ Tel._____

Morning_____
_____

Lunch_____ Tel._____

Afternoon_____
_____

Dinner_____ Tel._____

Evening_____
_____

Day 2

Hotel_____ Tel._____

Morning_____
_____

Lunch_____ Tel._____

Afternoon_____
_____

Dinner_____ Tel._____

Evening_____
_____

Day 3

Hotel_____ Tel._____

Morning_____
_____

Lunch_____ Tel._____

Afternoon_____
_____

Dinner_____ Tel._____

Evening_____
_____

Going "My" Way

Day 4

Hotel_____ Tel._____

Morning_____

_____

Lunch_____ Tel._____

Afternoon_____

_____

Dinner_____ Tel._____

Evening_____

Day 5

Hotel_____ Tel._____

Morning_____

_____

Lunch_____ Tel._____

Afternoon_____

_____

Dinner_____ Tel._____

Evening_____

Day 6

Hotel_____ Tel._____

Morning_____

_____

Lunch_____ Tel._____

Afternoon_____

_____

Dinner_____ Tel._____

Evening_____

Going "My" Way

Day 7

Hotel_____ Tel._____

Morning_____

_____

Lunch_____ Tel._____

Afternoon_____

_____

Dinner_____ Tel._____

Evening_____

_____

Day 8

Hotel_____ Tel._____

Morning_____

_____

Lunch_____ Tel._____

Afternoon_____

_____

Dinner_____ Tel._____

Evening_____

_____

Day 9

Hotel_____ Tel._____

Morning_____

_____

Lunch_____ Tel._____

Afternoon_____

_____

Dinner_____ Tel._____

Evening_____

_____

Index

• •

• N •

• T •